The Writings of Ivor Browne

STEPS ALONG THE ROAD –
THE EVOLUTION OF A SLOW LEARNER

ATRIUM

First published in 2013 by Atrium
Atrium is an imprint of Cork University Press,
Youngline Industrial Estate
Pouladuff Road, Togher
Cork, Ireland

All efforts have been made to seek permission for extracts included in this book
from published and unpublished copyright works. Sincere thanks to Vincent
Kenny, The Royal Society of Medicine Press, American Psychiatric Publishing, The
Irish Times, John Wiley & Sons Ltd., The American Journal of Psychiatry, Seven
Hats Media Ltd., The Irish Medical Journal, Columbia Press, Directions in Psy-
chiatry, The Royal Society of Medicine, The Lancet, Wolfhound Press, Heldref
Publications, and the Irish University Review.

British Library Cataloguing in Publication Data
A CIP catalogue record for this book is available from the British Library.

ISBN-978-185594-220-2
Printed in Malta by Gutenberg Press
Typeset by Tower Books, Ballincollig, Co. Cork
www.corkuniversitypress.com

The Writings of Ivor Browne

STEPS ALONG THE ROAD –
THE EVOLUTION OF A SLOW LEARNER

In memory of the late June Levine,
my wife and partner,
who gave me her love and support
for so many years

Acknowledgements

My deep appreciation to Michael Collins, Publications Director and Maria O'Donovan, Production Editor, both of Cork University Press, who worked so hard in the process and production of this work and to Gloria Greenwood for her dedication in editing this collection.

Thanks also to Frances Osbourne who was not only a great help with bringing to life so many of the early papers, but was a tower of strength in handling much of the administration of the professorial Department of psychiatry, UCD, which made it possible for me to find the time to write these papers. My thanks too to Jim Behan, David Meagher and Kevin O'Neill, who served successively as lecturers in the professorial unit, and were such a support in those difficult times.

These papers span more than fifty years of my life, my thinking, and my development. Those fifty years included the wonderful early years I spent with my four children, Garvan, Tierna, Ronan and Dara and I would also like to acknowledge the support of my former wife Orla who helped me to gain access, by scholarship from Ely Lilly, to undertake postgraduate study in Harvard in mental health which was a major contribution to my further career.

Much thanks also to Trish Ford, who has been my personal assistant for a good many years now since my official retirement in 1994, and who has been such a key help and support in so many ways. Thanks to Shay Ward, my untiring technical advisor.

Thank you also to Fintan O'Toole, who kindly agreed to write the Forword to this book, and to Fionnuala Flanagan for her kind support. I am also grateful to Dr Brendan Kelly and Dr Malcolm Garland for their comments.

Heartfelt thanks go to the many people who have contributed their thoughts and reflections to the individual papers that are included in this collection: Robert Whittaker, Paddy Doherty, Vincent Kenny, Mairead Leonard, Tony Boland, T.J. Kiernan, Erich Lindemann, Tom Murphy, Paul Kearns, Jim McMahon and Gillian Duffin, Carmel Semple, Ciaran Smith, and Stephen Costello.

My stepson Michael Mesbur is a constant source of inspiration for which I am eternally grateful. I would also like to thank my stepson Adam for his steadfast support to me which I greatly appreciate.

I also wish to honour those who shaped my thinking in the early days, and made such valiant efforts to educate me: Dr Joshua Bierer, Professor Gerald Caplin, and Professor Tom Hackett.

I want to make special mention of my old and dear friend Kevin Clear, now sadly deceased.

Special thanks to Colm Toibin and Catriona Crowe for their incisive and helpful support, and to Professor Austin Darragh for his patience and many years of friendship.

I am eternally grateful to Sahaj Marg, to its founder Shri Ram Chandra of Shahajanpur, also called Babuji, and to the current president Shri Parthasarathi Rajagopalachari, affectionately known as Chariji, who have both changed my life, in a fundamental way, and set me on the path of spiritual growth.

Thank you to the many people who have come to me over the years seeking help. You have given me inspiration and helped me to grow my ideas, which are finally seeing the light of day in these papers.

Many thanks to my son-in-law Martin Reid for his help, support and expertise in many things, especially in seeking out references.

Finally, my special thanks and eternal gratitude to my step-daughter Diane who has selflessly assisted me in each stage of this project, and in so many other ways, with love and patience.

Contents

Contents

Foreword

FINTAN O'TOOLE

Somehow you tried to be one human being working with another.
– Ivor Browne

Ivor Browne is one of Ireland's great liberators. Such a word is normally used only to describe those who furthered religious and civil freedom or political independence. But it applies here nonetheless – doubly so, in fact. Browne is a literal liberator: he was a key figure in the freeing of thousands of people from institutional incarceration, a process described in these crucial writings. That alone would make these papers highly significant social documents, as important in their own way as the archives of government departments or the makers of economic policy. (It is not entirely coincidental that he dates his own beginnings as a 'slow learner' in the field of psychiatry to 1958, the same year in which Kenneth Whitaker's programme of economic modernization began the transformation of the Republic.)

But Ivor Browne is a liberator in another sense, too. Alongside his pioneering work as a psychiatrist, he is one of the most important public intellectuals in Ireland in the second half of the twentieth century. Not merely for what he says but for the way he says it. Readers will find themselves in this volume encountering a free mind, one that is open, questioning, utterly unintimidated by orthodoxies and entirely comfortable with the way his ideas took him from the centre to the margins of his profession. It is not necessary to agree with everything – indeed with anything – he writes to be engaged and invigorated by the exemplary way in which he combines calm rationality with a fearless questioning of received wisdom about how humanity works and what happens when it doesn't. In his writings and speeches, the image of the godlike healer with all the answers is replaced by that of the explorer, entering into what is still the greatest terra incognita of all: the human mind. Browne has enough serene confidence not to

xi

worry about being out of step with current fashions of thought in his profession and enough awareness of the limitations of knowledge to remain deeply modest.

There is no false modesty, indeed, in this book's subtitle and its reference to the author as a 'slow learner'. For what we have here is not a retrospective account of Browne's career and thinking (he has already given us that in *Music and Madness*) but the organic imme-diacy of a man thinking on his feet. An important aspect of these pa-pers is that they are contemporary documents. They are not edited to remove material that may, with hindsight, seem embarrassing. It is interesting, for example, to note that 'homosexuality' is listed along with depression and psychopathic tendencies as a 'diagnosis' in one of the early papers. Equally interesting, of course, is that that same paper describes an experiment with LSD as a therapeutic aid – a practice that was by no means unique but that other psychiatrists tend not to talk about.

We do, however, get a profound sense of why experimental therapies were needed. Throughout the world, mental hospitals had become fearsome institutions in which people could be subjected to extreme 'cures' – insulin comas, lobotomies, massive doses of electro-convulsive therapy – with no proven therapeutic value and no concern for the rights and dignity of patients. Asking questions, not just about these practices but about the mechanistic models of the human personality that made them possible, was a moral duty.

And even more of a duty in Ireland than elsewhere. Ivor Browne was one of the first people to point out, in papers re-published here, that Ireland locked up a larger proportion of its population in mental hospitals than any other known society. In 1955, when he was just beginning on his journey in psychiatry, Ireland had 710 psychiatric beds per 100,000 people; the Soviet Union had 617; the United States 511; Northern Ireland 440; Scotland 436; Sweden 422; England and Wales 357 and Australia 332.

Browne captures here the sheer, dehumanising awfulness of what this meant for so many vulnerable people: 'When, in 1958, I first visited St Brendan's, the main mental hospital serving the greater Dublin area, I was appalled by what I found. All kinds of human beings jumbled in to-gether, the severely mentally handicapped, the epileptic, the frail elderly and severely disturbed, were all herded together in overcrowded wards often containing a hundred or more patients.'

At the heart of Ivor Browne's writing, there is compassion for people such as the 2,000 souls crowded into St Brendan's. But there is also the prophetic perception that this locking away of unwanted citizens (one per cent of the entire population was housed in mental hospitals, Magdalene laundries and industrial schools) did not make the rest of society healthy. Browne is in the tradition of Sigmund Freud in seeing the repression of unwanted memories or ideas as lying at the root of illness: 'the more society tries to get rid of something which is a part of itself and sweep it under the carpet, the more that problem will grow.' Looking back from 2013, it is easy to see all of this institutional incarceration as a way not of healing Irish society but of keeping it sick. But Ivor Browne was one of the people who saw – and said – this at the time.

Browne's raw compassion was allied to something else that shines through these pages – his sense of social justice. He spent fifty years as that most unfashionable of things – a public servant. In 1966, he became chief psychiatrist with what was then the Dublin Health Authority and a year later Chair of Psychiatry in University College Dublin. The normal path for him to follow would have been to exploit the opportunity thus created for lucrative and prestigious private practice. He chose instead to devote himself to the dismantling of the model of institutional care and to developing, against all the odds of official neglect, a community mental health service. (Apart from everything else, these papers also provide an insight into the institutional and political culture of the country: 'in Ireland, the adoption of a report does not mean any commitment of resources or real intent to implement its plans.')

That broad shift from big institutions to care in the community was, in the 1960s and 1970s, part of the mainstream international trend. It made Ivor Browne an important pioneer but still a broadly orthodox figure. What is really distinctive about him, however, is that he did not simply switch off his critical mind when the idea of 'community care' became standard official thinking. He challenges that model with the same courage and clarity – and the same core concern for the human beings caught up in the system – he had previously brought to bear on the old and discredited institutions.

Part of the 'slow learning' we can trace here is the realization that the mental hospital was not just a place apart: 'I thought that these human beings were simply forgotten by the world and did not realize that the mental hospital was intimately connected with so-called 'normal' society.'

From this stems one of Browne's most courageous contentions: his challenge to a simplistic notion that the aim of all treatment must be to get people back to a 'norm' which is defined by an ideal of family life in the community. On the contrary, he suggests that this aim can be both unrealistic and counter-productive. Unrealistic because so many people with mental illness do not in fact have 'normal' family lives. And counter-productive because, as he puts it, it means 'people in their twenties, thirties or even forties returning to ageing parents and to a setting where they have always been treated (and have behaved) as small children, locked once again into a parent–child relationship that was a major factor in producing their psychiatric breakdown in the first place'.

Everything in Browne's writing is rooted in a passionate belief in human dignity, expressed in his terms through the notion of a mature, independent human self. The Irish political philosopher Philip Pettit has defined freedom as 'non-domination', the state of not being subject to the arbitrary will of another. For Pettit, this is the core of what it means to be a citizen of a republic. Ivor Browne expresses at the micro level of the individual person what Pettit points to at the macro, political level. For him, too, mental health is a condition of 'non-domination'. At the heart of Browne's approach to psychiatry is the idea of arrested development, the belief that illness arises 'when the natural drive to mature, to become independent and self-directing, is frustrated'.

The most uncomfortable thought that Browne utters is that there is no easy distinction between families and institutions. 'Institutionalization is not just to do with large anonymous impersonal environments; the essence of it is whether you are able to run your own life or whether others are running it for you. If you hold up that criterion, then you will see true institutionalization happening right in the middle of families just as much as in mental hospitals.'

This is not a defence of large psychiatric hospitals (Browne did more than anyone else to empty those institutions in Ireland.) And it is not an attack on family life. It is, rather, a radical statement about what mental health looks like. It is not a utopian state of blessed-out happiness. It is simply the capacity to run one's life. Just as a republic is a state which allows us to run our collective lives with dignity and autonomy, mental health is a state which allows us to run our personal lives with dignity and autonomy. Browne is, in other words, a republican of the mind.

It follows from this that a model of psychiatry which relies only on the administration of drugs cannot succeed, a position that accounts for Browne's marginalization within psychiatry. He is not a psycho-pharmaceutical Luddite: he acknowledges that 'many of the psycho-active drugs are very useful'. He merely says that 'the full answer can never be pharmaceutical'. True healing cannot be administered in chemical doses but must involve 'psychotherapeutic and educative work to give a person competence for living and bring them to a state of independence'. It also follows that people who are mentally ill cannot be cured – they can only be helped to heal themselves. 'There is,' he writes, 'one universal limitation on any form of psychotherapeutic endeavour, that is the willingness and commitment of the person to go through the pain and suffering which is an inevitable part of any real therapeutic life change.'

In this, Browne's compassion is of the hard variety. It is tough love. He does not believe that people – and by implication societies – can get better because a great expert makes them so or because science suddenly solves the conundrums of the mind. 'Even at its simplest, any change involves two things – work and suffering. The deeper the change to be accomplished, the greater the amount of work and effort, pain and suffering, involved. People resist change for this very reason, even when they realize that change will have a positive benefit. Because of the mechanistic attitudes which have accompanied the enormous advances of science and technology, the western mind has succumbed to the illusion that there is a remedy for every ill and we expect to be able to avail of this without any effort or suffering on our part whatsoever.'

This message had a particular social resonance in the Ireland of the Celtic Tiger years. In a prescient talk given to the Irish Management Institute in 2001 and included here, Browne applies his idea of maturity and responsibility to the freedom that Ireland had gained by throwing off institutional repression and by achieving economic prosperity. He warns that 'the other face of freedom is responsibility for our behaviour and how we manage our newfound affluence'. He warned, too, of the 'arrogant, selfish, individualistic behaviour' that was a product of the boomtime ideology of letting it rip.

That behaviour had dire long-term consequences and it is interesting that Irish people now routinely use the term 'madness' when they describe those years. If there was, indeed, a kind of collective mental breakdown, there must also be a kind of collective cure. Ivor Browne's writings over fifty years tell us that we should not expect that cure to be delivered by some Messiah or to be administered through the drug of a hyped-up market. If we wish to live again in what Ivor Browne defines as mental health – 'a state of independence' – we will have to make it for ourselves. We can, though, take courage from this enlivening encounter with the workings of a free and independent mind.

Introduction

NOT too long ago I was sitting in my office looking for something when I came across this collection of my papers. These are articles on a variety of topics that I have written over the past fifty years. Some have appeared in journals or in the media, but the majority have never been published anywhere, and were often put together for talks or lectures that I had to give.

Looking through them, I thought to myself, what is the good of keeping all these old papers, stretching back over the years; it's time for me to throw them out and get rid of them once and for all. However, it's hard just to throw away what has been, after all, a major part of one's life.

Then a solution presented itself. I thought, I'll send them down to Cork University Press – who published my book *Music and Madness* – and ask them to look at them. Once they tell me they are not fit to publish, I'll let them get rid of them. To my great surprise and dismay, they wrote to say that they would like to publish them; not to try to edit and bring them up to date, but simply to deal with them as a historical record and publish them in chronological order, insofar as this is possible. So that is how I come to be writing this introduction.

When I wrote *Music and Madness*, part of my motivation, as well as attempting a critique of the current state of psychiatry, was to rid myself of all the garbage of my past. Now these papers have placed one further impediment in my path, but my ultimate purpose hasn't changed and I am still resolved, once these papers are published, to finally let go of the past, to come into the present and to celebrate just 'being' and, for the few years remaining to me, take each day as a blessing.

Whatever about that, now looking back, it was in 1956 that I commenced my first job in psychiatry in the Warneford Hospital in

Oxford. This was a small, fairly typical, conservative, British mental hospital, with an orthodox view of psychiatry as a medical speciality, believing that mental illness is just like any other illness and that it would eventually be shown to have an organic basis. I didn't feel that I gained much useful understanding from this psychiatric exposure.

There were two aspects of my experience there, however, that did have a profound effect on me. The Warneford had been a private psychiatric hospital, which had a tradition of serving Oxford University. By the time I went to work there it had been incorporated into the new National Health Service and was a public hospital, but the tradition of relating to the university still continued, and virtually all the patients were either students or academic staff of the university. Meeting these people was a revelation to me. To describe this awakening, I cannot do better than quote what I wrote in my book *Music and Madness* about this:

> Because of the attitude and derived thinking in the education system in Ireland . . . when I was growing up, I had always assumed that if any question arose, someone in authority would give you the answer. Until I came to Oxford it had never dawned on me that one could think independently about the nature of reality or come up with solutions oneself. But here in this hospital I was dealing with people who, although they were labelled as patients, had been selected as the most brilliant academics or students from schools all over Britain and elsewhere. Their attitude seemed to be starkly different. If a question arose, they asked themselves 'what do I think about it?' This struck me like a bolt from the blue and I began to think: 'if they can think for themselves, independently, why can't I do the same?' From that moment on, I began to think for myself, never again being willing just to accept, unquestioningly, the views of others.

There was an elderly psychoanalyst who was only there on sufferance because he was a friend of the medical superintendent of the hospital. He, too, gave me quite a different view of emotional disturbance as an understandable and adaptive response to traumatic and painful experiences. To quote once again what I said about this in my book, he

> was completely at variance with the conservative and orthodox views of the rest of the staff there. He gave me one piece of

advice that I never forgot: 'Don't accept any of the current theories or belief systems in psychiatry. Keep an open mind and
listen to the patients themselves. Eventually you will form your
own opinion about these questions.'

He also gave me a further useful word of advice, which is more
germane to our discussion here: that I should use every opportunity
that presents itself to start writing papers. I have often passed on this
advice to young training psychiatrists but they don't always hear it. I
have found that, if they don't start writing early in their training, they
seldom take it up afterwards, and lose a valuable opportunity to
develop their ideas and advance their career. I didn't actually write any
paper during that year, however, but in my next job, when I returned
to Ireland and was working in St John of God psychiatric hospital in
Dublin in 1957–8, I wrote a paper on 'The Acute Withdrawal Phase
in Alcoholism', which was published in *The Lancet*. This was a joint
effort with the consultant under whom I was working at the time, Dr
John Ryan. The psychoactive drugs were just coming in at the time
and we worked out a regime for helping to detoxify those who were in
the acute phase of withdrawal from alcohol. A paper of this standard
would not be published nowadays in a prestigious journal like *The
Lancet*, but it wasn't a bad effort for the time.

Looking back over these papers they seem, at first sight, to be just
a conglomeration of unrelated topics with little evidence of any relationship between them. However, on re-reading them I discern that
there is after all, at a deeper level, a theme running through most, if
not all, of them. Indeed, there are really three main aspects of this
central theme that are all interrelated. Over the years in writing these
various papers I was not fully conscious of this.

From what the physicists tell us, it seems that, at the most fundamental level, everything is interrelated and all that exists is energy
but, as the universe formed itself, subatomic particles began to separate out. These combined to form atoms and these in turn coalesced
into all kinds of molecules, until eventually life forms appeared. As
the universe and life has evolved, this movement can be discerned at
every level. A single entity – an atom, a molecule, a cell – replicates
itself or combines with others to form a multiple, and this then
further evolves to emerge as a unity at the next level, and so it goes
on. This is the underlying theme I feel I have been struggling to
understand for most of my life and it appears in various ways in most

of these papers: unity leading to diversity, then diversity leading to unity, at every stage.

For me this began, I believe, as part of my own difficult struggle to achieve some independence during adolescence from my over-involved parents, and to get some idea of who or what I was. Then, as a psychiatrist, I came across the same problem in most of the people coming to me for help, the struggle to achieve some independence and personal autonomy in their lives and to separate from their family of origin. Then I gradually came to realize that this is not just happening to individuals but at every level, from the family, out to society, and ultimately to the biosphere and beyond.

As I said, there appear to be three main aspects that relate to this theme: firstly, there is the importance of 'boundedness' – that is, the management of the 'boundary' around any living system; secondly, the question of 'responsibility' for all that is within us, and how evil only arises when we fail to take responsibility for both the positive and negative aspects of what we are – what Carl Jung referred to as the shadow side of ourselves; thirdly, there is our relationships with others, and with the surrounding environment.

A number of these papers represent my attempts over the years to examine these different aspects of this central theme, to look at the different levels of living system, from the individual to the family, and out to the various types of human organization that characterize our chaotic society at the present time. Related to this, in the paper 'The Madness of Genius', I tried to examine the nature of intuition, creativity and divergent thinking.

Then there are also a number of papers that relate, more specifically, to mental health. Several of these are concerned with the way psychotherapy works and with the importance of trauma in the causation of emotional distress, my concept of 'unexperienced experience' (unassimilated happenings), and how such experiences can be integrated to become memory. These may be of more interest to those working in psychiatry and related fields, as well as to those who have suffered at the hands of psychiatrists and are trying to free themselves from psychiatric medications and the damaging side-effects of such drugs. There are also a couple of letters to *The Irish Times* in answer to a debate on the question 'What is mental illness?' and another in response to a debate about the presumed efficacy of electroconvulsive therapy (ECT). Some of these papers will only be of historical interest but I felt they were worth including for that reason.

There are several papers that arose out of the work of the Irish Foundation in Derry in regard to the Troubles in the North of Ireland.

Finally there are a group of papers relating mainly to the question of spirituality, with which I have been increasingly involved for the past thirty years. Late in the day I have realized that our central purpose in this life is to try to learn not only to love but to 'become' love to the greatest extent possible.

1. The Management of the
Acute Withdrawal Phase in Alcoholism

IVOR W. BROWNE, JOHN P.A. RYAN
AND S. DESMOND MCGRATH

In Dublin in 1957–58, I wrote a paper on 'The Acute Withdrawal Phase in Alcoholism', which was published in *The Lancet*, 9 May 1959. This was a joint effort with the consultant under whom I was working at the time – Dr John Ryan.

Psychoactive drugs were just coming in and we worked out a regime for helping to detoxify those who were in the acute phase of withdrawal from alcohol.

THE alcoholic in an acute toxic state following prolonged excess is an unpleasantly familiar problem. We have been unfavourably impressed by the frequently vague and haphazard treatment of such cases in general hospitals, and even in specialized centres.

Standard textbooks tend to dismiss the management of the acute toxic withdrawal phase with references to small doses of insulin, paraldehyde sedation, and the use of concentrated vitamins (Mayer-Gross *et al.* 1954; Sargant and Slater 1954; Brain 1955; Cecil and Loeb 1955; Henderson and Gillespie 1955; Price 1956). The current literature of the subject varies widely in its approach, and there is what appears to us a mistaken preoccupation with single therapeutic agents such as chlorpromazine (Sainz 1957), promazine (Figurelli 1956), corticotrophin (Smith 1950), reserpine (Avol and Vogel 1955; Carey 1955) and vitamins (Armstrong and Gould 1955).

Most alcoholics present themselves for treatment only when drinking has become a pressing problem through extreme excess, when trauma or infection has supervened, or when long-continued indulgence has dangerously undermined health. Any uncertainty or hesitation in instituting effective treatment at this critical point may result in dangerous or even fatal complications, such as delirium tremens, status epilepticus or pneumonia. It may be valuable, therefore, if we describe a regime that we have found effective.

1

Development of Method

This regime was first used in this hospital early in 1955. For withdrawal symptoms, preliminary American reports (Cummins and Friend 1954; Aivazien 1955; Mitchell 1955; Schultz *et al.* 1955) had emphasized the advantages of chlorpromazine over the more established forms of sedation. We were impressed by its effectiveness, but we found that it gave still more favourable results if combined with a barbiturate.

The importance of vitamins in cerebral metabolism had become increasingly evident and Gould (Gould 1953, 1954; Armstrong and Gould 1955) had demonstrated that patients in toxic states responded to large doses of the B group with vitamin C. When a highly concentrated vitamin preparation for intravenous administration (parentrovite: 20ml. contains B_1 500mg, B_2 8mg, nicotinamide 380mg, pyridoxine 100mg, calcium pantothenate 10mg., dextrose 2g, and ascorbic acid 1000mg) became available, we tried it by itself and in conjunction with chlorpromazine and barbiturates. The results obtained with the combination were much better than those achieved using the vitamin preparation by itself.

This tentative approach led to the evolution of a well-defined regime which has remained essentially unaltered for the past three years. As the use of chlorpromazine was followed by jaundice in two cases, and as there was often severe pain at the site of its injection, a more recent phenothiazine derivative (promazine, 'Sparine') has been used instead. This is apparently free of these disadvantages (Fazekas *et al.* 1956; Mitchell 1956).

This method has now been employed in the management of 313 alcoholics suffering from severe withdrawal symptoms.

Method

A careful history is taken from a relative or friend and a physical examination of the patient is made. No alcohol is given after admission to hospital.

First 24 hours

An initial injection of 100mg promazine and 4g pentobarbitone is administered by the deep-intramuscular route into the buttock using separate syringes and needles (because mixture of these drugs causes

2

precipitation). Following this, 20ml parentrovite is injected intravenously. These do not normally take effect for about 30 minutes, and during this period the patient is encouraged to eat a light meal with liberal fluids. In view of the deep sedation normally produced, antibiotic cover is given as a routine, usually as 500,000 units of crystalline penicillin intramuscularly.

Injections of pentobarbitone, promazine and penicillin similar to the first are repeated after 8 and 16 hours, making three injections in all. The patient is kept propped up by pillows and is roused 4-hourly. Fluids are encouraged, to achieve a total intake of 2.5 litres in 24 hours.

Second 24 hours

Clinical improvement should now be definite, and intramuscular sedation is stopped. Pentobarbitone 3g and promazine 100mg are continued by mouth thrice daily. Antibiotics are now discontinued and a further intravenous injection of parentrovite 20ml is given. The patient is allowed to sit up and is permitted to visit the toilet. He is encouraged to take a light and nourishing diet. Should sedation at night be necessary, an additional 3g of pentobarbitone is given.

Third 24 hours

On the morning of the third day, the patient is usually anxious to be allowed up. He is encouraged to undertake light tasks about the ward and to mix with the other patients. Sedation is further reduced to sodium amylobarbitone 1g and promazine 50mg t.d.s. Parentrovite 20ml is given intravenously.

Fourth 24 hours

The patient is permitted to take part in all ward activities and to engage in occupational therapy. No more barbiturates are given and the dose of promazine is reduced to 25mg t.d.s. A concentrated vitamin preparation by mouth is substituted for the intravenous preparation (we use 'Omnivite', two tablets t.d.s.) and the patient is now ready for more specific treatment of his alcoholism. Promazine is discontinued after another day, while vitamin therapy is continued for 7 or 10 days.

The regime described above is adequate for the severe and chronic alcoholic but occasionally one may meet a patient in whom infection of the respiratory tract, trauma or mental and physical exhaustion has supervened. This situation may be followed by the appearance of alcoholic hallucinosis, toxic confusion, delirium tremens, or epileptiform convulsions. During the most dangerous period, 36–48 hours after admission, particular care should be taken, and the routine may be modified as follows:

1. The usual 24-hour period of intramuscular sedation is extended to 48 hours.
2. Parentrovite 20ml is given intravenously 12-hourly instead of 24-hourly.
3. Antibiotic cover is continued for 72 hours or longer, and if necessary is modified to deal with the particular infecting organism.
4. Corticotrophin 25 i.u. 8-hourly is given intramuscularly if alcoholic hallucinosis, toxic confusion, or delirium tremens has supervened. This is normally continued for 36 hours and then the dosage is gradually reduced.

In the present series, we admitted twelve such complicated cases. Ten were suffering from delirium tremens, one from status epilepticus and one from lobar pneumonia. A further ten cases became complicated during the first 72 hours after admission. Six developed lobar pneumonia, three delirium tremens and one major epileptic attacks.

Discussion

The physiological mechanisms underlying alcoholic withdrawal symptoms have not yet been fully determined, although several have been implicated. Thus, the combustion of carbohydrate by the brain may be impaired because of the deficiency of vitamins which are essential coenzymes in cerebral metabolism (Gould 1953; Armstrong and Gould 1955). There may be sudden failure of a partially successful abnormal pattern of cerebral metabolism which depends on the combustion of alcohol (Armstrong and Gould 1955). A further possibility is a sudden increase of cerebral irritation to critical levels. Our therapeutic approach has a twofold aim:

1. The restoration of normal cerebral metabolism by administering concentrated vitamins (with particular emphasis on the B group and vitamin Q and giving a rapidly utilized carbohydrate).
2. The control of cerebral irritation by adequate sedation. The use of corticotrophin is based on the hypothesis that delirium tremens is similar biochemically to addisonian crisis and is an

4

expression of adrenocortical exhaustion in response to continued stress (Smith 1950).

Our regime makes the withdrawal phase smooth and rapid and entails the minimum risk and discomfort to the patient. On the fourth day after admission, he is ambulant, non-toxic and fit for psychological therapy.

Our ten cases who were admitted in delirium tremens had all been suffering from this condition for 24 to 72 hours before admission. All responded well to the modified system of treatment (within 24 hours in most cases) and all were ambulant on the fourth day after admission. The three cases which developed delirium tremens in hospital did equally well. Five of the six cases of pneumonia occurred during the period before the administration of penicillin during the first 24 hours was made a routine procedure; all cleared up uneventfully with antibiotics.

It is noteworthy that, of the 313 cases treated, we admitted only ten who developed complications and none of these complications proved serious. Twenty-one out of the total of twenty-two cases considered to be complicated were ambulant on or before the sixth day after admission.

We have also found this regime very effective in the management of withdrawal symptoms in pethidine and morphine addiction, but our series of cases is small.

Summary

We have treated 313 cases of acute alcoholic withdrawal symptoms using a method which is reasonably simple, safe and satisfactory. The emphasis of our regime is on sedation with chlorpromazine and barbiturates, and large doses of a concentrated vitamin preparation; antibiotics are also given at first. Twenty-two of our cases were complicated by pneumonia, delirium tremens or epilepsy but our regime can be modified to deal with these, and none of the complications proved serious.

References

Aivazien, G.H. *Dis. Nerv. System*, 31, 57, 1955.
Armstrong, R.W., and Gould, J. *J. Ment. Sci.*, 101, 70, 1955.

Avol, M., and Vogel, P.J. *J. Amer. Med. Ass.*, 159, 1516, 1955.

Brain, W.R. *Diseases of the Nervous System*, London, 1955.

Carey, E.P. *Ann. N.Y. Acad. Sci.*, 61, 222, 1955.

Cecil, R.L., and Loeb, R.F. *Textbook of Medicine*, Philadelphia, 1955.

Cummins, J.F., and Friend, D.G. *Amer. J. Sci.*, 227, 561, 1954.

Fazekas, J.F., Shea, J., and Rea, E. *J. Amer. Med. Ass.*, 161, 46, 1956.

Figurelli, F.A. *J. Amer. Med. Ass.*, 162, 935, 1956.

Gould, J. *Lancet*, i, 570, 1953.

Gould, J. *Proc. R. Soc. Med.*, 47, 215, 1954.

Henderson, D., and Gillespie, R.D. *Textbook of Psychiatry*, London, 1955.

Mayer-Gross, W., Slater, E., and Roth, M. *Clinical Psychiatry*, London, 1954.

Mitchell, E.H. *Amer. J. Med. Sci.*, 229, 363, 1955.

—. *J. Amer. Med. Ass.*, 161, 44, 1956.

Price, W.F. *Textbook of the Practice of Medicine*, London, 1956.

Sainz, A.A. *Psychiat. Quart.*, 31, 275, 1957.

Sargant, W., and Slater, E. *Physical Methods of Treatment in Psychiatry*, Edinburgh, 1954.

Schultz, J.D., Rea, E.L., Fazekas, J.F., and Shea, J.C. *Quart. J. Stud. Alc.*, 16, 245, 1955.

Smith, J.J. *Quart. J. Stud. Alc.*, 11, 190, 1950.

2. An Experiment with a Psychiatric Night Hospital

JOSHUA BIERER AND
IVOR W. BROWNE

The article 'An Experiment with a Psychiatric Night Hospital' was included in the Proceedings of the Royal Society of Medicine in late 1959. It was written in conjunction with Joshua Bierer (1901–84), founder and long-time editor of the *International Journal of Social Psychiatry*. Bierer also pioneered the concepts of psychotherapy and the therapeutic community and founded the Marlborough Day Hospital in London.

EIGHTY million working days are lost in Great Britain every year due to psychiatric illness; in comparison, only seven million working days are lost through strikes. In 1952 a pilot project was established to determine how many working days could be saved by providing psychiatric treatment during the night for those patients who are still at work but in imminent need of help.

The night hospital occupies part of the premises of the Marlborough Day Hospital. It consists of three three-bed rooms and one single bedroom (used for emergencies or as a treatment room), one small surgery for the sister, a dining-kitchen, bathroom and two lavatories. It functions five nights a week from 6pm to 9am. One consultant psychiatrist is responsible for three nights and a second for two nights of the week. Each consultant has a registrar working with him. The registrar is not resident but is on call after he leaves at 10pm. One sister works two full nights (from 6pm to 9am) and two evenings (from 6pm to 10pm). A second sister works one full night and two nights from 10pm to 9am. A nursing orderly works three nights from 7pm to 11pm, and a ward orderly, who is responsible for the preparation of dinner and breakfast, for twenty hours a week.

The Experiment

Of the total number of 218 patients treated in two years, 76 were emergency cases (i.e. those kept in the hospital for one or two nights either as a safety measure or as part of their treatment, of which only five were kept for five nights) and fifty-four were treated with LSD and with individual psychotherapy by a consultant psychiatrist. He chose to treat the young to middle-aged and mainly professional men and women of good intelligence, personality and motivation, diagnosed as suffering from psychoneurosis.

The remainder were the more chronic patients, including the psychotic or the psychopath. To treat the latter type of patient with LSD appeared – according to literature – inadvisable, contra-indicated or even dangerous. Hoch *et al.* (1952) report that the mental symptomatology of schizophrenic patients was markedly aggravated by Methedrine and lysergic acid, and that they disorganized the psychic integration of a schizophrenic much more than that of a normal person.

Working Hypothesis

We thought this so-called 'disorganization of the psychic integration' must be a temporary removal of the ego-defences and possibly could be used therapeutically. It was presumed that group participation might provide the atmosphere of security and belonging in which the sensitized patient could achieve a deeper degree of insight. It was therefore decided to combine LSD, or LSD plus Methedrine, with group psychotherapy. The plan was to run several consecutive groups, two of which should meet five nights a week for the first four weeks, two for three nights a week, two for two nights a week and one for one night a week. The seven groups involved a membership of 103 patients but, as the sixth and seventh groups are still running, the report is confined to the first five groups, with a total membership of seventy-five. Tables I–III show the diagnosis, duration of symptoms and work distribution in the various groups.

TABLE I. DIAGNOSIS
Groups

	1	2	3	4	5	Total
Schizophrenia and advanced schizoid states	4	6	7	7	5	30
Depression	4	3	2	1	0	10
Psychopath	2	2	1	2	4	11
Hysteria	1	1	2	1	3	8
Anxiety	1	3	2	1	2	9
Homosexuality	1	2	0	0	4	7
Total	13	17	14	13	18	75

TABLE II. DURATION OF SYMPTOMS
Groups

	1	2	3	4	5	Total
Lifelong	1	4	4	6	5	20
Over 10 years	6	5	4	3	6	24
5–10 years	5	7	5	3	5	25
1–5 years	1	1	1	1	2	6
Total	13	17	14	13	18	75

TABLE III. WORK DISTRIBUTION
Groups

	1	2	3	4	5	Total
At beginning of treatment						
Working	9	11	9	5	9	43
Not working	4	6	5	8	9	32
Total	13	17	14	13	18	75
During treatment						
Got a job	3	5	0	1	6	15
Gave up work	0	1	2	0	1	4

The original policy of opening the night hospital only for patients in full-time employment was modified to admit a certain number of patients who were not working.

Objects of the Investigation

There were five main objectives of the investigation:

1. To discover whether it was contraindicated to give LSD plus Methedrine to the chronic patients, including psychotics, psychopaths and the emotionally immature.

In spite of the severity of illness there were no accidents, except for one girl who committed suicide, not under the influence of LSD, but on impulse in reaction to an unhappy love affair. On the other hand, for a long time we successfully supported a number of suicidal patients, including one who was a hopeless drug addict. He said that the group experience kept him going and that he was happier than he had ever been before, but when the group discontinued he relapsed and was transferred to a mental hospital, and later committed suicide.

Indications for LSD in this type of patient depended on: (a) the strong group cohesion which acted as a support; (b) the therapist's awareness of the psychopathology of the patient and his good relations with him; (c) the interruption of treatment with Largactil and, in some cases, hospitalization for 24 hours if necessary; (d) not giving LSD to a reluctant patient.

2. To find out if such a combination of treatments can be used with reasonable success with such chronic patients.

Even those patients who were working had manifested chronic symptoms for years. Of the seventy-five patients in the first five groups, none had shown symptoms for less than one year, only six for from one to five years and forty-four patients had had persistent symptoms for more than ten years.

TABLE IV. RESULTS
Groups

	1	2	3	4	5	Total
Stopped treatment	0	3	2	3	2	10
Suicide	0	0	0	0	1	1
Sent to mental hospital	2	2	2	1	0	7
Not improved	1	2	5	8	4	20
Slightly improved	0	3	1	1	2	7
Improved	7	5	3	0	5	20
Much improved	3	2	1	0	4	10
Total	13	17	14	13	18	75

Table IV shows that Group 4 produced no results and Group 3 small results. It was at first presumed that Group 1 produced better results because they met five times a week in the first month but Group 4 did not confirm this.

3. The third objective, regarding the optimum number of meetings a week, must be left unanswered for the time being.

4. To assess the effect of the constitution of a group on the curative result. Further work is necessary but it is clear that to include 50% of schizophrenics in a group markedly reduces the chances of success.

5. To find the optimum number for this particular kind of group. There was no general optimum, but each psychiatrist had *his* own optimum with each particular type of method of group treatment. The optimum for the therapist conducting this experiment was between twelve and fourteen members.

Effect

LSD acts as a strong disinhibiting factor, revealing material and traumata that have been deeply buried for a very long time.

An illustration is a young woman who, four years ago, at the age of twenty, married a man whom she loved very much. She wanted to have a family but whenever her husband approached her she experienced a complete vaginismus and it was impossible to consummate the marriage. She had prolonged outpatient treatment with drugs and psychotherapy without result and analytic treatment in our hospital did not unearth any relevant subconscious factor. However, under LSD in the presence of the whole group she disclosed that she had a great shock when she had a haemorrhage in school at the age of nine (i.e. experiencing an early menstruation without any preparation). A further shock occurred when her mother, who was sent for, told her: 'You will bleed like this throughout your life.' She interpreted this literally. Her mother also said: 'You must never go near a man.' After revealing this to herself and the group she became extremely vivacious and eloquent, and attempted to undress and make love to the therapist before the whole group, shouting continuously: 'I want my husband, I want my husband.' After another fortnight of syntho-analytic treatment the marriage was consummated, and she and her husband are now happily settled.

11

The second function of LSD is that it helps to produce an unusually intense, intimate and well-knit group atmosphere, which can help even those patients who have not taken LSD.

A woman of forty-two had been in a mental hospital four times and contends that her relapses occurred because, after the protection of hospital, she was unable to adapt to normal conditions. In the group she found the atmosphere and the support she needed. She has remained well for two years, held a responsible job, made good social relationships for the first time since her original illness and is engaged to be married. She feels that her greater stability has been achieved as the result of being part of the treatment group and that, through this, her last discharge from hospital was successful.

Another instance of a patient who had not taken LSD but was helped by the group atmosphere was a man of thirty-seven. He was referred to us complaining of irritability and inability to relax at intervals for the past six years, following an attack of viral pneumonia. Recently he had been upset by the noise of the four children at home and for six weeks had been living in quiet lodgings but he had not improved. This case has been puzzling. It was significant that this man had great control over a very strong temper and that he always left the room after a disagreement with his wife. It became clear to the group that he left his home and family because subconsciously he was afraid that he would no longer be able to control his temper. This assumption seemed confirmed when he told us spontaneously that his only friends were three convicted murderers, which influenced our decision to abstain from giving him LSD. The patient maintains that the group helped him to open up. He had always been a very silent man, unable to express himself, but now he can talk with his wife for hours on end. He has returned home and is happily settled there and in his work.

There are a number of patients who refuse LSD and there are some on whom LSD appears to have no effect. 'Burnt-out' schizophrenics fall into the latter category. There are others who react in a variety of ways where the therapeutic value must be considered doubtful. These patients may experience a distortion of colour, sound, time and of their own figures, or they may live through wonderful fantasies.

Finally, there is the case where it was difficult to define which factor produced an unexpected result (the abreaction or specific insight she gained from LSD), the atmosphere of the group, a strong attachment to the therapist, some other factor, or a combination of all these factors. This patient was a young woman of thirty. She had had three dreadful experiences in her life. She had been seduced by her father, been let down by a married man, and a priest with whom she was having an affair had died in her arms. She became a nun but after seven years had a schizophrenic breakdown. She was released from her vows and was so ill that she entered a mental hospital six times in five years. She now appears to be completely different. She is not only free of her symptoms and feeling well but is, for the first time in her life, holding down a responsible job.

Conclusion

We believe that the night hospital, although still in the experimental stage, is an important aspect of the part-time psychiatric service. The use of LSD as part of an active and interpretative dynamic psychotherapy seems to be indicated in acute neurotic cases and with some sexual difficulties. The experiment in LSD as part of individual and group psychotherapy in psychotic cases seems to be encouraging enough to be continued on an experimental basis. As to the use of LSD plus individual and group psychotherapy in chronic psychopathic and emotionally immature cases, nothing definite can yet be stated. There is no contraindication where LSD cannot be given, if certain precautions are taken. LSD should not be considered as a treatment in itself but as part of a system of treatment. It is too early to assess the number of working days which were saved. However, our experiment has convinced us that the night hospital can prevent some patients from experiencing breakdown by allowing them to remain at work and does not jeopardize their chance of promotion through absenteeism and the stigma connected with mental illness.

References

Becker, A.N. *Wien. Z. Nervenheilk.*, 2, 402, 1949.
Busch, A.K., and Johnson, W.C. *Dis. Nerv. Syst.*, 11, 241, 1950.
Condrau, G. *Acta Psychiat.*, *Kbh.*, 24, 9, 1949.
Deshon, H.J., Rinkel, M., and Soloman, H.C. *Psychiat. Quart.*, 26, 33, 1952.
Fischer, R., Georgi, F., and Weber, R. *Schweiz. Med. Wschr.*, 81, 817, 1951.

Forrer, G.R., and Goldner, R.D. *Arch. Neurol.Psychiat., Chicago,* 65, 581, 1951.

Frederking, W. J. *Nerv. Ment. Dis.,* 121,262, 1955.

Giacomo, U. de. *I Congr. Mondial Psychiat.* (Paris, 1950), 3, 236, 1952.

Hoch, P.H., Catiell, J.P., and Pennes, H.H. *Amer. J. Psychiat.,* 108, 685, 1952.

Hurst, L.A., Reuning, H., Van Wyk, A.J., Crouse, H.S., Booysen, P.J., and Nelson, G. *S. Air. J. Lab. Clin. Med.,* 2, 4, 1956.

Liddell, D.W., and Weil-Malherbe, H. *J. Neurol. Psychiat.,* 16, 7, 1953.

Mayer-Gross, W., McAdam, W., and Walker, J.W. *Nature, Lond.,* 168, 827, 1953.

Rinkel, M., Deshon, H.J., Hyde, R.W., and Soloman, H.C. *Amer. J. Psychiat.,* 108, 572, 1952.

Rothlin, E., and Cerletti, A. *Proceedings of the Round Table on 'Lysergic acid diethylamide and mescaline in Experimental Psychiatry',* Pharmacology of LSD-25, Grune & Stratton, New York, 1956.

Sandison, R. A., Spencer, A.M., and Whitelaw, J.D.A. *J. Ment. Sci.,* 100,491.

—, and Whitelaw, J.D.A. *J. Ment. Sci.,* 103, 332, 1954.

Savage, C. *Amer. J. Psychiat.,* 108,896, 1952.

Sloane, B.S., and Doust, J.M.L. *J. Ment. Sci.,* 100, 129, 1954.

Stoll, A., and Hofman, A. *Helv. Chim. Acta,* 26, 944, 1943.

—, Hofman, and Troxler, F. *Helv. Chim. Acta,* 32, 506, 1949.

Discussion

Dr J.T. Robinson (Horsham):

We have had some experience of LSD as an aid to individual psychotherapy but have not used it in group therapy. We became concerned at Roffey Park Rehabilitation Centre with some of the difficult patients – chronic neurotics, chronic psychosomatic disorders and personality disorders – who had received a wide range of treatment at many hospitals and outpatient clinics without any lasting benefit. On the basis of recent reports on LSD in such cases, we have in the past year done over 260 abreactions with doses ranging from 50 to 300μg on patients who were at Roffey Park for seven to twelve weeks. Since we have only been using this therapy for a short time, we can only refer to the immediate clinical results based on the capacity of the individual to go back to work and on symptomatic improvement.

The first problem is how LSD performs its alleged therapeutic role. It is obvious that the drug is a 'deep-seated' abreactive agent; i.e., able to produce the discharge of repressed experiences with an appropriate emotional response. The setting in which this response occurred may be the central reason for any alleged therapeutic value, the core being the relationship between the patient, the therapist and his assistants. In thirty-seven patients who have completed treatment, we have observed three types of reaction:

1. Those who had a good catharsis with the reliving of repressed experiences, twenty-two cases. Of these, twelve were much improved, able to discontinue treatment and to resume normal life on a level equal to that attained prior to illness, including a full return to work. Such patients were considered capable of enjoying all normal social relationships and family life, but only four were completely free from symptoms.
2. Those with unspecified response in which they have been able to express hostility and sibling rivalry without any repressed memories, six cases. Of these, three came into the category of 'greatly improved', with one completely symptom free.
3. Those who responded with no catharsis of any kind other than slight autonomic response and toxic effects, 9 cases. Of these, 4 were 'greatly improved' but only 3 were completely free of symptoms.

It would seem that not all patients who show really marked improvement and freedom from symptoms have a definite catharsis, including the recall of repressed memories with appropriate emotional response. Nor can we understand why some 50% with unspecified responses should get well and be symptom free, though probably factors other than LSD played a significant part. Similarly with those in whom only autonomic and toxic responses were experienced and no catharsis, factors other than LSD are clearly operating to lead to marked improvement in a high proportion of cases. One cannot disregard the fact that in Roffey Park all patients are given a thorough physical examination, that the whole centre is geared to a rehabilitation programme, including occupational therapy and encouragement of social participation of all patients and, in addition, following treatment, psychotherapeutic sessions are held the day after LSD. This must definitely affect the results.

Duration of Symptoms Prior to Admission

Twenty-four patients with symptoms present for between six months and three years prior to admission have completed treatment and been discharged. Of these, 50% were much improved or symptom free.

Those with symptoms of between three to fifteen years' duration number thirteen, and of these four were improved but only 1 was symptom free. Again, these numbers are too small to draw any definite conclusions but they seem to indicate that, the longer the duration of symptoms, the less effect LSD has in leading to a clinical improvement. In the particular group of patients with symptoms of over three years' duration, it is of interest that several produced no 'catharsis' and one of these was symptom free. It seems obvious that the more recent the onset of symptoms, the better are the results, and our impression is that there is considerable doubt as to the value of this treatment.

Dr Ling has emphasized how LSD speeds up the psychotherapeutic process but I am convinced that before any patient is given LSD there must be a thorough anamnesis of all environmental and personal factors. There must also be some understanding by the therapist of the underlying dynamics. Furthermore, it is necessary for the patient to have some intellectual insight through established psychotherapy prior to LSD therapy.

Not all patients benefit from LSD and, while the immediate results may be striking, it is the long-term progress that really matters; in this regard we have had no less than six patients in the last six months who had been given LSD for varying periods prior to admission but were no better as a result of such treatment. One of the difficulties about using LSD is that, like all other abreactive agents, those using it always seem to obtain material that they want and in which they happen to be interested, just as Freud, when he was interested in daughters sleeping with their fathers, got no fewer than tenconsecutive hysterics who remembered such events, which he afterwards realized was, of course, nonsense. Thus I am quite certain that many of the birth fantasies which are being reported are the result of the therapist's suggestion to the patient. It is of interest that we have had no birth experiences in any of our abreacted patients.

Of essential importance in the use of any abreactive drugs is the abreactor rather than the drug itself and this is, I feel, of even more importance in using a drug like LSD. As in every treatment, the attitude of the patient to the treatment is very important and may well determine the results. Also the patient's attitude to the therapist carrying out this role and the therapist's attitude to the patient are important. A further consideration, often overlooked and not measurable, is the intellectual insight which may not be obvious but which has been inculcated to some degree in the patient by previous therapies.

Dr Ling has stressed the importance of motivation and with this I agree. A point which may be relevant is that there is no evidence of the comparable value of LSD in the various social cultures nor between private patients who pay for their treatment and National Health Service patients. Those who can afford to pay for treatment and not have their treatment paid by others are men and women who have shown a capacity to live with their difficulties, indicating a basic stability of personality of some degree, which is important in treatment and is supported by a strong motivation to get well. Such people are seldom basically dependent types but usually have drive and aggression, demanding quick action. They will respond to any form of therapy but whether LSD is better for such patients than any other treatment has not in fact ever been statistically confirmed. The enthusiasm and suggestibility of the doctor using the drug has far more influence on the success of treatment than anything else.

Cases Who Do Not Respond to LSD

Dr Ling has given some contraindications to the use of LSD and to this I would add our experience with certain other types of cases which do not respond well to LSD:

1. One of the most difficult to treat is the patient with acute anxiety symptoms superimposed on a basically passive, dependent personality. Such patients are always insecure and vulnerable and LSD does not help them. In fact, the LSD experience arouses tremendous fears and makes such patients much more distressed and regressed. They can also be made extremely depressed and suicidal.

2. Another type is the long-term, parasitic, hysterical personality with hypochondriasis and paranoid features. Such patients are always demanding but LSD increases this and further stimulates their paranoid features. In fact, such patients should not be given LSD. One case that we had was sent to a mental hospital, where she will remain for a considerable time. There is

an added danger that in such patients the transference situation is very difficult to resolve.

3. The narcissistic, histrionic hysteric who is shy and fearful also regresses and becomes very much more dependent.

Obsessional Neurosis

We are not convinced of the value of LSD in the ritualistic, handwashing or ruminative obsessional neurosis. The characteristic psychopathology of these cases is their chronic inhibition and restriction of any capacity for emotional expression. Such patients are always indecisive, have a tremendous deep-seated hostility which is destructive and terrifying associated with a considerable fear of letting go lest they themselves suffer punishment. This destructiveness is usually directed against near loved ones and is therefore associated with considerable guilt, and there is a related basic incestual attachment to the parent of the opposite sex, jealousy and a desire for the death of the rival of the same sex. There is no doubt in my experience that LSD provides one of the most dramatic abreactions in such patients, to confirm Freud's observations in his classical description of the obsessional syndrome.

I do not consider that LSD has any effect at all on rituals or in assuaging guilt and it is almost folly to give LSD to any obsessional neurotic without a previous long period of psychotherapy based on a 'here and now' relationship and reactions between the patient and the therapist. I very much doubt that these abreactive drugs are short cuts to perform what psychotherapy should do.

We have used LSD alone and LSD with Methedrine and are convinced that Methedrine should never be used with LSD, in any case without a previous trial of LSD alone. The reactions to the combined therapy are always much more severe and the symptoms may be terrifying, not only to the patient but also to the staff dealing with these cases. Such patients, following LSD and Methedrine, require far more attention and reassurance.

LSD has never been compared with other drugs and used in controlled experiments. Until such a study is carried out, and this we are attempting to do at Roffey Park, we have no evidence that LSD has a greater value than other drugs, and at present there is nothing to indicate that it is in any way superior to other abreactive agents.

3. Psychiatry in Ireland

In 1960 I went to the United States on a scholarship to the Harvard School of Public Health. One of the participants in the Mental Health Group was a psychiatrist from India. What interested me was that at that time there were 20,000 mental hospital beds in the Irish Republic for a population of less than 3 million, and in India, where at that time the population was approximately 600 million, there were also 20,000 mental hospital beds. It was this fact that made me decide to write this paper which was published a couple of years later in the *American Journal of Psychiatry*.

SINCE my arrival in the United States, it has been said to me on many occasions: 'So you are a psychiatrist from Ireland. Surely they don't need psychiatrists over there. I thought that life in Ireland was so easy-going they wouldn't have any worries about mental health.'

And yet, when one begins to look more closely at the situation, it is found that approximately seven persons per 1,000 of the population in the Republic of Ireland – for the purposes of this paper, the six northern counties will be excluded – are currently hospitalized for mental illness. This is more than twice as high as the corresponding figure for the United States of 3.61 per 1,000, and is probably the highest figure in the world. An even more startling percentage is to be found in one county in the west of Ireland where 12.3 persons per 1,000 are in mental hospitals; that is more than 1% of the total inhabitants in that area. In a country with a predominantly rural society, where toleration of disturbed behaviour is probably high rather than low, such facts as these hardly suggest that the problem of mental illness is a negligible one or that there is much room for complacency.

Ireland is a small island, the western outpost of Europe – some 300 miles from north to south, nearly 200 miles from east to west. It is a country with an ancient civilization presenting many contrasts between the old and the new, ranging from the inhabitants of a modern European city like Dublin to the nomadic 'travelling' people who roam all over the country and whose way of life has probably changed little in over 1,000 years. In little more than a century, the population of Ireland has fallen from over 8 million to approximately half that number. Although for hundreds of years there has been some emigration, the more recent excessive trend was largely set in motion by the Great Famine of 1845–7, when in barely four years nearly a million people perished from starvation and an even larger number were forced to leave the country. The present population of the Republic of Ireland is just under 3 million (the population of the six northern counties is approximately 1,390,000).

A high rate of emigration alone is not sufficient to explain this marked reduction in population. Another factor is probably the annual marriage rate of 5.3 per 1,000, one of the lowest in the world. Contributing to this is the fact that one-quarter of the population do not marry at all and the average age of those who do is one of the world's highest – thirty-three years for men and twenty-eight years for women. These characteristics too are probably partly a result of the Great Famine, when the Irish people seem to have suffered a profound loss of confidence in the future. Prior to that period they had married at an early age.

In recent years there has been increasing evidence that the tide is turning against such all-pervading pessimism. Under the impetus of a rapidly growing industrialization and an improving economic position, an atmosphere of buoyant optimism is fast replacing the former cynical apathy. Already people are beginning to marry earlier in urban areas, the rate of emigration has fallen markedly in the past two years and a growing number of those who had left the country are returning home. Ireland is now about to enter the *European Common Market* and this will undoubtedly lead to widespread economic and social upheaval. These signs would seem to indicate that the country is approaching a period of rapid social change. This is already being mirrored by an increasing interest in mental health and a feeling that something must be done to provide more adequate psychiatric care. It seems, therefore, an appropriate time to review the current position of mental health services in Ireland.

Historical Background of Health Services

Considerable progress has been made in the past quarter-century in Ireland towards the provision of adequate health services and the achievement of reasonable standards of general health. During this same period, however, there has not been a corresponding activity in the sphere of mental health. Since the end of the Second World Warwhen, for the first time, the Department of Health became a separate entity (1947), a number of urgent health problems have been tackled with considerable success, notably the control of communicable diseases and the development of adequate maternal and child health services. In more recent years, the main emphasis has been placed on a campaign for the eradication of tuberculosis. Large regional sanatoria were erected, in addition to many smaller facilities. While this programme was still being carried out, new powerful anti-tuberculus drugs were introduced, with the result that a number of the newer sanatoria have never been fully occupied at any time since they were built. This lesson should serve as a warning to those who would suggest the construction of large new mental hospitals, for such structures are already contraindicated by present knowledge of the nature of mental illness, and are likely to become even more incongruous in the face of future therapeutic advances.

During the same period, there was an energetic hospital construction programme, as a result of which modern medical and surgical hospitals were erected all over the country. Ireland is now more adequately supplied with general hospitals than almost any other country in Europe. In contrast to this, the mental hospitals are almost without exception old and dilapidated. Although there should not be any shortage of accommodation (seven beds per 1,000 population), these institutions are in fact filled to capacity, and in many cases grossly overcrowded.

Perhaps at this point it is interesting to speculate as to why Ireland should have such a uniquely high mental hospital population. The reason which first suggests itself is that this is due, in large part, to long continued emigration of the more virile, healthy elements of the population. It seems to me, however, that a more likely explanation lies in the fact that the majority of the mental hospitals were built early in the last century, when the population was roughly twice as large as it is today. This, then, would provide an instance of what has often been noted by others: that the more psychiatric facilities there are available, the greater the number of patients who will be found to utilize them. In this way, the existence of a large number of mental hospital beds in a country may have an adverse rather than a positive effect upon mental health. If, as in many countries, an acutely disturbed psychotic can only find accommodation in the local jail he is likely, as soon as the acute episode subsides, to be returned to the community from which he came. Should there be a place for him in the mental hospital, however, he might well (until recently) remain there languishing on a back ward for many years.

Although there was considerable scope for development under the Irish Mental Health Act 1945, not a great deal has in fact been accomplished to date. Until recently, there was not much active treatment carried out in the mental hospitals and, even now, in a number of areas patients are given little more than custodial care. Up to 1945, nineteenth-century definitions, law and procedures still governed the care of the mentally ill. Patients were 'committed' to mental hospitals on warrants signed by peace commissioners, and there was provision for nothing between detention on such warrants and complete freedom. There was a system of 'trial discharge' but this did not work well in practice. The Mental Health Act 1945 (Amend. 1953), was for its time a progressive piece of legislation that made medical personnel responsible for certification of mental patients without resort to judicial process. It is worth noting here that in Britain the Irish Act of 1945 was severely criticized, mainly on the grounds that compulsory detention was effected on medical recommendation alone. It was only some thirteen years later, in 1959, that England and Wales adopted similar measures. The United States has not yet done so.

Present Position of Mental Health Services

In 1959, the total number of patients resident in mental institutions in Ireland was 20,609; of these, 19,590 were under care in the district (state) mental hospitals and 1,019 were resident in private, private charitable, authorized and approved institutions. During the year 1959, 8,569 patients were admitted to the district mental hospitals and, of these, 1666 were over sixty-five years of age. Any attempt at a breakdown into diagnostic categories must necessarily be somewhat inaccurate due to lack of uniform diagnostic criteria being applied in different hospitals. Figures are only available for the district mental hospitals but these are interesting in that they show such a high preponderence of psychotic disorders. It seems that in Ireland mental illness is not likely to come to public attention until it has reached psychotic intensity. Broken down into broad categories, these percentages are shown in Table 1.

TABLE 1.
DIAGNOSTIC CATEGORIES OF PATIENTS IN MENTAL HOSPITALS

Diagnostic Category	% of patients under care on December 1958	% of patients admitted during year ended 31 December 1958
Schizophrenic disorders, paranoid and puerperal psychoses	53.73	31.18
Manic-depressive and involutional disorders	15.53	33.78
Mental deficiency	10.61	3.45
Senile, presenile psychoses, organic & epileptic conditions	15.82	14.56
Neurotic disorders	2.21	9.76
Pathological and immature personality character disorders	1.48	2.00
Alcoholism	0.48	4.99
Drug addiction	0.04	0.24

The average cost of maintaining a patient in a mental hospital per year (estimated for the year ending 31 March 1959) is approximately $600; that is, less than $2 a day. The cost of a more adequate service would undoubtedly be higher if measured in this way over a given time. Of course, this would not necessarily be true if the cost of each patient's illness were measured as a whole, for with more active treatment the duration of complete financial dependence might not be so prolonged. In all events, the present maintenance per patient is extremely low and covers a bare subsistence level. In many instances, the actual living conditions for the patient are literally wretched.

Most of the mental hospitals are overcrowded and the number of well-trained psychiatrists is inadequate although increasing. Other personnel, such as psychologists, psychiatric social workers and occupational therapists, are almost non-existent. Psychiatric nurses are also in short supply and are, for the most part, inadequately trained. In the field of child psychiatry, there is only one child guidance clinic, which is working to full capacity. This is run by a religious order. Another guidance clinic is being organized at a children's hospital in Dublin but is not yet functioning on a full scale. It should be remarked in passing that these clinics follow the traditional pattern for a child guidance clinic in the United States. To my mind, this conception is outmoded, inappropriate and becomes ludicrously expensive when applied to a country such as Ireland.

Preventive psychiatry is almost completely undeveloped. There is little activity going on in the community, and not much work is being done in the area of mental health education. Although a few of the Dublin voluntary hospitals have psychiatric beds, there is no properly developed psychiatric department in a general hospital. An aftercare service has been started in connection with only one mental hospital.

The position with regard to mental retardation is little better. It is estimated that there are at least 2,000 persons in the mental hospitals who are there primarily because of mental retardation. In addition, there are approximately 25,000 mentally handicapped persons in the community, of whom about 7,000 probably require institutional care. To deal with this problem, there are fourteen residential centres, which provide accommodation for only 2,620 persons. With one exception, all these institutions are managed by religious communities. The government has no direct programme in this field.

There are only three active geriatric units in the whole country. Most old people are cared for in the county homes, or in mental hospitals, often under miserable conditions. Otherwise they have to be looked after at home. Efforts are being made at present to improve the county homes but little evidence of this can be seen as yet. There has been some development in the sphere of domiciliary psychiatry. In a number of districts, patients are now seen in their own homes by the psychiatrist or specially selected members of the nursing staff.

This is particularly aimed at the geriatric patients who at present occupy a large number of beds in mental hospitals.

In spite of this on the whole rather gloomy picture, there have been a number of more positive developments in recent years. There are two private mental hospitals in Dublin which have now achieved a high standard, comparing favourably with better psychiatric hospitals in Britain and the USA. The staff of these hospitals carry on active teaching and training programmes. Even in the district mental hospitals there has been a gradual change towards more active treatment. The number of patients admitted on a voluntary basis is increasing; during the year 1959, as many as 58.5% were voluntary. The number of psychiatric outpatient clinics, most of which are conducted by the mental hospitals, has grown rapidly during the past few years. At the end of 1959, there were ninety-two clinics in operation. Plans are now in progress for the opening of two day hospitals with a third to follow.

During the past year, the mental health services were discussed openly in the Dáil (parliament) for the first time. As a result of this, a commission of enquiry has been set up to examine thoroughly the whole problem. A similar commission has already been formed to investigate fully the allied question of mental retardation.

These sporadic but nevertheless quite definite evidences of progress would seem to indicate that the country is approaching a period of more active development in the sphere of mental health. As things stand at present, however, the mental health services in Ireland are in roughly the position of equivalent services in Britain and the United States in the period prior to the Second World War, when psychiatric outpatient treatment was rapidly developing and the whole child-guidance movement was taking shape. There is the important difference, however, that since then knowledge and understanding of the human personality and mental illness generally, as well as methods of treatment, have advanced considerably. A country such as Ireland is now in a position to draw on such experience and, hopefully, to avoid some of the mistakes that have been made by other countries during the past thirty years.

From the evidence produced by the tuberculosis programme in Ireland, it can be learned that the Department of Health is capable of making a concerted drive and investing sufficient capital to bring about significant changes in a particular sector of health. It would seem a pity if, when making efforts to raise the standards of mental health, Ireland were merely to follow slavishly the painful step-by-step progress already gone through by other countries more developed in this field, rather than make a radical departure from traditional faculties and procedures. Perhaps it is possible for a small country, in a relatively short time, to carry out successfully a plan of major development and reorganization within a limited field of health throughout the entire country. In a nation as large as the United States, on the other hand, it takes many years for a major change in the organization of a health service, however desirable, to gather momentum.

References

Hensey, B. *The Health Services of Ireland*, Alex Thorn, Dublin, 1959.

The Problem of the Mentally Handicapped, White Paper, Stationery Office, Dublin, 1960.

Report of the Inspector of Mental Hospitals, Government Publications Sales Office, Dublin, 1957.

Report of the Inspector of Mental Hospitals, Government Publications Sales Office, Dublin, 1959.

US Department of Health, Education and Welfare, Public Health Service, *Report of the Surgeon General's Ad Hoc Committee on Planning for Mental Health Facilities*, Public Health Service Publication 808, Government Printing Office, Washington, DC, 1961.

4. The Dilemma of the Human Family:
A Cycle of Growth and Decline

IVOR W. BROWNE
AND T.J. KIERNAN

The following article, 'The Dilemma of the Human Family: A Cycle of Growth and Decline', is reprinted from the *Journal of the Irish Medical Association*, vol. LX (Jan. 1967), No. 355, p. 1. The co-author is T.J. Kiernan, who was Irish Ambassador to the United States during the presidency of John F. Kennedy. At that time he became interested in the work of Carl Jung and wrote a Jungian commentary study on Irish mythological stories. The commentary was published in his book *The White Hound of the Mountain*. Because of this, he was interested in the whole developmental aspect of the family.

THE living organism is in a constant state of struggle, its situations constantly changing, its efforts for equilibrium continuously operating. When this struggle relaxes, something is wrong. It ceases only with death. The situation of the human family is analogous, with one important difference. The living organism is a unity where cooperation of the parts is normal and easy. The family is a unity of personalities where cooperation is at best an uneasy balance.

Holy scripture promises a reward to children who love their parents but not to parents who love their children. The need for parents to love and, therefore, protect their children furnishes the parent, particularly the mother, with an affective appetite which needs satisfaction through giving love and care to the child. The child's need is of a different order, for security of food, shelter, clothing and such basic necessities. This tapers off as development proceeds and a strong and seemingly genetic appetite makes itself increasingly felt, reaching its full expression as the child emerges into adolescence. This is no less than an appetite for freedom.

It is an appetite or urge not only for the limited measure of freedom meant by non-dependence, but is the mainspring of that idealism which often occurs at adolescence when the human person is endeavouring to make a new and difficult transition from that of dependent childhood to independent manhood and womanhood. This shifting of equilibria runs all through life and is the reason why life and struggle are necessarily co-existent; but in the human person there are certain major shifts which are critical to development (or, in the falling period of life, to decline, which is really another aspect of development, since on our planet growth is dependent on decay and is, therefore, a development from decay).

These major shifts, and in a very particular way the shift of adolescence, must have a marked effect on the family balance. Hence the dilemma of the human family, arising from the fact that the human family is a cycle of growth and decline, each cycle in turn making way for growth of new cycles derived from the original family but separate from it. Just as for the individual, the healthy norm is to 'grow old gracefully' and indeed gratefully, so also for the well-balanced family. So much of mental disorder is blamed on the stress of modern living (which is often, as put by an American beatnik, merely the stress of 'worms living in a jar of warm butter') that it is worth putting the human family dilemma in its wider context. One may go back before and beyond Abel and Cain and have a look at the international significance of the 'stepmother' in folklore. To illustrate from an Irish tale, 'The Golden Apples of Loch Erne', analysed by Heinrich Zimmer (1956): the good wife and mother dies; the king marries again, meaning the introduction of a stepmother for the good boy, who is a potential hero and who very much wants to take up the challenges of life which will make him what he wants to be, a hero. Every boy is a potential hero and every girl is a potential heroine. Likewise, every boy and every girl is good until a 'stepmother' is introduced to create disorder. What the old folk tales tell us is that every mother is a potential stepmother and every father a potential stepfather. The commentary on this tale by Kiernan (1962) in *The White Hound of the Mountain* explains:

> Since Conn's mother is perfect, it is necessary to introduce a crisis to separate him from her. In the original tale, she dies and is replaced by a stepmother. The real crisis, however, is in the forces of masculinity maturing in the boy. Adolescence is the cruel stepmother and in the folk-tale, adolescence is personalized in the negative-mother form, the mother who is no longer the safe bosom of love but the scheming enslaver.

Freud (1920), in introducing his concept of the Oedipus complex, was attempting to describe the same development of conflict but his theory is inadequate in two respects. First, it overemphasizes the sexual aspects, for this struggle is not essentially a sexual matter, although like every human phenomenon it may have sexual overtones. Later he tried to broaden his theory to include the female as well as the male by introducing his Electra complex, but this is even less convincing and there is a sense of desperation in these later attempts to force the full range of human experience into the confines of his original theoretical assumptions.

Secondly, Freud places the struggle back in early childhood and, although he was correct to stress the importance of these early years, it is nevertheless true that the conflict only has its beginning at this stage. It continues to make its presence felt throughout childhood and often reaches its climax at adolescence. In those uncommon instances where the Oedipal struggle appears to be evident in early childhood, it is as a rule forced on the child by very abnormal and immature parents; it is the parents who are the victims of the Oedipal complex rather than the children.

The real struggle which Freud tried to explain in this way is the outcome of the law affecting all living things, the cycle of growth and decay, that the flower must wither and the fruit disintegrate in order that the seed may be released to grow, signalling the beginning of a new cycle.

Universality of the Family

Although the human family can take many and varied forms from country to country and from age to age, there seems now to be fairly general agreement amongst anthropologists that the nuclear family – husband/wife and their immediate offspring – is universal and is to be found in all societies. Murdoch (1949), on the basis of a survey of 250 representative human societies, states: 'The nuclear family is a universal human grouping. Either as the sole prevailing form of the family or as the basic unit from which more complex familial forms are compounded, it exists as a distinct and strongly functional group in every known society.' It seems hardly likely that such a universal institution would exist and have endured throughout thousands of years unless it served some important function. If one looks at human society, it is not difficult to see that, in contradistinction to animals, the part of our cultural heritage transmitted genetically now comprises but a small fraction. Most of what we need to know for modern life comes to us through learning from one generation to the next. The family constitutes the main vehicle for transmission, it is the primary social unit from which all other social institutions have arisen and the fundamentals of learning are laid down within the family circle.

It has been said that in modern times, with the growth of urban life, the part played by the family has become of far less importance and that it is withering away. Closer examination reveals that this is far from the truth: with the decline of rural community and village life, and the weakening of certain forms of the extended family, the nuclear family has assumed a role of greater importance than ever before as the sole link between one generation and the next.

Owing to the complex nature of human society, as well as the greater relative complexity of contemporary human society, the child has to learn and absorb a much greater volume of knowledge than the child of any earlier generation. At the same time it is also true that the human infant is born in a more helpless condition, if you like at a more premature stage, than any other animal. Most other animals can stand or even walk on the day of their birth and after just a few weeks can make a fair attempt at self-preservation. The human infant is completely helpless and absolutely dependent on the care of its parents for several years. The human family, therefore, to fulfil its growth-producing and continuity-of-culture functions, has to endure over many years, to endure and itself undergo internal shifts of attitudes between its members. It requires strong bonds of love and attachment to sustain this organization and provide the necessary stability, elasticity and resilience.

The final aim of all this preparation is to produce an independent, free and self-sufficient human person. Herein lies the dilemma. An institution which has to achieve and maintain such stability over a long period cannot easily break up and relinquish its functions when the time comes for it to do so. The stability can easily become fixed, the essential elasticity and resilience be weak or missing, to produce a family which, in place of growing towards releasing the seed elements for new cycles of life, becomes ingrowing and loses the vital process. The surprising thing is not that pathological situations exist but that so many families are as successful as they are in carrying out their functions.

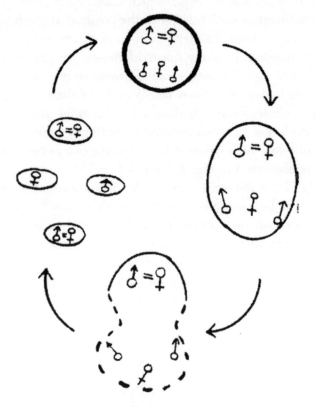

Fig. 4.1 Normal family cycle

Fig. 4.1 illustrates the cycle of growth and dissolution in a reasonably normal family. At the commencement the family is closely knit together by bonds of love and affection, as well as a strong commitment on the part of the parents to care for and educate their children. As the cycle progresses, the ties are gradually loosened, the child's range of experience and freedom of movement is broadened to the extent that he is capable of handling at each stage. With the emergence from adolescence into adult life, the emotional bonds uniting the family continue to grow weaker as the individual increasingly takes over his own freedom and self-determination. In no case does this evolution take place smoothly – it is always marked by struggle and conflict and is usually punctuated by periods of crisis, as at the commencement of school, during adolescence, or the onset of work or marriage. If the parents themselves are reasonably well-adjusted they are able to let go at each stage and eventually return to their investment in each other – to the position at the beginning of their marriage – their children going on to marry and establish fresh cycles. As happens in many normal families, the grandparents – as they will now have become – can continue to play a useful, if subsidiary, role in one of the new family cycles of their children.

When one looks at this diagram it becomes obvious that this healthy evolution may not proceed according to plan. At the risk of oversimplifying, such failure is likely to take one of two main forms. These are illustrated in Figs 4.2 and 4.3.

In Fig. 4.2 a failure is seen in the primary organization of the family at the beginning of the cycle. In these families there is poor stability and cohesion during the early years when the children are young and require most support. Consequently the child is not provided with clear guidelines within which to grow and mature, he does not receive the necessary love and interest to encourage him towards healthy learning nor does he experience the frustration and control essential to stable personality formation.

Fig. 4.2. Unstable family organization

Diverse factors can give rise to this sort of early family disorganization: death or absence of a parent, divorce, separation or open conflict between the parents; illegitimacy or any other reason condemning the child to institutional rearing where, in a monosexual atmosphere, the cold heavy hand of meaningless discipline is lowered on the child relentlessly; there can be a generally loose organization of the family arising from the cultural background as occurs in a delinquent sub-culture. Even in higher socioeconomic sectors of the community one finds parents who are so totally involved in their own careers as to virtually abdicate their role as parents.

This type of pathological family organization is not emphasized further – not because it is unimportant but because it has already been more than sufficiently stressed by others. Many studies (Glueck and Glueck, 1934; Otterstrom, 1946; Ahnsjo, 1941; Armstrong, 1932) have shown the association between this type of disorganized family background and delinquency, psychopathic personality and other forms of personality disorder. So much attention has been focused on disorganization of this kind that these broken homes or open conflict situations have come to be regarded as almost synonomous with family pathology.

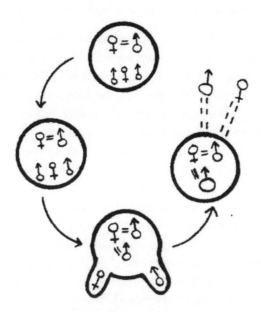

Fig. 4.3. Failed dissolution of family

33

Yet such homes really only represent one end of the spectrum. There is another side to the picture which is of at least equal importance: it, in a sense, represents the opposite extreme.

In the type of family depicted in Fig. 4.3, the family members are closely bound together – indeed often abnormally so – the parents often having poor contacts with the outside world. There are many variants of this type of family organization, some shown in Figs 4.4, 4.5, 4.6, 4.7 and 4.8, (see pp. 37, 39, 40) but the essential of it is a failure to loosen and dissolve the ties as the family progresses – a failure of separation.

> For the early years, when the offspring are infants or small children, there may appear to be little wrong – the home is stable and, while the children are still helpless and dependent, the mother (and father) may fulfil the role of parents reasonably adequately. In some of these homes, although there may not be open conflict between the parents, there is often a good deal of covert hostility and tension, or there may be simple spoiling of the child so that he is not subjected to limits of any kind and, consequently, experiences little stimulation towards maturation. But at this beginning stage the home may be reasonably satisfactory. It is only when the children attempt to move out and progress towards independence that trouble becomes manifest.

It is not, therefore, enough to speak of a home as being good or bad. The further question must be asked is it good or bad for the stage of the cycle which it has reached? What may be reasonably appropriate behaviour in a mother towards a six-month-old infant may be highly pathological behaviour if directed towards a twenty-six-year-old man. Yet this is characteristically the sort of thing found in many families with an adult schizophrenic: the mother or both parents behave towards him as if he were a small, dependent infant.

In such families as illustrated in Fig. 4.3, there is a failure to separate at each stage; a poor school attendance record or even school phobia may also be found. The mother is often anxious unless she can literally see her children and feels uneasy the moment they move out of sight. Consequently, they don't play with other children – they are denied the experience by which they would learn adaptive social behaviour. Hence they tend to remain asocial and isolated and are uneasy when away from home.

There may be a poor achievement record or, if they do well in school, they may often have their first breakdown at the first real separation from home – i.e. at the point where they should move from adolescence into adult life – perhaps failing to take the Leaving Certificate or to manage the first job away from home.

Case 1

D.D., an only child, was grossly spoilt and showed temper tantrums from an early age. Other children refused to play with her. As her mother said, 'maybe it is because she thought she could boss everyone the way she could boss us'.

She progressed well in school intellectually and obtained her Intermediate Certificate but, by now socially isolated, she avoided the other children in school. She left school at the age of sixteen because 'she didn't like it'. Soon after this she had her first breakdown – the classical hebephrenic type: grimacing, mannerisms, delusions and hallucinations. From this time she was hospitalized repeatedly up until one year ago, when she gradually deteriorated into a chronic, apathetic, schizophrenic state.

During her last three hospitalizations she showed considerable progress with activation or total push therapy but relapsed rapidly once discharged home, to the point where her mother would have to care for all her needs. On the last occasion, all contact with her mother was stopped and the patient was given typing training and discharged to a rehabilitation flat. She has now completed her training, is working in a secretarial post and has a boyfriend. She is able to spend weekends at home with her mother without any ill-effect, and is at present on no medication.

In other cases, the person may appear to separate for a time, even emigrate to another land but when, due to the underlying inadequacy in the personality, such a person breaks down and returns home, the old dependent relationship asserts itself.

Case 2

A Jewish girl treated in London, she, too, was an only child who had everything done for her to the point of complete dependence on her parents. She described how, at three or four years of age, she still had to be lifted over the saddle of the doorway leading to her room. On reaching adult life, however, she made a strong attempt to separate, went to the United States and married but, as might be expected, she made a bad choice and the marriage ended in divorce. Following this, she worked for a time but finally returned home to her mother. In graphic terms she described how in the first three weeks she and her mother raced each other in doing everything to see who would get there first. At the end of this time the patient gave up and quite quickly regressed to the position where the mother was doing everything for her, including feeding, washing and dressing her. Although the mother brought her for treatment, when after a time the attempt was made to activate the girl and get her to be more independent, the mother responded by becoming quite depressed and going down with severe migrainous headaches. It became quite clear that the mother needed her daughter to remain as a dependent infant.

As illustrated in the figure (4.3, p. 33), it is often only one child who shows the full pathology, the others making more or less satisfactory attempts at separation.

Setting down these two contrasting types of pathological family organization is a gross oversimplification, nor are they necessarily polar opposites. In fact, the different forms of family organization can be extremely complicated and many variations exist. It is quite common to find mixed forms containing elements of both types. For example, this is often seen in cases where the child is grossly spoilt when young – when no limits are placed on him during the early years – but where there is also a failure to separate later on and abnormal, possessive bonds are maintained when adolescence is reached giving, in a sense, the worst of both worlds.

There are many variants on this basic scheme of failure in separation, of failure of the parents to step down and for the family to progress through its natural cycle. Most represent a lack of balance in the family.

A few of these are illustrated in the following figures.

Fig. 4.4 (p. 37) depicts the weak, passive father with an overdominant wife. In such a family, the mother often invests too much of her life in the children because her husband has failed to supply a satisfactory relationship. Indeed, such mothers are often angry, restless and demanding (this being itself a direct response to the father's passivity), turning their children against the father, taking over all the decisions for the family, the father retiring still further into himself and becoming little better than a doormat around the house.

Fig. 4.5 (p. 37) shows another variant of this, the father who is not so much weak as absent – 'out drinking with the boys'. If there is

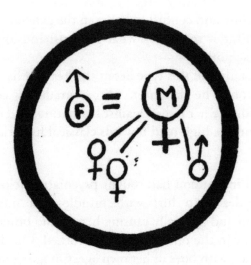

Fig. 4.4. Weak passive father

a picture characteristic of Irish culture, this is probably it. The male, doted on by his mother, reared in a monosexual atmosphere in school, who has never learned to form a friendship with the opposite sex of his own age, marries and takes a 'housekeeper' into his home, while he continues his friendship with his male friends – 'the lads'. She goes on to become the mother of his children, invests her life in these and so carries on the pattern into the next generation. In such

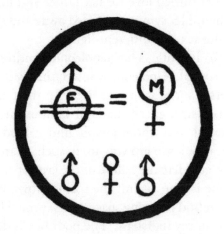

Fig. 4.5. Absence of a parent

a poorly balanced family organization there is a great danger of separation failure and confusion between the generations, of holding on to the children to supply what the husband and wife should provide for each other.

The weak father of this type lies at the heart of hysterical personality formation. The daughter, who is gradually conditioned to deride and ridicule her father against her natural and deeper need to love him, is on the high road towards classical hysteria.

Case 3

A girl treated in London had sought psychiatric help because of an irrepressible desire to flirt with middle-aged men, sometimes pinching them and generally causing herself and others considerable embarrassment in the office where she worked. On the other hand, she never mixed with boys of her own age. On going into her history, it was found that she had been a pet of her father's and was very close to him up to four years. Then, following a row between the parents (which was in no way the father's fault and was due to the mother's unfaithfulness), he was relegated to a subservient position in the home. The mother treated him like dirt and ridiculed him. This image of her father was taken on by the patient, who had little further to do with him. The situation remained unaltered up to the time the patient came for treatment as an adult. As part of her treatment a joint interview between father and daughter was arranged and the whole background reviewed. The effect was remarkable. The patient realized her buried love for her father and made friends with him there and then. Her symptoms faded away and she was now able to see the opposite sex in a different light.

Fig. 4.6 (p. 39): The title 'The Napoleonic Syndrome' is a reminder of the weakling son of Napoleon, whose father was probably one of the strongest personalities who ever lived. In the typical Napoleonic situation there is a strong, self-made or famous father and a timid, perhaps homosexual, son whom people find it hard to believe is his father's son. In reality, a son growing up in such an atmosphere has literally nowhere to go. Here the failure of the last generation to give way to the current one is seen again. The son is drowning in the father's reputation and can find no living space of his own. 'This is my son. He is going to follow in my footsteps.' The poor boy is doomed unless he can excel in some quite different direction. For example, the son of a

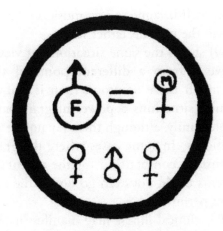

Fig. 4.6. Napoleonic Syndrome

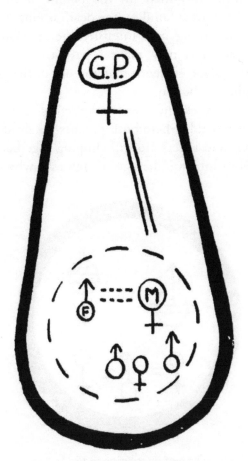

Fig. 4.7. Tied siblings

composer, who himself becomes a jazz musician, has to listen all his life to 'He's not half the man his father was'.

Fig. 4.7 (p. 39) shows the same situation but viewed from a different perspective – from a different point of the cycle. This constellation is much more common than is realized – in many pathological family situations a powerful grandparent effectively controls the whole family, although this may not be apparent unless looked for specifically. In some cases where the grandmother and child were in constant competition for the parent's attention, the middle-aged parents could not even go out in the evening without the grandmother's permission.

In such families clinical illness may manifest itself in any of the three generations: in the grandparent as a late involutional depression from feeling unwanted, in the parent or in the child. In potentially quite normal families, the death of one parent while the children are still young may intensify the relationship with the remaining parent and may make separation difficult later. For example, there is some evidence that absence of the father may lead to homosexuality in the son.

Fig. 4.8 illustrates another pathological constellation, not uncommon in Ireland, where both parents are dead and gone but several brothers and sisters are still clinging together ('keeping the family together') into middle age. If one asks why did you never

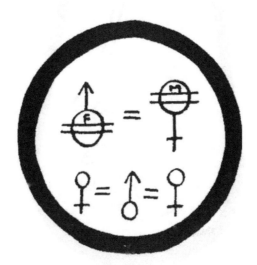

Fig. 4.8. Failure of dissolution in the last generation

marry, the response often is 'I couldn't. I had to look after my brothers.' Quite frequently in such cases, a late paranoid psychosis becomes apparent when one of the brothers finally marries after many years and the elderly sister has to get out of the house.

Discussion

Over the past twenty years there has been a considerable volume of research on the family and the part played by the family in schizophrenia in particular. Much of this work, however, has been concerned with the 'how' rather than the 'why' of family disturbance. There has been a preoccupation with the disturbed processes of communication existing within such families and much valuable work has been done in analysing the interaction going on between the family members. G. Bateson (1956) has described what he calls the double-bind situation. Lidz and others (1958) have referred to similar processes in their families and Britain Laing (1964) has described the process of 'mystification' as characteristic of the families of schizophrenics. All of these represent attempts to understand what is going on in disturbed families but they do not tell you *why* this disturbed interaction should exist in the first place. The tentative hypothesis put forward here goes some way towards correcting this deficiency. It is not suggested that any particular type of family organization leads inevitably to any single psychiatric diagnosis. On the contrary, abnormal family constellations cut across psychiatric diagnosis. It may well be true that only a genetic sub-group of the population is capable of developing schizophrenia but it is probably equally true that no one need develop the disease (except possibly in rare instances), that they will only do so if subjected to an abnormal family environment such as has been described, where the family is unable to loosen and dissolve. If this be true, then the environmental processes in the family represent a crucial aetiologic factor. This may be the point where genetic factors enter the picture: that the same constellation which in one instance results in a phobic neurosis may, in a different genetic population, give rise to a schizophrenic illness.

However, surely it may then be argued that it is not the family constellation which is important but rather the genetic composition of the individual which led him into schizophrenia and would have made him schizophrenic whatever kind of family he came from. The family disturbance is only an epiphenomenon: just one manifestation of the underlying genetic predisposition. This brings back the old either/or view of aetiology – of primary and secondary causes – and such a view of aetiology seems a gross over-simplification, particularly in relation to psychiatric illness.

It is more useful to think of 'cause' in psychiatric illness from an operational standpoint and of the factors underlying a psychiatric illness as forming a 'mosaic' of causality. In this way, any given causal factor can be examined to try to estimate its significance. Also, from the therapeutic aspect, it can be asked at what point in the causal chain is it operationally best to intervene. A pathological organization in a family is likely to give rise to some kind of psychiatric disturbance, but the exact form which the illness takes depends partly on genetic and other factors.

The studies of Brown and his colleagues (1959, 1962, 1963) showed that schizophrenics who were discharged to a neutral environment, such as a boarding-house, did better than those who returned to their families. Similar results were found by Freeman and Simmons in Boston (1963). Also, the findings of a number of earlier studies would seem to point in this direction, although the results are far from conclusive.

We have found, although as yet in only a very few cases, that, by actively separating the patient from his family, even to the point of allowing no visits while in hospital, several schizophrenics have shown remarkable improvement and the illness has gradually melted away. In other cases where the balance in the family has been askew, it has been possible to achieve significant results by bringing say, the father and daughter together, while keeping the mother away (in such a case the mother requires a lot of support).

This hypothesis may partly explain why results in serious psychiatric conditions, such as schizophrenia, have been so poor, for present-day psychiatric practice is to discharge the patient to his family as soon as he shows reasonable progress (although he may continue to be treated as an outpatient) and just as regularly he is found to relapse, often after only a few weeks.

Far from there being any air of caution about this, the whole philosophy of current social psychiatric thinking continues to re-emphasize the stereotype: 'if the patient is at home, keep him there at all costs, and if he is in hospital, get him home at all costs to his family'. Notice the curious absence of any time perspective in such thinking. The home, the family, is always 'good to go home to', whether it be a three-year-old child, a thirty-year-old male schizophrenic or an ageing fifty-five-year-old Irish bachelor. It is never questioned that what may be quite appropriate for the three-year-old may be highly pathological for the thirty-year-old schizophrenic.

If, however, this stereotype is examined critically and it is accepted that 'home' may not always be the best place for the patient, there will be far-reaching repercussions for the organization of services. It means that alternative accommodation as part of rehabilitation and range of hostels must be planned, not just for those who have no homes but for the many hundreds who need re-education towards independent living. At the same time, this combined with other measures – i.e. work and social rehabilitation techniques currently being developed – would lead to better results in schizophrenia. For the over-dependent, adhesive type of family described, by the time the patient has reached adult life, the ties binding him are not, as a rule, merely emotional ones. Because of a failure to separate and develop his own independence as he progressed through childhood, he has very often missed opportunities in school or later in training for a career. He may, too, be quite socially isolated. Thus, by the time he becomes a psychiatric patient, he is truly dependent on his family in every sense, not just emotionally but economically and socially as well – quite incapable of survival on his own. There is thus a major job of personality retraining to be accomplished and, whatever chance this may have of success, it is not likely to get very far if the patient is embedded in the bosom of his family and the old dependent attitudes are fostered daily.

There are also implications for mental health education. Some attempt is being made now to prepare people for the marital state by the provision of pre-marital courses. For many centuries Church and State have attempted to bring home to people their duties as parents by preaching and by legislation. Parents are told to care for and correct their children, to keep them from bad company, to send them to the right schools. Children are told to love, respect and obey their parents, but never a word is spoken to parents about the vital job of learning to separate from their children, or to children to help them towards this separation. This is the place where parents – given the nature of the family – are most likely to run into difficulty. The circumstances of life, in fact, often aid this separation unwittingly but there should be much more conscious awareness of this. Graded opportunities for separation should be built into the educational system and each child should be watched to see that this development is normal.

Summary

Some of the unique characteristics of the human family are examined here and a dilemma suggested. The resolution of this dilemma is marked by tension and crisis and, where it is not satisfactorily completed, may be highly correlated with various forms of psychiatric disorder.

References

Ahnsjo, S. *Acta. Paediat., Stockholm, 28*, Suppl. 31, 1, 1941.

Armstrong, C.P. *Six Hundred and Sixty Runaway Boys*, Boston, MA, 1932.

Bateson, G. *Behav. Sci.*, I, 251, 1956.

Brown, W.G. *Millbank Mem. Fd. Quart.*, XXXVIII, 2, 105–31, 1959.

Brown, W.G., Carstairs, G.M., and Topping, G. *Lancet*, ii, 685, 1958.

Brown, W.G., Monck, E.M., Carstairs, G.M., and Wing, J.K. *Brit. J. Prev. Soc. Med.*, 16, 55, 1962.

Freud, S. *A General Introduction to Psychoanalysis* (English translation), Permabooks, Garden City, New York, 1953.

Glueck, S., and Glueck, E.T. *One Thousand Juvenile Delinquents*, Cambridge, MA, 1934.

Glueck, S., and Glueck, E.T. *Ventures in Criminology*, 1966.

Kiernan, T. *The White Hound of the Mountain and Other Irish Folk Tales*, Devin-Adair, New York, 1962.

Kisher, K.P., and Strotzel, L. *Arch. Psychiat. Nervenkr*, 202, 1–30; 203, 26–60, 1961–62.

Laing, R.D., and Esterson, A. *Families of Schizophrenics*, vol. 1 of *Sanity and Madness in the Family*, Tavistock publications, 1964.

Lidz, T. *Schizophrenia and the Family*, 21, 1, 21–37, 1958.

Lidz, T., Terry, D., and Fleck, St. *Arch. Neural. Psychiat.* (Chic.), 79, 305, 1958.

Mark, J.C. *J. Abnorm. Psychol.*, 48, 185, 1953.

Murdoch, G. *Social Structure*, New York, Macmillan, 1949.

Otterström, E. *Delinquency and Children from Bad Homes: A Study of Prognosis from a Social Point of View*, Lund, 1946.

Simmons, O.G., and Freeman, H.E. 'Wives, Mothers and the Posthospital Performance of Mental Patients', *Social Forces*, 37, 158, 1958.

Tjetze, T. *Psychiatry*, 12, 55, 1949.

Zimmer, H. *The King and the Corpse: Tales of the Soul's Conquest of Evil*, Bollingen Series XI, New York, Pantheon, 1956.

5. The Therapeutic Community
Within Society

This article about the 'therapeutic community' was written in September 1968. At a mental health meeting in Maynooth attended by a number of psychiatrists, including Maxwell Jones – the first person to establish a therapeutic community in Britain – and Joshua Bierer, I presented this paper on the current development of community psychiatry in the Dublin area.

THE notion of the 'therapeutic community' has grown up over the past twenty years as a reaction to the custodial atmosphere of the traditional authoritarian mental hospital. The roots of the idea are by no means new and attempts to mobilize the inherent capacities of the mental patient go back to Pinel and earlier. The tendency of psychiatric environments to revert to the old passive authoritarian ways has been equally constant and history tells us all too clearly that this represents a perpetual danger.

Efforts to apply the principles of the therapeutic community since the Second World War have given rise to an extensive amount of literature on the subject (Jones, Cumming, Greenblatt, Levinson & Williams, Freeman, Crocket, Schwartz). Although it has not always been clear what precisely this concept has meant, its essential feature has been that it sets out, as Maxwell Jones puts it, 'to mobilize the interest, skills and enthusiasm of staff and patients and give them sufficient freedom of action to create their own optimal treatment and living conditions'.

Unfortunately, however, because the need to change the structure of the custodial mental hospital was the most pressing priority, efforts to study and create the therapeutic community have centred mainly on the hospital. It is worthwhile to examine a little more closely exactly what people were attempting to do when they set about creating a therapeutic community within the mental hospital.

Generally what was being aimed at was the creation within the hospital of an atmosphere which would more closely resemble life in the outside world. This meant the creation of a substitute world which tried to supply the essential elements of living, work and training, play and socialization, a personalized situation where both individual and group learning could take place.

As long as twenty years ago Bierer had proposed that methods of psychiatric care could be developed as alternatives to the mental hospital and, while his ideas of the day hostel and the psychiatric social club were taken up, these were considered as mere adjuncts of the mental hospital and no one seriously listened to his claim that the mental hospital as such was obsolete and unnecessary.

Now, today, the position of the mental hospital is as firmly entrenched as ever and all our thinking about mental health still presupposes its continued existence as the basic component of psychiatric care.

Since the work of Tooth & Brooke (1961) who, on the basis of an examination of trends in the mental hospital population, predicted a dramatic fall in the number of mental hospital beds in Britain to half their present number of the mid-1970s, controversy has raged about their predictions. Many have questioned the reliability of these findings and have argued that the number of beds required was likely to be greatly in excess of that estimated by the Ministry of Health (Gore & Jones, 1961; Gore *et al.*, 1964)

The relevance of this whole controversy is open to question. Those who accept the findings of Tooth & Brooke appear to believe that the large mental hospital, as we know it, will gradually wither away. Their opponents rightly point out that this is not happening and that, in fact, in some instances the number of beds required is on the increase. I suggest that this whole controversy misses the essential point, that the future existence of the mental hospital does not depend on any naturally occurring phenomena but is, on the contrary, an issue that rests in our own power to decide.

The alternatives which are usually presented by the present concepts of community psychiatry are that either the patient is cared for in a mental hospital or else is returned home and made the responsibility of his own family. If these are the only alternatives, then the mental hospital as we have known it must remain. However, if we are really serious about the dissolution of the mental hospital, we will have to create genuine alternatives within society which must be more than partial developments out from the mental hospital. Before attempting to formulate these alternatives, it is necessary first to know exactly what we are trying to replace.

It is generally assumed that the mental hospital is a coherent and well-defined entity; but in reality what is it? To take the group of public psychiatric hospitals in Dublin, which could be reproduced across the world as typical examples, of some 3,000 patients we find that approximately 750 are old people who are in hospital essentially because they are old. Another 500 to 600 are mentally subnormal and require institutional care. These two groups together make up well over a third of the total population. Of the remaining 1,700, about 1,200 are persons showing a chronic failure of adaptation – they have failed educationally, have poor social and work skills and were never able to compete in ordinary life. Even if some miracle drug were to appear tomorrow which would remove all their psychiatric symptoms, they would be quite unfitted to function in a normal living situation. We find, therefore, that out of our 3,000 places only 500 are occupied by persons with current psychiatric problems.

What at first glance appears to be an entity is, on examination, found to be a heterogeneous collection of human beings whose only common characteristic is their rejection by a society which has found no place for them, yet it is to this population that we have attempted to apply the concept of a therapeutic community. Surely the first thing that must be done is to define properly each component of the population. It scarcely needs to be argued that the old would be better cared for by a comprehensive geriatric service extending out into the community, while the mentally handicapped would similarly be more appropriately cared for by a service directed to their needs. For the remaining section of chronic adaptional failures, why cannot the essential elements of the therapeutic community be created in adjusted environments – work and training centres, hostels, day centres, social clubs, boarding houses and foster homes – within society.

These environments, distributed throughout the community, while providing an appropriate degree of asylum and support, would provide also the essential elements of living, work and training, play and socialization. They would give a much more appropriate setting in which to apply the principles of the therapeutic community of individual and group learning based on knowledge which has been painfully accumulated over the years by dedicated workers in mental hospitals, but which could never be applied with real hope of success within the unreal and substitute work of the hospital. Needless to say, this will involve psychiatric patients rubbing shoulders with the man in the street and will make demands on all of us in society, but we must remember that, like any other human being, the psychiatric patient has a right to participate in ordinary society in so far as he is able, and it should no longer be tolerable that he be excluded from society and shut away in the traditional manner.

It will naturally be asked how, without the mental hospital as we know it, one is to deal with the acutely disturbed patient and the more specifically medical dimension of psychiatric illness. For this, in my opinion, we need only short-stay active treatment units, specifically designed to provide only for the medical or hospital phase of treatment. In the context of modern psychiatry, where the grosser forms of disturbance and deviant behaviour can be controlled by drugs and other means, this hospital phase of illness should, in the vast majority of cases, be comparatively short.

To meet this need, units of fifty to one hundred beds, preferably in association with a general hospital or medical centre and situated within the area being served, would seem to be appropriate. Such units could in addition care for the relatively small residual group of patients suffering from brain damage or other chronic disability requiring continual attention in hospital.

It is on the basis of this concept of the therapeutic community within society that the future structure of the psychiatric services in the Dublin area is being planned. In Dublin a programme has been adopted to replace the traditional mental hospital complex with a series of decentralized psychiatric units based on the community and related to the population areas which they serve. This programme is to be implemented gradually, initially by the break-up of the large mental hospitals into sections, each serving its own catchment area. The next step is to move each of these sections – i.e. active treatment units of 50 to 100 beds – out into the area which they serve. This is being accomplished at present and involves the division of the Dublin area into seven sectors, two of these being operated by psychiatric services which have been traditionally private. Each area service will thus provide for all the psychiatric needs of approximately 100,000 population. The units envisaged will only supply the active treatment phase and psychiatric care.

St Loman's Hospital is the only section which, so far, is providing a fully self-contained service without a backlog of chronic patients. Our experience gained in the functioning of this section enables us to predict the needs of the psychiatric service in the future. The population being dealt with by St Loman's is approximately 170,000 and it has been found that the 170 adult beds available are more than adequate for the needs of the area. Thus, leaving aside the large chronic, immobile population already in existence within the psychiatric service, the functioning of the St Loman's area would indicate that bed needs in the future would be less than one per 1,000 of the population. In addition, in relation to these area units, it is our aim to develop the full range of special facilities to provide the type of adjusted environments about which I have been speaking in this paper. By the end of this year we will have about one hundred places occupied in hostels. This number is likely to increase to 300/400 over the next few years. Our hostel places will be matched by places in day care, work and training centres.

It remains to be considered what is likely to be the future outcome of the plans for development envisaged here. If, and only if, these developments – the break-up of the mental hospital system, the mobilization of community resources and the development of rehabilitation facilities within the community – are brought to reality, then it is likely that the present large chronic mental hospital population will gradually disappear. This is what we have already seen happen with tuberculosis. Twenty years ago the problem of tuberculosis in this country also seemed enormous yet, once effective services and rehabilitation were established, tuberculosis as a major problem ceased to exist within a matter of a few years.

In a similar way it is predicted that, once effective mental health services are created, the chronic mental hospital population will also disappear, even if it takes some years to accomplish this. Will this mean that the large-scale development, which is the subject of this paper, will no longer be necessary? Far from this being the case, all the indications are that these facilities and community resources will be required indefinitely.

Even though the chronic institutionalized psychiatric population may wither away, new psychiatric patients are constantly appearing from within society. Many of these persons who, although not institutionalized, have never functioned adequately (they have failed educationally, have poor social and work skills) are unable to compete in ordinary life. If these are not to become a new chronic institutionalized population, they too will need work training, education and to acquire social skills. It is important to realize, however, that these persons manifesting psychiatric symptoms and coming directly to the psychiatric service for help really form only a small part of a much larger pool of individuals who, whether or not they show psychiatric symptoms, have the common characteristic of failure to meet the competitive standards of modern society.

There is frequently much in common in the origins of their problems among those who have failed to learn how to live in society. This seems to apply whether they are the chronic schizophrenic, the chronic attender at the general practitioner's surgery or general hospital or out-patient clinic, the betting office loiterer and chronically unemployed or the recidivist petty criminal. All too often we find common factors such as a deficient home background, poor education, inadequate social skills and a generally poor level of independence.

Our society, from now on, will demand a much higher educational standard of all our citizens and with increasing affluence the gap between those who succeed and the social failures will inevitably widen. There are only two alternatives open to us: whether to allow this deterioration to continue, with perhaps an increasing number failing to find a place for themselves in society, or to provide an alternative pathway of training and functional education for those who have failed to succeed within our traditional system of education. The rehabilitation and re-education facilities proposed here could in future years provide the nucleus of such an alternative pathway in society.

What in fact will be happening as all this takes place is that our psychiatric service will be gradually transforming itself from one negatively concerned with mental illness into one which is positively directed towards mental health. And here, perhaps, we come to the most important reason of all for breaking up the traditional mental hospital system: in so doing we will be releasing the potential of upwards of 1,000 salaried workers – doctors, nurses and paramedical staff – to throw their weight behind others already concerned, in a general effort to turn our society as a whole into a more therapeutic community.

6. Human Beings, Their Surrounding Environment and Human Development

This paper was never published but was presented at an international meeting in Dublin in 1970 on the state of society at the time. It was attended by a diverse group, including economists, sociologists, community workers, etc. This paper was my first attempt to look at the direction I felt small, personal, human communities might evolve into in the future. This is a theme I revisit in some of the later papers in this collection.

TEILHARD de Chardin gave us a vision of the perfection of mankind, of the gradual and painful emergence of consciousness and reflection in the world. For the first time he showed us a direction in evolution, he put before us the concept of humans as the most elaborate synthesis yet achieved by the evolutionary process and their gradual but relentless progress towards perfection, their personal and spiritual growth leading to unification of all mankind in love. Over and over again in *The Phenomenon of Man* he stresses this aspect of synthesis: 'First the molecules of carbon compounds with their thousands of atoms symmetrically grouped; next the cell which, within a very small volume, contains thousands of molecules linked in a complicated system; then the Metazoa in which the cell is no more than an almost infinitessimal element; and later the manifold attempts made sporadically by the Metazoa to enter into symbiosis and raise themselves to a higher biological condition. And now as a germanization of planetary dimensions comes the thinking layer which over its full extent develops and intertwines its fibres not to confuse and to neutralize them but to re-enforce them in the living unity of a single tissue.' Or again, when speaking of humans: 'they represent individually and socially the most synthesized state under which the stuff of the universe is available to us.'

Yet barely fifteen years after de Chardin's death this wonderful message of hope giving meaning to the universe seems to be thrust back into his teeth, for although the technological and scientific progress he predicted has been more than realized, the personality of the human being has shown little evidence of change for the better. Indeed there is mounting evidence to suggest a change in the opposite direction. In the past twenty years we have witnessed as part of the vast urban explosion and industrial growth the breakdown of many of our inner cities – the very heart of our civilization – into something near total anarchy, an emergence of the impersonal and of individuals showing a failure of any standards of ethics and behaviour without parallel in recorded history or, for that matter, in any contemporary, so-called, 'primitive' society. To find an equivalent level of mores and behaviour we would probably have to go back to the first emergence of the human being as a hunter ape from the forests 50,000 years ago and we might not find it even then.

Surely to find such a rapid deterioration in our social and civilized values, even if this is not very widespread as yet, must make us pause and wonder: is it merely a coincidence that we see this happening in the midst of the full flowering of capitalism, with the growth of huge impersonal bureaucracies? Whether these take the form of the state capitalism of Russia or the huge industrial complexes and ever-growing civil service bureaucracy in our own countries is immaterial, for these apparent alternatives are but the two faces of the same monster – the dehumanized technology to which we are all increasingly subject.

Of course, de Chardin always saw clearly that the upward progress of humans towards perfection which he envisaged was in no sense inevitable and that humans could refuse to follow their true direction and to accept the responsibilities of increasing consciousness – could refuse to travel along the pathway of ever greater self-realization and fulfilment. He always saw the possibility of human beings going down a blind alley, of their submerging themselves again in the impersonal and turning their back on reflective awareness. This would not be the first time that evolution had turned down a blind alley; it happened with the great reptiles, with the beehive and ant-heap. Interestingly enough, what is happening to our civilization at the present time seems strangely reminiscent of the beehive type of development in evolution. I refer here to the sacrifice of flexible and diversified personal development to over-specialization and uniformity. The little evidence we have of China under its present regime suggests an alarming trend in this direction.

What has gone wrong? What is going wrong? This is the question which keeps coming back to haunt us. Why is the vision which de Chardin foresaw being submerged, and in danger of being lost, perhaps for ever, at a time when humans have greater affluence and technological development than at any previous time, and should be in a position to realize themselves as never before in history. If the perfection which Teilhard de Chardin led us to hope for is not happening, I think we seriously have to ask what is wrong in our modern technological development that is frustrating all our endeavours. What forces underlie the trend towards de-personalization and de-humanization which seems to be growing all around us and making the human being merely a pawn, a number in an impersonal world.

If we are to understand and find the answers to this dilemma, I think we must turn back to the development of human beings and our civilization. Originally, if we go back over our evolution, the information available for adaptation was that passed genetically. This was transmitted from one individual to another in the genetic code, and evolutionary progress took place principally through mutation and the process of natural selection. With the human, the situation is fundamentally different once the biological basis of human beings is genetically programmed. Most of what we would regard as the central characteristics of the modern civilized human – indeed more particularly the attributes we regard as the marks of civilization – are genetically only a possible or potential development. Ah, you may say, simply like growing a flower, when you have to supply soil, water, fertilizers, etc., to obtain a healthy plant. No: there is a fundamental difference when we come to consider human development. With a flower or one of the lower forms of animal life, all the essential characteristics of the plant or organism are already there, genetically programmed. When we turn to humans, the situation is completely altered: what we recognize as the 'self', the essential of our personality, is only there in potential and has to be built up from the experiences in which we are immersed from the moment of conception onwards. This is not merely a descriptive statement but literally means that the 'building-blocks' of the 'self' are digested and internalized from the surrounding environment. Most attempts to understand society and the effects of environment fail to realize this and take a cross-sectional view. They think of an environment as 'good' or 'bad', of an environment which, for example, depersonalizes or enhances participation. It may be asked, for instance of our housing or of conditions in a factory, whether they increase neurosis and frustration or lead to an increase in happiness and well-being.

In all this sort of thinking the assumption is made that humans 'are' themselves, that they may be affected for good or ill by their surroundings but their inner substance, what they 'are', is taken for granted as something 'given', something which is simply there. But are we warranted in making such an assumption? If there is any truth in what I have already said – that only the basic substrata of human beings is transmitted genetically, the potential for being 'human', that most of the behaviour and characteristics of the so-called civilized human being of the twentieth century are passed down from generation to generation culturally and built in through the process of learning – then are we in a position to assume that a human being is simply 'there', that he/she automatically becomes what he/she 'is'?

On the contrary. There is increasing evidence from biochemical studies, from storage of memory, from animal studies of learning and less pleasant evidence from sociological studies of the kind of human beings who are emerging from ghettos and inner cities, evidence to suggest that what we regard as the fully developed human personality, particularly in the dimension of the personal, has to be painfully 'built up' during development, and I mean literally 'built up'; that much of the very substance of personality is the product of the experiential ingredients which have been fed into it. If this view is correct, it means that we all have a terrifying responsibility towards each other. What I do, the way I live and behave, is what I will become. Much more important (and this is what is frightening) is the realization that the way in which I live and behave will be built into my children, constituting an important part of what they will become. The behaviour of one generation – the way in which they live – becomes the structure and very being of the next. I think it was to this terrible responsibility that we have for one another and for the generations to follow that Jesus Christ was referring when he said: 'And if anyone hurts the conscience of one of these little ones that believe in me, he had better have been drowned in the depths of the sea, with a mill-stone hung about his neck. Woe to the world, for the hurt done to consciences. It must needs be that such hurt should come, but woe to the man through whom it comes' (Matthew 18.6, 8).

But surely this is the way it has always been right back through history? As primitive human beings painfully groped their way forwards they learned from the world around them, very slowly at first, but over thousands of years they gradually and painfully built up their heritage of learning and eventually the whole process began to accelerate and increase, each generation passing on a little more to the next. As I have already said, this heritage was then transmitted to their children. In the beginning, all that was known was passed down within the family, literally from parent to child. As society developed, some of this information was preserved within the tribe or clan that formed the total social grouping at the time. It was passed from parent to child, from teacher to disciple.

We have in this the beginnings of education. It will be noticed that up to this point all the information, whether passed down within the family or within the small tribal society, had to be contained in the individual brains of each generation. In other words, although it was not transmitted by the genetic system, it still had to be absorbed and contained by the human organism personally. Once methods of recording information began to develop – at first writing, later printing and more recently modern techniques of recording, such as computers – then the possibility of storing information outside the human being became an increasing reality. This had its early beginnings some thousands of years ago with the preservation of a few highly treasured and closely guarded manuscripts, but it received a great impetus forward with the advent of printing prior to the Renaissance. In this century we are seeing an even greater acceleration in the various means of storing and recording information, so much so that the ability of the human brain to record and store our heritage has now sunk into relative insignificance when compared to the external means available. The upshot of all this is that there is now a tremendous increase in the amount of information available and the task of each generation to pass this on to the next is enormous. The part of this information which is stored and transmitted genetically is now but a tiny proportion of the whole, and even that proportion which is passed on culturally through learning from one human being to another and stored within the brain (that is, biologically) now forms only a very small part of the total mass of knowledge which is contained within modern society.

A parallel development has been taking place from early times in the acquisition by humans of skills and technical expertise. Just as the volume of knowledge available to them was slow to build up, so was their development of skills and creation of tools and implements. At first the only implement humans had were their bare hands and the only source of energy available to them was their own muscular strength. Later they domesticated other creatures, such as the dog and the cow, and put their energies to work for them; humans manufactured simple tools and weapons and gradually extended their domination over nature. Here too, in early times, their progress was very slow but as they discovered other sources of energy and learned how to utilize these, their skills and technology have developed at an increasing rate. In just the same way as with the expansion of knowledge, with the advent of the machine and the industrial revolution the part played by a human being as an individual in the midst of an enormous technology which he/she has created has sunk into insignificance. To an even greater extent, and in one situation after another, the human is being replaced by the machine, by automation, to the point where he/she appears to be almost dispensable in the face of a ubiquitous technology.

It is this enormous increase in the amount of knowledge and technology available which really underlies the phenomenon of specialization, which has developed in modern times. It is this too which constitutes the dilemma facing humans at the present time – how to make this enormous amount of information and expertise available to each generation and, more importantly, available to each individual person.

Here we have to be careful. It is true that society as a whole is richer than ever before – we know more and can do more. We have developed and are developing the means of storing this huge repository of information. We have developed and are developing the technology to utilize it. Large numbers of human beings are no longer faced with a life of sheer drudgery or, worse, of poverty and starvation. It should follow that each person is richer as a human being than he/she ever was before; but is this in fact true?

Unfortunately what we frequently find is a kind of poverty in the midst of plenty. I am speaking now in terms of the richness of the human personality and there is a sense in which the individual – say the Aran Islander or, for that matter, the ordinary tenant farmer in any part of rural Ireland of a generation ago, or again, in a different context, the Oxford or Cambridge don of a hundred years ago – was a richer person than many individuals at the present time.

What does this mean? Is it merely a harking back to 'the good old days', some vague nostalgia for a Celtic Twilight? I don't think so. The Aran Islander of a generation ago carried almost the whole of his culture within himself. Certainly the total culture was carried by a relatively small number of people forming an island or village community. What is more, the culture was holistic and well rounded, incorporating the full cycle of life.

The way of life was in a state of ecological balance with its surrounding environment – i.e. close to nature. The Aran man had to be in tune with nature, he had to be subject to it from the cradle to the grave, for he had not the technological means to ride roughshod over it as do modern humans, to their increasing peril. Were an atomic war to intervene, resulting in a large-scale destruction of our civilization, the Aran man, assuming he survived at all, could have reproduced his whole civilization again without difficulty, as he carried it largely within himself.

In contrast, take the factory girl from Ballyfermot or an individual from the Harlem ghetto and strip away the veneer of civilization, take away the support of the surrounding technology – the factory, the supermarket, the hospital, the school – and what is left? What can such an individual do? What does he/she know? How much of our enormous civilization and expertise do such individuals carry within themselves. The frightening answer comes back: almost nothing. Let us go further. We will not simply ask what such an individual knows, what he/she has or can do but what he/she 'is'. Again the frightening answer comes back: almost nothing. You will say, but what about all those who are well educated, the elite in our society? But is their situation so very different? The plastic surgeon, the business executive, the civil servant – they have a highly skilled expertise in one small area but how much of the 'whole' do they carry within themselves or understand? I am not sure the answer is very different.

This seems to be the situation we are facing. As our knowledge has increased, as our technology has developed, the place of each individual human being has become correspondingly diminished. It has obviously become impossible for each one of us to contain the 'whole' within ourselves and, as a result, we have largely given up the attempt, contenting ourselves instead with nibbling at a small piece. We have been forced to specialize and to split up our resources and ourselves into largely disconnected roles or functions. Early on, for instance in medieval times, when this process had not gone so far, things were not too bad. We had the tradesman and skilled artisan – the baker, the stonemason, the carpenter and so on – but these were holistic functions and, even though it was no longer possible for an individual to carry the whole culture within him/herself, at least these functions were carried on in a personalized developmental context close to the family and to village life: what was known was passed on from parent to child. Interestingly enough, at some of the historical peak points, such as the height of Greek civilization or of the Renaissance, a few of the most brilliant persons living – such as Socrates or Leonardo da Vinci – seemed to have been able to incorporate almost the whole of what was then already a complex civilization within themselves, thus realizing a development of personality and an attainment of wisdom which has probably not been equalled since. It is interesting, too, as Doxiadus points out, that the great cities of the past at their height – Athens, Italian cities like Florence or Venice, Paris – were all of a similar size and population; they were of human dimensions where people could walk and meet one another and where personal communication could still take place. However, with the growth of capitalism, the industrial revolution and the enormous expansion of our civilization that has taken place during the past 100 years or so, all of this has been swept aside. It is now, as I have said, quite impossible for one man to encompass the 'whole' within himself and we have simply given up any attempt to do so.

The worrying question, however, is what has been happening to us as individuals in the process? When one looks around it is clear that the skills and knowledge available to us have been divided up and then further subdivided to an even greater extent. It seems clear, to me at any rate, that this splitting process is taking place all around us and, what is more sinister, is now going on within each of us as individuals. Consider, for example: the amputation of the family's civic role from its nurturing role; the gulf between one generation and the next – between the adolescent and the adult, between the adult and the aged (in this regard it will be noted that the need for human relationships tends to be satisfied now by spreading out horizontally, as with the adolescent gang); the separation of work from leisure; the gap between man himself and the provision of his basic needs, such as health, education, welfare, housing (which more and more tend to be provided in a compartmentalized form – as if, for example, health was something quite separate from education – and to come from a remote source in which he has no direct participation).

In short, if we look at a modern person as an ordinary citizen, where he/she lives in the bosom of his/her family, and ask in this context what does he/she control? In what does he/she participate? What essential functions does he/she carry out as him/herself, other than the biological role of begetting children? Once again the frightening answer comes back to us – *almost nothing*. The modern human being knows and does many things but to an ever-increasing extent these are carried out as disconnected roles largely separated from one another. Less and less does he/she encompass anything within him/herself as a whole person. It is as if society were affected by a sort of cancerous process. The essence of cancer is not that it is an attack on the body by an invader from outside but rather that certain cells of the organism cease to obey the influence of the whole organism on its parts and go out of control. Such cells break free from overall control, serving their own ends and obeying their own internal mechanisms. They reproduce wildly at the expense of the rest of the body; living purely for themselves they continue to feed on the rest of the organism until they have destroyed it. Within our society, in a similar way, a human being has become split off from himself into disconnected roles and functions; in adopting one role that person finds that he/she is attacking him/herself in another. An example would be a worker in the building industry who goes on strike in the cause of a sectional interest and thus holds up the national housing programme. He/She may, in doing this, be depriving him/herself and his/her family of a dwelling in which to live. Modern society is full of such sectional interests, each attempting to achieve its short-term goals. The conflicting interests cannot but end up in the chaos and madness which we see all around us.

Our efforts as a society to deal with the problems thus generated are undertaken in the same schizophrenic manner. As the human being participates less and takes less and less responsibility for him/herself as a human being, he/she has to create an even more oppressive bureaucratic machine which doles out passive welfare to him and supplies his needs from a remote impersonal source. As this process continues to its logical conclusion, and it has nearly reached this point now, one half of the population will find itself caring for and treating the other half. The process cuts even deeper than what is suggested by this statement, for it essentially means that the human being will find him/herself being cared for and governed by an impersonal aspect of him/herself split off in the role of bureaucrat, civil servant and specialist. Within the cogs of this enormous bureaucratic machine that we have created, all personal motivation is lost and millions of pounds are consequently wasted. Meanwhile, as society as a whole becomes more frustrated and therefore 'sicker', the answer is always to set up more services and to split up more human beings into impersonal roles and functions, thus endlessly recreating the vicious cycle.

What then is left to the modern human being? Has he/she any longer a real place within his/her own civilization? What unique or essential quality, if any, does he/she still possess? From what has already been said, it seems clear that he/she is no longer of central importance as a storehouse of information; nor is he/she any longer of central importance as a 'doer' – automated technology is taking one function after another from him/her – and even where he/she does carry out a function he/she has already become an insignificant pawn or cog in a larger process.

The only real, primary and essential attribute left to a human being is creativity, and this, I believe, is the natural offspring of the 'personal'. I am convinced that these are inseparable – that creativity springs from the personal and that this is consequently the only important attribute left to humans, but then surely this was his/her really important attribute from the beginning. The individual's consciousness, his/her ability to reflect and to understand, has been the central human theme since we originally came into existence.

If this is so – and if de Chardin is right that human beings are the highest point of synthesis yet achieved within the universe and if the essence of this synthesis is the creative personal dimension – then surely we should ask what is necessary to nurture this personal growth in human beings. Moreover, if, as I have suggested, development is crucial, that a human being does not simply happen but rather that the self and the personality have painfully to be built up – have to literally grow out of the experiential ingredients to which they are exposed – then of course the importance of the surrounding environment and the milieu of human relationships in which learning takes place is highlighted, and the nature of our environment becomes of vital importance to our becoming what we are, or rather, what we could be. For the first time in history we must seriously ask ourselves what humans need in order to be themselves and to grow, what we require to develop into a true human being. Once and for all we must accept that, for the 'personal' to come into being, for humans to realize their full potential, we must grow in the context of a truly human 'personal' milieu. However, this is something we must *choose* soon. It is not a change that can take place across the whole of society at once, nor does it seem reasonable to expect that some kind of change of heart will take root within mankind *en masse*. Throughout history, thinkers and religious reformers have appealed to human beings to change for the better in this way but it has never happened and it seems hardly likely that it is going to happen now.

No! To think in this way would not only be useless but would misunderstand the very nature of the problem facing us. A change towards the personal, by very definition, cannot take place across society as a whole, for this could only result in a denial of the very personal dimension we are trying to promote. If there is to be any hope of change in this direction, fundamental to it must be the creation of some nucleus within which it can happen, some basic unit of society where these personalized processes can take root. However, this is precisely where humans appear to be at variance with the natural order. We have grossly interfered with the biological equilibrium controlling all living substances and have taken over to an ever-increasing extent our own destiny but we do not appear to be prepared to accept the self-discipline and control over ourselves that such a takeover presupposes if disastrous consequences are not to follow.

Early in our history, human beings followed the general principle of organizing themselves – into family, tribe, city – these gradually coalescing to form larger and more complex units of society. However, becoming aware of his/her new-found freedom he rode roughshod over any natural growth of this kind from tribal units to more definite molecules of society. Civilizations like those of the early Celts showed a quite sophisticated concept of decentralization, each tribal unit being virtually autonomous and complete within itself yet linked by a common culture, language, system of law, music and literature. These unified cultures, such as those of the Celts, the ancient civilizations of Africa and South America, were overcome by ruthless centralized powers like the Romans, the Spaniards and the British who, although more technologically efficient, were in reality much less civilized. It is not my intention to be taken as wishing for a return to the primitive, for this would seem to be neither possible nor desirable. On the contrary, it is only now in the midst of our modern technology that the opportunity is there for the first time to realize the full flowering of the 'personal' and creative potential within human beings. And it was essentially the as yet primitive state of technological development, the slow and inadequate systems of communication, which spelt the ruin of the early attempts to create a decentralized molecular form of society.

If we turn, however, to examine the rest of our world, the startling fact emerges that the whole stuff of the universe appears to be built up of units, or 'wholes', these combining to form at each level a genuine synthesis, a new pattern of organization, creating a larger and more complex 'whole'. This remarkable design seems to run right through, from the tiny Quark to the galaxy in outer space. As de Chardin has put it so clearly:

> After allowing itself to be captivated by the charms of analysis to the extent of falling into illusion, modern thought is at last getting used once more to the idea of the creative value of synthesis in evolution. It is beginning to see that there is definitely *more* in the molecule than in the atom, *more* in the cell than in the molecule, *more* in society than in the individual, and *more* in mathematical construction than in calculations and theorems. We are now inclined to admit that at each further degree of combination something which is irreducible to isolated elements emerges in a new order. And with this admission, consciousness, life and thought are on the threshold of acquiring a right to existence in terms of science.

Thus it seems clear that the whole process of evolution is concerned with the organization of energy through synthesis into the 'whole' at an even more complex level.

Somehow human beings must come back into tune with the basic order of the universe. It appears to be inescapable that this involves creating some basic module or unit of society within which human processes can grow and develop. Indeed there is some evidence that, in response to the growing impersonal horror which is already facing us on all sides, humans are already groping in this direction; over the past twenty years we have seen the emergence of the suburban shopping centre, the neighbourhood concept, the new town and, particularly here in Ireland, the growth of resident and community organizations and voluntary bodies of all kinds. But if this groping is to amount to anything and if we are to create a really basic unit of society, a much more radical departure than this is needed. It will have to be a truly conscious decision by humans, a specific reversal of the amoeba-like spread of contemporary society. It is not something which is likely to happen spontaneously or even to emerge gradually.

On the contrary, I believe we are approaching a critical point where either our society will make a big leap forward – of the same order as with the emergence of the first living substance on the earth – to create a truly new synthesis, or we will inevitably destroy ourselves and our civilization. However, this time the synthesis would have to be at the human level, a human molecule which will form the basic unit of a 'granular' society. Because this will represent a genuinely new synthesis at the human level, the forces holding it together, the energising principle organizing and maintaining it, must also be of a quite different order. The atom, the molecule, the living cell, each is maintained in existence by a pattern of forces, by energy in a form appropriate to its own level. When we come to a synthesis at the human level, it must be asked what form will the organizational forces now take, where will we turn to find an energizing principle that will maintain and vitalize our human molecule. It is true that in the human being the earlier electro-chemical forms of energy are still at work in the atoms, molecules and cells that go to make us up, but to bind one human being to another to create a true communion of human beings some new principle must be introduced.

To find the answer I believe we must turn once again to the personal dimension and look at the kind of bonds which operate in basic human structures already in existence, such as the family. Here we find the power of love and understanding ,psychological and emotional forces operating at the conscious level as between one human person and another. These, although incorporating physical–chemical forces, are quite distinct from anything which exists at lower levels of synthesis.

However, as is found in lower forms of synthesis – for example, with the atom or the molecule – the forces operating are not simply those of attraction. On the contrary, the individual components of, say, an atom maintain a dynamic relationship, always striving towards a stable arrangement, a state of balance between the forces of attraction and repulsion. So, too, at the human level there is a need for love, intimacy and separation – if you like, wherever there is love there is always, in some sense, hate. We see this within the family and for that matter within most human groups, where the need for intimacy, closeness and love is always balanced by the need to keep a measure of distance and separateness between oneself and the loved ones, the need at times for privacy, to separate and be purely oneself. I think if we are to make any progress with human relationships in society it is vital to understand this need for separateness, distinctness, uniqueness and personal development as the need for love and an intimate relationship. To return once again to de Chardin, in any domain

> whether it be the cells of the body, the members of a society or the elements of a spiritual synthesis – union differentiates. In every organized whole, the parts perfect themselves and fulfil themselves. Through neglect of this universal rule many a system of pantheism has led us astray to the cult of a great all in which individuals were supposed to be merged like a drop in the ocean or like a dissolving grain of salt. Applied to the case of the summation of consciousness the law of union rids us of this perilous and recurrent illusion. No, following the confluent or orbits or their centres, the grains of consciousness do not tend to lose their outlines and blend but, on the contrary, to accentuate the depth and incommunicability of their *egos*. The more 'other' they become in conjunction, the more they find themselves as 'self'.

Having got this far, I think it is possible to discern some of the general characteristics of a basic human module. One of the main difficulties is to find a suitable term to describe this, because we are concerned here with a grouping of human persons, and because the pattern of organization, the bonds maintaining it, must be energized and vitalized by *personal* forces of love and consciousness. In the Greek there seems to be no word for the person, or for the personal dimension, as such. Perhaps the word *tuath*, which was the basic political unit of ancient Celtic Ireland, comes closest to the concept I am trying to describe. A full description and understanding of a human module such as envisaged here must be the subject of major research and can only come from the application of a genuine science of human beings. At the same time, from all that has been said, I think it is possible for us to point to some of the basic and general characteristics that such a human module must have if it is to fulfil the function of a basic unit of society.

Tuath – General Characteristics

1. The tuath must be large enough to be viable, to be autonomous and self-containing for the basic functions of life:
   housing (design, build, land maintenance)
   education (directed to all age groups of the population)
   work and employment
   leisure
   family support and social welfare
   community health
   legal services
   administration and local self-government
   basic physical services (street cleaning, garbage, etc.)
   information and research
To maintain these basic functions, the *tuath* would probably need to contain between 30,000 and 50,000 persons.
2. The *tuath* must be small enough to enable personal human relationships to exist at all levels. This statement presupposes of course that it contains sub-units or sub-nuclei such as the neighbourhood group, the crèche, the club, right down to the fundamental human unit – the family. This would be on the same lines as the sub-units, sub-systems and molecules within the living cell.
3. The *tuath* must have a surrounding membrane providing a clear separation or boundary between itself and the rest of society. This would be partly geographical and spatial but, because as already

explained the organizational forces operating within the *tuath* are at a conscious level of human love and understanding, the boundary membrane must be mainly of a psychological nature or a barrier which would provide a protective mechanism, a semi-permeable membrane, to filter uncontrolled sensory bombardment and mass communication from outside. The question of a distinct and separate language is of fundamental importance here, although language is something which normally operates as a barrier at a national level rather than at the level of a basic module of society such as is described here. Nevertheless, if Ireland were to be the site for the first human experiments along these lines the Irish language, which is not at present spoken by the majority of the people in this country, could play a crucial role in the information of the surrounding membrane by being introduced as the everyday tongue of the members of each successive *tuath* as it is established. This would, as well as protecting the *tuath* from undue bombardment from outside, provide the means of gradually spreading the language until it became the spoken tongue of the entire population of the country. Just as the achievement of the cell membrane constituted a great leap forward with the emergence of the first living substance and allowed the heightening of intensity of various chemical processes to take place within the living cell and not to be lost by dispersion and diffusion into the surrounding milieu, so the surrounding psychological membrane of the *tuath* would allow an intensification of internal communication and human relationship, heightening the intensity of the human processes of love and ideas within. Thus, just to take one example, it would be possible to install a system of closed-circuit television to enable an enhancement of the internal communications within the *tuath* while restricting and controlling to some extent the input of national television bombardment from the outside. An essential part of the creation of this barrier or surrounding semi-permeable membrane would be the exclusion of the motor car as a means of transport within the *tuath* (see later).

4. At the same time the *tuath* must be an open system allowing the free exit and entrance of individuals to come or go between other human molecules. In other words, it would be the structure as a whole and the patterns of forces/bonds and relationships within it that would remain stable while, as is the case with atoms or ions moving in and out of a living cell, any given individual could leave

and be replaced by another from outside without disturbing the overall arrangement. It was the failure, I believe, to achieve such an open system that spelled the ruin of many primitive attempts at organizing society. Thus, in earlier times the village, parish or even the ancient city often tended to become ingrown and ossified by elaborate systems of blood ties, taboos and rigid patterns of behaviour of class and caste. As with the living cell, which constantly synthesizes and breaks down its large protein molecules and other structures, so in the *tuath* families should be moving through their life cycle releasing their seed elements to move freely to other *tuaths*, thus constantly synthesizing themselves and breaking down, without disturbing or damaging the overall pattern of organization and dynamic structure.

5. It follows from this, therefore, that the *tuath* must be built around the total life cycle containing all human elements from the cradle to the grave. From the beginning it must contain all age groups, both children and the elderly, with the basic social and architectural facilities to care for all of these. It is the failure to understand this total concept of humans within space/time which underlies the error in a number of political systems and philosophies, such as for example Communism, with its emphasis on the very practical concept of the human being as worker. This concept of the life cycle would enable education to be directed to the total life cycle (to the family as a whole) and would also allow remedial and health measures to be introduced to the family at the first appropriate operational point of intervention. As the priority in education and healthcare would now be the maximal development of the human person, and as it would be taking place in a personalized concept, there is no reason why these dimensions should not become liberalized and creative. The real purpose of education should now be for the individual to develop himself and only secondarily to learn how to utilize the storehouse of knowledge and to be able to manipulate and avail of the technology common to society as a whole. The present examination system could thus become redundant and many of the current problems of selection for university, etc., might be approached quite differently. In a different context, a life-cycle concept could be applied to work with a progression up the ladder of promotion occurring earlier in life and as a gradual scaling down on the other side, starting perhaps as early

as thirty-five to forty to less important posts, instead of the abrupt retirement to the scrap heap at sixty-five as at present.

6. Human beings must become central. They must be the first priority at all levels. Human freedom and basic human rights must therefore also be central, and the functioning of the *tuath* must be built on genuine democratic principles. All social classes should be represented and it would be hoped that the whole concept of class would become less significant. We have said that humans must be central therefore they must live and work within the *tuath*. However impractical it may sound, work and economic considerations must become a secondary priority. Thus we must first be concerned with human beings as they live within their family but for this to succeed work, factories and industry must be within easy reach of where they live. Similarly those supplying basic human services such as health, education and so on must also live within the *tuath* which they serve. This would ensure that the basic functions of life – working, leisure, rearing our children – are at last brought together in a unified way and lived out close to one another in a personalized form. Such an arrangement would also free humans once and for all from the slavery of the motor car. It should now be possible to have most functions of life, such as home and work, within walking distance of one another. Where transport is necessary, as in the case of a mother going shopping with several young children, it could be provided by a form of communal vehicle; for example, by a development from the present supermarket cart, providing a simple electrically powered vehicle that would move at 5 or 10 miles an hour, endangering no one. Sufficiently large numbers could be produced quite cheaply to allow it to function within the *tuath* as a common amenity owned communally.

7. When one *tuath* begins to grow too large through reproduction, it could divide in two, in a similar way to cell division – one half moving off to build a new unit.

8. If such a 'granular' or molecular structure of society were to take root, there would seem to be no need for urban sprawl and for the disastrous break between rural and urban development. Provided each *tuath* was linked to others by rapid transit systems, and hopefully these in time could be built underground, there is no reason why these units should not be evenly or relatively evenly spread across the country. At the same time, where it seemed desirable, by

grouping several units close to one another the real advantages of the city could be preserved and it would be possible still to have the excitement and life of a true city centre with such an arrangement.

9. Each *tuath* should have its own administrative heart and local self-government, this having full autonomous control of the basic functions of life for the unit. If then, as mentioned above, each *tuath* is linked to others by rapid transport systems and by rapid communication and information systems, and provided all this information and data is fed from each *tuath* to the central government, the latter could then take on a true planning function. Indeed its main function would now become that of planning and co-ordination, exerting an overall monitoring and control over the basically self-governing units. With such a system there should no longer be a need for the enormous civil service bureaucracy which we have at present. This could be streamlined so that present departments of state would become little more than efficient channels for policy to travel from the central planning group to the discrete and largely autonomous *tuath*. Democracy might for the first time have a chance in these circumstances of working from below upwards, the central planning group being fed, replaced and revitalized continuously from the periphery.

Conclusion

I am afraid all I have done is to attempt to sketch some general but fundamental characteristics of a human module – a very tentative outline – but I see no reason why a much more developed and detailed description could not be undertaken. This to my mind must involve the application of genuine human research to the human being, the application of the scientific method to the setting up of human experience or human laboratories. It may be objected that we already have the human and social sciences, but for too long these have studied human beings as if they were a purely natural phenomenon. Essentially their approach has been to go and observe people and see what they think, say and do. The trouble is that human beings are not in fact a natural phenomenon. They have, through a long and painful striving, largely created their own civilization and culture, but more importantly I believe that they have the ability to change and redirect their own destiny if they should so wish. If we compare the approach of social science to that of the physicist, it is clear that the latter operates in a quite different way. The true scientist, it seems to me, thinks and dreams, perhaps for years, and when he feels he has an idea or hypothesis he then constructs an experiment to test this and see to what extent it is true. If we were to turn this approach to the human being, I think we would then have something resembling a genuine human science. We would ask how should human beings develop, how should they build their society to enhance their personal and human qualities and then, having constructed a hypothesis or theory as to what human beings should be and what they should do, we would set up a human experiment along these lines and see how far it is successful, how far it would work. We could then compare this human experiment, and human beings growing and living within it, with society as it exists at present. I see nothing mechanistic in such an approach and it seems to me that in this way the scientific method could be applied to the human being while maintaining full respect for Christian ethical and human values generally. Would it be too much to expect our universities to develop in this way – real departments or human studies involving a number of disciplines and separate lines of thought. It is not my intention in any way to detract from the tremendous contribution that has been made by anthropologists and sociologists to our knowledge of mankind, but it seems to me that to observe human beings as they are can only be considered a part of the full spectrum of human experiments and that we must go beyond this and set up genuine human experiments so that the sociologists can then study the human being in the process of actively and consciously changing.

It finally remains to be asked where could such a development in society take place in the contemporary world. It would not seem that there are many countries where this is likely or even possible. Large technological countries such as the United States, Britain or West Germany would appear already to have so devitalized the personal dimension as to be unlikely soil in which a development of this kind might take root. Russia or China appear to have similar defects. In addition, from what is known they evidently lack the basic human freedoms necessary for such an experiment. It did seem that something along these lines was beginning to grow in Czechoslovakia but we saw only too tragically what happened to that development.

The countries of the third world, the Afro-Asian and so-called underdeveloped nations, on the other hand, appear to lack the necessary technological development. Most of their people are living at bare subsistence level and there would therefore seem little hope of building personalized society units for a long time to come.

We are left then with a number of small countries, such as the Scandinavian countries, particularly Finland, Israel, possibly Yugoslavia or Cuba, which have a reasonably developed standard of living and technology. These, because they are small geographically and in terms of population, and have each their own separate culture and language and are already somewhat more personalized in their organization of society. Interestingly enough, it is in several of these countries that a groping towards a 'granular' society seems to be taking place. In Finland there is the experimental town of Tapiola, which is apparently designed along these lines and is largely self-maintaining. In Israel we have the Kibbutz, which is probably the closest to a human module yet developed but the troubled political situation there may make further development in this direction very difficult. In Yugoslavia there seems to be a considerable growth of democracy at community level, worker participation in factories and so on and, provided the authoritarian and dictatorial qualities so far associated with Communist countries can be overcome, there may well be further developments in this direction there. Lastly we come to Ireland. Even amongst the group of countries just mentioned, Ireland seems to have unique possibilities. It still has links, even though these are tenuous, with the ancient decentralized Celtic culture from which it developed. Possibly as result of this, the personal dimension still seems to be stronger in this country than in any other. One indication of this is the number of creative authors and poets this country has produced over the past few decades. Over this period Ireland has probably produced more creative writers than Britain and the United States combined, and this out of a tiny population. Of all forms of creative endeavour, poetry and prose are probably the most personal and individual. Ireland has a population of barely three million, but even now 50% of these are not yet urbanized. The parish and village structure of community life here, although in many ways now debilitated, is still largely intact and has a unique pool of voluntary effort. In recent times there has been a tremendous growth and emergence of local community associations and voluntary organizations of all sorts. For all of these reasons I feel this country has a unique opportunity to make a radical change within its society – a radical change of direction should it only wish to do so. However, forces of influence pouring in from outside are enormous and this change, if change there is to be, has probably only ten, at most twenty years, within which to happen. I believe that, unless Ireland shakes itself out of its lethargy and actively halts its passive downward progression towards the impersonal, following relentlessly behind the United States and the nations of Western Europe since the advent of the Common Market, Ireland as a recognizable and in any sense separate entity will have ceased to exist within twenty years.

7. Psycho-Social Problems and the General Practitioner

The following address was delivered at the Medical Union's Annual General Meeting in Sligo on 27 September 1973.

ON reflection, a better title for this paper would have been 'Human Bio-Social Problems and the General Practitioner', for in real life we do not find any such thing as a purely psychic or psycho-social problem; all the things which happen to us are experiences involving our whole being. Take a typical neurosis, agoraphobia, which we would ordinarily think of as a purely psychiatric condition. The person finds himself compelled to avoid certain external situations. If he attempts to face these situations, he experiences certain unpleasant 'symptoms'. These symptoms, when he describes them to us, we recognize as manifestations of 'anxiety' or 'fear' but if we look closely at what is happening we find they are mainly physiological: in unpleasant sensations we experience fear in the stomach, in feeling weakness of the knees, cold sweat, the heart racing and so on. The summation of these experiences we recognize as the psychic awareness of 'anxiety' but the total experience which we are talking about is not merely psychic it is an experience of our whole being. The same is true of any other 'psychic' experience we like to think of, whether depression, guilt, elation, anger or whatever.

But I am going ahead of myself. What has all this to do with the General Practitioner? I think it brings to the fore some of the fundamental questions about the nature of illness or health. I imagine your response would be 'surely any fool knows what illness is'. But do we? My impression is that, when we say we understand something – as, for example, what health or illness is – this understanding rests not on a well-thought-out logical basis relating back to first principles but rather is more likely to depend on what has been happening in the area of activity in question; what developments have been taking place, for example, in medicine, over the preceding period. It is these activities and developments which tend to supply the materials out of which we build our concepts of reality. It is not so much, therefore, that the actual reality of something like illness or health changes but that our idea of what these are is influenced by an emphasis in a certain direction due to developments that have been taking place over a preceding period of time.

If we look at the growth of medicine over the last hundred years it can be seen that there were enormous achievements along certain lines of development. With the introduction of asepsis and anaesthesia into modern surgery, there were great successes in the early years in dealing with burns, injuries, excision of diseased parts of the body, reparative operations, etc., moving on to the more creative and reconstructive forms of surgery being undertaken at the present time. Likewise, there were marked achievements in medicine which led to the virtual elimination of whole groups of diseases, such as smallpox, lobar pneumonia, diphtheria, tuberculosis, etc., which have been brought under control by inoculation, vaccination, public health measures and more recently by the development of antibiotics and other therapeutic measures.

In these fields of endeavour, the successes related mainly to external assaults on the human being, injury or infection. Out of these advances grew an understanding of what it is felt constituted illness and, following from this, by a process of elimination emerged a concept of health (although this was much less clear as a state which is assumed to be present when one is not ill). However, if we turn now to the major hazards to health facing western society at the present time, we find these are utterly different from those which faced clinical medicine during the period of great expansion and successful intervention in the latter half of the nineteenth century and early years of this century, when the major infections and surgical conditions were being conquered. Therefore, although the real nature of health and illness has not changed, our idea of what these are will have to alter radically if we are to tackle successfully the problems facing us today, which are quite different in character to those of fifty years ago. Let me illustrate this change with but one example: the EEC. The Experts Research Committee has recently reported to the Commission that:

Following a detailed analysis, which took into account the criteria mentioned above, the following subjects were considered to be of high priority:

1. metabolic and psychosomatic factors in cardiovascular diseases;
2. environmental and genetic factors in respiratory diseases;
3. psychosomatic, metabolic and environmental factors in digestive diseases;
4. embryotoxic, genetic and environmental factors in congenital disorders;
5. psychological, physiological and metabolic aspects of ageing; and
6. psychological, toxic and environmental factors in road traffic accidents.

Now what does this mean? In what way do these disorders mentioned by the EEC group differ from those which formerly preoccupied the attention of medicine? There are several important ways in which they differ. No simple single cause is found. Many interacting causal factors, both genetic and environmental, appear to be concerned. There is a difference, too, in the nature of some of the causal factors that have been elicited. Take, for example, lung cancer or cardiovascular disease. Suggested causal factors such as smoking, excessive food intake and low-energy output, chronic stress or frustration, etc., are not in fact organisms or chance occurrences which come upon us out of the blue; they are human behaviours. Smoking or eating are things which one does, which one learns, and the origin of this learning is often in early childhood, but the key factor which now enters the picture is that of *time*. All of these conditions which have now become a health priority in western countries develop slowly over many years, often from imperceptible beginnings early in life. In their beginnings there are signs that the bodily responses to emotion brought about by stress are becoming less flexible and adaptive. Heightened activity and increasing sensitivity of bodily processes – blood pressure and glandular activity – can be detected. At the same time, psychological functioning is manifestly less effective and coping skills are diminishing.

If this is true then, ultimately, illness is the outcome of the influence upon us of the surrounding environment; it is the product of the attitudes and practices of society, of parents and others, which impinge upon us and provide the raw materials out of which we grow and develop. I am convinced, therefore, that if we are to understand the major ills affecting man in modern society, then it is essential for us to grasp two fundamentals. First, the dimension of time. These are processes that grow and develop slowly over time; the illness, therefore, is not to be found at the beginning but rather at the end: the overt illness is the end point of a process and of course at this stage it may not be fully or even partly reversible. Second, each of us forms a continuum with our surrounding environment, each of us is the outcome of all the influences which surround us from birth onwards as we grow and develop. Nowhere more than here is the statement true that 'no man is an island'. Our genetic endowment is moulded and shaped by the surrounding environment as we develop and by the influence of all those persons – our parents and others – who are close to us.

It was in this sense that I meant my alternative title – 'Psycho-Social' or 'Bio-Social Problems'. All illnesses are partly social in origin and are the results of the attempt of each of us to adapt to and deal with the environment in which we live.

The question arises here: is man capable of adapting to any kind of environment? Over the long stretches of evolutionary time, the genetic endowment of man has been moulded and shaped by the surrounding milieu of this planet, so that the human nature to which we are all heirs is now suited to, and in tune with, the natural surroundings of this world. However, this is where the difficulty arises, for in the past few hundred years human beings have grossly interfered with and radically altered this natural order and hence the question arises – can man adapt satisfactorily to the artificial man-made environment in which most of us are now forced to live? In his recent work, *So Human an Animal*, René Dubos addresses himself to this problem:

> On the one hand, the genetic endowment of *homo sapiens* has changed only in minor details since the Stone Age, and there is no chance that it can be significantly, usefully, or safely modified in the foreseeable future. This genetic permanency determines the physiological limits beyond which human life cannot be safely altered by social and technological innovations. In the final analysis, the frontiers of cultural and technological development are determined by man's genetic make-up which constitutes his own biological frontiers.

It would be a rash person indeed who would put a limit on the adaptability of man. Every time in the past that it has been said – 'human beings will never be able to do that' or 'we have reached the limits of human endeavour' – someone has come along to prove that man could accomplish that very thing. Human beings have landed on the moon, have shown that they can live in outer space, can climb the highest mountain or penetrate to the bottom of the sea, but what has become very clear – and there is increasing evidence to support this – is that, the further man departs from his natural environment, the higher the price he has to pay, in whatever terms we like to measure this, to achieve this departure. In space, this can be seen in the technological cost, in the huge expenditure of energy and so on, but it has also become apparent that prolonged exposure to environmental extremes – such exposure to emotional or sensory deprivation; being a prisoner of war or a concentration camp; a natural catastrophe such as flood or earthquake; torture – involves strain and brings in its train a personal cost, a physiological price that has to be paid in psychosomatic stress, seen in the increased incidence of a wide range of illnesses and premature termination of life.

This seems to be the situation we are in, and indeed moving further into all the time. We are paying an exorbitantly high price in terms of physiological, social and personal breakdown for the kind of society we have created, which is largely inimical to man's nature. We are in an inflationary position where every year the cost in economic and, much more important, in human terms goes higher. Our behaviour, that is the behaviour of society as a whole and of the medical profession in particular, can be likened to that of a farmer who uses his land to grow high-priced crops and livestock for short-term gain without any thought to plough back some of his resources into fertilization, rotation of crops and so on; pouring all that he has into high-priced technological machinery to enable him to more rapidly and completely harvest his gains. Or again, to the owner of a car-hire firm who, putting a new fleet of cars on the road, fails to take any care as to how they are driven or serviced. When asked why he neglects the new vehicles in this way, he pleads that he has no alternative, as all his maintenance resources are deployed carrying out expensive repairs to the old fleet of cars to try to keep them functioning on the road for a little while longer. These hypothetical situations are not strictly comparable but may perhaps help to illustrate the point I am trying to make. I think it will be agreed that neither the farmer nor the manager of the car-hire firm would remain long in business were they to behave in this way. Yet this is almost exactly the way our health services and the medical profession behave at the present time. Of the approximately £100 million which we spend yearly on health services, by far the largest portion goes into hospital care and increasingly expensive specialist medicine and surgery. We appear to make great heaps of our resources around the gateway of death in an attempt to close it but we are no nearer to closing it nor ever will be, for the simple fact is that all of us have to die. I want to emphasize that I am in no way espousing the cause of euthanasia or questioning any real effort to save life, but sooner or later we will have to face honestly where the priorities in health lie, and how we are going to deploy most effectively the limited resources available to us. It was in this sense that I used the analogy of the car-hire firm for if, as I have suggested, we view illness, particularly the major problems facing us today, such as cardiovascular disease, degenerative conditions, psychiatric disorders and so on, as developing along a time scale, with their beginnings taking shape in the developmental processes of early life, then the blunt fact of our health services and of the behaviour of the medical profession in this country, as indeed in most other countries, is that almost all our resources are poured into attempting to arrest and treat illness at a late stage, when much of the process is already irreversible.

Our efforts, therefore, are directed at a point where the illness has become overt and is fully developed, when it is largely irreversible and when the processes of decay and disease, through maladaptive living, are already well advanced in the patient (for at this stage he is a patient rather than a person) and when at best, even utilizing the most expensive techniques available to technological and specialist medicine, we can only hope to drag the patient on for a few years of poor and failing health. Thus, if we stand back and look at the situation with cold logic, it must be admitted that the medical profession and our health services generally are geared to intervene in the process of illness when it is too late to do anything really effective; at the end rather than at the beginning; at the most costly point in the time scale. This is medical and economic madness. It is no wonder that the costs of health services are escalating out of sight in all western countries at the present time, for (except for some simple and rather primitive public and child health measures) we are not providing health services, only services for sickness.

In this and in other countries, we are often inclined to think that the major expenditure of public monies goes into industrial and economic development but who are the wealthy, the powerful, the people of high status in our society? Certainly we think of the big business interests, those in the government and high places but also I think we must admit that, as professionals, we are usually numbered among this group. We may not always be wealthy but society tells us that we are of high status; indeed, we often look down even on the business man. Even though, as individuals, some of us may not be personally wealthy, where do the wealth and resources of our contemporary society lie? On the one hand they are concentrated in big business and in the giant corporations or state bureaucracies, and on the other side nowadays there is nearly as great a concentration of wealth and resources in the social services – health and social welfare departments, hospitals and so on. The human and social services are booming growth industries at the face of capitalism, caring for and maintaining at subsistence level thousands of casualties produced by our aggressive competitive form of society. It appears to me inescapable, therefore, that whenever one of us sits down in our nice hospital-family-practice or other office, with one of our titles of doctor, social worker/priest, lawyer/judge, we set out, in our white coat, wig and gown or other uniform, to 'help' some other person who is likely to be poor, shabbily dressed or, if not actually in a state of poverty, certainly of low status – a patient, a client, a problem, a delinquent – then, as surely as we sit in a room behind our desks peering at him through dark-rimmed glasses, punctuating our questions or examination with 'hm! hm!', we are doing a violence *to* him. Whatever else we may do *for* him, we are damaging his autonomy and self-respect and therefore damaging him as a person, to the extent that we fail to recognize him as an equal, independent human being.

I can almost hear some of you saying, this may be all very well, perhaps there is some truth in it, but it is all very theoretical. What relevance has this for me as an ordinary working practitioner? It seems to me that what I have been saying has very real and practical implications for medicine at the present time, and for that matter for any practising doctor for, while the approach to health assessment and adaptation to the environment can be as sophisticated as we like to make it – and there is an enormous explosion of new knowledge now becoming available in this area, involving the growth of a whole new technology of endocrine and behavioural investigation – the essential of what I am speaking about is really very simple. It means exactly this: we need to change from diagnosis of a state of illness to diagnosis of the state of health of the person. This may not sound like very much but I put it to you that, if we are really serious as doctors about the need for such change, it will involve turning our whole health services and the medical profession upside-down. If we are honest, the job of a doctor at present is to decide whether or not a person that comes to see him is ill. We really make very little judgement as to what is the state of health of the person, what is his general state of adaptation to his environment when he comes to see us, and what are the implications of this for his future.

I have no neat formula to put forward as to what a full diagnostic assessment of health would consist of as, although knowledge in this area is expanding rapidly, our understanding of health as distinct from illness is still in an early stage of development. As I have said, the techniques of psycho-physiological and endocrinological measurement and investigation are becoming very sophisticated and new technological developments are appearing almost daily. Our research workers in the Department of Psychiatry under the direction of Dr Cullen are studying and developing these on a systematic basis and it seems clear that unprecedented new horizons in the development of community medicine and primary health care are opening up. All that I am attempting to do here – and indeed I would not feel competent to do any more – is to indicate broadly what such a change of approach, from concern with illness to an emphasis on health status, would involve. The kind of diagnostic approach I have in mind, therefore, I would see as being concerned with the following areas:

1. An assessment of the physiological functional status of the person, including cardiovascular function, endocrinological profile and availing of pre-diagnostic screening techniques of the Mediscan type to the level of sophistication which is available. In such an assessment, any evidence of abnormal reaction to stress, danger signals for the future or of course any evidence of overt illness would be looked for.

2. An assessment of the current level of anxiety of the person and, where possible, measurement of sensitivity to stress at a pre-symptomatic stage.
3. An examination of the adaptive behaviour of the person, not so much in the sense of whether this is good or bad but rather a description of the kind of way the person adapts to life and to stress. This would involve an assessment, be it a rough assessment, of their personality development and of the kind of learning and experience to which they were exposed during their formative years, leading to the patterns of adaptive behaviour which they now show.
4. An assessment of the interpersonal relationships and the social context within which the person is attempting to adapt to life.

It should be stressed that, in assembling this kind of pre-symptomatic profile, as much attention would be given to the positive aspects of the person as well as the negative symptoms. I believe that such a diagnostic assessment, even if this were only attempted on a fairly rough clinical level, would provide a totally different kind of information to the present 'medical' diagnosis and would bring to light early signs for the future. It would also provide information as to the kinds of social and interpersonal situations the person would, in the future, be likely to adapt to successfully or alternatively run into trouble. For example, such an assessment would be able to indicate that a person who appeared at the time of examination to be managing life quite successfully might, perhaps in ten years' time, run into serious trouble when faced with retirement. Information of this kind, therefore, would open the possibility for remedial and preventative action to be taken.

Lest there be any misunderstanding, I want to emphasize here that the diagnosis of illness – where this is found to be present – would remain an important part of the overall assessment and, where an overt illness is found, obviously the more effective the intervention of curative medicine and efficient specialist treatment the better. What I *am* saying is that, in this kind of approach, the diagnosis of illness would only be a part – and, increasingly, as we intervene in the developmental process of disease at an earlier stage, a subsidiary part – of the overall diagnosis of a state of health. Another thing that should be said here is that, in my opinion, if we are serious about achieving this redirection of our health services it is not more psychiatry that we need, for I do not accept that a health assessment and intervention approach of this type is the province of psychiatry but rather a different kind of generalism – if you like, a new form of primary health care – involving community physicians with a much wider range of skills and competence than exist at present. If we are honest, I think we will have to face that the present generation of doctors, and this includes most psychiatrists, simply were not given the training and have not got the range of skills and competence to undertake the kind of job that I am proposing here.

This means that, even if major reallocation of resources in the health services were effected so as to allow a greater emphasis on health and prevention rather than treatment of sickness, there does not exist at present a generation of doctors appropriately trained to translate such a health policy into reality. What is implied here is that, if we are really serious that such a change of direction in the implementation of our health services is necessary, then it must be accompanied by a radical reorganization of the medical curriculum and the process of training in our medical schools, both undergraduate and postgraduate.

I would go further and say that, even if such a transformation in the training and skills of the medical profession is effected, I do not believe that a single isolated doctor working on his own, no matter how differently and competently trained, could undertake satisfactorily the implementation of a health policy of this kind. I think there needs to be, in addition, a major reorganization in the structure and administrative framework of our health services, particularly in primary health care. I believe that this will involve some or all of the following changes:

1. The development of a health team that will include, in addition to the community physician, social workers, psychologists, a very differently trained type of district nurse and active participation by the community itself.
2. That this health team would have responsibility for a definite catchment area and population, with a definite responsibility for these persons and families, whether in sickness or in health.
3. That the services provided in a health district would radiate out from a properly equipped diagnostic health centre. Such a centre could be available to each health district or supply several districts as indicated.

4. That an appropriate number of these health districts would then be brought into relation to, and have available to them, the technological and specialist facilities of a general hospital or poly-clinic.

To sum up, I would like to emphasize that all I have attempted to do here is to try to give some rough indication of the kind of changes of direction that I believe are required of our health services if we are to address ourselves effectively to the major hazards to health facing western society at the present time. I hesitate, somewhat, to remind you of Lincoln's famous utterance – 'that we can fool some of the people all the time' – I do not need to complete the quotation but I think its meaning for the medical profession is clear: while we may be turning out doctors with competence suitable to the late nine-teenth century, if we do not, as a profession, alert ourselves and genuinely set about facing the problems of the latter part of this century, society is likely to quietly pass us by and look for help from someone who will.

8. Macra na Feirme: To Farm
or Not to Farm

The next piece was written on 7 November 1974. As part of the work for the Irish Foundation for Human Development, we were asked to consult with Agricultural Inspectors to suggest ways in which they might be able to assist farmers with the human problems that were arising as a result of the introduction of the Common Agricultural Policy.

This paper was never published but I presented it at a meeting in the Department of Agriculture with about 500 participants. I received a standing ovation from the audience because I spoke about the misgivings that many of them had about the current policies. Shortly after this, I was informed of a decision by the Department of Agriculture that I was never to be allowed to speak there again!

Introduction

I AM beginning to believe that farming in this country must be in a bad state when one of the leading farming organizations feels the need of a headshrinker to come to talk to them. Now, right at the beginning, I want to make clear that I know nothing about agriculture or farming and therefore if I say some things which seem contentious or even foolish, perhaps you will be kind enough to excuse these on the plea of ignorance.

Economic Realities

Hearing almost daily about the difficulties under which farmers in this country are labouring, I felt some time ago, I should try to understand what I could about the programmes of the European Economic Community (EEC) for the future of our agriculture, and the common agriculture policy. As far as I can understand it, the economic constraints upon us within the EEC will demand a programme of modernization and rationalization (to use some of the typical jargon phrases) to bring our farming units up to a competitive size. This policy is based on the premise that farmers and farm workers should receive incomes which are equivalent or comparable to those received outside agriculture. This comparable income in 1973 was calculated to be approximately £1,800 per annum. In that year it was estimated that approximately 20% of farms in the Republic had obtained comparable incomes. From this point of view, farms are classified into three groups:

1. commercial farms – i.e. those already providing a viable income;
2. development farms – i.e. those which it is hoped with development could in time provide comparable incomes;
3. transitional farms – this category appears to include the vast majority of farms under 50 acres, where there does not appear to be a reasonable hope of their becoming competitive.

From what I can gather, the EEC will assist those in category 2, development farms, with grants and other forms of support to help them to reach commercial status; this they will do, it seems to be implied, at the expense of the transitional farms, which will get no help whatever and will be literally squeezed out of existence. Thus, farmer will be set against farmer and very considerable numbers will have to leave the land, to seek alternative employment, or go into retirement. Of course, this trend has been evident for some years. Estimates show that the agricultural labour force has been declining in this country by 11,000 per year from 1966–1972. Also a high proportion of farmers are single and in the higher age groups. It is hoped that many of these will go into retirement, allowing their land to go to more efficient and younger farmers. The EEC will encourage retirement with pension schemes from the age of fifty-five upwards. This seems an excellent way to encourage premature senility and to enhance our geriatric problem. All of this policy appears to be aimed at creating fewer, larger, more efficient and highly mechanized farms which will specialize in one line of production, whether beef or dairying, and will resemble the factory assembly line, depending heavily on fertilizers and pesticides.

Human Realities

These then are the economic realities about which we are told, which have to be faced whether we like it or not. I know that, if I tried to ignore them, you would very quickly remind me of the fact that they are there and will not go away. But there are other realities about ourselves as human persons which I feel I have a right to talk about. These, too, are real and will not go away. In fact, evidence is now coming in from all over the world that is telling us that they represent a much deeper reality about man's situation in the world at the present time. It is quite impossible for me to go into all this evidence here, but what I would like to do is to put briefly before you our position as human beings in the world at the present time as I see it.

Ourselves in Relation to the Environment

The more we look down deeply into ourselves, understand our physiology and the way our bodies work, the more clear it becomes that we are designed to live in a very direct relationship to nature and to the environment. When I say 'designed', I mean that over several million years of evolutionary struggle and interaction between man and nature what we are, the way in which we function, right down to the structure and function of the cells which make up our bodies, has been hammered out so as to fit a life of struggle with nature, with the natural world as it existed undisturbed in this planet until recent times. What does this mean? It means a number of things: that it is of the essence of our being to struggle with nature; that we have a vital need to directly experience growing and living things, to mould and do things with our surroundings. For a human being to be sane and healthy, he must directly control his own life, have control over his own destiny. This is another way of expressing that it is of the very essence of our being to be free, to have the personal freedom to control our lives. It follows that, if we are to have this direct relationship to the environment, that environment must be understandable; we must relate to a whole world, so that all the essential aspects of life bear a clear relationship to one another – work, play, the provision of shelter, the growing of food, the making of the utensils and tools we use, other living creatures and nature in general. All of these must bear a clear relationship to each other, forming a whole world, small and intimate enough to be understandable in human terms.

Ourselves in Relation to Others

Another vital aspect of this holistic understandable world within which we need to be is our relationship to each other. This is the second reality which I believe we cannot afford to ignore – *our fundmental need to relate to each other as persons*. Now for this to happen, the number of persons who form any primary social setting must be quite small. Clearly there are several levels of intimacy; perhaps the most intimate relationship of love can only fully happen between two persons. Intimate friendships can exist within groups of three or four, perhaps even five or six, persons and we know now from the study of group relations that, once the number of participants in a group exceeds ten or twelve, the character of the relationship changes, the level of intimacy lessens, and it is no longer possible to have direct face-to-face relationships of all the members to each other. Nevertheless, within a stable community it is probably still possible for human beings in some way to relate to each other as persons, up to several hundred, perhaps even up to a few thousand people in a town or village and its hinterland, where the roots with the past and the territorial relationships are clearly identifiable. Beyond this, however, it does seem quite clear that personal relationship is lost, and we begin to move into the impersonal collective where human beings are aware of one another as anonymous units.

This is the 'mass culture' with which we are so familiar in our modern cities. My point is that, once human beings lose this direct personal relationship to each other, and to the environment, they begin to lose touch with themselves, cannot recognize who they are and are no longer able to remain sane and healthy. We have allowed the impersonal, the mechanized mass-society, where most of us now exist, largely, as machine components, to enter so deeply into our lives that we are no longer able to perceive the cause of our malaise. We are not even *aware* of our deep need for personal relationships. What appears to be urgently needed, then, is for man once again to grow more small, personalized human settings, primary human communities where people can know each other as persons, where women have true equality with men, and human beings once again have control over the essential functions of their lives. What is quite clear is that such a consciously accepted free, personalized and cooperative form of social organization is quite incompatable with the ruthless competitive ethos of western society, where personal advancement and success can only be conceived as happening at the expense and disadvantage of someone else.

Ourselves in Relation to Our Past and Future

None of us simply come into existence *now*. Unless we can be related to our past, where we came from, and have a clear relationship to our children who will come after us, we are again unable to clearly identify who or what we are. A human being has to be born and to be grown: we do not simply happen. Nor do we remain for long as aggressive, energetic and competitive adults, but have to grow old and die; this is the cycle of life in which all of us are embedded. If a child is to grow into a healthy human person, the relationships about which I spoke under the previous two headings – to the environment and to other persons within a holistic world of understandable proportions – are even more vital to the developing child. The isolated family where the father disappears for most of the time to a workplace that has no meaning and where the child is confined within a concrete box amidst thousands of other boxes does not make up the kind of understandable world or human relationships about which I am speaking. Thus we come upon a fundamental human need here once again: for all the ages of the life cycle to bear a clear relationship to one another, if we are to make sense of ourselves and not to have disturbed children, vandalizing adolescents and hoards of isolated wretched middle-aged and demented old people.

Now these realities seem to me to point unrelentingly to the need for a fundamental change within society, one to do with man himself. They seem to point unmistakably to the fact that we have allowed an enormous separation to take place between the human being as a person and the corporate, industrial and economically dominated society which we have created; that we badly need now to get down to the job of creating, in a new form, primary social units of society. These, if there is any truth in the realities to which I have been referring, will have to be small personalized human communities where human beings would learn to cooperate rather than compete with one another. I am not suggesting that we would be confined within such human modules but rather that, were once such a personalized human base established, then we could cross the boundaries of these personalized communities to relate to other communities and persons and thus to build up the fabric of a radically different kind of society.

. . . That Is the Question

These two sets of realities seem to be in stark contradiction: the economic realities, as manifested in EEC directives; and the 'human realities' to which I have referred above. Have we arrived then at an impasse which can in no way be reconciled? Before throwing up our hands in despair, let us look again at these so-called 'economic realities' as laid down for us by those who 'know' in the European community. Here I would like to quote from a recent interview with Sicco Mansholt. It was he, you may remember, more than anyone who put together the blueprint for agricultural policy in the EEC, although now some years later he appears to be a sadder and wiser man. These are some of the things he has to say:

> Five million people have been leaving the land in Europe every ten years for the last twenty-five years. But it was mainly the young people, leaving the old ones on the land. Small farms couldn't give farmers a living. The EEC plan gave young farmers a chance to stay on bigger farms. It was politically impossible to double prices, the only alternative was to increase production per acre by mechanization, intensive use of pesticides and fertilizers. But this is anti-ecological. Bigger farms are better since in theory, farmers can undertake recycling of wastes. But there is no research on ecological recycling in agriculture. Now with the energy crisis, I agree people will have to start returning to the land in Europe. As for the third world, 'modern' agriculture is a disaster. Multinational companies operating there should be putting small farmers under contract, instead of having huge monocultures.

This all follows from the madness of 'growth' economics – 'increase the gross national product by efficient production and increased exports, thus giving everyone higher incomes'. Listen again to what Mansholt has to say about 'growth':

> Ever since 1968, I have been convinced we have to stop growth not only for ecological reasons but because of the enormous gap between developed and developing countries. The increasing gap is proof of our economic failure. Our politicians say that we must grow in order to help the third world grow; that is a lie, the opposite is true. There are not many resources left for the third world, and they are the bigger losers in our present economic system.

This from the man who was, after all, the main architect of the common agricultural policy of the EEC.

It is openly admitted that the fruits of this policy when once fully implemented will mean that something like 120,000 farmers in the Republic will be driven off the land. Let us leave aside for the moment the human implications of this and simply ask, where are they going to go? We are told complacently that they will be given jobs in industry. This, imagine, in a situation where we have at this moment an official figure of 73,000 unemployed, a world-wide economic depression already more severe than that of 1929, and where businesses are running into trouble all over the country. But do I dare to suggest that the pundits of the EEC, and our own agricultural authorities, could be wrong? After all, these policies represent the fruits of some of the greatest brains in Europe. Could these even be very stupid policies? Were it not for some of the things which are already happening to our agriculture and our beef trade as a result of these very policies, one would surely not dare to harbour such thoughts. But then one hears of a small farmer in Mayo taking his calf to the town to sell and his wife asking him to pick up a chicken for dinner in the supermarket while he is there; he manages to sell his calf for a £1 and pays £1.50 for the chicken for dinner. When the policies of the 'mass-society' lead to this degree of absurdity, does one need to say any more?

We are told that the common agricultural policy is to ensure that those farmers who remain on the land have a higher income, comparable to that of other sectors in society. This seems only fair and reasonable, but I find myself asking 'What is income, what does it mean'? Really! I am beginning to think I must be stupid; I always thought that real income not only means what we earn, but also what we spend, what we produce ourselves and how we use it.

Indeed I find in my own life that it seems to matter little nowadays how much I earn, but it makes a great deal of difference how I use what I have. If I economize and avoid buying things that I do not really need, if I grow my own vegetables, make my clothes and car last a little longer, and shop carefully where things are cheap – this is what makes the difference. How much use then is 'income' to a farmer if he produces only one product, say beef, and has to buy everything else he needs at exorbitant prices? As I said at the beginning, I know little or nothing about agriculture, but I remember a farm where I used to go as a child: on that farm they produced everything they needed: meat, vegetables, eggs, dairy produce. They even had their own flour milled at the local mill and produced the wool of which their clothes were made; they literally only had to buy a few things like tea and tobacco. I know I will be told it is not economic to do so but I wonder, when you think of examples like those I have mentioned.

(I would like to state clearly here that I am not against the EEC as such. I voted for joining the EEC and would do the same again. But to my mind the real reasons for us to be part of the European Community are cultural, not economic. It has enabled us to break out of the total mental straitjacket of domination by England in which we were caught. After nearly 500 years we are becoming culturally part of Europe once again, linked to the mainstream of European thought and culture.)

Is there then any way out of the mass of contradictions, any way that we can hold on to some human values and ordinary sanity and at the same time meet the economic requirements of modernization, technological efficiency and rationalization of our agriculture? I am afraid I have a simple mind but it seems to me that the only way out of this dilemma is *cooperation with one another*. I get the impression that the mention of cooperatives is something of a dirty word nowadays but before condemning the notion let us allow our imagination to run free for a few moments. Suppose a number of small farms were to come together, they would at least then be able to meet the requirements of the EEC for a farming unit of economic size – the combination of say ten small farms would provide a unit of more than 100 acres. By pooling their resources they could then qualify, I presume, for grants and other EEC schemes to allow them to modernize, buy machinery and create an efficient operation. However, the matter does not rest there. It seems to me they could at the same time build in their own life-support systems. For example, each family could retain a small area of land on which to grow their own vegetables and they could, either separately or by combining together, supply themselves with dairy produce, free-range chickens, fruit trees and so on. I may be very wrong but I cannot see why these essentials for home use and survival could not be produced while at the same time the cooperative specializes in one dimension such as beef or dairy produce along modern lines of efficiency. Let me take one more fanciful example. If the cooperative were to buy one large deep freeze, they could, by killing an occasional beast, supply all the personal needs of all the families in the cooperative. It is not beyond conceiving that, were there an old watermill in the area, this could be got going again to mill flour for the home use of the cooperative. Think what this sort of thing would mean in terms of the human realities about which I spoke earlier, of the holistic world and meaningful relationships that would once again be introduced to the children growing up in such a settlement.

Ah, but you will say that cooperatives have been tried and they simply don't work. This may be true but I think there are three important reasons why cooperatives were never fully successful in the past:

1. Until now there was no real pressure on human beings in a country like this to cooperate with one another. Of course, in the old Celtic world there was a great deal of cooperation and the structure of Celtic society was essentially on a decentralized model with a lot of tribal cooperation. But at that time communications and technology were simply not sufficiently developed, nor was man's conscious awareness and understanding of himself mature enough for such a system to work satisfactorily. In recent times, however, western society has been so dominated by a ruthless individualism and competitiveness that any spirit of cooperativeness had little chance of success. Now the situation has once again radically changed and I would predict to you that every year the pressure on all of us to work cooperatively with each other will grow steadily greater. As the mass economic society breaks down – and it is already breaking down – each community, whether rural or urban, will have to think seriously about building in its own basic life-support systems, growing its own essential foodstuffs and providing its own housing, etc. Now I honestly believe that the sooner groups of farmers in this country start to come together to work cooperatively, the better it will be. This brings me to the second reason why I believe cooperative endeavours have not, on the whole, succeeded in the past.

2. If the idea of cooperation is to work this time, I think it cannot be by organizing along one simple dimension as, for example, the cooperative creamery. This time it must be about cooperation for the whole of life. We are talking about a cooperative human

community, a community that would be responsible not only for providing its basic life support but that would also involve cooperative housing and responsibility for its own education, and I would also see such a community perhaps running a factory, or a fishing cooperative, or whatever. Thus the rigid division between what is urban and rural could be broken down. Now, once we say this much we are talking about cooperative endeavour at several levels, for example a number of basic cooperative farming and living units grouped around a village or town, perhaps with one or several small industries, the larger community, again on a cooperative basis, taking responsibility for its own housing, education and other essential aspects of ordinary living.

3. What was not understood in earlier attempts to form cooperatives was the amount of work and effort that has to be put into human relationships. If there is to be success, it is only in recent years that systematic work and research has begun to be seriously applied to the understanding of human group behaviour and human relationships. We are just beginning to realize how complex and difficult these relationships are and probably the most serious task for mankind in the next few generations will not be the mastery of economic or environmental difficulties but attempting to grapple with the problems of human behaviour and our relationships with each other, which now represent the main factors underlying all our other difficulties. Funnily enough, it is right at the opposite pole to the sort of cooperative effort about which I am speaking here – that is, in the world of business, in the giant multinational corporations – that the question of human relations is being taken really seriously. Much of the time of higher management nowadays is spent on the problems of personnel and staff relationships. A lot of work has been done and a good deal is now understood that could be utilized in human living situations, had we a mind to do so. Like the reference in the Gospel to the unjust steward, we could learn much from the business world were we of a mind to apply it to totally different purposes. The strange thing is that, when we turn from big business to the sensitive world of human living, pitifully little effort and resources are brought to bear on what one would have thought were vital questions for human beings to address and try to solve – marriage and family relationships, the education and

development of our children and learning to live corporatively in relation to each other.

There is another important aspect of this same question which I believe will have to undergo radical change if we are to make progress: that is our attitude to ownership and private property; our preoccupation with what is 'mine' as against the other person's. Now I am not taking any idealogical stand on this issue (I no longer have any faith in ideologies). I would rather point to the fact, and I think it is undeniable, that individual private ownership is fast ceasing to exist, to have any meaning, in the world. Take the typical urban dweller in this country, whether his dwelling belongs to the state, or he is struggling to buy his own house, which in fact for most of his life is the property of either the building society, the bank or the insurance company. He works either in a business corporation whose ownership probably rests outside the country, or in a state or semi-state department. In either event he has no ownership or personal control over his working life or what happens to him, he is merely a cog ground between giant wheels. Another example is this very EEC agricultural policy we are discussing for, if the small farmer is foolish enough to give up his tiny holding, what will he have? What will he be? If he is lucky enough to get a factory job, he will, as already mentioned, find his destiny controlled by a multinational corporation outside the state where at any time he can be thrown out of work if they decide to close a 'non-viable' subsidiary. Otherwise he will have a miserable, quickly worthless, pension or dole and will find himself another human fragment thrown on the geriatric scrapheap. The only possible way out of this trap that I can see is for small farmers to group themselves as quickly as possible on a cooperative basis, when they will at least have some joint ownership and control over their lives. I seem to remember that Jesus Christ once said something about loving our neighbour as ourself. I don't remember his saying anything about the sacredness of private property. Don't let us delude ourselves: as I have said elsewhere, state socialism and capitalist big business are not opposites, they are simply two faces of the same impersonal corporate monster which is enslaving us.

Let me end by quoting once more from Sicco Mansholt in his interview with the *Ecologist* where, speaking of ruthless, selfish competitiveness which follows from the preoccupation with private ownership, personal power and dominance by economics, he says:

> We have to get to no-growth, dematerialize our society, have greater equality, abolish private cars. I will have to take a cut in my living standard myself. We must teach our children quite differently: at present, as I see with my five-year-old grandson, they are being programmed at school to take part in the economic rat race. People are defined by their occupation, not their talents or inclinations. We must have a society in which people say, when you ask them what they do, 'I go fishing', 'I play the piano', instead of 'I am a banker' or 'I am an unskilled worker'.

9. Mental Health
and Illness

The article 'Mental Health and Illness' was never published, but I gave a talk on it on 8 May 1976. I am not sure where this was – it may have been at a meeting in Wexford. In this paper I refer to the numbers of patients in Irish Mental Hospitals in comparison to other Western countries and I discussed the relationship of this to the dependency culture resulting from our troubled history.

IRELAND is not a well nation. There is no point in searching for a healthy nation to hold up by comparison. Let it suffice to say that our mental health is below par, way below par, and will continue to be increasingly so unless we are prepared to face the reality that we are responsible for our own mental health. For example, the studies of Dr Dermot Walsh show that there are between three and five times as many patients (depending on age and diagnostic category) in Irish mental hospitals as in British hospitals. Mental illness, with its painful symptoms of depression, anxiety and loss of autonomy, is not visited upon us. It is not caused by an unknown virus or a bug that anyone can catch. It does not come from outside ourselves, nor does it exist independently of our relationships with other people. Mental illness can happen to anyone only in so much as everyone exists in relation to others. We make each other sick. Simply, we allow ourselves to become ill and continue in this state. People are the cause of mental illness. One can say kindly that illness is caused by the pressures of this or that. Who causes the pressures? Who creates the stress factors and the difficult relationships which bring about ill health? Therefore, people cause mental illness.

The sooner we accept that we make each other sick – almost inevitably – and set about the avoidance of this fact, the sooner we will be addressing ourselves to the solutions rather than the problems of our lives. We could have a healthy nation. We could see a rapid decline in emotional suffering among our population, a lessening of dependency on alcohol and tranquillizers and faceless authority, but we must first, every one of us, take personal responsibility for our own mental health and that of our family and community. Miracle drugs and modern treatment can heal acute pain, making it possible perhaps, for the patient to rise once more to a fighting state, but there is no pill or potion to restore mental health. There is no treatment that gives a person back autonomy, no trick for establishing self-esteem, no healing possible in which the sick person does not take responsibility. I know there are people walking around who think they are well because drugged they feel less pain, but they are not cured by medicine. They are simply in a sort of cold storage for the day when they will be able to take hold of their lives and relish the living of them, whatever the difficulties. I do not deny the existence of genetic or bio-chemical determinants of mental illness. It is my view in the majority of cases that these act as background influences rather than directly causing illness, as such. Most mental illness cannot be cured by medicine, and there is certainly none that will prevent its onset. There are organic factors in all mental illness, and mental factors in all physical illness, but these factors are only rarely the main character of the illness. We can learn to take control of so-called biochemical factors of mental illness.

Everyone in this country is subject in greater or lesser degree to the apathy, helplessness and loss of autonomy born of oppression. It is no use, however fashionable, to say that this oppression is behind us. It is seen most clearly in our unawareness of personal responsibility and in our unawareness of our potential as a people and as persons. Our past as a nation has been so crushing and so painful that we are too inclined to rush blindly ahead and leave it behind us. The fact is that we cannot go ahead in any real sense unless we can identify where we are, in relation to where we have been. Who are we now? What sort of a society are we prepared to put our backs into? Or are we only concerned with aping our oppressors by proving to ourselves that we are the same as they were and can use the same methods of oppression on each other? After fifty years of independence, we are still afraid to cast off the security of oppression. However, our fear of freedom, our inability to believe in ourselves, is costing us dearly. It is fast getting to the stage when we must face the past squarely, the better to be able to deal with it and then throw it off as totally unsuitable for the needs of the Irish people. That way spells mental health. Continuing as the architects of our own oppression would be a deliberate bid for the dependency of illness.

When I speak of the past, I refer to our years under colonial domination since the break-up of Celtic society. Instead of linking up with the good of our Celtic heritage when we were able to, we forgot about it. It is time we returned for the good things we were forced to leave behind; our past must be linked up with the present for the sake of the future. Youth, at least, is sick of our pseudo-past, sick of our dependency on anyone and everyone who will lord it over us, and the health of this nation lies with its youth. Our young people are ready and willing to accept responsibility for themselves and the nation, if they could only get their parents and their grandparents off their backs. It is hard for them to see the way so long as their elders keep proclaiming how change is so difficult and almost everything is impossible.

Meanwhile we must confirm youth, let youth have its head and responsibility, if we are to avoid their joining in a few years the dependent hundreds of thousands who can only exist with the help of alcohol and drugs. It is no use telling youth not to drink as much as we do, not to depend on pills as much as we do, if we prevent them from ever acting in their own right. The alternative to autonomy is dependence, and the long continuum of dependency in our culture can be seen in our drinking and dependence on tranquillizers and antidepressants; in the inability of the Irish family to let go of its members' freedom; the failure of man to relate to woman as an equal partner, thus forcing the mother to latch on to her children and the whole stereotype of the Irish mother-son relationship, where sons in turn force their wives to become mothers and housekeepers. This can be seen in the final oppression of women and children – it is the women who feed on tranquillizers, literally thousands in every housing estate. How can we allow our children to think independently and act in freedom without their behaviour becoming an accusation to our serf-like colonial dependence? So we have to hammer them in school into subservience, teach them that they can never have an independent thought but only regurgitate the derived thinking that all of us take in from outside.

We are mentally healthy to the degree to which we manage ourselves – to the degree to which we take responsibility for all our actions in what we are and what we do. Naturally there seems to be a deep thrust in us to grow and develop, to take hold of ourselves, to take responsibility for the management of our lives as we mature; a deep thrust, if you like, towards freedom – for there can be no freedom without responsibility. This appears to be the crucial difference between the immature and the mature. Were it not so, it is hard to see why we should ever emerge from the state of dependency in which we are born. Every infant is born totally dependent and, were it not for this deep thrust to take charge of ourselves, we would remain in this totally dependent state. Yet we accept that any living creature, particularly the human being, struggles to crawl, to stand, to walk, to hold a spoon, to feed themselves. All of this is a primary urge to take hold of life, to master it, and thus to achieve freedom.

Freud said 'mental health was the ability to love and to work'. This may not be a perfect definition but it does grasp the two primary dimensions of all living creatures to feel and to act. To act without feeling is insufficient, to feel without acting is not enough. For good mental health, thinking, feeling and action are co-related and must be in balance. It is then not surprising that there is so much depression and anxiety amongst women. Women are expected to feel, tolerated to think, but seldom allowed to act. I no longer believe that we can talk of the mental health of an 'individual', be it man, woman or child, out of relation to the family with which he or she grows and develops, or of that family climate other than in the context of the total society within which we live as persons and families. Objecters may say that we have had our own government now for some sixty years, and how therefore can I still talk of colonial attitudes in our society, but if we look more closely we will see that these attitudes have in fact never changed because the institutions which maintain them did not basically change. The resolution to which we came in the early years of this century was so partial that it had little or no effect on any of the institutions of our society. Our government departments remained essentially colonial civil services almost incapable of taking independent action and, after sixty years, still effectively awaiting orders from London; our business and economic institutions remained essentially in foreign hands and under foreign control and, when in 1820 the British finally accepted Catholic emancipation, they perpetuated in more subtle form their imperialist and colonial control, handing our education from primary to third level into clerical hands, to intensely conservative priests who, whether they realized it or not, became agents not of Rome or the Vatican but of colonial oppressors who developed an Irish replica of the sexually segregated British public school, who indoctrinated us and our children with subservience and dependence at every level. We, as adults, are fed into the institutions – the civil service, the Church, the businesses and professions, the trade unions – to maintain the dependent colonial relationship for yet another generation. In the last decade we have widened this relationship of dependence to the EEC and to the multinational corporations, so that it is now questionable to what extent we either own or control any aspect of our country. If, as a society, we cannot take hold of ourselves so as to be effective in the running of our affairs and the management of our economy, and if we adopt a relationship of dependency on other countries and outside economic forces, then is it any wonder that the individual can find no place or room to act; that when in this country someone comes up with a creative idea, all those around him set themselves energetically to the task of denigrating that idea, of finding reasons why it could never work?

We have a hundred ways in this country of undermining a person who wants to act, whether by ridicule or by showing how it is impractical: 'It would be useless to try to do that here'; 'ah sure you could never get that going, how would you ever get it to start?'; 'sure you would never get the backing or resources to do that here' and so on. These attitudes run through everything, from the red tape of our civil service departments right through to the public house – 'come on and have a jar and don't be coddin' yourself'. The views of Murphy of McGill University are of interest here. He feels that the 'double-bind' theory in relation to schizophrenia could be operating in Ireland. His theory proposes that 'social situations . . . are schizophrenia-evoking if they persistently confront people with tasks requiring the interpretation of ambiguous, conflicting or otherwise complex information'. In Irish society such tasks are imposed not just by deliberate ridiculing but by a style of conversation that is witty and evasive, and by a tendency to perceive all the available alternatives in a forced choice situation as bad.

You can see this attitude in our willingness to invest in anyone but ourselves, in the get-rich-quick attitudes of the gombeen man, in the attitudes of dependency in the west, the dole, our willingness to act as the agent, the bailiff, for the outsider, never to stand in solidarity with each other to make an authentic statement on independence. In my view, this country represents a dependency culture, by which I mean a society that fails essentially to take responsibility for itself, fails to state itself in the light of its history and its true needs, fails to be self-directing and to manage itself. Further, this dependency culture permeates right down through society, through its institutions to the family and finally to the individual. Consequently, the Irish family also is characterized by dependency and tends to stifle independence and freedom in its members, and each individual, to a greater or lesser degree, tends to manifest dependent behaviour. Furthermore, this dependency culture running through our society forms a continuum which operates in both directions, so that the culture as a whole tends to mould each family and individual into a position or role of dependence, while each individual, having been moulded and developed in the family and in the school in a dependent way of behaving, in turn informs and fills every level of society, all its institutions of church, business and state, with dependent roles, attitudes and behaviours, thus perpetuating the culture of dependency in the society as a whole.

On referring again to the primary thrust or need within each human being to become free, autonomous and independent, it surely becomes clear that mental health for the individual must be synonymous with his being free and independent, having autonomy and taking responsibility for managing himself and his relation to the environment and to other persons. Let us now hold this yardstick up to the notion of therapy or treatment and what conclusions are we forced to draw? The traditional political viewpoint would tell us that the doctor treats the patient, that he takes responsibility for treating the patient's sickness and curing him. Thus it seems that the doctor takes responsibility for all sickness. I am a professor of mental illness. If mental health implies a person who has autonomy, who is self-directing and manages himself in freedom and independence, then how can a doctor or psychiatrist take responsibility for this? The doctor may attempt to treat an illness but only the person himself can take responsibility for his mental health. There appears therefore to be a fundamental contradiction in the notion of treatment – of me as a physician treating another person.

If we examine the notion of treatment, even at the level of a simple physical illness such as a broken bone, the surgeon can set the bone in position but it is the person's own internal curative processes that heal and unite the fracture. If we examine almost the entire spectrum of illness, I think we will find that the procedures of medicine and surgery usually take this form of assisting or aiding the natural healing processes of the body. Were these not to exist or were they to fail, there is seldom much that the physician can do on his own. It would seem that there are two positions which can be taken up by the therapist and which lead inevitably to a kind of absurdity. We can tell a person seeking help to pull themselves together and stand up and deal with their own problems. However, if the person in need of help were able to do this, they would hardly have come complaining in the first place. Our population would already, by definition, be mentally healthy, and there would be no need for psychiatrists or mental health services. At the other pole, if the physician or psychiatrist takes total responsibility for another person's mental health or for the treatment of his illness, then by definition he must interfere with and destroy that person's autonomy and remove from them the responsibility for managing themselves. Yet we said that this independence and autonomy is synonymous with and at the very heart of what we mean by mental health, therefore the doctor who treats another person's illness, and takes responsibility from them, inevitably must do so at the cost of their mental health and of making them dependent. This is the dilemma which we find to be manifested at every level of our mental health services; it is the tragedy underlying our mental hospitals which represent, par excellence, dependency cultures, where anyone who enters them, whatever else may happen to them, become more dependent, less able to care for and take responsibility for themselves with each day that they reside there.

What then can be said of therapy? Between these two polarized positions there is perhaps left the statement, 'helping people to help themselves'. It seems to me that it is only in this middle ground that the possibility of a therapeutic relationship can exist. There are obviously certain exceptions to this, for some people are so demented, damaged or disabled that they have to be totally cared for, but these are a minority and with their exception all real therapeutic effort can only mean a person or a physician helping another person to help themselves. This implies extreme care and diffidence about invading another person's autonomy – or the taking over of their normal responsibilities for themselves. As therapists we often have to do this temporarily, where person's have become acutely disorganized, incompetent and unable to manage their own lives. However, the moment we do so, and depending on the degree to which we do so, we take on the delicate and difficult task of transferring back to that person their own responsibility for themselves. It is in this delicate arena that the whole skill of psychotherapy – and the art of healthy living – lies.

A number of possibilities now emerge within these relationships, for one ordinary person can in fact help another to help themselves. What's more, the health-giving relationship can be mutual, thus there can be an interdependence among persons without any connotation of dependency in a damaging sense. What is more, a physician, psychiatrist or mental health worker can adopt a role not only of helping a person to help themselves but of helping a community of persons to help themselves, and thus foster a therapeutic mutuality or interdependence. This allows for another possibility in regard to that minority of persons already mentioned who are so damaged physically and mentally, disabled or demented, as to require partial or total care. Rather than seeing professionals, nurses or doctors or the state assume responsibility for such people, the alternative possibility exists of a personalized community taking responsibility for those handicapped or disabled persons who are unable to help themselves. Thus the notion of responsibility, of independence or mutual interdependence, can be seen to be capable of operating at every level of society. However, such a notion of community mental health could only operate in a personalized communal setting and within a community that had already adopted a position of self-direction, taking responsibility for its own management. Coming full circle, we can now ask whether Irish society as at present constituted can be said to be capable of improved mental health. I think this is the measure against which we have to judge ourselves at every level of Irish life. We can institute mental sickness services. We cannot claim to be creating services for mental health. The status quo depends upon an apathetic and dependent population for its very existence.

The complexities and tyranny of dependency as expressed in the lives of most women have not yet been recognized for their contribution to ill health. Motherhood is considered a natural cornerstone upon which the family and society is founded. Every woman can be a mother, we accept, and every mother is naturally a good parent, we believe. Whether we believe it or not, we do nothing to equip a woman for her role in the family while still insisting that this is where her role should be. The supposition would seem to be that a person's potential is completely determined by their sexual role. And yet the Irish mother, especially a mother of many, will say she lives for her children. I put it to you that the woman who lives for her children also lives through them, and is in fact the worst possible parent for a child to have, creating dependency and never wanting to let go. In terms of mental health and development, the adequate parent must be the one who is fulfilled as a person and brings this fulfilment to the role of parenting the child. However, women in our society are not encouraged to fulfil themselves as people. They are expected to be women first – which means a servicing role in relation to the rest of us – and people second, if at all. In fact the woman who does not accept a helpless subservient role is still considered odd or selfish. Until she insists on her own autonomy and takes responsibility for herself, she will find it difficult to shape the mental health of her children or to be a free part of the society in which she lives. Women will play an enormous part in the shaping of Ireland's future. Their influence will be seen in the development of truer human relationships and in humanizing our structures and institutions. In fact, if women were to take hold of their autonomy and stop letting men run everything, especially women's lives, I would predict a rapid decline in depression and anxiety among women.

It is easy to scoff at the more newsworthy antics of women's lib, but it is in the area of sexuality and the relationship between the sexes that we must search for solutions in the future. Indeed, what we are facing now at the human level is the struggle and tension of sexuality – of male and female become conscious. As human beings over the span of human history, what have we done with this tension, with this divided state of the sexes? It would seem that we have further polarized it; we have extended sexual difference into many areas of life that are not primarily to do with sexuality. We have subscribed to the delusion that the male is only maleness and the female only femaleness. It is only now beginning to be gropingly understood that these gender relations are present in all living creatures, that each person contains within him or herself both the female and male dimensions, and that therefore there is no such thing as a total female or male. Each person contains their opposite sexual orientation. The sexual difference is really one of degree rather than of kind. This has important practical implications for society and development, for it means that we must begin to understand the reality of what is femaleness or maleness and to recognize what is conditioned imbalance within ourselves. These are not mystical qualities but are practical realities in terms of hormones, of feelings, attitudes and behaviours, and the balance between these extremes is going to be of vital importance in how we deal from now on with the changing world around us. I would suggest that the male qualities of competitiveness, aggressiveness and dictatorial behaviour are probably less adaptive in the context of modern civilized living, while the gentle, caring, mothering qualities of the female may be much more useful.

It is against this background that some of the traditional developmental customs and mating practices we questioned – where boys are trained from their earliest years to deny almost totally their feminity, while girls are discouraged from development in many areas of activity traditionally associated with the male – it seems that we should be working towards now is a much better balance within each person, woman or man. Young people are beginning themselves to teach us about this, refusing to have their sexuality polarized and increasing areas of dress, behaviour, occupation and sport are being degendered. Also boys and girls are relating much more to each other as persons and sexual activity is not nearly as sectored off from other aspects of life as before. All of these developments are hopeful signs for the mental health of men and women for the future, for much excessive drinking, sexual deviancy and uncontrolled aggression, which have been widespread, are related to the harsh polarization of sexuality.

Right back to primitive tribal times, it is the woman who has sustained and provided the basis for both the family and subsistence culture which was generally prevalent until recent times; she has done this precisely because she was in a subservient caring role. Once she is no longer prepared to shoulder this burden, then everything else must change. This is another factor that has been imperceptibly influencing many of the changes which have taken place in Europe and the rest of the western world since the Second World War, and has only recently been working its way to the surface, so that the full impact of the refusal of women to continue in their traditional role is only now beginning to be experienced. We cannot keep them in that role, essentially cut off in vast housing areas, by numbing them with tranquillizers. They will have to decide for themselves, and be allowed to decide for themselves, what sort of society they wish to live in.

Women, especially urban women, cannot be expected to continue for long in their current subservient role in the family, the family which has lost all power, its functions passing increasingly from people to bureacracies, where even the ordinary phases of the life cycle are increasingly defined as problems. We have the geriatric problem, the adolescent problem, the problem of the pre-school child, the problem of the young mother, and many more. In fact it was as recently as the eighteenth century that we began to separate children from adults and put them in institutional boxes such as kindergartens or schools. The segregation of the old into senior citizens' homes or resorts is still more recent and results, in large measure, from the outward migration of young married couples to the suburbs. Thus increasingly we have a clear geographical segregation by age, most marked in the United States but already evident in Europe: suburbs for the young marrieds, campus towns for our youth and resort communities for the old people. In such communities a child may never – or almost never – have any experience of communicating with a person over sixty years of age, or an old person may never have the chance to aid the upbringing of small children.

The isolation and break-up of the nuclear family are further compounded by the removal of the husband from the family circle; by his being forced to spend more and more time at work, usually at a distance from home, so that he largely ceases to exist as far as the rest of the family are concerned. For many ambitious businessmen and professionals, work commitments may eat into evenings and weekends; and, as more and more wives also pursue careers, the same pressures affect them also. Each partner finds relationships at work more meaningful and work life more interesting generally than home life. They come together briefly each evening but find it too exhausting to build a relationship so they bury themselves in the passive entertainment of television. Small wonder that so many marriages end in breakdown, with increasing numbers – already one in seven in the United States – of one-parent families.

Thus, in a literal sense, the family ceases to exist. Traditionally the task of the family when it was still an integral part of the tribal circle and had not yet deteriorated into an isolated nuclear unit – the interpersonal relationships between parents and children, the work of development – went on continuously throughout the day as part of the normal processes of living and surviving. This no longer happens; the isolated family becomes more relevant. Naturally, problems of development result: problems of sexual identity, problems of marital relationship, all to be resolved by professionals. Thus more and more human beings must take on one-dimensional roles, as professors or technicians, to help solve the problems. However, this in turn takes more and more people away from the primary living situation into an isolated artificial activity – work – and from an existence as a whole person into a specialized one-dimensional role.

In a sense we might be said to have the worst of both worlds in this country at the moment. For, while the new influences associated with modern urbanization that I have been describing – of isolation and breakdown of marriage and the nuclear family – are flowing in on us, we are still carrying with us the old problems of coming from a dependent colonial society. These older, more familiar problems, which perhaps are most obvious along the western seaboard, are in fact still endemic across the whole country, even in our suburban housing estates around Dublin – the pattern of late marriage, or no marriage at all, giving the middle-aged bachelor or spinster, and the rigid ingrown family structure, unable to let go of its children; the wife who is turned into a mother; all that I have spoken of already in this paper, the apathy, depression, the uniquely high rate of schizophrenia and, underlying it all, the preoccupation with alcohol. Now, alongside these more familiar problems, we have flowing in the new sickness of late twentieth-century decadent capitalist western society, all the sequelae of the mass society – the alienation and loss of identity, the meaningless aggression, vandalism and escalating crime statistics, the stress disorders, the breakdown of family life and marriage, the thousands of housewives on tranquillizers, the choked polluted cities with rotting centres, the dehumanization and mechanization of agriculture, with thousands leaving the land – all this is being added unto us.

Nevertheless, the picture is not all black, for at least the new influences have broken down or are in the process of breaking down many of the old static, rigid patterns. The dependency on an autocratic Church, on the gombeen man, the blinkered mental horizon that could not see beyond the English Channel, the narrow frozen attitudes to sexuality, the need to denigrate and feel ashamed of everything Irish – all these are in question, or are being questioned. Our young people, especially our young women, are better educated and have more understanding than ever before and are, I believe, capable at last of taking on freedom and independence could they but see clearly the way to do so.

I believe we are now at a crucial turning-point for the future of this island and its people, one which we will have to decide, one way or the other, within the next ten to fifteen years.

We can drift on and watch the emergence of a new culture of dependency for the coming generation – pauperized peasants on the back of Europe – spawning a new breed of gombeen men, shonings and toadies, but this time as agents of the multinationals, mining and oil companies, or of the new overlords in Brussels who appear to be successfully continuing the destruction of our traditional rural way of life begun by the landlords of the past. In that situation we would once again lose all self-determination, would not own or control a stick or a stone in our own country, and reap a new crop of stress and mental disorders, alcoholism and alienation, while yet another generation of our children will be forced to leave Ireland, this time to go across Europe as migrant workers.

There is another course open to us. Instead of drifting helplessly along, we have it in our power to take control of our own destiny, to grasp our inheritance. This is a fertile island with a small population capable of supporting itself in a good standard of living but in order to do this we need to create personalized, cooperative and self-directed communities on a human scale, with men and women equal, sharing the tasks of living in an atmosphere of love, and making their first priority the rearing of strong and healthy children. It is my opinion that, in such a setting, where society and its individual members accept responsibility for themselves, few would need to feel alienated, anxious, depressed or mentally ill, and those few would be accepted as the concern of all. We could then truly be said to live in the shelter of each other.

10. The Family in
Western Society

The following piece, 'The Family in Western Society', was written on 1 August 1975. This paper was never published but was written for a talk that I gave some time in 1975.

MOST people in this country or elsewhere would, I think, agree that the family is a basic social institution in our society, perhaps the primary social unit. The constitution of Ireland has this to say about the family in Article 41:

1. The State recognizes the Family as the natural primary and fundamental unit group of Society and as a moral institution possessing inalienable and imprescriptible rights, antecedent and superior to all positive law.

2. The State, therefore, guarantees to protect the family in its constitution and authority, as the necessary basis of social order and as indispensable to the welfare of the Nation and the State.

3. In particular, the State recognizes that by her life within the home, woman gives to the State a support without which the common good cannot be achieved.

4. The State shall, therefore, endeavour to ensure that mothers shall not be obliged by economic necessity to engage in labour to the neglect of their duties in the home.

If the family has this central place in our society, then one would expect it to have some important functions for which it is responsible. Article 42 of the Constitution, regarding education, has this to say about the family:

The State acknowledges that the primary and natural educator of the child is the family and guarantees to respect the alienable right and duty of parents to provide, according to their means, for the religious and moral, intellectual, physical and social education of their children.

Much has been written, of which this statement is but one example, of the many functions that have been attributed to the family at one time or another. Let us try to ascertain what these functions might be. There would appear to be two main groups of tasks for which it is felt the family should have a major responsibility:

1. Those more obvious and visible functions relating to survival.
2. A group of less visible, subtle and more intimate functions to do with personal relationships and the development of our children.

Commonplace, Visible Functions Relating to Survival	*Deeper, Less Visible Functions of Intimacy, Relationship and Development*
Procreation	Primary relationship between woman and man; i.e. between parents
Security: protection from disaster	Relationship of mother to infant in the womb: peace, stability and security
Clothing: protection from exposure	Intimacy: development in the child of a basic capacity for intimacy, in touching, feeling, relationship with parents in the first year of life
Provision of shelter: housing	Laying down the foundation for sexual identity
Maintenance of basic health	Laying down the foundation for personal identity
Education of offspring: spiritual, moral and social	On this secure base to then provide a setting for the child to grow in independence: freedom to experience the world and to learn by doing
Leisure: time and space to play	Providing the child with the basic knowledge and information for living
	Providing a setting in which the child can develop the capacity for personal relationships; this involves initially the relationship with both parents and siblings, and later with a widening circle of friends
	Finally, to help the young person to progress to a position of confidence, independence and mature responsibility

Fig. 10.1. The family: a cycle of growth and decline

If we go back to primitive cultures, or even further to the societies of primates and other higher animals, we find that the primary social unit is in fact a group of families, living and working together (developed out of the extended family), which addresses itself to the task of survival. On through history, until recent times, this has been the pattern. The primary social unit for survival and for transmission of the culture has always been a group of families. This has taken various forms at different times, from the extended family, the hamlet, the village, the small market town with its hinterland, the cluster of neighbourhoods making up the human city with its pedestrian centre, such as the city-state of ancient Greece or renaissance Italy. To my limited knowledge of human history, it is not until we come to modern society that we find the isolated nuclear family as it exists today. If this is the reality, then I think one has only to pause for a moment to realize that, however much we may preach about the sacredness of the family as 'the fundamental unit group of

111

society', this isolated, fragile social unit is clearly quite unable, on its own, to sustain virtually any one of the functions already mentioned and is in a quite ineffectual position to undertake the responsibilities that are being laid at its door.

This is true, with perhaps one exception: that of procreation, the act of conceiving a child. This function the isolated nuclear unit can undertake without assistance and, unfortunately, it exercises this ability all too frequently, as is demonstrated by the overpopulated state of the world. This one exception aside, it may well be asked where or to whom does the isolated family turn for help in facing its tasks of survival, and the development of the coming generation. Most of the previous organic or personally based forms of society have been pushed aside and allowed to decay or to disappear altogether.

What groupings have taken their place? As the situation polarizes and all the intermediate networks of society are allowed to decay, we are left with, on the one hand, the isolated nuclear family and, on the other, the state, with government departments growing every-where and extending their tentacles to every aspect of life, the multinational and giant corporations, the massive bureaucracies of organized religion, the trade unions and the professions. The isolated family therefore has no choice but to offload its essential functions on to one of these impersonal state, commercial or professional organizations. This polarization is taking place in virtually every developed country in the world.

This is the real struggle that has been going on in the world during our time; not the apparent battles between right and left, between socialism and capitalism, between church and state, but the relentless transfer of power and control from the peripheral to the central, from the small to the large, from the personal to the anony-mous and institutional. This is the real change that has been taking place and it still continues, intensifying with every year that passes. Small private businesses amalgamate to form corporations, corpora-tions merge to form multinationals, government departments expand to take over control of more and more areas of our personal lives, even national governments are superseded by supranational federations and so on.

Not surprisingly, given the personal nature of human beings, all of this leads to problems, and once this polarization has begun it sets up a progressive chain reaction. It would seem that this is what has been happening in Western society now for some generations. While I don't say that this is historically exactly how things have happened, it is possible, for descriptive purposes, to discern several consecutive phases in this process.

Phase I

Because the family cannot manage the ordinary tasks necessary for survival, for which it has traditionally been responsible, these are passed on and one after another necessarily become defined as problems for society. These problems then have to be tackled either by the state or by some other impersonal, corporate or voluntary institution. Responsibility for education and preparation for life is passed on in turn to the crèche or pre-school, the school, the university, with their supporting educational authorities and the Department of Education. Responsibility for maintenance of basic health is passed on to the crowded doctor's office, the impersonal outpatient clinic and sterile hospital ward, backed by health boards, professional, medical and nursing organizations, and the Department of Health. Responsibility for the provision of food and the necessities of life is passed on to mechanized agricultural and manufacturing industries, with their attendant problems of food distribution, dehumanized supermarkets, human alienation and environmental pollution. And so we can go on, listing in turn each of the basic functions of survival and ordinary living.

Let us look in a little more detail at one of these functions – the provision of shelter and protection of the family from disaster. There is a need for security against fire or accidents, to guard against sickness and have something to fall back on in our old age. In addition, some try to ensure that they will have the wherewithal to educate their children, and every family of course has to try to provide itself with a house or flat to live in. In primitive times, habitation and such protection from disaster as was possible were provided by the tribe as a whole, working in some form of mutual cooperation. Nowadays, however, we expect a much more complete protection from every kind of disaster – from sickness, death or injury to the breadwinner – and of course we expect a house to live in. But where is all this to come from? Clearly the single family is in an even less satisfactory position to provide the protection for itself from all these hazards than was the tribal group, and it hardly seems feasible for husband and wife to set about building their own house with their bare hands before raising a family.

So, once again, the responsibility has to be passed on to the speculative builder, to county councils and the Department of Local Government. Building societies, banks and multinational insurance companies now come into the picture. But the loan for our house or the pension we receive on retirement are not given to us for nothing. On the contrary, for many of us the reality is that we struggle for most of our lives to pay off the loans and the interest and keep up with the insurance premiums, devoting a considerable proportion of our human energy and total working life to this purpose, gaining in the end of all a poorly designed and badly built home and a miserable pension which, by the time we get it, is eaten away to almost nothing by inflation.

Nor does the matter end there, for our human energy, transformed through work into loan payments, premiums, paid in month by month, year by year, cannot simply be left to lie dormant. It has to be put to use, to ensure the survival and maintain the profits of the building societies and insurance corporations, and safeguard the security of their clients. For this reason it cannot be used to build better communities, or to provide a better life for those of us who contribute. Instead it has to be invested where the smallest risk is entailed and where it will earn the highest possible financial return. This, as far as my simplistic mind can understand, appears to be in financing giant office blocks, high-class apartment dwellings, luxury flats and large suburban shopping centres, which apparently bring the most profitable returns for investment.

Unless my poor understanding of economics is leading me astray, when I look around a city such as Dublin and see grotesque prestige office blocks appearing everywhere, replacing beautiful Georgian houses or more humble homes once occupied by ordinary people, and when I find myself angry and wanting to protest at the destruction of a living city, I am forced to a rather frightening and uncomfortable conclusion. It becomes apparent to me that what I see is not simply the doing of wealthy property developers but is largely financed by you and me, as we find ourselves forced to lay aside family responsibilities. Thus we attempt to achieve a wretched habitation to live in and some miserable security for our old age. In this way each of us is doing our bit to destroy and pollute the very city we live in.

It may be objected that this does not apply to the ordinary working man, who does not bother much with life assurance, voluntary health insurance and so on, nor does he as a rule purchase his own home, but if we look again I think we will find that he too gives his life blood to finance expensive shopping centres and supermarkets, which are the first amenities to appear in every public housing estate. He too pays rent, rates and taxes, ultimately to build and maintain the public housing in which he lives and to finance the social welfare and state health benefits, family allowances and so on which are, after all, only another form of insurance and which he ultimately receives grudgingly back from the government, having first of all paid the salaries of thousands of dubiously efficient civil servants in the departments concerned.

Having put our shoulder to the wheel to finance all these ventures, both commercial and state, the little human energy we have left over to devote to our families and to ordinary living is quickly mopped up in the building of churches and schools which, we are told by the hierarchy, it is our duty to provide for ourselves and our families.

Phase II

As this process of transfer of responsibility for basic functions from the 'personal' to the 'bureaucratic' continues and as the organic fabric of family life begins to break up, more problems emerge. What were ordinary stages of the life cycle now become defined as problems – we hear of the geriatric problem, the problems of adolescence, the problem of pre-chool children and so on. In fact the separation of children from adults as a distinct category and the placing of them in institutional boxes of kindergarten, school, etc., began as early as the eighteenth century. More recently we have seen the segregation of the elderly into ghettoes, institutions and, through the movement out of young married families to suburban housing estates, their relegation to derelict centre city areas where they are dumped in isolation. This same movement of young married couples to the suburbs is, of course, itself a major factor in the creation of the isolated nuclear family, the problem which has been the central theme of this paper.

This isolation and break-up of the nuclear unit has been further compounded by the progressive removal of the husband or bread-winner from the family circle, by his being forced to spend more and more time at work, usually at a distance from home, so that he largely ceases to exist as far as the rest of the family is concerned. For many 'go-ahead' young businessmen, professionals and others, this involvement characteristically extends to taking in evenings and weekends for meetings, management and training courses, etc. This process is now affecting wives also as more and more of them go out to work. In many urban settings adolescents are now increasingly separate and alienated from all other age groups, whether this takes the form of the school dropout or the more vicious aspect of the adolescent gang. It is estimated that there are now 10,000 to 14,000 young people highly organized in ruthless teenage gangs in New York city alone, heavily armed and involved in serious crime, including murder, on a regular basis. Another example of this fragmentation of the life cycle is the young, single, working adult, or university student, both women and men, living in flatland, frequently fresh from the country and more isolated from family or other human relationships than ever before.

What does all this do to the family as a social unit, and more particularly what effect does it have upon the deeper, less visible, intimate tasks of the family which were referred to earlier? For, while it may have been possible, if not desirable, for the family to hand over responsibility to impersonal organizations for the more commonplace functions of survival, no one has as yet claimed to have found a satisfactory substitute for the carrying out of the intimate and subtle tasks of relationship and development. Nor has it been suggested that these can or should be handed over to anyone else.

On the contrary, it seems clear now that satisfactory development depends ultimately on an open loving relationship between the parents, out of which will grow naturally the right sort of healthy, trusting and intimate relationship between parents and children. This deeper aspect of the work of the family is embedded in the primary relationship and love between the parents, as has been stressed by the newer theology of marriage since Vatican II. The loving relationship between man and woman is the vital thing from which all else in marriage and family life follows. When all the jargon has been put to one side, this is the simple fact which emerges from all the study and knowledge of human development that has grown up over the past fifty years. There is, quite simply, no substitute for these kinds of positive, loving relationships if we are to grow healthy children.

We are further told that the early months and years of relationship with both parents, even extending back to the relationship between mother and infant in the womb, is crucial to the growth of intimacy, basic trust and to the development in the child of a clear personal and sexual identity.

But what is the situation we find? In the United States, one out of seven families is now a one-parent family and similar trends are already apparent here. Either one parent is absent altogether or the father is away all day at work leaving a lonely, frustrated wife at home, isolated, on tranquillizers, in a poorly designed box of a house, among hundreds of others, in a dehumanized housing estate. Or, as is perhaps more likely nowadays, both parents are at work, leaving the children in a crèche or in the hands of some more or less unsatisfactory parent substitute.

Frequently each partner finds relationships with friends at work to have more meaning, and life generally in the work setting to be more interesting than the relationship which they have with each other at home. They come together for an hour or two in the evening to re-establish contact with each other in a vacuum, and perhaps with less and less in the way of mutual common interests. Even here the pain of trying to work at reopening and building a relationship each evening, which has already, perhaps, less meaning than what has been happening during the day, can be avoided by burying themselves in the passive entertainment of television, the peripheral terminal of the corporate outside world piped directly into every home.

This is the shambles of broken and fragmented relationships that we call the family in contemporary society, the sacred institution which is supposed to pass on the subtle and delicate message of life to the coming generation.

Once the family has given up the attempt to take direct responsibility for the ordinary jobs of living, such as providing food, shelter and so on, it would seem that these deeper, more intimate aspects of family life must in turn break down, for there is now no setting within which these subtle relationships – between husband and wife and flowing from that the relationship with the children – can happen, for the parents are largely separated from one another and the children, once they reach pre-school age, are also separated from their parents. This crucial fact seems to have been missed in all the hypocritical talk about the importance of the family. In primitive or tribal society, the interpersonal relationships between parents and children, and the work of development, went on more or less continuously throughout the day, while the group as a whole carried out the ordinary tasks of living and surviving. We continue to talk about the family, and about development, as if this were still the case, when in fact most contemporary families, as a set of ongoing relationships, don't exist at all for most of the time.

So now we get problems of development. The establishment of personal identity becomes a problem. There are problems with sexual identity, and the marital relationship itself becomes a major problem. We hear of marital therapy, the professional finally invading even the marital bed, followed relentlessly by the technician. The sexual act itself becomes a technical matter to be 'tuned' and adjusted like a motor car engine, following which, presumably, all will be well. Childbirth, too, which for countless thousands of years was a natural event of life, has now also become a technical problem to be managed under hygienic conditions in the depersonalized sterile atmosphere of the large maternity hospital, in the midst of medical technology where even the time of arrival of the infant is the subject of medical intervention, and where the father first sees his child through a glass screen behind which the baby is held up, out of a row of identical-looking infants, by a nurse with a masked face.

Phase III

As more and more problems are generated in this way and attempts have to be made to solve them by the impersonal bureaucratic forces of society, more and more human beings (at first largely men, to be followed later by women) have to leave the family circle and take on one-dimensional roles or professions, or become technicians to help solve them. I mean something quite specific by this that there is a transfer of each of the following:

- *Time*   from the home or community to more and more time spent at work

- *Personal identity*   from existence simply as a human being to identity with a role, such as nurse, computer programmer, lab technician, doctor, etc.
- *Location*   from the home setting to being physically located at a distant place of work
- *Human energy*   from a low input in the home community setting to a higher and higher input in the world–role setting
- *Being*   from a whole human person in relation to the world and to other human beings, to becoming a 'component' or 'segment' in a process
- *Human relationships*   from being centred primarily on the marital partner, children, friends and neighbours, to relationships in the work setting with colleagues, workmates, secretaries and others
- *Sexual activity*   from home to work – e.g. from wife to secretary – manifesting itself in an increasing rate of marital breakdown

Thus the endless splitting process of specialization, moving on to ever finer sub-specialization, is now ushered in. However, to become professionals and technicians equipped for their roles, people have to acquire skills, and this involves training. Somewhere along the assembly line, the individual's personal life becomes firmly attached to the role, profession or trade.

The training has to be certified, there is the graduation ceremony, and then the person becomes a social worker, a technician, a lawyer and so on. These no longer are simple descriptions of what the person *does* but rather of what he/she *is*, the most real part of him/her ('I am assistant-secretary in the Department of —'), often leaving very little of the person to be a husband or wife, mother or father. The process does not end there for, as degrees, diploma, and qualifications take over, testing procedures and examinations, by means of which people are certified, assume a dominant place. These now become the main determinant of training programmes, of courses which increasingly have to be tailored to prepare people for 'the examination'. What is more, entrance criteria now have to be developed, to ensure the fitness and acceptability of those who are to enter. The Leaving Certificate comes to dominate all education in schools from childhood onwards. Thus, as the chain-reaction turns full circle, all of life becomes a treadmill of teaching courses, examinations, certification, one human being competing ruthlessly with another to gain acceptance to a 'role', to sneak a place for themselves as a 'component' on the assembly line. Those who do not make it – and, given the ever more oppressive criteria for entrance and acceptance, these are increasing in number – are considered as refuse for the human scrapheap, to be the 'redundant', the 'passive social welfare recipients', the 'chronically unemployed', the 'poor', and the 'sick', the 'chronic attenders' in hospital outpatients and doctor's offices, the 'delinquent', the 'vagrant' and the 'petty recidivist' criminal. Of course, if we had not all of these, what would we do with all the social workers, doctors, nurses and charitable voluntary workers?

And so the wheel turns full circle. As the turning of ordinary life and the different stages of the life cycle into problems has got under way, ever more problems are generated. The turning of human beings into roles and technicians to deal with them creates ever more roles and sub-roles; specialization leads to sub-specialization, and certification to further certification, examinations, setting of higher standards and even more oppressive entrance criteria. All of this supplies the nourishment to ever-larger corporations and bureaucracies, to the endlessly growing government departments and legions of civil servants, these in turn filling the multiplying office blocks with which we are choking our cities.

This is why I found myself, when trying to grasp a picture of contemporary society, forced to the analogy of cancer. However, the analogy would not be accurate if we think of a person with, say, cancer of the lung alone. The spectre of contemporary Western society is rather more analogous to a person with raging cancers growing in virtually every organ of the body.

Can this cancerous dissemination be halted? Is there any way for human society to get itself off this treadmill, to free itself from the relentless process in which all of us seem to be trapped? Strangely enough, my feeling is one of optimism, because I think the very cancerous process which I have been clumsily trying to describe is choking and destroying itself, that the very process of pollution, waste, over-population, malnutrition, choked cities and traffic chaos, alienation and dehumanization is already forcing mankind to seek alternative ways of living, indeed that this search has already begun.

And remember that these pressures on humanity are probably only just beginning. As the noose tightens and the situation worsens, I believe that the search for alternative ways will become intensified and more widespread.

I might be accused of representing in this paper everything in dark, negative terms whereas, in fact, I see much that is positive. The ordinary contemporary woman or man (and I think this is particularly true of young people) is more gentle, less aggressive, more understanding, more considerate towards children, more humane, with more tolerance and concern for others probably than ever before in history. It is in this that I see hope.

Alternatives to our present society will come when they will come. Could it be that the 'alternative', when it does come, may be almost frighteningly simple? Perhaps the apparently hopeless complexity of our present situation is itself the result of the very way we have been doing things. When the pressure on human beings builds up sufficiently and when enough people become aware of the need for change, then the change will come, so there is not much sense in trying to picture what future society will be like until the time arrives. Nevertheless, I would like to take a look into the future and to outline some very tentative criteria that, it seems to me, will have to apply in some form if human beings are really to change their mode of living.

The change will involve a further development of technology. There will not be any question of our going back to some primitive idyllic state of the past. In my opinion we will not solve our problems by going backwards but rather by advancing further to a post-industrial society with the development of ultra-technology. I think this is already beginning to happen. Many of the technological processes now available could already be decentralized and, where it was once necessary to make and assemble things on a large, noisy factory floor, flexibly decentralized parts of such work could now be done at home, or by people working together on a village green. It is not so much technology which is now standing in our way as archaic institutions like civil service departments and multinational corporations that are already outmoded and choking themselves to death and are only awaiting further human enlightenment in order to be scrapped. This would mean that much technology could either be carried out completely automatically, with the involvement of very few human beings, or, where human beings are involved, much more flexibly related to ordinary human living.

Many of the intermediate forms of society that have been allowed to decay or disappear will have to emerge once again, appearing in new forms, not simply repeating what they were, and avoiding some of the mistakes that virtually ordained their breakdown. If we are to think clearly about this, it is essential that we try to see mankind in its true historical perspective. The following passage written by the archaeologist Glyn Daniel may help us to do this. Referring to the long history of early man he says:

> What is perhaps most dramatic as we reflect on this long process is the length of time which the earlier stages have taken. No one suggests that the so-called Neolithic revolution – the change to a food-producing economy based on cultivation and domestication – started anywhere in the world before ten to twelve thousand years ago, and until recently this date would have been given as nearer six to seven thousand years ago. Yet man himself – man by definition as *homo sapiens* – was in existence six hundred thousand years ago. We as food producers with a life built on villages and cities have only been in existence for one sixtieth of man's time on earth. Do these figures of thousands of years mean anything to you? Think of the face of a clock, and of a minute hand going round for an hour. Fifty-nine minutes of that hour represents man the food-gatherer, man in the stage of Palaeolithic savagery, man in the Old Stone Age. In the last minute but one we see him pointing at Lascaux and Altamira and Niaux, but it is only at the beginning of the last minute that we see him gaining control over the cultivation of grain and the domestication of animals – it is only then that the Neolithic revolution takes place, and only in the last half-minute that the social, material, and cultural changes we call civilization occur. Egypt, Sumeria, Greece, Rome, Christianity, Buddhism, the pre-Columbian civilizations of America – all these have occurred in that last half minute of man's long life on earth. This does not mean that they are irrelevant, but it does mean, at least to me, that their relative importance is less. You remember the philosophy which George Borrow put into a sentence in *Lavengro*: 'There's night and day . . . sun, moon, and stars . . . likewise a wind on the heath, brother.' True, but to me it is a wind that blows from ancient, dimly apprehended, prehistoric heaths, and that tells us that man is very old, and that the present with its

ideological conflicts, its threats of destruction by nuclear warfare on the one hand and by overpopulation on the other is not necessarily the end of existence, an existence that is already sixty times as long as the beginning of agriculture and nearly a hundred times as long as the inventions of writing and formalized religions.

It would seem, then, that our main task is not to recreate the past but to join ourselves once again to the main stream of human history. As I have tried to emphasize in this paper, the basis of human society for by far the greater part of its existence was the small, personalized human group; that is, a tribal circle or group of families living in some form of communal arrangement. As I see it, our task is to rejoin this main stream, but now by creating totally new forms of personalized human networks. In these circumstances I think the family will once again take its place as the core of the personalized human group, but that it would not now be dominated by blood ties or necessarily be built up out of the extended family or biologically related clan as of old. This time the primary living unit would be groups of adults and children of all ages but not necessarily blood-related. This would provide a background cellular network to society that would allow a much freer movement of persons or whole families from one living group to another, analogous to the movement of molecules in and out of cells in the living body. This would particularly apply to the adolescent or young adult stage of the life cycle, but the movement of individuals or families should not reach such a degree that it would disrupt the background cellular network.

Whatever form the basic network may take, one fundamental point seems clear. In any new alternative society there would need to be a clear distinction between the primary living units – i.e. groups of families living in some form of communal or cooperative relationship who would be responsible for personalized tasks relating to the basic life support and survival of the group, but whose priority would be specifically about living, relating and human development, as against other levels of society whose primary concern would be with centralized, coordinating functions in relation to production, the use of heavy technology and other tasks to do with the survival of society as a whole.

Thus, society would probably need to be built up organically out of a number of levels or human groupings, of varying size and function. A great deal of work would now have to be invested by society in matching and allocating the many functions to be undertaken – living, loving, relating, procreating, producing food and goods necessary for survival, economically utilizing energy and technology – of matching all of these to the appropriate level or societal grouping which is to be involved. In this way, in the primary living network, it should be possible to bring together in a holistic personal form the various basic functions of human living, of developing and of the different ages of the life cycle. Only by this means could the less visible, subtle, functions of the family and of personal relatedness mentioned at the beginning be made possible once again.

However, this is to be redone, I believe it will involve the scrapping or reshaping of most of the present institutions and organizations to create more flexible task-oriented structures, many of which at more central levels would be temporary and impermanent – groups brought together on a temporary basis to carry out a specific project, such as the development of a nuclear reactor or rapid transit system serving a region.

Somehow or other, it will be necessary to separate the knowledge and expertise available to society from the personal lives of the individuals who are going to use such knowledge. Techniques and skills necessary for human living should no longer be attached rigidly to roles, professions, technicians, etc., but be more freely and flexibly available to groups of persons living in cooperative communities. Many jobs in the human or social services, now hived off, could be taken back into the basic living group. Tasks now done by nurses, teachers, clergy, social workers, doctors, could be done by ordinary people as part of their daily life in the living group. Similarly, tasks such as sanitation, garbage disposal, street cleaning, parks maintenance, policing, administration of justice and so on could be done by the members of the living unit for themselves. These tasks and the work of survival could become again the setting for human relationships and development, the notion of 'the job' as a separate activity disappearing from many areas of human life. This would make possible, too, the scrapping of much institutional education – i.e. that of schools and universities in their present form – so that education would once again become an integral part of living, all age groups making use of and enlarging the pool of knowledge available.

Finally, to achieve this, it appears to me that two major obstacles will have to be overcome: the total emphasis on individualism and selfish private ownership, and the difficulties involved in cooperative relationships in groups. This does not mean the loss of the personal, or of ownership and participation, with transfer of all power and decision to dehumanized state control, but rather some form of more cooperative, communal ownership, participation and control in a setting of human and personal relationships. Thus the great Jewish philosopher, Martin Buber, writing in 1938 and seeking a third alternative says, the first step 'must be to smash the false alternative with which the thought of our Epoch is shot through – that of "individualism" or "collectivism"'. He goes on:

> The fundamental fact of human existence is neither the *individual* as such nor the *aggregate* as such. Each, considered by itself, is a mighty abstraction. The individual is a fact of existence in so far as he steps into a living relation with other individuals. The aggregate is a fact of existence in so far as it is built up of *living units of relation*. The fundamental fact of human existence is *man with man*. What is peculiarly characteristic of the human world is above all that something takes place *between* one being and another the like of which can be found nowhere in nature. Language is only a sign and a means for it, *all achievement of the spirit* has been incited by it. *Man is made man* by it; but on its way it does not merely unfold, it also decays and wilts away. It is rooted in one being turning to another as another, as this particular other being, in order to communicate with it in a sphere which is common to them but which reaches out beyond the special sphere of each. I call this sphere, which is established with the existence of man as man but which is conceptually still uncomprehended, the sphere of '*between*' though being realized in very different degrees, it is a primal category of human reality. This is where the genuine third alternative must begin.

His last words are: 'We may come nearer the answer to the question of what man is when we come to see him as the eternal meeting of the One with the Other.'

11. The Human Group –
A Living System

The following paper was never published. It was written for a talk in 1977, at a fairly early stage in my reflections on the 'human group'. I was interested at this time in the societies of the social insects – termites, ants and honeybees.

> 'There is a light that shines beyond all things on earth, beyond us all, beyond the heavens, beyond the highest, the very highest heavens. This is the Light that shines in our heart.'
>
> (Chandogya Upanishad)

THERE is a growing awareness among individuals at the present time of the need to live more in tune with nature, each other and our fellow creatures. That we will do this only by making *being* a priority and *doing* a by-product, albeit totally necessary, would seem to be an inescapable conclusion. To be is the primary task of a human being; any doing or function which deprives him of his consciousness as a being is destroying him as surely as slow starvation. Unconscious doing, or rather functioning to the detriment of being, has left the world in a state of rising anxiety over our dwindling resources: Is our planet running down? Are we going to choke ourselves to death? What about the oil, minerals, etc.? And suppose our sources of energy last, what about the mounting dangers of pollution, our dying lakes and rivers and our decimated fish stocks? With this the spectre of famine comes ever closer. Already, we are told, two-thirds of the world's population is hungry, with the population explosion and more and more mouths to feed melting food supplies.

All of this we hear *ad nauseam* but is the problem really one of insufficient natural resources? Is there really not enough food to go around? Does the problem actually lie in the environment which is being relentlessly polluted? In considering these questions, we always seem to turn our eyes outwards from ourselves but who is it that

126

makes the decisions about the use of natural resources and about the purposes for which they are used? Who decides to burn oil in automobiles rather than to make fertilizers? Who is it that pollutes the rivers, lakes and seas? Who is responsible for the beef mountain in Europe while children in Ethiopia grow thinner each day? The fact is that there are still ample natural resources in the world for all our needs; we could easily feed the present world's population were we to use our technology and present understanding of food production for this purpose. Even if the world's population reaches four thousand million before it stabilizes, as has been predicted, it should still be possible to feed this number if land and other resources were used intelligently. What is more, with the understanding gained in recent years of the balance of nature and the world's ecology, it would be quite possible to do this without overusing fertilizers and insecticides and thus damaging the ecological balance.

So, as always, the problem seems to come back full circle to ourselves, to the way we utilize our human energy.

Whatever about the balance of energies in the cosmos as a whole it seems evident that, in our immediate physical environment on this planet, the laws of thermodynamics are relentlessly at work – the planet is running down, natural resources are being gobbled up at an accelerating rate and, with each reaction, entropy is increasing. Nevertheless, in the midst of this, biological life has appeared and has been growing continually, becoming ever more complex, alive and conscious and concentrating more energy into itself. In this there consists a strange contradiction to which Teilhard de Chardin referred again and again in the last years of his life.

> On the one hand, we have in physics a matter which slides irresistibly, following the line of least resistance, in the direction of the most probable form, of distribution, and on the other hand, we have in biology the same matter drifting (no less irresistibly but in this case in a sort of 'greater effort for survival') towards ever more improbable, because ever more complex, forms of arrangement.

Thus we find, as he said, a fundamental contradiction between physical entropy and biological 'orthogenesis', with increasing complexity and concentration of energy in a living substance that has reached full flood with the emergence of human life, consciousness and the enormous technological complexity of modern society. In another essay written shortly before his death he returns to this question:

> However, it may well be, perhaps, that this contradiction is a warning to our minds that we must completely reverse the way in which we see things. We still persist in regarding the physical as constituting the 'true' phenomenon in the universe, and the psychic as a sort of epiphenomenon . . . if we really wish to unify the real, we should completely reverse the values – that is, we should consider the whole of thermodynamics as an unstable and ephemeral by-effect of the concentration on itself of what we call 'consciousness' or 'spirit' . . . In other words, there is no longer just one type of energy in the world: there are two different energies – one axial, increasing, and irreversible, and the other peripheral or tangential, constant and reversible. And these two energies are linked together in 'arrangement', but without nevertheless being able either to form a compound or directly to be transformed into one another, because they operate at different levels.

It seems clear, then, that the essential problem of energy does not lie in the physical domain, in the control of natural resources, pollution and so on. It is rather a matter of whether we can control and manage human energy, with its accompanying consciousness, both in ourselves as individuals and, perhaps more urgently, as a collective in the corporations and institutions of society.

It is the emergence of consciousness in the world and, hence, of human freedom that lies at the heart of our dilemma and it is the management of this consciousness and freedom that is central to all our difficulties. This is true, not only of our actions and behaviour as individuals but, to an even greater extent and in a much more important way, to our behaviour as members of human groups; to the role we play as part of the various institutions, corporations and organizations of society to which we belong. It is at the level of the group, at the level of societal institutions, that things really seem to pass out of our control.

If the whole question of energy comes back to the human being rather than the human by-product of function or technology, we must first define 'being' as a living system. Illuminating findings are now available from Maturana and Varela in their work on autopoietic systems. It is an interesting coincidence that some of this work was carried out in Chile under the Allende regime, which for a few years seemed to be addressing itself to the creation of a living society.

First let me explain the word autopoiesis. *Poiesis* is defined as a combining form which produces, and *auto* refers to self, therefore an autopoietic system is, literally, a self-producing system; i.e. any living thing. The aforementioned authors say:

> A living system is specified as an individual, as a unitary element of interactions, by its autopoietic organization which determines that any change in it should take place subordinated to its main-tenance, and thus sets the boundary conditions that specify what pertains to it and what does not pertain to it in the concreteness of its realization. If the subordination of all changes in a living system to the maintenance of its autopoietic organization did not take place (directly or indirectly), it would lose that aspect of its organization which defined it as a unity, and hence it would dis-integrate. Of course it is true for every unity, whichever way it is defined, that the loss of its defining organization results in its dis-integration. The peculiarity of living systems, however, is that they disintegrate whenever their autopoietic organization is lost, not that they can disintegrate. As a consequence, all change must occur in each living system without interference with its func-tioning as a unity in a history of structural change in which the autopoietic organization remains invariant. Thus ontogeny is both an expression of the individuality of living systems and the way through which this individuality is realized. As a process, ontogeny, then, is the expression of the becoming of a system that at each moment is the unity in its fullness, and does not constitute a transit from an incomplete (embrionary) state to a more com-plete or final one (adult).

A human being is autopoietic or self-referential, whereas a machine is allopoietic, defined from outside, according to its function. For example, a car does not exist for its own sake but because of the task for which it is designed. Neither does it exist in relation to other cars.

Much of the recent research into human behaviour is reinforcing the essentially homeostatic nature of a living system. A living crea-ture only functions satisfactorily when it has autonomy, that is when it takes responsibility, otherwise it becomes allopoietic or dependent, defined from without. Seligman, in his work on learned helplessness, has demonstrated this across a wide range of species including human beings:

> Helplessness is a disaster for organisms capable of learning that they are helpless. Three types of disruption are caused by uncontrollability in the laboratory; the motivation to respond is sapped, the ability to perceive success is undermined and emotionality is heightened. These effects hold across a wide variety of circumstances and species and are prominent in *homo sapiens*.

If this applies to an individual, does it also apply to a group? More important, what happens to a person in a group? How much autonomy is lost, what is gained? Can a group also be described as a living system?

Viewing a human group in this way is really seeing it as one example of a general principle. Wherever we look in the universe at an element, we find on closer examination that we are examining a system composed of sub-elements or sub-systems. If we look inside these, in turn, we find that they too are systems with a complete inner world of components or sub-units, of which they are comprised and whose movement and behaviour they regulate. This principle appears to apply whether we look at an atom composed of electrons, protons and neutrons, a molecule composed of atoms, a cell with its nucleus and molecular systems, an organ in the body composed of clusters of specialized cells, and so on to solar or stellar systems, nebulae. In every case, we find the system with an internal dynamic arrangement of balancing elements which are under the control of the whole, and which is bounded. It is this boundary which appears to be crucial, for it distinguishes what is within the system from what is without. This boundary has to be actively and dynamically maintained; if the boundary is weakened and invaded, the system will not endure. As long as the system can dynamically sustain its boundary, and hence its internal organization, it can become a component or sub-unit of a larger or more complex system, and thus an ascending or hierarchical order of wholes can be built up.

From this point of view, when we speak of a human individual it is, in a sense, a misnomer, for a human being also is a group, a system of complex dynamically interacting elements. We can postulate that a human being too has a boundary, partly material – i.e. the skin – but also in terms of personality – a dynamic psychic barrier. As with other systems in the world we know, it is the management of interactions taking place across this boundary that is crucial to the health and stability of an individual.

When looking at the individual and a group of which he is a member, we are dealing with two interacting but separate systems functioning as self-regulating wholes. There is clearly a relationship between the intra-psychic processes going on inside the individual member and the effect of these as they cross the boundary of the individual on the behaviour of the group as a functioning entity and, reciprocally, the behaviour of the group as a functioning whole has its effects on the internal physiological and psychological function within the individual. In creating and regulating its internal organization – that is, the dynamic relationship between its members – and in its external behaviours and interactions with the outside world and with other groups, the group makes use of the repertoire of behaviours available to it through its members, depending upon their individual characteristic, their personality type, sex and general consciousness.

The statement that a human group is an entity or self-referential whole – that is, a whole reacting back upon itself whose primary task is its own stability and survival as a dynamic system – would seem to be outrageous. One's immediate response is to say 'I am a separate person, an individual in my own right, I'm not simply part of a herd, a part of a group to be forced to behave purely to serve its ends. I'm not simply a passive component of some organization or institution'. I think the reason this statement appears to be so outrageous is because of the reference point from which we start. As human beings, we characteristically begin from the assumption that each of us is a totally separate individual; after all, we have known ourselves from our early years, as far back as we can remember; we can move about freely and experience that we are in control of our own behaviour. I know what I am and what is outside of myself – not me. Without rejecting this important reality and awareness of ourselves as individuals, it must nevertheless be questioned whether this statement of individuality is in fact truly our starting point, either in terms of our personal development or of our historical evolution as a species.

From the moment of conception, each of us begins life not simply as a separate individual but in intimate relation to another – the dyad of foetus and mother. Our earliest origin as a human organism, the development of our endocrine and nervous systems, the determining of our sexuality, all happen in intimate relation to our mother, to her circulating hormones. From birth onwards, this interpersonal setting expands characteristically to a relationship with three or more others – father and siblings. As one of the social mammals, all our development from this point onwards takes place in a context of group relationships; at first that of the nuclear family, later expanding to include teachers, friends and so on. The whole formation of our personality, all our behaviour and the emergence of our individuality, grows out of this interpersonal setting, is called forth through our intimate relationship with others, so that our emotional responses, the functioning of our endocrine system, the ways in which we behave, are all elicited by and happen in response to other human beings.

Turning to our evolutionary origins, the world of lower animals reveals some rather startling facts. It must, of course, be stated that any direct comparisons between, for example, the societies of the social insects and the human species is hazardous and must not be pressed too far. Many of the insect societies are very ancient compared with the mammalian group (termites can reach back over two hundred million years and a younger branch, such as the bee, has been in existence for over forty million years). These social insects took a separate pathway very early on, and greatly pre-date human evolution. Their societies are relevant to the study of man and his society and, in relation to their starting point, could be considered more stable and developed than ours. They could, in a sense, be considered as adults, while we – that is, the mammalian group – are, by comparison, children; for this reason, no direct comparisons between the social insects and ourselves can be made. Nevertheless, something occurring at one point in evolution is worth noting, for it may represent a general principle, and it may occur in some form, perhaps under very different circumstances, elsewhere among living creatures.

With this reservation, it is informative to note that Rémy Chauvin, one of the world's greatest authorities on insects, has to say about the society of bees:

> Many biologists, myself among them, are tending more and more to alter their concept of the bee as an isolated insect. What sort of an individual is it that can live only a few hours out of contact with its fellows? Surely some essential factor is missing,

as in the case of those tissue cultures which degenerate and take the form of ordinary connective tissue when separated from the parent body. Suppose the bee to be no more than an abstract idea in our minds, suppose insect societies to be not societies but organisms of which the bees, the ants, the termites are all cells? This would merely presuppose that the intercellular relationships are less well defined than in our own bodies; the 'cells' could detach themselves temporarily from the organism to go and search for food, defend the colony against attack, etc. . . . And all the comparisons that have been made, or could be made, between human society and that of bees would come from a basic misunderstanding of the true nature of bees.

He continues:

Let us accept, then, this hypothesis of the hive as a super-organism where the individual bee is just a detachable part with little importance, almost without separate existence. Those wooden boxes at the bottom of our garden, from which the foragers leave, then take on a more disturbing aspect. Inside each one is a fairly bulky animal weighing 4 to 5 kilos (there are 10,000 bees to the kilo), provided with a supporting apparatus (the wax comb), and hermaphrodite reproductive organs: the ovaries of the queen and the testicles of the male . . . Respiration of this animal is assured by the fanning of the ventilating bees, who blow out spent, or too humid air, at times with sufficient force to flutter the flame of a candle. There is a circulation, in fact a very active one, as has been shown by experiments with radio-isotopes. It is true that it does not work through veins and arteries, but the *buccal* exchange of food and social hormones is a perfect substitute. The *production of heat* is one of the most important social functions, and it is characteristic of bees . . . In a hive, under normal conditions the temperature is 34°C and it is kept within half a degree of that, as with man . . . There remains then only one big and inevitable question if we wish to push this suggestion of a super-organism to its logical conclusion: where is the nervous system? Where is the brain?

Further on, Chauvin has this to say in answer to this question:

An ant, which has far fewer nerve cells than a rat, cannot be so flexible in its behaviour as that creature. Nevertheless, there is an exception: the social insects. If, in fact, the little brains can

133

interconnect, pool their resources and all work together, they can work on a far superior level. All the more in that there are over 60 to 70,000 workers in the hive, and as many brains as there are workers. To be better understood, I must make a comparison with the big electronic calculating machines. We know that their memories are made of rings of ferrite joined in a complicated system. Let us suppose that an engineer, told to make one of these machines, had but one ring of ferrite: he could do nothing. If he had ten or a hundred he would be hardly any further advanced; but if he had several thousand, then he could connect them up and make the machine's memory out of them. A thousand units acquire a value and significance of their own which ten or one hundred do not have. Let us now suppose that the little ferrite rings are provided with legs, move about and only come back to join the whole on special occasions: you would then have a machine very like a hive.

So the remarkable fact which emerges from the work of Rémy Chauvin and others is that, for the highly developed societies of the social insects, the evidence would suggest that it is more logical to regard the social group, that is, the bee hive or ant nest, as the living creature rather than the individual bee or ant. The isolated insect on closer examination is much more analogous to an individual cell in our own bodies, with the single difference that the insect is geographically mobile.

An even more striking example is to be found when we turn to those strange creatures known as slime moulds, particularly to the species *dictyostelium disocideum*, which has been the subject of intensive study by Raper, Bonner and others. Here we are faced with the creature (perhaps it would be truer to say creatures), which passes at different stages in its cycle from amoebic unicellular organism to a multicellular state and back again.

While in their free living state, each amoeba lives alone. When there is a plentiful supply of food and other appropriate conditions, it multiplies by simple cell division once every three or four hours. Inevitably, this geometrically expanding population uses up the available food supply. This ushers in a complete change in behaviour.

As the food dries up the amoeba begins to form aggregations: first, a few individuals cluster around a dominant individual, and this group then joins others until clumps of organisms form. The clumps now begin to join one another and a mound forms as groups of amoeba pile on top of one another. This mound gradually rises into the shape of a slime mould. It eventually topples over on its side, looking like a small, slimy slug. This slug begins to migrate across the forest floor to a point where, hopefully, more favourable conditions prevail. At this point, this slug is known as a 'migrating pseudoplasmodium', leaving a trail of slime behind it.

As the slug migrates, it continues to attract other amoeba. These join the mass and become immediately incorporated within it. Estimations about the size of the population vary but generally it is thought that some half a million amoeba are involved.

It was found that the slug's migration responded to light and warmth and that the slug narrowed into a point at its front end. The point apparently guides the migration of the entire body and if this tip is cut off the slug, and the community, is deprived of its leadership, and migration stops. The decapitated body ceases migration, and no longer responds to light. The amoebae crowd forward and collect in the rounded body.

After migrating for a time in the direction of light and warmth, this slug now ceases its movement and enters into another phase called 'culmination' (the formation of the fruiting body). The slug gradually erects itself once again until it is standing on its tail. A group of cells near the tip of the pseudoplasmodium become rounded off and enlarged. The group is either round or oval in shape; the oval shape gradually assumes a form, bellied at the bottom and coming to a point at the top. As the belly forms, a waist also appears. This waist gradually lengthens and becomes a stalk and this brittle stalk continues to rise. It now tends to become more spherical in shape, either in a straight or wavering line.

Normally the end of this culminating stage produces a brittle form only half an inch or so high. The pod at the top of the stalk is known as the spore mass. What actually happens, however, is that amoeba from the apical tip migrate down through the forming fruiting body, thus erecting the stalk. As the process occurs, the slug first points its tip upward and stands on its end. The uppermost front cells swell with water and become encased in a cellulose cylinder forming the stalk. Each amoeba in the spore mass now encases itself in cellulose and becomes a spore. When the spores are dispersed each can split to liberate a tiny new amoebae. Thus the cycle begins again.

Although the societies of higher animals, closer in an evolutionary sense to ourselves, are historically less ancient and their social organization is not so stable or highly developed as that of the insects, many similar instances of group-dependent behaviour and the effect on the individual of the social group can be cited. This is true of many forms of fish and birds, as well as mammals, and is particularly so of the social primates, such as apes and baboons. When we look at the dominant group behaviours of many of these animals, we can observe with interest that they bear a striking resemblance to the group behaviours which emerge during a group-relations conference following the method developed by A.K. Rice and which Bion described as 'basic assumption' activities of a group. With many animals there is a preoccupation with establishing a territory and forming a boundary to the group. There is also the work of internal organization within the group – the question of dominance, the formation of a hierarchical relationship or pecking order, the selection of a leader: i.e. the emergence of an alfa male. There is the handling of aggression between members of the group and of sexual relationships and reproduction. The group will consolidate itself against an outside aggressor, protect its younger and weaker members and organize itself for fight or flight as the situation demands. These major group behaviours of many of the social animals correspond closely with the three basic assumptions cited by Bion as characteristic of human groups – i.e. that of dependence, pairing and fight/flight – and also to the work of A.K. Rice on the formation of boundaries in and between groups.

The hypothesis is, therefore, that with human beings, as with many other higher or lower animals, the group is a living system. It has its own internal organization and emotional life and behaves as a living entity; it establishes a boundary to distinguish itself from what is outside and functions as a self-regulating system whose primary aim is to preserve its own stability and ensure its continued existence. Much of this behaviour takes place outside the conscious awareness of the individual members of the group. Thus, a human group has its own primitive behavioural and emotional life which is normally outside the conscious control and direction of any of its individual members.

While Maturana and Varela stop short of the question whether human societies are, or are not, biological systems, Stafford Beer – who writes the preface to their work – leaves us in no doubt as to his conclusion:

I am quite sure of the answer: yes, human societies *are* biological systems . . . Any cohesive social institution is an autopoietic system – because it survives, because its method of survival answers the autopoietic criteria, and because it may well change its entire appearance and its apparent purpose in the process. As examples I list: firms and industries, schools and universities, clinics and hospitals, professional bodies, departments of state, and whole countries.

If this view is valid, it has extremely important consequences. In the first place it means that every social institution (in several of which anyone individual is embedded at the intersect) is embedded in a larger social institution, and so on recursively – and that all of them are autopoietic. This immediately explains why the process of change at any level of recursion (from the individual to the state) is not only difficult to accomplish but actually impossible – in the full sense of the intention: 'I am going completely to change myself.' The reason is that the 'I', that self-contained autopoietic 'it', is a *component* of another autopoietic system. Now we already know that the first can be considered as allopoietic with respect to the second, and that is what makes the second a viable autopoietic system. But this in turn means that the larger system perceives the embedded system as diminished – as less than fully autopoietic. That perception will be an illusion; but it does have consequences for the contained system. For now its own autopoiesis must respond to a special kind of constraint: treatment which attempts to deny its own autopoiesis.

Consider this argument at whatever level of recursion you please. An individual attempting to reform his own life within an autopoietic family cannot fully be his new self because the family insists that he is actually his old self. A country attempting to become a socialist state cannot fully become socialist; because there exists an international autopoietic capitalism in which it is embedded, by which the revolutionary country is deemed allopoietic. These conclusions derive from entailments of premises which the authors have placed in our hands. I think they are most valuable.

*   *   *

'When Cain beat out his brother Abel's brains, his maker laid great cities in his soul.'

Robert Lowell

If I am correct in supposing that a human group, being composed of human individuals who are themselves autopoietic units, is indeed a living system, then, by Varela's definition of the essential nature of a living system, a human group must show the same characteristics. That is, a first priority for any human group must be its own preservation and existence. It must be first and foremost concerned to preserve its own being and anything which threatens this will be reacted against in a total way. Secondly, and very definitely in that order of priority, a human group like any other living system will have to undertake certain tasks in order to survive. Just as, for example, an animal must eat to survive, so a human group or organization will have to undertake one or more working functions if it is to maintain its existence. This will constitute the primary task of the group as defined by A.K. Rice: i.e. that task which a group must undertake at a given time if it is to survive. But this is something which a group *does*, and such a task therefore is not a part of the essential definition of what it *is*. This then is the crucial differentiation that we must make if we are to understand properly the human group as well as the individual. This statement alters completely the order of priorities of human groups and societies, and asks fundamental questions about the kind of organizations, corporations, government departments and so on that we have been creating for the past century or more. If the essential definition of a human group is its own being, and its existence is of its very nature its first priority, then surely it is important that we be aware of this fact.

Human individuals being autopoietic tend, of their very nature once they form into groups, to try to create self-producing wholes; that is, to try to form living systems whose primary purpose is to *be*. From what has already been said, it will be seen that this will be true irrespective of the ostensible purpose for which the group is formed, whether it be a group of football supporters or a company to make washing machines. This, it would appear, is the central problem of human society in the world today. For the past few hundred years the human organizations that have been coming into existence have increasingly been for the purpose of *doing*. We have been literally as human beings imitating the machines we have created – we have been organizing ourselves around the tasks to be done rather than simply to be and to live.

As a result of this we have increased productivity and have

undoubtedly improved human standards of living, at least in the west. This has created aspirations for better living standards, for more time to *be* rather than simply to *work*, so that, as individuals, we are more conscious than ever before of the possibility of enjoying life in a human way. However, by a strange paradox, we find ourselves hoisted on our own petard, because the organizations and institutions we have created to give us this better standard of living have now taken on their own existence and are controlling and dominating us as allopoietic components. In other words, we find ourselves increasingly the slaves of the structures we have set in motion – we are working and existing for them, rather than they for us. This is a cruel contradiction but the evidence that it is so is all around us. The terrible problem of our cities is but one example of this, where cities like the Paris or London of a couple of hundred years ago were places primarily for *being,* where people lived out their lives through the entire life cycle. Now they have become places for *doing,* where the heart of the city is filled with office blocks that become a dead world when night falls.

Almost nowhere today in modern western society do we find whole communities, but rather monstrous aggregations. Set up originally for the purpose of carrying out some task such as making motor cars or dispensing social welfare, they have very often broken free of their original purpose and exist merely to *do* and make everything. These pseudo-communities show all the characteristics of a cancerous growth in a living body, reproducing wildly at the expense of the rest of the body. Modern society is full of sectional interests, each attempting to achieve its own short-term goals, resulting in the chaos that constitutes modern society.

The reverse organization that is necessary is for *being* rather than *doing.* The *part* cannot be healthy if the *whole* is sick; there is no hope for the individual unless the group is formed correctly. This hypothesis should not be taken to imply any diminution of the existence or importance of human individuality, but rather it would say that the emergence of the conscious self-directing human individual is a triumph arising out of the group, that the social group is more ancient and that full human individuality is a relatively recent and still developing phenomenon. If this is correct, we have been putting the cart before the horse in terms of our human development. We may have to retrace our steps and accept the power and influence of group behaviour on each of us as individuals. We will have to try to understand this as it manifests itself in our organizations and institutions, the better to develop ourselves as individuals and realize our full potential as human beings. Far from our individuality and consciousness being of lesser importance than group forces these group forces are, in their present state of comprehension, largely blind and primitive. Hope for the future lies with the individual, with the further development of consciousness, with a greater understanding of the forces which operate in the creation and functioning of human groups, and of an acceptance of our personal responsibility, as individuals who have an extra-personal existence as members of a living society. Perhaps in this way we can bring about the birth and natural growth of groups and institutions whose primary concern is *being* rather than *doing*.

References

Beer, S. 'Preface', in Maturana and Varela, *Autopoiesis and Cognition*, 1980.

Bion, W.R. *Experiences in Groups*, Tavistock Publications, 1961.

Bleibtreu, J. *The Parable of the Beast*, Paladin, 1970.

Bonner, J. 'A Descriptive Study of the Development of the Slime Mould Doctyostelium', *American Journal of Botany*, 27, 437, 1944.

Bonner, J.T. 'Differentiation in the Social Amoebae', *Scientific American*, December 1959.

Bonner, J.T. 'Epigenetic Development in the Cellular Slime Moulds', *Symposia of the Society of Experimental Biology*, vol. 18 (Cell Differentiation), Cambridge University Press, NY, 1963.

Chauvin, R. *Animal Societies*, Sphere Books, 1971.

Maturana, H., and Varela, F. *Autopoiesis and Cognition*, 1980.

Raper, K.B. 'The Communal Nature of the Fruiting Process in the Acrasiaeae', *American Journal of Botany*, 27, 437, 1940.

Rice, A.K. *Learning for Leadership: Interpersonal and Inter-group Relations*, Tavistock, 1965.

Seligman, M.E.P. *Helplessness: On Depression, Development, and Death*, Freeman & Co., San Francisco, 1975.

Teilhard de Chardin, P. *Activation of Energy*, Collins, 1978.

The Upanishads, trans. J. Mascaró, Penguin, 1965.

12. Towards a Healthy
Society

This paper was never published but was the subject of a talk I gave in Wexford on 11 June 1979. It was around this time that I first encountered the work of the two Chilean biologists, Umberto Maturana and Francisco Varela, and their concept of autopoiesis, which is fundamental to the understanding of human group organization.

THE first thing I want to say is that, in my opinion, we are moving away from, not towards, a healthy society. This at least as I see it is the position at the present time, that there is a fairly rapid movement away from anything that could be called sane or healthy in our society. In this paper I would like to say why I believe this to be so, and also to express my hope that this may be only a temporary situation, that we are in fact seeing the last days of an era in western society, indeed that we are already seeing the beginnings of a very radical change that is going to alter the very basis of all that we thought most stable and permanent in our western world.

My purpose in raising this subject is not to get involved in an anti-technological medicine debate; the knocking of orthodox medicine and psychiatry has been a little overdone of late. Indeed in recent years I have found myself developing a growing respect for the achievements of modern medicine: the foot of a deformed child which can be turned around by a paediatric surgeon so that the child can grow up healthy and strong like other children; the harelip which can be repaired so as to leave no traces; the young father of a family who, by receiving a kidney from a relative, can once again lead a normal life and be a father to his young children; the bringing under control of infections that would certainly be fatal with antibiotics therapy; the ability of a modern personality to blossom out and lead a full creative life. Many of these everyday events in contemporary medicine would seem like miracles to our forefathers. This is not to mention the achievements of public health and preventive medicine, which have virtually eliminated a whole range of infectious diseases which took the lives of millions before they reached adult life, so that it was only the lucky person who got beyond twenty or thirty years of age. No, I think it is quite wrong to make little of these advances and the skills which we now possess. There is nothing to decry in these achievements in themselves; more than enough knocking of orthodox medicine has been done by Illich and others. What is wrong is not the existence of modern technological medicine, but the way in which we as a society order our priorities, where we place our primary emphasis. Modern medicine can treat any illness or at least greatly enhance the human body's ability to deal with them, but it has little to say to the development of, or maintenance of, health.

Let us go right back to the beginning. What do we actually mean in ordinary terms when we say someone is healthy? When we say to someone, 'You're looking very well'? One thing it cannot mean is that that person is free from disease. Such a statement might be true of a healthy child, but, once we pass even twenty years of age, our bodies usually show the ravages of various disease processes, our teeth are decayed, our lungs, cardiovascular system and other organs are almost inevitably showing signs of damage. We frequently see even more obvious evidence of disability, such as a missing eye, a damaged limb or impaired respiratory function, but such a person is often going contentedly about their daily life and, if asked, would described themselves as healthy. So what do we mean? It seems to me that we mean something that is essentially simple, that in operational terms, in everyday life, we say we are healthy and experience ourselves as healthy when we are able to manage ourselves, and are able to cope with ordinary life as it comes to us. We may or may not have disease of some kind or another present within us. For all we know we may within a week have had a heart attack or a brain hemorrhage, so that some disease process may already be well advanced within us. Nevertheless, until some evidence of this comes to the surface that interferes with our management of our everyday life, we are, at least in terms of an operational definition, healthy both in our own eyes and in the eyes of those around us.

You may respond by saying that in such a person the impression of health is only an illusion, but I would still contend that that person is in a state of health – they are in a state of adaptation and equilibrium with their surrounding environment. A little later they may not be. The time factor enters in here and, of course, if we look at our state of health over time, then in a sense all notions of health are a delusion, for, given enough time, we are all going to reach a state of ill-health, we are all going to die. So I find it hard to escape from a definition that health at any given moment is our state of coping, of being able to manage ourselves.

But is there something deeper here? Is there a deeper sense to which health is synonymous with self-management and autonomy? Is there some ordering principle within each of us, some integrating principle, which maintains control over our parts, and ourselves, and which, when it weakens, when it begins to lose its hold over the ordered maintenance of our parts, allows the disintegration and disorder to affect organs or cells in our body, so that they may either die or go their own way, reproducing themselves at random and out of control – i.e. the part growing itself at the expense of the whole; that is, cancer.

What is the unifying principle that I have suggested underlies the concept of health? The work of Varela and Maturana is interesting here. As cyberneticists and biologists they were interested to try to ascertain the essential definition of a living mechanism or system as distinct from a man-made machine or a system which is dead. This is an urgent question. Some of the more recent computers are taking on characteristics which are similar to, if not identical with, those of living creatures. Already we know computers can take on certain functions and operations well beyond the capacity of the human brain, so their question was: what is the essential defining characteristic of a living system?

After a penetrating analysis they came up with the conclusion that the essential or central characteristic of something that is alive is that it is *self-requiring* and *self-producing*; the term they coined for this is autopoiesis – 'auto' meaning self and 'poiesis' meaning to produce (i.e. self-producing). According to this view, then, the essence of something that is living is that it actively maintains and produces itself, that its first priority is to maintain itself in existence. We are now making a much more fundamental statement, for this view would argue not only that self-regulation and self-management are the essential basis of health, but that this is so because this characteristic forms the essential basis of what it is to be alive.

143

If this viewpoint has some credibility, then I think it has far-reaching implications for those of us working in the health professions: in medicine, surgery, psychiatry and so on. If the essence of health and living is the responsibility of each of us for ourselves, then what is the proper role of the therapist or professional? This takes us back to the beginning. We know that medicine can achieve or do many wonderful things, but how do we reconcile this with the essential job of each person to maintain their own health? This is what I was referring to above when I said that our ordering of priorities and our general emphasis was out of line, rather than that there was anything wrong with the specific skills and techniques of medicine in themselves. I would suggest that what emerges from all this, at the very least, is a yardstick by which we can judge what we are doing.

If a person comes to us for help at the end of whatever treatment we undertake, we can ask the simple question: Is the person, as a result of our intervention, returned to a state of self-management or autopoiesis or are they less independent than they were before? We may have successfully treated one or more disease processes, but if, at the end of it all, the person is less able to fend for themselves and to manage, then, using this criterion, we have rendered them less healthy than they were before our intervention began. We see this happening so frequently, particularly in the care of the elderly, where a person is admitted to hospital with some specific complaint, then, while they are there, in the course of routine examination and diagnosis other pathological processes are found, which in turn demand further intervention, surgical operations and so on. We see this person months later having been treated for the complaint for which they entered, and several other complaints as well. He or she entered hospital as a self-reliant independent old person but leaves as a decrepit dependent invalid, never again able to manage for themselves.

If the treatment has been successful – i.e. medical science has done everything possible to bring the person up to scratch – how is it that the person's health has diminished? For, by my definition, no matter what bones are mended or pathological condition is put right, the person has been rendered sicker than they were at the start if they are less able to cope and less capable of self-management, not just temporarily in a convalescent state, but for ever more.

That kind of trade may even save a life, but is it a fair bargain? Would it not be better not to be treated at all, rather than be rendered helpless by the stay in hospital? One see this very markedly in the elderly and psychiatric patient, but also right across the board in medical practice. How does it come about? All hospital staff wish to see improvement in a patient. Everyone, with few exceptions I would say, works towards that end. Everyone is happy to see a patient leave their care improved. However, too often, during all the caring, something is lost. Something vital to health. Something vital to the living being in any state. We come again to autonomy. The autopoiesis is lost. The person becomes dependent. Learning dependence in sickness, the person stops coping. Really, the hospital institution is very like the family that will not let its child grow up but overprotects, prevents growth in case it might be painful. All of us working in the psychiatric field understand what eventually happens to such a child, the destructive dynamics of such a family group.

What is the alternative? How do we help people to help themselves? How do we protect growth? How do we respect a person's autopoiesis, even when they are very sick and helpless? The answer is by always addressing ourselves to the person, the living essence, not by concentrating on the elimination of the complaint or problem so that the autopoietic system, which is the human being, becomes secondary.

As I said in Sligo in 1976, our population would already, by definition, be mentally healthy, and there would be no need of psychiatrists or mental health services, if sick people were able to do without us. I often wonder, though, who needs who most: the patient the doctor, or the doctor the patient. It's one of those haunting thoughts that creeps in unbidden, but one must, in all honesty, confront it and deal with it. I think we unconsciously like to believe that all this is soluble at the level of the individual. It is not. The individual doctor is a person, good bad or indifferent. The medical group is something else – that's to do with allopoiesis – and we'll come back to that later. Not *autopoiesis* mind but, *allopoiesis*.

Meanwhile, let's think again about the doctor or nurse who takes total responsibility for another person's health or for the treatment of his illness. By definition, he must interfere with that person's autonomy and remove from them the responsibility for managing themselves. Yet we agree that autonomy is at the core of our health.

So here lies the dilemma that is manifested at every level of our health services, the tragedy underlying our mental hospitals, which represent, par excellence, dependency cultures, where everyone who enters them, whatever else may happen to them, become more dependent, less able to care for and take responsibility for themselves, with each day they are there.

As I have said on other occasions, this is where we must come full circle and ask ourselves whether Irish society as at present constituted can be said to be capable of improving health, especially mental health. The status quo depends upon a pathetic and dependent population for its very existence. Quite simply, then, the job of medicine and the therapist is to help the patient to help him or herself, but this implies a radical change. For a start it demotes the doctor as godly, the nurse as guardian angel. It is a radical change that threatens egos throughout the medical profession and it is therefore understandable that we have been so slow to make this change. This radical change has already begun to happen widely in other countries; and even here, with the setting up of women's self-help groups, therapy groups and family planning clinics, as well as the older AA-type organizations.

But much more must come. The change towards a healthy society must involve the sharing of knowledge of the management of health and healthy growth. It means taking a lot of the mystique out of medicine. It means imparting knowledge and making it available early in life, through education and other means, to children and young persons as they are growing up. During the past year we have, in fact, seen a great deal of information being dispersed through TV, radio and medical columns. This change does not mean giving up or repudiating any of the skills and useful techniques of medicine, but it is only through this sort of dispersal of knowledge that we will be able to speak of health rather than sickness. And where we will see anything like a move towards a healthy society.

No Man is an Island

Thus far I have only spoken of the essential self-reliance and self-regulation of the person, indeed of any living system, and said that this is synonymous with being healthy. In fact it is the essential characteristic of being alive. However, I immediately find it necessary to qualify this statement, for we are not alone and we do not live in a vacuum. This autopoiesis of the individual is not complete and is conditional upon our relationship to each other in the groups and organizations within which we live and upon our relationship to nature – that is, to the world, to the biosphere within which all of us have our being.

There is an apparent contradiction here, on the one hand to say that our essential nature is autopoietic – when we continually create and manage ourselves – while on the other hand to say that we are dependent on each other and the world around us. In fact I would put it to you that both statements are correct within their proper context; that each of us is a separate living system, independent and autopoietic within itself, responsible for all our parts and the cells which constitute us.

I said early in this talk that we would return to the word allopoietic. We know by now, I hope, that an autopoietic system is one such that the product of its processes is itself existing for its own sake in creation; i.e. a dog is a dog, or a leopard a leopard, and a human being is a human being, not a doctor or a garage attendant. The human part is all, it comes first last and always. The function of doctoring or garage-attending is a learned function that does not and cannot reproduce itself. A person exists to live, to be, before any function.

An allopoietic system is one such that the product of its process or processes is something other than itself. Both words derive from the Greek verb *poinein*, which means 'to produce'. So an autopoietic system is a self-producing system and an allopoietic system is one that produces something else; such as a factory that produces a motor-car. Now the idea of allopoiesis begins to explain a lot of things about group behaviour and the evolution of society, which we have never understood.

For instance, a member of a caring profession is respected for his or her work and philosophy in relation to society. A nurse nurtures, a teacher cares for the child, whereas suddenly a body of nurses or teachers can do something ruthless and seemingly out of character. (Bear in mind that I am choosing these two professions because I have to choose someone, it is nothing personal.) How can it be that this group of respected people can display this kind of behaviour? The answer is that a person is able to control his behaviour as an individual, but his behaviour may be totally altered within a group, even to his own amazement.

Just as the human being has a controlling influence over all of his parts – that is, all of the cells that are in their turn separate living systems – so the group or organization has a controlling influence on its parts – that is, on the human individuals of which it is composed – and this is why our autonomy as individuals is only partial or conditional. Human individuals, being autopoietic, tend, of their very nature, once they form into groups, to try to create self-producing wholes – that is, they try to form living systems whose primary purpose is to be.

From what has already been said, it will be seen that this will be true irrespective of the ostensible purpose for which the group is formed, whether it be a group of football supporters or a company to make washing machines, a charity, or a trade union. This, it would appear, is the central problem of human society in the world today. For the past few hundred years the human organizations that have been coming into existence have increasingly been for the purpose of doing. We have been literally, as human beings, imitating the machines we have created; we have been organizing ourselves around the tasks to be done rather than simply around being and *living*.

If we could make a clear-cut distinction between, on the one hand, a human autopoietic system – that is, a system of which the primary purpose is the accomplishment of human life in its fullness – and, on the other hand, an allo-system – that is a working group or team or organization of human beings whose primary purpose is the performance of some task that subserves the elaboration of the autopoiesis of some superior human group, say a community or a nation – then we would have a comparatively simple classification. However, even a very brief foray into the territory we are exploring reveals that human allo-systems can rarely be confined to a single specified objective.

We shall refer to this intrusion of autopoietic drives into the allo-systems as 'pseudo-autopoiesis' and, to refer briefly to systems so affected, we shall use the label 'pseudo-systems'. Institutions that, at first glance, seem to be characteristic pseudo-systems are very prominent in modern western society and are powerful mutilators of the drive towards supranationalism. It may even be that pseudo-systems have achieved such dominance and power that the true autopoiesis of whole cultures and civilizations, not least our own, is being seriously diminished and threatened by them.

At the threshold of intelligence is mammalian life, where extremely complex physiological systems have been elaborated by the systematic organization of the cells; the behaviour patterns of a dog, say, or a dolphin or even of chimpanzee, are very much more rudimentary then the systems that sustain its life. At the very pinnacle of intelligent life we encounter human beings, with their elaborate mammalian physiology and, in addition, their marvellous nervous systems, which give us memory, our imagination, our awareness of time and of infinity, our vaulting intelligence and creativity. However, the very complex groups in which we are organized seem limited to behaviours that scarcely rise above the instinctive responses of the beasts – aggression, dominance, suppression, acquisition, conflicting and counter-productive enterprises lacking either rational coherence or subtlety. In the whole course of history it is difficult to call to mind instances in which either nations, states or societies of any complexity have behaved in a genuine spirit of altruism or even with an intelligent appreciation of their long-term advantages.

An understanding of human auto- and allo-systems and of the relationship between them may lead to a deeper understanding of the nature of the crisis through which we are living. If it does, it may help us individually to maintain a balanced mind in a period of great stress. That is a gain in itself; but it is also a significant contribution to the solution of some of the major human and global problems of the present day.

My theory is that modern groups tend to dehumanize the individual, to destroy his autopoiesis. It would follow that much of our behaviour, which we interpret as originating with ourselves, is in fact under influence from the higher-order system and therefore a behaviour of the group. I believe this in fact to be the case. It would further follow that, if our health or ill-health is largely the result of our behaviour, then our health as individuals would be again largely determined by the group organism of which such of us form a part. So finally the statement has to be made that, if the whole, that is the group, organism (organization or institutions within society) is not behaving in a healthy way, then that behaviour will inevitably affect the health of the individuals within it. In other words, much of the stress to which we are subject as individuals has its origin in the influence on our behaviour coming from the higher-order systems. And that is why as individuals we find it so hard to take effective action in regard to it. We are at the mercy of forces which as individuals we do not control. These forces often have a decisive effect on our behaviour and therefore on our health, that is upon the function of our organs and cells, emerging finally in what we know as the stress disorders.

What is the characteristic of these societal allopoietic organisms that appears to be generating so much stress, both for the individual and in the world at large? Here we have to take a look, I think, at the nature of these structures and the way in which they have grown up historically and developed up to the present time. Most of the organizations and institutions which make up contemporary society have the distinguishing characteristic that they were set up originally to carry out some function or task. This is true whether they be private, entrepreneurial, industrial-type organizations, trade unions or state institutions such as government departments, semi-state bodies and so on. In this regard they are in marked contrast to the main societal groupings which existed in former times. In earlier times, most of the latter were natural living groups, such as families, tribes, villages, towns etc., which grew up naturally and organically out of the biological nature of the human species. They were similar, therefore, to the natural groups of other animals such as primates, mammals and birds, etc., their primary purpose was not 'to do' but rather 'to be'. They were there primarily to fulfil their own existence and only secondarily undertook whatever tasks were necessary to ensure their survival and continued existence. They were, in short, autopoietic in the full biological sense.

We are not machines. We cannot make ourselves into other than what we were created as if we are to be healthy living systems. We must perform tasks, but if we exist only for the performance of these tasks we are fighting against ourselves. Our groups will have to be living groups, set up in the first instance to be rather than to do, for that is the nature of a living system. If we continue to use people as parts of a machine, we will continue as we are going.

We are going to be forced to retrace our steps. This is no pipe-dream of mine. The more our allopoietic systems, our task groups, destroy the world with pollution, depletion of natural resources, violence, congestion, over-production, the more the individual is replaced and made redundant by automation, the more relentlessly we will be forced towards the creation of living groups that are truly autopoietic, biological realities.

150

Nature will not forever accept our arrogant behaviour, riding roughshod over the natural ecological balance of the biosphere. Nature's reaction has been apparent for years and becomes increasingly so. More and more human beings are finding that, each time they try to get away with some short-term, selfish solutions, the unwelcome side-effects come home to roost.

I am not suggesting that we return to the past but we will have to learn humility. We will have to rush forward to a post-industrial society where we learn to manage the group systems that we create. These will have to be true biological autopoietic entities designed for living. Hopefully we will move on to the development of a lighter more advanced, more automated technology that can be used to serve mankind not to dominate it; which is in harmony with nature.

I am not being idealistic when I say that human beings will choose of their own free will to create such a world. I am saying that nature will force us, relentlessly, to do so. Either that or we will destroy ourselves and the delicate living envelope on the surface of this planet along with us.

It is only when we are forced towards the creation of a sane world that fosters the *being* and potential of all the creatures living in it – then and only then will we be moving towards the creation of a healthy society. My hope is that this day may not be too far distant.

13. Minorities

I was asked by *The Furrow* magazine to write this article to promote the launching of an issue of *Crane Bag* dealing with minorities. In my paper, written on 7 May 1981, I started with a poem by Bobby Sands, who had died on hunger strike. However, because of the political tensions surrounding his death at the time, *The Furrow* magazine refused to publish the article unless I removed the reference to Bobby Sands. This I refused to do, and the article was never published.

I am very happy to have been asked to help with the launching of the current issue of *Crane Bag*, which deals with 'minorities'. The question of minorities within our society is a subject that has always interested me, but I now see it from rather a different point of view to that which I think is usual. When the question of minority groups such as the travelling people, the mentally ill or the Protestant minority is raised, it is usually in the sense of seeing them as a problem apart from ourselves, a group existing somewhere in society that has to be dealt with but for which I am not personally responsible.

To my mind, to look at things in this way is to misunderstand the true nature of what is involved. The reality represented by the various minorities is not something external to me, something out there in society, but is intimately related to what I am, to what is inside me. This may seem a strange thing to say, and implies a rather different view of what a human being is from what is perhaps the way we normally understand ourselves. We usually think of ourselves as something solid: I am an individual, a self, a person with a strong ego, a sort of core within me that enables me to withstand the buffeting of life around me/myself.

I want to put forward a very different conceptual model of ourselves as human beings, which may not itself be totally correct but which I find operationally more useful for understanding what is going on between the individual and the various groups, families and organizations that make up the society of which he/she is a part. I see a human being as a living system, as a piece of reality separated from the rest of reality by a boundary, by a surrounding skin or envelope. This external boundary is not simply the physical barrier of our skin but is, so to speak, a living membrane separating what is inside from what is outside and managing the dynamic interactions which take place between these two realities. When we think of all that takes place during development and of all that the growing child takes in from its parents and family and of the interaction of that family with the outside world, it is not so strange to state that the internal reality of that individual, when they reach adult life, is not really different from the reality of the external society. All the confused jumble of ideas, views, emotional attitudes, beliefs, prejudices, fears and hatreds which we find, say, in contemporary Irish society are really to be found in the same confused chaotic mixture within each of us. The only thing which separates one reality from another is the semi-permeable membrane around each of us that enables us to recognize what is within: a self. From this point of view I think it is more useful to think of ego function as the boundary system by which we manage the transactions between ourselves and the outside world.

If I look honestly at myself, I have to admit that I contain an aspect of most, if not all, of the minorities that are dealt with in the present issue of *Crane Bag*. I am part homosexual, part female, half a Protestant; I will be old and have been through the throes of adolescence; I am a frustrated artist and failed musician; like most people I have felt the desire to travel the roads and have at times experienced rejection by society; and certainly I have within me the anxieties, the depressions and, lurking beneath, the madness of the mentally ill. The question is not so much that all of this reality is within each of us but how we deal with it, whether we accept or reject it.

To understand this further, it may help to turn to Freud's concept of psychological defences, the elucidation of which was perhaps his greatest contribution. If we have within us some emotional attitude, wish or part of ourselves that we do not find acceptable, for which we are not prepared to be responsible and are not willing to 'own', there are several typical ways of dealing with this aspect of unwanted reality. We can use the mechanism of repression, so that what is not wanted is shut out of conscious awareness and made to appear not to exist. It takes a lot of energy to maintain such a repression and frequently a second mechanism is invoked to project outwards on to somebody else that which has been repressed and denied: 'this badness and these hated feelings are not in me, they belong to those people out there'. It appears to me that this process lies at the very heart of our ways of dealing with minority groups. Typically, of course, there is a third step in this process for, having got rid of what we do not want and located it firmly in others, the next step is to reject or destroy the minority in whom we have placed the unwanted aspect of ourselves and thus be rid of this evil altogether.

It will be noticed that we have moved imperceptively from the individual to the group but, in my view, just as individuals are living systems so too are groups, organizations, families, clubs and societies, towns and villages and ultimately a whole society or nation itself. These, too, behave and defend themselves as individuals and use similar mechanisms for projecting what is bad and unacceptable on to others as does a single human individual. A family, group or organization also has its boundary membrane by which it distinguishes what is not part of itself. It is not so strange, therefore, that societies or parts of societies have the same confused chaotic reality within them and deal with what they do not want by similar mechanisms.

A third and typically modern way in which we deal with all the unwanted minorities is by reduction of difference, by assimilation. We deny their right to be different and assimilate them into ourselves, as we are doing here with the travelling people, or as often happens now with different cultural religious or ethnic groups. We simply say that such differences are irrelevant and have no right to exist and make them disappear, which is very similar at a societal level to repression in the individual for, while it may remove the unwanted problem, it results (as is the case with repression) in an impoverishment of the richness of cultural diversity in society as a whole. I was made acutely conscious of this recently when visiting India, where many cultures, races and religions live together side by side, tolerating each other without making the exclusive statement 'because I am such and such or believe such and such, therefore you are wrong and must be destroyed'. While India has many terrible problems, this tolerance of enormous cultural diversity made me realize the degree of intolerance and boring uniformity, through destruction of difference, that is characteristic of western societies.

The fatal weakness of the use of these defences is that, no matter how much we repress and try to make disappear, or project out on to others, the unacceptable parts of ourselves, all of this effort is in fact illusory, for we do not actually rid ourselves of what is within us. On the contrary, these unwanted parts of ourselves, which are now defined as evil are, because they are hidden, given free rein to grow and multiply unimpeded within us. The interesting thing is, had these aspects of our reality been consciously accepted as part of the richness and diversity within us (and remember I am speaking here of either the individual or the group) and had we taken responsibility for owning them, then they could have been seen as good and wholesome and the bad or evil need not have become a reality or have grown either within or without. A perfect example of what I mean was to be seen in Hitler's Germany. Had the Jews been accepted as part of German society they would have made, and had been making, an immense contribution to the scientific and cultural life of that society but, because they were stigmatized as 'bad' and rejected, the very evil that was projected on to them grew within the Nazi party itself, and we know how real and terrible that spectre became in concentration camps and warfare as the years went by.

The treatment of the mentally ill by society perhaps exemplifies better than any other issue the relationship of a minority to the whole of society, and how this relationship of the part to the whole comes right back into the very core of each of us. There is what at first sight seems an extraordinary conspiracy in almost every society across the world to deny the existence of mental illness and to shut those who suffer from it out of sight and try to make them disappear. Just to illustrate this, let me mention the observation that virtually everyone in the Dublin area has heard of St Brendan's or, as it is known parochially, 'the Gorman', but the surprising thing is that you will find very few who can tell you where Grangegorman is. Moreover, that whole section of the city within which the hospital is situated has been allowed to deteriorate, whole areas of it falling into decay and looking like a wasteland. It is almost as if, were this part of the city to be developed, then people would have to admit that places like Grangegorman and Mountjoy Gaol actually exist. Yet St Brendan's Hospital is only the same distance from the GPO in O'Connell Street as St Stephen's Green. What a contrast there is between these two parts of the city! If we now look inside at the sort of people who are deposited in a hospital such as Grangegorman, and this is true of old-style mental hospitals across the world, we find that it is a human warehouse, not simply for the mentally ill but for all kinds of people who are rejected and unwanted by society – the old, the poor and uneducated, the mentally handicapped, the chronic sick, the deprived and antisocial, as well as those who suffer from psychiatric illness.

In his article in the current issue of *Crane Bag* on 'The Insane as a Minority', Walter Lonenz puts his sense of the relation of the mentally ill to the rest of society very succinctly:

> But in one sense, these worlds of the majority and the minority are perhaps not that separate at all. Or rather, the world that we have declared as 'insane' is holding a mirror to the face of our society, and as we perceive a divided and fragmented picture of ourselves we begin to wonder if it is the cracks in the mirror that cause the fragmentation or whether we stare indeed at a true image of our own fragmentation.

Here he pinpoints that what we do to the mentally ill in society is ghettoize them and make them disappear which is, as I have already pointed out, the same essential mechanism of repression that each of us uses in ourselves as individuals. Further, I believe that the real reason we continue to do this to the insane in our society is because each and every one of us is deadly afraid of the madness which lurks in the depths of our own being. Nevertheless, I am convinced that this deeper unconscious and primitive part of ourselves is not necessarily mad and frightening in a negative sense, were we only prepared to accept that it is there and to open ourselves up more fully to it. Certainly this part of ourselves is not subject to the ordinary narrow rules of reason and masculine logic by which we normally control our lives and our society. Rather, it is the intuitive part of our nature and from this deep well within us emerges creativity, so that the creative aspects of science, the arts and the fantasies and magical ideas which constitute what we call insanity are close relatives, easily merging one into the other. It is my impression also that somewhere down in these depths within us, from whence springs our creativity, we touch the reality of the spiritual and the universal source of all things.

From this point of view, the criticism that *Crane Bag* is too involved with social and political issues is to my mind incorrect, for at this deeper level the social and political issues affecting our society are not really different from the arts and the insights of science. Indeed it could be said that the real task of the artist is always to take a step ahead of mediocrity into the unknown and to make us constantly re-examine our mundane view of reality and the norms by which we live. So that the true artist is always essentially political and a social activist, for to create a new art form is always to break with conformity with the forms, norms and rules that have been accepted up to that time. That is why a creative genius is seldom understood or accepted within his own time and is usually at best dismissed as a fool or at worst condemned as evil or insane.

Another important concept makes its appearance here: the notion of personal authority and responsibility. When I mentioned that, in my view, the ego should mainly be seen as a function of the boundary of the living system (whether this be an individual or a group), in the management of the interactions between what is inside and outside the system, I had this in mind as the exercise of authority. However, the crucial question here is where this 'authority' or 'control' lies. Psychologists in recent years have coined the term 'locus of control' and asked the question whether this lies within the living system or individual or outside it. From what has been said, it will be clear, that this question is vital. If the locus of control lies outside any living system, whether individual, group or society, then that system will have no control or personal authority over itself. It will then be directed from outside by other or larger systems than itself. This is a crucial question for any person or society, whether they exercise their personal authority and are self-directing, taking responsibility for all that is within them, or whether they are directed from outside.

From the point of view of tolerance of its minorities the Irish, and Irish society, may be seen to have some special characteristics. It will be clear from what has been said so far that, given human nature, the existence of minority groups will tend to be a universal problem within any society but, for two main reasons, arising from its historical context, I believe Irish society is likely to have special difficulty in relation to tolerance of its minority groups.

Centuries of colonial domination here have left a cultural legacy where, even after sixty years of partial freedom, Irish society still tends to see authority (the locus of control) as located outside itself; that is to experience itself as 'other directed'. The other reason why this is so lies in the special position of the Roman Catholic Church in this country. Presumably because of its long years of religious persecution, when it represented the only lifeline of the people, the Church holds a very intimate and central position in Irish society. When the British granted Catholic emancipation in the early years of the nineteenth century, they in fact made available to themselves a more powerful means of colonial domination over the hearts and minds of the people than they had ever wielded up to that time. For the Church, however intimately it may be built into the fabric of Irish society, drawing its priests from the people, takes its ultimate authority from outside the country. This has been used in collusion with British colonialism over and over again in the last hundred years to frustrate any attempt at the growth of a full national identity, which would draw together Irish people of various religious dominations. We have had an upsetting and painful example of this within the past few weeks in the visit of the Papal Emissary to a hunger striker in Long Kesh to try to persuade him to give up his fast. There was no equivalent visit from Rome to the British government to try to persuade them to change their frozen colonial attitude, which has remained obdurately unchanged now for over sixty years.

There has been, nevertheless, some evidence in recent years of a change on the part of the Irish clergy and bishops to free themselves from this authoritive relationship to Irish society, as is evident from the article on Church–State relationships in this issue of *Crane Bag*. Strangely enough, it is Irish society rather than the Church itself which tends to keep forcing us back into the same 'other directed' relationship. I believe this is because of our fear and unwillingness as individuals and as a society to take on our own personal authority, to make a conscious break with the old institutionalized colonial relationships. There are signs, however, that the third generation since the revolution, and the young people coming on, may be free enough and conscious enough within themselves to accomplish what the idealists of 1916 were unable to grasp fully, and what the maimed country-town shopkeeper generation, clinging meanly to survival during the 1930s and 1950s, lost sight of altogether. It may be hoped that the new generation, better educated and more conscious, now emerging into a European context, may finally be able to free themselves enough to take on their own self-direction and to create a fuller, more human identity that is able to accept within itself all the streams and minorities that go to make up Irish society today.

14. The Canute Syndrome

This paper was never published but was the subject of an interview published in the *Irish Independent* on 29 September 1986 and also in the *In Dublin* magazine.

WORK, and the methods by which wealth can be distributed, are relentlessly changing – terrifyingly, for many people. There are now in excess of twelve million people unemployed in Europe. Even as I write, that figure will have increased. A large proportion of these people will never again have a job, in the sense of being employed eight hours a day, five days a week.

It is simply impossible to redress the imbalance created by technology and other factors and return, however slowly, to full employment for those who have until now been given the expectation of employment in their future. So, after all the shouting and promises, blaming and disclaiming has piled confusion and increased stress upon the problem, we are, at the end of it all, bound to find an alternative solution to unemployment other than jobs for everybody. Sooner or later we must apply ourselves to this task. It may as well be sooner. Personally I feel comforted to find myself no longer a voice crying in the wilderness, saying that employment as we knew it is slipping away. Others are saying it, even politicians are beginning to admit to it. It may lose them votes but those in power will never again be able to create enough jobs to go round.

There never were enough jobs anyway. Less than one-third of the population were in jobs when employment was high: just over one million. Of these, less than half (approximately 500,000) are engaged in producing the wealth that we all share. So all the wealth which is available is produced by less than one-sixth of the population. The rest could be made redundant very quickly, their jobs in reality existing as a means of distributing wealth. Yet the job is considered as the only legitimate way of distributing wealth.

The number actually engaged in the production of wealth is quite small. Let me illustrate this with some simple statistics:

Total population		3,500,000	
Total number at work	Male	827,800	
	Female	322,500	1,150,300
			(i.e. less than one-third of the population)
Those not at work	Unemployed	200,000 +	
	Sick and Disabled	80,000	
	Smallholders	20,000	
	Total Unemployed	300,000	
	Students	180,000	
	Home Duties (almost entirely female)	640,000	
	Retired	180,000	1,300,000
			(i.e. more than one-third of the population)
Under fifteen			1,030,000

In fact, for the majority of our citizens, wealth is already distributed through other channels: the dole, old-age pensions, single-parent allowances, etc., but all of these are given grudgingly and those receiving them are defined as of low status and denied self-esteem. Our society still works by the nineteenth-century Poor Law concept – those who 'make money' are good; the rest are failures, or at least undeserving dependants. Ideally we must find a way for all our citizens to have a basic standard of living with the freedom to earn creatively on top of that.

The effects of unemployment are so painful in our present set-up that it is small wonder it is so difficult to get enough people to listen or to explore alternative methods of distributing the nation's wealth. Anyone who is currently unemployed or runs the risk of being unemployed is inclined to have tunnel vision, with employment at one end and disaster at the other. People are shunted into this tunnel by society's attitude to jobs which obviously, in a transitional period, must be to save as many as possible.

The ill-effects of unemployment have been shown in several recent studies. There is the sequence of downward social mobility due to loss of work; strong association with illness; likelihood of mortality greatly increases; suicide and homicide increase within a year of increasing unemployment; cardiovascular mortality worsens two or three years after high unemployment.

There are three stages of unemployment described:

1. Firstly, after the initial shock, there is a short-lived sense of release or a holiday period, the person being freed from stress and the constraints of work; brooding and real worry have not yet begun.

2. The second stage sees the development of anxiety, self-doubt and urgent attempts to find work. Social activities and pastimes become reduced due to demoralization. Shortage of money and the lack of social opportunity that go with work take their toll. The person retreats and home becomes like a prison rather than a sanctuary from work. Depression occurring soon after loss of a job is more likely with the middle-class professional worker who is accustomed to stability of employment. Anxiety and agitation often predominate, with depression.

3. Stage three follows continued unemployment over a year or more and is most likely to occur in lower-paid workers used to endemic unemployment. This person may resign him or herself to the situation, lowering their expectations and allowing life to become structured around a much lower level of psycho-social functioning. There may be clinical depression, with feelings of sadness, hopelessness and self-blame, lethargy, lack of energy, loss of self-esteem, insomnia, withdrawal and poor communication, loss of weight, suicidal thoughts, impulsive (sometimes violent) outbursts and an increase in the use of tobacco and alcohol. An increase in health problems is likely, the subconscious value of the person being: 'it is better to be sick and unemployed than healthy and unemployed.' There may be asthmatic attacks, skin lesions, backaches and headaches. Depression and physical disorders can also manifest in the spouse and children, particularly those under twelve years.

Given these serious and multiple effects of chronic unemployment, the clear implication and usual response of politicians is that something desperate must be done; somehow or other more jobs must be created. However, there a number of factors which lead to a very different conclusion, a conclusion which shows that, while endeavouring to hold back the tide of unemployment, some new alternatives must be found before the inevitable waters overtake most of our population.

Among the factors which must be faced and accepted before any conclusion for long-term solutions can be drawn are:

1. Over one million of our population of approximately three and a half million in the Republic are under fifteen years of age. In the next twenty years, up to the turn of the century, 50% of the population of this country will be under twenty-five. With little possibility of emigration, this means a large increase in the number seeking employment.

2. Women are gaining equality in society as part of the workforce. Released from excessive child-bearing, they no longer accept domesticity as the only trade open to them. The number of women seeking employment is reaching 50% in some professions. Moreover, one hardly needs a crystal ball to see the time when homemakers will finally demand a labourer's wage, like everybody else.

3. The new technologies bringing about automation in a wide range of industries are only beginning to bite. This factor is, for the moment, being artificially delayed due to political and trade union pressures. These efforts are buying us time but, given the capitalist system, the time will inevitably run out. The extension of these technologies is unavoidable. While it is true that the introduction of the micro-technologies is giving rise to new industries and thus employment, this falls far short of redressing the balance of redundancies caused by the extension of these same processes.

4. Even if it were possible to increase industrialization to the enormous extent necessary to create enough employment (let us not suggest anything as ridiculous as 'full employment'), this would have disastrous consequences in terms of pollution and damage to the environment, traffic congestion and urban decay in cities.

With twelve million unemployed in the EEC, the social consequences of this so-called structural unemployment are already apparent: widespread poverty, delinquency, vandalism, alienation with loss of personal identity as manifested in violence, a widespread increase in hard-drug addiction, alcoholism and attempted suicide.

For the first time in the last couple of years, some people in key positions began to take a fresh look at the problem. We cannot find answers to this frightening problem while we continue to ask the wrong questions. The dilemma is made worse by the way in which we are construing reality.

The solution is not to be found along traditional lines, or overnight. The EEC Study Group, of which I was a member some years ago, on 'New Characteristics of Socio-economic Development' made the point that the market economy, which it referred to as the first sector, can provide wealth and, given modern technology and automation, can without difficulty satisfy all our needs for material goods, but this will happen at the cost of an ever-diminishing pool of jobs. This is similar to the point made recently by the IDA. The state sector, which the committee referred to as the second sector, has increasingly been given the task of controlling the excesses of the market economy and of providing the bulk of our social services. That is, it has been given the role of dealing with all the problems created by the market sector. The traditional response to rising unemployment has been to increase expenditure in the second sector, creating jobs in the social services.

It has become quite clear now that this method of creating full employment will not work either. It is disastrous for two reasons: firstly, because to create the many thousands of jobs that will be necessary over the next decade if full employment is to be achieved will entail an enormous expenditure, pushing up inflation and destroying the competitiveness of the market sector; secondly, because the making of thousands of jobs in the social services means necessarily the creation of a culture of dependency.

What this involves, quite brutally, is that for every caring role that is brought into existence, dozens of people must be defined as problems, casualties and failures in order to provide the work. This completes the vicious cycle of the culture of dependency, where a diminishing élite are defined as good. They compete frantically for the diminishing number of productive jobs or for the status roles of caregiver (doctor, social worker, welfare officer, prison governor, civil servant, etc.) while increasingly large sections of the population have to be defined as bad, failures, sick, delinquent, disabled, alcoholic and so on, to prop up the system and enable it to continue to function. This is too high a price for any society to pay and can only lead ultimately to collapse.

As an example of the above, approximately 10% of our population are in the range of normal to mild mental handicap. The simple jobs by which many of these people would have lived have either disappeared or are now going to people who would previously have considered (with their qualifications) such jobs beneath them. People who are unable to compete in the new job market will fail but are intelligent enough to get into crime and other social difficulties. We can choose whether to provide them with a context wherein they can be useful members of society or to define them as problems for the health service or the prisons, in either case costing the state enormous expenditure.

The way out of our dilemma is to break out of the straitjacket of traditional modes of thinking. We have to look towards those neglected aspects of society which the aforementioned EEC Study Group identified as the 'third sector'.

Ever since the beginning of this century, thinkers and activists like Horace Plunkett and others, in this country and elsewhere, have seen the possibility of a different kind of society but they were ahead of their time. Thus the 'third sector' has remained weak because the time for its emergence was not yet ripe. Nevertheless, there is a considerable amount of activity already taking place at this level in most western countries. This can be seen in the various forms of cooperative movement: in agriculture and housing, etc.; in widespread attempts at community development; in attempts to develop 'small technology', harnessing wind, water and solar energy; and in the development of small craft industries. The emergence of the third sector can also be seen in all the self-help activities, in sports, health and fitness, leisure and cultural activities, in the attempts to improve the environment and quality of life and in personal development of ourselves and our children as better and fuller human beings.

Since, as we know, the nation's wealth is produced by less than one-sixth of the population, the distribution of that wealth for the survival of all seems to be more relevant than job creation. We cannot have enough jobs. What will we do with our time? How will we live? We have to find alternatives for those ousted from jobs.

Pretending we do not have to change our ways of distributing wealth is bound to make change harder over a longer painful period of time. Change is happening anyway. Our only chance of lessening the trauma of a transition period is in having a hand in it rather than merely suffering it to happen to us.

For a start, we must do away with our 'Poor Law' attitude to the dole, which defines a person as bad and a failure if they do not have a 'job' in the old sense. Rather, what must be done is to separate the concept of 'work' from the notion of a 'job' for which one is paid. Thus working should be part of the whole of living. There is no foreseeable limit to the amount of work and human development to be undertaken in this sense as part of living. It is only the tasks rigidly defined as jobs in industry and mechanized agriculture that are diminishing.

What is necessary then is to press on to a post-industrial stage, developing fully automated sophisticated ultra-technology and communications systems. This will produce the excess wealth and material goods, although there will be fewer jobs, to provide an adequate standard of living for the whole population. A new means of distribution of this wealth, other than through paid employment, is the key which must be found; and some form of basic minimum income to which all citizens and families are entitled must be introduced. People will receive this not because they work but because they are members of society. If this can be achieved, then people will be freed from many dehumanizing occupations that can now be carried out by automated technology in order to undertake all sorts of creative activity and work in the development of themselves as better and fuller human beings.

It might be objected that, if these objectives could be achieved and the majority of human beings no longer had to be employed to gain the means of survival, then human beings would become lazy and indolent, sitting around doing nothing, waiting to be supported by the state. However, I would like to point out that there is now overwhelming evidence, both from animal behaviour studies and human research that all living creatures, and more particularly human beings, are by their very nature active, inquisitive and goal-seeking. There is a very basic drive in all living creatures and particularly in humans to understand and organize our environment and ourselves to become involved in play, activity or work if left freely to themselves to do so.

In modern society we not only deny many people an opportunity to earn a living in a job, we also deny them access to the basic essentials for any productive activity they might wish to undertake. These essentials are: access to resources (a plot of ground for instance), working space, materials, tools and education in skills, and sufficient working capital investment to begin an enterprise. It is relevant that Marx based his whole philosophy on the proposition that humans are realized (made real) in their work. To alienate a man from his work, Marx maintained, is to alienate him from his humanness. This may be the ultimate root of the vandalism that is so prominent a feature of our society.

Most important of all is to have faith in the basic goodness of the people. If, having denied them the opportunity to get a job, we do not then grind them down into poverty and herd them into an impoverished environment but rather secure them in human dignity, people will respond by engaging, on their own initiative, in a wide variety of activities that are life-enriching. These would include gardening and other food production, crafts, small industrial undertakings, arts, education and a host of cultural activities. Already there is evidence that many individuals are operating in this way to supplement the allowances made under one heading or another by the state. The job is not the only way of life. It was not in the past and will not be in the future.

I was reminded recently of the powerful and intimidating hold of the Calvinist ethic when I heard Margaret Thatcher praised as a workaholic. She finishes her day at 2am. and resents going to bed because of the interruption in her work. She sleeps uneasily and is up again at 6.20am. One could be forgiven for thinking that the world might be a safer and better place were such people to spend more time in bed.

It is clear that this change to an alternative approach to these problems cannot take place across the whole of society, everywhere, at once. There will inevitably have to be a fairly long period of transition. It would seem sensible, therefore, to consider the setting up of one or more pilot projects where a new form of approach could be tried and experimented with. I would like to see a brain-storming group set up of economists, politicians, trade unionists, community organizers, psychologists, psychiatrists, theologians, philosophers, etc., to produce emergency and long-term alternatives to current increasing unemployment.

The question is how can this be achieved when education and human development are always taking place within the context of the present society and within the group culture that already exists. This, if we think about it, always inevitably produces more of the same. There have been, over the past thirty years, many attempts to introduce innovative educational and community development projects in many parts of the world. I have been involved in several of these experiments. Our experience has been similar to that of many others. Somehow the efforts to bring about change seemed to be dissipated out into an ever-widening circle so that, while for a time there may be enthusiastic endeavour for change within the experimental project, this dribbles away into the wider community and it soon becomes painfully clear that, in order for the experiment to work and have an enduring effect, a change would need to be brought about in the whole society. What happens, in fact, is that the effort for change simply disappears into the ever-widening pool of society and everything gradually drifts back to the status quo.

A second outcome that is often seen is where a group withdraws from the community and an attempt is made to create the perfect alternative society. A commune or closed-off artificial community is established which breaks all connection or interchange with the rest of society. While perfection and peace may appear to reign for a short time, inevitably the closed society begins to stagnate and decline, the activity dries up and eventually the whole thing withers and dies, or worse.

It is here that the illuminating insights of Teilhard de Chardin and the more recent pioneering and meticulous work of Prigogene *et al* on self-organizing, non-linear systems help us to understand more clearly why these innovative attempts to bring about real social change and human development have had so little long-term success up to the present and why, in spite of so much idealistic endeavour, everything seems relentlessly to drift back to square one.

The second law of thermodynamics states that every physical process will result in a net decrease in the amount of order (hence a net increase in the amount of disorder) in the universe as a whole. Entropy (from the Greek *entropian*, meaning evolution) is that quantity which indexes the amount of disorder in a system at any given time. The second law thus implies that every physical process will result in an irreversible increase in the amount of entropy in the universe as a whole, over time. Entropy, therefore, sometimes has been referred to as 'time's arrow'. Since its formulation, this law has appeared to most physicists to be one of the greatest achievements of theoretical physics, one of the cornerstones of our understanding of the physical world. It was thus thought to be universal in its application. It seemed evident then that, in our immediate physical environment, on this planet the second law of thermodynamics is relentlessly at work. The planet was running down, natural resources being gobbled up at an accelerating rate and, with each reaction, entropy was increasing. Then de Chardin drew attention to a strange paradox which, although it was not appreciated at the time, fundamentally altered this whole concept of the universe. He pointed out that, in the midst of this dissipative view of the world, biological life has appeared and has been growing continually, becoming ever more complex.

From this point of view, if we take a fresh look at the world, the startling fact emerges that the whole stuff of the universe appears to be built up of units – 'wholes'. These combine to form at each level a genuine synthesis, a new pattern of organization creating a larger and more complex 'whole'. This remarkable design seems to run right through from the quark to the galaxy in outer space.

Ilya Prigogine, in his work on the characteristics of self-organizing systems which he calls irreversible non-linear transformations under conditions far from equilibrium, has dealt with this much more systematically and in far more detail. Most biological, psychological and social systems are neither isolated nor closed. They are, instead, thermodynamically open systems. An open system is one which is capable of exchanging both energy and matter with its environment. When the principles underlying the second law are extended to these systems, a new set of properties emerge which were not formerly apparent. These new properties include capacity for 'self-organization' – that is, for a 'spontaneous' shift from a lower to a higher level of organizational complexity. Prigogine has named such self-organizing systems 'dissipative structures'. We can say that each such locally developing system achieves an increase in structural order and complexity only by 'ingesting', 'digesting' and 'assimilating' the negative entropy (i.e. the orderliness previously possessed by the structure in its surrounding environment) and by 'excreting' back into that environment 'waste products' that are higher in positive entropy (i.e. disorderliness) than those which it initially ingested.

Taking this basic work on self-organizing systems and applying it now to the question of human development – that is, to the question of how we can bring about change at the level of society – a quite different approach to the problem begins to become apparent.

It appears to me inescapable that if we are to have any hope of educating for real human development, of bringing about real human change, this will only be possible if we find ways to create bounded human systems. But these must be open systems with semi-permeable boundedness so that exchange with the surrounding environment (i.e. society) can be managed and controlled sufficiently to allow self-organization, growth and development to go on within the system and not to allow this to be simply dissipated into the surrounding society.

What I now see is the possibility, difficult though it may be, and however much the scales are tilted against it, of setting up islands, human networks, bounded both spatially and psychically, where a truly human education can begin and where real personal growth and development can take place in a context of personal relationships. Much of the knowledge and understanding necessary to set up such bounded human systems is now available as never before.

If these 'human islands' are to achieve anything, they must involve the whole person and the whole life cycle from cradle to grave. Both male and female dimensions of sexuality must find their expression in each person, and both women and men must be able to participate fully and equally and each make their full contribution to the whole. There must be places where all can come to live and to learn, to work and to play and, more importantly, simply to 'be'.

It is quite clear now that no partial concept of education, such as our present school system, can ever really achieve anything different. It can only further reinforce the schizophrenic splitting process which is more and more affecting all aspects of our society. New curricula, smaller classes, and all the other current slogans for progress, all mean nothing and will achieve nothing. The expertise and understanding of the good teacher is another matter and these human skills will have a vital place within the self-development context of a bounded, human, living system.

Another important concept makes its appearance here. I tried to clarify this in a recent paper on 'minorities', in which I said:

In my view, the ego should be mainly seen as a function of the boundary of the living system (whether this be an individual or a group) in the management of the interactions between what is inside and outside the system. I had this in mind as the exercise of authority. But the crucial question here is where this 'authority' or 'control' lies. Psychologists in recent years have coined the term 'locus of control' and ask the question of any living system of individual, whether this locus control lies within the system or outside it. From what has been said, it will be clear if we think about it that this question is vital. If the locus of control lies outside any living system, whether individual, group or society, then that system will be directed from outside by other or larger systems than itself and will have no control or personal authority over itself. This is a crucial question for any person or society, whether they exercise their personal authority and are self-directing, taking responsibility for all that is within them, or are directed from outside.

The question of taking responsibility for all that is within us, the negative as well as the positive, is absolutely crucial. Many human groups and societies in the past have deteriorated and destroyed themselves because, in trying to be perfect, they have denied in themselves, or projected on to others, the negative aspects and evil that they could not accept in themselves and for which they were unwilling or unable to take responsibility. In the same article, I tried to deal with this.

The fatal weakness of the use of these defences is that no matter how much we repress and try to make disappear, or project out on to others, the unacceptable parts of ourselves, all of this effort is in fact illusory, for we do not actually rid ourselves of what is within us. On the contrary, these unwanted parts of ourselves which are now defined as evil are, for the very reason that they are hidden, given free rein to grow and multiply unimpeded within us. The interesting thing is, had these aspects of our reality been consciously accepted as part of the richness and diversity within us (and remember I am speaking here of either the individual or the group) and had we taken responsibility for owning them, then they could have been seen as good and wholesome and the bad or evil need not have become a reality or have grown either within or without.

If the bounded human system that I am proposing is to have success as a 'human island' where real change and growth can take place in the midst of a fragmenting and deteriorating society, then all these issues will have to be faced and worked at unflinchingly.

As an example, I am presenting the following proposal for a project which I hope to implement on the site of St Brendan's Hospital as soon as possible. We are currently working at getting the money to put this into action. The goal is to turn St Brendan's and all its unused resources into a living, breathing, learning centre to which large numbers of the larger community will come. We hope to see St Brendan's come alive rather than continue as a stagnant pool of dependency which is too often a dumping ground from our 'healthy' society.

15. How Does Psychotherapy Work?
Part I. The New Science Paradigm for Psychotherapy Theory

IVOR W. BROWNE AND VINCENT KENNY

Vincent Kenny and I were asked by Dr Frederik F. Flach, MD, to write two papers on the way psychotherapy works for his ongoing Professional Development programme in New York entitled 'Directions in Psychiatry'. The following two papers were published in the journal *Directions in Psychiatry* (vol. 5, lesson 3) in December 1984.

Flach later included these two papers in a book he edited on the subject of psychotherapy.

Editor's Note

IN this chapter and the following, the authors explore the question that recurrently haunts even the most experienced clinician: does psychotherapy really work? Do the hours, weeks and years we spend carrying out this modality really have a healing influence?

The approach they take is not, however, statistical. Rather, they emphasize that many of the traditional methods in research may be simply inadequate to the task for confirming – or denying – the importance of psychotherapy. They divide scientific endeavour into past – dominated by Newtonian concepts that deal in measurable forces of cause and effect – and contemporary (and future), which began with Sadi Carnot's formulation of the second law of thermodynamics, to the effect that any isolated physical system will proceed spontaneously in the direction of ever-increasing disorder. Darwin, de Chardin and Einstein continued the evolution of vision and thought that moved away from the idea of the material world being a comfortably ticking clock to be repaired when out of order to an indeterminate interweaving of interdependent interrelationships.

Studies of psychotherapy following the Newtonian model have been singularly inconclusive. Some, such as those of Eysenck, suggest psychotherapy is totally ineffectual; others give the appearance of proving the efficacy of one psychotherapeutic approach over all others; some suggest that every form of psychotherapy is equally effective.

The authors offer a fresh, challenging view of psychotherapy and redefine the nature of psychotherapy as a way to help patients who are in psychological distress because their personal theory of reality has failed to reconstruct their view of the world and consequently help them reorganize themselves in a new and different way. The concept of open systems suggests an active principle emerging in matter characterized by change, instability and continual fluctuation; at bifurcation points fluctuations destabilize the current organization of the system, which may then disintegrate into chaos or suddenly reorganize itself into a higher level of organization. The purpose of psychotherapy is to facilitate a constructive outcome for such an event when the individual cannot do so on his own.

Introduction

To find the answer to the question 'How does psychotherapy work?' we must first ask another question: 'Why, after more than half a century, do we not have an answer to the question 'How does psychotherapy work?' The answer to this question probably lies in the inappropriate application of Newtonian science to the area of human experience. Part I of this chapter explores the tacit assumptions and problems inherent in the old science and outlines the essential ingredients of the new science paradigm. Part II outlines the application of the new science outlook to psychotherapeutic practice and attempts to illustrate how psychotherapy works within this framework. We will begin with a brief historical review of the major conceptual landmarks on the way from Newtonian to systemic theory.

Galileo (1564–1642)

The scientific revolution began with Nicholas Copernicus, who first proposed that the earth was no longer the centre of the universe but merely one of a number of planets circling a star. This theory was published in 1543, the year of his death. The real change in scientific thinking, however, was ushered in by Galileo. He not only confirmed the work of Copernicus but for the first time combined scientific experimentation with the language of mathematics. Galileo stated that science should restrict itself to studying the essential properties of material bodies: shapes, numbers and movement; i.e. that which can be measured and quantified. In doing this he was very aware that this did not represent all of reality and that the science he suggested did not deal with other aspects such as experience, quality or values. Nevertheless, the views he put forward represented the dominant features of science throughout the seventeenth century and still remain as important criteria in scientific work today.[1]

Francis Bacon (1561–1626): Classical Empiricism

Francis Bacon was the father of empiricism, a pragmatic view which has dominated the British tradition in science ever since. Bacon is also of particular interest in that he established the strongly masculine influence we associate with scientific endeavour. As attorney-general at the time of James I, Bacon had the task of conducting the trial of suspected witches. It is not surprising that, when addressing himself to nature, which has always traditionally been considered female (e.g. Mother Earth), he used phrases such as 'torture nature's secrets from her' or 'to make a slave of nature'. We see here the idea that we can interfere as we like with nature, make her do as we want, and we can see this influence still at work today in medicine and psychiatry and in the deterministic notion of 'giving' a person a 'course' of psychotherapy as if it were a form of medicine to make them do our bidding.[2]

René Descartes (1596–1650): Classical Rationalism

Both Bacon and Descartes split the person into a 'higher' and 'lower' self. Baconian observation and Cartesian intellect acted as the 'higher' self which discerned truth, as opposed to our 'lower' self (prejudiced, irrational) which promoted error. Descartes started from a position of doubting all things until he came to something he could not doubt – himself as a thinker. This gives rise to his famous phrase, *Cogito ergo sum*: 'I think therefore I am.' Here we have the separating of mind from matter. He said 'there is nothing included in the concept of body that belongs to the mind; and there is nothing in that of mind that belongs to the body'. This fundamental division between mind and matter has had an enormous effect on western thought and plagues medical thinking to this day. More than anything else, this has made it difficult for us to think rationally about psychotherapy, and many westerners think of their bodies simply as something which transports their 'real' (thinking) self; i.e. their mind. Descartes' greatest contribution was probably the use of analytical methods of reasoning. This was extremely valuable and underlay most of the advances in the development of scientific achievement for the next 300 years. Unfortunately, overemphasis on this Cartesian method has led to the ubiquitous attitude of reductionism in science, the idea that all natural phenomena can be understood by breaking them up into smaller parts. We have thus arrived at a view of causality, that disturbance of the 'whole' will always be explained by a malfunction in one of its parts. It is the model which is used in attempts to study and understand how psychotherapy works. Descartes' clockwork, a mechanistic model of nature, has had a major effect on biologists, physicians and psychologists for the past 300 years, indeed right to the present day. Unfortunately, the kind of illnesses and health problems affecting us in the late twentieth century do not yield their secrets to this kind of reductionist thinking.[3]

Isaac Newton (1643–1727)

The conceptual framework created by Galileo and Descartes was completed by Newton, who developed a consistent mathematical formulation of the mechanistic view of nature. From the second half of the seventeenth century to the end of the nineteenth century the Newtonian, mechanistic model of the universe dominated all scientific thought. Newton created a new mathematical method (i.e. differential calculus) to describe the motion of solid bodies. He used this to formulate the exact laws of motion of all bodies under the influence of the force of gravity. The great significance of these laws lay in their universal application where the universe was seen as a vast machine operating according to exact mathematical laws. The unique importance of Newton's work was understood by his contemporaries. The natural sciences, as well as the humanities and social sciences, all accepted this mechanistic view of classical physics as the correct description of reality and modelled their own theories accordingly. Whenever psychologists, sociologists or economists want to be scientific, they always turn to the basic concepts of Newtonian physics and base their research on them.[4]

After Isaac Newton, scientists believed they had laid bare the laws governing the universe and that all happenings were understandable at last in terms of strictly determined laws of cause and effect. By identifying all of the 'inputs' in any situation one could determine precisely the result that would follow. The existing uncertainties and areas of incomplete knowledge would be conquered by the steady growth of scientific knowledge. Our understanding of nature would be complete, including the complex area of human existence, the treatment of disease and the phenomenon of madness.

Thermodynamics (1824): 'The Science of Complexity'

The formulation of the laws of thermodynamics constituted the first great break with the static, reversible world of Newton and classical dynamics. The first law is concerned with the conservation of energy. It states that the total energy involved in a process is always conserved. In 1824 Sadi Carnot formulated the second law of thermodynamics, which stated that any isolated physical system will proceed spontaneously in the direction of ever-increasing disorder. In the 1850s Rudolf Clausius introduced a new concept which he called 'entropy' to measure the degree of evolution of a physical system. Thus entropy can be seen as a measure of disorder. Boltzmann developed this work further, demonstrating that irreversible thermodynamic change is a change towards states of increasing probability. This move to explain a physical concept in terms of statistical probability marks a sharp departure from Newton. With the help of probability theory the behaviour of complex mechanical systems can be described in terms of statistical laws. Thus, in any isolated system made up of a large number of molecules, the entropy (or disorder) will keep increasing until the system reaches a state of maximum equilibrium. This introduced for the first time into science the notion of irreversibility and, as Eddington called it, 'the arrow of time'. Nothing could ever be the same again.[5]

Charles Darwin (1809–1882)

Charles Darwin brought together an array of evidence to create a theory of evolution with a firm biological footing. Darwin's *Origin of the Species* had the same all-embracing effect on subsequent biological thought as Newton's *Principia* had earlier on astronomy and physics. Once again the concept of irreversibility and an 'arrow of time' was emerging but now as an evolving and ever-changing system in which complex forms of life developed from simpler structures. At first Newtonian scientists tried to dismiss this development as unimportant accidents and peculiarities of nature but by the end of the nineteenth century the classical dynamics of Newton were already losing their central role as the fundamental theory of natural phenomena.[6]

Pierre Teilhard de Chardin (1881–1955)

Teilhard de Chardin's major work was in geology and palaeontology. He tried to integrate his philosophical and scientific insights into a coherent world view. This view shows remarkable compatibility with recent systems theory. He emphasized that evolution proceeds in the direction of increasing complexity with an attendant rise of consciousness. This he called the 'law of complexity-consciousness'. He defined consciousness as 'the specific effect of organized complexity', a view similar to that of Gregory Bateson. He also saw the manifestation of mind in larger systems and postulated that, as human evolution progresses, human beings 'pressing up against' one another cover the planet with a web of ideas for which he coined the neologism 'noo-sphere'. He viewed the growing tensions between the physical and biological sciences as follows: on the one hand, we have in physics a matter which slides irresistibly, following the line of least resistance, in the direction of the most probable forms of distribution; and, on the other hand, we have in biology the same matter drifting (no less irresistibly but in this case in a sort of 'greater effort for survival') towards ever more improbable, because ever more complex, forms of arrangement.[7]

Albert Einstein and the Quantum Physicists

Albert Einstein produced two papers in 1905 which marked the beginning of twentieth-century scientific thought. One dealt with the theory of relativity and the other with a new way of looking at electromagnetic radiation, which was to form the foundation of quantum theory. As Capra describes it, 'The new physics necessitated profound changes in concepts of space, time, matter, object, and cause and effect; and because these concepts are so fundamental to our way of experiencing the world, their transformation came as a great shock.'[8] The material world, which had been viewed as a comfortably ticking clockwork mechanism, was now transformed into a complex and indeterminate interweaving of interdependent interrelationships.[9]

While psychologists were struggling to exclude consciousness from their fields of study, the quantum physicists such as Max Planck, Heisenberg and Niels Bohr were eagerly building into their experiments the human relational features of consciousness, intentionality and subjectivity. In experiments of subatomic particles, it became clear that the answer, when obtained, depended critically on the initial conditions, the way the experimenter framed his question, and upon his position as a participant observer. The human observer was now seen as being part of the observation process and of what he was observing. The world was now seen as sets of interrelations and not merely as static separate entities. It is only recently that such thinking has begun to appear in biological and applied sciences. These continue to be dominated by reductionistic thinking. In the psychotherapeutic literature, for example, we see how a rigid Newtonian view of linear causality is applied, fruitlessly, to the question of effectiveness in psychotherapy.

Ilya Prigogine (1917–)

For the last two decades Prigogine and others have been bringing about the same kind of radical change in our thinking at the macroscopic level that the quantum physicists did during the early years of this century. In 1977 Prigogine was awarded the Nobel Prize for his work on the thermodynamics of non-equilibrium systems. In his work on the characteristics of self-organizing systems – which he calls irreversible, nonlinear transformations under conditions far from equilibrium – he dealt very systematically with a complex interdependent holistic view of the universe. As Prigogine puts it, 'Our vision of nature is undergoing a radical change toward the multiple, the temporal and the complex'.[10] It would seem then that we are living in a pluralistic world and there is not simply one way of understanding reality. In some aspects of the universe we see processes which appear to operate like machines. These closed systems now appear to form only a small part of the physical universe. When we turn to open systems we find what appears to be an active principle emerging in matter which, far from being orderly and stable, is characterized by change, instability and continual fluctuation. Such systems exchange energy or matter with their environment. When the principles underlying the second law of thermodynamics are extended to these systems, a new set of properties emerges which was not formerly apparent. These new properties include capacity for 'self-organization'; i.e. for a spontaneous shift from a lower to a higher level of organizational complexity. Prigogine has named such self-organizing systems 'dissipative structures'. We can say that each such locally developing system achieves an increase in structural order and complexity only by 'ingesting', 'digesting' and 'assimilating' the negative entropy (i.e. the orderliness previously possessed by the structure in its surrounding environment), and by 'excreting' back into that environment 'waste products' which are higher in positive entropy (i.e. disorderliness) than those which it has initially ingested. He has shown that, as the input of energy into such a dissipative structure is increased, and as it moves further from equilibrium, it is likely to be characterized by continual fluctuation. This in turn can give rise to increasing turbulence and now and then cause a fluctuation so powerful that it destabilizes the pre-existing organization. This is what Prigogine refers to as a 'bifurcation point', at which time it is inherently impossible to determine in advance in which direction the change will move. The system may disintegrate into a chaotic state or suddenly reorganize itself into a quite fresh, more differentiated, higher level of order or organization which then takes on the characteristics of irreversibility. This process of order and organization arising spontaneously out of disorder and chaos, through a process of self-organization, has deep implications for the whole of psychotherapy and for personality change and development in relation to life crises.[11]

Humberto Maturana and Francisco Varela (1970)

The Chilean biologists, Maturana and Varela, have asked the questions: 'What is it to be alive?' 'What is the essential difference between a machine and a living organism?' They have arrived at a similar formulation to that of Prigogine, stating that the essential characteristic of life is a state of self-organization. The term they coined for this is 'autopoiesis' – 'auto' meaning self, and 'poiesis' (from the Greek root, *poinein*) meaning 'to produce'; i.e. self-producing. According to this view, the essence of something which is living is that it actively maintains and produces itself, that its first priority is to maintain itself in existence. This is in contrast to other structures such as machines which they term 'allopoietic', meaning that they do or make things other than themselves, and are made by others. Maturana gives the example of a donkey as an autopoietic system which, when harnessed to a cart, becomes an allopoietic machine but which on being unharnessed becomes autopoietic once more. Essential to this notion of self-organization is the concept of boundedness. It is by virtue of our boundary that we can distinguish what is outside from what is inside, what is self from non-self. As Varela points out, an interesting characteristic which follows is that living creatures essentially relate to themselves. This is all the more true as the complexity of self-organization increases. At the human level we find a living system which is in an enormously complex state of communication with itself and hence manifests consciousness. Varela illustrates the operational closure of the living system as follows:

> For example, if we were to travel with the nerve activity originating at the retina into the cortical area (of the occipital lobe), we would find that for each fibre from the retina entering this piece of cortex, 100 other fibres enter at the same spatial location from all over the brain. Thus the activity of the retina at best sculpts or modulates what is going on internally in the high interconnection of the neural layers and nuclei.

What this means quite simply is that, if we ask the question 'What causes a given activity in our nervous system or any action of the whole human being?', the answer is quite simply the nervous system and the human organism itself. No longer can we talk of some external input 'causing' us to behave in a specific way. There are simply no direct linear correlations between the outside and the inside, between the inputs and the outputs. From this point of view, an input from the outside world can be no more than a perturbation, which meets a very complex world of communication busily creating its own reality. The most that can be achieved is for the input to perturb the equilibrium and the state of self-coherence of the organism so that it must readjust its state of self-organization, perhaps with the conclusion that it acts in a particular manner. Here is one aspect of indeterminacy in that the living organism relates to the outside world only indirectly through the altering of its own state of self-coherence. Thus the organism may completely ignore the input altogether.[12] This has obvious implications for research in psychotherapy, since it means that studies which ask questions from the viewpoint of linear causality can only arrive at meaningless results. This is not to say that the study of psychotherapy is impossible but rather that we will have to approach it from a completely different perspective, that of the constructivist philosophy which builds in probability theory and the uncertainty principle. In dealing with living creatures we are involved in a form of circularity where the organism essentially relates to itself, and where simplistic notions of causality must be abandoned.

The Psychotherapy Research Literature

Almost half a century of 'scientific' research into psychotherapy has brought us no nearer to answering the question 'How does psychotherapy work?' Research efforts have cast more confusion than clarity on the other fundamental question 'Is psychotherapy effective?' In a review of psychotherapy research studies Eysenck[13] stated that there was no empirical evidence to demonstrate that psychotherapy had any significant effectiveness in treating patients. Since that time there have been numerous publications attempting to refute his claim: Meltzoff and Kornreich;[14] Bergin;[15] Luborsky, Singer and Luborsky;[16] Smith and Glass;[17] Bergin and Lambert;[18] and Smith, Glass and Miller.[19] These studies have not managed to scientifically demonstrate the effectiveness of psychotherapy to a degree that would satisfy critics such as Eysenck,[20] Kazdin and Wilson,[21] and Rachman and Wilson.[22] The area is characterized by unseemly and unscientific internecine criticism and accusations; for example, of selective bias in studies chosen for analysis. There is a tendency for researchers with a behaviour therapy bias to 'prove' that behaviour therapy is superior to psychodynamic and psychoanalytic therapy; e.g. Rachman.[23] On the other hand there is a tendency for the psychodynamically biased researchers to 'prove' that psychodynamic therapies are indeed effective. There are many outright contradictions arising here, partly from the 'scientific' approach used and partly from the unacknowledged personal nature of 'knowing' or 'proving' anything. Thus we have Bachrach[24] asserting that psychoanalysis leads to psychotherapeutic benefits, while Garfield,[25] commenting on the research findings of behaviour therapists such as Eysenck and Rachman, states that, 'With regard to psychoanalysis, they find no acceptable evidence to support it as an effective treatment, a conclusion that is difficult to refute.' It is evident, thirty-three years after Eysenck's initial attack, that this area of research is a morass of unrecognized value-system bias. As Rosenthal[26] demonstrated, experimenters will often find what they set out to find. It is also becoming apparent that psychodynamic psychotherapists cannot hope to find an answer from within the double-bind that Eysenck put them in originally. His challenge is of the variety 'Have you stopped beating your wife yet?'. Eysenck demands an answer within his reductionistic and logical positivistic framework and, while this may suit the mechanistic behaviour therapy approaches, this Newtonian view of science defeats the very subject matter attended to by psychodynamic therapists; for example, emotions, the mind, the unconscious, dreams, etc.

The Dodo Verdict

Many of the psychotherapy research studies which showed a high effectiveness rate – Meltzoff and Kornreich;[27] Luborsky, Singer and Luborsky;[28] and Bergin and Lambert[29] – gave rise to feelings of unease when it began to appear that all psychotherapies seemed to be effective. Moreover, they appeared to be equally effective and, further, that it did not seem to matter what specific techniques were used, how often the treatment occurred, or even how well-trained or experienced the therapist was. In *Alice's Adventures in Wonderland* the Dodo, having presided over the chaotic Caucus-race, was unable to decide who had won and consequently concluded that 'everybody has won, and all must have prizes'. This statement provided an ironic subtitle to the paper written by Luborsky *et al.*[30] These findings, while cheering to practising clinicians, have done nothing to alleviate doubts regarding the credibility of the psychotherapeutic enterprise.[31]

Many of these problems stem from attempts to apply an inappropriate mechanistic model of science to the subject matter of psychology and psychotherapy. In attempting to work within the Newtonian approach, academic researchers have either completely excluded the most interesting and important aspects of human nature (e.g. the mind is systematically excluded by behaviourists) or they have attempted, vainly, to capture a reduced and often caricatured version of important human experience within the mechanistic model, a task akin to that of trapping a flow of water in a fishing net. As Wittgenstein pointed out, 'the existence of the experimental method makes us think we have the means of solving the problems which trouble us; though problem and method pass one another by'.[32] The absurdities of this type of research are such that it now takes an army of researchers and a vast amount of money and time to even begin to answer questions regarding the effectiveness of psychotherapy. In discussing the National Institute of Mental Health (NIMH) project to compare three different approaches to unipolar depression, Garfield comments that 'This project in its first phase is estimated to cost $3 million. If we were to conduct such a study for the 200 different forms of psychotherapy with several of the major disorders, it would probably take hundreds of years as well as a good share of our federal research budget.'[33]

Future research in psychotherapy must take place within the new science paradigm.[34] Only by a return to the experiential and essentially personal nature of psychotherapy can we hope to begin influencing clinical practice – which has largely continued to ignore the academic–scientific debate about psychotherapeutic effectiveness. As Smail points out, 'research in psychotherapy tends to destroy the significance of findings concerning the personal nature of the therapeutic relationship precisely through attempting to mechanize them'.[35]

The Need to Change to a Constructivist Outlook

In discussing the philosophy of radical constructivism, Ernst von Glasersfeld[36] introduces the idea that the best we can ever hope to aspire to in our knowledge of the real world is to discover what the world is not. More succinctly, not only does the world not tell us what it is, neither does it tell us what it is not. It only reveals to us that certain aspects of our human endeavours are possible or viable. When we learn this, we are learning only about ourselves in the world, and not about the world we inhabit. Underlying this proposition are two further propositions: namely that (a) we cannot know the world directly and (b) we personally construct our view of the world.

These statements are a radical shift away from the traditional realist epistemology which held the view that human knowledge of the world related to the actual world in a picture-like or representationalist correspondence (or match) between the two. As Glasersfeld puts it: 'The metaphysical realist looks for knowledge that matches reality in the same sense as you might look for paint to match the colour that is already on the wall you have to repair.'[37] The constructivist epistemology, on the other hand, holds that the relation between human knowledge and the world is not that of matching but rather that of fitting. Glasersfeld uses the metaphor of a key fitting a lock. A key fits a lock if it serves to open it. Many different keys with alternative shapes can serve to open the same lock. Within this metaphor, the relationship between human knowledge and the world we live in is the same as that which exists between a burglar and a lock which he must open in order to proceed. As we have seen above, scientific theories are no longer regarded as 'wrong' or 'right' or 'true' or 'false' but rather as being useful, relevant and viable or not.

George Kelly[38] proposed a theory of personality which viewed each person as if he were a scientist, constructing theories about the world and testing out such theories through his behaviour. Each individual's personal theory of the world can be seen to fit the world to one degree or another, and to work usefully for the individual most of the time. Psychological disturbance can be defined within this view as when the person's theory no longer fits satisfactorily with 'reality'. The person's outlook or the conceptual 'goggles' through which he views the world leads him into difficulties with the world. Things are not as he perceives them. Psychological distress is therefore a signal that his theory fails to make adequate sense of his world. Therapy consists in aiding the patient to actively reconstruct his view of the world, thereby reorganizing himself in a different way.

That reality can disprove our theories is obvious. What is perhaps not so obvious is the fact that we cannot ever 'prove' a theory.[39] What is often not fully appreciated is that having been informed by reality that our theories do not fit, we are no wiser as to what actually constitutes that reality as to what it is. Thus, each 'breakthrough' in science, each 'discovery' that is made, does not actually push back the frontiers of reality but rather is a statement about the internal consistency and validity of the theories we have constructed in our attempts at explaining reality. Thus, while we may come to know what is not the case, our theories as to what is the case must remain for ever mere conjecture.

Our theories of the world not only describe the world but also dictate how we will experience it. As Glasersfeld says: 'The world we experience is, and must be, as it is because we have put it together in that way.'[40] Just like any good burglar, this view of reality encourages one to carry many alternative 'keys' about one's person to ensure that obstinate locks will yield to one's probings. At the heart of Kelly's[41] personal construct psychology we find the philosophical notion of 'constructive alternativism'. This states that whatever exists may be reconstrued. It states that man does not have to be a victim of his biography or his circumstances but that he may enslave himself with his interpretation or his construction of his circumstances. Our outlook on reality therefore may be liberating or imprisoning.

Summary

Classical science thought it had found eternal laws where all processes were reversible and static but what has now emerged as the dominant view involves time and evolving systems. Where once there 'appeared to be a universal symmetry, recent scientific developments have shown symmetry-breaking processes at all levels from elementary particles up to biology and ecology. Our outlook on nature is changing radically towards plurality, temporality and complexity. It would seem then that we are living in a world where there cannot be simply one way of understanding reality. In a small degree some aspects of the universe appear to operate as stable machines. However, with open systems we find what appears to be an active principle emerging in matter which is characterized by change, instability, and continual fluctuation. A bifurcation point is reached when fluctuations destabilize the current organization of the system. Issues of 'being' and 'becoming' are raised here in the context of the indeterminate nature of the 'choice' of direction the system will take. The system may disintegrate into chaos or suddenly reorganize itself into a quite fresh, more differentiated, higher level of organization which then takes up the characteristics of irreversibility. These processes of increasing organization arising spontaneously out of chaos through a process of self-organization have direct applicability to human change processes and are readily illustrated within the framework of crisis theory.

Conclusion

There are a number of important questions raised by the foregoing, for example how well do modern theories of psychiatry fit with human reality? Ever since David Rosenhan's[42] study illustrated how the making of the psychiatric diagnosis invented, rather than described, a reality wherein any patient behaviour (even normal behaviour) was seen as disturbed, many clinicians have begun to question the self-fulfilling nature of such diagnostic practices.

TABLE I. SUMMARY OF THE DICHOTOMIES BETWEEN
THE OLD AND NEW SCIENCES

Epistemological Position	
Old	*New*
Discover world	Invents world
Match	Fit
Absolute truth	Usefulness/viability
Accumulative fragmentalism	Alternate constructivism
Reductionism	Constructivism (Holism)
Reversibility	Irreversibility
No time	Time dimension
Verification	Falsification
Initial conditions specify outcome	Impossibility
Analysis	Synthesis
Symmetry	Asymmetry
Absolute knowledge	Uncertainty

Image of the Person	
Old	*New*
Finished product	Process
Determined by inputs	Self-organization
Linear cause and effect	Boundedness and circularity
Object	Reflexive subject
Separate entity	Intersubjective process
Objective observer	Participant–observer (experiential)
'Value-free'	Value context
Man as machine	Man as scientist
Passive	Active
Mechanism	Humanism

If we are concerned with constructing an alternative theory to fit reality better, then such a theory has to encompass many of the issues raised in the above discussion. Such a theory must encompass the view of the person as a process who exists in time and who is embedded in a causal, interactional and intersubjective context within which he actively creates or invents his own world and his image of himself in that world. Such a theory must also be reflexive in that, since we are what we study – i.e. we are the same type of phenomenon as our patients – our theory must apply equally to ourselves as to our patients, rather than having a double standard where we use one theory to fit our patients and another to fit ourselves. Furthermore, any such theory must recursively explain itself. Since there is no one reality that we can find a 'match' for, then we need to develop the discipline of theoretical plurality or what Kelly called constructive alternativism.[43]

References

1. S. Drake, *Galileo Studies*, University of Michigan Press, Michigan, 1970.
2. F. Bacon, *Philosophical Works*, ed. J.M. Robertson, Routledge, London, 1905.
3. R. Descartes, *Philosophical Works*, Cambridge University Press, New York, 1931.
4. I. Newton, *Isaac Newton's Philosophiae Naturalis Principia Mathematica*, London, 1687, eds. A. Koyrae and B. Cohen, Cambridge University Press, New York, 1972.
5. I. Prigogine and I. Stengers, *Order Out of Chaos*, William Heinemann, London, 1984.
6. C. Darwin, *The Origin of Species*, Mentor, London, 1958.
7. P. Teilhard de Chardin, *Activation of L'Énergie*, Harcourt, Brace, Jovanovich, San Diego, CA, 1963.
8. F. Capra, *The Turning Point*, Flamingo, London, 1983.
9. B. Hoffman and H. Dukas, *Albert Einstein*, Viking Press, New York, 1972.
10. Prigogine and Stengers, *Order Out of Chaos*, William Heinemann, London, 1984.
11. I. Prigogine, *From Being to Becoming: Time and Complexity in the Physical Sciences*, Freeman & Co., San Francisco, 1980; G. Nicolis and I. Prigogine, *Self-Organization in Nonequilibrium Systems*, John Wiley & Sons, New York, 1977.
12. F.J. Varela, *Principles of Biological Autonomy*, Elsevier, New York, 1979; F.J. Varela and H. Maturana, 'Living Ways of Sense-making: A Middle Path for Neuroscience', paper presented at the International Symposium on Disorder and Order, Stanford University, Palo Alto, CA, 1981; H. Maturana and F. Varela, *Autopoiesis and Cognition*, Boston Studies in Philosophical Science, vol. 42, D. Reidel, Boston, 1980.

13. H. Eysenck, 'The Effects of Psychotherapy: An Evaluation', *J. Consult. Clin. Psychol.*, 16, 319–24, 1952.

14. J. Meltzoff and M. Kornreich, *Research in Psychotherapy*, Atherton Press, New York, 1970.

15. A.E. Bergin and M. Lambert, 'The Evaluation of Therapeutic Outcomes', in A.E. Bergin and S.L. Garfield (eds), *Handbook of Psychotherapy and Behavior Change*, John Wiley & Sons, New York, 1971.

16. L. Luborsky, B. Singer and L. Luborsky, 'Comparative Studies of Psychotherapy: Is It True that "Everybody Has Won and All Must Have Prizes"?', *Arch. Gen. Psych.*, 32, 995–1088, 1975.

17. M. Smith and G. Glass, 'Meta-analysis of Psychotherapy Outcome Studies', *Am. Psychol.*, 32, 752–60, 1977.

18. Bergin and Lambert, 'The Evaluation of Therapeutic Outcomes'.

19. M. Smith, G. Glass and T. Miller, *The Benefits of Psychotherapy*, Johns Hopkins University Press, Baltimore, MD, 1980.

20. H. Eysenck, 'An Exercise in Mega-silliness', *Am. Psychol.*, 33, 517, 1978.

21. A. Kazdin and G. Wilson, *Evaluation of Behavior Therapy: Issues, Evidence and Research Studies,* Ballinger, Cambridge, MA, 1978.

22. S. Rachman and G. Wilson, *The Effects of Psychological Therapy*, 2nd edition, Pergamon Press, New York, 1980.

23. S. Rachman, *The Effects of Psychotherapy*, Pergamon Press, New York, 1971.

24. H. Bachrach, 'The Efficacy of Psychotherapy', Lesson 17 in *Directions in Psychiatry*, vol. 4, The Hatherleigh Co. Ltd., New York, 1984.

25. S. Garfield, 'Effectiveness of Psychotherapy: The Perennial Controversy', *Professional Psychology: Research and Practice*, 14, l, 35–43, 1983.

26. R. Rosenthal, *Experimental Effects in Behavior Research*, Appleton-Century Crofts, New York, 1966.

27. Meltzoff and Kornreich, *Research in Psychotherapy*.

28. Luborsky and Singer, 'Comparative Studies of Psychotherapy'.

29. Bergin and Lambert, 'The Evaluation of Therapeutic Outcomes'.

30. Luborsky and Singer, 'Comparative Studies of Psychotherapy'.

31. M. Parloff, 'Psychotherapy Research and Its Incredible Credibility Crisis', *Clin. Psychol. Rev.* 4, l, 95–109, 1984.

32. L. Wittgenstein, *Philosophical Investigations*, Blackwell, Oxford, 1968.

33. Garfield, 'Effectiveness of Psychotherapy'.

34. P. Reason and J. Rowan (eds), *Human Inquiry: A Sourcebook of New Paradigm Research,* Wiley & Sons, Chichester, 1981.

35. D. Smail, 'Learning in Psychotherapy', in P. Salmon (ed.), *Coming to Know*, Routledge & Kegan Paul, London, 1980, p. 175.

36. E. von Glasersfeld, 'An Introduction to Radical Constructivism', in P. Watzlawick (ed.), *The Invented Reality*, Norton, New York, 1984.

37. Ibid.

38. G. Kelly, *The Psychology of Personal Constructs*, 2 vols, Norton, New York, 1955.

39. K. Popper, *The Logic of Scientific Discovery*, Hutchinson, London, 1972.

40. von Glasersfeld, 'An Introduction to Radical Constructivism'.
41. Kelly, *The Psychology of Personal Constructs*.
42. D. Rosenhan, 'On Being Sane in Insane Places', *Science*, 179, 250–58, 1978.
43. Kelly, *The Psychology of Personal Constructs*.

16. How Does Psychotherapy Work?
Part II. A Systems Approach to
Psychotherapy Practice

VINCENT KENNY AND IVOR W. BROWNE

A New Paradigm for Psychotherapy

THE previous chapter raised the issue of what is reality and what is illusion. It was argued that there is a large gulf between the view of reality inherent in the Newtonian mechanical model on the one hand and the experience of reality as humans live it on the other. Psychotherapeutic research framed within the old physics model has failed completely to grasp the experiential richness of the psychotherapeutic venture as well as having failed to say anything sensible about the varieties of psychotherapy in practice. Living on the cutting edge of a new scientific paradigm is not a comfortable place to set up house. The attempts to date to transfer concepts such as homeostasis, equifinality, etc., have largely been 'lipservice, rather than an actual development in theoretical elaboration'.[1] Even the issue of deciding what constitutes the component units of a human system is a complex one. While there is a certain reluctance[2] to extrapolate from biological systems to human societies, Stafford Beer leaves one in no doubt as to his conclusions:

> I am quite sure of the answer; yes, human societies are biological systems. . . Any cohesive social institution is an autopoietic system – because it survives, because its method of survival answers the autopoietic criteria, and because it may well change its entire appearance and its apparent purpose in the process. As examples I list: firms and industries, schools and universities, clinics and hospitals, professional bodies, departments of state, and whole countries.[3]

This chapter will attempt to spell out in some detail the implications of the new science paradigm for psychotherapy practice and how changes may be effected within the psychotherapeutic context. To begin this task we must spell out what it means to be a living system.

Definition of a Living System

The basic principle of a living system is that of self-organization. This means essentially that its order in structure and function is not imposed by the environment but is established by the system itself. Thus something can be held to be 'alive', to be an 'organism' if, and only if, it fulfils the following five conditions:

1. It contains a number of elements.
2. These elements are involved in a dynamic process of interaction and interrelationship.
3. It is separated from its environment by a boundary of its own elements such that it permits transactions of import and export across the boundary; i.e. it is an 'open system'.
4. It maintains and renews (regenerates) its own elements by its own internal processes. Living organisms continually renew themselves; cells breaking down and building up structures, tissues and organs replacing their cells in continual cycles of regeneration. Nevertheless the living system maintains its overall structure and integrity in space. Its components are continually renewed and recycled but the pattern of organization remains stable.
5. Living systems show a tendency to transcend themselves. As Capra says, 'To reach out creatively beyond their boundaries and limitations to generate new structures and new forms of organization. This principle of self-transcendence manifests itself in the processes of learning, development and evolution.'[4] Thus living systems not only tend to change and adapt but also to reproduce themselves and thus to ensure the survival and evolution of the species.

If these are the essential characteristics which describe what it is to be alive, then they must apply to every living being whether plant, animal or human. But it is important here to note the interesting characteristics of living systems; i.e. that they tend to form a hierarchical order of one living system within another. Thus the basic living system out of which all superordinate systems are constructed is the cell. The most common form of life on this planet is still the unicellular organism or amoeba but over the long course of evolution nature has found ways for cells to combine to form new multicellular living systems such as a bee, an ant, a baboon, or a human being.

In Kelly's *The Psychology of Personal Constructs*[5] this superordinate hierarchical arrangement is replicated within each person's system of constructs or theory of the world. The way we think about the world is conceptually organized in a hierarchical manner, so that certain constructs or concepts are superordinate to (i.e. control) other constructs which are subordinate. The superordinate constructs of the system tend to be those core constructs concerned with the maintenance of the 'self'. The criteria for a living system obviously applies to one's personal construct system, since in Bruner's terms, 'You are your constructs'.[6] Thus, properly speaking, we do not 'have' a theory or map of the world with which we try to fit, rather we *are* our map, we *constitute* our theory, or our theory constitutes us. It is *we* who fit the world or not. Therefore, taking a closer look at the psychological (construct) system which we constitute in terms of the five criteria of the living system we find the following:

1. The construct system contains a number of components. We have thousands of verbal labels within our communication and labelling system.

2. Constructs are interrelated and intercorrelated to one degree or another. Thus whenever we describe somebody as sincere, we also imply that the person is likeable, trustworthy, worth knowing, etc. Our abstract (verbal) system of anticipation hangs together in an intercorrelated pattern.

3. The construct system has a semipermeable boundary so that we are variously open to the validational experiences of the environment. However, sometimes we can act in a hostile[7] manner whereby we attempt to force reality to conform to our expectations of it. Such a person has a poor fit with the world. Since they do not fit it, they try to force it to fit them.

4. The construct system maintains and regenerates itself by its own internal processes, by redefining itself more clearly, by engaging in 'fine tuning', by improving prediction of events.

5. The living construct system has a tendency to transcend itself. As Epting puts it, 'In construing one must reach out beyond what exists at present to that which is emerging and

becoming.'[8] Kelly's psychology of constructivism encourages one to transcend the obvious and to come to grips with the unknown.[9]

If we keep in mind the criteria of a living system it can be seen that they have a wide range of applicability. Throughout nature many examples of a third order of living system can be found. The most highly organized examples of these exist among the social insects – the termite mound, ant heap, or the beehive. The important thing to note here is that these third-order systems fulfil the definition of a living system just as completely as do the individual bees or ants of which they are composed and it has therefore increasingly been accepted by entomologists that, for example, a beehive or termite mound must truly be classed as a living creature in its own right.[10] In a similar way, although the process has not as yet developed so highly, various birds, fishes and mammalian groups can also be recognized as forming third-order systems, such as a colony of baboons, a gorilla or human family, or a human village. These too may be understood as separate living beings. Beyond this, further superordinate living systems can be discerned: ecosystems and, finally, the living envelope covering the surface of the entire planet – the biosphere, maintaining itself (until recently at any rate) as a delicately balanced self-referential living system.

In all of these situations where we find one living system existing within another, as in the case of the cell within our own bodies, or where a third order is involved – the cell within the body of a bee, the bee within the body of the beehive – we find the superordinate system is in a position of influence over the primary or secondary systems of which it is constituted. Each system retains its proper integrity as a living system on its own level but nevertheless its autopoiesis is depressed and transmission and exchange across its boundary are increased to a significant degree under the influence of the superordinate system. An important point should be clarified here in considering superordinate human living systems. The fact that one as a human individual may be under the influence of a superordinate group system should not in any way be taken to mean that the superordinate system is necessarily more developed or more conscious than the individual living system of which it is constituted. On the contrary, all the evidence would suggest that the individual human person is by far the most complex and highly developed form of life of which we have any knowledge on this planet. Most human systems are by comparison primitive, largely unconscious and comparatively simple in their range of behaviours; nevertheless they do have a powerful superordinate influence on the human individual in them. As Stafford Beer remarks:

> It means that every social institution (in several of which any one individual is embedded at the intersect) is embedded in a larger social institution, and so on recursively – and that all of them are autopoietic. This immediately explains why the process of change at any level of recursion (from the individual to the state) is not only difficult to accomplish but actually impossible – in the full sense of the intention: 'I am going completely to change myself.' The reason is that the 'I', that self-contained autopoietic 'it', is a component of another autopoietic system.[11]

To say how psychotherapy works, we must take into account the criteria for a living system not only in relation to the interpersonal/social interfaces within which the individual system exists, but also in relation to the intrapersonal system through which the individual interprets and constructs the meaning of the perturbations arising from his interrelationships.

Definition of the Therapeutic System

Different levels of living systems are involved in the psychotherapeutic enterprise. Each clinician must deal with systems from the cellular–biological level, through the personal–psychological level, to the psychosocial and sociocultural levels. These systems are organized hierarchically with lines of influence moving up and down the total hierarchy. We cannot deal with an individual in isolation from the systems in which he is embedded contextually. Each individual joins his family and grows up within a family context co-evolving with the other family members. The family system co-evolves within the context of other neighbourhood family systems within a community/cultural/national identity, etc.

Even were we to 'completely' remove the individual from his living context we still could not treat him in isolation since, firstly, he carries within himself the coherence of his co-evolved self-organization. The holographic conceptualization of the family or group implies that the whole family has its 'existence' within each person. Thus, even when dealing with an 'individual', we may be working with the representation in that person of the total historical family constellation. Secondly, the therapist necessarily forms a relational dyad, or a new system within which both will co-evolve a new coherence together.

Just as the client brings a context with him, so too does the therapist who lives within similar systems. Furthermore, the therapist is influenced by the immediate work hierarchy of the clinic wherein the consultations take place. This in turn must exist within other umbrellas, the parent hospital, the culture of the medical profession, the overall Department of Health structures, policies, etc.

Maturana[12] describes these interactions between different systems as 'structural coupling'. This will occur between any two systems over a period of time. This can be seen every time a newly-born infant is brought home to join his older siblings. There follows a time of turbulence after which a new family coherence is achieved. Bateson also referred to this movement towards internal consistency as 'self-healing tautology'.[13]

Consider individual therapy from this new standpoint. It can now be seen that what is involved in setting up a therapeutic relationship is indeed the creation of a new living system, within which the individual boundaries are lowered and both exchange and change are now possible under the influence of the superordinate system; i.e. a group of two. This is all the more true if one member of the new system is skilled in and not threatened by the task of lowering the individual boundary and allowing projections and introjections to flow across from one person to the other – to empathize and make conscious for both what is hidden and unconscious.

One of the primary questions for the therapist in each new case is 'At which of these possible levels will intervention be most effective to the point that it can influence this system?' For a variety of therapists who have a specific commitment to particular therapeutic strategies this question is answered all too automatically. For example, the family therapists tend to see the most appropriate level to join as being the 'family'. In psychoanalysis and behaviour therapy the level of joining dictated by the approach is largely that of the 'isolated' individual. For marital therapists the selected system level is the 'couple', and so on.

The manner in which we define what constitutes a 'system' at the different levels is purely theoretical. Our theory may fit effectively or not. If we find our efforts are unsuccessful we should seriously question the manner in which we decide that this particular segment of reality (e.g. defining the family systems as 'those members who live in the same house') is an effective way to define the going 'system'. Where therapists are over-committed to one view, one theory, one set of tactics, then they are unlikely to question their basic approach, which sees them working at the same level of 'system' all the time.

Interpersonal and Intrapersonal Systems

A main point of discontinuity in defining levels of system can be found with the 'individual system' on one side of the divide and couples, families, groups, etc., on the other side. This is a major dividing line between those biological/psychological approaches which are intrapersonal and those which are interpersonal. In systems terms the main difference lies in the type of components which go to make up the system. At the individual level the components are various theoretical constructs postulated to describe and explain psychological functioning. Thus we have terms such as 'cells', 'organs', 'neural connections', 'ego', 'needs', 'personal constructs', etc. On the other side of the divide the components are whole individuals who make up a family, etc. Family therapists attempt to change the family system by influencing the actions of individual members, while intraindividual therapists attempt to change the person's self-organization by dealing with his personal constructions, meanings, etc. Both endeavours are similar in that they may attempt to promote change in the overall organization of the system by changing the structural components. Both may work equally on the whole in order to have a recursive impact on the components. Both tend to precipitate the system (individual or family) into a state of flux or disorganization as a prelude to emergent change in the form of a new state of self-organization. Both recognize the hierarchical lines of influence in attempting to restructure the whole by working on the parts, or change the parts by working on the whole. In this way the overall level of coherence of the system is altered. 'Coherence simply implies a congruent interdependence in functioning whereby all the aspects of the system fit together.'[14] In any given situation it may be more appropriate to work with the individual, couple or family. In a given case at various times we may choose to work with different levels of these systems in sequence or concomitantly.

The Problem of Fit

In what way must the epistemological position of 'fit' influence clinical practice? The answer, as we shall see, is that the concept has extensive implications for etiology, diagnosis and treatment. Shotter[15] outlines three major areas of 'fit' which must be considered: (i) mind-to-world fit, (ii) world-to-mind fit and (iii) mind-to-mind fit. To avoid any mind–body duality we must simply substitute the word 'person' for the word 'mind' in the above.

These three areas cover the realms of anticipation, feedback and communication. Psychotherapy involves all three at many different levels. Etiology may be viewed as the story of where the person's beliefs or anticipations (person-to-world fit) broke down. Diagnosis (and much else in psychotherapy) depends on the level of communication between therapist and patient (person-to-person fit). Treatment involves evoking reality-contact and facing the vicissitudes of invalidation from reality experience (world-to-person fit).

Suicide can be seen to involve all three types of fit. One form of suicide occurs in the context of personal confusion about the world (poor person-to-world fit). The person experiences invalidation and absence of gratification (world-to-person fit). Finally the person is isolated from anyone whom he feels could understand him (person-to-person fit), and so he decides to kill himself.

How Do Symptoms 'Fit'

From an etiological point of view, it is important to consider the role of symptoms as an attempt to personally organize oneself or reach a state of coherence. It is notable that many patients arrive in a state of relative incoherence. The individual must 'fit in' with his family. When his person-to-world fit breaks down and symptoms develop we must consider how his symptoms (as new person-to-world projects) help him to make better sense than did his old outlook. It is also important to ask what type of (family or other) reality is he failing to fit into? Do his symptoms raise particular questions about the form of reality he is attempting to make sense of? In other words, his symptoms are 'symptoms of' the difficult reality to which he is trying to fit himself, or to which he is attempting to join himself as a complementary piece of the overall family jigsaw. In this sense his symptoms may point to the elusive nature of the family reality he is attempting to predict and fit. This is commonly seen in the case of pathological communication systems which use the double-bind.[16] No matter what the patient attempts, he finds his fit is 'wrong' even when it seems to be 'right'. However, the person never gives up the attempt to reach a co-evolved coherence and, in pursuing the search for meaning, may strike upon certain unusual theories or outlooks which seem to him to fit the family facts. Such theories are commonly diagnosed as 'delusions', 'hallucinations', 'madness', etc.

Watzlawick[17] quotes a number of noncontingency experiments (i.e. where the subject's behaviour in attempting to solve a task has no connection with the feedback he receives) to illustrate the human struggle to make sense of events when our person-to-world fit has no symmetry with the world-to-person fit. Consequently, the person must develop a rather idiosyncratic and sometimes bizarre outlook in order to encompass the noncontingency feedback. Watzlawick states, 'once we have arrived at a solution – and in the process of getting there, have paid a fairly high price in terms of anxiety and expectation – our investment in this solution becomes so great that we may prefer to distort reality to fit our solution than sacrifice the solution'.[18] Thus the subject's new person-to-reality fit becomes rhetorical and encapsulated. Every therapist is familiar with the apparently incorrigible nature of certain delusions. This coherence reached by the patient becomes more so with practice.

Coherence evolves in the direction of that to which we must relate. The system can in one sense be seen as a specialization of interaction. The more one repetitively practises, the more coherent one becomes. Thus, the family doctor tends to develop a very ossified and stereotyped consultation pattern[19] using the same phrases and sequences of clinical interpersonal behaviour. Those who repetitively practise sports develop a coherence in relation to the behaviour sequences needed. The anorexic develops her speciality in relation to food and weight. Psychotherapists who specialize in treating psychotic patients tend to develop an obvious coherence in that direction (H.S. Sullivan, Fromm-Reichmann, R.D. Laing).

Many clinicians who feel that the person-to-person fitting required in treating psychotics is impossible to achieve are criticized by Fromm-Reichmann, where she says that the fault lies in the therapist's personality, not in the schizophrenic's.[20]

Playing an effective role in relation to another person is defined by Kelly[21] in person-to-person fit terms. He says that to the degree that we can accurately construe the other person's constructions about us we can play a role in relation to him. Even if we disagree with the other person's outlook (e.g. a particular delusion) we may evolve a complementary fit with the other person and be able to effectively communicate and develop a relationship with him.

'Too Close a Fit'

The fear which many clinicians experience in this area is that of being 'sucked into' the patient's madness. In the nonpsychotic sphere the family therapist fears being 'enmeshed' in the family system to the point where he becomes neutralized by the family and then acts merely as an additional component. He has become part of the problem instead of part of the solution. The therapist has co-evolved a coherence with the family system rendering him therapeutically neutral. An image we may use from lower down the system hierarchy is that of the action of phagocytosis occurring at the cellular level. When a phagocytic cell encounters some foreign matter it quickly engulfs, breaks down, neutralizes and incorporates the foreign substance within itself. Thus, the therapist can no longer create 'inputs' or perturbations from the outside since he is now firmly placed inside the family cell. The therapist's system has become 'at one' with his environment. He now fits the family.

This phenomenon explains why family therapists like to work in teams[22] (where certain members are 'isolated' from the family system acting as supervisors-from-a-distance) and why Tavistock group methods insist that the therapist 'sits on the boundary' of the group[23] – a form of therapeutically 'sitting on the fence'.

The Issue of Change: How to Precipitate It?

Another implication of these views is that the patient is not necessarily seen as a 'victim' and the family as a 'procrustean bed' upon which unwitting victims are 'stretched to fit'. Rather the whole family is a mutually determined coherence of all the individual parts. Each individual fits with the family reality to one degree or another. As Niels Bohr's principle of complementarity obviated the arguments as to which view of light (wave versus particle theory) was 'correct', so we must view the complementarity of relationships within the family and avoid the attribution of 'blame'. The family does not 'cause' an individual to become schizophrenic. Many clinicians still think in causal terms in relation to psychological processes.[24] For example, a patient is obsessive 'because' he fixated at the anal stage of development. A young girl is anorexic 'in order to' bring her parents closer together. A child is acting out 'because' his mother does not love him, and so on. It is clear that such attributions of 'cause' or 'purpose' are in the eyes of the beholder. It is this form of causal thinking that leads to convictions that one person more than another is 'to blame' for psychopathology. Consequently, interventions are often directed more towards such a 'causal figure' than others.

Reflexively, we must apply the same type of analysis to our own interventions. Rejecting the linear causal view we must admit that psychotherapy is not something that you can do to someone else. It is not a mechanical skill that can be reliably 'applied to' psychopathology. Rather it must involve co-evolving a coherence with the patient in such a way that we provide an experimental context within which he may begin to alter his current level of self-organization. To this end the therapist will spend a lot of time extricating himself from the patient's attempts to co-evolve a coherence that is similar to one already existing in his life.

The issue of transference relates centrally here. If the patient can set up a relationship with the therapist on the basis of his existing self-organization, then he has little need to revise his system or to change it in any way. One of the first perturbations provided by the therapist is, therefore, that of being elusive, or 'difficult to pin down'. Within this model one would rarely discuss food intake with an anorexic, since she has already evolved a 'starvation coherence'. Speaking to her within her reduced frame of reference is merely helping her practise 'more of the same'.[25] We have all seen cases of 'borderline' anorexia being admitted to an anorexic ward and emerging several weeks later as a fully committed anorexic; i.e. one whose system has reached a new level of coherence oriented around food and weight.

The theory of learning implicit here is that 'you become what you do'. We have seen how this works for producing psychopathology, but the same principle applies to re-learning more 'adaptive' or 'fitting' behaviour. One of the main roles of the therapist is to persuade the patient into taking novel actions through which he may transform himself. Since novelty is a spontaneous experience and, since we cannot intend to be spontaneous, we can see once again how the causal model of 'doing' therapy to the patient breaks down. This is one of the junctures in psychotherapy where the risk factor enters, since for the patient it is a case of 'leap before you look'. To aid this process the therapist must engage in a type of 'instruction' which Vygotsky[26] defines as 'that which marches ahead of development and leads it; it must be aimed not so much at the ripe as at the ripening functions'. This is not to say that the therapist must give instructions in the form of directives or advice but rather – from the Latin *instruere* meaning to build up – to structure a context for the patient's self-experimentation. Such personal experimentation often provides the bifurcation points for self-reorganization.

Destabilization

Having accurately subsumed and understood the complex self-organizational style of the patient and the consequent significance of the symptoms used, we must then decide how to destabilize his current organization. This consideration applies equally to individuals, couples or families. There are many techniques evolving, especially in certain schools of family therapy,[27] which aim to destabilize the going system with the hope that it will reorganize itself in an alternative manner. At a less haphazard level, Milton Erickson[28] specialized in framing a destabilization in such a manner that the patient moved through an oscillation to a more predictable but still indeterminate bifurcation.

Thus the perturbation put into the system by the therapist must take cognizance of (a) the current state of self-organization – i.e. the construction style of the contract system; (b) the intensity of destabilization needed; (c) likely construction the person will make of the perturbation from the therapist; (d) the possibilities of perturbations arising from inside the construct system itself.

It is here that the concept of crisis enters the therapeutic arena.

Crises can be precipitated by sudden change in the external world, such as sudden death of a dear one (as described by G. Caplan), or through a developmental change affecting the internal state of coherence as in pregnancy, childbirth, or adolescence – the developmental crises emphasized by Erik Erikson. In both of these types of crisis a destabilization occurs spontaneously without any influence from a therapist. The concept of crisis intervention is to avail of this state of fluctuation and the approach of a bifurcation point when the system (person, family, etc.) is in a chaotic state, to try to move it (influence it) towards a better (higher) state of self-organization. These are the times when a person is in a receptive state to accept help and is open to the possibility of change in the state of self-coherence. Thus the possibility of therapeutic intervention is enhanced.

It should be remembered that the system is in a continual process of flux and of self-perpetuation and self-organization. It is not a fixed frozen entity but rather a living organism. Again this applies as much to a family group as to an individual. Here we can see that the old idea of direct causality is no longer present. This assumption of causality is still very prevalent in psychiatry where we see attempts to change the biochemical balance of the system or where ECT is used as a direct shocking perturbation as if this could somehow determine that the system would realign itself in a 'proper balance'. This assumes again that there is an absolute whereby one can tell what a proper balance consists of, and that a direct linear causality can be appealed to. In criticizing technical approaches to therapy that emphasize control and the use of technique, Keeney states that 'a therapist who sees himself as a unilateral power broker or manipulator is dealing with partial arcs of cybernetic systems. Such a position threatens the recursively structured biological world in which we live. Only wisdom, that is, "a sense or recognition of the fact of circuitry" (Bateson, 1972, p. 146), can safely and effectively deal with ecosystems.'[29]

Summary

The object of psychotherapy is to precipitate new movement in the patient and in his life. New movement will be carried forward by changing the person's inner self-organization. It is the new organization that will take the person forward to his future rather than entrap him in the endless present of his psychopathology. In order to begin this process we must first accurately subsume the complex state of the person's current level of self-organization. Very frequently we see that patients have organized their lives around the practice of a particular symptom, for example 'doing' anorexia or 'doing' hypertension. One of the important changes in our thinking as clinicians must be that of moving from the use of static nouns to action verbs. Thus it is becoming popular in family medicine to think of a patient as not 'having' hypertension but rather to be 'hypertensing'. Similarly in psychiatry we must begin to see patients actively doing their pathology as opposed to being victims of socioculture sanctions on the one hand or genetic/biochemical accidents on the other. From the Kellian point of view, the most important human task is that of making sense of one's world.[30] Very often, the sense one makes is that he is 'unable to cope', that he is 'mad', that he is 'depressed', etc. Thomas Szasz has described professional activities in relation to life problems as merely sanctioning a way for the person to escape his responsibilities.[31] Within the proposed model such therapist–patient collusion is understood as a particular type of co-evolved coherence which 'makes sense'.

Apart from changing our thinking from using nouns to verbs, and to seeing the intrinsic sense-making of a patient's symptoms – for example, Haley discusses the symptom as a strategy[32] – there are other changes in conceptualization and approach that are important to achieve if the new science clinician is to reflect the implications arising from the systems view of the world. What are these other pragmatic/conceptual changes? In the first place our view of diagnosis ceases to be something that is a fixed reality. Diagnosis becomes instead a fluid way of planning treatment rather than a static 'pigeon-holing' of a person. It has been shown that the diagnostic label a patient receives on entering an institution is not the same diagnostic label he will hold some years later.[33] Thus even within the unchanging world of an institution, somehow the quasiscientific diagnostic category manages to shift over time. The one thing we do know about human beings is that they change over time, often despite themselves. We must learn to see the person plotted along a time-line of personal history and extending along the same arrow of time into the future. As clinicians we are therefore concerned with the pathways which the patient may have available to take him into his future. Much of George Kelly's work focused on this issue.[34] The philosophy of constructive alternativism tells us that any construction we make of reality (e.g. a diagnosis of a patient) is only one view or opinion on the matter. Other diagnosticians may well, and very often do, diagnose the person differently. We must reconstruct our diagnostic language so that it is constituted by a more fluid process-oriented language which can allow the person to move and change within the categories we prescribe. We must be prepared to see when our diagnosis does not fit the reality of the patient. The way we invent reality in the form of our constructions of patients must be seen as just that, an invention rather than a fact.

References

1. M. Elkaim *et al.*, 'Openness: A Round-Table Discussion', *Fam. Process*, 21, 1, 57–70, 1982.
2. Ibid; H. Maturana and F. Varela, *Autopoiesis and Cognition*, Boston Studies in Philosophical Science, vol. 42, D. Reidel, Boston, 1980; H. Maturana, 'The Biology of Cognition', in Maturana and Varela, *Autopoiesis and Cognition*, 1980.
3. S. Beer, 'Preface', in H. Maturana and F. Varela, *Autopoiesis and Cognition*, Boston Studies in Philosophical Science, vol. 42, D. Reidel, Boston, 1980.
4. F. Capra, *The Turning Point*, Flamingo, London, 1983.
5. G. Kelly, *The Psychology of Personal Constructs*, Norton, New York, 1955.
6. J. Bruner, 'You Are Your Constructs', *Contemp. Psychol.*, 1, 355–6, 1956.
7. Kelly, *The Psychology of Personal Constructs*.
8. F. Epting, *Personal Construct Counselling and Psychotherapy*, John Wiley & Sons, Chichester, 1984.
9. G. Kelly, 'The Psychology of the Unknown', in D. Bannister (ed.), *New Perspectives in Personal Construct Theory*, Academic Press, London, 1977.
10. R. Chauvin, *Animal Societies,* 1st edition, Sphere Books, London, 1971.
11. S. Beer, 'Preface', in H. Maturana and F. Varela, *Autopoiesis and Cognition*.
12. H. Maturana, 'Biology of Language: The Epistemology of Reality', in G. Miller and E. Lenneberg (eds), *Psychology and Biology of Language and Thought*, Academic Press, New York, 1978.
13. G. Bateson, *Mind and Nature: A Necessary Unity*, Dutton, New York, 1979.
14. P. Dell, 'Beyond Homeostasis: Toward a Concept of Coherence', *Fam. Process*, 21, 1, 21–41, 1982.
15. J. Shotter, 'Understanding How to Be a Person', in E. Shepherd and J.P. Watson (eds), *Personal Meanings*, John Wiley & Sons, London, 1982.
16. G. Bateson *et al.*, 'Towards a Theory of Schizophrenia', in G. Bateson (ed.), *Steps to an Ecology of Mind*, Granada, London, 1978.
17. P. Watzlawick, *How Real Is Real? Confusion, Disinformation, Communication*, Vintage Books, New York, 1977, p. 54.

18. Ibid.

19. P. Byrne and B. Long, *Doctors Talking to Patients*, HMSO, London, 1976.

20. F. Fromm-Reichmann, *Psychoanalysis and Psychotherapy: Selected Papers*, University of Chicago Press, Chicago, 1959, p. 177.

21. Kelly, *The Psychology of Personal Constructs*.

22. L. Hoffman, *Foundations of Family Therapy*, Basic Books, New York, 1981.

23. A.K. Rice, *Learning for Leadership: Interpersonal and Intergroup Relations*, Tavistock, London, 1965.

24. Dell, 'Beyond Homeostasis: Toward a Concept of Coherence'.

25. P. Watzlawick, J. Weakland and R. Fisch, *Change: Principles of Problem Formation and Problem Resolution*, Norton, New York, 1974.

26. L.S. Vygotsky, *Thought and Language*, MIT Press, Cambridge, 1972, p. 104.

27. Hoffman, *Foundations of Family Therapy*; M. Selvini Palazzoli *et al.*, *Paradox and Counter-Paradox*, Jason Aronson, New York, 1981.

28. J. Haley (ed.), *Advanced Techniques of Hypnosis and Therapy: The Selected Papers of Milton R. Erickson, MD*, Grune & Stratton, New York, 1967.

29. B. Keeney, *Aesthetics of Change*, Guilford Press, New York, 1983.

30. Kelly, *The Psychology of Personal Constructs*.

31. T. Szasz, *The Myth of Mental Illness: Foundations for a Theory of Personal Conduct*, Hoeber & Harper, New York, 1961.

32. J. Haley, *Strategies of Psychotherapy*, Grune & Stratton, New York, 1963.

33. J. Coulter, *Approaches to Insanity: A Philosophical and Sociological Study*, Martin Robertson, London, 1973.

34. Kelly, *The Psychology of Personal Constructs*.

17. Thomas Murphy:
The Madness of Genius

This paper was published by the *Irish University Review* in 1987 in a tribute edition to Tom Murphy.

Tom Murphy is one of Ireland's premier playwrights who has worked closely with the Abbey Theatre, Dublin, and Druid Theatre, Galway. He was born in Tuam, County Galway, in 1935. His first successful play, *A Whistle in the Dark*, was performed at the Theatre Royal Stratford East in London in 1961 and caused considerable controversy both there and in Dublin when it was later given its Irish premiere at the Abbey, having initially been rejected by its theatre director. Considered along with Brian Friel as Ireland's leading living playwright, his works have since been performed frequently in the West End and throughout Ireland, and he has influenced the work of younger playwrights like Conor McPherson and Martin McDonagh. In 2001 he was honoured by the Abbey Theatre by a retrospective season of six of his plays. *A Whistle in the Dark*, *Famine* and *Conversations on a Homecoming* were produced as a cycle by Druid in 2012, known as DruidMurphy, a story of emigration. The cycle toured to London and New York, as well as a nationwide tour of Ireland, before winning multiple awards at the prestigious Irish Times Theatre awards, at which Murphy's *A House*, produced by the Abbey in 2012, was also an award winner. *The Irish Times* declared 2012 'the year of Tom Murphy in Irish theatre'.

ART is triumph over the impossible. It is almost impossible to fulfil creative talent; in fact it *is* impossible, because recognition of talent within oneself seems to come hand-in-hand with a critical faculty. The artist has an awareness of excellence, of perfection always out of reach but attracting compulsively the focus of intense strife. It is towards perfection that the artist is drawn with a mystical sense of urgency and relentlessness. It is as if what he is struggling for is not his but only something for the production of which he is responsible, something which he is charged to drag out into the light of day. You may call it perfection, source, or grace, if you will; and, once aware of its existence, how can the artist be satisfied with less? Whether agnostic or atheistic, the artist strives towards perfection as the goal of life. His work seldom comes close enough to his goal or his expectation of art's potential to satisfy him. It is said of Charlie Parker, perhaps the most creative jazz musician of them all, that, when asked what he considered his finest recording, he replied, 'Man, I haven't made it yet'. This seems to be almost universally true of the artist, whether painter, poet or playwright. What he has done may be good enough, better than anything he has done before, even better than every other artist who has tried to do the same thing, but if he is a true artist it still will not be good enough. Perhaps that is why, when asked what he admires most, Tom Murphy points to children, God's creation. Perhaps that is why he also marvels at pregnancy. He says he loves just to be near a pregnant woman, to experience the atmosphere which she creates around herself. Tom feels creativity is central to the life force. More than that, it translates life itself. When asked why he wrote plays, which are so difficult to write, 'in retrospect, impossible tasks', Tom Murphy replied: 'It's my way of answering back'. Answering whom, or what? 'Everything', he said.[1]

The truly creative writer has to opt out of normality, leave the 'nine-to-five logical brain', to go down into the creative source. Artists never seem to know where what they find within themselves has come from. This seems to be, as has often been remarked, the aspect of genius comparable to madness, or near to madness. It comes from the same depth, the same level of awareness, the root of things, mysticism.

Tom Murphy himself has told me that he does not know where the speech 'Down in the forest', delivered by Edmund in *The Morning after Optimism*, came from, nor does he understand to this day what it means:

> Down in the forest . . . I saw her. And my being fed to regeneration. And the meaning of everything became clear and unimportant. And once I closed my eyes to trap the angel self within me, but all of me had fused to become one sensitive eye, drinking in God, or was I radiating Him? or was I Him? . . . Then . . . (*he shivers*) Down in the forest . . . I lay upon the fallen leaves, the only noise was dying hushed derision. And then the quietness

208

of a smile, so strange and still, no sound to cheer the accomplishment of journey's end, for my mission was quite done. And then
I looked up to see a crow alighting from a tree, to perch upon my
breast. I wondered at his fearless apathetic eye more beadier than
fish's fixed on mine; and I wondered at his mystery purpose: 'Twas
not good. The caked offal on his beak was grey, and then he ope'd
it up to show the stiffened corpse of maggot for a tongue. I knew
that birds are sometimes known in vagary to offer their own store
to human kind, and so I thought I would accept, to please the
crow for he was dark, his succulence, his relish, my disgust. And
then I checked my mouth to find that it was shut as in paralysis.
And then – O God! – my eyes I found were open with such taut-
ness: they were gaping bulges wide. And though I would I could
not race my fear towards liberating climax, to release me in a roar.
And on and on the insult of my tightened lips I stared back, in the
innocence of silent nightmare. And then he pecked; I was so
young, and that was that.[2]

Tom Murphy gets down to that level only after frustration and
long periods of confusion, depression, anxiety and antisocial existence. Nothing seems to be happening until it happens. Tom can
drift on for a year or two, apparently doing nothing, frittering away
his time, deeply dissatisfied with himself and his life, but all the time
the deeper realms of his mind seem to be struggling, toiling, germinating, until a new creation works its way to the surface and another
play is born. When an artist is working in this way he appears to be
using the intuitive dimension of the mind, a mode of consciousness
akin to dreaming; what has, perhaps over-simplistically, been referred
to as right-sided brain activity. This would seem to be a quite different mode of consciousness from the nine-to-five, so-called
'rational' mode of thinking in which most of us spend our normal
everyday waking existence. It is the mode of consciousness from
which the poets find their inspiration.

Poets have said it is a matter of finding the poem. It is as if the
completed work is there all the time but the poet has to find his or
her way to it, chip away at the dross to expose the art in its wholeness. It is like cutting a diamond, which on the outside is dull and
opaque but holds the jewel within.

It is important to remember that none of us is a stranger to the
world of fantasy, to this alternative mode of consciousness. Indeed, we
spend almost a third of our lives in this realm of fantasy when we

dream in sleep. This is also the mode of consciousness used by those we term psychotic, those the world calls mad. They, too, predominantly use this dream-like fantasy side of the brain because of a variety of factors, even genetic, influencing their early development. There is a failure to clearly differentiate self, to evolve a separate person capable of achieving adult independence. This has a twofold result: on the one hand, because no clear self emerges, there is a failure to develop the ordinary coping skills, the necessary skills for living which enable one to manage life. So it is not possible to achieve a reasonable self-esteem and standing within the consensus of reality we all share. On the other hand, again because there is no clear boundary around the self, no clearly separate person, it is much easier to slip into the fantasy mode of consciousness (which all of us know well in childhood and adolescence) and to build within this fantasy world the self-esteem and status all of us seek in this world, whether mad or not.

It is in this way that the psychotic builds his delusional world in which he is a famous astronaut, scientist, artist or saint. It is not the desire to be special or successful and recognized as outstanding that is unusual or abnormal. No, the difficulty of those we see as insane is their failure to distinguish one mode of consciousness from the other, so that the exalted position they build for themselves in fantasy is not shared by those around them; hence they are called mad. Herein lies the paradox. The artistic genius and the psychotic have in common their existence in the alternative reality, the intuitive, fantasy mode of consciousness, the deeper dreaming other world, but they differ starkly in the use they make of it. Every genius, every great artist, has learned the trick of being able to differentiate these two (and perhaps other) modes of consciousness. What is more, someone like Tom Murphy is able, albeit sometimes with great difficulty, to move from one to the other. While the psychotic is terrified to face ordinary reality and to tackle the anxiety of practical day-to-day living, the writer, playwright or poet, when he actually gets down to writing, not only emerges into an everyday work habit but characteristically works harder and shows greater self-discipline in organizing his day than the rest of us.

I have never met an artist who did not work hard. The greater the artist, the more powerful seems the drive to work. There are, of course, people with lesser talents who are driven to work hard enough to make something of their lesser gift by an ambition which has another source, but the true artist is obsessively creative, even when not working, not producing anything. Tom Murphy as a playwright works cruelly hard when actually getting things on paper, but he is never wholly at peace, I think. At a deeper level his mind is working all the time, even when not writing, draining his energy, and in my experience of him he is tormented by conscience too much of the time. Creative artists are their own cruellest taskmasters. They never let up on themselves and much of their behaviour can be traced back to what Freudians have called the wisdom of the unconscious; by that I mean that even when they are not aware of accomplishing anything, and in Tom's case when he is often disgusted with himself for 'dossing' and wasting his time, the deeper struggle and search is going on unabated, out of ordinary consciousness. The creative drive seems to come from their belief that they should be doing what they do because they cannot help it anyway. And I've never met an artist who felt that he or she accomplished enough or that what they did was as good as it might have been. It is in this relentless dedication to work and struggle that the creative artist is at the very opposite pole to the psychotic, and certainly to most of those we call schizophrenic or mad whom I have met in my clinical practice.

Not only does creative writing seem to emerge out of struggle, it seems to me to need conflict and confusion from which resolution can be sought. Suffering? I believe that the great artist is born but takes advantage of sufferings. This is neither to say that suffering is always creative for, indeed, suffering and poverty destroy many people and kill creativity, nor that suffering makes the artist, but that the genius is one who seems to be able to use suffering creatively, as grist to his mill. If you believe that the soul is older than one lifetime perhaps the creative artist is one who has reached that point where he or she clearly recognizes the goal of human life. If there is any truth in the theory of Karma, then the soul actually chooses the setting, the context, the family and so on in which to work out its destiny. In this sense perhaps the artist chooses the form, the life's journey, as the quest for the truth. Be that as it may, the artist will use whatever material and life experience most claim his attention, that upon which he is most compelled to focus. It is generally suffering that most acutely claims our attention and focuses our being, more than comfort, joy or even passion.

Writers like Tom Murphy so not simply write autobiographically as such, yet the raw material of their work comes from their own experience, or something that fascinates them so much that they fantasize it as their own experience. In Tom Murphy's plays all of the characters seem to be, in one way or another, aspects of his own self. What has fascinated me is the immediacy and extraordinary detail from which someone like him, if there is anyone like him, seems to be able to draw from that experience of family and early life. For many years now I have worked with helping people to work through and fully experience painful and traumatic situations, such as death of a loved one, childhood sexual abuse, abortion or loss of a baby by adoption, or even their own birth, which happened many years before.

Having been led astray for a long time by Freud's notion of 'repression', I have finally come to realize that, when a person, particularly in early life, is faced with an experience that is extremely painful, that threatens to engulf him or her, rather than go through the pain and the suffering at that time, the person brings into play a capacity we all appear to have: to inhibit, to deny, to quite simply put the experience on ice, so that it remains unlived, held out from us, waiting to be experienced with all its pain and immediacy at some later time. Many persons carry such inhibited experiences through life, or years later work them through (with the help of a trusting relationship) with all the immediacy, detail, pain and suffering as if the experience were happening right at that moment, and in this way they manage to become more at ease within themselves. It seems to me that unresolved situations of this kind are the creative artist's meat. The artist dramatizes them, painfully experiences them and works them through; hence the detail and the extraordinary immediacy that great writers are able to bring to their work. They are literally living out and experiencing for the first time the shut-off pain and suffering of many years before, albeit in fictional or dramatic forms. In this way resolution, for whatever reason, by the artist is a move towards health, not madness, even if the artist appears to be quite mad at times. This may be why some writers appear to have only one great book in them, after which the unresolved experience becomes only ordinary memory: the immediacy, the passion, is gone. Others, like Tom Murphy, seem to be able to go on year after year, struggling with the main themes of their lives, working at bringing out ever more fully the twisted relationships of family and parents they knew many years before but were unable to resolve and which are, of course, archetypal and universal in their application. It is for this reason that the creative artist may need to be wary of psychotherapy, or of entering any sitaution that might too easily resolve the pain and suffering of the past and leave him bland and well-adjusted.

In Ireland there has been a great oral literary tradition in the distant past, yet in recent centuries the native Irish, when they were most downtrodden, were not producing great writers. The first great Celtic revival of the nineteenth century was mostly the work of Anglo-Irish artists like Yeats and Synge, who came from well-to-do families and had opportunities for education and so forth. It seems that for great writings to emerge and to become possible it is necessary to rise up a bit from the abject poverty of the Irish native peasant a hundred years ago so that one can at least afford a pencil or pen.

In his essay 'The Divided Mind' Thomas Kinsella points to this dilemma facing the Irish writer, even though for an artist like Tom Murphy this is probably not a conscious struggle:

> In all this . . . I recognize a great inheritance and simultaneously a great loss. The inheritance is certainly mine but only at two enormous removes – across a century's silence and through an exchange of worlds . . . I recognize that I stand on one side of a great rift and can feel the discontinuity in myself. It is a matter of peoples and places as well as writing – of coming from a broken and uprooted family, of being drawn to those who share my origins and finding that we cannot share our lives.[3]

It is only in the last generation or two that we have seen the emergence of such as James Joyce, Patrick Kavanagh or Tom Murphy, who come from a specifically native Irish tradition. The paradoxical aspect, however, is that the affluence that produces a word processor may not produce work as good as did the pencil. Comfort seems to be anathema to art: bland comfort, middle-class contentment and mediocrity produce lack of awareness; affluent materialism seems to spell the death of creativity.

Suffering is the cutting edge of genius and it may not be an accident that the long history of hundreds of years of suffering, struggle and poverty of the Irish has resulted in Ireland producing most of the great writers and playwrights in the English language during the last century, from a tiny population compared to Britain or America. It is hard to imagine a James Joyce or a Sean O'Casey or a Tom Murphy emerging from a well-adjusted, affluent, middle-class, Scandinavian-type family and educational environment.

Tom is drawn to those who share his origin, identifies with them, as Richard Kearney says in his introduction to *The Irish Mind*:

> The Irish mind does not reveal itself as a single, fixed, homogeneous identity. From the earliest times, the Irish mind remained free, in significant measure, of the linear, centralizing logic of the Graeco-Roman culture which dominated most of western Europe . . . In contra-distinction to the orthodox dualist logic of *either/or*, the Irish mind may be seen to favour a more dialectical logic of *both/and*: an intellectual ability to hold the traditional oppositions of classical reason together in creative confluence.[4]

Tom Murphy says that writing plays is his way of answering back. I think he means answering the power of God. It all seems mindless, chaotic, without reason, unless one identifies with it, accepts that one is part of it, part of the ongoing creative happening, and then it doesn't have to make sense at all. One simply contributes to the whole. In *Bailegangaire* he has this to say, as Mommo quotes her father:

> 'I have wrestled with enigmas (*all*) my life-long years. I've combed all of creation', that man intoned, 'and, in the wondrous handiwork of God, have found only two flaws, man an' the earwig. Of what use is man, what utility the earwig, where do they either fit in the system? They are both specimens desperate, without any control, and therefore unfree. One cocks his head', says he, 'the other his tail. But God will not be mocked. Especially when He was so clever at creating all things else. Still, God must have said, I'll leave them there an' see what transpires'. An' says me father (*she winks shrewdly*) 'maybe the earwig isn't doin' too bad at all'.[5]

I recall Tom telling me how, years ago, when standing urinating in a street in a London suburb, he suddenly roared at the sight of the little houses, each one the same. He was enraged by the sameness of the houses belieing the magic of the individual, mocking the human being, mocking Tom who knows that he is not ordinary, enraged that in any event it is a desperate thing to put a person in a box, for a person to put himself in a box. By answering back, Tom Murphy avoids roaring his rage at man's helplessness in the context of the ultimate. The houses in that street were to Tom a symbol of human potential distorted and he roared at the trap, the threatening claustrophobia, as he pissed against a tree.

To be ordinary is to live without wonder. To be beyond wonder, not to recognize the wonder in others, to be one of the herd and let it all pass, even life itself, without noticing or uncovering the truth, is to be as good as dead. The part of Tom that wrote plays such as *A Whistle in the Dark* roars, but 'roaring on stage' as it were, which helps the rest of us to see and interpret and be involved in the experience of being alive. We feel that we have 'roared' too. The overt and sickening violence of the characters in *A Whistle in the Dark* is his way of bringing to the surface the hidden violence and covert aggression in so many Irish families. In the polite middle-class Ireland of today, our tendency is to say, 'Oh, no, we are not like that', but at a hidden level, in our families, are we not?

The artist may be taken aback by what he has spoken aloud. He usually does not know why those things choose him nor why he chooses them. Often his characters appear to confront him rather than rise out of his imagination. He cannot simply accept; he must triumph over the impossible, express it all so that the blind are nudged, the numb awakened and we are forced to be aware. Yes, 'there's the truth' or 'that isn't the truth'. The truth may not be complete but, because it *is* the truth, the artist will let it stand, truth in its incompleteness. A question. In being an artist, Tom Murphy is true to himself, therefore his own experience will be drawn upon again and again, however brilliantly disguised. He draws on this material even without knowing it or recognizing it at a conscious level. His conflicts are resolved or attempted again and again but never abandoned. He is a man of his time, yet timeless and, above all, a man with a sense of place. Tom Murphy is, first and last, a child of the west of Ireland, utterly normal in that context, sane without the dull connotation that description holds for me, for too sane a perception is often 'madder' than a touch of insanity. Too much 'sanity' is seen to smother creativity and I celebrate the human facility for creative 'madness'; call it individuality. Tom Murphy is an outstanding artist and a special Irish individual who brings us all recognition of the uniqueness of the 'mad' Irish.

References

1. Personal interview.
2. Thomas Murphy, *The Morning after Optimism*, Mercier Press, Dublin and Cork, 1983, pp. 44–5.
3. Quoted by Richard Kearney, Introduction, in *The Irish Mind Exploring Intellectual Traditions*, Wolfhound Press, Dublin, 1985, pp. 10–11.
4. Ibid., p. 9.
5. Thomas Murphy, *Bailegangaire*, Gallery Press, Dublin, 1986, p. 72.

18. Psychological Trauma, or
Unexperienced Experience

Stanislav Grof came to Ireland in the 1980s to run several work-shops, in which I was involved, on his method of 'holotropic therapy', and I came to know him well. As a result of discussions we had at that time, I submitted this article to the journal *ReVision, The Journal of Consciousness and Change*, with which he was associated. It was published in spring 1990 (vol. 12, no. 4).

> I call this sphere . . . the sphere of 'between'. Though being real-ized in very different degrees, it is a primal category of human reality. This is where the genuine third alternative must begin.
>
> Martin Buber (1938)

MY thesis is such that it is hard to understand why it is not already part of our everyday knowledge. Simply, when some-thing happens to us, we do not experience all of it at once. Experiencing is a process that takes place over time. It involves neu-rophysiological and somatic work on the part of the person to whom the experience happens. Further, the amount of work that is involved depends on how serious the nature of this external challenge is and several other internal factors that I will go into later.

I have perused much of the voluminous literature that has appeared in recent years in relation to post-traumatic stress disorder as well as the literature on traumatic neurosis written during the nine-teenth century, and yet this simple awareness that experiencing something is a process that takes place within us over time seems to have been missed. Simply, when something happens to us we do not experience all of it at once. This is all the more strange because, if we consider our everyday experience of life, we know that if something disturbing happens to us – say, for example, an unpleasant argument with someone on a Friday afternoon – we may find ourselves going over and over it during the weekend, unable to escape the unpleasant feeling attached to it or resolve the problem, but then, having slept on it for a couple of nights, we wake up on Monday morning no longer troubled, even though we may have had no further communication with the person involved. Somehow the problem is now solved. This to me is clear evidence that some work has been going on within us during this couple of days so that the experience is now integrated into ourselves, is becoming memory, and has moved from something in the present, something unsettled and current, into the past.

There appear to be two main reasons why this simple phenomenon of everyday experience has been overlooked. The first reason involves certain historical factors that surrounded the early work of Sigmund Freud, now just a hundred years ago, for it was he who first clearly drew attention to the whole issue of traumatic neurosis. The second reason has to do with the way in which we use language. I would like to deal with each of the reasons for this oversight in more detail.

Historical Development of the Concept of Traumatic Neurosis

From ancient times, the adverse emotional effects of trauma have been well recognized by philosophers and writers, but in the psychiatric literature the earliest reference I can find is that of Briquet who, in 1859, first put forward the notion that hysterical symptoms came as the result of traumatic events. It was he who first formulated the concept of dissociation. Around the same time, Auguste Ambroise Tardieu (1818–1879), who was professor of legal medicine at the University of Paris, first raised the question of child sexual abuse. His *Étude Médico-Légale* (a medico-legal study of assaults on decency) was published in 1857; it drew attention, for the first time, to the frequency of sexual assault on children, mostly young girls. In France during the years 1858–1869, there were 9,125 persons accused of rape or attempted rape of children. The vast majority of the cases Tardieu described involved children between the ages of four and twelve, and almost all of them were girls. His was a medico-legal study and offered no implications as to the psychological effect of such trauma. This would have to wait.

I should mention here that Tardieu was a medical specialist who did not doubt the authenticity of the sexual assaults on children that he was called upon to deal with by the courts. However, within thirty years, his successors, Alfred Fournier (1832–1914) and P.C. Brouardel, who was dean of the faculty of medicine during the period when Freud was in Paris, took a starkly different view, casting serious doubt on the reality of sexual abuse of children. Articles by Fournier ('Simulation of Sexual Attacks on Young Children', 1880) and Brouardel ('The Causes of Error in Expert Opinions with Respect to Sexual Assaults', 1883) had a major effect on all later thinking. To give just one example of these views which, as I say, were current at the time of Freud's stay in Paris, here is a quote from the Brouardel article:

> Hysteria plays a considerable role in the genesis of these false accusations, either because of the genital hallucinations which stem from the great neurosis or because hysterics do not hesitate to invent mendacious stories with the sole purpose of attracting attention to themselves and to make themselves interesting.

Freud later had a change of heart about sexual abuse. He would have been only too familiar with the views of Fournier and Brouardel when the pressures came upon him to change his mind in regard to the reality of sexual abuse of children and his theory of seduction in the genesis of hysteria and other adult neuroses. Yet again, in our time, this debate regarding child sexual abuse is coming full circle.

From a different source, physicians such as Dr Jacob Mendez da Costa (1871) were beginning to describe the traumatic effects of war experiences. Da Costa studied a group of physically sound, yet symptomatic, American Civil War veterans; these men complained of palpitations, increased pain in the cardiac region, tachycardia, cardiac uneasiness, headache, dimness of vision and giddiness. He found no evidence of myocardial disease and labelled the condition 'irritable heart', which became known as da Costa's syndrome. Following the First World War, Sir Thomas Lewis (1919) described a group of soldiers with a similar cluster of symptoms; he called this the 'soldier's heart or the effort syndrome'. Oppenheimer (1918) referred to similar psychoneurotic and cardiac manifestations in soldiers of the First World War as 'neurocirculatory asthenia'.

It was Charcot (1825–1893) who first related the symptoms of dissociation to brain changes following a traumatic event. This paved the way for Freud's early theories as to the importance of seduction and child sexual abuse in the aetiology of hysteria and other neuroses. Freud was in Paris from October 1885 until February 1886 to study under the great French neurologist. In discussing the seduction theory in 1914, Freud wrote, 'Influenced by Charcot's use of the traumatic origin of hysteria, one was readily inclined to accept as true and aetiologically significant the statements made by patients in which they ascribe their symptoms to passive sexual experience in the first years of childhood – to put it bluntly, to seduction.'

In the years following his return to Vienna, Freud began serious work on his theories of the traumatic origin of the neuroses. This was the period of his fruitful collaboration with Joseph Breuer. In their preliminary communication, printed in *Studies in Hysteria* (1893), Freud and Breuer stated that 'traumatic experiences owe their pathogenic force to the fact that they produce quantities of excitation and these in turn call for discharge in accordance with the principles of constancy'. They maintained that affect remains attached to the memory and that these memories were 'found to be astonishingly intact, to possess remarkable sensory force and when they returned they acted with all the affective strength of new experience'. Although the writers use the term *memory* here, they were describing the retrieval of *experience* – or the *present*, in the sense in which this word is used in this paper.

This brings me to a central question about Freud's work, to which for many years I could find no answer. In 1959, when I was working in London with Joshua Bierer, I was first introduced to the study of the possible therapeutic effects of LSD. I witnessed patients powerfully experiencing traumatic events that had taken place many years before as if they were happening at that moment. Later, when in the United States for the first time, I laid hands on Freud's early papers (written in the years 1893–1896) and was astonished to find him describing virtually identical scenes that his patients underwent in the process of analysis. In 'The Aetiology of Hysteria' (1896), which was presented to the Society for Psychiatry and Neurology in Vienna on 21 April, Freud said:

> We must take our start from Joseph Breuer's momentous discovery; the symptoms of hysteria (apart from the stigmata) are determined by certain experiences of the patient which have

operated in a traumatic fashion and which are being reproduced in his psychical life in the form of mnemic symbols.

Freud went further and, in doing so, parted company with Breuer, for he insisted that 'whatever case and whatever symptom we take as our point of departure, in the end we infallibly come to the field of sexual experience'. In this way, he was hoist with his own petard, and he prepared the way for the difficulties in which he soon found himself, for he went on:

> The two investigators as whose pupil I began my studies on hysteria, Charcot and Breuer, were far from having any such presuppositions; in fact they had a personal disinclination to it which I originally shared. Only the most laborious and detailed investigations have converted me, and that slowly enough to the view I hold today. If you submit my assertion that the aetiology of hysteria lies in sexual life to the strictest examination, you will find that it is supported by the fact that in some eighteen cases of hysteria I have been able to discover this connection in every single symptom, and where the circumstances allowed, to confirm it by therapeutic success.

In a paper published even earlier in the French paper *Revue Neurologique* on 30 March 1896, Freud enlarged on this:

> In none of these cases was an event of the kind defined above [seduction in childhood] missing. It was represented either by a brutal assault committed by an adult or by a seduction less rapid and less repulsive but reaching the same conclusion.

Freud then anticipated objections that would undoubtedly be raised when he asked: 'How is it possible to remain convinced of the reality of analytic confessions which claim to be memories preserved from the earliest childhood and how is one to arm oneself against the tendency to lies and the facility of invention which are attributed to hysterical subjects.' The answer he gives is striking, in view of his later volte-face, and is worth quoting in full:

> The fact is that these patients never repeat these stories spontaneously, nor do they ever in the course of the treatment suddenly present the physician with the complete recollection of a scene of this kind. One only succeeds in awakening the psychical trace of a precocious sexual event under the most

energetic pressure of the analytic procedure and against an enormous resistance. Moreover, the memory must be extracted from them piece by piece and while it is being awakened in their consciousness they become the prey to an emotion which it would be hard to counterfeit.

What I could not understand at the time, and which remained a question with me for many years afterwards, was how in little more than a year Freud apparently underwent a complete change of heart, something he confided in a letter to Wilhelm Fliess, who was his closest and most trusted friend at that time. In his biography of Freud, Ernest Jones describes dramatically what happened:

> Up to the spring of 1897 Freud still held firmly to his conviction of the reality of child traumas, so strong was Charcot's teaching on traumatic experiences and so surely did the analysis of the patient's associations reproduce them. At that time doubts began to creep in although he made no mention of them in the records of progress that he was regularly sending to his friend Fliess. Then quite suddenly he decided to confide in him 'the great secret of something which in the past few months has gradually dawned on me'. It was the awful truth that most – not all – of the seductions in childhood which his patients had revealed and on which he had built his whole theory of hysteria, never occurred. The letter of September 21st 1897, in which he made this announcement to Fliess, is the most valuable of that valuable series which was so fortunately preserved.

Much later, in *The History of the Psychoanalytic Movement* (1914), Freud wrote the following:

> When this ideology broke down under the weight of its own improbability and contradiction in definitely ascertainable circumstances, the result at first was helpless bewilderment. Analysis had led back to these infantile sexual traumas by the right path and yet they were not true. The firm ground of reality was gone. At that time I would gladly have given up the whole work just as my esteemed predecessor Breuer had done when he made his unwelcome discovery. Perhaps I persevered only because I no longer had any choice and could not then begin at anything else . . . If hysterical subjects trace back their symptoms to traumas that are fictitious then the new fact which emerges is precisely that they create such scenes in

fantasy, and this psychical reality requires to be taken into account alongside practical reality. This reflection was soon followed by the discovery that these fantasies were intended to cover up the auto-erotic activity in the first years of childhood, to embellish it and raise it to a higher plane and now from behind the fantasies, the whole range of a child's sexual life came to light.

What was this new evidence under which Freud's theory of childhood sexual trauma broke down? No answer to this was forthcoming until, in the early 1980s, Masson published the full correspondence from Freud to Fliess, certainly the key parts of which had been suppressed up to that time. In his book *The Assault on Truth*, Masson also made clear for the first time the degree to which Freud had been ostracized by his medical colleagues following the presentation of his paper 'The Aetiology of Hysteria' to the Society for Psychiatry and Neurology in Vienna in April 1896. In one of the unpublished letters to Fliess, Freud had this to say: 'A lecture on the aetiology of hysteria at the Psychiatric Society met with an icy reception from the asses, and from Kraft-Ebbing the strange comment, "It sounds like a scientific fairy tale". And this after one has demonstrated to them a solution to a more than thousand year old problem, a "source of the Nile".' In a further letter to Fliess, on 4 May, Freud wrote, 'I am as isolated as you could wish me to be; the word has been given out to abandon me and a void is forming around me.'

Masson also brought to light for the first time the strange story of Emma Eckstein. She was one of Freud's first analytic patients. Because of his idealized view of Fliess at the time, Freud agreed to let the Berlin ear-nose-and-throat surgeon operate on the nose of his patient. Fliess had the crackpot theory that the nose and the sexual organs were intimately connected and that sexual problems could be cured through nasal surgery.

In the first week of February 1895, Fliess arrived in Vienna and operated on Emma Eckstein. He left soon afterwards. The operation was not a success, and the patient developed a purulent discharge with intermittent haemorrhage; her condition deteriorated so markedly that Freud had to call in another surgeon. Freud described this in a letter to Fliess: 'I asked Rosannes to meet me. We did so at noon. There still was moderate bleeding from nose and mouth, the fetid odour was very bad. Rosannes cleaned the area surrounding the opening, removed some sticking blood clots, and suddenly he pulled out something like a thread, kept on pulling and before either of us had time to think at least half a metre of gauze had been removed from the cavity. That moment came a flood of blood. The patient turned white, her eyes bulged and she had no pulse.' The letter goes on to describe how extremely shaken Freud was, and yet he is at pains to exonerate Fliess and assure him that he was not in any way to blame for carrying out this, to say the least, ethically dubious operation.

The relapsing course of Emma Eckstein's illness continued for a number of months. Masson points out that Freud's concern was not primarily for her health but rather for Fliess's reputation. Emma, however, gradually recovered, and then we find perhaps the most surprising turnabout of all in this strange saga. In an early letter following the operation, Freud was lamenting to Fliess 'that this mishap should have happened to you, how you will react to it when you hear about it, what others could make of it, how wrong I was to urge you to operate in a foreign city where you could not follow through on the case, how my intention to do the best for this poor girl was insidiously thwarted and resulted in endangering her life – all this came over me simultaneously.'

Then, on 16 April 1896, Freud told Fliess that he had found 'a completely surprising explanation of Eckstein's haemorrhages which will give you much pleasure. I have already figured out the story . . . I should be able to prove to you that you were right, that her episodes of bleeding were hysterical, were occasioned by longing and probably occurred at the sexually relevant times'. On 4 May, Freud explained further: 'so far I know only that she bled out of longing. She has always been a bleeder, when cutting herself and in similar circumstances . . . When she saw how affected I was by her first haemorrhage . . . she experienced this as the realization of an old wish to be loved in her illness . . . [T]hen in the sanatorium, she became restless during the night because of an unconscious wish to entice me to go there, and since I did not come during the night she renewed the bleeding as an unfailing means of re-arousing my affection.' So what had been a life-threatening complication of a botched operation was changed in one masterly stroke to fantasy bleeding out of her longing for Freud himself. Freud showed himself on a number of occasions during his lifetime capable of turning a former position upside-down. He not only resolved a painful position, which had caused him considerable anxiety and guilt over a number of months, and exonerated his friend and himself from any responsibility for, or recrimination over, the mess; this new 'insight' also opened the way to turn painful reality into fantasy and to blur the distinction between them. Thus, inadvertently and I am sure unconsciously, he found the means to rehabilitate himself in the eyes of his medical colleagues so that he, a Jew, could once again find himself accepted among the conservative medical establishment of Victorian Catholic Vienna. It was shortly after this that he began to have serious doubts about the reality of seduction and child sexual abuse on which rested his whole theory of the aetiology of hysteria, and a little more than a year later, in September 1897, we find him writing the extraordinay letter to Fliess already quoted above.

Although in this way Freud rehabilitated his social and medical position, I feel he did so at the cost of several fundamental errors. First, in claiming, as distinct from Breuer, that the underlying trauma in the aetiology of hysteria and other neuroses was always sexual, involving abuse of small children, he left himself little room to manoeuvre and made certain that his views would be attacked from all sides. We now know that this was incorrect and that a whole variety of traumata occurring in childhood and later – such as unresolved grief, various physical assaults, operations and injuries, experiences of war and natural disasters, and so forth – can give rise to problems and neuroses in adult life. Second, had Freud been aware of the thesis that I am putting forward – that experiencing is a process involving work over time and that only at the end of that process has the experience been integrated into the self as memory – then he could have answered the arguments that were raised against him and that he eventually accepted and used against his original theory. I do not feel that Freud is to be criticized for not being aware of this possibility, for most of what we now know of the neurophysiology of the brain, of the relationship of the cortex to the primitive brain, the limbic system, and of its interconnections with the whole endocrine and autonomic nervous system, was still largely unknown at that time, but his most serious error was made in 1897 regarding Emma Eckstein, when he blurred the distinction between reality and fantasy. I believe that Masson was quite correct (although he has been vilified from all sides by psychoanalysts and others) in seeing this change in position on Freud's part as pivotal. Indeed, I am convinced that the later development of psychoanalysis and the whole psychotherapeutic movement has remained in a state of confusion because of this right up to the present day. I do not mean to detract in any way from Freud's later achievements and those of other creative geniuses in the psychoanalytic movement (such as Carl Jung) but simply to stress that to blur the distinction between external reality and fantasy was in itself a tragedy.

In that same critical letter to Fliess in September 1897, Freud demonstrated clearly his fundamental change of position when he stated: 'Then, the certain insight that there are no indications of reality in the unconscious, so that one cannot distinguish between truth and fiction that has been cathected with affect. (Accordingly, there would remain the solution that the sexual fantasy invariably seizes upon the parents.)' And further down in the same letter: '. . . it seems once again arguable that only later experiences give the impetus to fantasies which hark back to childhood'. To confirm that this became increasingly Freud's position, let me quote from a letter Freud wrote to Lohenfeld, which the latter published in 1904 in a paper on psychic obsessions:

> As a rule it is the experiences of puberty which have a harmful effect. In the process of repression these events are fantasied back into early childhood following the pathways of sexual impressions accidentally experienced during the illness or arising from the sexual constitution.

Or again, from Freud's introductory lectures on psychoanalysis (1916):

> If, in the case of girls who produce such an event in the story of their childhood, their father figures fairly regularly as the seducer, there can be no doubt either of the imaginary nature of the accusation or of the motive that has led to it . . . [U]p to the present we have not succeeded in pointing to any difference in the consequences, whether fantasy or reality has had a greater share in the events of childhood.

These later statements of Freud's were a direct reversal of the very arguments he put forward in his original paper on the aetiology of hysteria (April 1896), where he stated that 'we have learned that no hysterical symptom can arise from a real experience alone but that in every case the memory of earlier experiences awakened in association to it plays a part in causing the symptoms'. Further on in the same paper, Freud wrote:

> [O]r again, let us take the instance of a young girl who blames herself most frightfully for having allowed a boy to stroke her hand in secret, and who from that time on has been overtaken by neurosis . . . [A]nalysis shows you that the touching of her hand reminded her of another, similar touching which had happened very early in her childhood and which formed part of a less innocent whole, so that her self-reproaches were actually reproaches about that *old* occasion.

Freud continued, '[O]ne has an impression indeed, that with hysterical patients it is as if all their old experiences . . . had retained their effective power as if such people were incapable of disposing of their psychical stimuli . . . You must not forget that in hysterical people when there is a present day precipitating cause, the old experiences come into operation in the form of unconscious memories.'

So we see that Freud had completely reversed his position (although it took him a number of years to fully do so), had changed real events of childhood into fantasies, and had blurred the distinction between these. As already quoted, he had explained this change later in 1914 – 'When this ideology broke down under its own improbability and under contradiction in definitely ascertainable circumstances. . . .' – but what was this evidence and this contradiction? Nowhere did he actually give any evidence to explain this change of heart, except in the original letter in 1897 to Fliess where he wrote: 'Then the surprise that in all cases, the father, not excluding my own, had to be accused of being perverse – the realization of the unexpected frequency of hysteria, with precisely the same conditions prevailing in each, whereas surely such widespread perversions against children are not very probable.' But this is precisely what the disclosures from all parts of the western world during the past number of years has shown to be so – that sexual abuse of children (in the vast majority of cases of girls), back to their earliest years, is extremely common, with figures as high as one in ten being cited in the general population. Freud's earliest intuition has indeed been proved correct after all, although the same old forces of male-dominated society are trying once again to minimize or even deny these disturbing findings.

Unexperienced Experience

Before going on to the second reason why I feel that the true nature of 'experiencing' something has been neglected and misunderstood, I must refer to another fundamental aspect of this problem. If 'experiencing' is a process, if after a short time all experiences were integrated into long-term memory, the hypothesis I am raising in this paper would have little practical importance, but if the process of 'experiencing' can be blocked at an early stage and the inchoate experience can remain in this state for months, years, or indefinitely, then an entirely different situation is involved.

Modern human beings have retained, to a surprising extent, the bodily constitution, physiological responses and emotional drives that we have inherited from our Palaeolithic or Stone Age ancestors. What is even more surprising is that a large and functioning part of the human brain belongs to an earlier lineage of our ancestors; namely, the reptiles and mammals. While these inner regions, collectively called the limbic system or temporo-limbic system, have been somewhat overshadowed by the development of the neo-cortex, and of course are now intimately interconnected with the latter, they are not to be outdone, as they not only harbour the instinctual and emotional drives but maintain all the vital survival functions of the body. In a sense, the neo-cortex sits astride the primitive brain like a rider on a horse and tries to direct it with tenuous reins. Remarkably, most of the time this partnership works out well enough, considering the rider's inexperience, but in a sizeable minority of situations, given the marked change in modern human conditions, this uneasy partnership runs into difficulties.

In the late 1920s, Walter Cannon studied the psychophysiological aspects of trauma. He termed these phenomena *homeostasis* and demonstrated how, when a living creature was faced with a threat to its physical integrity, it responded to the challenge with what he called a 'flight or fight' response. This involved a mobilization of the neuro-endocrine system (with an outpouring of adrenalin) and of the sympathetic nervous system. The organism was thus prepared for flight or fight with a general physiological arousal – exaggerated respiration, dilation of the arteries to the skeletal muscles, increased heart rate and cardiac output, and so forth.

For some reason, he failed to draw attention to an equally ancient and basic strategy for survival that is seen in many species as we go down the evolutionary ladder to even the most primitive organisms. That is, the capacity, when faced with an overwhelming external threat against which there would be no possibility of either flight or fight, to 'freeze' or 'play dead' – that is, the ability to inhibit or suspend all reaction that would normally be appropriate. Pavlov (1924) perhaps came closer than anyone else to an awareness of this phenomenon when he described how some of his dogs were accidentally trapped in their cages when the Neva River flooded Leningrad. The water entered Pavlov's laboratory and nearly reached to the top of the cages containing his dogs. All the dogs had met the frightening experience with initial fear and excitement, but after their rescue some were in a state of severe inhibition, stupor and collapse. According to Pavlov, the strain on the nervous system had been so intense that the fearful excitement aroused had resulted in a final emotional collapse. However, it would seem more likely that the animals had gone into a state of inhibition in order to protect their nervous systems from going through an experience that would have threatened disintegration.

Every child is aware of this capacity in many animals to inhibit or suspend a serious external threat. We have all seen how the spider (or the caterpillar or the hedgehog) will curl itself into a ball when threatened but this reaction has been described as as far down the evolutionary scale as the amoeba by the biologists Max Hartmann and Ludwig Rumler. In a series of experiments, they exposed amoebas to a variety of stimuli. Depending on the quantity and quality of these stimuli, the amoebas reacted in one of two ways. Either they sought these stimuli (moved towards them) or they avoided them and assumed a spherical shape (played dead). So it would seem that this is a basic capacity in living organisms, and it is not unreasonable to assume that, like other survival mechanisms, it is to be found in some modified form also in human beings, precisely because it has survival value. But like so many of our primitive reactions, it is likely that this capacity has been modified to serve a different purpose in modern human conditions.

What I am suggesting is that the capacity to suspend and inhibit an overwhelmingly threatening experience may now serve a quite different purpose. Instead of a way of avoiding external danger, it is now utilized to deal with the threat of internal destabilization: whenever we are faced with an overwhelming experience that we sense as potentially disintegrating, we have the ability to suspend it and 'freeze' it in an unassimilated, inchoate form and maintain it in that state indefinitely, or for as long as necessary. Our biological structure seems able to specify in advance that to fully experience the meaning of the threatening encounter would destroy or disintegrate its core organization. The clinical evidence would suggest that this capacity to suspend the progress and integration of experience in some way involves the limbic, or temporo-limbic, system for it is this part of the brain that controls the vegetative nervous system through which we express all our emotions and that is still responsible for the basic mechanisms of survival.

In this regard, it is interesting to refer to Wilder Penfield's (1959) experiments involving direct electrical stimulation of the temporal cortex and hippocampal area of the brain. Penfield pointed out that 'the patient has usually recognized that this was something out of his own past. At the same time he may have been acutely aware of the fact that he was lying upon the operating table'. Thus one patient, when the superior surface of his right temporal lobe was being stimulated, cried out, 'Yes Doctor, Yes Doctor. Now I hear people laughing, friends in South Africa'. Penfield continued, 'Some patients call an experiential response a dream. Others state that it is a "flashback" from their own life history.' All agree that it is more vivid than anything that they could recollect voluntarily.

Another patient (Penfield and Jasper 1954, 137) 'was caused to hear her small son, Frank, speaking in the yard outside her own kitchen, and she heard the "neighbourhood sounds" as well. Ten days after the operation she was asked if this was a memory. "Oh no," she replied. "It seems more real than that." Then she added, "Of course I've heard Frankie like that many, many times – thousands of times." This response to stimulation was a single experience, her memory of such occasions was a generalization.'

Further on, Penfield had this to say:

> When, by chance, the neurosurgeon's electrode activates past experience, that experience unfolds progressively, moment by moment. This is a little like the performance of a wire recorder

or a strip of cinematographic film on which are registered all those things of which the individual was once aware – the things he selected for his attention in that interval of time . . . Time's strip of film runs forward, never backward, even when resurrected from the past. It seems to proceed again at time's own unchanged pace.

The anticipation of the potentially disintegrative effect of the external threat, were it to be fully experienced, is probably achieved through the initial expression of emotion and painful feeling, for it is thus that we are able to recognize the significance of threatening or traumatic events. The 'unthinkable' has occurred, and the fear engendered elicits a primitive defensive manoeuvre. It is a desperate attempt by the individual to forestall a crisis by making the intrusion of threat inadmissable by a process of inhibition. The critical work of working through the experience is suspended, thus subverting assimilation, integration and adaptation. This state of 'suspended animation' produces the symptoms of emotional blunting and numbing and the other clinical phenomena as listed in the *Diagnostic and Statistical Manual of Mental Disorders* (DSM III). As the process of experiencing tries to happen and the inevitable leakage of emotion occurs, panic attacks, agitation and restlessness supervene. Because the original traumatic event has been actually perceived, and a trace has been laid down (in some form of unstable, short-term storage) but not worked through in reflection to long-term memory, it remains 'active' and, again, in spite of denial, it leaks, breaks through, and causes 'flashbacks' on the screen of perception. This in turn triggers a painful emotional response, which is once again blocked and suspended as in the original event. Thus, from both the cognitive and emotional systems leakage occurs, necessitating their immediate shut-off. These vicious cycles repeat ad infinitum, leaving the individual feeling fatigued, worn out, anxious, fearful, experiencing vivid nightmares, complaining of poor concentration and attention span, and all the other phenomena as listed in the DSM.

On Our Everyday Use of Language

Let me turn now to the second reason why I feel that the true nature of 'experiencing' something has been neglected and misunderstood. In spite of the confusion engendered by Freud's early difficulties and the ensuing development of psychoanalysis, the very real effects of traumatic situations on human beings simply would not go away. The phenomenon described by da Costa in 1871, and by Oppenheimer and Lewis following the First World War, as 'irritable heart', 'effort syndrome' and 'neurocirculatory asthenia' surfaced again during the Second World War but now, with the better understanding of neurosis that had developed since the work of Freud and others, the phenomena encountered were described as 'traumatic war neurosis' or 'combat neurosis' (Kardinder & Speigel, 1947). Others used terms such as 'combat or battle stress', 'battle fatigue', 'combat exhaustion' and 'acute combat reaction' (Grinker & Spiegel, 1945). Erich Lindemann (1944) published his seminal paper, 'Symptomatology and Management of Acute Grief' following the Coconut Grove fire in Boston and, a little earlier, Kardiner (1941), under the term 'physioneurosis', for the first time described the full picture of what has since been enshrined in the DSM III as post-traumatic stress disorder.

In all of these descriptions, and in many others that have appeared since then in regard to natural disasters, accidents, child sexual abuse, kidnappings and rape, to mention but a few, we repeatedly find descriptions of how the traumatic 'memories' are '*re*-enacted', '*re*-experienced', or '*re*-lived'. The fundamental error that I am struggling to demonstrate is all contained in this prefix *re* and in the use of the term *memory*, or *repressed memory* for, once we use these words in this way, we already are making the assumption that the traumatic event has been fully experienced and is now integrated in the self as 'memory'. This is precisely the assumption, however, that I believe we are not entitled to make for it assumes, be it all inadvertently, that experiencing and the transfer of information into memory happens 'all at once' rather than that it is a process involving work that takes place over time.

I cannot illustrate this better than by quoting at some length the diagnostic criteria of post-traumatic stress disorder as laid out in the DSM III (revised edition):

1. The person has experienced an event that is outside the range of usual human experience and that would be markedly distressing to almost anyone, e.g. serious threat to one's life or physical integrity; serious threat or harm to one's children, spouse, or other close relatives and friends; sudden destruction of one's home or

community; or seeing another person who has recently been, or is being, seriously injured or killed as the result of an accident or physical violence.

2. The traumatic event is persistently re-experienced in at least one of the following ways:

   (a) recurrent and intrusive distressing recollections of the event (in young children, repetitive play in which themes or aspects of the trauma are expressed)

   (b) recurrent distressing dreams of the event

   (c) sudden acting or feeling as if the traumatic event were recurring (includes a sense of reliving the experience, illusions, hallucinations, and dissociative [flashback] episodes, even those that occur upon awakening or when intoxicated)

   (d) intense psychological distress at exposure to events that symbolize or resemble an aspect of the traumatic event, including anniversaries of the trauma

3. Persistent avoidance of stimuli associated with the trauma or numbing of general responsiveness (not present before the trauma), as indicated by at least three of the following:

   (a) efforts to avoid thoughts or feelings associated with the trauma

   (b) efforts to avoid activities or situations that arouse recollections of the trauma

   (c) inability to recall an important aspect of the trauma (psychogenic amnesia)

   (d) markedly diminished interest in significant activities (in young children, loss of recently acquired developmental skills such as toilet training or language skills)

   (e) feeling of detachment or estrangement from others

   (f) restricted range of affect, e.g. unable to have loving feelings

   (g) sense of a foreshortened future, e.g. does not expect to have a career, marriage, or children or a long life

4. Persistent symptoms of increased arousal (not present before the trauma), as indicated by at least two of the following:

   (a) difficulty falling or staying asleep

   (b) irritability or outbursts of anger

   (c) difficulty concentrating

   (d) hypervigilance

   (e) exaggerated startle response

   (f) physiologic reactivity upon exposure to events that symbolize or resemble an aspect of the traumatic event (e.g. a woman who was raped in an elevator breaks out in a sweat when entering any elevator)

5. Duration of the disturbance (symptoms in B, C, and D) of at least one month.

As a description of the clinical picture presented by those who have been traumatized, and where the trauma remains unresolved, this could hardly be bettered, for it describes clearly all the essential clinical features – were it not for the fatal intrusion of the apparently innocuous syllable *re* over and over again. It is important to realize, however, that, while the clinical picture of post-traumatic stress disorder delineated in the DSM III is accurate and comprehensive, it provides no understanding as to why the clinical phenomena should occur.

This is essentially the same difficulty that Freud faced in his early work for, although he clearly described the clinical symptomatology and furthermore correctly stressed the importance of early sexual traumata in many of these cases, he was unable to explain why people were adversely affected and emotionally crippled many years after the events in question; nor was he able to explain why some people were affected adversely and others were not, by the same traumatic situation. Had he had available to him our present understanding of neurophysiology with all its endocrinological ramifications and had he been aware of our capacity to suspend the processing of experience in its early stages, he would have been able to answer the attacks of his critics and, in spite of the ostracism and social pressures upon him, he might never have succumbed to the temptation to renege on his original theory of early sexual traumatization.

What then is the clinical evidence of the hypothesis that I am putting forward?

1. First of all there is the clinical picture that these people present as very fully and comprehensively described in the DSM.

> *Section A.* This section simply points out that these events, for the reasons listed, are such that it is likely they 'would be markedly distressing to almost anyone'.
>
> *Section B.* If one thinks about it, this only makes sense if the traumatic experience has not yet fully happened for the person. Had it been fully experienced, why should it need to be re-experienced? In particular, for the first time, this makes clear why events that

symbolize or resemble an aspect of the traumatic event would tend to 'activate' the process of 'experiencing' and the movement of the suspended information through the brain.

Section C. Again we can now see why there should be avoidance of stimuli associated with the trauma; also, numbing of general responsiveness for these behaviours is essential if the process of experiencing is not to be set in motion. It is possible now to understand the need for restriction of activities and the danger of feeling any emotion. It is also for the same reason that we find 'psychogenic amnesia', both cognitive and emotional. (And, as we shall see later, this amnesia disappears when the experience is fully worked through into memory.)

Section D. We can also understand now why there should be symptoms of increased arousal, for the suspension of the natural process of experiencing has to be actively maintained and blocked; there is a constant tendency for 'leakage' to occur and for the experience to begin to move, at any time of night or day, with activation of the limbic system and emotional discharge – hence, the increased arousal and hypervigilance.

Section E. The duration of the disturbance will be for as long as the experience is suspended – for months or years or even a lifetime.

2. When, by whatever means, an altered state of consciousness is achieved (hypnoid or dreamlike state), the person moves into a full 'experience', living through the original traumatic event as if it were happening at this moment and manifesting the full emotional response that would have been appropriate at the time when the event took place; that is, when the suspended encounter is triggered, the threatening event is experienced as happening *now*, in full present time. This is exactly the type of catharsis that Freud described in his early papers and that has been described by Sargent (1976) and many others since that time. They all make the mistake, Freud included, of referring to these 'experiences' as 'memories re-experienced', but the descriptions bear no resemblance to remembering in the sense in which we would ordinarily use that term.

3. When, as part of therapy, the person has 'gone through' the traumatic experience one or more times to the point where it has been fully experienced, the traumatic event moves from the present to the past. It is now an ordinary memory (albeit not a very pleasant one) like any other memory. The person is no longer concerned

with it nor troubled by it. There is no longer any amnesia, and the full story can be recalled at will. The experiential catharsis is finished and will not appear again in therapeutic sessions.

4. When one elicits the account of the original traumatic event from the person concerned, it is found that he or she did not experience the appropriate emotion that would be expected at the time but was in a state of 'psychic numbing', both during and after the event in question.

5. During therapy, it frequently happens that a person starts to experience something of which he or she had no previous inkling whatsoever, either cognitive or emotional. The person may have had some knowledge of a more recent traumatic event, and when this new experience supervenes, he or she is completely taken by surprise. In these situations, what comes first is very often an intense emotional and bodily experience, but neither the person nor the therapist will have any idea what the extreme emotional and physiological reaction means. It is only in the days following the session, and sometimes only after three or four full therapeutic sessions, when most of the work of 'experiencing' has taken place, that the story unfolds bit by bit, and it is only then that the person will be able to say what the traumatic experience is all about. Not only will he or she then know the nature of the traumatic experience, but typically every minute detail of what happened will now be available to the person as if what took place happened only yesterday, although the actual occurrence may have been many years before in childhood.

6. If one follows the patient over the coming weeks and months it will be found that, while the traumatic experience is now readily available to consciousness, just like any ordinary memory, the clarity and detail begin to blur and merge with other childhood memories, and it loses its characteristics as a distinct experience.

7. Finally, there is the same old question as to how we can know whether these traumatic events really occurred and are not simply fantasies. First of all, there is the internal consistency of the traumatic account, once this has been elucidated and becomes available to consciousness. This was lucidly argued by Freud in his original paper on the aetiology of hysteria before he inexplicably reversed his opinion and joined the opposition. In many instances, it is

simply not possible to verify the story because the other partici-pants in the drama are no longer available, may be unwilling to speak, or are actually dead but, in a sizeable minority, there is someone available who was a witness to the event and who is willing to cooperate. Where this has been so, I have found that, in every instance, the traumatic events that the patient has now brought out through experience, and of which they may have had no former knowledge whatever, turn out to be true.

Because of the above diverse clinical evidence, I feel that the hypothesis put forward in this paper is soundly based. Furthermore, I believe it is a hypothesis that is capable of being scientifically veri-fied and tested in neurophysiological terms although, given the present state of our knowledge, this is still likely to present difficul-ties. We are at present just beginning to look at a number of neurophysiological parameters. It may be that part of the way in which we block or suspend the integration of painful experience is by the release of endorphins. On the basis of this hypothesis, we have been giving moloxone to some subjects prior to the experiential session, and the clinical evidence so far suggests that the blocking of endorphin sites in the brain does facilitate the release of painful experience. It is our intention now to carry out a double-blind trial to further elucidate this question.

We have now begun to look at the possible role of central nora-drenergic, Alpha 2 receptors and also serotonergic and cholinergic receptors. A particularly hopeful line of investigation would be to undertake positron emission tomography, injecting the altered glucose at a point where the person is experiencing a suspended traumatic episode, which might have occurred many years previ-ously, in an attempt to show in what part of the brain activity is going on.

All of this work is only a tentative beginning, but I am hopeful in regard to the future, for in recent years there has been a virtual explo-sion of knowledge of biochemistry and neurophysiology of the central nervous system, and almost every week one hears of new advances.

Therapeutic Aspects

Before ending, I would like to say a word about the therapeutic aspects of this work. Any method that brings about an altered state of consciousness of a hypnoid or dreamlike kind (the similarity of such altered consciousness to temporal lobe epileptoid states has been noted) will open the way to the movement of inchoate experience through the brain into memory. This therapeutic work of experiencing can surface, therefore, in the course of a wide range of therapeutic procedures:

1. In psychoanalysis of the various theoretical traditions or in analytic psychotherapy.
2. In various forms of group therapy, perhaps with particular reference to Gestalt therapy.
3. In family therapy.
4. During hypnosis or, more specifically, hypnoanalysis.
5. In the course of behaviour therapy programmes – flooding, reciprocal inhibition and so forth.
6. In the course of various somatic therapies, such as bioenergetics, rolfing, or other forms of deep massage. (It should be remarked here that there is clearly a peripheral extension into the muscles and bodily organs from the endocrine and autonomic nervous systems, with interconnections back to the limbic system and hence, ultimately, to the cortex. Wilhelm Reich was the first to draw attention to this muscular or character armouring, and it is not difficult to see that a pressure on, or a stimulation of, a muscle or bodily organ may activate a suspended experience and set in motion movement of information through the central nervous system.)
7. Exposure to the site where a traumatic event took place or to events or places that symbolize or resemble an aspect of the traumatic event.
8. The use of psychedelics or other chemicals that induce an altered state of consciousness or the use of various procedures that have been known to tribal communities from ancient times (procedures that utilize music, rhythm and dance, with often fatigue and deprivation of sleep). The use of various methods of sensory deprivation will give similar results.
9. Finally, methods more specifically geared to this end, such as holotropic therapy, developed by Christina and Stanislav Grof (1988), from their study of the above methods used by so-called primitive societies, involving hyperventilation accompanied by evocative music and other sounds.

While, as I have said, a state of altered consciousness with activation of suspended, unresolved experience can occur inadvertently in any or all of the therapeutic procedures listed, in most instances this occurs haphazardly, is unreliable and, because what is happening is not clearly understood, is not differentiated from other aspects of therapy. For a therapeutic approach of this kind to be effective, therefore, the first prerequisite is a proper understanding of what is meant by the 'experiential' component of therapy as put forward in this paper. This dimension of psychotherapy then can be clearly distinguished from other aspects of therapeutic work that are equally valid and necessary in their own right, for simply to fully experience a suspended and unresolved trauma is not the whole of therapy.

If a person is to become fully well, then the constricted patterns of living, attitudes and behaviours that have developed over the years in an effort to maintain the inhibition and avoid the pain of experiencing the trauma that has been suspended will also have to change. These do not automatically disappear because the original traumatic experience has now been fully resolved.

There is, therefore, a place, once the experiential aspect has been taken care of, for the use of various cognitive and behavioural strategies, such as assertiveness and vocational training, in order to help the person to bring about significant change in his or her patterns of living and relationships.

Experiential work, then, can never be considered as more than part of therapy and must, I believe, always be undertaken in the context of a trusting therapeutic relationship. It is, however, important that we know *what* we are doing and *when* and that the proper sequence of therapeutic approaches is put in place. In persons who have a history of unresolved traumatic experience, it is not only useless but cruel to try to help them, through cognitive or behavioural methods, to change their attitudes and living patterns, when they are exploding with unresolved painful experience.

Unfortunately, there are several other complications if one is getting involved in this type of work. In situations where there has been a sudden catastrophe, traumatic war experience, or a sudden loss of a loved one affecting persons who up to then had a reasonably normal adaptation, it can be quite simple to bring the person through the painful unresolved experience so that he or she can resume an everyday way of life. However, what we have been finding in dealing with the long-term, chronic cases of post-traumatic stress disorder going back to childhood is that there is not simply one traumatic event but a whole series of painful insults, going back to the earliest years (just as Freud pointed out in his original early papers), and that these traumatic events tend to follow a theme, such as child sexual abuse, repeated rape and so on, or a series of painful losses of dear ones, or again a succession of repeated physical insults; so that the person suspends or inhibits one traumatic insult after another until, with the holding back of the final trauma, the nervous system is literally exploding. It is usually also found that only one or more of the more recent traumata are available to consciousness and there is little or no awareness of all that has gone before, right back to early childhood. It is because of this fact that most of the post-traumatic stress literature is pessimistic about intervention in these chronic cases whereas, in fact, the task is essentially the same. It simply means that the work and suffering to be endured is to be more tedious and prolonged, but there is actually no alternative to guiding the person through a whole chain of unresolved experiences, for until this is done there is no hope of real improvement or recovery.

Another difficulty one encounters is that, where there is a secret in the family that other members are unwilling to face honestly, then in my experience the unfortunate patient can be blocked from progress no matter what experiential therapeutic approach is undertaken. In these cases, through family therapy or by whatever means, it is essential to try to open up the hidden area and collusion going on within the family where it is often seen as necessary to hold the patient in his or her sick and painful state as scapegoat and guardian of the secret. It would be nice if this work were simple and straightforward and just involved the experiencing of one traumatic event, but then life is seldom like that and, in the end, it is worth going through the full rigours of therapy with the person so that he or she fully experiences all that has been blocked, even if this takes several months or a year or more, rather than condemn the person to a lifetime of chronic illness, constricted lifestyle, or even suicide and death, for these are the alternatives.

Finally, let me return to another serious shortcoming in the description of post-traumatic stress disorder as in the DSM III and most of the other post-traumatic literature. The DSM III defines this disorder almost entirely in terms of the characteristics of the external traumatic event. This is emplified in the statement that the person has experienced an event that is 'outside the range of usual human experience and that would be markedly distressing to almost anyone'. The manual of the American Association of Psychiatry gives a long list of 'stressors' that may help to produce what they call post-traumatic stress disorder. It is interesting to note that the stressors or events are all inherently life threatening. What is not taken into account is the internal set of the individual at the time the event occurred; this is a function of all the learning and experience of that individual up to that time, including of course whether there have been previous insults or experiences of a similar kind that were blocked or suspended (something that Breuer and Freud had noted). Thus it is possible for events that are not inherently life threatening in themselves to be perceived by a particular individual as threatening disintegration and thus as being unacceptable. In other words, it is as if the person has knowledge of the implications of an event for his or her total being in advance of its being experienced. Instead of integrating the components (both external and internal) of the event, the person retains these subsidiaries in an unorganized or inchoate form. In Michael Polanyi's terms, there is no movement from the parts to the whole. By refusing to integrate the particles of the encounter, the person never consciously identifies the threatening experience.

In Conclusion

In this paper, I have attempted to deal with one, rather mundane, aspect of this work. There are much wider and deeper implications that relate to the trauma of birth – to the experience of the birth/death dimension and to the question of the collective unconscious as described tentatively by Carl Jung (1959). His insights have been extended and further clarified by the significant contributions of Stanislav Grof, both in regard to the trauma of birth and his work on transpersonal experiences. This work will, I believe, be seen in time as a major contribution to this field and will establish him as the true successor to Carl Jung. These wider aspects, however, go well beyond the scope of this paper.

What I am attempting to describe here, then, is, in Martin Buber's words, 'the sphere of "between"'. It is not to be understood, therefore, in the language and concepts of the behaviourists – that is, in terms of conditioned responses, reciprocal inhibition and so on – nor can it be understood in terms of the usual psychodynamic theories or the current concepts of cognitive psychotherapy. In the post-traumatic stress literature, attempts are made, unsuccessfully, to explain the clinical phenomena along both these lines of approach. It is our hope that the ideas put forward here will act as something of a bridge between psychodynamic theory on the one hand and some of the current concepts of cognitive and behavioural psychotherapy on the other.

Perhaps, if these ideas are well founded, their importance lies more in what they exclude than in what is covered. My hope is that they may also help to clarify those aspects of psychiatry and psychotherapy to which they do not apply.

To put it in simple terms, what is being put forward here is essentially a cognitive process, the question of how information moves or is moved through the central nervous system when an event is being experienced. It is as if a piece of the external world, which is now within the person but is not part of that person, constitutes a continuing focus of stress acting from within. This internalized stressor now exists outside of time, in an unstable state and, unless and until it is fully experienced, it will continue to exert its effect indefinitely. Clearly, if this is the case, the individual is going to have great difficulty in sustaining this suspended internal reality against evidence from the outside world. Thus, inhibition and the subsequent constriction that occurs serve the function of a refusal to acknowledge a certain reality in the outside world. The views of the Chilean biologist Francisco Varela (1988), although written in a different context, would seem to be particularly appropriate here:

> Our cognitive relationship with the world is neither one of picking up information and processing it and having some kind of output or result, nor is it one of having some very smart and rich network inside. This is not to say that I don't believe in some kind of sense of reality. Clearly existence is there. That's to say, is neither here nor there, it is an emergence . . . [E]xistences are not a matter of the inside mapping the outside and the outside mapping the inside, nor the inside constructing the outside, but in fact this stable dance which is multiple.

References

American Psychiatric Association, *Diagnostic and Statistical Manual of Mental Disorders*, 3rd edition, Washington, 1987.

Briquet, P. Traite *Clinique et thérapeutique de l'hystérie*, Balliere, Paris, 1859.

Brouardel, P.C. 'The Causes of Error in Expert Opinions with Respect to Sexual Assaults', *Annales Medico-Psychologique*, 3rd series, 10, 60–71, 148–79, 1883.

Buber, M. 'What Is Man?', in *Between Man and Man*, Macmillan, New York, 1965, 1938.

Cannon, W.B. *Bodily Changes in Pain, Hunger, Fear and Rage: An Account of Recent Researches into the Function of Emotional Excitement*, 2nd edition, Appleton-Century-Crofts, New York, 1929.

Charcot, J.-M. 'The Aetiology of Hysteria', *Acta Psychiatrica Scandinavica*, 43, 144–62, 1967.

da Costa, J.M. 'On Irritable Heart: A Clinical Study of a Form of Functional Cardiac Disorder and Its Consequences', *American Journal of the Medical Sciences*, 61, 17–52, 1871.

Fournier, A. 'Simulation d'attentats venériens sur de jeunes enfants', *Annales Medico-Psychologiques*, 53–67, 374–86, [1880] 1883.

Freud, S. 'Studies in Hysteria', in J. Strachey (trans. and ed.), *Complete Psychological Works*, vol. 2, Hogarth Press, London, [1893] 1954.

—. 'The Aetiology of Hysteria', in J. Strachey (trans. and ed.), *Complete Psychological Works*, vol. 18, Hogarth Press, London, [1896] 1954.

—. 'Heredity and the Aetiology of Neuroses', in J. Strachey (trans. and ed.), *Complete Psychological Works*, vol. 3, Hogarth Press, London, [1896] 1954.

—. 'History of the Psycho-analytic Movement', in E. Jones, *The Life and Work of Sigmund Freud*, Pelican Books, London, [1914] 1964.

—. 'Introductory Lectures on Psychoanalysis', in J. Strachey (trans. and ed.), *Complete Psychological Works*, Hogarth Press, London, [1916] 1959.

Grinker, R., and Spiegel, J.P. *Men Under Stress*, Blakiston, Philadelphia, 1945.

Grof, S. *Realms of the Human Unconscious*, Viking Press, New York, 1975.

—. *Beyond the Brain*, State University of New York Press, Albany, NY, 1985.

—. *The Adventure of Self-Discovery*, State University of New York Press, Albany, NY, 1988.

Hartmann, M., and Rumler, L., in M. Sharaf, *Fury on Earth: A Biography of Wilhelm Reich*, Andre Deutsch, London, 1983.

Jones, E. *The Life and Work of Sigmund Freud*, Pelican Books, London, 1964.

Jung, C.G. 'The Archetypes and the Collective Unconscious', in *Collected Works*, Bollingen Series XX, vol. 9.1, Princeton University Press, Princeton, NJ, 1959.

Kardiner, A. *The Traumatic Neuroses of War*, P. Hoeber, New York, 1941.

Kardiner, A., and Spiegel, H. *War Stress and Neurotic Illness*, Harper, New York, 1947.

Lewis, T. *The Soldier's Heart and the Effort Syndrome*, Hoeber, New York, 1919.

Lindemann, E. 'Symptomatology and Management of Acute Grief', *American Journal of Psychiatry*, 101, 141–8, 1944.

Masson, J.M. *The Assault on Truth*, Penguin Books, Middlesex, 1985.

Oppenheimer, B.S. 'Report on Neurocirculatory Asthenia and Its Management', *Military Surgeon* (now *Military Medicine*), 42, 7–11, 1918.

Pavlov, I.P. *Conditioned Reflexes and Psychiatry*, Lawrence & Wishart, New York, London, [1927] 1941.

Penfield, W., and Jasper, H. *Epilepsy and the Functional Anatomy of the Human Brain*, Little, Brown & Co, Boston, 1954.

Penfield, W., and Roberts, L. *Speech and Brain Mechanisms*, Princeton University Press, Princeton, NJ, 1959.

Sargent, W. *The Mind Possessed*, Pan Books, London, 1976.

Sharaf, M. *Fury on Earth: A Biography of Wilhelm Reich*, Marek, London, 1983.

Tardieu, A.A. 'A Medico-Legal Study of Assaults on Decency', in J.M. Masson, *The Assault on Truth*, Penguin Books, Middlesex, [1857] 1985.

Varela, F. 'Mind and Nature', lecture given at a conference in Hanover, 1988.

19. A Granular Society

This paper was published in a book entitled *Across the Frontiers: Ireland in the 1990s*, edited by Richard Kearney and first published in 1988. Also included in the book is an article by our new President, Michael D. Higgins.

IN 1992 we are told that Europe will be taking a further step towards political and economic integration. There will be free movement throughout the community with the abolition of customs and national borders. This is to be welcomed and is simply part of a wider and very gradual movement on the surface of our planet (at times an almost imperceptible movement) towards the creation of one single, global society. This movement can be discerned in a number of areas: the rock music culture has become virtually international and it has become increasingly hard to tell the place of origin of the songs, music, accents, dress and appearance of groups, etc.; the growth and expansion of transnational companies which neither know nor respect any national boundaries and which have set up technological, transport and telecommunications systems that are increasingly worldwide. Here too we see the global linking up of diasporas, of scientific research right across the world, of intellectual endeavour of many kinds and the growth of a world literature. These are but a few examples of an increasingly manifest global world culture.

If this movement towards a united states of Europe and, on a wider scale, towards a global world culture, however much it is to be welcomed from one point of view, is not to be very destructive in other ways to our fundamental nature as living human beings, then it implies and indeed demands an equally imperceptible and penetrating movement in the opposite direction, towards decentralization and the emergence of strong, much more autonomous regional and local structures.

If I were asked why I see such a reverse development as a necessary balancing evolution, I would point to our inherent biological nature. In the end of all we are living creatures, we still retain our animal nature and, although human beings are perhaps the most adaptable of all living species, we are nevertheless not capable of adapting to simply any kind of circumstances. The human being is a living system, like all other living creatures and, what is more, like many other species we are intensely social animals. We begin life in relationship and, just as we require essential nutritional ingredients if we are to remain healthy, we need to be embedded in intimate and personal social relationships throughout our lifetime, otherwise we become mad.

So, if this process of centralization towards a united states of Europe, and ultimately towards a global society, is to go ahead without any counterbalancing movement towards decentralization, then a point will be reached (as is already evident in the USA) where there is nothing between the isolated human individual and enormous conglomerations of literally millions of people. This inevitably leads to the feelings of alienation and anhomie already so prevalent among the young in contemporary society, where so many of them experience a sense of isolation and pointlessness and have no sense of future or purpose in living. What every day becomes more urgently necessary, then, is the emergence of a counterbalancing process of decentralization across society. And this is particularly necessary at the regional and local level.

The Nation State: Before and After

For some hundreds of years now European society has experienced an undue emphasis on the nation state, defined by geographical borders. This has manifested itself in the cult of nationalism, with all its attendant wars, bloodshed and intolerance of the rights of other nations. It might be argued that it was always so but this is not true. In earlier tribal cultures, such as (to take but two examples) the Bambuti in the rainforests of the Congo, or the ancient Celtic civilization which spread right across Europe, there was no clear nationhood or fixed geographical borders. However, this did not simply mean they were a group of disconnected warring tribes. In societies such as these there was a clearly unified culture, with a common language, religion, laws and crafts and artefacts, so that an individual pigmy, for example, could be taken from his own local tribal group and moved, perhaps 1,000 miles, to another tribal cluster where he would rapidly feel completely at home, recognising everything and able to communicate freely with his neighbours. The same was largely true in Celtic society, where a bard or a lawyer could travel freely from one end of Ireland to the other and right through Scotland, from one distinct tribal kingdom to another, but always finding himself in a continuous, understandable culture, language, system of law, etc.

The fairly recent development of the nation state in Europe and elsewhere, therefore, has been damaging not only to the possibility of a wider union of peoples (such as a united Europe) but has also led, since the Industrial Revolution, to the dismemberment and virtual disappearance of regional and local societal structures. I am thinking of the loss of autonomy and vibrant life of provinces (to be able to recognize the difference between a person from Connaught, and someone from Leinster or Dublin), local towns or city states such as Venice or Genoa in Italy, villages, tribal clusters and extended families, in which the individual was ultimately embedded and could recognize and know him or herself. All of these smaller societal entities have withered, indeed have virtually disappeared in recent times, losing all the richness of difference or diversity, colour and intimate personal relationship characteristics of local life. It is out of such local autonomy and relationship that person-hood, with all its loving, hating intimacy and creativity, emerges. Without this, the essence of what is to be human will wither and die.

This is not to say that such a counter-development of decentralization (allowing for appropriate centralization even up to the global level) should mean the disappearance of nationalism or the nation state altogether, but rather that this level should diminish and lessen in influence so as to bring the hierarchy of societal structures or living systems into harmony, so that no one dimension of society cannibalizes or expresses itself to the detriment and proper life and autonomy of the levels below or above it. What is valuable about national identity or the notion of nationhood is really a cultural statement, defined by language, music and other cultural characteristics as well as by geographical location. And, indeed, to be Irish, French or Italian can extend beyond geographical boundaries so that one can think of, for example, the greater Irish nation perhaps encompassing as many as seventy million people, able to link themselves in one way or another to a common ethnic culture, while the Irish nation state is only a small island with less than five million people.

To look to the emergence of such a process of decentralization is not simply a hopeless dream or harking back to a sentimental past. On the contrary, there is an increasing awareness and evidence of such a movement in a number of European countries at the present time. In countries such as Italy, Germany or Switzerland, such a healthy regional and local emphasis has always remained strong and now, in France, Spain and here in Ireland, a renewed awareness of the importance of such decentralization is clearly discernible. Within the past year several Irish members of the European Parliament – John Hume, Eileen Lemass, Mary Banotti and others – have put forward and have had accepted plans for regional development and new growth of local structures. Such movements are still weak when compared to the overweaning forces of centralization but there is no doubt about the growing awareness in Europe of the need for such a development.

All over the European countries communities are stirring and, although this movement remains incipient, the voice of ordinary people looking once again to have a personal responsibility and control over their lives is beginning to be heard. Nor are such movements purely local or isolated: there is frequently an awareness and even an intercommunication with similar movements in other parts of the world. For example, in Ireland we see the conscious application of liberation theology, which had its origins in South America, now becoming a driving force here in projects with the unemployed, the travelling people and other disadvantaged groups in our society. What is emerging ever more clearly from community projects and movements which are beginning in the alienated ghettoes of the inner cities across Europe is that there can be no hope for the individual person who is marginalized to gain a foothold in society, to learn the skills they need if they are to have a decent life and if they are to have any self-respect or personal autonomy, unless they can feel themselves part of a bounded community of human size, where personal relationships are possible.

Community Projects

To take a concrete example from my own professional experience: a fundamental principle of the democratic psychiatric reform which is under way in Italy, and which has also been clear to some of us in Ireland for a number of years, is that any training that will enable the disadvantaged young person of our inner cities, who is demotivated and alienated to learn what he/she needs to know to find a place in society, will fail unless such training is part of a social contract to the community; unless the activity through which the skills are being acquired is also providing a service or fulfilling a useful function for the community in which that person lives.

This is what has been happening, for instance, in the inner city project in Derry, which has been under way now for nearly ten years and where upwards of 500 unemployed young people who dropped out of school are revitalizing the old inner city: rebuilding old, derelict buildings, setting up small craft industries and undertaking a range of useful community services, so that what was a dead, bombed-out city following the 'Troubles' is now throbbing with life and enterprise. A similar project is now getting under way in the north-west quadrant of the inner city of Dublin, which has been run down and virtually derelict for many years. Out of a community of approximately 20,000 there are some 5,000 unemployed, many of whom are at risk for social or psychiatric breakdown. The whole area is in urgent need of major urban renewal. The local Stoneybatter community have already produced an excellent development plan, to chart the way forward, but on their own have little hope of fully realizing this potential. What is proposed now under the heading of the 'Brendan Project' is a joint effort between rehabilitation and mental health professionals on the one hand working with the community on the other.

The idea is to create, in this quadrant of central Dublin, a living city for the future but one which is designed to help the local community to break out of the poverty trap. The project will be primarily a cultural undertaking: the creation of a living city, celebrating the arts, music, drama and sporting activities of all kinds, with some economic and commercial underpinning to create a rounded development. It will be an urban development for the next century, built by the disadvantaged and unemployed *for* the disadvantaged and unemployed. It will be for the people, by the people and of the people – for those who live in it and for those who will come to enjoy it from other parts of the greater Dublin area. There seems little doubt that such a development would attract major international interest among architects, social planners and socially minded industrialists. There is also little doubt that it would merit substantial funding from the European regional fund and other international financial sources.

What will make this project unique, should it get under way, and an interesting example of the concept of devolution being put forward in this paper is that, while it will be a truly local communal endeavour on the one hand, it will at the same time be linked with a wider European perspective. For it is also proposed that it will participate in the Greater European Project (GEP) which is soon to commence and will be centred on the concept of 'habilitation' and skills for living, these to be applied both to the disadvantaged unemployed and at risk population and to new chronic psychiatric patients, who are now the central problem facing community psychiatry. This GEP is to include projects from Italy, Germany and possibly northern Greece, and Ireland (through the Brendan Project) has been invited to become an active participant. Thus we have here an example of a movement which on the one hand is truly local in character, centred on personal communal development, but at the same time is part of an integrated European-wide endeavour involving similar local projects in a number of member states.

Interconnections

These are but some examples, among many, which I feel illustrate well both the opportunity and the difficulty inherent in any attempt to bring about human change. Whether we are talking about change in a human individual or in society, the question which must be asked is – how can this change begin? During this century, fundamental changes have been taking place in our scientific understanding of the world and our view of the nature of reality. Fritjof Capra describes this change in our scientific world view in the following way:

> The material world, according to contemporary physics, is not a mechanical system of separate objects but rather appears as a complex web of relationships. Sub-atomic particles cannot be understood as isolated, separate entities but have to be seen as interconnections, or correlations, in a network of events. *The notion of separate objects is an idealization which is often very*

useful but has no fundamental validity. All such objects are patterns in an inseparable cosmic process and these patterns are intrinsically dynamic. Sub-atomic particles are not made of any material substance. They have a certain mass but this mass is a form of energy. Energy, however, is always associated with processes, with activity: it is a measure of activity. Sub-atomic particles, then, are bundles of energy or patterns of activity . . . The world view of modern physics is holistic and ecological. It emphasizes the fundamental inter-relatedness and interdependence of all phenomena and also the intrinsically dynamic nature of the physical reality. To extend this view to the description of living organisms we have to go beyond physics.

The more we understand of the nature of reality and of ourselves as human beings, the clearer it becomes that everything is interconnected, that there is no such thing as a separate human individual or community. If we apply this view to society, then it inevitably follows that what is taking place in one part of society, as for example joyriding, gang rape, vandalism, or vicious attacks on old people around the countryside, must be ultimately related and interconnected with what is happening in other sectors which we ordinarily think of as normal healthy society – the apparently genteel life that goes on in better-off middle-class suburbs. If there is any merit in such a view, then we must all have a share in the responsibility for the vicious and sordid activities which are daily going on in some of the more deprived and disadvantaged sections of our society. We have to ask the question how far all of us are dumping the negative aspects of ourselves into others and using certain persons or groups in society as scapegoats. This should in no way be interpreted as meaning that these people have not their own proper share of responsibility for what they are doing, or that there are not some very vicious human beings around, but nevertheless we still have to ask in what way have we all, society, contributed to this viciousness. How do we maintain it? I will resist the question 'Why?'

Herein lies the dilemma. If we take this statement seriously, and so often we see this work out in practice, for one human individual to really change would involve the family and community in which he/she is embedded also changing fundamentally, and for this change to really take root would imply a similar change in the wider society, indeed in human society as a whole. But reciprocally the whole of human society cannot change unless real change takes place in the heart of each individual who makes it up. This is the human merry-go-round on which we appear to have been stuck for thousands of years. On the one hand we have appeals from the various religions to each of us to change our ways, but if you examine this proposition honestly it becomes quite clear that one cannot really change as an individual unless the society out of which we emerge changes also. On the other hand we have political reformers and revolutionaries who have perennially attempted to create a more humane society by introducing a new political system or different ideology but this always founders on the bedrock that the individuals who have to operate this new system haven't really changed and hence everything goes back once again to where it was.

It may seem a trifle far-fetched to put the problem in this way but, if one looks around the world at all the attempts over the last half-century to bring about real change in human society, we will see how often what looked like hopeful and enthusiastic experiments withered away after a time and merged back eventually into the same old status quo. This lesson has been repeated but not learned over and over again. So, looking at the situation from this aspect brings one back relentlessly to the conclusion that real human change is impossible. No part can change unless the whole changes and the whole cannot change unless there is change in the parts. Is there any way out of this impasse?

The Human Group in Systems Theory

Each of us is conceived and born already in the context of relationship and, from the very beginning, each of us emerges out of some form of primary human group; at the very least a nuclear family. In fact, almost always some form of wider communal setting is also present within which the family rests. That is, we are already embedded in a society, in a culture, and in fact this primary group culture, if we think about it, extends back in some form unbroken to the very dawn of human history. While the life of the human individual is finite and represents only a transitory moment in the evolutionary time-scale, the human group, in whatever form this may take at a given time, is not finite and has had an unbroken continuous existence stretching back over two to five million years since the very first appearance of *homo sapiens* on this planet. Indeed it now seems very likely that what passed across from the pre-human to the human species was not some remarkable individual mutation but rather the crossing over of a group of hominids to finally achieve fully conscious human status. So, as far as we can discern through the mists of the dawn of human history, at no point do we find first the individual and then the emergence of the group or community, but rather always the human group, some form of primitive society in which the individual is embedded. Indeed, the emergence of the highly sophisticated, conscious, individual human person out of the primary human group has been a long and painful process and represents a crowning achievement of only fairly recent times.

So we arrive at a position where it must be accepted that there is no such thing as a separate human individual; first and last, we find the individual person embedded in some form of primary social unit. The fundamental question which faces us then is 'what is the nature of the human group?' Is it simply a collection of individuals or is it some form of 'separate being' which has an existence in its own right, distinct from the individuals who make it up? Whichever way we answer this question will alter the very basis of our thinking about ourselves. Fortunately we are not simply shooting in the dark, for the work of a number of scientists in recent years is helping to illuminate our understanding of this and a number of related questions. Most of this work falls within the sphere of what has loosely been called General Systems Theory.

A system may be defined as an integrated whole that derives its essential properties from the inter-relationship between its parts. A system, therefore, cannot be understood by analysing the parts of which it is made up but rather by focusing upon the dynamic inter-relations and inter-dependencies between its parts. All throughout nature we find examples of systems both in the living and the non-living world, but our concern here is with living systems.

The basic principle of a living system is what the Nobel Prize scientist Ilya Prigogine refers to as 'self-organization'. The work of Maturana and Varela is also of fundamental importance here; they have termed this principle 'autopoeisis'. By a penetrating analysis, they have shown that the essential characteristics of anything which is alive is that it is self-regulating and self-producing; the term they coin for this is 'autopoiesis' – 'auto' meaning self and 'poiesis' (from the Greek root *poinine*) meaning to produce, i.e. self-producing. According to this view, then, the essence of something which is living is that it actively maintains and produces itself, that its first priority is to maintain itself in existence. Thus, a living organism, as Fritjof Capra says, is a self-organizing system, which means that its order in structure and function is not imposed by the environment but is established and maintained by the system itself. This theory maintains, then, that any subject of study can be held to be 'alive', to be 'living', to be an organism if, and only if, it fulfils the following conditions:

1. It contains a number of elements.
2. These elements are involved in a dynamic process of inter-relationship.
3. It is separated from its environment by a boundary of its own elements such that it permits transactions of import and export across the boundary; i.e. it is an open (not closed) system surrounded by a semi-permeable membrane.
4. It maintains and renews (regenerates) its own elements by its own internal processes. Living organisms continually renew themselves, cells breaking down and building up structures, tissues and organs replacing their cells in continual cycles, and so on. Nevertheless the living system maintains its overall structure and appearance. Its components are continually renewed and recycled but its being – the pattern of organization – remains relatively stable.
5. Finally, living systems show a tendency to transcend themselves, as Capra says, 'to reach out creatively beyond their boundaries and limitations to generate new structures and new forms of organization. This principle of self-transcendence manifests itself in the process of learning, development and evolution.' Thus, living systems not only tend to change and adapt but also reproduce themselves and thus ensure survival and evolution of the species.

So much then for the definition of a living system but, if these are the essential characteristics which describe what it is to be alive, then they must apply to every living being – whether plant or animal, a single-celled organism, a dog, a monkey or a human being. But there is something important to be noted here, and indeed this is the essential aspect which I wish most to emphasize, for it relates specifically to the central theme of this paper: this is the interesting characteristic of living systems that they tend to form a hierarchical order of one living system within another. Thus the basic living system making up all supra-ordinate systems is the cell. The most common form of life on this planet is still the unicellular organism or amoeba but, over the long course of evolution, nature has found ways for cells to combine to form new multicellular living systems, such as a bee, an ant, a baboon, or a human being but, here and there in the multitude of forms which life takes, we find a third order of living systems coming into being. The most highly organized examples are to be found among the social insects – the termite mound or ant heap, the beehive – and this is hardly an accident, for, in terms of evolutionary history, these organisms are many millions of years older than, say, the mammalian group to which we belong. The important thing to note here is that these third-order systems fulfil the definition of a living system just as completely as do the individual bees or ants of which they are composed and it is therefore increasingly being realized by entomologists that, for example, a beehive or termite mound must truly be classed as a living creature in its own right.

In a similar way, although the process has not as yet developed so highly, various birds, fishes and mammalian groups must also be recognized as forming third-order systems, such as a colony of baboons. Where we find this happening, as in the case of the cell within our own bodies, or where a third order is involved – the cell within the body of a bee and the bee within the body of a beehive – we find the supra-ordinate system is in a position to influence over the primary or secondary systems of which it is constituted. Each system retains its proper integrity as a living system at its own level but nevertheless its autopoiesis is depressed and transmission and exchange across its boundary is increased and, to a significant degree, under the influence of the supra-ordinate system.

Beyond this, further supra-ordinate living systems can be discerned ecosystems such as the coral reef, where many species of both plant and animal life live in a balanced co-existence or symbiotic relationship; another example would be the teeming life of the African plains and finally there is, of course, the living envelope covering the surface of the entire planet – the biosphere, maintaining itself, until recently at any rate, as a delicately balanced, self-referential living system. One point should be clarified here in speaking of supra-ordinate human living systems. The fact that a higher order of living system may exist and that, as a human individual, I may be under the influence of a supra-ordinate group system, should not in any way be taken to mean that the supra-ordinate system is necessarily more complex or more highly developed than the individual living systems of which it is constituted. On the contrary, all the evidence would suggest that the individual human person is by far the most complex and most highly developed form of life of which we have any knowledge on this planet. Most human third-order living systems are by comparison primitive, largely unconscious and simple in their behaviours; nevertheless, they do have a powerful supra-ordinate influence on the human individual within them.

Questions of Minorities

Like many in the 1960s, I had idealistic hopes of society breaking up and reconstituting itself in a granular form, creating an enlightened, loving form of society. These idealistic visions of a transformed society have not come to pass. Transformation has indeed been taking place and high-order human systems have mushroomed and spread throughout most of the world, growing more enormous and powerful with each passing day. However, these are huge, mindless, bureaucratic systems, composed of human beings but not in any sense embodying enlightened or loving human values – transnational corporations, state departments, insurance empires, international banks and others – all impersonal, all anti-human and destructive of the total environment of the planet.

From this point of view, the Irish and Irish society may be seen to have some special characteristics. It will be clear from what has been said so far that, given human nature as it is, the existence of minority groups will tend to be a universal problem within any society but for two main reasons, arising from its historical context, I believe Irish society is likely to have special difficulty in relation to tolerance of minority groups within it. Centuries of colonial domination here have left a cultural legacy where, even after sixty years of partial freedom, Irish society will tend to see authority (the locus of control) as located outside itself: that is, to experience itself as 'other directed'. The other reason why this is so lies in the special position of the

Roman Catholic Church in this country. Presumably because of its long years of persecution, when it represented the only life-line of the people, the Church holds a very intimate and central position in Irish society. When the British granted Catholic emancipation in the early years of the nineteenth century, they in fact made available to themselves a more powerful means of colonial domination over the hearts and minds of the people than they had ever wielded up to that time for the Church, however intimately it may be built into the fabric of Irish society, drawing its priests from the people, takes its ultimate authority from outside the country. This has been used in collusion with British colonialism over and over again in the last 200 years to frustrate any attempt towards the growth of a full national identity which would draw together Irish people of various religious denominations. We had an upsetting and painful example of this some years ago in the visit of the Papal emissary to a hunger striker in Long Kesh to try to persuade him to give up his fast. There was no equivalent visit from Rome to the British government to try to persuade them to change their frozen colonial attitude which has remained obdurately unchanged for over sixty years.

There is, nevertheless, some evidence in recent years of a change on the part of the Irish clergy and bishops to free themselves from this authoritarian relationship with Irish society. Strangely enough, it is Irish society rather than the Church itself which tends to keep forcing us back into the same other-directed relationship. I believe this is because of our fear and unwillingness as individuals and as a society to take on our own personal authority, to make the conscious break with the old institutionalized colonial relationships. There are signs, however, that the third generation since the revolution, and the young people coming on, may be free enough and conscious enough within themselves to accomplish what the idealists of 1916 were unable to grasp fully and what the maimed country-town shopkeeper generation, clinging meanly to survival during the 1930s and '50s, lost sight of altogether. It may be hoped that the new generation, better educated and more conscious, now emerging into a European context, may finally be able to free themselves enough to take on their own self-direction and to create a fuller more human identity which is able to accept within itself all the streams and minorities which make up Irish society today.

Exchange Entropy: Towards an Open System

What, you may well ask, is the relevance of all this to human change and development? Well, as already stressed, this must necessarily involve bringing about change within society. The question is, how can this be achieved when education and human development are always taking place within the context of the present society and within the group culture which is already there. This, if we think about it, always inevitably produces more of the same. There have been over the past thirty years many attempts to introduce innovative education and community development projects in many parts of the world. Our experience has been similar to that of many others. Somehow the efforts to bring about change seemed to be dissipated out into an ever-widening circle so that, while for a time there may be enthusiastic endeavour for change within the experimental project, this dribbles away into the wider community and it becomes painfully clear that, if the experiment were to take and have an enduring effect, this would involve bringing about a change in the whole society; what happens, in fact, is that the effort for change simply disappears into the ever-widening pool of society and everything goes back to where it started.

A second outcome which we have often seen is where a group withdraws from the community and an attempt is made to create the perfect alternative society – a commune or closed-off artificial community is established which breaks all connection or interchange with the rest of society. While perfection and peace may appear to reign for a short time, inevitably the closed society begins to stagnate and decline, the activity dries up and eventually the whole thing withers and dies, as happened with Synanon in California and, all too horribly, in the Jim Jones experiment ending in mass suicide in Guyana.

It is here that the illuminating insights of Teilhard de Chardin and the more recent pioneering and meticulous work of Prigogine *et al.* on self-organizing, non-linear systems help us to understand more clearly why these innovative attempts to bring about real social change and human development have had so little long-term success up to the present and why, in spite of so much idealistic endeavour, everything seems relentlessly to drift back to square one.

The second law of thermodynamics states that every physical process will result in a net decrease in the amount of order (hence a net increase in the amount of disorder) in the universe as a whole. Entropy (from the Greek *entropian*, meaning evolution) is that quantity which indexes the amount of disorder in a system at any given time. The second law thus implies that every physical process will result in an irreversible increase in the amount of entropy in the universe as a whole, over time. Entropy has, therefore, sometimes been referred to as 'time's arrow'. Since its formulation, this law has appeared to most physicists to be one of the greatest achievements of theoretical physics, one of the cornerstones of our understanding of the physical world. It was thus thought to be universal in its application.

It seemed evident, then, that in our immediate physical environment on this planet the second law of thermodynamics was relentlessly at work – the planet was running down, natural resources were being gobbled up at an accelerating rate and, with each reaction, entropy was increasing. Then de Chardin drew attention to a strange paradox which, although it was not appreciated at the time, fundamentally altered this whole concept of the universe. He pointed out that, in the midst of this dissipative view of the world, biological life has appeared and has been growing continually, becoming ever more complex, alive and conscious and concentrating more energy unto itself. He referred again and again to this in the last years of his life:

> On the one hand, we have in physics a matter which slides irresistibly, following the line of least resistance, in the direction of the most probable forms of distribution. And on the other hand, we have in biology the same matter drifting (no less irresistibly but in this case in a sort of 'greater effort' for survival) towards ever more improbable, because ever more complex, forms of arrangement.

In another essay, written shortly before his death, he returned to this question:

> However, it may well be, perhaps, that this contradiction is a warning to our minds that we must completely reverse the way in which we see things. We still persist in regarding the physical as constituting the 'true' phenomenon in the universe, and the psychic as a sort of epiphenomenon . . . If we really wish to unify the real, we should completely reverse the values – that is, we should consider the whole of thermodynamics as an unstable and ephemeral bi-effect of the concentration on itself of what we call 'consciousness' or 'spirit' . . . In other words there is no longer just one type of energy in the world: there are two different energies,

one axial, increasing, and irreversible, and the other peripheral or tangential, constant, reversible. And these two energies are linked together in 'arrangement', but without, nevertheless, being able either to form a compound or directly to be transformed into one another because they operate at different levels.

From this point of view, if we take a fresh look at the world, the startling fact emerges that the whole stuff of the universe appears to be built up of units – 'wholes'; these combine to form at each level a genuine synthesis, a new pattern of organization, creating a larger and more complex 'whole'. This remarkable design seems to run right through from the quark to the galaxy in outer space. In *The Phenomenon of Man*, Teilhard had this to say:

> After allowing itself to be captivated by the charms of analysis to the extent of falling into illusion, modern thought is at last getting used once more to the idea of the creative value of synthesis in evolution. It is beginning to see that there is definitely more in the molecule than in the atom, more in the cell than the molecule, more in society than in the individual, and more in mathematical construction than in calculations and theorems. We are now inclined to admit that at each further degree of combinations something which is irreducible to isolated elements emerges in a new order. With this admission, consciousness, life and thought, are on the threshold of acquiring a right to existence in terms of science.

In the same chapter he makes an important qualification of this emphasis, which is very much to the point in our consideration here of the question of a 'granular' society, when he says:

> In any domain – whether it be the cells of the body, the members of a society, or the elements of a spiritual synthesis – union differentiates. In every organized whole, the parts perfect themselves and fulfil themselves. Through neglect of this universal rule, many a system of pantheism has led us astray to the cult of a great 'All' in which individuals were supposed to be merged like a drop in the ocean, or like a dissolving grain of salt. Applied to the case of the summation of consciousness, the law of union rids us of this perilous and recurrent illusion. No, following the confluent orbits of their centres, the grains of consciousness do not tend to lose outlines and blend but, on the contrary, to accentuate the depth and incommunicability of

their *egos*. The more 'other' they become in conjunction, the more they find themselves as 'self'.

Ilya Prigogine, in his work on the characteristics of self-organizing systems (what he calls irreversible non-linear transformations under conditions far from equilibrium), has dealt with this much more systematically and in far more detail. He points out that a thermodynamically isolated system is one which neither energy nor mass can enter or leave. In actual practice, the only truly isolated system possible is the universe as a whole. The thermodynamically closed system is one which energy can enter and leave but matter cannot. A well-sealed steamboiler, whose water can be heated or cooled but cannot escape, is an example of such a closed system. It was specifically to explain certain properties of such 'steam engines' that the second law was first devised. Most biological, psychological and social systems, however, are neither isolated nor closed. They are, instead, thermodynamically open systems. An open system is one which is capable of exchanging both energy and matter with its environment. Such open systems have always been viewed as anomalous from the point of view of classical thermodynamics. However, when the principles underlying the second law are extended to these systems, a new set of properties emerge that were not formerly apparent. These new properties include capacity for 'self-organization' – i.e. for a 'spontaneous' shift from a lower to a higher level of organizational complexity. Prigogine has named such self-organizing systems 'dissipative structures' and says they are capable of 'exchange entropy', since they can maintain their organizational complexity only by continually dissipating the positive entropy which they produce back into the environment. We can say that each such locally developing system achieves an increase in structural order and complexity only by 'ingesting', 'digesting' and 'assimilating' the negative entropy (i.e. the orderliness) previously possessed by the structures in its surrounding environment, and by 'excreting' back into that environment 'waste products' which are higher in positive entropy (i.e. disorderliness) than those which it initially ingested.

Towards a Self-Organizing System

Taking this basic work on self-organizing systems and applying it now to the question of human development – that is, to the question of how we can bring about change at the level of society – and taking Maturana and Varela's concept of autopoiesis into consideration, a quite different approach to the problem begins to become apparent.

It appears to me inescapable that, if we are to hope to educate for real human development, to bring about real human change, this will only be possible if we find ways to create bounded human systems. But these must be open systems with semi-permeable boundedness so that exchange with the surrounding environment (i.e. society) can be managed and controlled sufficiently to allow self-organization, growth and development to go on within the system and not to allow this to be simply dissipated into the surrounding society.

My position is that there is a vast reservoir of untapped energy, ability and creative potential in any human individual but most of this potential usually lies dormant and is not available to the person. There is always untapped potential. If, however, this human potential is to be realized, then two fundamental issues have to be faced and tackled.

The first is personal authority. Most human beings, particularly in this post-colonial country, fail to establish any reasonable degree of personal authority. By this I mean that they have little awareness as to who or what they are and that most of the decisions concerning their lives are being taken by authorities outside of themselves, their family, state or corporate organizations, many of whose centres of power are operating from outside the country altogether.

Many of our school-leavers, particularly those coming from socially deprived areas, are almost devoid of self-direction. Throughout their schooldays rote knowledge has been fed into them. They may have become literate or have developed some specific skills but all of this is derived from outside of themselves and they can seldom make a statement as to who or what they are or ask questions of the world in which they live.

The hypothesis presented then, is that, unless the centre of control is discovered by each of us within ourselves, there is no possibility of the emergence of creativity, of the realization of the potential within us, of taking a fresh look at the world so that we can create new forms of work and activity.

This is a crucial question for any person or society, the question of personal authority and self-direction. Human beings are intended to take responsibility for all that is within them. Direction from outside is a sick symptom for the person or society, a symptom of lost autonomy, lost power. This is mainly a function of the boundary of a living system (whether this be an individual or a group) in the management of the interaction between what is inside or outside the system. The crucial question is where this 'authority' or 'control' lies; to be self-directing, or self-motivating, lies at the very heart of what it is to be alive, to be human.

The second essential principle is that the person begins to understand and take responsibility for the role each of us has to play as part of a group, a member of society. The essential thing that has to be learned here is that within society, in the families and groups within which we live, each of us tends to be given a role with an expected set of attitudes and behaviours which are often quite different from the way we see ourselves as individuals. People are often only dimly aware of being made to behave in this way, of the role they are given by the group, such as peacemaker, rebel, leader, follower, the talker or the silent one, etc. One has the unpleasant feeling of being forced to be someone one does not wish to be, over and over again, in the various groups we participate in as we go through life. The crucial learning here, which again can only take place within the space of a managed bounded human system, is to become aware of the characteristic ways in which we participate and relate with others and to start to take responsibility for this.

In contemporary western society, this element is almost invariably seen in competitive terms, a world of winners and losers. More and more in our society, we see the few who struggle their way to the top, who find a comfortable place for themselves, and the many for whom society has no place.

The learning of our involvement with groups within which we live is absolutely crucial if people are ever to change to a more cooperative way of functioning. To me, it is quite clear now that any alternative strategy of work and living will have to emerge from such a cooperative base, and will only be possible with human beings who have some understanding of these realities.

It should now be clearer why it is necessary to establish a bounded living system, a 'human oasis', where the group is managed so as to provide a space for its many parts. This removes the outside controls which are normally present in society, so that a young person is left face to face with his or her own behaviour. If they have not, up to this time, learned any skills in managing themselves, usually a good deal of confusion and uncertainty will result. The setting has to be managed so as to provide, within the limits of tolerance, sufficient emotional space and freedom for individuals to experience themselves and their behaviour.

Not having the resources within themselves for self-direction and self-management, they may become highly anxious. This may manifest itself in destructive, anti-social or other forms of acting-out behaviour but, providing that the group setting as a whole can be managed, the natural tendency in all of us towards self-management and creative expression will come to the surface.

A change towards the personal, by very definition, cannot take place across society en masse, for this would only result in denial of the very personal dimension we are trying to enhance. If there is to be any hope of change in this direction, fundamental to it must be the creation of some nucleus within which it can happen, some basic unit of society where these personalized processes can take root.

The Granular Society

This time the synthesis must be at the human level, a human module which will form the basic unit of a 'granular' society. Because this will represent a genuinely new synthesis at the human level, the forces holding it together, and the energizing principle organizing and maintaining it in being, must also be of a quite different order. The atom, the molecule, the living cell, each is maintained in existence by a pattern of forces, by energy in a form appropriate to its own level. When we come to a synthesis at the human level, it must be asked what form will the organizational forces now take, where will we turn to find an energizing principle that will maintain and vitalize our human module. It is true that in the human being the earlier electro-chemical forms of energy are still at work in the atoms, molecules and cells which go to make us up, but to bind one human to another, to create a true communion of human beings, some new principle must be introduced.

To find the answer, I believe we must turn once again to the personal dimension and look at the kinds of bonds which operate in basic human structures already in existence. Here we find the power of love and conscious understanding, psychological and emotional forces operating at the level of consciousness as between one human person and another. However, as is found in lower forms of synthesis, for example with the atom or the molecule, the forces operating are not simply those of attraction. On the contrary, the individual components of, say, an atom maintain a dynamic relationship, always striving towards a stable arrangement, a state of balance between the forces of attraction and repulsion. So too, at the human level, the need for intimacy, closeness and love is always balanced by the need to keep a measure of distance and separateness between oneself and loved ones – the need at times for privacy, to separate and be purely oneself. I think, if we are to make any progress with human relationships in society, it is as vital to understand this need for separateness, distinctness and uniqueness and personal development as the need for love and intimate relationship.

This living human system then must have a surrounding membrane providing a clear separation or boundary between itself and the rest of society. This would be partly geographical and spatial but because, as already explained, the organizational forces operating are at the level of consciousness, of human love and understanding, the boundary membrane must be mainly of a psychological nature, which would provide a protective mechanism, a semi-permeable membrane, to filter uncontrolled sensory bombardment and mass communication from outside.

Just as the achievement of the cell membrane constituted a great leap forward with the emergence of the first living substance and allowed the heightening intensity of various chemical processes to take place within the living cell and not to be lost by diffusion into the surrounding milieu, so the surrounding psychological membrane would allow an intensification of internal communication and human relationship, heightening the intensity of human processes of love and ideas within.

At the same time, this bounded system must be an open system, allowing the free exit and entrance of individuals to go or to come from other human modules. In other words, it would be the structure as a whole and the patterns of forces/bonds and relationships within it which would remain stable but, as is the case with atoms and ions moving in and out of the living cell, any given individual could leave, being replaced by another from outside, without disturbing the overall arrangement. What I now see is the possibility, difficult though it may be, and however much the scales are tilted against it, of setting up islands, human systems, bounded both spatially and psy-chically, where a truly human education can begin and where real personal growth and development can take place in a context of personal relationships. Much of the knowledge and understanding necessary to set up such bounded human systems is now available as never before but this time we must learn from nature and from what biological systems have to teach us, through the slow painful process of evolution, stretching back over millions of years. We must learn what the living cell and other living systems had to learn – that a boundary must be created but one which allows and manages appropriate exchange with the environment and is neither too open nor too closed. We must not make the mistake of the communes of the 1960s, which shut themselves off from the world to create the perfect society and then withered and died.

If these 'human islands' are to achieve anything, they must involve the whole person and the whole life cycle from the cradle to the grave. Both male and female dimensions of sexuality must find their expressions in each person, and both women and men must be able to participate fully and equally and each make their full contribution to the whole. They must be places where all can come to 'live' and to 'learn', to 'work' and to 'play', and, more importantly, simply to 'be'.

It is quite clear now that no partial concept of education, such as our own present school system, can ever really achieve anything different; it can only further reinforce the schizophrenic splitting process which is more and more affecting all aspects of our society. New curricula, smaller classes and all the other current slogans for progress all mean nothing and will achieve nothing. If the bounded human system which I am proposing is to have success as a 'human island' where real change and growth can take place in the midst of a fragmenting and deteriorating society, then all these issues will have to be faced and worked at unflinchingly.

This growing voice calling for decentralization and devolution coming from many parts of the world should not be misunderstood as a regression to parochialism or some form of primitive tribal culture. There can be no question of humanity turning backwards; on the contrary, the growth of consciousness, education and under-standing, the vastly increased potential for personal relationship, have all become possible with the growth of modern technology and com-munications. What is required is a further development of technology and even more advanced systems of communication but a technology utilized economically with careful management of scarce energy resources, subjugated to serve the genuine needs of human beings. This would allow further automation of heavy technology, thus permitting human beings greater freedom to develop the primary infrastructure of society. Were such an infrastructure of personalized human modules (basically self-running neighbourhoods and communities) to be built up, then central functions could look very different. While it is impossible at this stage to say exactly what form these would take they should be able to take on more of a coordinating role, guiding and influencing the basically self-running local structures, planning for the future and supervising central technology. The present top-heavy Civil Service and government departments, and multi-state bureaucracies, such as that in the EEC headquarters in Brussels, could thus be vastly trimmed down and hopefully replaced, to a greater extent, by impermanent working parties, task groups and planning think-tanks. These could come together to do a job and then break up. Human beings could thus preserve much more of their individual and group energies for the primary human structures of society concerned with ordinary living.

This groping for a different way is appearing in various countries and under the guise of differing ideologies but I think a much deeper logic than any of the present political or philosophical systems is at work, a deeper logic which is coming from the sheer necessity for human beings to resolve their relationship to the world, and to each other, if they are to survive. Humans who, for almost the total period since they first appeared on this planet, have been struggling with nature are now – as the pressure of the human layer covering the surface of the earth increases – coming face to face with themselves. This is the crux of the human question, which has totally altered within the last hundred years. It is one on which our health and sanity and, unless we can solve it, the continued existence of human life on this planet depends.

20. *To Be or Not to Be*
(Doing vs Being)

This is a section from the first draft of my book *Music and Madness*; it was not included in the final publication. In this section I am concerned with the current state of society, the problems of pollution and the general ecological deterioration of the planet.

> All fixed, fast frozen relations, with their train of ancient and removable prejudices and opinions, are swept away, all new formed ones become antiquated before they can ossify. All that is solid melts into air, all that is holy is profaned, and man is at last compelled to face with sober senses his real conditions of life and his relations with his kind.
>
> All old-established national industries have been destroyed, or are daily being destroyed. They are dislodged . . . by industries that no longer work up indigenous raw material, but raw material drawn from the remotest of zones; industries whose produces are consumed, not only at home, but in every quarter of the globe. In place of the old wants, satisfied by the productions of the country, we find new ones, requiring for their satisfaction the products of distant lands . . .
>
> Karl Marx, *The Communist Manifesto*, 1848

ENTER homo sapiens. For the greater part of the two million years or more since human beings appeared on this planet, tribal or hunter-gatherer clusters lived in a more or less harmonious relationship with all the other living systems within the biosphere. Of course, violence and the continuous cycles of creativity and destruction were always present in nature, and human communities were no exception. Nevertheless, because of their relative powerlessness throughout all of this period, human beings were not in a position to disturb or interfere with the overall balancing forces of nature, or the stability of the biosphere.

267

Conventional wisdom dates the beginnings of fundamental change in this relationship with the advent of the Neolithic revolution, which occurred somewhere between six and ten thousand years ago. I have long suspected that the early human civilizations of the Middle East and those of Central and South America were not the beginning of modern civilization as has been suggested. Indeed, recent work would suggest that the great cities around the Indus and Saraswatti rivers in northern India were considerably earlier, going back as far as 7000 or 8000BC. However, there is now a considerable body of evidence to suggest that none of these civilizations, even that of the Indus valley, of which we have archaeological and historical knowledge, may have been the beginning.

We know now that, prior to the meltdown following the last glacial maximum, which occurred somewhere between 17,000 and 10,000 years ago, there were extensive coastal areas of dry land in various parts of the world – around northern and southern India, in the Mediterranean and the Persian Gulf as well as in the Atlantic – which were submerged during that period. All over the ancient world there are stories of great floods and it may well be that there were advanced human civilizations in these coastal areas which were destroyed at that time. This would mean that the great civilizations which we know about were not the beginning but rather grew up from the few survivors of these earlier civilizations. I mention this possibility because it could well be that history will repeat itself and that we are approaching another period of natural destruction of our present civilization.

Whatever about that, it is from this time onwards that the change in human consciousness, and all that has followed from this, began to slowly develop. It was only from the Renaissance period, however, with the changes in scientific thinking and technological development in Europe, that our interference with the delicate balance of the natural world began to accelerate. Following on from the reductionist legacy of Francis Bacon and Descartes, the male thrust for power, fanned by selfishness and greed, moved into the ascendant. The first expression of this was the colonial expansion of the European nations – the Spanish and Portuguese, followed later by the French, British, Belgians and others. These colonial powers destroyed, pillaged and raped civilized and highly developed societies in Central and South America, in Africa and Asia. They enslaved and wiped out whole populations in their lust for power and insatiable greed, to take for themselves the wealth and resources of these lands. They took over, and developed enormously, the obscenity of slavery, shipping millions of black slaves to the Americas.

Then, at the beginning of the nineteenth century, further development of technology ushered in the Industrial Revolution, first in Britain and then in the rest of Europe and the United States. The Industrial Revolution brought with it the growth of all kinds of *purposive* organizations – government departments, banks, larger and larger schools, colleges and universities, hospitals and voluntary organizations. The driving force behind this was partly philosophical. Following the reformation in Protestant countries like Switzerland and Britain, the Calvinist and Puritan ideology saw industrious work, worldly success and the material rewards resulting from this as a sign of divine predestination. From this came the Protestant work ethic, what has become known as the Wasp Culture: White, Anglo-Saxon, Protestant.

Most significant was the emergence of the first generation of corporate enterprises. One of the first of these was the British East India Company, which was given a Royal Charter by Queen Elizabeth I. With the help of the psychopathic personality, Clive of India, this became so powerful that it finally controlled most of India, even running its own private army. There was an ironic sequel to this. The East India Company fell into debt and to help it financially the British government imposed a tea tax on its American colonies. The response of the residents was the famous Boston Tea Party, which threw the corporation's tea into the harbour, and this led on to the American Revolution. Because of what had happened, after the revolution the American fathers of the new nation went to great lengths to draw up a constitution, which would place ultimate authority with the people, maintaining tight control on private corporations. Near the end of the Civil War, President Abraham Lincoln, who was deeply concerned about this very issue, wrote a letter to a colonel fighting in his army:

> We may congratulate ourselves that this cruel war is nearing its end. It has cost a vast amount of treasure and blood . . . it has indeed been a trying hour for the Republic; but I see in the near future a crisis approaching that unnerves me and causes me to tremble for the safety of my country. As a result of the war,

corporations have been enthroned, and an era of corruption in high places will follow, and the money power of the country will endeavour to prolong its reign by working on the prejudices of the people until all wealth is aggregated in a few hands, and the Republic is destroyed. I feel at this moment more anxiety for the safety of my country than ever before, even in the midst of war. God grant that my suspicions may prove groundless.

His words were indeed prophetic.

The introduction of mass production methods by energetic and ambitious entrepreneurs like Henry Ford and others, as well as those who became known as the 'robber barons', such as Carnegie, Rockefeller, etc., created the first great industrial empires. The latter were not so much hard-working entrepreneurs as opportunists who cornered the market on certain key resources such as steel and oil.

The main point I want to make is that, although these men may have been ruthless and following in the footsteps of the colonial Conquistadors, the industrial empires they created were personal to them and controlled by them personally. Indeed, several of them in their later life became great philanthropists. Their efforts were a response to the aspirations of an expanding industrial society, whether it was a desire for machinery of all kinds, for new forms of transport – the railways, the motor car – or for key resources such as oil and steel. Nevertheless, the enterprises they established were still limited, in that they operated within national borders and were usually involved in producing one commodity, such as the Ford motor car.

By the dawn of the twentieth century, all of this began to change. As Noreena Hertz, in her book *The Silent Takeover*, describes it:

> By the end of the nineteenth century governments in Europe and the United States had begun to accept that they had respon-sibilities beyond those of internal order and external security. There was a growing realization that capitalism was responsible for great cruelties and a sense that the state should play a role in alleviating the harshest elements of the system through some sort of social intervention. And this nascent feeling gained pace over the first half of the twentieth century, through the Wall Street Crash and the Great Depression, then World War Two, events which brought the first mass unemployment, and then even wider human suffering . . . By the middle of the last century most developed states had begun to establish systems of

social security and welfare themselves . . . The dominant mindset was that no citizen was to be allowed to fall below a minimum standard of overall wellbeing . . . Not only did the state become the main provider of welfare during the post-war period, it also became the key economic actor . . . And neo-classical liberalism – a system that had largely left the market alone to regulate economic life – was displaced, in the west at least, by Keynesian economics.

In spite of these efforts in western democracies to create a more humane society, during this same period a quite different generation of corporate enterprises had been making their appearance. This was the arrival on the scene of the giant transnational corporations. By the late 1970s, disillusionment had set in with the idea of the welfare state and big government, which had given rise to the growth of enormous state bureaucracies, unwieldy civil service departments and inefficient public enterprises. Keynes, a man whose teachings had been adopted wholesale by the west in an attempt to rebuild a world shattered by war and to establish a secure capitalist bloc as a bulwark against communism, was relegated to a footnote in history. The watershed came in 1979 and 1980, with the election first of Margaret Thatcher and then of Ronald Reagan, politicians from the new right who enthusiastically advocated the free market and were determinedly hostile to the concept of an interventionist state. Rejecting Keyensianism, the grocer's daughter and the Hollywood actor embraced the views of economists such as Milton Friedman and Frederick Hayek (Hertz).

As the authors of *Gaian Democracies*, Roy Madron and John Jopling point out: 'since the late 1970s, neo-liberal economic ideology has shaped the policies of almost all western democracies. Its principles include the primacy of private property, economic growth, the need for free trade to stimulate growth, competition, the unrestricted "free market", privatization and the absence of government regulation. The theory is a highly selective interpretation of the classical, mainstream tradition of economics.' They continue: 'This economic ideology is not an accident. It is a result of a concerted, well financed, utterly determined and increasingly globalized campaign, led originally by the Austrian economist Frederick Von Hayek, his colleague Milton Friedman, and other members of the so-called "Chicago school". It is the theory of economics deliberately developed to serve the interests of the owners of capital.' This is in fact harking back to the ideas of Adam Smith in the eighteenth century, which first introduced the theme of laissez-faire. He also first introduced the concept that prices would be determined in 'free' markets by the balancing effects of supply and demand.

This creed of free-market capitalism, Anglo-American style, was soon disseminated across the world. Aided by developments in communications and the media, which ensured that ideas quickly spread, and by the single-mindedness of the neo-liberal international lending institutions, the IMF and the World Bank, who were promoting the so-called 'Washington's Consensus', capitalism's foot soldiers marched from Latin America to East Asia, India and most of Africa, from old and declining capitalist nations such as the UK, to vigorous capitalistic economies with strong traditions of regulation such as Germany, and eventually even to the former command economies of the communist world. The 'market' became the catch-phrase of the 1980s and 1990s as liberalized states bore witness to the benefits of the capitalist system (Hertz).

All of this coincided with the collapse of communism in the Soviet Union in 1990. Since then, globalization has had a free rein and is spreading its tentacles all over the planet. This is what the authors of *Gaian Democracies* term the 'global monetocracy', the true purpose of which they say is that of money growth in order to maintain the current 'debt-based money system'. Almost all the money we use (i.e. all except the notes and coins, which today are about 3% of the total) came into existence as a result of a bank agreement to make a loan to a customer at interest. This is why it is called 'debt-money'. This system has several extremely important consequences. First it gives the bank a free lunch. They are, in effect, able to print money and lend it out at interest. That the governments of 'western democracies' permit the banks to continue to enjoy this massive subsidy, and for this extraordinary privilege to be off the agenda of public debate, is a tribute to the power of the 'elite consensus'.

Secondly, the effect of this method of creating money is that the economy has to grow in order to avoid collapsing. The fact that the necessary growth can be achieved only by increasing the total level of debt makes the economy heavily dependent on confidence. People borrow when they are optimistic about being able to repay with interest. Businesses borrow when they want to expand.

Confidence in the future is self-fulfilling; so is the lack of it. The economy therefore constantly moves between boom and bust; it is systemically unstable (Madron and Jopling).

Looking at these economic developments from a systemic perspective and how they impinge on us as human beings, a rather different picture begins to emerge. For me, it comes down to the question of 'doing vs being'. These business enterprises, which eventually grew to become the giant transnational corporations of today, originally started in response to the materialistic demands of an expanding industrial society. The same could be said of the government departments and all the other organizations that have grown up over the past hundred years.

What is less often recognized is that, over the same period, the age-old forms of human community such as the original tribal settlements, feudal clusters and, more recently, villages and small towns have largely disappeared. These natural human settlements, even the cities of the past, developed in relation to natural resources primarily in order to *be*. What they did and what they produced in order to survive and maintain themselves in existence was secondary to the main thrust – to *be*. Thus the celebration of life and of their *being* was central to their existence. For many thousands of years, indeed for the major part of the two million years or more since human beings first made their appearance on this planet, this delicate balance of human settlement versus the natural environment was maintained in a relatively harmonious relationship with nature, through network cycles of negative feedback. This is not to say that such human settlements were perfect. War and violence in the desperate struggle for survival often marred them.

Over the past two centuries, however, all of this has changed: first the tribal settlements, then the villages and the small towns have largely disappeared or have altered their character totally as part of the giant urban conurbations which now exist. The extended family, too, has gone and even the nuclear family is now under threat. Giant corporations, bureaucratic state departments and organizations of all kinds have taken their place. These are primarily task-oriented enterprises, concerned with *doing*. Yet, because they are composed of living human beings, they inevitably tend, as they progress and grow, to take on the characteristics of a living system. Thus we find giant corporations becoming involved in functions

273

related to the life cycle – providing housing for their workers, crèches, swimming pools and fitness clubs, and various other social and community-like activities. In this way, they take on more and more the characteristics of self-organizing living systems.

However, because they depend ultimately on tasks or production of some kind and must satisfy the financial concerns of their share-holders, if the value of their shares on the stock exchange fall or their cash-flow fails for even a few weeks, they can go out of existence, with the loss of thousands of jobs and all the other human activities which are the lifeblood of a living community. For this reason, they can never be more than 'pseudo-living' systems and can never embody the full definition of a genuine living system, like a town or village that has come into existence primarily to celebrate its own *being*.

As I mentioned earlier, a third-order system of this kind, however powerful, because it is of recent origin, is essentially a new beginning. Therefore, these 'blind monsters', even though they have entangled thousands of sensitive, sophisticated, conscious human beings within them, are only capable of quite primitive behaviours, similar to the dinosaurs of the ancient past – they can show *fight* or *flight,* take over another corporation or be taken over, expand and grow or retreat and go into decline. In this way we can see them, in their pursuit of eco-nomic growth, destroy whole indigenous communities in developing countries; they can put an aged widow out of her tenement flat, where she has spent a whole lifetime, in order to demolish the building. Yet the human beings working in such an organization as individuals in their ordinary life outside would never behave in such an insensitive fashion. This kind of primitive, insensitive behaviour is just as true of trade unions, social welfare departments or health boards as it is of transnational companies. I think this fact is fre-quently misunderstood. People would say that individual teachers who have dedicated their lives to educating children would never deny these young people say, a summer programme, but the teachers union can do precisely this. I could provide examples of this kind of behaviour by organizations and corporations ad nauseam, but I think the point I am making is clear enough.

A strange twist enters the picture here, which I didn't realize until recently. As I have mentioned already, the fathers of the American constitution were extremely concerned to protect the ordinary American citizen from the power of unbridled corporations.

Abraham Lincoln, in the letter that I quoted, shared this concern. I am indebted to Paul Kingsnorth, in his book *One No, Many Yeses*, for this insight. Although in the late nineteenth century there was, obviously, no knowledge of systems theory, or of my view that giant corporations are a form of 'pseudo-living' system, yet what happened would suggest that those involved already had this awareness.

After the war, Lincoln's fears that corporations would be 'enthroned' began to be realized – and the means of their coronation was to be the courts. A series of court cases, brought by corporations with the specific intent of bending the law to their advantage, saw judges granting more powers to corporations by way of generous or downright suspicious interpretations of the constitution. The most notorious court decision came in 1886, when the innocuously named 'Santa Clara County vs Southern Pacific Railroad' case was interpreted to mean that a corporation was a 'natural person' under the constitution. A further raft of court cases confirmed the new concept of 'corporate personhood', and corporations began to claim constitutional rights. The Supreme Court ruled that the fourteenth amendment to the constitution now gave a corporation – legally a 'person', after all – the right not to have its 'privileges or immunities' 'abridged': no state shall 'deprive any person of life, liberty or property without due process of law'. By 1876, another US President, Rutherford Hayes, was lamenting the coming-to-pass of Lincoln's prophecy: 'This is a government of the people, by the people and for the people no longer,' he said. 'It is a government of corporations, by corporations and for corporations.'

If we look back for a moment at primitive cultures, we find that the primary social unit is a group of families, living and working together, which addresses itself to the task of survival. On through history, until recent times, this has been the pattern. The primary social unit for survival and for transmission of the culture has always been a group of families. This has taken various forms at different times, from the tribal settlement, the extended family, the hamlet, the village, the small market town with its hinterland, to the cluster of neighbourhoods making up great human-sized cities of the past – such as the city states of ancient Greece or Rome, Paris, London, or Dublin – at the high point of their development, before they became oversized anonymous conurbations. It is not until we come to modern society and the much-lauded phenomenon of globalization that we find the isolated nuclear family as it exists today. I think one has only to pause for a moment to realize that, however much we may preach about the sacredness of the family as the 'fundamental unit of society', this isolated, fragile social unit is clearly quite incapable, on its own, of sustaining virtually any of the basic functions of survival, and is in quite an ineffective position to undertake the responsibilities that are being laid at its door.

It may well be asked where, or to whom, does the isolated family turn for help in facing its task of survival, and for the development of the coming generation. Most of the previous organic or personally based forms of society have been pushed aside and allowed to decay or disappear altogether. What, however, has taken their place? As the situation polarizes we are left with, on the one hand, the isolated nuclear family and, on the other, the state – with its government departments growing everywhere and extending their tentacles into every aspect of life – the transnational and giant corporations, the massive bureaucracies of organized religion, the trade unions and organized professions. The isolated family, therefore, has no choice but to hand its essential functions on to one or other of these impersonal state, commercial or professional organizations.

This is the real struggle that has been going on during our time as the spectre of globalization spreads across the world in all directions: not the apparent battles between right and left, between socialism and capitalism, but the relentless transfer of power and control from the peripheral to the central, from the small to the large, from the personal to the anonymous and institutional. This is the real change which has been taking place, and it is still intensifying with every year that passes. Small private businesses amalgamate to form corporations, corporations merge to form transnational companies, government departments expand to take over control of more and more areas of our personal lives and even national, supposedly democratic, governments are superseded and become the lackeys of the 'blind monsters' we call transnational corporations. Not surprisingly, given the personal, self-organizing nature of human beings, all of this leads to problems and, once this polarization has begun, it sets up a progressive chain reaction. Because the family cannot manage the ordinary tasks necessary for survival for which it has traditionally been responsible, these are passed on and, one after another, necessarily become defined as problems for society. These problems then have to be tackled either by the state or by some other impersonal, corporate or voluntary institution.

Let us take just one example: the provision of shelter and protection of the family from disaster. In primitive times, habitation and such protection from disaster as was possible was provided by the tribe as a whole, working in some form of mutual cooperation. Nowadays, we expect a much more complete protection from every kind of disaster – from sickness, death or injury – and, of course, we expect a house or apartment to live in, but where is all this to come from? Clearly, the single family is in an even less satisfactory position to provide protection for itself from all these hazards than was the traditional community. So, once again, the responsibility has to be passed on to the speculative builder, to county councils and departments of local government.

Building societies, banks and multinational insurance corporations now come into the picture, but the loan for our house or the pension we receive on retirement are not given to us for nothing. On the contrary, for many of us the reality is that we struggle for most of our lives to pay off the mortgages, loans and interest and to keep up the insurance premiums. Thus we devote a major proportion of our human energy and total working life to this purpose, gaining in the end of all a poorly designed and badly built home and a pension which, by the time we get it, is often eaten away by inflation. Nor does the matter end there, for our human energy, transformed through work into insurance premiums, mortgages and loan payments, cannot simply be left to lie dormant. It has to be put to use, to ensure the survival and to maintain the profits of the building societies and insurance corporations and to safeguard the security of their shareholders. For this reason, it cannot be used to build better communities or to provide a better life for those of us who contribute. Instead, it has to be invested where the smallest risk is entailed and where it will earn the highest possible financial return. This appears to be in financing giant office blocks, high-class apartment dwellings for the wealthy and large suburban shopping centres, which apparently bring the most profitable returns for investments.

When I look around a city such as Dublin and see grotesque prestige office blocks appearing everywhere and find myself getting angry and wanting to protest at the destruction of a living city, I am forced to a rather frightening and uncomfortable conclusion. It becomes apparent that what I see is not simply the doing of wealthy, foreign property developers but is steadily contributed to, and very largely financed by, you and me. In this way, each of us is doing our bit to destroy and pollute the very city we live in.

As more and more problems are generated in this way, attempts have to be made to solve them by the impersonal bureaucratic forces of society. Thus human beings have to transfer an increasing amount of time from the home or community to more and more of their lives spent at work. There is constant traffic chaos and people are spending longer and longer in their cars trying to get to and from work. Young couples are moving further and further out, travelling up to 50km or more to get to and from work. This adds several hours on to the length of the working day. The cost of mortgages means both partners now must work outside the home, with the additional cost of child-care. Thus people are subjected to an increasingly stressful lifestyle in order to survive. The evidence of this is all around us – the excessive use of alcohol, particularly among young women, and other forms of substance abuse, comfort-eating leading to obesity, and suicide, which is now the commonest form of death in young men in this country. We are seeing a marked increase in violence on the streets, road rage and so on. What is alarming about this is the anonymous nature of it. Most people who are attacked are just making their way home and are attacked often by several others who don't even know them. These attacks are usually not for money or to settle a grievance but simply to satisfy meaningless aggression. There seems to be a great deal of undirected frustration and anger out there among the young.

At a deeper level, there has been a marked shift from existence simply as human beings to identification with a role. The endless splitting process of specialization, moving on to ever-finer, sub-specialization, means that somewhere along the assembly line the individual's personal life becomes firmly attached to the *role*, profession or trade. These no longer are simply descriptions of what a person *does* but rather of what they *are*, the most real part of them. Little is left over to be a citizen or a person. The process does not end there, for in modern society we find ourselves entrained in numerous roles, often in contradiction with one another. As degrees, diplomas and qualifications take over, testing procedures and exam-inations, by means of which persons are certified, assume a dominant place. These now become the main determinants of training programmes, of courses, which increasingly have to be tailored to prepare people for 'the examination'. What is more, entrance criteria now have to be developed to ensure the fitness and acceptability of those who are to enter. The Leaving Certificate, or graduation from school of whatever type, comes to dominate all education in schools from childhood onwards as, without it, all vocational avenues into adult society are closed.

Thus as the chain-reaction turns full circle, all of life becomes a treadmill of teaching, courses, examinations, certification, one human being competing ruthlessly with another to gain acceptance in a 'role', to sneak a place for themselves as a 'component' on the assembly line. Those who do not make it – and, with globalization, given the evermore oppressive criteria for entrance and acceptance, these are an increasing number – become the refuse for the human scrap heap, the 'redundant', the 'passive social welfare recipients', the 'chronically unemployed', the 'poor', the 'sick', and the 'chronic attendees in hospital outpatients and doctor's offices', the 'delinquent', the 'vagrant' and the 'petty recidivist criminal'. Of course, if we had not all of these, what would we do with all the social workers, doctors, nurses and charitable and voluntary workers? As the turning of ordinary life, and the different stages of the life cycle, into problems takes place, ever more problems are generated. This necessitates turning more and more human beings into 'roles', as technicians to deal with them. All of this supplies the nourishment to ever larger corporations and bureaucracies, the employees of which fill the office blocks which are choking our cities.

Then there are the wider effects of globalization on the environment. As the authors of *Gaian Democracies* point out, this is the inevitable consequence of a system in a state of positive, reinforcing feedback. Over 11,000 species of plants and animals (all of which have as much right to live on the planet as we do) are now known to face a high risk of extinction, including 24% of all mammals and 12% of all bird species. In the last thirty-two years the impact of amplified man has resulted in a 35% deterioration in the earth's ecosystems. Forest cover has shrunk by 12%, the oceans' biodiversity by one-third and freshwater ecosystems by 55%. Data for 350 kinds of mammals, birds, reptiles and fish disclose that the numbers of many species have more than halved. E.F. Schumacher, back in 1973, in his classic book *Small Is Beautiful*, had already pointed to the dangers which lay ahead: 'Today we are concerned not only with social malaise but also, most urgently, with a malaise of the ecosystem or biosphere which threatens the very survival of the human race.'

In his more recent book, *The Hidden Connections*, Fritjof Capra summarizes the prevailing view of international globalization:

> According to the doctrine of economic globalization – known as 'neo-liberalism', or 'the Washington consensus' – the free trade agreements imposed by the WTO on its member countries will increase global trade; this will create a global economic expansion; and global economic growth will decrease poverty, because its benefits will eventually 'trickle down to all'.

In the same chapter he further states:

> The process of economic globalization was purposefully designed by the leading capitalist countries (the so-called 'G-7 Nations'), the major transnational corporations and by global financial institutions – most importantly, the World Bank, the International Monetary Fund (IMF) and the World Trade Organization (WTO) – that were created for that purpose.

The reality of what is actually happening could hardly be more different. The authors of *Gaian Democracies* provide some alarming statistics. In the USA, 10% of the population controls 90% of the nation's wealth. Between 1988 and 2000, the average pay of America's top ten executives increased from $19.3 million to $154 million, while the majority of Americans lost income. At the latest count, 497 billionaires share the planet with 1.6 billion people living in extreme poverty. In many countries, black women living in rural areas are the worst affected by extreme poverty. Finally, 40% of the world's people suffer from micronutrient deficiencies.

In his book *The Myth of Development*, the Peruvian Oswaldo De Rivero has analysed the experience of all so-called developing countries under globalization; thirty-seven now have non-viable economies. There is another large group in Latin America, Asia and the Middle East that are incubating symptoms of non-viability. The two groups have in common 'an export structure that is technologically functional with the global economy'. Within the current system, there is no prospect of providing jobs for 700 million unemployed workers. The greater part of humankind continues to exist with low incomes, in poverty, technologically backward and governed by authoritarian regimes or, at best, in low-powered democracies. For a great many countries, their only hope will be merely to survive, in some manner, the challenges of the technological revolution and global competition. If their situation should worsen, they could implode into violence, as ungovernable chaotic entities, as has already happened with some countries in Africa, the Balkans, Asia and Latin America.

The authors of *Gaian Democracies* go on to point out that these very gloomy assessments are echoed by the International Monetary Fund (IMF) and the World Economic Outlook Report 2000. This noted, despite the spectacular economic growth of the past century, the quality of life of one-fifth of the world's population has actually regressed in relative, and sometimes absolute, terms. This spreading poverty in the midst of economic growth was described by the IMF's deputy research director, Flemming Larson, as 'one of the greatest economic failures of the twentieth century'.

Paul Kingsnorth, in his book *One No, Many Yeses*, sums up the statement behind globalization:

> the pursuit of this dream, we have been assured for years, is the best – the only – way to meet every challenge facing humanity, from abolishing poverty to preventing environmental catastrophe. Sit back, let the market work its magic, watch the cake grow, eat until you are full. Yummy. And yet almost three decades of chasing this dream have shown it to be a nightmare for much of the world. Compare, for instance, the world today with the world as it was before the neo-liberal experiment began in the 1970s. Measured in conventional economic terms, we are certainly richer. Gross world product in 1960 was $10 trillion; today it is $43.2 trillion – over four times as high. Where that wealth has gone though is another matter entirely. In 1960, the 20% of the world's population that lived in the rich industrialized countries of the west had 30 times the income of the poorest 20% of humanity. Today, we have 74 times as much. A stunning 2.8 billion people – over half the world's population – live on less than $2 a day, and this figure is 10% higher than it was in the late 1980s. The richest 1% of the world's population receives as much income as the poorest 57%. The richest 10% of the population of just one country – the USA – have a combined income greater than the poorest 2 billion people on earth. The assets of the three richest people on the planet are more

than the combined GNP of all the least developed countries put together.

Work – Life – Balance

A range of innovations are being researched and applied, such as new ways to organize work, develop and meet individual and business needs, flexible work arrangements, part-time options, telecommuting, a compressed work week, job sharing, and a recognition that the needs of people may change at different stages of the life cycle. The importance of showing respect for equality of opportunity for all staff places joint rights and responsibilities on workers and managers to find workable solutions: stock options for staff at all levels; employers to adopt a management style that reflects respect for work life; managers to be encouraged to experiment with new ways of doing things; two-way communication, between employer and employee; a shared vision where both employer and employee share responsibility and benefits; staff training, training for managers, counselling services, contracts of employment being made clear and employees understanding their statutory rights.

The needs of people with caring responsibilities are also being considered, in particular working parents. This may involve a focus on women and equal opportunities, paid maternity and paternity leave, financial assistance for childcare, on-site childcare centres, pre-natal care, parenting support groups and elder care assessment and case management, etc.

Such policies have been shown to improve staff well-being and quality of life and are not having a negative effect on productivity and profitability. Research in many business and organizations has demonstrated that there is increased staff loyalty and commitment, reduced staff turnover with a saving on recruitment costs, increased productivity, reduced absenteeism, reduced training costs and an enhanced corporate image, which is a plus factor with customers helping to cultivate new consumer markets.

Tinkering with the Problem

There seems to be no doubt that such innovations and staff-enhancing policies, where they can be applied, are beneficial in the workplace but these attempts to humanize the environment and relationships at work are only tinkering with the problem. They will do little to alter the ills in our society. Indeed, such policies all boil down to attempts to create the sort of environment and human relationships which would have existed in an ordinary village or small country town in former times. None of this is having any effect or likely to have any effect on the alarming and negative aspects of our consumer society, to which attention has already been drawn. Also, when such considerations are discussed, it is almost always in relation to the needs of, and effects on, adults whose personalities are already formed. It is an entirely different matter when the requirements of human development and the needs of children are taken into consideration.

When I was a child, we went every summer to the farm down in County Wexford where my father was born and raised, and his ancestors before him. That's more than half a century ago now. I still remember the joy of being in direct contact with nature, with trees and fields and growing things. On that farm they produced nearly everything they needed. They had their own vegetable garden, which supplied all the vegetables they required. They had cows, sheep, ducks and free-range hens to provide their meat, dairy produce, eggs and so on. They grew their own grain. The wheat was sent to the water-powered mill less than a mile away, from which the sacks of flour were returned and stored in the granary. From this they made their bread and cakes. They had a small dairy, where they separated out the cream from the milk and churned beautiful country butter. There was an orchard with apples, pears, plums and currants from which they made jams and desserts. All this provided a full, nutritious and varied diet. This was a reasonably prosperous farm, which provided virtually all the needs of those living there. They only had to buy a few things, like tea, clothes, etc. The culture was one of an extended family with farmworkers, a couple of servants, children and adults. All the relationships, human and economic, were close at hand, within a radius of a few miles. This was a world of direct face-to-face contact with friends and neighbours, comprehensible to a child. I can still feel that sense of belonging. It helped set me up for life.

Contrast this with our present society, where the economic interconnections extend over thousands of miles, and yet where we are lucky if we even know the name of the person living next door or in the next apartment. Everything that farm produced was organic. This was typical of mixed farming, which was fairly general around the country at that time. Think what a favourable position we would be in now if this were still the current form of farming here, when organic produce is at a premium and is being sought after all over Europe. If only we could have managed to avoid the madness of the Common Agricultural Policy, with its total preoccupation with mechanized farming. We know now how badly this has backfired, with its beef and dairy mountains, which nobody knows what to do with.

It would be neither possible nor desirable to turn the clock back and to attempt to re-create the community life of former times but the fact remains that, the more we look deeply into ourselves and understand our physiology and the way our bodies work, the clearer it becomes that we are formed to live in a very direct relationship to the natural environment and to each other. For us to be sane and healthy, we must relate to a holistic world, so that all the essential aspects of life bear a clear relationship to one another. This is the very essence of our 'being' as living creatures to be self-organizing. And that in turn implies a reasonable degree of personal freedom and control over our lives. It follows that the context within which we need to have our 'being' must be intimate enough to be understandable in human terms. An essential part of this is our fundamental need to relate to nature and to each other as persons. I mentioned some of the innovations being introduced into businesses and institutions. These more human and compassionate interventions, which the corporate world is being forced to introduce if it is to survive, simply represent a watered-down version of our basic human needs but, if our fundamental need for an understandable world of human size is essential for us as adults, how much more vital and urgent is this for a child's development.

None of us simply come into existence as adults, already formed. On the contrary, we are formed out of the matrix of relationships and environmental influences which we absorb from the moment of conception onwards. If these influences are remote, anonymous and fragmented, as is increasingly the picture in our economically driven society, then the adult who emerges will show the negative characteristics that are becoming more evident daily among the younger generation of our society. Nor does the matter rest there for, as one generation succeeds another, this deterioration in behaviour and ethical mores will become ever more manifest.

A quarter of a century ago, I wrote a paper on the decline of the nuclear family, which was evident to me even then. There I said:

> It seems clear now that satisfactory development depends ultimately on an open, loving relationship between parents, out of which will grow naturally the right sort of healthy, trusting and intimate relationship between them and their children. This is the simple fact that emerges from all the studies of human development, which have been carried out over the past fifty years. There is, quite simply, no substitute for positive loving adult relationships if we are to grow healthy children.

Further on in this paper, I continued:

> What is the situation we find now? Either one parent is absent altogether or the father is away all day at work leaving a lonely frustrated wife at home sitting isolated, often on tranquillizers, in a poorly designed box of a house, or, as is perhaps more likely nowadays, both parents are at work leaving the children in a crèche or in the hands of some more or less unsatisfactory parent substitute . . . frequently each parent finds relationships with colleagues at work to have more meaning, and life generally to be more interesting than the relationship which they have with each other at home. They come together for an hour or two in the evening to try to re-establish contact but perhaps with less and less of mutual common interest. Even here the pain of trying to keep open a relationship which has less and less meaning can be avoided by burying themselves in the passive entertainment of the television; the peripheral terminal of the corporate outside world piped directly into every home. This is the shambles of broken and fragmented relationships which we call the family in contemporary society, the institution which is supposed to pass on the subtle and delicate thread of civilization to the coming generation.

When I wrote this back in 1975, I was accused of being negative and overly pessimistic but, in view of all that has happened since, I think few would argue that my prediction was far off the mark.

Human Needs

The human 'needs' that we have in order to live a full and fruitful life are actually relatively few. The difficulty is that our economically driven society has filled us with all kinds of 'wants', for things we do not actually need, nor do they in the long run contribute to real contentment or happiness. In order to increase production, these 'wants' are constantly stimulated by mass advertising and hence a vicious circle is established. With our present technology, let alone the developments which are around the corner, the human needs of the entire world population could be met with a mere fraction of the present industrial output but, of course, if this were to happen, we are told it would have a disastrous effect on jobs. This is why we have constant demands from economists for an increase in the economic growth rate and politicians here congratulating themselves if the growth rate is increasing. This same economic growth and over-production is, however, directly causing all the ills – pollution, global warming, etc. – that are threatening the very existence of life on this planet. The logical flaw behind all this thinking is the belief that the only way to distribute wealth is through jobs and employment. As the ecological pressure due to this economic, materialistic madness, and all the other negative aspects of globalization increase, I believe we will be forced to seek alternative ways of approaching these dilemmas.

Mae-Wan Ho, in her book *Genetic Engineering: Dream or Nightmare*, puts this craziness in perspective:

> the microbes do not compete, each against the other. On the contrary, they engage in unbridled cooperation, sharing even their most valuable assets for survival against the onslaught of selfish, myopic human beings. It is high time we put this 'warfare with nature' mentally behind us and started learning in earnest how to live sustainably and healthily with nature.

Enough is Enough

Given this disastrous picture across the world, the situation is rapidly polarizing. When one hears of 'globalization' it is usually assumed that this refers to the picture I have been describing. In fact, there are in reality two forms of 'globalization'. One is enormously powerful and is being spearheaded by the 'blind corporate monsters', which are locked into a state of positive feedback and are running rampant across the world, destroying everything ecological in their path. It has taken several hundred years of desperate struggle by reformers and ordinary people to establish some semblance of representative democracy among various countries, mainly in the west, but sadly such democracy that we have has become virtually irrelevant. Most national governments are now simply the lackeys of the corporate free market and it makes little difference which political party one votes in when the election comes around every few years.

However, there is another form of 'globalization' which is working away beneath the surface. This constitutes a new and quite different form of democracy. Little pockets of spontaneous activity have been emerging across many areas in the so-called developing nations – from the rebel Zapatistas in the Chiapas area in the rain-forest remnants of southern Mexico, to 'Operation Khanyisa', the campaign against disconnection of electricity by Eskom, the electricity utility in Soweto in South Africa. More and more of these pockets of spontaneous resistance by ordinary people, poverty-stricken peasants and others, are appearing every day. Similar pockets of spontaneous activity are arising in many of the wealthy developed nations as well: places like California, at the forefront of the capitalist dream. More and more young people, highly educated scientists and academics, are becoming disillusioned with what they see happening in the world.

Eco-villages are sprouting up everywhere, both in third-world countries and in the developed west. When I first heard of these movements, I thought that this is too peripheral – too little too late – to have any real effect on the way things are progressing but every week now one hears of hundreds of these 'little streams' that are coalescing and interconnecting in all sorts of ways to become a vast river, now involving some millions of ordinary human beings who are echoing to the cry of the Zapatistas – *Ya basta* ('Enough is enough'). Every time the WTO, the IMF, or the world leaders representing the G-8 nations attempt to meet, they are now met by many thousands of demonstrators, who make it increasingly difficult for them to get on with planning the next step in the destruction of this planet.

These new experiments and the creation of human-sized communities and protest movements are no longer isolated from one another. They are fast creating networks across the globe. With mobile phones, email and the internet, constant interaction and communication between human beings everywhere is now a reality. These innovations are very different from the hippie communes of the 1960s, which closed themselves off from the world in an attempt to create the perfect society, then withered and died. The current protest movements, involving many thousands of demonstrators, are ordinary people with no particular axe to grind – members of trade unions, environmentalists, politicians, anarchists, church representatives, middle-aged anti-debt campaigners and many thousands upon thousands of non-aligned but passionate people. What is unique about this movement is that no one person or organization is in charge.

The same is true of the eco-villages and ecological groups which are springing up everywhere. These should not be misunderstood as a regression to parochialism or an attempt to return to some form of primitive tribal culture. On the contrary, they are using some of the most advanced forms of architectural design and technical expertise for achieving 'sustainable living'. Nor is there any evidence of this groundswell being led by charismatic leaders or fixed ideologies. Indeed, it is simply groups of ordinary people taking power back for themselves where they live in order to survive. There can be no question of humanity turning back; on the contrary, the growth of consciousness, education and understanding, the vastly increased potential for personal and global relationships, have only become possible with the growth of modern technology and communications. What is required is a further development of technology and even more advanced systems of telecommunication, but this time a technology hopefully utilized more economically, with careful management of scarce energy resources, subjugated to serve the genuine *needs* of human beings.

If these 'human islands' are to have a real possibility of a transformation of society, this time they will need to involve the whole person and the whole life cycle, from the cradle to the grave; for women and men to participate equally, each making their full contribution to the whole. Women form half of the human race and, if full equality and balance were to be achieved between the sexes this, of itself, would alter everything in human society. Thus, if these new attempts to create human communities are to succeed and to spread, they must be places where all can come voluntarily to live, to love, to learn, to work and to play; and even more importantly, to be; to leave if they wish or move on to another community.

These efforts towards the creation of real community are only a trickle as yet and are having no discernible effect on the power system of corporate society but, as the pressure of the destructive influence of our present way of life on the environment and the biosphere builds up as a result of overproduction and economic growth, pollution, global warming, waste and traffic congestion, etc., one can see the possibility, difficult though it may be, of a real transformation of humanity beginning to emerge. The critical question is, can it take hold in time?

There is also the question of maintaining our essential technology and developing what is yet to come, for all this development of sustainable communities is only possible because of our present communication systems – the internet, mobile phones, broadband, etc. – which enable these living systems to be 'open' and constitute a worldwide movement. There is no reason why this should not be possible, along the lines of the way space technology is organized, with many small, decentralized units working as a network to assemble the finished products. At present, millions of messages are swirling around the surface of the planet. It could be that we are on the verge of the biosphere becoming conscious of itself. Taking as a starting-point the statement of Gregory Bateson that 'mind is the aggregate of differentiating parts' and de Chardin's concept of 'complexity-consciousness', it seems clear that the more complex the interactions in any living system the more the mind will develop and the more conscious the system will become. In this sense, from time immemorial, consciousness has been increasing in the biosphere but it may be that now, with human beings as the 'leading shoot', mind and self-reflexive consciousness is beginning to manifest. De Chardin spoke of human beings 'pressing up against one another' around the globe. The question is, as the complexity of all kinds of communication between people increases, will Gaia begin to manifest not only consciousness but self-consciousness?

Peter Russell, author of *The Awakening Earth*, proposed that we are moving towards a human quantum leap, towards a relatively sudden synchronization to produce a super-consciousness or universal mind, which would then regulate and bring about a more wholesome change in each of us as individuals. His view is that this would happen when a sufficient number of individuals synchronize through some form of meditation. It may well be that meditation and other forms of spiritual practice will have a role to play in this change. It is estimated that, in the United States alone, some twelve million people are now meditating regularly, not to mention all those involved in various forms of yoga and Buddhist meditation in India and the Far East generally. However, if such a quantum leap is to take place, it will involve not only direct interactions between human beings but also those mediated through the communication technologies already mentioned. It may well be that, in the midst of all the chaos of human activity at present, this is the really significant change, taking place imperceptibly in the world, beneath the surface of our awareness, and that some form of super-consciousness is developing in the biosphere. Looked at from this point of view, it could be that all the problems of human disorganization we see around us are a temporary phenomenon, because we are still at an early stage in this process.

Maybe we won't make it this time. Maybe there will be a period of widespread natural upheaval, with major destruction, and it will only be when the next civilization dawns (hopefully a purer, simpler one, based on spirituality) that the quantum leap will be achieved. It seems to me that this may be what Teilhard de Chardin envisaged with the coming of the noosphere.

Much madness is divinest sense –

To a discerning eye –

21. Management of Responsibility

This paper was not published. It arose as a result of the Tavistock Group Conferences that we ran in Dublin during the late 1970s on the theme of responsibility and leadership. This paper, written in February 1980, represented my views as a result of those experiences.

WHEN a group is formed, once the process of transaction commences between the individual elements and a boundary is drawn around this process then, given that these elements are living biological units, a higher-order system inevitably begins to come into being. Within this system the individual elements – that is the human units which make it up – can no longer be considered as separate entities. Some degree of merging necessarily commences and transactions begin to take place across the boundaries of the individual elements as the new higher-order system begins to organize itself and create its own being; that is, the process of autopoiesis of this new system begins to take place. Nevertheless, to describe it in this way or in this order of sequence is already incorrect, for it suggests that our existence as humans first begins as separate individuals, whereas in fact we enter life already embedded in a group setting. We come into being within a higher-order system such as a family, tribe or community, etc. Our individual being only emerges gradually out of the group matrix, nor could we even come into existence other than out of a process of relation within a higher-order group system. This is simply to point out that human reproduction is not a function of the individual autopoiesis but of the autopoiesis of the group.

This qualification having been made, it is nevertheless true that once individuals have come into existence then the process of forming higher-order group systems is continually taking place. Once a group is formed, there is inevitably some degree of merging or blurring of the boundaries between individuals. This allows a transfer and exchange of energy between individuals to take place, within the newly-formed boundary of the higher-order system; i.e. the group. This transfer of what is normally inside one individual into another would appear to take several forms. There can be coalescence of emotion, so that the whole group takes on a characteristic emotional tone – whether of anger, sadness, elation or whatever but a transfer of emotion can also take place into one particular member. This person then appears to carry emotion of a specific kind for the group as a whole, whether of pain, anger or sadness, while other members appear to show and experience less feeling than usual and may feel quite apathetic and disinterested. Thus a shift of energy, as well as feeling, appears to take place, so that one person or a pair carry all the activity, thinking or leadership for the group at a particular time; or a particular individual may find his attitudes or his views changing as the group moves on. He may find himself believing and hence behaving in quite a different way to what he or others would have expected of him as an individual separate from the group process.

Wherever we look in reality, whether inside an atom or inside a human being, we find opposing positive and negative forces. These are held in dynamic balance with varying degrees of stability. This would seem to be a basic principle of reality. If we look at any particular reality we inevitably find these opposing dynamic forces existing within a boundary. In any particular body or thing, not only do the opposing forces balance one another but they are bounded so that they do not normally spill over from one body into the next.

There are several comments to be made about this. This balancing of energies or forces has been found to be the nature of reality, in so far as we can discern it, inside the atom. It was also the underlying principle discerned in ancient times by the Taoist sages and in eastern philosophy generally. In very early times these ancient scientist–philosophers in India and in China came on this principle of a balance of forces or energy within all reality. These energies have been given various names – positive/negative, right/left, male/female, good/bad, etc. – but the essential point in reality is, as a Taoist would put it, 'Every reality is in a state of contradiction trying to resolve itself'.

Therefore, a state of opposing forces is always attempting to unite but the moment it joins it is already dividing again. This, as I say, appears to be the nature of reality as we know it, at least in this world: always changing, always balancing, and always attempting to resolve and unify but always dividing. Perhaps behind this, as the Taoists would say, there is an unchanging reality on which our effervescent changing reality rests but this is not something that we can discern directly.

If we speak of any particular thing and identify it as a separate body or system, then we must involve the other crucial principle of boundedness. It is not that the nature of reality differs within the specific thing or system but what enables us to identify it as a separate entity is its boundedness. The balancing energies are bounded and therefore do not merge with the rest of reality, so the concept of boundary is fundamental to the definition of any system that can be identified as something separate.

The next matter for consideration is that there are not simply things or bodies but things within things, bodies within other bodies; i.e. there is in nature a hierarchical order of systems. Once a system has been formed, once a piece of energy has been bounded, then the body or system can become the unit or building block of the next order system. Thus the atom becomes the unit out of which the molecule is built up, the molecule becomes the unit out of which the cell is created, and so on. I think the essential thing to understand here is that, while one system or body may form the basic unit or building block of another system, this does not mean as a rule that the energy is simply merged or that this first-order system loses its boundary and therefore ceases to exist as a separate entity. No, it remains as a system within a system. Nevertheless, it is now a unit (and therefore the energies within it) under the influence of the higher-order system. The degree to which this happens will depend on the overruling power of the higher-order system and the degree to which the boundaries of the units are lowered or weakened by this influence. The evidence would suggest that the balancing forces within any given system, whether in subatomic physics or in human gatherings such as football crowds or mobs, that the energies which are held in control by being bounded within a given system are not minor forces. Rather, when boundaries are smashed or weakened and these energies are allowed to coalesce and go out of balance, enormous quantities of energy may be released, as can be seen in an atomic explosion.

The point is that the same fundamental principle would appear to be operating in all of reality, in atoms or molecules or, at the biological level, in living cells, insects or humans. In all of these situations frightening energies and forces can be released when the discrete bounded and dynamically balanced systems are allowed to merge and coalesce. The formation of higher-order systems out of these delicately balanced, bounded units is fine so long as the energy is contained and properly controlled at each level. When this fails for any reason, frightening energies can be unleashed. These then coalesce and flow upwards to throw pressure on the boundary at the next level, where it must be held if it is not to flow onwards again, like water bursting a dam or a river overflowing its banks.

To turn to the human situation, I think this is the process which is at work when we deal with a human group vis à vis an individual: the transfer of emotion or energy from one person to another within a group setting. We also have to address the question of human leadership and what its function is, as well as the significance of human culture as a binding force and its function in providing boundedness for human groups, institutions and ethnic systems.

To put it quite simply, each of us has to realize, and accept, that we contain both good and bad, are capable of aggression or gentleness. Hence the responsibility must rest on each of us to control our own boundary and to manage and take responsibility for the positive and negative forces that exist within each of us. It is the task of each human being to take responsibility for all of these painful and conflicting emotions, attitudes and behaviours which go to make up the human condition.

If this is so, the next question that must be asked is what happens if a person fails to take responsibility for all that is in them. This, of course, has been the perennial problem. The difficulty is not so much that none of us is perfect but that, characteristically, we are not willing to accept the fact. Very few of us will willingly accept responsibility for the negative and less pleasant side of ourselves. Very few are willing to accept the fact that this is what we have to painfully manage and struggle with all the days of our lives. If one had to pick a central characteristic of us as human beings I think this would be it. All of us want to see ourselves as perfect, as containing all that is good; we will go to almost any lengths to turn a blind eye to our seamy side and to try to get rid of it.

Now this must be a very basic characteristic of human beings, and the mechanisms by which we try to rid ourselves of these negative aspects must also be very basic. It was in this area that Freud perhaps made his greatest contribution when he elucidated the various defence mechanisms, particularly that of projection. Of course others, like denial and repression, are also at work. An important point should be noted here, however, that these mechanisms of projective identification are characteristically used in a context of relationship. And, of course, therefore, they are learned and brought into being, right from the earliest stages of development in the family, from the very beginning of life.

I will return to the developmental aspect later, but the point I want to stress here is one which Freud and others did not emphasize when dealing with the defence mechanisms. These defences typically occur in a context of relationship; that is, like most other human activity, they are worked out within the group. In other words our management of all that is in us does not happen in isolation. In a sense, if we were totally isolated we would have no choice but to contain everything within ourselves. No, this process, like almost everything else, takes place within a higher-order system – i.e. the group, whatever that may be. It is when a higher-order system is formed and the boundary drawn around it that the individual boundaries tend to become more permeable, some degree of merging or coalescence takes place and therefore transfer of elements from one person to another becomes possible and more freely available. It is in this context of the higher-order system, then, that we can project unwanted parts of ourselves on to others, or alternatively take their feelings and attitudes into ourselves. The danger is, and of course this is what typically happens, that, if we are not conscious of this possibility, then it happens apparently automatically outside of our awareness. These unwanted energies or forces, these negative aspects of the individual, are now able to circulate freely within the group. In this way they can be lodged in some weaker, susceptible, indeed often willing, individual who then becomes the victim or scapegoat and is left carrying these negative energies.

The process does not end here, however. If we now turn to the human group, which is essentially a new entity, this higher-order system will typically behave in the same way as the single individual. It will want to keep all that is good and positive to itself and get rid of the evil negative aspects, which it does not want to own. This is true whether we're dealing with a married couple, a family, an extended family, village, a business, or a government department.

In fact, not all groups do behave in this way. The old-style extended family or tribe (for example, an Irish village or a Jewish ghetto) knew very well that all was not perfect in it and in fact spent much of its time and energy dealing with and putting up with its less savoury aspects and members. This is where humour and making the best of it is often one of the great and heroic characteristics of the human race. As I say, it is often seen at its best in oppressed ghettoes or other ethnic groups. This may indeed be why some of the world's greatest comedians have come from oppressed cultures like the Jewish ghetto or Harlem.

While some human groups have been forced to deal with all that they are and to manage themselves as best they can, others, particularly if they were dominant and aggressive, have followed a quite different path. I am thinking here of some extreme fundamentalist religious groups, or the behaviour characteristic of Fascist totalitarian regimes. In these situations the regime or orthodoxy sees itself as all good, as free from sin, saved and righteous, and then attempts to project or export out across its boundary all that is bad, sinful or evil.

A culture that adopts this position is indeed in a dangerous state, for the attempt to expel all evil does not succeed but, characteristically, because it denies the evil within it, has the effect of unleashing horrible excesses and evils from within the group itself. We have seen the terrible results of this all too often. In the Spanish Inquisition, in Hitler's Germany, in the excesses of some of the Communist regimes, in the McCarthy era in the USA and, more recently, in such examples as the warped religious sect that ended its days in British Guyana. But we also see this process at work more parochially and nearer home, in a less gross and obvious way, in many of the groups and institutions in which we live and work. It is very interesting to analyse what happens in these situations and to examine the crucial function of leadership in this context. However, first I wish to return to the formation of these mechanisms in early development.

Early development examined from this point of view throws some interesting new light on these issues. Melanie Klein, a developmental theorist, has developed her object relations theory, which incidentally has been the cornerstone of the Tavistock group theorists such as Wilfred Bion. Melanie Klein states that, very early, in the first few months of life, the infant takes in good and bad aspects of key parts of the mother, such as the breast. He then projects these outwards to gradually build up good and bad objects in external reality. Although she uses what is to me rather strained and obscure psychoanalytical terminology, she nevertheless points to what I believe is an important truth. The child begins to build a construction of reality and, groping towards a picture of the external world, is formed out of an intimate relation first to the mother and then to the other key figures in the family group. It is out of this primal cluster of relationships that individuation takes place. A separate person gradually differentiates out, becomes bounded and builds up a unique eternal reality.

So once again we see the individual is formed and differentiates out of the group. The important contribution of Melanie Klein is that she stated that this reality is created out of the positive and negative aspects of the external world and the intimate human relationships in which it is bathed. The child incorporates the positive and negative dimensions, good and bad, love and hate, and has to integrate these within itself, creating a picture of the external world, a world composed of these positive and negative elements. The personality thus gradually forms a boundary between itself and external reality, and painfully learns to manage the transactions that continually have to take place across that delicate boundary.

This differentiation, separation of the self and the building up of a personality, although in the nature of things always difficult, can happen reasonably smoothly if the parents are managing the group space of the family effectively. To put this more correctly, if the parents are managing the contradictory and opposing forces within them responsibly, if they are keeping a reasonable balance within themselves and in the family, then that reality is coming to the infant and the child across the boundary of the parents in a reasonably balanced way. Of course, this is mediated mainly through the mother initially in the very early phase of development. Even then, what she gives to the child is affected by what is happening in the relationship between her and the husband and older children in the family, if any. So we see that the task of the family and of the parents is to provide a space or a setting in which the positives and negatives of reality and of the surrounding world flow into the developing infant in a gentle, balanced way. Provided this is happening, the child can commence its differentiation in a satisfactory way. The child can thus avoid the vicious circle of introjection and projection back into the parents and the outside world, such as Melanie Klein describes in the distorted family situations which she attempted to analyse.

Because Freudian thinkers were so concerned to point to the developmental stages, the complexes and mechanisms which they considered universal principles, they tended to speak of them as applying equally in all persons and situations. The difficulty with this is that, if these factors apply universally and equally to everyone, how can they be made to explain the differences and the pathological situations which arise? This difficulty emerges once again in the writings of Melanie Klein. In fact, concepts like the Oedipus complex or projective identification only give rise to serious problems where there is a major failure of management within the family. This will only occur where parents are unable, for whatever reason, to manage their boundaries responsibly and are projecting unwanted parts of themselves into the child and into each other. This is a rather long-winded way of saying that, if the parents are reasonably normal human beings and are able to manage their behaviour responsibly, the child will be reasonably normal and be able to differentiate itself so as to form a separate balanced personality at the appropriate time. In the family, parents should provide the leadership function. Sometimes the father, sometimes the mother but perhaps at its best this happens when the function is shared in a balanced way between the parents.

To return to the question of leadership, at first sight we would tend to think of a leader as a focal point or centre around which the group can organize itself, and of course this is true. This can be seen clearly in the case of chimpanzees, where the dominant ape, once he has established his position, appears to do little or nothing. He becomes what is very clearly a centre around which the troupe organizes itself and carries out its various functions and behaviours. Most of these functions are enacted through subdominant males or females who discipline adventurous juveniles as the situation demands. The alpha male only intervenes where there is a serious disruption in the order of things or where there is a direct threat to his leadership. We think therefore of the leader as managing the group space so that the internal processes of interaction and group life can be carried on. He also has to manage the external boundary so that the group as a whole can behave and take action in relation to the surrounding world.

It should be remembered, of course, from our examination of primates and other mammalian groups and from what can be learned from primitive human societies such as the Bamabute (Pygmies), that not all groups or societies are organized around a simple dominant leader. There are in fact various forms of internal organization within groups, within living systems, clusters of families, flexibly shifting leadership for different purposes and so on. It will be noted, however, that these more flexible forms of internal organization are to be found in small tribal or extended family societies such as the hunter-gatherers. Here the primary group is small enough for every member to be able to see and directly relate to every other, as in a Pygmy village. A person seeking to deal with an issue has only to stand in the centre of the clearing to be able to address the entire gathering. However, once the size of a group or organization moves beyond this point, the mobilization around a single leader tends to emerge.

At first sight we think then of the leader as managing the positive and negative forces within the group, resolving contradictions and continually working to restore and maintain a state of uneasy balance within the group. However, there is a subtle twist to the working of this process, which was not for a long time apparent to me. Describing the situation in this way would suggest the function of the leader as managing something external to him/herself, but, once the leader has emerged, once the function of leadership has been differentiated out by the group, then that leader becomes the stage on which the contradictions and struggling forces of the group are acted out. It is within the very person of the leader that the core of the struggle between the opposing energies takes place. Like most things, as soon as one points to it, it can be seen that there is already an unconscious awareness within society that this is the reality. When two leaders such as Haughey and Thatcher or Kennedy and Kruschev meet, everyone is aware that the struggle is enacted in a very personal manner. The result will depend very much on the personal qualities, the emotional conflicts and the personality strengths or weaknesses of each of the two leaders concerned. In a strange way, Cuchulain and Ferdia or David and Goliath fighting it out hand to hand is not so primitive or far distant from our contemporary situation as we would like to imagine. A very primitive example of what I am attempting to describe can be seen in the life of the slime mould. Once certain cells take on cephalic functions to become the head of the minute slug, which is formed out of single-celled organisms, they then become differentiated out, in a sense as leaders. They become, so to speak, the seeing eye of the multiple organism, although up to that point they were no different from any other of the single cells when they took unto themselves this function. However, if the head is destroyed, then the recently formed slug is no longer able to function and rapidly disintegrates. It would appear that there is a very interesting and deep process involved here. For example, at the human level, I believe an analogous situation can be seen in the relationship of Hitler to the German people. Once they had personified in him all their responsibility and initiative, he was the only one who retained any real decision-making powers. Indeed it may be that he was consumed by all the energy and powerful forces thrust upon him by the whole of German society. And as he was driven mad by the German people, his decisions became increasingly irrational, while those around him, the generals and others who would normally have been leaders, became quite impotent to do anything to help themselves.

One could point to many similar instances from despotic regimes. One thinks of Napoleon's marshals, who behaved like nincompoops once he had sucked all their ability and potential leadership into himself. The statement of de Valera, that when he wanted to know the needs of the Irish people he looked into his own heart, was therefore perhaps closer to the truth than even he realized. Needless to say, for a society to personify all of its responsibility and capacity for action and decision in one frail human being, however great he may appear to be, is to place itself in a very perilous situation. Yet there is little doubt that, with the mass organizations that we have saddled ourselves with in the modern western world, we have little choice but to trap ourselves over and over again into situations of this kind.

There is a strange paradox here that runs through all of these processes that I have been attempting to elucidate. Several individuals emerge and coalesce to form a group, which takes on its own being and becomes a living system. This group entity then centres itself and personifies itself into a single individual that it creates as leader. Then most of the important decisions and questions for the life of that group take place in, and indeed are acted out within, that individual person. This is a strange paradox, and one that could well merit deep and serious consideration.

22. Guided Evolution of a Community Mental Health Service: The Dublin Experience (*A Personal Odyssey*)

This paper, written in January 1985, was not published. I wrote it to describe the development of the Psychiatric Service in the Eastern Health Board area at that time.

This paper is the first of three papers dealing with the general area of community psychiatry and chronicity.

MANY talented and dedicated women and men have participated in the Dublin Community Psychiatry Experiment, in so far as this has succeeded. My only contribution has been to keep a guiding hand, from time to time, on the direction of its flow.

Introduction

When, in 1958, I first visited St Brendan's, the main mental hospital serving the greater Dublin area, I was appalled by what I found. All kinds of human beings jumbled in together, the severely mentally handicapped, the epileptic, the frail elderly and severely disturbed, were all herded together in overcrowded wards often containing a hundred or more patients. Any real therapy was quite impossible and patients were constantly being moved from one ward to another to make room for those pressing in from the outside world. I remember that evening making a commitment, deep down, without being consciously aware that I was doing so that somehow, some day, I would return to do something about the plight of these people. But I did not understand! I thought that these human beings were simply forgotten by the world and did not realize that the mental hospital was intimately connected with so-called 'normal' society. I was naïve enough to believe that, if the community at large were made aware of the state of our mental hospitals and of the people in them, they would insist on something being done about it.

301

Although I left the country shortly afterwards for further training abroad, the year 1958 remains a turning-point for me and indeed in considering how best to present this paper I find that the evolution of the psychiatric services breaks down naturally into three ten-year periods: 1958–1968, 1968–1978 and the present decade, 1978–1988. During each of these three periods critical changes in direction have taken place which seem to be part of the natural evolution of Irish society on the one hand and of developments in the mental health services on the other. I propose therefore to present this paper through these three periods.

Historical Note

Before doing so it may be helpful to look briefly at the growth and development of the main mental hospital in Dublin at Grangegorman over the preceding one-hundred years, from its origins in 1814 as the centre of an institution-based mental hospital system. I feel that this is worthwhile, for it illustrates a trend which could be seen in most western countries from the beginning of the Industrial Revolution when, with rapidly expanding urban populations, a way had to be found to contain the increasing numbers of unwanted and disadvantaged people for whom no place could be found in a ruthless industrial society. The creation of the new mental hospitals provided a ready solution to this problem and the provision of these institutions was undertaken with extraordinary zeal and rapidity during the first half of the nineteenth century. Wherever we find such a policy of containment and human warehousing, a similar picture is always to be seen.

From its foundation in 1814 as the Richmond Lunatic Asylum in Dublin the number of inmates grew rapidly, so that by the 1840s and 1850s more buildings had to be constructed on what is now the west side of St Brendan's Hospital to relieve the situation of overcrowding. The numbers continued to grow and by the 1890s had so outgrown even the capacity of the greatly enlarged institution that the adjoining prison buildings of the Grangegorman General Penitentiary had to be taken over to accommodate patients. Further temporary buildings had to be erected, so that by December 1900 a total of 2,254 patients were accommodated throughout the complex.

In 1903 a new hospital in Portrane in north County Dublin was completed. However, the number of patients continued to grow and in 1930 further buildings of the North Dublin Union (the Workhouse) were taken over to accommodate an additional 320 patients. The patient population of the two large mental hospitals was now 3,837. This total complex, known as the Grangegorman Mental Hospital, catered for the city and county of Dublin, County Wicklow and County Louth. In the 1930s a new hospital was opened to serve County Louth, but in spite of this the number of patients in the Grangegorman/Portrane complex continued to grow. By 1958, the year in which I first saw St Brendan's, the population of that hospital was 1,973, with a slightly greater number housed in the hospital at Portrane, making a total mental hospital population of approximately 4,000 patients. At this time the population of the greater Dublin area was approximately 735,085.

Throughout the post-war period public health authorities in Ireland had been more concerned with the ravages of tuberculosis than with the unhappiness and disability generated by mental illness. As part of a programme designed to eradicate the plague of tuberculosis, a major building programme got underway. By the time most of the projected sanatoria had been built, however, tuberculosis had been brought under control, so that many of the newly provided beds were never occupied. In the Dublin area some of these were availed of to relieve the situation in St Brendan's. However, despite the fact that some 500 beds were provided in former sanatoria, by December 1965 the population in St Brendan's had dropped by only 345 to 1,628.

By this time it was manifest that so long as the traditional centralized institutional-based and medically understaffed containment programme continued and the district mental hospital remained the only facility for the provision of psychiatric care, this tendency to keep on filling up would continue. This is for the very simple reason that the more society tries to get rid of something which is a part of itself and sweep it under the carpet, the more that problem will grow. The picture in the rest of Ireland mirrored that of Dublin. By 1900 the nation as a whole could boast of five psychiatric beds per 1,000 of population. With further population decline and demographic changes leading to greater dependency, particularly in western areas, these numbers were to rise still higher, until by 1958 the figure stood at seven per 1,000 of population and in certain western areas of the country was as high as thirteen per 1,000; that is, more than one in every hundred persons was resident in a mental hospital. This situation was sufficient to spur governmental action, so that in 1961 a Commission of Enquiry on mental illness was instituted. It reported in 1965 but, as is usual in Ireland, its proposals were never translated directly into government action.

Following the Second World War, revolutionary changes began to take place in the treatment and management of psychiatric illness, including the advent of psychoactive drugs. In Europe, in Britain and a little later in the USA and elsewhere, these changes became manifest in a widespread movement towards providing care for psychiatric patients in the community, with a corresponding reduction of numbers in the mental hospitals. From about 1955 onwards this movement began to spread rapidly but its beginnings did not reach Ireland until between 1958 and 1960. It was from this time that a reduction in numbers in the large mental hospitals in the Dublin area first made an appearance. Even then the change was slow to get off the ground and the next ten years may be regarded as a germinating phase in which the concepts which would bring about a fundamental change in the psychiatric services gradually took shape.

1958–1968

1961 saw the first break with the old mental hospital system when St Loman's, a disused sanatorium, was opened as a small psychiatric hospital with a community-oriented treatment policy. In 1962 I returned from the United States and, with a few other rebel psychiatrists, joined the staff of that hospital. In 1965 Dr Dermot Walsh and I formulated a plan for the future development of public psychiatric services in the Dublin area. We were impressed by the *psychiatrie de secteur* which had been established under Lebovici in the 13th arondissement in Paris and by de Ajaiuagerra's pioneering efforts in the city and canton of Geneva; also by the unit system pioneered by Humphrey Towers in Britain. Influenced by these ideas, the plan put forward suggested the decentralization of the psychiatric services for the greater Dublin area, and the setting up of a number of community-based psychiatric teams, each serving a geographical sector.

The following year, 1966, I was appointed Chief Psychiatrist to the then Dublin Health Authority (now the Eastern Health Board) with charge of all the public psychiatric services for the area. When a year later I was appointed to the Chair of Psychiatry in University College Dublin I was very soon faced with a dilemma – a parting of the ways. An opportunity presented itself to establish a prestigious Professorial Unit in one of the major teaching general hospitals. This, had I availed of it, would have provided the opportunity to create a high-standard professorial unit with a good level of practice and research, as well as prospects for a lucrative private practice. This would have enabled me to develop a psychotherapeutic approach and to train psychiatrists, medical students and other personnel in what were then new and different approaches to current psychiatric practice in Ireland at that time.

All of this sounds eminently reasonable but if one examines psychiatric services around the world where prestigious teaching units of this kind have been established that do not relate to the main public psychiatric services, one will find the same phenomenon constantly recurring. What characteristically happens is that the professorial teaching unit becomes an elite service which caters for the 'good' patient; i.e. the acutely ill patient who usually manifests neurotic or depressive illness and has a good short-term prognosis. These patients tend to be better educated, middle-class and generally come from the more advantaged strata of society. By contrast, the 'bad' patient – usually from a socially deprived background, who is often unemployed, has poor social and work skills and is more often psychotic, with an illness that is chronic in type and who may have additional complicating factors such as old age or mental handicap – is typically transferred on for care and treatment by the public psychiatric services, unless they show some rare and interesting clinical features, in which case they may be retained in the teaching unit for some time before being passed on. (I saw this situation recently illustrated only too clearly in the professorial teaching unit in Athens. This unit provides an acceptable level of service and research but has little connection with the two large public hospitals in the city, where there is a very poor standard of care; nor is there any real rotation of psychiatric trainees or other personnel between the two services.) What happens when this kind of development is followed is that the young psychiatrist in training learns to distinguish between the 'good' and 'bad' patient and, while he may receive an acceptable level of training, tends to move towards a mainly private-oriented psychiatric practice (of which there is usually a well-developed complementary dimension to such prestigious centres), so that the public psychiatric sector is left grossly understaffed, with poorly trained psychiatric personnel, providing a miserable standard of care.

This was then the position in Dublin in 1967 and, had I availed of the opportunity provided by the Chair of Psychiatry to follow this direction, I think we might well now have a situation in Dublin where there would be one or two prestigious professorial units in general hospitals but the mental hospital system would have remained custodial and cut off, perhaps with an even larger inpatient population than were resident at that time. (It should be remembered that the population of the Greater Dublin area has almost doubled in this period.) Perhaps even more important is the fact that the community psychiatric services which, with all their faults, now represent the main psychiatric service for the eastern region would have remained poorly developed or nonexistent. For all these reasons, therefore, I chose a second alternative and, indeed, even looking back in the light of all that has happened since, were I faced with the same situation again I would make the same choice.

The second alternative was to firmly centre my position as Chief Psychiatrist and the Professorial Chair in the public psychiatric service. This made possible, with all its disappointments and shortcomings, the development of a community psychiatric framework for the eastern region. The disadvantage of following this line of development – and there is always a negative aspect to any decision – was that it was not possible to concentrate as much as one would have liked on the quality of psychiatric practice or the standards of psychiatric training. The difficulty here is that, although a community psychiatric framework was introduced, most of those who emerged out of the mental hospitals to minimally staff the new psychiatric districts were not only insufficient in number but were trained in the old custodial institutional methods of care and treatment. I did not appreciate the significance of this at the time.

1968–1978

This brings me to the second ten-year period, commencing in 1968 when a start was made on the development of a community psychiatric service. The plan adopted at that time by the authorities recommended that the area being served by the traditional mental hospitals should be split up into a number of psychiatric sectors, each of which would develop a comprehensive range of alternative facilities, including inpatient beds for acute and long-stay patients in each psychiatric sector, with continuity of care – whether in hospital or in the community – being provided by the psychiatric team serving that district. It was intended that these community-based services be developed as an alternative to the traditional large mental hospital.

It should be pointed out that this plan was generated during the economic boom period of the 1960s; what in Ireland is known as the Lemass era. There was a mood of optimism and hope; we were to reach full employment with jobs for everyone; at last Ireland was on the move. Although it was not obvious at the time, widespread demographic changes were taking place in Irish society. Emigration had virtually ceased and a population explosion was on the way. Many Irish emigrants were returning home to take part in the new industrial development.

This mood of general optimism was reflected in psychiatric circles. There was enthusiasm for industrial therapy and patients were to be trained for realistic work in the new factories that were springing up everywhere. During this period also there was hope that increased finance would be directed towards the development of what had, until then, always been the 'Cinderella' services – psychiatry, geriatrics and mental handicap. Consequently I was naïve enough to believe that, when the authorities and public representatives accepted enthusiastically a community psychiatric plan, it meant that there was a real intention to implement it. I did not realize then that mental hospitals do not come into existence by chance. There are processes continually at work, with many ramifications throughout society, against the acceptance back into normal life of those who have already been rejected by the community. I did not realize that the traditional mental hospital, as we have known it in the west, is not in fact something separate from the rest of society. It represents one end of the spectrum of an interconnected process which runs through every aspect of society, from the individual to the family to the wider community; from the suburban homes of the wealthy to the poverty-stricken ghettoes of the inner city. The traditional mental hospital is not a place where those who are suffering from mental illness come to be treated, to be returned cured and well again to the community. No, it has simply been a receptacle where all those for whom society has no place are dumped to get them out of sight – the aged, the mentally handicapped, the epileptic, the disturbed and all those who lack the competence and wherewithal to gain a foothold in the ruthless, competitive, capitalistic environment we euphemistically term 'Christian' society. For these reasons, and because the essential resources to develop a community psychiatric service were not made available, progress was much slower and less satisfactory than was anticipated.

Emulating ideas that were current in Britain, we would at that time, had we been able, have created large all-purpose psychiatric units in the general hospitals of fifty to one-hundred beds. These were to have constituted the core of our new service around which ancilliary day-care and hostel facilities would hopefully develop later. Instead we were forced to do things piecemeal, availing of any opportunity as it arose. Wherever a large house, an old school, a nursing home or unused hospital unit became available it was acquired, often without any financial involvement, as day or residential accommodation and put to use as part of the overall objective. The basic idea of developing services by sector was there from the beginning but the facilities in each area were established quite haphazardly rather than in an ordered way and were often far from ideal. This is how things took shape.

Another aspect of this attempt to try to make the best use of whatever facilities were already in existence was the integration with the public psychiatric services of private psychiatric facilities wherever possible. As a result of the progressive and open-minded attitude of several of these private organizations, which were already operating services at a better level than the public service, three of our psychiatric districts were now integrated with and operated on a subcontract basis by, either in part or wholly, these private agencies. This had the further advantage of avoiding the development of a two-tier service in the Dublin area. In addition it was possible to rationalize the mental handicap services and to create the beginnings of a geriatric service within the four main quadrants of the Eastern Health Board area, although the further development of these was slow and lagged behind for some years to come.

What evolved then was a more flexible range of small and decentralized facilities in each sector, linked together and operated by a single psychiatric team. What gradually emerged was a rather different picture of community psychiatry from that which had developed elsewhere. Ironically, because of all the delays and lack of financial resources to implement our initial plans, we were able to learn from the mistakes of more affluent societies and avoid some of the pitfalls into which they had fallen.

From this experience I learnt an important principle about the nature of planning. Until then, as is still current thinking in most administrative circles, I had assumed that one sat down with one's colleagues and worked out a comprehensive and detailed plan for the next five or ten years, which was then to be implemented as a fairly rigid set of guidelines. I did not appreciate that, in dealing with societal institutions and indeed human society as a whole, one is involved with 'living systems' which are not static and inert but manifest their own dynamic growth and evolution. It is hopeless therefore to make detailed plans as to how things will develop. Rather, all that one can do is to identify the general direction and long-term goal one is attempting to reach and then move on to the next immediate step. In the light of how this turns out, one tries to guide the evolution of the process in the general direction one is attempting to reach, and reciprocally the long-term objectives which had been identified usually themselves undergo a considerable modification in the light of this same experience.

As the development of the psychiatric services painfully evolved during the early 1970s it was possible to clarify, to some degree a perennial confusion which had arisen again and again in the debate surrounding community psychiatry. Those who are convinced that we must retain the traditional mental hospital as the basis of our psychiatric services always assume that the alternative is to put people out on the streets, to place them in sub-standard nursing-home accommodation where they would be even more institutionalized than they were in mental hospitals, or to send them home where they would be a source of disturbance and pain to their relatives, often rapidly relapsing in the very environment that had played a large part in their becoming ill in the first place. I want to state emphatically that this is not the alternative that has been proposed in the mental health programme being implemented in the Dublin region. What we have been attempting to do is to provide an alternative place for every patient who has not either died in hospital or made a sufficient recovery to lead an independent life in the community.

By the late 1970s the inpatient population of the two large mental hospitals had been almost halved, from just under 4,000 in 1958 down to 2,300 but, since the plan to sectorize psychiatric services had got actively underway in 1968, over 800 alternative residential places had been created, of which 250 were in hostels and group homes and the remaining 550 in small decentralized inpatient units in the various sectors. During that period approximately 550 places had also been provided in day hospitals, day centres and workshops. From a situation where there was only one child guidance clinic in the Dublin region, run by a voluntary agency, a fairly comprehensive range of day treatment centres for children were developed in the various sectors. Also, two residential units for children and adolescents were provided. These developments were carried out with the cooperation of both public and private agencies along the lines already achieved for adult services.

Nevertheless, since 1968 a number of factors had intervened which militated against the full implementation of the plan to decentralize psychiatric services and close down the traditional mental hospitals:

1. During the period when this change was being attempted, the population of Dublin had increased rapidly and had nearly doubled since 1959.

2. With the establishment of the Eastern Health Board, the functional area was enlarged to include Counties Wicklow and Kildare.

3. By the time the community psychiatric development should really have been getting underway (and remember that in Ireland this was taking place nearly ten years later than in countries like Britain and the United States), we were entering the early 1970s and the prolonged recession ushered in by the first of several oil crises was already upon us. Thus by 1978 only approximately 50–60% of the necessary alternative facilities had actually been provided. These developments were uneven and in no psychiatric sector was there a sufficient range of the necessary facilities to provide an adequate service for a catchment population without reliance still on the traditional mental hospital.

4. Perhaps most importantly, it was not appreciated that, unless the flow of patients into the old facility – that is, St Brendan's – was controlled, the creation of new and alternative services would simply deal with the new population who would use them. It would not affect the use of the traditional facilities.

5. The parallel services for mental handicap and the elderly remained relatively undeveloped so that, while there was a considerable reduction in the number of psychiatric patients, both by reducing beds and reducing overcrowding, the number of elderly and mentally handicapped remained virtually unchanged. Further, if the composition of the population of St Brendan's was examined it would be seen that we were dealing with an ageing population, so that out of a total patient population of approximately 1,100 almost half were over sixty-five, a further 200 were between the ages of fifty and sixty-five and only 300 were under the age of fifty.

6. Because of structural changes affecting society and the nature of technology, the numbers of unemployed were rising and standards of living were dropping, resulting in increased pressure on the psychiatric services and admissions, particularly among the elderly.

7. At that time I also had no awareness of the nature of living systems; of the strength with which a living institution like a traditional mental hospital will resist change and its dispersal into the community and will manifest its strong will to survive by maintaining itself as far as possible as it is.

8. In the meantime, because the mental hospital had not faded away as rapidly as anticipated, together with the increase in population in the region and other factors mentioned above, overcrowding was becoming a serious problem once again. Also, the old buildings were deteriorating, so that staff morale had reached an all-time low. This was in spite of the fact that the financial investment that had been put into shoring up the old buildings over the past ten years would have been more than sufficient to create the necessary alternative community facilities, had the money only been spent at the right time and in the right place. It will be remembered that in 1968 St Brendan's had been subdivided into three sections with three separate admission units, serving three of the psychiatric

sectors in central Dublin. This was done along the lines of the unit system because, at that time, these sectors did not have admission facilities outside. By 1978, although inpatient units had emerged in each of the three sectors, these were still not sufficiently developed to handle the flow of patients seeking admission, so that the overflow still had to come into St Brendan's. This particularly applied to the elderly. Hence once again the spectre of overcrowding was raising its ugly head.

In 1978 all these factors culminated in something of a public crisis about deteriorating conditions in the old mental hospital. For one whole week it dominated the headlines in the Dublin newspapers and eventually the Minister for Health had to visit the hospital to restore public confidence.

It was factors such as these I believe that led to the disillusionment and backlash against community psychiatry which began to appear in the US, Britain and other European countries during the 1970s. This was the time of editorials with headlines such as 'The rootless wanderer', 'Does the community care?' and the general resentment at patients being pushed out on to the streets without preparation and without any suitable alternative facilities being provided for them.

1978–1988

The direct intervention by the then Minister for Health acted as something of a catalyst which set a number of subsequent developments in motion. A fundamental reappraisal of the situation was undertaken. I once again took over direct control of St Brendan's as it became clear that the institution was not simply going to fade away. The first step was to deal with a number of the factors mentioned in the previous section. The problem of controlling the inflow into the hospital was dealt with by the creation of an Assessment Unit under the direction of Dr A. McGennis, with eight beds, separate from the Admission Units. Almost from its beginnings in the early nineteenth century the people of Dublin, through their various channels, had always decided who should be admitted to the hospital; the hospital itself had never had any effective control of its boundary. This was not something unique to Dublin but has been commented upon universally in psychiatric circles across the world – that, whenever a new service such as a psychiatric unit in a general hospital is set up, it tends to attract a new population, while the old clientele still tread the well-worn pathway to the traditional mental hospital. This is one of the reasons why community psychiatric projects have often appeared to fail. Since the Assessment Unit was set up in St Brendan's, however, and all patients who present at the hospital are held overnight until next morning, when they are either sent home or passed on to their appropriate sector service, it has been found that the catchment areas are now undertaking the work for which they were established in the first place. This is so even though they do not possess anything like the full range of facilities which would enable them to provide an adequate service. For the ten years preceding the establishment of the Assessment Unit on 1 April 1979, the admission rate had been running at over 2,000 patients per year. In 1978 the number of direct admissions to the hospital was 2,676. By 1980 this figure had dropped to 1,558. Needless to say, this made a significant difference to overcrowding in the hospital and allowed a breathing space to carry out further reorganization within the institution.

One chronic problem was the influx of inappropriate groups of patients into the ordinary admission wards; i.e. the homeless, those suffering from chronic alcoholism and the elderly:

1. A special service was established for dealing with the homeless under the direction of Dr J. Fernandez. He set up a case register and followed admission patterns and the movements of these people around the various hostels in the city centre. A small inpatient unit was provided for those requiring admission and a day centre was established for them in the grounds.

2. For some years we have had an alcoholic unit and a large outpatient programme for alcoholics within easy reach of the hospital. Nevertheless, during the 1970s many alcoholics, like the homeless, constituted a revolving-door population who drifted into the admission units, leaving again after a few days or weeks without having gained any material benefit from the experience. Indeed it was clear that to be able to dry themselves out as inpatients only served in many instances to reinforce their drinking patterns. Since the establishment of the Assessment Centre alcoholics are seldom admitted and, having been dried out overnight, are referred on to the alcohol programmes. Follow-up studies would seem to indicate that the

therapeutic results are at least as good, and indeed may be significantly better, than when the majority of them gained admission to hospital.

3. The sections of the hospital on the east side of the road were already largely filled with elderly patients and these older parts of the hospital were now formally designated as geriatric accommodation, with the idea that any elderly patients presenting would be admitted directly there, leaving the west side of the hospital free to concentrate on more specifically psychiatric work. Right up until the present, however, this arrangement has not fully succeeded because of the lack of properly organized geriatric and psychogeriatric services outside, hence increasing numbers of elderly persons have been presenting for admission. Thus the geriatric sections of the hospital are constantly full and old people, often simply in need of physical geriatric care, continue to crowd into our psychiatric admission units. This remains a continuing problem up to the present.

Having gained some control of the inflow to the hospital and carried out internal reorganization along these lines, it was possible to empty and demolish the main building on the west side of St Brendan's. This symbolically represented a turning-point in the continuing struggle with institutionalization. Following this, a project team was established with the full agreement of the Minister for Health in 1981 consisting of officers of the Department of Health and the Eastern Health Board. Its terms of reference were as follows:

> To establish the whole question of the future of St Brendan's Hospital and its role in the context of continuing development of community services.

As a result of its deliberations it was decided that all the old buildings remaining on the east side of the road should be demolished and replaced by small thirty-two-bed psychogeriatric units, to be strategically situated, on a decentralized basis, out in the various sectors of the Greater Dublin area, where high concentrations of old people are living to be within easy reach of these and their relatives. This will involve the relocation of some 400 elderly persons as well as over one-hundred mentally handicapped patients and will constitute the basis of a psychogeriatric dimension to the overall geriatric services for the Eastern Health Board region. When these ten thirty-two-bed psychogeriatric units are built over the next four years, with appropriate accompanying day accommodation together with additional accommodation for approximately one-hundred mentally handicapped patients, St Brendan's will at last have been reduced to a hospital of manageable proportions.

Over the past six years, while all of this change and planning has been taking place, I found my view of the St Brendan's complex undergoing a radical reappraisal. The whole question for me seemed to turn upside down. For the past twenty years I had very largely seen only the negative face of St Brendan's and had felt a sense of despair that anything positive could ever be done with such an institution. Over this period I had been pointing out the folly of attempting to prop up an outdated institution whose buildings had long since served their purpose and whose philosophy was totally contrary to my concept of what a mental health service should be. I had felt pessimistic that, in the face of an ingrained institutional mental climate, it would ever be possible to change staff attitudes and patterns of behaviour and hence I thought the only solution was to phase out the old institution entirely and replace it with a ring of community psychiatric sector services. I had thus often contemplated selling the entire site to help finance the community psychiatric programme.

Now that a solution was at last coming into view I found myself taking a fresh look and it gradually began to dawn on me that right here in central Dublin was a site of 70 acres of fine green open space, the largest open area left in the city, and that moreover this had hundreds of skilled workers, mostly nurses, as well as psychiatrists and various paramedical disciplines, if only these could be retrained and take on different roles.

Throughout the 1960s and '70s I had believed that the job of psychiatry was to help people to return to 'normal community life' outside and had not questioned that there was a 'normal community' for people to return to. I had not realized that any real community life, in a modern conurbation such as Dublin with in excess of 1,000,000 people, was already largely destroyed and that, as we entered the 1980s, there was evidence on all sides of a disintegrating society. In common with other western countries one sees soaring crime rates, constant vandalism and predatory behaviour, widespread abuse of drugs and alcohol and alienation of whole sections of the population, such as the young, the chronically unemployed, the travelling people, those made redundant and much of the elderly population.

Once the building programme of small psychogeriatric units and the accommodation for the mentally handicapped has been completed and four new twenty-five-bed admission units have been built to replace the remaining old buildings on the west side, St Brendan's Hospital, as such, will have come down to a reasonably sized unit of 150–200 beds. By that time St Ita's will have become mainly a centre for the mentally handicapped, with a large day-care programme and a residential unit of 400 beds. In addition, the district psychiatric unit for north County Dublin will be situated in St Ita's, with one-hundred beds.

In the meantime, over the next four years, it is expected that there will be a further increase in the range of alternative facilities throughout the psychiatric sectors. This will bring the total number of residential places, including inpatient units, group homes and hostels, to 1,495 and the total number of day places to approximately 1,000.

Given the population of the Eastern Health Board, now in the region of 1¼ million, there is a need to further subdivide several of the psychiatric sectors, creating three additional sectors. This will bring the total number of psychiatric sectors in the Greater Dublin area, with counties Wicklow and Kildare, to twelve. One of these areas which needs to be divided is Dublin north-west, and this will give an opportunity to create a new psychiatric sector in the immediate vicinity of St Brendan's Hospital.

Thus I see the remaining units comprising the new St Brendan's Hospital, with 150–200 beds, forming a suitably sized district unit to serve the north of the city and the districts of Cabra and Finglas, with a population of something over 100,000 persons. This hospital section will only take up to 10 to 15 acres and will be redesignated as the new St Brendan's Hospital. The remaining 50 to 60 acres of the larger St Brendan's campus will thus be left free for alternative development. An elaborate site control plan has been completed, designating the area to remain as hospital development, and the rest of the concourse is now seen as available for multi-purpose development. It is envisaged that the main offices for Health Board administrative staff will be constructed there, also a sports complex for Eastern Health Board staff and perhaps a regional training school for psychiatric nursing. Even allowing for these developments, ample room is still available on the campus for development of a different nature.

Mental Health in the 1980s: A New Challenge

In excess of 300,000 persons are now unemployed in the Republic, if one includes those on chronic sickness and disability benefit. The direct cost of this to the nation is now in excess of £600,000,000 per annum, and the indirect cost is far greater. Each one of these citizens is potentially at risk for mental and physical breakdown, drug abuse, alcoholism, crime and vandalism. The families stricken by unemployment are also likely to manifest problems, to fail educationally in school and hence to become eventually at risk for any or all of the problems mentioned. There is in addition the enormous loss of productivity. Such a large section of the population could be making a huge, positive contribution to the welfare and productivity of the country as a whole but, because of Poor Law legislation and attitudes to social welfare, they are denied the opportunity to do anything useful as long as they are recipients of financial benefits from the state.

Moreover, for some years now the population of the Republic has been increasing rapidly. With diminishing emigration and a continuing high birth rate, over one million of our population of approximately 3½ million are now under fifteen years of age. In the next twenty years, up to the turn of the century, 50% of the population of this country will be under twenty-five. This inevitably means a massive increase in the numbers seeking employment. In addition, with pressure from the EEC, women are gaining equality in society as part of the workforce. Released from excessive child-bearing, they now no longer accept domesticity as the only trade open to them. The number of women seeking employment is thus reaching 50% in a number of occupations and professions. Finally the new technologies bringing about automation in a wide range of industries are only beginning to bite. This factor is, for the moment, being artificially delayed by political and trade union pressure but such efforts are only buying time and, given the capitalist system, the extension of these technologies is inevitable.

Taking these separate factors into account it thus seems quite clear that the major challenge facing the mental health services over the next ten years will be the large population of unemployed and alienated persons and their families who are at risk for various forms of mental breakdown. Obviously I do not purport any more than anybody else to have any ready-made solution to this horrendous dilemma but it is abundantly clear that the conventional psychiatric services will have little to offer in stemming this tide and it does seem appropriate that we in psychiatry should try to gear ourselves up to make some form of even partial response to this onslaught which is about to descend upon us.

To this end a number of us have been giving thought to the creation of a pilot project in social welfare based on the campus at St Brendan's as the centre of an evolving network of training and enterprise centres which are already developing throughout the inner city. If this comes to pass, St Brendan's will have changed from being a large, custodial institution for the unwanted of society to an open centre where eventually hundreds of people, both patients and others, would come each day from the outside world to become involved in some form of mental health and productive activity, developing themselves more fully as human beings. This evolving network would, needless to say, avail of various training agencies already in the field, such as Anco and the Youth Employment Agency, and others which will undoubtedly develop over the next few years. The entire project would thus be directed towards the unemployed and 'at risk' population of young people in the city centre and surrounding areas.

A beginning has already been made in this direction, for in 1980 a local branch of the Mental Health Association was formed, based in St Brendan's, and this group has planned and is about to embark on the provision of a 'National Mental Health Resource Centre', which will be erected on the St Brendan's campus and will provide a range of social, educational and work facilities to begin the kind of activity contemplated. A small EEC project for the resocialization and vocational training of chronic psychiatric patients has also begun on the site and this is developing new approaches to the education and personal development of those who have become demotivated and alienated from society. At present this programme is working with persons who have spent many years in hospital but will soon be extended to those designated as 'revolving door' patients. Even though many of these people manage to stay out of hospital for long periods, they nevertheless lead impoverished, restricted, isolated lives – a burden to themselves and their families. Thus it is hoped to make a beginning towards a growing network of alternative contexts where young people and those not so young can come to build a place and a future for themselves; in effect, a sort of university for ordinary poor people – if you like, a new form of 'asylum', but this time, instead of a closed system to contain those not wanted by society, we will be creating an open system where perhaps as many as 1,000 people will come each day to enrich their lives and to engage in enterprising and productive activity. Thus it is to be hoped we will see St Brendan's come alive and turn all its unused resources into a living, breathing, learning centre to which large numbers of the wider community will come, rather than remain a stagnant pool of dependency which for too long has been a dumping ground for those who are not wanted by our 'healthy' society.

Back to Square One

This brings me almost full circle back to my starting point. When, in 1966, I took on the role of Chief Psychiatrist it was necessary, as I have described, to lay down a basic framework within which community psychiatric sector services could develop. This framework is now well established, so inevitably the role of a post such as mine, whose powers were only advisory from the beginning, is now in question. There is now a group of capable and talented clinical directors, each in charge of his own sector or area of specialization, so there is little sense in my trying to look over their shoulder or in any way attempt to directly interfere with the running of their services. Nevertheless, there is still much work to be done throughout the service generally to achieve satisfactory standards of practice and provision of a sufficient range of facilities in each psychiatric sector so that these can offer a full independent mental health programme for the communities they serve.

With at most five to ten years of active working life remaining, I have to ask what, if any, final contribution my role can make to the further development of the mental health service. In attempting to answer this question it seems to me that the only useful role of a post such as that of Chief Mental Health Advisor (which is the effective nature of my job) is one of influence, concentrating on training and, where feasible, demonstration of new approaches to therapy and practice. In addition, with a largely decentralized sector service there would seem now to be an urgent need for the development of an effective data and monitoring system, to identify where there are gaps and deficiencies in the service as a whole.

Within the next year or so the professorial headquarters of University College Dublin are to move directly on to the main university campus and this will provide the opportunity to establish a prestigious teaching, research and demonstration centre which can hopefully then exert a general influence on the raising of standards of psychiatric practice in the region as a whole. This sounds perilously close to the kind of development described earlier in this paper, against which I turned my face in 1968, but I believe the situation now is very different. The main psychiatric service for the region is now firmly centred in the public service, with strong connections to each of the psychiatric departments in the three medical schools, and it would be virtually impossible now for it to drift back to the kind of private/public, two-tiered dichotomy that I feared at that time.

What I would propose, then, is that the Dublin South-East psychiatric sector, within which the main university college campus is situated and which has a population of manageable size – approximately 100,000 – should be declared a demonstration area. This would enable the nagging question to be answered once and for all whether a community psychiatric service, if properly organized, can provide an acceptable and effective service to a catchment population for which it is responsible, without the support of the traditional back-up mental hospital. This is a question which, to my knowledge, has never been fully or satisfactorily answered to this day anywhere in the world.

If one looks at community psychiatric developments around the world over the past thirty years the story is always the same. While one may find highly developed specific units – here an excellent general hospital psychiatric unit, there a first-class community mental health centre or day hospital – virtually never in my experience does one find a balanced development with the full range or both inpatient and community facilities necessary to provide an adequate service for a sector population. Even more rarely does one find these appropriately staffed by properly trained community personnel, and all of this backed by an effective research and evaluation system.

It so happens that in the Dublin South-East sector we have, for the first time, the opportunity to achieve this. Once the agreed facilities to be developed in my professorial headquarters on the main university campus have been provided, this sector will have the following range of community and inpatient facilities:

1. A professorial department with Community Psychiatric Demonstration unit and supporting Research and Development (R & D) and evaluation facilities.
2. An inpatient psychiatric unit of fifty beds with accompanying day and outpatient facilities at Vergemount Hospital.
3. A well-developed general hospital psychiatric unit and clinical professorial centre with twenty-eight beds in the large teaching general hospital at St Vincent's, Elm Park, complete with the day hospital being constructed at present.
4. A well-developed psychiatric day hospital with large hostel attached at Mountpleasant Square.
5. A pre-vocational and vocational training centre – the Thomas Court centre – providing a comprehensive range of activities and skills in living in the Liberties area of Dublin.
6. Psychiatric hostel accommodation (additional housing will have to be acquired to bring the hostel accommodation up to a satisfactory level).
7. A comprehensive child and adolescent centre at Orwell Road.
8. A joint assessment unit for the elderly at St Vincent's Hospital, Elm Park, backed up by a high-quality geriatric unit, and these supported by medium- to long-stay geriatric units in Vergemount Hospital, as well as two units that are about to be constructed there for the management of the disturbed elderly.

I feel with some confidence that this reasonably comprehensive range of facilities, which will have an inpatient complement of something less than one bed per 1,000 population, can provide the basis for a definitive demonstration of the community psychiatric concept. It is important to emphasize however that, for this demonstration to succeed, three basic elements are absolutely essential:

1. The necessary minimum range of community and inpatient facilities.
2. An adequate complement of staff; these can more than be provided by the running down of the institutional services in St Brendan's. More importantly, all personnel must be appropriately trained to undertake community psychiatric work. It is quite useless to operate community psychiatric facilities and undertake community mental health work with personnel who have little psychotherapeutic understanding and who have been trained in the traditional, institutional, organically oriented mental illness services.
3. A properly organized system of research, monitoring, review and evaluation of the operation and demonstration sector and of the psychiatric service as a whole.

Conclusion

Finally it would be our intention to undertake basic research into new methods of treatment of some of the major psychiatric disorders such as schizophrenia, depression and brain failure in the aged. I am hopeful that if we have correctly trained personnel, operating from the right sort of facilities, it will be possible to bring about something of a therapeutic breakthrough in a number of these areas. If my intuition is correct, such improvements in therapy with a reduction in chronicity would result in enormous savings in the mental health budget of a country such as ours.

All that will be possible in the time remaining to me will hopefully be to set the stage for these developments and, even if only some of these expectations meet with success over the next generation, this will be for me a satisfactory termination to what has been something of a personal odyssey over the past thirty years.

23. 'Community Care' or Independence?

This paper, the second dealing with the psychiatric services, was presented on the occasion of the twenty-fifth anniversary of the Mental Health Association of Ireland.

D R JOHN Connolly in his paper spoke of the widely differing meanings of and attitudes towards the concept of community care but, to paraphrase the words of Humpty Dumpty in *Alice in Wonderland*: 'When I use a word . . . it means just what I choose it to mean – neither more nor less.'

The original pioneers of the community movement in psychiatry – Joshua Bierer, Maxwell Jones, T.P. Rees and particularly the work of Basaglia in Italy – saw this movement as primarily the democratization of human relationships and the breaking down of the contradictions within society which created total institutions such as mental hospitals, orphanages, prisons, etc. They saw this movement as a struggle towards independence and self-esteem for those human beings we call patients to enhance their independence and bring about a real change in their quality of life, so that they might become full persons in society. As he said, for many this definition of community care has changed subtly over the years to become a debate about moving people from the large mental hospital to the community; thus the mental hospital has become identified with 'institutionalization' and the 'community' with 'normal life'.

I was an active participant in this debate, from its beginnings in this country, after my return from the USA in 1962. When Dermot Walsh and myself produced the first plan of the development of a community-based psychiatric service in the Eastern region, we suggested a general framework of psychiatric districts for the entire health board area. The basic idea was to relate psychiatric personnel and services to population areas rather than, as in the past, to

323

hospitals – close to where people lived, so that treatment would be provided as part of normal life, thus avoiding, as far as possible, institutionalization.

Dr Connolly referred to the fact that there are 'excellent models of good practice in community care abounding throughout the world' but, when I took up the post of Chief Psychiatrist of the Eastern Health Board (back then, the Dublin Health Authority) in 1966, although innovative developments were already underway in a number of countries – the USA, Britain, France and especially Italy – nowhere in the world was much more advanced than we were and information about these developments only became available much later. Hence we had to depend largely on our own ideas and resources to guide us.

When I put forward a formal plan along these lines in 1967, I was naïve enough to think that, because it was enthusiastically received and adopted at both local health board and departmental level, there was a real intention and commitment to implementing it. Had I then the political astuteness and wisdom of hindsight, I would have realized that, in Ireland, the adoption of a report does not mean any commitment of resources or real intent to implement its plans.

I have often asked myself since, if I were beginning over again, what would I do differently? It is easy now, with the build-up of a whole infrastructure of community facilities and trained psychiatric personnel, to think what one could do, but at that time there was literally nothing but the two mental hospitals, with over 4,000 inmates, with totally institutionalized staff as well as patients. (To give an idea of how bad things were, the first advertizement we put out for trainee psychiatrists attracted five applicants, of whom four were either alcoholics or drug addicts.) So, no matter how one approached the problem, it was not easy to make a start. Nevertheless, if I had realized then the true situation I think I would still have come up with the general framework but I would have approached the problem differently in at least two respects. I would initially only have tried to implement the plan in one pilot area, concentrating all the available resources there so as hopefully to demonstrate real success. Secondly, on the basis of this innovation, I would have gone about the selection of personnel, particularly those in a leadership role, much more slowly and carefully, so as to bring in people who really believed in a radically different community approach, concentrating them in the demonstration area, and then only widening the programme to include other areas when those who were converted to the new approach on the basis of the successful implementation in the demonstration district could be deployed in other areas. Perhaps if we had gone about it in this way, the change to a community-based service would not have taken so many years. But I wonder!

However, enough of the past. Let us turn now to where we find ourselves at present. In the Eastern region, the demise of the large mental hospital is nearly complete and in the rest of the country things are moving in the same direction, in some areas more quickly than others. At present, from over 2,000 patients in 1960, St Brendan's has reduced to something over 300 – of whom half are over sixty-five years of age – and St Ita's has become mainly an institution for the mentally handicapped, with only about a hundred active psychiatric patients. By the time I retire in 1994, St Brendan's will have virtually ceased to exist (indeed, I expect to be one of the last patients to leave!). Most of the psychiatric service is now concentrated in the various psychiatric districts, in a wide range of community facilities, and this has been achieved mainly by transfer of personnel from the mental hospitals themselves, with relatively little additional input of resources from the Department of Health over the years. Also, in Dublin there is not, as in other cities such as London, New York or San Fransisco, a large problem of homelessness of ex-psychiatric patients. In recent years, the success of this transition has been largely due to the unstinting commitment and efforts of Michael Walsh since he became Programme Manager.

So, from this point of view, the programme of reform to a community-based psychiatric service, even if it took somewhat longer to implement than elsewhere, could be viewed as a considerable success. I feel, however, that we have to look below the surface and ask some critical questions. For instance, are the forms of practice now being undertaken close to the community very different from what went on in the traditional mental hospital? Is the hierarchical nature of human relations between staff and patients really different from what it was in the mental hospital? We still have large, overcrowded outpatient departments, with the psychiatrist giving only two or three minutes to each patient. Undoubtedly there are changes, and changes in behaviour are still going on but, by and large, I am afraid to say that the answer to these questions is in the negative.

Even more serious is the question: is there a hidden reservoir of new chronicity building up in the community? The government policy document 'Planning for the Future' said that we should try to get patients back to normal life in the community – to their families, but, if we look below the surface and ask what this actually means, for most of those who have a serious mental illness, such as schizophrenia, this does not mean returning to their wife and children, for the large majority of such people are single and indeed have never reached full adulthood. So, we have the strange contradiction of people in their twenties, thirties or even forties returning to ageing parents and to a setting where they have always been treated (and have behaved) as small children, locked once again into a parent–child relationship that was a major factor in producing their psychiatric breakdown in the first place. This, in the over-simplified definitions of community care, is said to be a return to 'normal' community life.

In raising this question, I am not simply returning to the old debate about sick families of schizophrenogenic parents. Undoubtedly some of these families are unhealthy or could be described as sick but that is not the issue. What I am speaking about is something much simpler: the question of whether it can be considered normal or healthy for any of us who have reached our adult years to return to live in our parental home when inevitably the relationship will tend to return to that of parent and child. For many of us it is difficult, and frustrating even, to return to the parental home for a few days at Christmas.

This brings us to yet another question. Does institutionalization only happen in large custodial mental hospitals or similar institutions? The answer to this is that it does not. The worst instances of institutionalization I have come across have been persons incarcerated within their own families – young schizophrenics and others presenting to psychiatry for the first time. What the mental hospital usually does is simply offer a postgraduate training, completing the process that the family has initiated. Once we look at what institutionalization actually is – i.e. a state of dependency, not to be in charge of one's own life and destiny – we see that in this state everything is controlled by others and managed by them; it is, in essence, a state of 'learned helplessness'. Once this is understood, it is obvious that it can happen anywhere, indeed particularly in the family where we all begin life as babies in a helpless state. It is when the natural drive to mature, to become independent and self-directing, is frustrated and the person grows on into adolescence and adult life, that the true picture of institutionalization becomes apparent.

It follows from this that simply to remove mental hospitals and to send the inmates out into the community does not in itself deal with institutionalization; only psychotherapeutic and educative work to give a person competence for living and bring them to a state of independence will achieve this. Institutionalization, therefore, can continue 'alive and well' in a high-support hostel or day hospital or on returning a person to their home and family in the community, just as much as in a mental-hospital setting.

So, this is the critical issue that underlies the whole question of new chronicity or what has been called the 'new long-stay' patient. The other half of this problem is that many such patients, because they never achieved real adult status in the first place, lack the necessary skills and competence and even personal identity which would enable them to live independently even if they were willing to separate and leave their parental home. 'Planning for the Future' suggested that we would need a bed complement in some form of 0.27 per 1000 for the new long-staypatients, but I feel that this may be a serious underestimate of the new chronicity which is building up in the community and which may only surface in the years to come when, for example, parents die or are no longer capable of looking after these adult/children who are in a state of arrested development in their homes.

Thus, unless there is a real change in our methods of working, I see psychiatry moving into a blind alley, faced on the one hand with maintaining patients on long-term pharmacotherapy, with all that this implies in terms of increasing side-effects or, on the other, the likelihood of relapse in a person who is frustrated at being stuck at home with no possibility of an independent future.

Looking at the situation in this way exposes another question which has interested me for some time. If we look at services for the mentally handicapped where there is no question about the genetic/medical/organic deficit which is present we find that because, as a rule, nothing much can be done about the underlying disability, these services have for many years now geared themselves up for a sophisticated educational and developmental approach with a whole infrastructure of teachers, remedial work, physiotherapy, etc. Also, they have access to their clientele from early childhood onwards. If we compare this to the psychiatric service where the first breakdown usually emerges in late adolescence or early adulthood and where, therefore, if you were to have an effective remedial or rehabilitation programme (that is a broadly based restitutive educational input), you would need an even more sophisticated, highly geared, educational infrastructure to speed up the whole process of arrested development, we find patients engaged in folding garbage bags or other mindless activities. It is when we hold this yardstick up to our community psychiatric services that the picture looks considerably less satisfactory.

It is here that I think we should pay tribute to the Mental Health Association of Ireland, whose twenty-fifth anniversary we are celebrating, for they have been almost alone in fostering an educational, rehabilitative and preventive approach.

Finally, then, I feel it is important to state that we are not at the end of a revolution, of a period of reform, but rather that we are at the beginning of a new epoch in psychiatric development. We are standing on the threshold of a really radical revolution in the nature of psychiatric services. It is my fervent hope that we will have the courage to grasp this opportunity.

24. New Chronicity

This is the third paper in the series dealing with Psychiatric Services in the Eastern Health Board Region. The first paper is entitled 'Guided Evolution of a Community Mental Health Service', followed by 'Community Care or Independence'.

This was a talk given at a seminar run by the organization 'GROW'

I AM pleased and honoured to be here because I have admired GROW's work for a good few years and I have had a number of dialogues with Con Keogh whom I have great respect for. This, of course, means I am a deviant like the rest of you, because the orthodox people do not even ask me to talk anymore. Anyway, the reason I wanted to look at this question is because I think it has been something of an assumption that everything is developing nicely and that mental hospitals are going down in number and we are getting all the mentally ill back to a healthy community life. I have spent a great part of my life struggling with mental hospitals; they are definitely closing and that is a very good thing. Nevertheless, it does not follow that everything is right. There is the hidden problem of the people who would in the old days have gone into mental hospitals and probably stayed there – the whole question of where are they now and what is happening to them. That is what I really want to look at.

If we look at what we call the 'new longstay', these would be people who are under thirty-five years of age and have been in hospital for one to five years – that is the usual definition of the new chronics rather than the old ones, who have been there for twenty/thirty years. Below thirty-five years of age, the people we call schizophrenic comprise 88% of the total number.

What I mainly want to talk about is this group aged under thirty-five, who are becoming the new chronics or the new longstay (the names are not very nice), people who are still continuing to be a

329

problem. As you can see, the majority of them are schizophrenic. A small number of cases that we call 'organic syndromes' are probably the truly new chronics, in the sense that they won't ever be able to be dealt with purely in the community, but these are a small number and it could be asked whether they should be included in the psychiatric field at all. Although these may show behavioural disturbances, the problems they are suffering from are mainly neurological, like brain damage from motorbike accidents, or those who damage their brains from drink. So there will be a small number like these who will need full institutional care of some kind but probably only fifty to a hundred beds in a whole area like the Eastern Health Board region. It is important to realize that they are there and that they do need care. Nowadays, a better term for them is the young chronic sick, like those in the late stages of multiple sclerosis and, as I say, it is questionable that we should be considering them to be psychiatrically ill, although some of them will show severe behavioural disturbances.

The bulk of the problems I want to consider fall under the heading of what we call 'schizophrenia' or allied conditions in the younger age group; also some of the very chronically neurotic people and particularly people who have been chronically depressed, whose moods swing. Some of these can be equally chronic. In the government policy document 'Planning for the Future', which is the nearest thing we have to an official document, it was suggested that for people like this we were going to need 0.27 beds per thousand. I know it doesn't sound very much but that would be 2.7 beds per ten thousand or twenty-seven beds per hundred thousand. In the area in which I have been working in the Eastern Health Board region, we have about twelve areas of roughly 100,000. Once you look at it, then you realize that you are looking at roughly 300 places – which is really a mental hospital again. Hopefully we won't be talking about a mental hospital but, whatever we are talking about, if these people are going to become chronic and unable to live an independent life (which is really what orthodox psychiatry is saying), then they are going to need maximum care. Whether you have them in a high-support hostel, which is the new version of the mental hospital, or in some smaller mental hospital, they are still going to need considerable care. They are going to cost a great deal of money and resources, because, whichever way it turns out, it is going to cost nearly as much to run a high-support hostel as it is a mental hospital ward. So we are talking of a very serious problem: first of all for the people concerned but also for the country. I also wonder if this is not an underestimate, because many people who are in hospital for a short time and then discharged to the so-called community are actually becoming chronic in their parental families.

The changes that are taking place in St Brendan's, are fairly typical of the changes that are happening generally in Europe. When I started out, there were 2,000 people in Grangegorman. They will be putting me out in 1994 – but by 1995 I think it will come very close to being empty. There are about 350 patients left at the moment and over half of those are already geriatric. The problem of the mental hospital is being solved in that sense and I think psychiatry should be congratulating itself, but of course the question we have got to ask is: is there a real shift, is there a real change in the way people are being treated and in the relationship of professionals to the psychiatrically ill?

When I worked with Joshua Bierer in London back in 1959 the question of community psychiatry then was really a question of changing this relationship, democratizing it. In other words, instead of dealing as a doctor with a patient you did things to, somehow you tried to be one human being working with another. That is very much the way GROW works. As this process has gone on, it has become more and more a question of emptying mental hospitals, that the mental hospital is bad and the community is good. Over the years the assumption has grown that the institutionalization that occurs among patients is to do with large mental hospitals, and there is no doubt that this is true.

The assumption, though, is that before that, people were not institutionalized, but some of the worst cases of institutionalization I have seen have come directly out of families. Institutionalization is not just to do with large anonymous impersonal environments; the essence of it is whether you are able to run your own life or whether others are running it for you. If you hold up that criterion, then you will see true institutionalization happening right in the middle of families just as much as in mental hospitals. I remember one girl I dealt with back in 1959 who was being washed, fed with a spoon and dressed by her mother, although a few years earlier she had held down a good job in New York.

If you read a document like 'Planning for the Future', there is a lot of talk about getting people back to the normal environment – the normal environment being the community. If you actually look closer, for the adult schizophrenic this usually means going back to their parental home, but is it ever normal for a twenty-five-year-old to be living in their parental home when most of us who are living out in the world can't usually stand it for a few days at Christmas. I am not in any way blaming parents. I am simply saying that we want to look a lot closer at what we mean when we are talking about community. To me the real issues are to do with dependence versus independence. I will come back to this later.

I just want to make a short digression into history. It is interesting that St Brendan's is as near to the GPO as Trinity or St Stephen's Green and yet most of the people in Dublin do not know where it is. This says something about what we do with people we do not want. We make the assumption that we are making steady progress and are now much more enlightened than we were, say, a hundred years ago. If you actually look at the history, this is very questionable. If you go back to the time of Samuel Wriggley – who was a layman, not a psychiatrist – who ran St Brendan's with his wife, he had virtually every patient doing some kind of work or industrial therapy and there was very little restraint. The man who followed him was a Doctor Lawlor, who introduced education to St Brendan's and, in that period, around 1856, all the patients were going to school, doing the full National School curriculum; there were a number of teachers in the hospital. The interesting thing is that there were very few suicides, there was no mechanical restraint and very few people were actually locked up in those two periods. The main thing to remember is that, as the situation became more medicalized, the numbers started to go up and the emphasis moved away from that so-called moral stage. Thus more attention was paid to medical intervention and more and more patients were restrained and there was increasingly more physical treatment and, eventually, drug therapy.

What is the true nature of mental illness? Is it primarily that persons fail and are unable to manage life and find a place for themselves in society because they are mentally ill? This would be the orthodox position up to the present and, in fact, it is more entrenched than it ever was. So it is possible to say about a person: 'He can't succeed. He is a schizophrenic.' But my question is: is it more correct to say that they have become mentally ill because they have failed, through lack of social and living skills, to manage life and to make the transition into adult life as self-directed individuals? In other words, have they had to choose the pathway of mental illness because they were failing to develop into adults who have the range of skills and coping mechanisms to be able to manage life? That question, in the traditional psychiatric mode, seems to me to be virtually never asked. It is obviously not totally one or the other position. I am not denying genetic elements and that some people are perhaps more vulnerable than others. However, when you have said all that, it does not follow that these are the primary causes of mental illness as such. My position would be that there is still a choice there for the person with the right help from those around them whether or not they go down that pathway; in other words, mental illness is the result of many things but I would say that it is primarily a psychosocial situation. Were we to look at most schizophrenics, or most of those chronically mentally ill – the new ones that we are talking about – and remove the symptoms by some miracle and ask how well is that person equipped for life, we would find a person who has a range of deficits that make it impossible for them to take on independent living. If this is so, then the full answer can never be pharmaceutical. If you need to be able to mend a lawnmower or speak French and run a computer in order to do your job and also to be able to care for yourself personally and you have not got those skills, there will never be a pharmaceutical that can teach you those things.

This seems to me to be where the whole problem is getting confused because the medical assumption is that, if we get rid of the symptoms, then we will have a normal person. There is also the assumption that before they became mentally ill they were normal. The way we respond to this, I think, determines the kind of psychiatric service we will have and the sort of approach we will have to the psychiatrically disturbed.

If we take the medical approach, these disturbances will be diagnosed within a psychiatric framework as symptoms of an underlying disease and will be treated mainly by corrective pharmaceutical methods or by the actions of the professionals, by the actions of doctors. Inevitably, this approach sees patients as victims of their chemistry, or the way, if you like, their mental machine is working. Therefore they can have no control over themselves. Once we say this, we are obviously embarked on a self-fulfilling prophesy. So, if a medical student breaks down as a schizophrenic and we say that he is now mentally ill and could not possibly continue in medicine, we have already made it true that this person cannot go back and do medicine. In believing this, we have already had a powerful effect on the future potential of that person. These are some of the introgenic, self-fulfilling prophesies that I think GROW are struggling against.

In contrast to this view, would it not be true to say that the large majority of those who have failed in the past or are failing at present have become mentally ill because they have failed to find an enriching context within which to make the transition to adult life. There is a myth in society that we automatically grow up, automatically emerge as independent adults. If we look at our own lives or look around us, we will recognize that this is a big struggle and, particularly in the aggressive sort of competitive society that we have now, is becoming a more difficult struggle, so that it is not even just a small minority who fail any more – every Leaving Certificate student is asking 'Will I get a place, will I make it?' Therefore, unless people have developed a full range of coping skills, they are immediately in trouble in our society. I feel that this is what is not being looked at honestly and I think, when it does happen, we medicalize it, and in fact therefore increase the problem. Even if the more obvious symptoms of illness were miraculously removed, we would still have a person who showed a range of personal, social and work skill deficits that would make it impossible for them to manage everyday life. This is a situation which, to my mind, simply is not looked at by orthodox psychiatry, and I am asking why it has not been highlighted until now. I think it is because we have seen such people as ill, mentally disabled, of poor genetic stock. It is not just the psychiatrically ill that this applies to. The sociopathic failures move along the same pathway and end up in jail and of course some of these populations are transferable: we close mental hospitals and the prison population goes up. This is essentially a pessimistic view of society and one that robs the person of any control in the situation, of any choices. It is a mechanistic view of the person as a machine, where everything is determined.

Is it any wonder then that such persons arrive at the door of a psychiatrist or drift into an anti-social pathway of drug abuse or vandalism, eventually ending up in prison or a mental hospital or as a premature death on the street? This is very much the problem we are facing. If we look at a place like New York, mental hospitals are again closing down but there are thousands of people on the streets living miserable lives or dying of substance abuse.

Systemic Thinking

If we look at science over the last two or three hundred years, since the Renaissance, people in the medical profession, whenever a problem occurs, are still asking what part of the person is not functioning and thus making their behaviour disturbed. The question always seems to be framed in this way. In the hard sciences like physics and chemistry there has been a revolution that has changed all that. Now we find people in those fields thinking along lines like 'chaos theory' and a whole view of indeterminacy is entering into the picture. However, the medical profession and other professions like sociology and economics are still thinking in the old, deterministic way and seeing this as the scientific approach. This may be an appropriate way to think about ordinary working machines – if your car is not working you search to see what valves are giving trouble, and this works for your motorbike or most mechanisms of that kind – but, when we are dealing with living creatures, this way of looking at things does not give the whole answer. More and more of the illnesses we are dealing with now (not just psychiatric illnesses but heart disease and many others) are forms of chronic illness that result from the lifestyle of the person. They are something that the person lives and does. So you could argue that a person is living high blood pressure, they are not catching it like the common cold. While the mechanistic approach works for a lot of areas, I think we need to look in another way at where most of the current serious health problems and certainly most of the psychiatric problems are concerned. The way in which a person lives and behaves has an effect on their parts. This is the essence of systemic thinking: the whole is not understandable in terms of the parts that make it up.

So the way in which we live and behave will affect our cells and organs right down to the neuro-transmitters. To quickly take just one or two examples: if you decide to drink heavily, that is a behaviour that you choose; or if you choose to smoke and you go on doing it long enough to affect your heart and brain, eventually all your parts become diseased. However, you cannot talk about smoking in the same way that you talk about the TB bacilius because smoking is something that a person lives and does. If I am right in thinking this, then it implies that we need to change our whole way of looking at the seriously mentally ill person. It is a question of asking what is the schizophrenic going to do about themselves in their own life, not about how people are going to care for and 'treat' this patient.

I have struggled with people who are defined as schizophrenic or whatever and have had some successes with helping certain individuals but I have also wondered why I didn't succeed better. I was putting forward a belief system. Now you see that that is not good enough and even all the work GROW is doing still won't affect or change the orthodox psychiatric mind. What I am proposing now is a study taking say twenty or thirty schizophrenic patients, or those who come into that broad group that constitute the 'new chronics', and asking what can we do in the sense of a broadly based education programme – essentially what GROW is doing. The study would also have a contrasting control group, who would be matched, and these would be left to the traditional treatment methods (which is quite ethical because that is what official psychiatry says is the appropriate treatment). It would be interesting to follow those two groups and then see after two or three years if there is a difference in outcome. I cannot say that this is more than a hypothesis but if I am right in thinking along this line then the basic question we would be asking is whether it would be effective to work with people using an educational approach, with respect as human beings, in order to help them to change themselves. If we can do that in any way effectively, perhaps we can show a big difference. Remember, the present situation means that we are only keeping people out there in the community by maintaining them with large doses of pharmaceuticals, usually in their parental families. This is a blind alley: every year now more and more side-effects are manifesting and yet orthodox psychiatry has no other alternative but to go on using those drugs indefinitely, on a long-term basis. Unless we take this battle into the heart of psychiatry using their language in this sort of controlled study, I do not think they are going to listen.

Summary

We need to ask what can this person do for society rather than asking how can society care for them. In other words, you do not set a limit on the potential of the person. At present all of the professional world applies limits but if a person starts with such a limit (this person can't go further than folding garbage bags), then obviously they can't go any further because the power is in the hands of the professionals: so we take off the limits. That is the first point.

The other fundamental point is that, even if we have a whole context of services to bring a person through to independence, the process should still rest on a personal relationship, which would not be psychotherapy in the traditional sense but would mean the person would have an advocate, a trained therapist who is there in the background working with the person. A combination of this and an organization such as GROW would be the ideal.

If I look at most people labelled with schizophrenia, they are like children, they have not developed into rounded adults, so an essential part of this idea would be to help the person move from a child's to an adult position – i.e. from the position of dependence to independence – which means doing the work of separation out of the parental home. I say 'work' because both the individual and their parents will have to work at this. When we actually look at psychiatry, the opposite is happening, and people are being returned to their parental homes.

We will, however, need to give them the coping skills to enable them to live separately. Now most of the people who come in diagnosed as having schizophrenia or allied conditions haven't got those skills, so it is unrealistic to expect them to simply leave home. It is not fair to expect them to leave home unless they can gain those skills. I would not want to start the study I have proposed here unless there can be a systematic set of facilities, starting with personal development and moving on to workshop places and somewhere alternative to live. If I look around the present psychiatric services, this is missing. It is missing because of the enormously powerful caucus of medical nursing services aligned with the drug companies; and this is where all the money is going.

You can see this very clearly if you compare our psychiatric services to mental handicap services, where there is no question about the medical deficit for the person who is genetically damaged. From early in life they go into a very high-powered educational system. If we look at such services, we find teachers, bodyworkers, physiotherapists, a whole group of skilled educational people. If we turn to psychiatry, we find people folding garbage bags, and this to me is not an accident. So we need to set up a context similar to mental handicap services. I have talked to the Programme Manager, who is very willing to try and set this in place and I also know a few people interested in the project. When I look back, I realize that any time I have failed to help people with these problems it is always because I couldn't achieve the next step: when they were ready to leave home I couldn't get them a hostel place; if they got a place in the hostel they had nothing to do during the day. I would spend my time trying to match these facilities so they came together at the right time but in the meantime the person would relapse. When you hold this up to our psychiatric services, they look pretty pathetic.

We need to sit down with these people, as I would with a medical student, and work through their problems. And of course the other half of the disturbance profile is the addiction of solving the problems that most of us have to work at in life through fantasy. Of course, if you can be John Q from outer space or the papal legate or, as one fellow signed himself into hospital, Jesus Christ – address heaven – you do not have to bother with the Leaving Certificate. When life gets difficult, that person wheels in the delusions as, if you can be someone very important and have a mythical self-esteem, you do not have to struggle with ordinary life. Stan Grof drew a nice cartoon showing a mystic hanging out of a tree and a schizophrenic in a strait-jacket on the ground and the schizophrenic is saying 'How come I'm a schizophrenic and you are a mystic?' and the mystic says 'I know who not to talk to'. That, in a way, sums up the whole nub of this talk. If we are to succeed in helping such people, we really need to educate them to understand what it is to hallucinate and how we perceive the world and so on. This would mean they could not let themselves away with these dishonesties. Remember, a lot of mental illness is a dishonesty.

That is why organizations like GROW are so important. They are working away, with little help or encouragement, with those who have been diagnosed as mentally ill, to help them to face the truth about themselves and their families and to ask the world to deal fairly and truthfully with them so that they can find a place for themselves in the sun.

25. Mental Illness
– *Letter to* The Irish Times

This letter was published in *The Irish Times* in November 2006 in response to a piece by Breda O'Brien, 'The Minister's View on Mental Illness', which was subsequently described as 'downright irresponsible' by a group of six professors of psychiatry. I felt obliged to respond to what is now becoming a national debate about the nature of mental illness.

M ADAM, – Having read the letter from the group of six professors of psychiatry in response to the piece by Breda O'Brien, 'The Minister's View on Mental Illness', and their further letter of 24 November, I do not share the view that the Minister's remarks were 'downright irresponsible'. I feel obliged, therefore, to respond to what is now becoming a national debate as to the nature of mental illness.

It seems an obvious thing to say that, before and after birth to adult death, human beings experience things that cause them suffering. But this is a fact of life that is often overlooked. Some can bear more than others, some understand more than others, but suffering is a part of life and may become so unbearable that we want to fix it. At that point we look for help, usually from a doctor, and often find that our feelings are called 'mental illness'. Because of the mechanistic attitude which has accompanied the enormous advances in science and technology, the western mind has fallen into the illusion that there is a remedy for every ill. The belief has grown up, especially in the west, that it is the doctor who cures. The body is seen as a machine with which something has gone wrong, and the doctor's job is to deal with it. We have tended to fall into the error of thinking that the psychiatrist cures the patient. When applied to psychotherapy, or for that matter to psychiatry generally, this is an erroneous notion. In dealing with psychiatric illness, there is no treatment that you can apply to a person which brings about real change in them. The person has to undertake the work themselves and this involves pain and suffering. It remains true that the only lasting positive change anyone can make is within him/herself. The deeper the change to be accomplished, the greater the amount of pain and suffering involved. People resist change for this reason, even when they realize that change will have a positive benefit. By giving tranquillizers and relieving symptoms, something has been achieved temporarily. In fact, no real change has taken place, and sooner or later most will slip back to where they were, with a recurrence of their symptoms, and the added burden of the horrendous side-effects which most of these drugs inflict. Many drugs are useful on a temporary basis but they are not treatments for specific 'psychiatric diseases'. However, no psychiatrist who deals with the full range of psychiatric disturbance could manage completely without them. The question is whether they are given as a treatment themselves or as an aid to working in psychotherapy with the person. At times, the drug is the only way of facilitating the initial contact so that therapy can begin. It is not the drug, it is the message which accompanies the drug which is really damaging. Typically, if a person is 'clinically' depressed they are told that, whenever they feel a depression descending on them, they must contact their psychiatrist and commence the appropriate medication. It is because of this, more than anything else, that many people are gradually entrained into a pathway of illness. Perceiving themselves as 'ill' and helpless, they move into a state of chronic ill-health. Clusters of symptoms tell one little about the cause or the natural history of these so-called 'disorders'. They have a more ominous significance, however, for, once you can name symptoms as a 'disease', you have created an apparent reality. Then, if you have a specific 'disease' due to some, as yet, unidentified underlying biochemical abnormality, there should be a 'specific' remedy to deal with it. This suits the pharmaceutical industry perfectly. Unfortunately, most psychiatrists have taken this great falsehood on board. If you think about it, all that drugs can do is temporarily reduce the symptoms to make life bearable. No drug can teach you what you need to know to manage life or have a personal identity. Often in life we cannot see how we got to where we are, or why we continue to make the same mistakes no matter how hard we try. If a person could undertake whatever change is necessary to successfully manage their life, there would be no need for a psychiatrist or therapist. Of course, the person who comes to our aid need not be a professional; indeed, a great deal of helpful intervention is carried out by self-help organizations such as Alcoholics Anonymous, GROW, etc., but in many situations a friend is not enough and the objectivity and understanding of a person with experience and training is necessary. The sad fact is that most psychiatrists have not undergone a real training in psychotherapy, so they depend on others such as psychologists, social workers, etc., to do it for them.

I see the essential role of the professional, then, as a guide, to help the person to map out the situation in which they find themselves, not to do the work for the patient, but to provide the 'context' within which they can find their own truth. At the deepest level, this work is of a spiritual nature.

Perhaps the most important thing of all is to provide hope to enable the person to see that you believe that change is possible, and that they can do it. Finally, I agree with the six professors that the resource allocation for mental health services is grossly inadequate and needs to be radically improved. However, in my opinion, before such increased resources come on-stream, an official inquiry should be set up to investigate the efficacy of current psychiatric practice, which is evidently failing, and that this should be done by an independent scientific body. Further, I feel their brief should include an examination of the separation of the pharmaceutical industry from academia and all research which is carried out by psychiatric departments on their behalf.

Yours etc.
Ivor Browne
Professor Emeritus
University College Dublin
Ranelagh, Dublin

26. Electroconvulsive Therapy (ECT)
– *Letter to* The Irish Times

This letter was published in *The Irish Times* in June 2008. It resulted from the response of the Irish College of Psychiatrists to a letter on electroconvulsive therapy (ECT) by Dr Michael Corry, where they stated that 'ECT is still a valuable psychiatric treament'. I stated that 'I would beg to differ'.

MADAM, – The response to the article on electroconvulsive therapy (ECT) by Dr Michael Corry from the official voice of psychiatry on 28 June, speaking on behalf of the Irish College of Psychiatrists and the Irish Psychiatric Association, is headlined 'ECT still a valuable psychiatric treatment'. I would beg to differ.

Nearly three years after I commenced training in psychiatry, towards the end of 1968, as I stated in my book *Music and Madness*: 'I began to have deep reservations about the efficacy of ECT and the long-term damage which can ensue from this procedure. I was becoming increasingly uneasy about these crude forms of physical intervention; my feeling was growing that there must be a more humane way to work in psychiatry.'

As I gradually reached the 'use of reason' as to the true nature of mental health, I came to a decision. This was not an ideological position; it has always been my view that the ultimate priority is that we do whatever we can to help the person we are dealing with. But I decided that I would only countenance giving ECT to a patient if I could find no better alternative and if their very survival was at stake.

That was forty years ago and I have never had to give anyone ECT since that time, even though over all those years I have dealt with the full range of psychiatric disturbance. There were occasionally very difficult situations where, for example, someone was refusing food and in danger of dying, but I always managed to find an alternative.

Back in those days I was not yet fully aware of the extent to which punitive procedures had been meted out to psychiatric patients over several centuries, frequently without their consent. I knew of the purging, the bleedings, the swinging chairs, freezing baths, the beatings and so on that were perpetrated on those psychiatrically disturbed during the eighteenth and nineteenth centuries but I didn't realize that these same abuses continued on in different forms throughout the twentieth century right up to the present day. We have had the débâcle of lobotomies, deep insulin coma therapy, etc., and ECT all, one after the other, being shown to be highly damaging and therapeutically ineffective.

But the situation is much worse than this. By 1939 the plan to murder many mental patients in Germany was put into operation, with the support of most of the professors of psychiatry and senior psychiatrists. 'By September 1941, over 70,000 mental patients had been killed with carbon monoxide . . . the total figure for Germany alone is well over a quarter of a million' (*Models of Madness*, eds John Read, Loren R. Mosher, et al.). The entire procedure, which was later utilized in the Holocaust, had already been developed by psychiatrists.

In Canada, Dr Ewen Cameron, at McGill University's Allen Memorial Institute, instituted a method of 'complete depatterning' of the personality of his patients (frequently without their consent), to return their minds to a state of 'tabula rasa'. He then intended to recreate an entirely new personality, which was absurd and of course a total failure. To achieve this, he used continuous electroshock, giving a terrifying 360 shocks to each patient, combined with an array of drug therapies and sensory deprivation. At this time he was at the pinnacle of his profession, being at various times president of the American Psychiatric Association, the Canadian Psychiatric Association and the World Psychiatric Association. This vicious programme was funded by the CIA and the methods he pioneered have formed the basis of the interrogation, rendition and torture being carried out by American intelligence to this day.

Over many years, studies of ECT have shown no long-term benefit, only a temporary relief of symptoms due to confusion and brain damage. Some early studies utilized a simulated ECT control group and found no significant difference between the two groups. However, later studies justified the exclusion of any control group on the plea of 'ethical difficulties'; i.e. of withholding a treatment 'known' to be effective, thus 'begging the question' and deciding the very result that required to be demonstrated.

When will psychiatrists finally accept that we are dealing with sensitive, delicately poised human beings, not machines to be tinkered with; that the very definition of life is one of self-organization and self-management? The only real lasting change comes when we help a person to bring about the painful work of change within themselves.

Yours etc.
Ivor Browne
Professor Emeritus
University College Dublin
Ranelagh, Dublin

27. 'Unassimilated Happenings'[1] and the False Memory Syndrome

This paper and 'Healing the Trauma' were never published, although I did send them to the *American Journal of Psychiatry*, not realizing how much thinking had changed in the USA. They had dismissed the previous emphasis on psychoanalysis and dynamic psychiatry and shifted to a narrow medical view of psychiatric illness, claiming that it was all 'biologically based'. When I was in the US in 1960, every professorial chair was headed by a psychoanalyst. By the time I submitted these papers, there was not a single psychoanalytical professor and the major centres all across the country were headed by neurophysiologists and pharmacological psychiatrists.

Not only did they refuse to publish the papers but they also rubbished the theories that I was proposing, saying there was no evidence to support these ideas.

THE main concern of this paper is the way in which human experience is processed and integrated into the central nervous system and in particular the impact of psychological trauma. This was the subject of two previous papers,[2] and the more complete hypothesis presented here is based on extensive clinical work with psychologically traumatized patients. To put it in its simplest form, when an event takes place in the external world we do not fully experience it as it happens, although we do undoubtedly register it and take an impression of the raw experience as it is taking place, otherwise the event would no longer exist within us once it has happened in the external world. Evidence exists for this registration, in that many years afterwards a traumatic event may be recalled in complete detail in what Horowitz termed a 'video-tape of the mind'.[3] In other words, experiencing something fully and turning it into memory is a process that takes place over time. This involves neurophysiological and somatic work proportional to the degree of

345

disturbance and threat that the traumatic event poses to the integrity of the organism concerned.

The fact that a traumatic event can reappear after many years, when the person had no conscious recollection of it until then, immediately raises the question whether some or any of such activated experiences are genuine recollections or fantasies. This question is of particular concern in the light of recent revelations regarding over-enthusiastic therapists in the States and elsewhere and the widespread debate in regard to the 'false memory syndrome'. We will return to this question later in the paper but in order to do so it is first necessary to address the main concern of this paper and describe more fully what we mean by 'unassimilated happenings'. For, depending on whether or not this hypothesis is sound, the whole basis of the debate surrounding the so-called 'false memory syndrome' will be altered.

It has long been recognized that, when a living creature is faced with a threat to its physical integrity, it responds to the challenge with the noradrenergically mediated 'fight or flight' response.[4] In situations where defensive or evasive actions are not possible, it appears that an organism has at its disposal an equally ancient and basic strategy for survival; that is, the capacity, when faced with an overwhelming external threat, to 'freeze' or 'play dead'.[5] This involves the operation of a primitive biological, adaptive response which acts at the level of the limbic system (outside of conscious awareness or control) and blocks, partially or completely, the processing and integration of the experience.

The potentially disintegrative effect of the external threat is signalled by the initial surge of emotion which occurs as the event is appraised by the primitive brain. It would seem that it can be only thus that the significance of dangers or threatening events are recognized. This primitive biological response is widespread in nature and constitutes a highly effective survival manoeuvre when 'fight or flight' is not possible. Similar to other survival mechanisms in lower animals, this 'freeze response', while present in human beings, appears to have been modified to serve a somewhat different purpose in modern human conditions. As well as being a way of avoiding external danger, it may now be used to deal with the threat of internal destabilization: whenever we are faced with an overwhelming experience which we sense to be potentially disintegrative, we have the ability to suspend it in an unassimilated, inchoate form and to maintain it in that stage indefinitely. Our biological structure seems to be able to specify in advance that to fully experience the meaning of the threatening encounter would destroy or disintegrate its core organization. The clinical evidence would suggest that this capacity to suspend the progress and integration of experience in some way involves the limbic system, for it is this part of the brain that controls the vegetative nervous system through which we express all our emotions and that is responsible for the basic mechanisms of survival.[6]

Eccles[7] lays particular emphasis on the role played by the limbic system in processing information. It was postulated that short-term memory storage may occur within the sensory association areas of the cerebral cortex, information passing from them to the limbic system. This primitive part of the brain may function as some form of selection and appraisal unit. For long-term memory storage to take place, information would have to be processed through the limbic system itself and from there would be transmitted to the cortex and back to the limbic system again. Thus, what was proposed is that a circular form of interaction between the primitive brain and the cortex may occur until ultimate long-term storage is achieved.

Over the past twenty years there have been major advances in understanding the anatomical components of the brain's memory system, particularly of the structures in the medial temporal lobe. Studies of human patients had already strongly suggested that the hippocampus may play a crucial role in memory.[8] In 1957, Scofield and Milner[9] described a profound and selective impairment in human memory after bilateral surgical removal of the medial temporal lobe. Since then, other cases of human patients with selective damage to the hippocampus and related areas have been described.[10] More recent work with primates has identified neuro-structures that contribute to memory, has traced their connections and, to a considerable extent has demonstrated how they interact as memory is stored, retrieved or linked with other experience.[11]

Mishkin and Appenzeller proposed that, to produce severe amnesia, damage to both the hippocampus and the amygdala is required in both humans and monkeys. Evidence from animal experimentation and clinical work with various kinds of brain damage and dementia support these findings.[12] It was also suggested that bilateral removal of both amygdala and hippocampus result in an animal that is unable to process any new experience, although removal of one or other structure alone only brings about partial impairment.

A theory proposed by Squire and Zola-Morgan[13] suggests that memory is not a single faculty but is composed instead of multiple separate systems, only one of which is impaired in amnesia. In human amnesia, the ability to acquire information about facts and events (declarative memory) is impaired but not the capacity for skill learning, certain kinds of conditioning and habit-learning, as well as the phenomenon of priming. They point out that 'in the case of non-declarative memory, experience alters behaviour non-consciously without providing access to any memory content'. On the other hand, declarative memory is accessible to conscious recollection and available to multiple response systems.

More recently, the central importance of the amygdala in memory has been challenged by research which has demonstrated that it is not the amygdala but the surrounding cortical areas (which in earlier work were damaged together with the amygdala) which are critical to the production of amnesia – i.e. the entorhinal cortex, together with the adjacent anatomically related perirhinal and parahippocampal cortices.

Furthermore, it is suggested that these cortical areas adjacent to the hippocampus are not simply a conduit for connecting neocortex to hippocampus but are important for memory function. The implication is that information from neocortex needs not reach the hippocampus itself in order for some memory storage to occur. These considerations explain why memory impairment is increased by damage to cortical structures in addition to the hippocampus.

A conclusion drawn from this work is that the amygdala is not a component of the medial temporal lobe memory system and does not contribute to the kind of (declarative) memory that depends on this system. It is also suggested that the amygdala is important for other functions concerning conditioned fear and the attachment of affect to neural stimuli. The amygdala may also have a broader role in establishing links between stimuli, as in making associations among sensory modalities. Mishkin and Appenzeller had also pointed to these functions of the amygdala: 'Parts of the amygdala on which sensory inputs converge send fibres deeper into the brain to the hypothalamus which is thought to be the source of emotional responses.' They state further that:

> it is possible that the amygdala not only enable sensory events to develop emotional associations but also enable emotions to shape perception and the storage of memories . . . Circuitry exists that could give the amygdala this gatekeeping function.

It is particularly interesting also to note from their work that:

> Together the evidence suggests the possibility that opiate-containing fibres run from the amygdala to the sensory systems, where they may serve a gatekeeping function by releasing opiates in response to emotional states generated in the hypo thalamus.[14]

One crucial aspect that is missing from this current research into memory is the hypothesis that the primitive brain has the capacity to block this whole memory processing system when the living organism is faced with an overwhelming threat or traumatic experience which it is not capable of integrating at that time. The evidence would suggest that the amygdala mediates the association of memories formed through different senses and that it has 'direct and extensive connections with all the sensory systems in the cortex'.[15] In identifying these emotional connections of the amygdala complex, we are perhaps getting closer to a possible site for the blocking mechanism which is activated when a living organism is faced with an overwhelmingly traumatic experience.

The functions of the medial temporal lobe memory system have been summarized by Squire and Morgan:

> Cumulative and systematic research with monkeys and related research with humans has identified the components of the medial temporal lobe memory system: i.e. the hippocampus, together with adjacent, anatomically related cortex. This system is fast, has limited capacity, and performs a crucial function at the time of learning in establishing long-term declarative memory. Its role continues after learning during a lengthy period of reorganization and consolidation whereby memories stored in neocortex eventually become independent of the medial temporal lobe memory system. This process, by which the burden of long-term (permanent) memory storage is gradually assumed by

neocortex, assures that the medial temporal lobe system is always available for the acquisition of new information.[16]

It is important to stress that the limbic system has not only connections with higher brain centres, but also has intimate connections with the vegetative nervous system and therefore with the body as a whole.[17] These connections include a pathway through the hypothalamus and the pituitary, which controls the entire endocrine system; the second main pathway is through the autonomic nervous system, and the third route involves all the voluntary nervous system connections.[18] Clinical observations from the various forms of body work and somatic manipulation would suggest that there is a direct connection between the changing of particular somatic patterns which had developed following the inhibition of specific traumatic events and their release and opening up as a result of such bodily manipulation.[19] This would suggest the possibility of a feedback loop from connections in the soma, through the autonomic and voluntary nervous systems and the psychoendocrine system back into the limbic system and from there to higher cortical centres, forming an entire experiential cycle, all parts of which are intimately interconnected.

The question remains how experience and information are processed through the primitive brain into memory and more particularly the manner by which this processing can be blocked in the face of overwhelming traumatic insults. Recent neurobiological findings, rather than weakening the validity of psychological observations, complement them[20] and indeed point towards possible mechanisms for such a blocking process. Much of the literature focuses on changes in the hypothalamic, pituitary adrenal axis.[21] These suggest enhanced sensitivity of the negative feedback mechanism in post-traumatic stress disorder. Conversely, studies of major depressive disorder demonstrate decreased sensitivity of this axis.[22] This feedback mechanism operates through the pituitary hypothalamus and hippocampus. It has been shown that stress produces site-specific dynamic changes in glucocorticoid receptors in the brain, particularly at the hippocampus.[23] These receptors appear to have an important role in HPA dysregulation in post-traumatic stress disorder[24] and are opposite to those receptor changes found in major depressive disorder.[25] The number of glucocorticoid receptors strongly correlates with post-traumatic stress disorder symptoms but not with depressive symptoms.[26] Several studies have alluded to both the overlap of symptoms between major depressive disorder and post-traumatic stress disorder[27] and the high incidence of co-morbidity.[28] The evidence is strong, however, that post-traumatic stress disorder is a distinct entity[29] and that neurobiological changes are not due to adjunctive symptoms of depression.

Studies of acute stress generally show raised levels of both cortisol and norepinephrine.[30] However, these two responses can be dissociated under certain conditions.[31] It is striking that post-traumatic stress disorder patients have low stable cortisol levels at the same time that they have markedly increased urinary catecholamines.[32] Indeed, this has been suggested as a possible means of differential diagnosis of MOD and post-traumatic stress disorder.[33] A possible explanation for this phenomenon can be found in psychoendocrine research. The use of psychological defences can exert a strong suppressive effect upon urinary cortico-steroid levels[34] and the relationship between effectiveness of defences and adrenal cortical activity has been confirmed in other studies.[35] Chronic stress in the neonatal period has been shown to have profound effects on subsequent HPA responses to stress,[36] with lower base line corticosterone and attenuated corticosterone release to novel stress.[37] These changes appear to reflect state and trait characteristics[38] with altered responsiveness of key systems such as the receptor adenylate cyclase subunit.[39] This supports the theory that a pre-traumatic history increases vulnerability towards developing post-traumatic stress disorder.[40]

Psychophysiological studies have demonstrated high levels of sympathetic nervous system activity in post-traumatic stress disorder.[41] The primary source of noradrenergic innervation of the limbic system is the locus coerulus.[42] It exerts a hierarchical control over the ANS and is intimately involved in stress responses.[43] It also has a role in memory retrieval facilitation.[44] It has been postulated that a neurophysiological analogue of memory can be produced by extreme stress[45] such as that thought to be of primary importance in aetiology of post-traumatic stress disorder. The locus coerulus is also involved in sleep regulation;[46] its activity markedly increases during REM sleep.[47] It is thus plausible that both the flashbacks and nightmares characteristic of post-traumatic stress disorder are related to potentiation of LC pathways to the hippocampus and amygdala[48] or

351

that post-traumatic stress disorder may fundamentally involve a disturbance of REM sleep mechanisms.[49]

In the light of neurophysiolgical work described in relation to memory, a more hopeful line of enquiry would seem to lie with further investigation of the role of the hippocampus and, perhaps even more strategically, the amygdala complex.

Mishkin's work suggests a crucial role for the amygdala in gate-keeping, a function which is possibly mediated by opiate-containing fibres. Indeed, a possible connection between the 'numbing' symptoms of PTSD and possible opiate mechanisms has been noted,[50] as has the phenomenon of stress-induced analgesia mediated by endogenous opioids.[51] Stress-induced analgesia has been noted as early as 1946[52] and, more recently, studies of stress in animals have demonstrated activation of opiate receptors in a manner analogous to repeated application of exogenous opiates.[53] This can be reversed by Naloxone.[54] Symptoms of opiate withdrawal can be produced by both Naloxone injections or cessation of the stress; indeed, parallels have been drawn between the symptoms of opiate withdrawal and PTSD.[55] This may explain the phenomenon of addiction to trauma, where victims of trauma repeatedly place themselves in situations reminiscent of the trauma,[56] such as the case of an abused child provoking or seeking subsequent abuse.[57]

Although much of this work on memory is still speculative, one fact appears to stand out – that damage to tiny areas in the primitive brain, such as the hippocampus, leads to a total inability to process any new information whatsoever, although information stored in the memory banks from the past may remain relatively intact.

To summarize, then, the essence of this hypothesis:

1. The integration of experience into the self is a process taking place over time.
2. This involves neurophysiological and somatic work.
3. When a person is subjected to a serious traumatic event, an immediate, non-conscious, biological mechanism is invoked, which may suspend the experience, either partly or completely blocking further processing and integration into long-term memory.
4. The degree to which an event is threatening or traumatic does not depend simply on the nature of the external event but is also a function of the internal set of the individual at the time

the event occurs. This is a function of all the learning and experience of that individual up to that moment, including, of course, whether there have been previous insults or experiences of a similar kind which were blocked or suspended, or indeed other predisposing life events.[58] The traumatic event therefore is the meeting point of the external event and the internal set of the individual, involving all of the learned past up to that time.

5. It is now as if a piece of the external world is within the person but not part of them. This internalized 'stressor' now exists outside of time in a potentially unstable state. The person retains these subsidiaries in an unorganized or inchoate form, some of which may be represented somatically as well as centrally. In Michael Polanyi's terms, there is no movement from the parts to the whole.[59] By this biological refusal to integrate the particles of the encounter, the person may never consciously identify the threatening experience; it is as if it had never happened.

6. In situations such as this, where an experience is blocked or suspended, it may be held in that state for years or even a lifetime. Where an earlier experience has been inhibited or suspended in like manner, later events of this kind will also be blocked, thus building up increasing pressure on the primitive medial temporal lobe memory system, until activation occurs.

7. If activated later by some life event, the experience (or experiences) leaks, breaks through and causes 'flashbacks' on the screen of perception. In spite of denial, this triggers a painful emotional response (symptoms) which once again the individual attempts to block and suspend, as with the original event, but now only partially successfully.

Janet and Freud

In recent times there has been renewed interest in the work of Pierre Janet.[60] Freud and Janet were contemporaries: Freud (born 1826) was three years older but Janet, who died in 1947, outlived him by almost eight years. Although they never met, they were well aware of each other's work and in the early years the general direction of their work was very close. Indeed, in those years each paid tribute to the work of the other. In a letter to Fleiss,[61] Freud stated: 'Our work on hysteria has at last received proper recognition from Janet in Paris', and Janet praised the work of Breuer and Freud as follows:

> We are glad to find that several authors, particularly M.M. Breuer and Freud, have recently verified our interpretation, already somewhat old, of subconscious fixed ideas with hystericals.[62]

Janet's first major work *L'automatisme psychologique*[63] pre-dated the first writings of Breuer and Freud in 1895 by several years. In that work he developed the concept of dissociation (*desaggregation*), which had originally been introduced by Jacques Moreau. He suggested that in various neurotic conditions ideas and cognitive processes could become detached from the mainstream of consciousness, whereupon they had the power to form neurotic symptoms and, in some cases, secondary personalities. Some years later in a famous series of lectures entitled 'The Major Symptoms of Hysteria' delivered to Harvard Medical School,[64] he described the major symptoms of hysteria: 'Somnambulism, fugues, multiple personalities, convulsions, paralysis, blindness and loss of speech', as well as digestive and respiratory difficulties. In the last chapter in that book, having reviewed and criticized the many unsatisfactory definitions of hysteria by previous workers, he defined the condition as follows:

> Hysteria is a form of mental depression characterized by the retraction of the field of personal consciousness and a tendency to dissociation and emancipation of the systems of ideas and junctions that constitute personality.

In a later work, *Psychological Healing*, in the section headed 'Unassimilated Happenings', after giving several case illustrations he described the effects of psychological trauma as follows:

> All the patients seem to have had the evolution of their lives checked: they are 'attached' upon an obstacle that they cannot get beyond. The happening we describe as traumatic has been brought about by a situation to which the individual ought to react. Adaptation is requisite, an adaptation achieved by modifying the outer world and by modifying oneself. Now, what characterizes these 'attached' patients is that they have not

succeeded in liquidating the difficult situation . . . strictly speaking, then, one who retains a fixed idea of a happening cannot be said to have a 'memory' of the happening. It is only for convenience that we speak of it as a 'traumatic memory'. The subject is often incapable of making, with regard to the event, the recital which we speak of as a memory; and yet he remains confronted by a difficult situation in which he has not been able to play a satisfactory part, one to which his adaptation has been imperfect, so that he continues to make efforts at adaptation.[65]

Here, although he is using rather different language, he says that 'one who retains a fixed idea of a happening cannot be said to have a "memory"'. He says it is only for convenience that we speak of it as a 'traumatic memory'. This is clearly relating to the idea of suspended or unintegrated experience, as is the title of his section 'Unassimilated Happenings'. Janet, however, appeared to have made little use of these insights as, when he discusses therapeutic intervention, he continues to refer to 'memories' or 'traumatic memories'. Although he saw some value in the reintegration of consciousness and the retrieval of 'traumatic memory', he felt the usefulness of this was quite limited and could have negative and dangerous implications. In discussing dissociation of memories, he says: 'There came under my observation a good many instances of traumatic memory which were extremely dangerous although there was no apparent disorder of the individual.' He goes on:

When memories become subconscious it is because they conflict with the subject's other ideas and feelings. If we drag them back into a consciousness which will not tolerate them, they will soon be driven out again and we shall have to begin the whole process once more . . . Moreover I have myself had to combat my patient's traumatic memories which were not cured by the reintegration of consciousness.

Janet countered the truth of unpleasant traumatic memories by offering the person, under hypnotic suggestion, more pleasant but nevertheless false alternative versions of what happened in the past.

With the emphasis he placed on traumatic antecedents, dissociation and what he called the retraction of the field of personal consciousness, Janet offered a model of psychological trauma which remains valid today. However, he failed to explain why dissociation happened in the first place and, when faced with this question, he invoked the 'degeneracy' concept,[66] which was prevalent during the nineteenth century. He stated: 'The starting point of hysteria is the same as that of most great neuroses, it is a depression, an exhaustion of the higher functions of the encephalon.' As Nemiah puts it: 'What is it that leads in the first place to the lowered psychic energy that comprises the ego's binding power and permits dissociation to occur?'[67] For Janet, the answer was basically a genetic one: 'Because of their heredity, certain individuals are born with an inherently insufficient amount of that energy.'[68]

Freud's great contribution, in his early work, was to point to the importance of affect, to which Janet paid little attention, and to the role of catharsis in the treatment of hysteria. Like Janet, Breuer and Freud were convinced that this condition could be the result of traumatic experiences: 'Hysterics suffer mainly from reminiscences.' They also referred to the fact that these 'memories' were 'found to be astonishingly intact and to possess remarkable sensory force, and when they returned they acted with all the affective strength of new experience'. But they saw not only the importance of the cognitive aspect but also the affective component that was associated with it:

> We found to our great surprise that each individual hysterical symptom immediately and permanently disappeared when we had succeeded in bringing clearly to light the memory of the event by which it was provoked and in arousing its accompanying affect, and when the patient had described that event in the greatest possible detail and had put the affect into words. Recollection without affect almost invariably produces no result.[69]

The other great contribution which Freud made was to point to the importance of sexual abuse and incest in the early years in the genesis of hysteria. Although he initially erroneously attributed all cases to sexual trauma, recent history has nevertheless proved him right in bringing to light the frequency of sexually abusive relationships in childhood and how damaging these can be in their psychological consequences. The circumstances surrounding Freud's abandonment of the 'seduction theory' were described in detail by Masson[70] when he released the hidden correspondence of Freud to Fleiss. In April 1896 Freud presented his paper 'Aetiology of

Hysteria'[71] to the society for psychology and neurology in Vienna and he described to Fleiss[72] what happened:

> A lecture on the aetiology of hysteria to the psychiatric society met with an icy reception from the asses and from Kraft-Ebbing the strange comment 'It sounds like a scientific fairy tale' – and this after one has demonstrated to them the solution to a more than a thousand-year-old problem, a source of the Nile.

To illustrate the degree to which he was ostracized following this, a month later, on 4 May, he wrote: 'I am as isolated as you could wish me to be, and a void is forming around me.'[73] This, coupled with the debâcle surrounding Emma Eckstein, resulted a little more than a year later in his deserting his whole position when he wrote the famous letter of 21 September 1897 to Fleiss: 'When this ideology broke down under the weight of its own improbability and contradiction in definitely ascertainable circumstances . . .'[74]

The development of psychoanalysis and its widespread popularity virtually eclipsed the work of Pierre Janet so that, when he died in 1947, his death was not even reported in the media. When one combines the contributions of Pierre Janet and the early work of Freud and Breuer, it is extraordinary how close they were to the thesis being presented in this paper. Indeed, had they had access to our present understanding of neurophysiology, of the functions of the limbic system and all that is emerging in the sphere of psychoneuroendocrinology, it seems likely that one or other of them would have come upon the hypothesis of the biological suspension of experience.

That psychological trauma can lead to enduring consequences is now widely accepted in the syndrome of post-traumatic stress disorder. The essential aspects of this condition were described by Kardiner[75] and constituted what he called a 'physioneurosis', including both psychological and physiological criteria. DSM III-R emphasizes the importance of the external event in PTSD:

> the person has experienced an event that is outside the range of usual human experience and that would be markedly distressing to almost anyone, for example, serious threat to one's life or physical integrity; etc.[76]

This definition was framed largely around the experiences of the Vietnam War[77] and it was as a result of this catastrophic experience that the syndrome finally gained popular acceptance. The importance of childhood trauma leading to chronic PTSD in adult life is now recognized,[78] but what remains unclear is the process involved when an individual is exposed to an overwhelming traumatic experience.

The Cycle of Traumatic Experience

The Traumatic Event

The concept of experience as a cyclical process was introduced by George Kelly,[79] who emphasized the importance of the individual's own construct system in the 'production' of the experience (Fig. 28.1). Although frequently thought of as a cognitive psychologist, Kelly himself refuted this and allowed for the possibility of somatic or biological constructs. The immediate non-conscious discrimination made by the individual between 'allowable' and overwhelming events can be seen as a biological construct and corresponds to the stage of anticipation. In the case of ordinary non-threatening events, investment and encounter occur almost instantaneously and the cycle is rapidly completed.

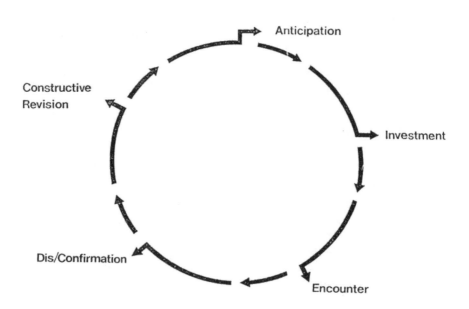

Fig. 27.1. Cycle of Experience (G. Kelly)

With traumatic events, several factors combine to determine whether the initial suspension or freezing which occurs is maintained indefinitely or is followed by full progression through the experiential cycle (Fig. 28.2). A hypothetical example of the latter would include a sexual assault on a child occurring in the context of a warm loving family, where she is able to tell her parents what has happened, and is provided with the support and validation to be able to express the emotion and distress appropriate to the experiences involved. In such cases, there are not likely to be any long-term ill-effects. The expression of emotion necessary to allow integration of the experience happens naturally and all that remains is likely to be a memory of an unpleasant event, but one which is easy to recall and does not give rise to any problems later in life.

In a different context, there may be little trust, warmth or security, as for example where there is alcoholism, marital conflict or, as is perhaps most typical in cases where chronic PTSD develops later, simply a family where the open expression of emotion is forbidden.[80] Obviously worse, of course, is the situation where physical or sexual abuse, incest, etc., is occurring within the family itself, being perpetrated by a father or near relative. To illustrate the situation where

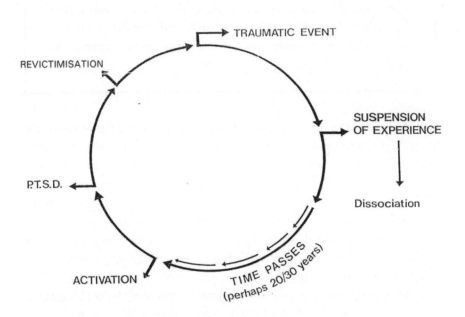

Fig. 27.2. Cycle of Experience

the expression of emotion is discouraged, let us cite an actual case which presented to our service some years ago.

CASE ILLUSTRATION

A young woman in her early thirties presented with a hemi-pareis following the death of her father, to whom she was very close. This had been preceded some months before by the death of her husband, who was a violent alcoholic. This woman had a strong, resolute personality and had coped for years with a very painful and difficult domestic situation. On her very first visit, having been put into regression under hypnosis, she went spontaneously not to the death of her husband or her father, but to a day at the seaside with her mother and siblings when she was nine years of age, when word was brought to them that her older brother, who was swimming on another part of the beach, had drowned. The mother got herself and the children into a taxi to go to tell their father, who worked in a bank in the town nearby. On the way, our patient burst into tears of grief, whereupon her mother turned on her and shouted 'Stop that crying! You'll upset your father'. The little girl stopped crying instantly and from that moment onwards had no recollection of the entire event until it was revealed under hypnosis many years later.

These contrasting scenarios illustrate a number of points which recur again and again in cases of chronic post-traumatic stress disorder. First of all there is the initial traumatic event, but this occurs in a context where the appropriate expression of emotion is not possible and typically against a background of a tough, coping atmosphere where tenderness, weakness or emotional expression are discouraged or not tolerated. So we have two factors here. First of all the nature of the event itself, which is often sudden and unexpected, the time and context in which it occurs simply making it impossible for the appropriate expression of emotion, but also the sociocultural background, usually of the family, which generally discourages the expression of emotion.

The suspension or freezing of the experience itself can take several forms, from a complete blocking of the entire experience in both its cognitive and emotional aspects to a partial suspension of the event. Where there is a complete suspension, the person goes into a numbed state, so that there is an inhibition of all activity as well as feeling. This may perhaps explain a question that has often been asked: why a strong, healthy woman, who may even have become an expert in self-defence, can be raped helplessly and shows no resistance to her attacker. The explanation would seem to be that, in the face of the threat of such a horrible experience, her entire being goes into a state of inhibition so that she is unable to take any effective avoidance action. This total response, as already mentioned, would seem to be part of an ancient survival mechanism – that of playing dead – which would have saved the living creature from being noticed and therefore enabled survival. As already stated, it now has the function of preventing disintegration of the living system but, in terms of the external threat, as in the example mentioned, can of course be counter-productive, preventing the person from protecting themselves.

A quite different kind of response is seen where, after a first stirring of emotion, there is a complete inhibition of all feeling but not of action, leaving the person free to take whatever measures are necessary for survival. This mechanism of 'psychic numbing' or 'emotional inhibition' must have saved countless lives in the past but, short of actual survival, it is also an essential device to enable individuals to deal with the practical problems which arise following a tragedy. For example, a woman whose husband dies suddenly may have to make arrangements for a funeral, deal with business problems, the question of a will, inheritance and so on; or, to take another example, where a young woman awoke on the tenth floor of a hotel to find the whole building shaking in an earthquake: she got out of bed quickly, dressed herself and remembers quite specifically feeling no fear while she ran downstairs out of the building into safety. A few days later, after it was all over, she went into a state of shock and experienced extreme panic, with her whole body shaking.

Thus, for temporary reasons, this denial of emotion is an important adaptive response and, in many instances, after a few weeks or months when the time is right, the person will spontaneously or with therapeutic help do the emotional work necessary for full integration of the experience. However, for a significant number this does not happen and the inhibition remains indefinitely. In some cases we find the process which Laing[81] described so eloquently, where not only is the experience cut off and not available to consciousness but the fact that it is cut off is itself cut off, so that the individual now has no awareness that the traumatic event ever took place.

Dissociation

Another situation to be considered is where there is not simply a single major traumatic event but where the trauma is ongoing and the person is subjected to the same traumatic experience again and again, as is the case, for example, of incestuous abuse by a father of a daughter within the family, which often commences in infancy and continues at regular intervals for many years. In these cases, not only is there an inhibition of the experience of the trauma but the child is faced with an impossible situation to adapt to. The process of dissociation described by Janet may then ensue, with a splitting of the personality. As one subject described it, 'the good little girl' – i.e. the 'visible' personality – continues with relatively normal, although constricted, development, such as attending school and other acceptable behaviours, while 'the bad little girl' continues to be subjected to incest and identifies herself with these behaviours, perhaps even, in some cases, indulging in abusive behaviour herself in later years. Where such dissociation is full-blown, we see the development of multiple personalities[82] and the other manifestations of classic hysteria.[83]

Activation

Whilst DSM III-R de-emphasized the distinction between acute and delayed-onset PTSD,[84] there is increasing evidence that a long period (often of many years) may ensue, following the traumatic event, before the emergence of the acute symptoms of PTSD.[85] During this 'latency' period there is evidence of constriction and avoidance behaviour in the person's life pattern, and also of chronic depressive symptoms with lack of spontaneity for life. This is something which was already clear to Pierre Janet – that in the majority of these instances the mechanism of dissociation was working effectively.

Indeed, during this phase the person would appear to be going on with a reasonably normal way of life, although they may have a deep sense of depression, a general feeling of lacklustre and, as already mentioned, may exhibit a rather constricted life pattern. Many of these people show an acute sensitivity as to what situations to avoid yet they will typically have no knowledge whatever as to why they are avoiding certain places or situations. For example, a woman who was raped many years ago in an elevator may be terrified of elevators and seized by intense panic at the thought of entering one but have no knowledge that she was ever raped or why she is terrified at the very thought of entering an elevator.

On going back carefully over all these cases, we found that in almost every instance they have been largely symptom-free for many years, managing to finish school, go to work and, even in cases where there had been severe sexual abuse, to marry and have children. In virtually every case, something happened which 'activated' the inhibited experience, so that by the time they presented they were in an active state of post-traumatic stress disorder. The occurrence which will cause this 'activation' may be another trauma of a similar kind. For example, a woman who was sexually abused as a child may, in adult life, be raped, or a person who lost their mother in infancy may, in adult life, have another loss, as for example their husband, and this activates the earlier traumatic experience. But the activation need not result from a further serious traumatic episode. It can be something as simple as a television programme about sexual abuse, or simply the first night in the marriage bed. Such 'activating' events may be entirely normal and not the least bit distressing for the vast majority of human beings but because, for this person, they touch the sensitive blocked-off experience they may be catastrophic and unleash the full-blown symptomatology of PTSD which was lying dormant up to that point.

CASE ILLUSTRATION

Mrs Y, a thirty-four-year-old housewife, presented to our service with a three-month history of increasing irritability, social withdrawal and depression; this was associated with intrusive recollections of an episode of sexual assault when she was fourteen by her adoptive father. She had no previous psychiatric history and had been happily married for thirteen years with two children. She described being well until the visit of an old schoolfriend three months previously. During the visit, her friend used a pet name to address her which had only previously been used by her adoptive father. From this point she described worsening symptomology, culminating in her seeking psychiatric help. On interview at this point she was aware of only one incident of sexual abuse. She commenced therapy and, in a short time, an extensive, rather sadistic, history of physical and sexual abuse emerged, extending back to early childhood. This involved both her father and dizygotic twin sister, for whom she described herself as having an intense dislike for as long as she could remember. She denied ever having known why this had been the case.

This activation is something which Freud pointed to quite clearly in his early work in the paper 'The Aetiology of Hysteria', where he says:

> we have learned that no hysterical symptom can arise from a real experience alone but that in every case the memory of earlier experiences awakened in association to it plays a part in causing the symptoms . . . or again let us take the instance of a young girl who blames herself most frightfully for having allowed a boy to stroke her hand in secret and who from that time on has been overtaken by neurosis . . . analysis shows you that the touching of her hand reminded her of another, similar touching which had happened very early in her childhood and which formed part of a less innocent whole, so that her self-reproaches were actually reproaches about that old occasion . . . one has an impression indeed, that with hysterical patients it is as if all their old experiences . . . had retained their effective power as if such people

were incapable of disposing of their psychical stimuli . . . You must not forget that in hysterical people when there is a present day precipitating cause, the old experiences come into operation in the form of unconscious memories.[86]

This question of activation of the blocked experience is of great importance, for it explains clearly for the first time why so many cases of chronic traumatic neurosis only present for treatment as an acute syndrome in adult life.

Post-Traumatic Stress Disorder

Now we move on to the next stage of the cycle. Once activation has taken place, the individual is in a dysfunctional state. They are now experiencing the full-blown picture of PTSD and are unable, on the one hand, to fully 'live' and integrate the blocked-off traumatic experience of many years earlier but equally they are now unable to maintain the 'freeze' and full inhibition of the experience which they had maintained until now so as to be able to manage to cope, in some fashion, with ordinary everyday life. As Horowitz pointed out, they typically oscillate in a biphasic pattern between the intrusive experience with high arousal and an exhausted constricted state, often diagnosed as depression. It is at this point that people usually look for help. Unfortunately the help which is likely to be available is that of traditional psychiatric care, which usually takes the form of psychopharmalogical intervention or, worse still, this combined with therapies such as ECT. Whatever diagnosis the individual may present with – and this can cover a wide range of symptomatology, from depressive manifestations, high arousal, anxiety, neurasthenic and psychosomatic symptoms, to substance abuse[87] or atypical psychotic features[88] – and whatever rationale may be used to support these diagnoses and interventions, the inevitable result is one of aiding and abetting the individual's unsuccessful attempt to reinstate the inhibitory defence which once enabled them to struggle on through life. At best, such medication (or illicit substance abuse) brings some temporary relief but again, inevitably, post-traumatic manifestations break through with all the usual sequelae of relapse, recurrent hospitalization, self-destructive behaviour and attempted suicide.

False Memory Syndrome

For generations, the abuse of women and children, both physical and sexual, which was carried out mainly by men, was a dark secret. It was only through the struggles of the feminist movement and the courage of some paediatricians and a few psychiatrists that, finally, over the past thirty years this abuse, and the full extent of it, was brought into the light of day. Until then, there was a 'culture of silence' within families and elsewhere, which meant that victims had nowhere to turn. And because, if our hypothesis is correct, in order to survive they had suspended the traumatic experiences and then dissociated, they usually knew nothing of what had happened to them. These experiences were hidden as a 'frozen present', unless they were activated later by some similar event. Even then, because of the culture of silence within society, the flashbacks and other symptoms which they suffered were likely to be dismissed or misdiagnosed, so they were still not heard. Also, because they had spent a lifetime building up defences to keep these experiences at bay, they were only too ready to disavow them if they were met with scepticism or ridicule. 'If it did happen, it happened years ago, so forget about it and get on with your life!'

Unfortunately, when the wall of silence was finally broken, this brought in its train a number of over-enthusiastic therapists, counsellors and others who, because those who have been traumatized and abused tend to present with a characteristic cluster of symptoms, saw abuse lurking below the surface in many situations where in fact no abuse had actually occurred. They actively suggested this to patients and, particularly with the use of methods such as hypnosis, highly suggestible subjects complied with the production of pseudomemories. Thus innocent parents and others were wrongly accused and the wheel turned full circle, giving rise to the debate that has become known as the False Memory Syndrome, and to organized groups of parents and others attempting to protect themselves from false accusations.

Since this debate arose, a number of papers have reported studies showing the dynamic nature of long-term memory. These make the point that, when such a memory is retrieved, it is reassembled from a number of inputs in different parts of the brain, from various times in the past, and is therefore essentially a new creation. These studies have demonstrated convincingly that both children and adults can and do distort past memories and, if subjected to suggestive influence (particularly the use of hypnosis), can invent occurrences which have never happened. However, if the hypothesis presented in this paper is well founded then these studies are missing the essential point. For the experiences we are dealing with in this instance are not long-term memories, nor indeed memories in the accepted sense at all but the suspended 'frozen present'; that is, experiences that have never been processed into memory and that in an emotional sense have not yet been experienced.

Over the past five years we have worked with 180 cases, who were referred to us because they were thought to have suffered traumatic experiences in the past, mainly sexual and/or physical abuse during childhood. Having carried out a review of these cases, we found they broke down as follows:

Total	True	FMS	Unclear	Dropped out
180	110	6	53	11

Because we were operating a careful diagnostic assessment and only taking on those who satisfied several diagnostic criteria, as can be seen in the large majority, the traumatic history turned out to be correct. This was so in that either there was corroboration from parents, siblings, other relatives or neighbours who were aware of what was going on at the time, or the abusive experience was already activated by some more recent event, so they were presenting for therapy with partially clear recollections and flashbacks of what had happened to them many years before.

To illustrate the sort of confirmation we have had from relatives in almost a third of our cases, let us look at a case which presented to our service some years ago.

CASE ILLUSTRATION

A couple presented with marital disharmony, but it was soon clear that the dissatisfactions of the wife were out of proportion and were not explainable in terms of the marital interaction. They clearly related to problems in the woman's own personality. While no clear history of trauma in her childhood was forthcoming, it was decided, with her agreement, to undertake some deep experiential work to see if there were factors in her early life of which she was unaware.

CASE ILLUSTRATION (*cont.*)

From the very first experiential session (utilizing music, hyperventilation and body work), she went into a deep altered state and seemed to be struggling to free herself from being trapped in some way. She continued in this way for about twelve sessions, struggling to get free. Then in one session, having started in the usual way, she began to suffocate, turning black in the face and causing us considerable alarm. She came to no harm, however, and, when the session terminated, she said she had experienced a feeling of being trapped and unable to breathe and she felt she was approximately six months old.

As it happened, her parents were still alive and she was going to visit them that weekend in County Donegal. When she asked her mother about what she had experienced, at first her mother was very defensive and angry, refusing to talk, but then she broke down and told her what had happened. They were small farmers and, when the patient was a baby, they had had no one to mind her when they were out working in the fields, so they used to strap her into her cot. One day when she was about seven months old they came back to the house and found her twisted up in the blankets. She was suffocating, black in the face, and almost died.

Once the patient retrieved this death-threatening experience, with some more work, she rapidly recovered and the original marital disharmony that brought them to us was easily resolved.

As the table (on page 367) shows, we also found a small number whose story, with patient handling, finally broke down. These differed from the other cases, in that their behaviour in experiential sessions was atypical and they usually presented their story pat, in a complete form outside of experiential work. There were a number which remained unclear in spite of all our efforts to reach a conclusion as to the validity of their story, and finally some who dropped out of therapy early on before any decision could be reached as to the nature of their problem.

Discussion

It is not our intention to claim that the hypothesis presented in this paper is necessarily correct. What we are saying is that it is a reasonable proposition and, more importantly, one which is capable of being rigorously tested. Research to establish whether this hypothesis is valid could be carried out with animals in addition to humans and, we believe, would be a fruitful area of study for neurophysiologists: to follow on from the work already referred to in this paper, which has been carried out on the formation of declarative memory and the functions of the medial temporal lobe.

There are many examples in lower animals of the use of this 'freeze response' as a survival mechanism. Pavlov described how some of his dogs were accidentally trapped in their cages when the Neva River flooded St Petersburg. The dogs met the frightening experience with initial fear and excitement but when they were rescued were in a severe state of 'inhibition, stupor and collapse'. We can see this same response in many animals when faced with a serious external threat from which they cannot easily escape. The spider or the hedgehog will curl itself into a ball when threatened, and this reaction has even been described in the amoeba by the biologists Max Hartmann and Ludwig Rumler. They exposed amoebas to a variety of stimuli and the amoebas reacted in one of two ways. Either they sought out these stimuli, or they avoided them and assumed a spherical shape – 'played dead'.

Research with human beings who have been traumatized in early life, and where the processing of this into memory has been suspended, could be even more fruitful. The recent development of chemical probes and the newer imaging techniques such as MRI and positron emission tomography have made it possible to investigate the function of discrete areas of the limbic brain and cerebral cortex. We were just commencing research in this area when, unfortunately, one of the authors reached retirement age and, because the Health Board failed to appoint a replacement, the unit had to close.

So all we have to support this hypothesis at present is the clinical evidence from our work with patients. What we have found is that the majority of our cases are genuine. Not only are the recollections true but they are accurate as to detail which is often quite irrelevant to the traumatic experience itself. For example, in one case where a patient was being gang-raped in a field, she saw a cow standing nearby when she was experiencing the event in an altered state during therapy. In other cases subjects will describe details of the furniture in the room where a traumatic episode took place or other background information which is very different from the sort of composite recollection which a person will provide from long-term memory when, for instance, they are describing their schooldays. Such suspended experiences are often related to the evocative nature of smell. Smell seems to have a particular relation to the limbic system and will often evoke an experience with all the immediacy of the present, as if it were happening at that moment.

Another way in which these suspended experiences differ from long-term memory recall is that frequently neither the person nor the therapist has any idea what the first intimation of a recollection from many years before of an intense bodily experience means. We have typically found that what we thought the patient was experiencing was quite wrong. It is only as the experience unfolds with further work that the story gradually emerges which underlies the initial bodily reaction. It can be seen, therefore, how critically important it is to use an experiential method that avoids, as far as possible, influence or suggestion from the therapist as to what the patient's experience is about but rather to let what lies below the surface emerge naturally.

There is one further important aspect of the cycle of experience which remains to be dealt with. This is the strange phenomenon that those suffering from PTSD, far more frequently than could be explained by mere coincidence, appear to get stuck in a 'fixed role' or 'life theme' in which the same form of traumatic experience will happen again and again. For example, if a child is physically abused in his family, this pattern will continue into adult life in various forms and he is even likely to become abusive himself. We will discuss this in more detail in a second paper, 'Healing the Trauma'.

References

1. Janet, P. *Psychological Healing: Historical and Clinical Study*, Macmillan, New York, 1925.
2. McGee, D., Browne, I., Kenny, V., McGennis, A., and Pilot, J. 'Unexperienced Experience: A Critical Reappraisal of the Theory of Repression and Traumatic Neurosis', *Irish Journal of Psychotherapy*, 3, 7–11,

1984; Browne, I. 'Psychological Trauma or Unexperienced Experience', *ReVision*, 12, 21–34, 1990.

3. Horowitz, M.J. *Stress Response Syndromes*, New York, Jason Arronson, 1976.
4. Cannon, W.B. *Bodily Changes in Pain, Hunger, Fear and Rage: An Account of Recent Researches into the Function of Emotional Excitement*, 2nd edition, Appleton-Century-Crofts, New York.
5. Pavlov, I.P. *Conditoned Reflexes and Psychiatry*, Lawerence & Wishart, London, 1961.
6. Guyton, A.C. *Physiology of the Human Body*, 6th edition, Saunders College Publishing, 1984.
7. Eccles, J.C. 'An Instruction Selection Theory of Learning in the Cerebral Cortex', *Brain Research*, 127, 327–52, 1977.
8. Squire, L.R., and Zola-Morgan, S. 'The Medial Temporal Lobe Memory System', *Science*, 253, 1380–6, 1991.
9. Scofield, W.B., and Milner, B. 'Memory Loss Caused by Bilateral Medial Temporal Lobectomy', *J. Neurol. Neurosurg. Psychiatry*, 20, 11, 1957.
10. Victor, M., Angevine, J.B. Jr., Mancall, E.L., and Fisher, C.M. 'Memory Loss with Lesions of the Hippocampal Formation: Report of a Case with Some Remarks on the Anatomical Basis of Memory,' *Arch. Neurol.*, 5, 244–63, September 1961; Woods, B.T., Schoene, W., and Kneisley, L. 'Are Hippocampal Lesions Sufficient to Cause Lasting Amnesia', *J. Neurol. Neurosurg. Psychiatry*, 45, 243–6, 1982; Cummings, J.L., Tomiyasu, U., Read, S., and Benson, D.F. 'Amnesia with Hippocampal Lesions after Cardio-pulmonary Arrest', *Neurology*, 34, 679–81, 1984.
11. Mishkin, M. 'A Memory System in the Monkey', *Philos. Trans. R. Soc. London*, 298, 85, 1982.
12. Mishkin, M., and Appenzeller, T. 'The Anatomy of Memory', *Scientific American*, 256, 80–9, 1987.
13. Squire and Zola-Morgan. 'The Medial Temporal Lobe Memory System'.
14. Mishkin and Appenzeller. 'The Anatomy of Memory'.
15. Ibid.
16. Squire and Zola-Morgan. 'The Medial Temporal Lobe Memory System'.
17. Snell, R.S. *Clinical Neuroanatomy for Medical Students*, 2nd edition, Little Brown, 1987.
18. Ibid.
19. Mindewell, A. *Working with the Dreaming Body*, Routledge & Kegan Paul, London, 1985; Bordella, D. *Lifestreams: An Introduction to Biosynthesis*, Routledge & Kegan Paul, London, 1987.
20. Nemiah, J.C. 'The Varieties of Human Experiences', *Brit. J. Psych.*, 154, 459–66, 1989.
21. Kudler, H., Davidson, J., Meador, K., Upper, S., and Ely, T. 'The DST and Post Traumatic Stress Disorder', *Am. J. Psychiatry*, 144, 1068–71, 1980; Yehuda, R., Southwick, S.M., Mason, J.W., and Giller, E. 'Interactions of the Hypothalamic–Pituitary–Adrenal Axis and Catecholaminergic System in Post Traumatic Stress Disorder', in: E.L. Giller (ed.), *Biological Assessment and*

Treatment of Post Traumatic Stress Disorder, Washington DC, American Psychiatric Press, 117–184, 1990; Dinan, T.G., Barry, S., Yatnam, L.N., Mobayed, M., and Browne, I. 'A Pilot Study of a Neuroendocrinological Test Battery in Post Traumatic Stress Disorder', *Biol. Psychiatry*, 28, 655–72, 1990.

22. Yehuda, R., Giller, E.L., Southwick, S.M., Lowy, M.T., and Mason, J.W. 'Hypothalamic Pituitary–Adrenal Dysfunction in Post Traumatic Stress Disorder', *Biol. Psychiatry*, 30, 1031–48, 1991.

23. Tornello, S., Orti, E., DeNicola, A.F., Rainbow, T.C., and McEwen, B.S. 'Regulation of Glucocorticoid Receptor in Brain by Corticosterone Treatment of Adrenalectomixed Rats', *Neuroendocrinology*, 35, 6, 411–17, 1982; Sapolsky, R.M., Krey, L.C., and McEwen, B.S. 'Stress down Regulates Corticosterone Receptors in a Site Specific Manner in the Brain', *Endocrinology*, 114, 1, 287–92, 1984; McEwen, B.S., De Kloet, E.R., and Rostene, W. 'Adrenal Steroid Receptors and Actions in the Nervous System', *Physiol. Rev.*, 66, 1121–88, 1986.

24. Meaney, M.J., Aitken, D.K., Van Berkel, C., Bhatnagar, S., and Sapolsky, R.M. 'Effect of Neonatal Handling on Age Related Impairments Associated with the Hippocampus', *Science*, 239, 766–8, 1988.

25. Gormley, G.J., Lowy, M.T., Reder, A.T., Hosrelhorn, V.D., Antel, J.P., and Meltzer, H.Y. 'Glucocorticoid Receptors in Depression, Relationship to the Dexamethasone Suppression Test', *Am. J. Psychiatry*, 142, 1278–84, 1985; Whalley, L.J., Borthwick, N., Copolon, D. 'Glucocorticoid Receptors and Depression', *Br. Med. J.*, 292, 859–61, 1986.

26. Yehuda, R., Lowy, M.T., Southwick, S.M., Shaffer, D., and Giller, E.L. 'Lymphocyte Glucocorticoid Number in Post Traumatic Stress Disorder', *Am. J. Psychiatry*, 148, 4, 499–504, 1991.

27. Dinan *et al.* 'A Pilot Study'; Helzer, J.E., Robins, L.N., Wish, E., and Hesselbrock, M. 'Depression in Vietnam Veterans and Civilian Controls', *Am. J. Psychiatry*, 135, 526–9, 1979; Sierles, F.S., Chen, J., McFarland, R.T., and Taylor, M.A. 'Post Traumatic Stress Disorder and Concurrent Psychiatric Illness: A Preliminary Report', *Am. J. Psychiatry*, 140, 1177–9, 1983; Pitts, F.N. Jr. 'Post Traumatic Stress Disorder: Editorial', *J. Clin. Psychiatry*, 46, 373, 1985.

28. Southwick, S.M., Yehuda, R., and Giller, E.L. 'Characterisation of Depression in War-related Post Traumatic Stress Disorder', *Am. J. Psychiatry*, 148, 179–82, 1991; Davidson, J., Swartz, M., Stork, M. Krishnan, R.R., and Hammett, E. 'A Diagnostic and Family Study of Post Traumatic Stress Disorder', *Am. J. Psychiatry*, 142, 90–3, 1985.

29. Yehuda *et al.* 'Hypothalmic Pituitary–Adrenal Dysfunction'; McEwen et al. 'Adrenal Steroid Receptors'.

30. Mason, J.W., Giller, E.L., Kosten, T.R., Ostroff, R.B., and Podd, L. 'Urinary Free Cortisol Levels in Post Traumatic Stress Disorder Patients', *J. Nerv. and Mental Disease*, 174, 3, 145–9, 1986.

31. Mason, J.W. 'A Review of Psycho-endocrine Research on the Sympathetic–Adrenal Medullary System', *Psychosom. Med.*, 30, 631–53, 1968.

32. Mason, J.W., Mangan, G.F., and Brady, J.V. 'Concurrent Plasma Epinephrine,

Norepinephrine and 17-hydroxycorticosteroid Levels during Conditioned Emotional Disturbances in Monkeys', *Psychosom. Med.*, 23, 344–53, 1961.

33. Kosten, T.R., Mason, J.W., Giller, E.L., Ostroff, R.B., and Harkness, L. 'Sustained Urinary Norepinphrine and Epinephrine Elevation in Post Traumatic Stress Disorder', *Psychoneuroendocrinology*, 12, 1, 13–20, 1987; Mason, J.W., Giller, E.L., Kosten, T.R., and Harkness, L. 'Elevation of Urinary Norepinphrine/Cortisol Ration in Post Traumatic Stress Disorder', *J. Nervous and Mental Disease*, 176, 8, 498–502, 1988.

34. Friedman, S.B., Mason, J.W., and Hamburg, D.A. 'Urinary 17-hydroxycorticosteroid Levels in Parents of Children with Neoplastic Disease', *Psychosom. Med.*, 25, 364–76, 1963.

35. Katz, J., Weiner, H., and Gallagher, T.E. 'Stress, Distress and Ego Defenses: Psychoendocrine Responses to Impending Breast Tumor Biopsy', *Arch. Gen. Psychiatry*, 23, 131–42, 1970; Knight, R.B., Atkins, A., Eagle, S.J., Evans, Finkelstein, J.W., Fukushima, D., Katz, J., and Weiner, H. 'Psychological Stress, Ego Defenses and Cortisol Production in Children Hospitalized for Elective Surgery', *Psychosom. Med.*, 41, 40–9, 1979; Poe, R.O., Rose, R.M., and Mason, J.W. 'Multiple Determinants of 17-hydroxycorticosteroid Excretion in Recruits during Basic Training', *Psychosom. Med.*, 32, 369–78, 1990.

36. Hess, J.L., Denenberg, V.H., Zarrow, Y., and Pfeifer, W.O. 'Modification of the Corticosterone Response Curve as a Function of Handling in Infancy', *Physiol. Behav.*, 4, 109–111, 1969.

37. Levine, S., Haltmeyer, C.G., Karas, G.G., and Denenberg, V.H. 'Physiological and Behavioural Effects of Infantile Stimulation', *Physiol. Behav.*, 2, 55–9, 1967; Haltmeyer, G.C., Denenberg, V.H., and Zarrow, M.X. 'Modification of the Plasma Corticosterone Response as a Function of Infantile Stimulation and Electric Shock Parameters', *Physiol. Behav.*, 2, 61–3, 1967.

38. Williams, R.B. 'Neuroendocrine Response Patterns and Stress: Biobehavioural Mechanisms of Disease', in R.B. Williams (ed.), *Perspectives on Behavioural Medicine: Neuroendocrine Controls and Behaviour*, Academic, New York, 1983; Kosten, T.R., Jacobs, S., Mason, J., Wahby, V., and Atkins, S. 'Psychological Correlates of Growth Hormone Response to Stress', *Psychosom. Med.*, 46, 49–58, 1984.

39. Leher, B., Ebstein, R.P., Shestatsky, M., Shemash, Z., and Greenbeg, D. 'Cyclic AMP Signal Transduction inPost Traumatic Stress Disorder', *Am. J. Psychiatry*, 144, 101324–7, 1987; Lerer, B., Breich, A., Bennett, E.R., Ebstein, R.P., and Balkin, J. 'Platelet Adenylate Cyclase and Phosphopase c Activity in Post Traumatic Stress Disorder', *Biol. Psychiatry*, 27, 735–40, 1990.

40. Malloy, P.F., Fairbank, J.A., and Keane, T.M. 'Validation of a Multimethod Assessment of Post Traumatic Stress Disorder in Vietnam Veterans', J. Consult. Clin. Psychol., 51, 488–94, 1983.

41. Blanchard, E.B., Kolb, L.C., Pallmeyer, T.P., and Gerardi, R.J. 'A Psychophysiological Study of Post Traumatic Stress Disorder in Vietnam Veterans',

Psychiatr. Q, 54, 4, 220–9, 1982; Brende, J.D. 'Electrodermal Responses in Post Traumatic Syndromes', *J. Nerv. Ment. Dis.*, 170, 352–61, 1982.

42. Grant, S.J., Redmond, D.E. Jr. 'The Neuroanatomy and Pharmacology of the Nucleus Locus Coerulus', in H. Lal and S. Fielding (eds), *Pharmacology of Clonidine*, Liss, New York, 1981.

43. Redmond, D.E., and Krystal, J.H. 'Mechanisms of Withdrawal from Opioid Drugs', *Annu. Rev. Neurosci.*, 7, 443–78, 1984.

44. McNaughton, N., and Mason, S.T. 'The Neuropsychology and Neuropharmacology of the Dorsal Ascending Noradrenergic Bundle: A Review', *Prog. Neurobiof.*, 14, 157–219, 1979.

45. Delaney, R., Tussi, D., and Gold, P.E. 'Long Term Potentiation as a Neurophysiological Analog of Memory', *Pharmacol. Biochem. Behav.*, 18, 137–9, 1983.

46. Ramm, P. 'The Locus Coerulus, Catecholamines, and REM Sleep: A Critical Review', *Behav. Neur. Biol.*, 25, 415–48, 1979.

47. Steriade, M., and Hobson, J.A. 'Neuronal Activity during the Sleeping–Waking Cycle', *Prog. Neurobiol.*, 6, 155–376, 1976.

48. Ross, R.J., Ball, W.A., Sullivan, K.A., and Caroff, S.N. 'Sleep Disturbance as the Hallmark of Post Traumatic Stress Disorder', *Am. J. Psychiatry*, 146, 6, 687–707, 1989.

49. Reynolds, C.F. 'Sleep Disturbances in Post Traumatic Stress Disorder: Pathogenetic or Epiphemomenal: Editorial', *Am. J. Psychiatry*, 146, 6, 695–6, 1989; Van der Kolk, B., Greenberg, M., Boyd, H., and Krystal, J. 'Inescapable shock, neurotransmitters, and addiction to trauma: Toward a Psychobiology of Post Traumatic Stress', *Biol. Psychiatry*, 10, 314–25, 1985.

50. Pitman, R.K. 'Self Mutilation in Combat Related Post Traumatic Stress Disorder', *Am. J. Psychiatry*, 147, 1, 123–4, 1990.

51. Maier, S.F., Davies, S., and Grau, J.W. 'Opiate Antagonists and Long Term Analgesic Reaction Induced by Inescapable Shock in Rats', *J. Comp. Physiol. Psychol.*, 94, 1172–83, 1980.

52. Beecher, H.K. 'Pain in Men Wounded in Battle', *Ann. Surg.*, 123, 96–105, 1946.

53. Christie, M.J., and Chesker, G.B. 'Physical Dependence on Physiologically Released Endogenous Opiates', *Life Sci.*, 30, 1173–7, 1982.

54. Pitman, R.K., Van der Kolk, B.A., Orr, S.P., and Greenberg, M.S. 'Naloxone Reversible Analgesic Response to Combat Related Stimuli in Post Traumatic Stress Disorder', *Arch. Gen. Psychiatry*, 47, 541–4, 1990.

55. Kosten, T.R., and Krystal, J. 'Biological Mechanisms in Post Traumatic Stress Disorder Relevance for Substance Abuse', *Recent Developments in Alcoholism*, 6, 49–68, 1988.

56. Solursh, L. 'Combat Addiction Post Traumatic Stress Disorder Re-explored', *Psychiatr. J. Univ. Ottawa*, 13, 1, 17–20, 1988.

57. Lynch, M., and Roberts, J. *Consequences of Child Abuse*, Academic Press, London, 1982; Green, A.M. 'Self Destructive Behaviour in Battered Children, *Am. J. Psychiatry*, 135, 579, 1978.

58. Solomon, Z., and Flum, H. 'Life Events, Contact Stress Reaction and Post Traumatic Stress Disorder', *Soc. Sci. Med.*, 26, 3, 319–25, 1988; Miller, T.W., Kamenchenko, P., and Krasniasnski, A. 'Assessment of Life Stress Events: The Etiology and Measurement of Traumatic Stress Disorder', *Int. J. Soc. Psychiatry*, 38, 3, 215–27, 1992.

59. Polanyi, M. *Personal Knowledge*, University of Chicago Press, 1974.

60. Nemiah, J.C. Janet Redivivus: 'The Centenary of *L'Automatisme Psychologique*', *Am. J. Psychiatry*, 146, 12, 1527–9, 1989; Van der Kolk, B.A., and Van der Hart, O. 'Pierre Janet and the Breakdown of Adaptation in Psychological Trauma', *Am. J. Psychiatry*, 146, 12, 1530–40, 1989.

61. Freud, S. *The Origins of Psycho-analysis Letters to Wilhelm Fleiss, Drafts and Notes: 1887–1902*, Basic Books, New York, 1977.

62. Janet, P. *État Mental des hystériques: Les accidents mentaux*, Rueff, Paris, 1894 (English translation, 1901).

63. Janet, P. *L'Automatisme psychologique: Essai de psychologie experimentale sur les formes inférieures de l'activité humaine*, Felix Alcan, Paris, 1889; Paris, Société Pierre Janet/Payot, 1973.

64. Janet, P. *The Major Symptoms of Hysteria*, Macmillian, New York, 1925.

65. Janet. *Psychological Healing*.

66. Dowbiggin, I. 'Degeneration and Hereditarianism in French Mental Medicine 1840–1890', in F. Bynum, R. Porter and M. Shepherd (eds), *The Anatomy of Madness*, Tavistock Publications, London, 188–252, 1985.

67. Nemiah, J.C. 'The Unconscious and Psychopathology', in K.S. Bowers and D. Meichenbaum (eds), *The Unconscious Reconsidered*, Wiley, New York, 1984.

68. Pick, D. *Faces of Degeneration: European Disorder 1848–1918*, Cambridge University Press, Cambridge, 1989.

69. Freud, S. *Studies on Hysteria*, in *Complete Psychological Works*, vol 18, trans. and ed. J. Strachey, Hogarth Press, London, 1893.

70. Masson, J.M. *The Assault on Truth*, Penguin, Middlesex, 1984.

71. Freud, S. *The Aetiology of Hysteria*, trans. and ed. J. Strachey, Hogarth Press, London, 1890.

72. Masson. *The Assault on Truth*.

73. Ibid.

74. Freud. *The Origins of Psychoanalysis*.

75. Kardiner, A. *The Traumatic Neuroses of War*, Hoeber, New York, 1941.

76. American Psychiatric Association. *Diagnostic and Statistical Manual*, 3rd edition revised, American psychiatric Association Press, Washington, DC, 1987.

77. Van Putten, T., and Emory, W.H. 'Traumatic Neuroses in Vietnam Returnees', *Arch. Gen. Psychiatry*, 29, 695–8, 1973.

78. Gelinas, D. 'The Persisting Negative Effects of Incest', *Psychiatry*, 46, 312–32, 1983.

79. Kelly, G. *The Psychology of Personal Constructs*, vols 1 & 2, Norton & Co., New York, 1955.

80. Kiser, L.J., Ackerman, B.J., Brown, E., Edwards, N.B., McColgan, E., Pugh, R., and Pruitt, D.B. 'Post Traumatic Stress Disorder in Young Children: A Reaction to Purported Sexual Abuse', *J. Am. Acad. Child Adolesc. Psychiatry*, 27, 5, 645–9, 1988.

81. Laing, R.D. *The Voice of Experience*, Allen Lane, Penguin Books, 1982.

82. Merskey, H. 'The Manufacture of Personalities: The Production of Multiple Personality Disorder', *Brit. J. Psychiatry*, 160, 3, 327–41, 1992.

83. Moscarello, R. 'Post Traumatic Stress Disorder after Sexual Assault: Its Psychodynamics and Treatment', *J. Am. Acad. Psychoanalysis*, 19, 2, 235–53, 1991.

84. Watson, C.G., Kucala, T., Manifold, V., Vason, P., and Juba, M. 'Differences between Post Traumatic Stress Disorder Patients with Delayed and Undelayed Onsets', *J. Nervous and Mental Disease*, 176, 9, 568–72, 1988.

85. APA. *Diagnostic and Statistical Manual*.

86. Freud. *Aetiology of Hysteria*.

87. Penk, W.E., Robinowitx, W.R., Patterson, E.T., Dolan, M.P., and Atkins, H.G. 'Adjustment Differences among Male Substance Abusers Varying in Degree of Combat Experience in Vietnam', *J. Consult. Clin. Psycho.*, 49, 426–37, September 1995.

88. Van Putten and Emory. 'Traumatic Neuroses in Vietnam Returnees'.

28. Healing the Trauma

The next paper was written, in June 1995, with David Meagher, Kevin O'Neill and Miriam Gannon. While the previous paper, 'Unassimilated Happenings', presents the theory of unexperienced experience, this second paper deals with the therapeutic aspects and the methods of treatment involved.

POST-TRAUMATIC stress disorder, although only formally recognized in DSM III in 1980,[1] is now recognized as a disorder causing significant psychiatric morbidity, often of a chronic nature.[2] Recent epidemiological studies indicate a lifetime prevalence ranging from 1% to 9%.[3] Despite this growing interest, reflected in a rapidly expanding body of research, many aspects of this disorder are not fully understood, including diagnostic, aetiological and management issues. DSM III-R de-emphasized the distinction between acute and delayed onset PTSD.[4] There is increasing evidence that a long period (often of many years) may ensue, following the truamatic incident, before the emergence of the acute symptoms of PTSD. A wide diversity of therapeutic strategies have been suggested[5] and it is generally accepted that a multifaceted eclectic approach is best adopted by the clinician, drawing from various psychotherapeutic and pharmacological strategies.[6] Applying this principle over a period of four years, we have developed such a therapeutic approach.

This therapeutic strategy is by no means original and, like most contemporary forms of therapy, it has drawn heavily on the therapeutic foundation laid down by a succession of great pioneers – from the early work of Freud,[7] Janet[8] and Jung,[9] on to others like Wilhelm Reich,[10] Feldenkrais,[11] Perls,[12] Stanislav Grof[13] and many others. While fully acknowledging these contributions, our most significant teachers have been the patients themselves. It is from these, more than from any other source, that we are continually learning and developing.

Undoubtedly, the central influence from which our therapeutic programme had its beginnings has been the seminal work of Stanislav Grof and his development of what he calls 'holotropic therapy'. In *The Adventure of Self-Discovery*, Grof describes the roots from which this method was developed:

> The holotropic strategy in therapy in the broadest sense is characteristic for many different approaches, including various shamanic procedures, aboriginal healing ceremonies, the healing trance dance of the Kung bushmen and other groups, rites of passage, psychedelic therapy, certain forms of hypnosis and other experiential psychotherapies, and for different spiritual practices. However, I would like to reserve the term holotropic therapy for our treatment procedure, which combines controlled breathing, music and other forms of sound technology, and focused bodywork.[14]

The majority of the patients who have gone through the therapeutic programme were suffering from severe, intractable psychiatric illness, having been in treatment or hospitalized for many years. The prognosis for such patients was, by general consent, extremely poor and, if they had not undertaken this treatment programme, it is likely that they would have remained in psychiatric care indefinitely.

As our work with long-term seriously disturbed patients has continued to develop, we have realized that the experiential component, although a central and vital part of the programme with such patients, is nevertheless only one component in a series of systematic steps in the full spectrum of therapy.

Diagnosis and Assessment

We have evolved four main criteria which should be present if patients are likely to benefit from this form of therapy. These are:

1. A previous history of trauma. Although frequently described in war veterans,[15] a diversity of stressors have been described: incest,[16] rape,[17] severe burns,[18] accidental fire disasters,[19] assault,[20] or even occupationally induced trauma.[21] Although there may be only an isolated episode occurring more recently in late adolescence or adult life which is available to conscious recall, this frequently represents only one part of multiple traumatic incidents reaching back into childhood.

2. PTSD symptomatology as listed in DSM III-R. The structured clinical interview for PTSD (SIPTSD)[22] or structured clinical interview for DSM III (SCID)[23] enables current and lifetime diagnosis of PTSD. These characteristic symptoms such as flashbacks, high arousal, intrusive nightmares, etc., will appear when activation has taken place as described in part one of these two papers. Prior to this, only recurrent depressive episodes with a rather constricted lifestyle may be present. It should be noted that PTSD may be masked by a secondary disorder being used to cope with the symptoms of the primary stress disorder; as described by Kardiner and Spiegel[24] this has been noted in relation to substance abuse.[25] In addition, there is much overlapping between post-traumatic symptoms and those of other disorders[26] such as depression,[27] antisocial personality[28] and in particular borderline personality.[29] Indeed, character change is to be expected after exposure to overwhelming personal disasters.[30] Finally, traumatic imagery is frequently misunderstood, resulting in the misdiagnosis of a variety of psychotic conditions, in particular schizophrenia and LSD abuse.

3. Highly organized ego defences, often accompanied by strong and effective coping mechanisms; these patients often struggle on against what seem insuperable odds.

4. There is one universal limitation on any form of psychotherapeutic endeavour, that is the willingness and commitment of the person[31] to go through the pain and suffering which is an inevitable part of any real therapeutic life change. We will return to the question of this category of patients who are unsuitable for this form of therapeutic intervention later in this paper.

Patients for whom this form of therapy is applicable fall into two quite distinct groupings, shown in Fig. 28.1. In this figure, human adaptation is illustrated along two axes: coping skills and defences. On one axis we have weak versus strong coping and on the other highly organized defence versus low defence organization. From this four groups emerge:

A. The first group are those we would normally regard as healthy; they are able to cope with appropriate action or emotional response, depending on what the situation or life challenge demands. Where the situation – such as tackling a job, facing an examination or other practical life challenge – demands an active

Personality types as a function of defence and coping skills

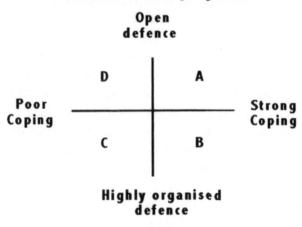

Fig. 28.1

response, they meet it with the appropriate action, but, where they are presented with the situation of loss – i.e. a broken love affair, death of a husband or close relative – they are able to deal with it by the appropriate emotional response, working through the grief or pain necessary to resolve the trauma. On the other axis they show a low defence organization, being open and flexible without need of highly organized defences.

B. The second group are those persons who show a strong level of coping but one that is rigid and inflexible. On the other axis they will present a highly organized and rigid defence system so that their lifestyle will tend to be constricted and one that avoids any situation where an open feeling response is indicated. These characteristics are frequently reported in victims of trauma.[32] This is the category of patients who are most suitable for, and will tend to show the most favourable response to, this form of therapy. Their powerful coping strengths give them the commitment to struggle through and experience whatever painful traumas of their earlier life they have to face. Indeed, such people, far from being weaker or more vulnerable than the average, typically show enormous strength and courage in their struggle to carry on in the face of terrible life experiences. Suprisingly, these patients often report very little alteration of psychosocial functioning.[33]

CASE ILLUSTRATION

One patient had a life of unbelievable misery in being raped and sexually and physically brutalized by her brothers and their friends in the neighbourhood from early childhood. When she reached adult life and was attending college, she had to face further insults. Her brother, who was her main abuser, used to arrange parties where he and his friends would gang-rape her, yet the next morning she would be up and dressed and in punctual attendance at her lectures. How many of us, in the face of such continuous brutalization, would be able to carry on, apparently coping with ordinary life?

C. In this group we find those who would generally be described as having anti-social or borderline personality disorders. On one axis, these too will have a highly organized defence system, but characteristically their defences will be of a more primitive kind and there will be a question mark over their ability to trust.[34] They will therefore tend to test any situation or relationship by anti-social behaviour to see whether they will be rejected yet again. This may take the form of self-destructive or aggressive acts and this kind of behaviour is particularly likely when unresolved experience surfaces in therapy. On the other axis, they have poor coping skills for managing life and difficulty in concentrating or sticking at a task which may be routine or boring, as is inevitably involved in most types of occupation. They are also likely to have poor educational and occupational skills. This group will be more difficult to manage in therapy. Nevertheless, it is possible to work with these cases if they have a validating, but also supportive, network along the lines of a therapeutic community.[35] The positive aspects of social support on a sufferer's ability to cope with PTSD have been commented on in a number of studies.[36] With the help of the supportive network as they gradually work through their unresolved traumatic experience, and as they learn to trust in the context of a consistent therapeutic relationship, they become able to undertake training and rehabilitation that will give them the coping skills for independent living as illustrated by the dotted line in Fig. 28.2.

D. In this group are those who not only have weak coping skills, but also have poorly organized defences. Many in this category will not fit the four criteria already cited for this form of therapeutic programme. The common characteristic of this group of patients is their childish dependency, their inability to bound themselves and their lack of commitment to any programme of therapy; thus, even where there is a history of traumatization, when this is activated they are unable to work with it and simply regress further into primitive psychotic defences.

The Therapeutic Cycle

Let us turn now to Fig. 28.2. This is shown initially in linear form in order to illustrate more clearly the different phases of therapeutic intervention. On the vertical axis we have a combination of coping strength and the degree of organized defensive structure, while on the other axis time is shown. These therapeutic stages should not be seen as relating to specific periods of time, for the length of time of any given phase will depend upon the individual characteristics and needs of the patient concerned.

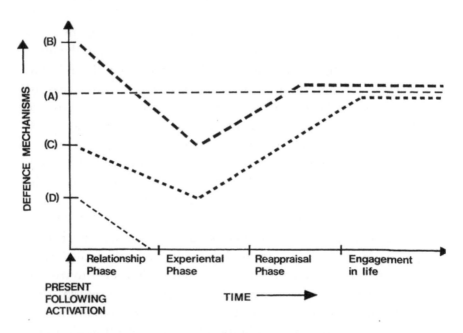

Fig. 28.2

The dotted line A acts as a reference point and represents the level of coping and the defence structure of a person who is managing everyday life and is in no particular need of therapy. In group B the patient is starting from a point of highly organized defence. They tend to present when the symptoms have been activated[37] and they are finding that they can no longer cope as they formerly could, and so on to the group C and D as described in the text.

Relationship Phase

The first step is to offer them a personal therapist, who will create a trusting therapeutic relationship and continue to work with them throughout all phases of their therapy. The special sensitivity of trauma victims to their therapist has been frequently emphasized. It is also important in this initial phase to negotiate as firm a commitment as possible, sharing with the patient information regarding what is involved in this therapeutic journey. This initial phase of establishing a trusting relationship and negotiating a firm commitment usually takes a matter of some weeks, but it may take much longer; in one case it took almost a year before the patient established sufficient confidence to move on to the experiential phase of therapy. As can be seen from the figure, at this time there is little change in the level of coping or opening up of the defences and the person is encouraged to continue working and maintain their normal activities as far as possible. During this period the therapist would ordinarily see the patient for an hour once or twice a week.

Experiential Phase

When the therapeutic relationship is sufficiently established we move on to the experiential phase. Up to twelve people may participate simultaneously in the therapeutic session which takes place one afternoon each week. However, patients usually attend on alternate weeks, as we find it normally takes a fortnight for the person to integrate and process the experiences which surface during a therapeutic session. This enables us to work with two groups, comprising upwards of twenty-four patients, each group attending on alternate weeks. At times, patients may attend less frequently, particularly towards the end of therapy, but in some instances they need to come every week for a time, when the pressure of unresolved experience emerging necessitates this.

Once the patient enters the experiential phase, they have much greater difficulty in managing everyday life, the symptomatology becomes more severe, and there is a general personality regression as illustrated in Fig. 28.2. They now resemble more closely the patients in group C: they have the same sense of worthlessness and often exhibit the same self-destructive behavioural problems.

Our general policy, wherever possible, is to work with them as outpatients, helping them to maintain normal life and relationships as far as they can. However, when the regression is at its height, it may be necessary to manage them on a brief inpatient basis, whilst encouraging them to take responsibility for themselves as soon as possible. This is particularly likely to happen following an experiential session, when a number of patients may stay in the hospital overnight, or for a day or two, until they have integrated the experience sufficiently to be able to cope again.

The session commences at approximately 2 p.m., each patient lying on a mattress, separated from each other by a reasonable distance so that they can move freely during the session. Each patient is attended by a trained 'sitter', who remains with them continuously throughout the session and cares for all their needs. The sitter's task is to see that the patient does not injure themselves and to encourage them in whatever way is appropriate to engage as fully as possible with their experience. The sitter does not interfere any more than is absolutely necessary with the person's spontaneous experience in this altered state of consciousness. The experiential session continues naturally for approximately three hours, although the time the patient remains in the altered state of consciousness may vary from person to person, some continuing on for a longer period; we allow each person to emerge naturally from their experience.

The therapeutic session moves through four broad phases:

1. A short initial period of relaxation lasting ten to fifteen minutes. The person lies on their back with eyes closed, palms upwards, in as open a position as possible. A relaxation tape is played, starting with the feet and moving through all the muscle groups of the body, breathing slowly and deeply but gently, from the abdomen and as far as possible emptying the

mind and focusing solely on the breath. The relaxation is accompanied by a background of quiet, gentle music.

2. As the relaxation ends, the participants are asked to increase the rate and depth of their breathing until they are breathing as rapidly and deeply as possible, to the accompaniment of tapes of gradually accelerating sounds of breathing and heart-beats to assist the subjects in achieving full hyperventilation. At the same time, the power and strength of the music is increased, rising to a full evocative pitch. A wide range of music is used, from strident symphonic pieces to various ethnic recordings such as African drumming, Sufi breathing or Tibetan chants. For most subjects, the period of active hyperventilation only lasts fifteen to twenty minutes, by which time they have entered a state of non-ordinary con-sciousness. This active stage with evocative music is then continued for approximately an hour.

3. By this time, most subjects are well into the experience and are in a well-established altered state of consciousness. During the third phase, the music is altered to a more gentle, floating, con-tinuous sound. This keeps the participants in the altered state of consciousness and allows them to continue whatever they are experiencing without too much strident interference.

4. After approximately two hours, as the patients are beginning to show signs of emerging from the experience and returning to ordinary consciousness, the music is changed to create a gentle peaceful atmosphere. This helps participants to return to ordinary waking consciousness in a quiet, peaceful state, with a sense of completion. To assist this, a terminating medi-tative tape is played.

We have developed a sophisticated sound system including tape decks, CD players and a mixer. This enables us to mix different sound modalities, providing a highly evocative background for the patients' hyperventilation. This combination brings most subjects into an altered state of consciousness. Once an altered state is achieved, the inner knowledge of the person brings unresolved expe-rience to the surface. It is as if the psyche knows which experience needs to be worked. No prompting or suggestion is necessary, as the process works quite automatically. It is important to emphasize here that what emerges is the raw experience that was laid down at the time the event took place. Typically, neither the subject nor the therapist has any idea what this experience is about until the story begins to unfold over the days or weeks to come. Indeed, it is often only after the subject has worked the experience through over several experiential sessions and the emotional component has been fully lived that the story of what happened becomes totally available to memory recall. Once this has been achieved, this particular item of experience will no longer cause problems for the person and will simply be a rather unpleasant memory which can be recalled at will without any undue emotional response.

This experiential phase can last from a period of weeks to, more usually, several months and in particularly difficult cases even up to a year or two. The duration is directly proportional to the amount of traumatic experience which the person has endured during their lifetime.[38]

Where the patient has difficulty with the basic approach of hyperventilation and evocative sound in achieving a non-ordinary state of consciousness we use a number of other modalities:

1. *Focused bodywork*.[39] This is only used in a non-intrusive manner, specifically with the agreement of the subject when they feel blocked energy or tension in some part of the body. It is often particularly useful towards the end of the session, when the full resolution of what has been experienced has become localized in some particular part of the body. The subject is then asked to bring their full awareness to that part of themselves so that nothing else exists and then to increase the sensations of tension while gentle pressure is applied. This pressure and focusing is maintained until the emotion associated with it surfaces and the person is then instructed to express this as fully as possible. This catharsis is often accompanied by the emergence of blocked information about some significant traumatic experience. In the application of this focused bodywork we have drawn on various traditions, such as bioenergetics,[40] cranio- sacral therapy,[41] Feldenkrais,[42] Hakomi,[43] amongst others. These various disciplines contain many common elements. The essential principle is to support and enhance the experience which is occurring spontaneously for the client, but never to intrude our preconceived notions upon them.

2. *A psychedelic agent.* We use the dissociative anaesthetic Ketamine in small doses. We only utilize this intervention where the person is unable to achieve a non-ordinary state of consciousness with the breathwork or focused bodywork. Ketamine is given by deep intramuscular injection; we use dosages in the range of 30–100 milligrams (approximately one-tenth the anaesthetic dose). Ketamine is a short-acting substance, the experience usually terminating within an hour.[44] Sometimes a repeat dose is necessary to fully resolve the experience which has emerged. Frequently we find that, when a person has achieved an altered state of consciousness with the help of Ketamine, they are able to return in the next session to the breathwork and progress satisfactorily with this alone. It should be stressed that there is no experience which occurs following the administration of Ketamine which has not also been found as part of the breathwork with evocative music. This once again illustrates the principle that it is the state of non-ordinary consciousness, not the route by which this altered state is achieved, which is important.

3. *Hypnosis.*[45] Where some patients are too highly disturbed and defended initially to allow themselves into hypnosis, once they have opened up with the breathing and music it is then possible to induce a hypnotic trance. This is useful because often in the experiential session the patient has a powerful catharsis or bodily experience but is unable to elucidate a clear story as to what actually happened. Under hypnotic regression, they are frequently able to recount the full details of the traumatic event but not the full catharsis of the experience. Thus, by combining the two modalities, it is possible to bring the person through the full experience, both the emotional catharsis and the detailed story of what happened. This seems to be necessary if full processing into long-term memory is to take place.

4. *Artwork and creative expression.*[46] Patients are encouraged to paint or sculpt their experience when they return to ordinary consciousness at the end of the experiential session, although not all subjects are sufficiently composed to be able to do this at the time. For this reason we encourage them to continue with artwork and to write out the experience during the week following the experiential session. This greatly helps with the integration and further elucidation of the experiences.

5. Lastly, where all else fails, or as a further aid to the full integration of the experience, it is often helpful to bring the person to the site where the traumatic event occurred, for example to the scene of a rape, or to the grave of a deceased relative to intensify the grieving process.

In the week following the experiential session, the subject sees their own individual therapist at least once or twice to continue the work of integration in face-to-face psychotherapy.

Reappraisal Phase

Prior to beginning therapy, and indeed often for most of their lives, persons who have been traumatized or abused over many years will typically have a very negative self-image. They think they were only fit to be treated in this way, that they are bad. They may have self-destructive motivation either to mutilate themselves or to end their life. As already pointed out, when they first present for therapy they are unaware of most of their traumatic history and major areas of their personality are dissociated, so they do not know why they have all these negative feelings about themselves. It is only when, in an altered state of consciousness, these major dissociated areas of their personality become accessible to them that they can begin to take responsibility for all that they are. Where there is a long history of abuse dating back to childhood, the dissociated dimension of their personality may have become abusive to others yet they have been unable to take responsibility for this because the visible personality had no knowledge of what was taking place.

It is only as the experiential phase proceeds that the person is able to begin to take responsibility for the dissociated dimensions of their personalities and to draw these together for the first time to become a whole person under conscious control. It is then that a reappraisal of their situation becomes possible; they can begin to see that it was not they who were bad or worthless but that anyone who was subjected to such brutal traumatic experience would have reacted in the same way. The abuser, particularly if it was the father, who is seen as omnipotent and perhaps even idealized, can now be seen for the weak, pathetic creature that he was. In this way, if not forgiveness at least reconciliation and acceptance become possible. It is not a case of rewriting the story or denying the facts of the terrible things that happened, as suggested by Janet, but rather of altering our relation to and our attitude towards what took place so that we are able to free ourselves from it and to take responsibility for our feelings and our future behaviour.

While the traumatic experience is unfolding and all the pain and anguish which was suspended is being felt, the person is clinically much worse than they were when therapy began. It is only when such reappraisal of the past takes place that we begin to see a real therapeutic change for the better.

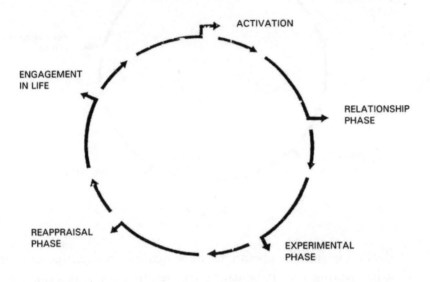

Fig. 28.3

In the early days, we thought that the experiencing of the trauma was the whole of therapy. It is only gradually and primarily through learning from the work with our patients that the successive phases of the full spectrum of therapy have become clear to us. Fig. 28.2, depicting the several phases of therapy in a linear fashion, does not accurately represent what is happening. These phases should be shown as a cycle, as in Fig. 28.3. Thus, reappraisal is quite different from the experiential stage. It takes place to a greater extent in ordinary consciousness and is part of the patients' work with their personal therapist. This is essentially a cognitive phase and represents a change in concepts and attitudes in the way the person has always looked at life. Just as during the experiential phase there is a movement of the traumatic experience from the present into the past, there is now a movement of the person and of their view of themselves from being fixated on the past to a state of 'being' in the present. At this point we see the prospect of real life-change coming from the perspective of the future.

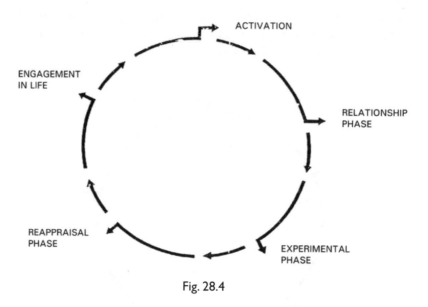

Fig. 28.4

Regarding this therapeutic cycle, which has evolved for us over time in working with patients, we recalled that the pioneering psychologist George Kelly had also seen his work with clients in the form of 'a cycle of experience'.[47] We thought it would be interesting, therefore, to see if the stages in his cycle of experience showed any similarities with those that have emerged for us. In Fig.28.4, we show his cycle of experience as compared to our therapeutic cycle and, although he uses different descriptive terms, the similarity is striking. Where we start with *activation* he uses the term *anticipation*, his *investment* is our *relationship* phase, our *experiential* phase is his *encounter*, our *reappraisal* is described by him as *dis-confirmation*: either the patient confirms their previous anticipation that things will always be the same or they dis-confirm their previous experience, realizing the possibility of real change. This leads to his *constructive revision*, which we describe as *engagement in life change*. The fact that, quite independently, we arrived at similar stages in the therapeutic progression suggests that these phases have some validity.

Provided that there is the basic commitment on the part of the patient, with the various procedures available to us we can usually enable the patient to open up their traumatic experience. However, when they become too open and regressed, filled with self-rejection and hopelessness, our main difficulty more recently has been in helping them to 'close'. Originally, we thought that all the traumatic experience had to be worked through before any reintegration of the personality could take place. A number of patients became so open and overwhelmed by the traumatic experience that they were unable to learn how to organize the newly-revealed traumatic experience, so that they were virtually unable to make any progress.

Once the cyclical nature of the therapeutic process, with its successive phases, became clear we realized that, as soon as the patient has processed a sufficient amount of the traumatic experience to ease the symptomatology and to allow them to cope with ordinary life, it is possible to enable them to close earlier. They are then able to engage in reappraisal and return to ordinary living but with the understanding that this does not mean that therapy is finally completed. This does, however, give them a break in order to be able to integrate their personality and avoids the danger of too much regression and the possibility of becoming too open and so over-exposed that they are unable to learn or usefully process any experience.

If, having suspended the experiential aspects of therapy, they remain well and are able to get on with reappraisal and engagement in normal life, so much the better and they will not require any further therapy. If, on the other hand, further traumatic experiences come to the surface and the PTSD symptoms return, then it is simply a matter of going round the cycle once again. What we have found, however, is that when patients need to return in this way, they tend to move through the stages of the cycle much more quickly and usually two or three more experiential sessions is sufficient to clear the newly-emerged traumatic experience so that they can return quickly to normal life once again.

Thus one patient suspended experiential work in order to take her final nursing examination and, having worked for a time, then returned in order to complete her therapy.

CASE ILLUSTRATION

A patient with a lifelong history from early infancy of brutal sexual abuse by her father had, after a lot of painful experiential work, apparently recovered fully and had returned to work successfully for almost a year. Then her post-traumatic symptoms returned and she came back to us almost as bad as ever. Prior to this, she had given an account of how her father had died from an acute heart attack while she was out at the shops and, on her return to the house, she had seen the ambulance waiting outside to take him away.

When her symptoms returned, however, and she undertook further experiential sessions, the story which emerged was quite different. It seemed that, having returned to work and normal life for a time, her personality integration was now strong enough to be able to experience the full horror of what actually happened. On the day her father died, when she was ten years old, she was actually in the house with him and he was forcing oral intercourse on her when he collapsed with an acute heart attack, pinning her underneath him with his erect penis in her mouth so that she was unable for some time to free herself. When she did succeed in struggling out from under him, she ran in panic out of the house and down to the shops, from which she returned some time later, with the brutal event completely obliterated from her mind, to find his body being taken away in the ambulance. Thus, with the altered truncated version of what had actually happened and the unexperienced horrible event in cold storage, she was able to go on with her life in some sort of fashion.

With regard to the difficulties of achieving closure, we have found that one useful approach, utilizing hypnosis, is to provide the person with a safe place to which they can retreat when the pressure of traumatic experience becomes too great.[48] It is important to ensure that the safe place that they choose does not turn out to be a location in which they were abused in the past. For this reason it is often better to establish with them some haven from their present life, such as a restful spot by the sea, or a secret place in the woods, or a quiet room where they feel totally safe which has no connection whatever with their traumatic past. Under hypnosis, they can then be given a signal that will immediately transport them to this haven and a secure boundary can be drawn around it so that nothing painful or traumatic from their past can ever enter this space. For those who can utilize this imagery, this can be a useful safeguard and an aid to 'closure'.

We have also tried various forms of medication. We have found antidepressants[49] and benzodiazapines[50] to be the most useful, particularly in ameliorating intrusive symptoms; this is in keeping with the current body of research.[51] More recently, we have had some success using the serotonin-specific re-uptake inhibitor Fluoxetine, which is consistent with the findings of McDougle *et al.*[52] amongst others.[53] Neuroleptics appear to have a poorly defined role in the treatment of PTSD and have been of limited value to us. Whilst pharmacological interventions enable limited symptomatic relief, they do not treat the underlying pathological process;[54] they may, however, play a useful adjunctive role in the treatment of PTSD, augmenting psychotherapeutic interventions.[55]

A recent development is Shapiro's work with eye movement desensitization,[56] utilizing rhythmic sacadic eye movements while holding in mind the most salient aspect of a traumatic experience. Although we have only limited experience of this method as yet, along with other authors[57] we have found it a useful method for achieving 'closure'.

Engagement in Life

We have found that even when patients have fully worked through all their traumatic experience and have completed the task of reappraisal, full recovery does not take place until they have moved the 'locus of control' into themselves and taken over personal direction of their life. Until now, the control of their life has either been in the hands of others, of family members or those around them, or they have been driven by the pressure of the unresolved frozen traumatic experience and the careful avoidance of anything that might bring this to the surface.[58]

Another difficulty has arisen where, although a good therapeutic relationship may have been established and the person is achieving an altered state of consciousness in the experiential sessions and indeed appears to be going through the full emotional experience of their traumatic past, still they are failing to make progress. When this occurs, it frequently happens that the block is at the next level of living.[59] If we take the view that the person is a living system, but also that the family too is a living system in its own right with its own separate life and existence,[60] if the trauma is unresolved at this level and if what happened in the past is still a secret and cannot be spoken of in the family, then the patient who is still functioning as part of that living system will be unable to free themselves and progress.[61]

At this point we have found that the only way is to bring together as many members of the family as are available, face to face with the patient, to open up the secret and if possible get an admission of the truth. What we typically find is that there is not only a secret which cannot see the light of day but also a myth, created many years before, that if these things were ever spoken of, some calamity would happen, somebody would break down or be destroyed.[62] This is unlikely to have any basis in reality now, whatever may have been the situation in the past. Usually, if what happened can be brought into the light of day, not only is it a validation for the patient but it is a general relief to all concerned. This can apply not only in cases where there has been physical or sexual abuse but in other traumatic situations such as loss of a baby or a miscarriage, or loss of a parent in the patient's early years.[63] In any of these circumstances, where the event is denied by the parents and hence by the family as a whole, the patient may unwittingly take on the role of scapegoat and guardian of the secret. In tackling this situation, it is obviously most satisfactory when the truth can be brought out and accepted by all but, even when other members of the family refuse to acknowledge what took place, it can still be beneficial if the patient can face them openly with the truth, or even write an account and send it to them where they refuse to be involved. By this means the patient is now left to carry what belongs to him or herself and is no longer tied into the secret, being free to get on with his or her own life.

Full recovery then can only take place when the person engages with life on a different basis, trying out new social behaviour and undertaking activities which until then had spelt danger and had to be strenuously avoided. It is this move from a rigidly defended narrow way of life to a much more flexible set of attitudes and behaviours, including the taking on of full personal autonomy, which permits one to talk in terms of full recovery or cure. For those patients who fit the picture of group B, it is this achievement of a flexible healthy way of life and full personal autonomy that is all that is required. They are likely already, because of their strong coping ability, to have a reasonable education and training and to have a job to return to.

However, when we turn to those patients in group C, much more is usually required. They are likely to come from a deprived social background, or to have been institutionally reared. They will have wide-ranging deficits in social behaviour and will usually have poor concentration and vocational skills, necessitating the full spectrum of vocational training if they are to reach any degree of reasonable independence in life. This means that the later stages of their therapy will necessitate rehabilitation and vocational training resources. This implies that the full therapeutic programme for such patients will be extended by several years, but it is important to realize that these later stages do not involve hospitalization or a major strain on health service resources; they can be undertaken with hostel care and the resources provided by the state under social welfare and vocational training. It should be further emphasized that, if this rehabilitative task is not undertaken, then such patients are likely to be a millstone around the neck of the psychiatric and other health services, causing management problems far in excess of what their numbers would suggest.

One final point that should be noted here is that, in bringing the person through a cycle of successive therapeutic phases, we are moving from one mode of therapy to another, each of which has often been thought of in the past as a complete form of therapy in its own right – psychodynamic psychotherapy, cognitive therapy, behaviour therapy and so on. We believe our therapeutic programme illustrates that these are not completely separate forms of treatment (as, for example, when one hears someone describe themselves as a cognitive therapist) but rather phases in the cycle of therapy to be applied at the point where the client needs a particular approach. Thus, initially we are involved with the patient in what might look like a traditional psychodynamic therapeutic relationship, moving on then when the time is right to the experiential phase, followed by the reappraisal period and the use of what would ordinarily be described as cognitive therapy and, finally, on to a form of behavioural psychotherapy, when the client is engaged in active 'life change'. Therapy should thus be appropriate not to the belief system or to the skills possessed by the therapist but to the needs of the patient at a given time in the psychotherapeutic process.

Conclusion

It is perhaps time then to consider the point we have reached in this work. We have developed a clear and consistent theory as to the genesis of traumatic neurosis which is described in the first of these two papers. We have also developed a therapeutic programme that promises considerable success for those who have a reasonable commitment to going through the painful work of change and who fulfil the four criteria for selection laid down at the beginning of this paper. This brings us then to the question of research to validate the therapy we are putting forward.

The systematic evaluation of a therapy which is lengthy and involves several distinct stages presents major difficulty when it comes to choosing a research methodology. Ideally one would like to have a matched control group of patients that undergo the same diagnostic assessment as the treatment group but it is difficult to see how this is ethically possible. One possible approach to the problem is to utilize a small -N design including control conditions rather than control subjects, effectively using the patient as their own control.[64] This is particularly applicable to the client group we are working with, as they typically have long histories of illness and show little change or improvement prior to presenting for this form of therapy. Preliminary work on a number of patients who have been through the complete therapeutic programme suggests that this approach is feasible and worth pursuing on a larger scale.

At the end of the first paper we touched upon the question of revictimization.[65] This is the peculiar fact that many of the patients fitting the general pattern of PTSD seem to be moving along a 'track', as if there were a theme running through their life so that they continue to be subject to the same kind of traumatic experience over and over again. For example, where there is sexual abuse early in childhood we find the person being abused by others in adolescence and then often subjected to rape or other types of sexual abuse again and again in adult life. In a similar way, we find patterns of loss or somatic illness running through a person's life. In all of these instances it is as if the individual lives out a theme that the external world continually plays back to them. Usually this phenomenon, which we believe is now quite widely recognized,[66] is explained in terms of the early learning and personality identification which the person takes into themselves so that they adapt with an 'enabling' attitude and evoke a reciprocal response in those who carry a complementary tendency. We see this, for instance, in the daughters of alcoholics who frequently in adult life will be attracted by, and attractive to – and indeed often marry – alcoholics. A similar arrangement of mutuality has been noted in battered wives and those who brutalize them.

There is little doubt that this view represents part of the explanation for such fixed behaviour and repetitive traumatization, but, when one examines the life history in such cases carefully, it becomes apparent that there is more to it than this. In case after case we have found occurrences happening which could conceivably be due to coincidences but, when these happen again and again, the odds against their happening by chance would be enormous. It was this phenomenon that Carl Jung adverted to in his essays on synchronicity. The ancient Yogic philosophy of Karmic transmission[67] would represent another possible explanation of these strange repetitive interactions. Stanislav Grof, in his writings, has also drawn attention to these obscure linkages, which he refers to as a co-ex system,[68] and points out that the theme usually extends into the transpersonal area, the person often going into experiences that are not from their present life but have all the immediacy and vividness of real experiences. In our work, too, we have frequently found the subject going into an experience which seems to be from a former lifetime but which follows the theme of their present lifetime and carries all the conviction of reality, the suffering, detail and painful emotion that one would expect were it an early experience from their present life. Whatever position one may take on these experiences, we have found over and over again that it is only when a patient has fully lived through one or more of these transpersonal episodes that they are able to free themselves from endlessly repeating the same form of traumatic experience and to take a genuinely new direction in life. It is not appropriate, however, to go further into this matter here, as these questions go well beyond the scope of the present papers, but it is our hope to return to these interesting questions, involving a wider view of reality and its implications for this work at a later date.

References

1. American Psychiatric Association, *Diagnostic and Statistical Manual of Mental Disorders*, 3rd edition, Washington, 1987.
2. Davidson, J. 'Drug Therapy of Post Traumatic Stress Disorder', *British Journal of Psychiatry*, 160, 309–14, 1992.
3. Breslan, N., Davis, G.C., Andreski, P., and Peterson, E. 'Traumatic Events and Post Traumatic Stress Disorder in an Urban Population of Young Adults', *Arch. Gen. Psychiatry*, 48, 3, 216–22, 1991; Davidson, J.R., Kudler, H.S., and Smith, R.D. 'Treatment of PTSD with Amitriptylline and Placebo', *Arch. Gen. Psychiatry*, 4, 259–69, 1990.
4. Watson, C.G., Kucala, T., Manifold, V., Vassar, P., and Juba, M. 'Differences between PTSD Patients with Delayed and Undelayed Onsets', *J. Nervous and Mental Disease*, 176, 9, 568–72, 1988.
5. Duckworth, D.H. 'Post Traumatic Stress Disorder', *Stress Medicine*, vol. 3, 175–83, 1987.
6. Scrignar, C.B. *Post Traumatic Stress Disorder Diagnosis, Treatment and Legal Issues*, 2nd edition, Bruno Press, New Orleans, LA, 1988.
7. Freud, S. *The Aetiology of Hysteria*, trans. and ed. J. Strachey, Hogarth Press, London, 1980.
8. Janet, P. *Psychological Healing: Historical and Clinical Study*, vols I and II, Macmillan, New York, 1925.
9. Jung, C.G. *Collected Works*, Routledge & Kegan, England, 1963.
10. Reich, W. *Character Analysis*, Farrar Strauss Girouse, New York, 1949; Boadella, D. *In the Wake of Reich*, Coventure, London, 1976.
11. Feldenkrais, M. *Body and Nature Behaviour*, International and University Press, New York, 1970.
12. Perls, F., Hefferline, R.F., and Goodman, P. *Gestalt Therapy*, Julian Press, 1958.
13. Grof, S. *The Adventure of Self Discovery*, Albany New York State, University of New York Press.
14. Ibid.
15. Atkinson, R.M., Sparr, L.F., Sheff, White, R.A., and Fitzsimmons, J.T. 'Diagnosis of Post Traumatic Stress in Vietnam Veterans: Preliminary Findings', *Am. J. Psychiatry*, 141, 5, 694–6, 1984; Solursh, L. 'Combat Addiction Post Traumatic Stress Disorder Re-explored', *Psychiatric Journal Univ, Ottawa*, 88, 13, 1, 17–20.
16. Lindberg, F.H., and Distrad, L.J. 'Post Traumatic Stress Disorders in Women Who Experienced Childhood Incest', *Child Abuse Negl.*, 9, 3, 329–34, 1985.
17. Holmes, M.R., and Lawrence, J.S. 'Treatment of Rape Induced Trauma: Proposed Behavioural Conceptualization and Review of the Literature', *Clinical Psychology Review*, 3, 417–33, 1983.
18. Blank, K., and Perry, S. 'Relationship of Psychological Processes During Delirium to Outcome', *Am. J. Psychiatry*, 141, 843–7, 1984.
19. Duckworth, D.H. 'Psychological Problems Arising from Disaster Work', *Stress Med.*, 2, 315–23, 1986.

20. Davis, R.C., and Friedman, L.N. 'The Emotional Aftermath of Crime and Violence', in C.R. Figley (ed.), *Trauma and Its Wake*, Brunner/ Mazel, New York, 90–112, 1985.

21. Schottenfeld, R.S., and Cullen, M.R. 'Occupation Induced Post Traumatic Stress Disorders', *Am. J. Psychiatry*, 142, 2, 198–202, 1985.

22. Davidson, J., Smith, R., and Kudler, K. 'Validity and Reliability of the DSM III Criteria for PTSD: Experience with a Structured Interview', *Journal of Nervous and Mental Disease*, 177, 336–341, 1989.

23. Spitzer, R.I., and Williams, J.B. *Structured Clinical Interview for DSM III-R, Patient Version*, New York State Psychiatric Institute, Bionetrics Research Department, 1985.

24. Kardiner, A., and Spiegel, H. *Stress and Neurotic Illness*, New York, Paul B. Hoever, 1947.

25. Van Putten, T., and Emory, W.H. 'Traumatic Neuroses in Vietnam Returnees', *Arch. Gen. Psychiatry*, 29, 695–8, 1973.

26. Penk, W.E., Robinowitx, W.R., Patterso, E.T., Dolan, M.P., and Atkins, H.G. 'Adjustment Differences Among Male Substance Abusers Varying in Degree of Combat Experience in Vietnam', *J. Consult. Clin. Psycho.*, 49, 426–37, 1981.

27. Kudler, H., Davidson, J., Meador, K. Lipper, S., and Ely, T. 'The DST and Post Traumatic Stress Disorder', *Am. J. Psych.*, 144,8, 1068–71, 1987; Southwick, S.M., Yehuda, K., and Giller, E.I. 'Characterization of Depression in War Related Post Traumatic Stress Disorder', *Am. J. Psychiatry*, 148, 2, 179–83, 1991.

28. Walker, J.I. 'Vietnam Combat Veterans with Legal Difficulties: A Psychiatric Problem?', *Am. J. Psychiatry*, 138, 1384, 1981.

29. Coors, P., Bowman, E., Pellow, T., and Schneider, P. 'Post Traumatic Aspects of the Treatment of Victims of Sexual Abuse and Incest', *Psych. Clinics of North America*, 12, 325–35, 1989.

30. Lindy, J.D., and Titchner, J. Acts of God and Man: Long Term Character Change in Survivors of Disaster and the Law', *Behavioural Science and the Law*, 1, 85–96, 1983.

31. Block, S. *What Is Psychotherapy?* Oxford University Press, 32–3, 1982.

32. Corcey, M., Santiago, J.M., and McCall-Perez, F.L. 'Psychological Consequences for Women Sexually Abused in Childhood', *Soc. Psychiatry*, 21, 129–33, 1986; Holmes, M.R., and St Lawrence, J.S. 'Treatment of Rape Induced Trauma: Proposed Behavioural Conceptualization and Review of the Literature', *Clinical Psychology Review*, 3, 417–33, 1983.

33. Roca, R.P., Spence, R.J., and Munster, A.M. 'Post Traumatic Adaption and Distress Among Adult Burn Survivors', *Am. J. Psychiatry*, 149, 9, 1234–8, 1991.

34. Blake-White, J., and Kline, C.M. 'Treating the Dissociative Process in Adult Victims of Childhood Incest: Social Casework', *Journal of Contemporary Social Work*, 384–402, 1985.

35. Clark, D.H. 'The Therapeutic Community', *Brit. J. Psychiatry*, 131, 563–4, 1977.

36. Egendorf, A. *Legacies of Vietnam: Comparative Adjustment of Veterans and Their Peers*, Washington DC Government Printing Office, 1981; Keane,

T.M., Scott, W.O., Chavoya, G.A., Lamparski, D.M., and Fairbank, J.A. 'Social Support in Vietnam Veterans with PTSD: A Comparative Analysis', *J. Consult. Clin. Psych.*, 53, 95–102, 1985.

37. Pitnam, R.K. 'Post Traumatic Stress Disorder, Hormones and Memory', *Biol. Psychiatry*, 26, 221–3, 1989; Goodwin, J. 'The Aetiology of Combat Related Post Traumatic Stress Disorders', in T. Williams (ed.), *Post Traumatic Stress Disorders of the Vietnam Veteran*, Disabled American Veterans, Cincinatti, 1980; Marafiate, R. 'Behavioural Strategies in Group Treatment of Vietnam Veterans', *Clin. Psych.*, 53, 95–102, 1985.

38. Solkoff, N., Gray, P., and Keill, S. 'Which Vietnam Veterans Develop Post Traumatic Stress Disorder?', *J. Con. Psychol.*, 42: 687–98, 1986; Greer, B.L., Wilson, J.P., and Lindy, J.D. 'Conceptualization PTSD: A Psychosocial Framework', in C.R. Figley (ed.), *Trauma and Its Wake*, Brunner/Mazel, New York, 53–669, 1985.

39. Lee Hoi, M., and Gregory, W. *Chinese Massage Therapy: The Handbook of Therapeutic Massage*, Routledge Kegan Paul, London, 1983; Mindwell, A. *Working with the Dreaming Body*, Routledge S. Kegan Paul, London, 1985; Emerson, P., and Williams, R. *Infant and Children Refacilitation*, Institute for Holistic Education, University of Surrey, 1984.

40. Boadella, D. *Lifestreams: An Introduction to Biosynthesis*, Routledge & Kegan Paul, London, 1987.

41. Chaito, L. 'Cranial Osteopathy', in *Osteopathy*, Thorsons, 1982.

42. Feldenkrais. *Body and Nature Behaviour*.

43. Kurtz, R. *Body Centred Psychotherapy: The Hakomi Method*, Life Rhythm Publications, 1990.

44. Vickers, M.D., Schnieden, H., and Wood-Smith, F.G. *Drug in Anaesthetic Practice*, 6th edition, Butterworths, London, 1984.

45. Spiegel, D. 'Hypnosis in the Treatment of Victims of Sexual Abuse', *Psychiatric Clinics of North America*, 12, 2, June 1989; Nash, M.R., Lynn, S.J., and Givens, D.L. 'Adult Hypnotic Susceptibility. Childhood Punishment and Child Abuse: A Brief Communication', *Int. J. Clin. Exp. Hypnosis*, 32, 1, 6–11, 1984.

46. Kellog, J. 'The Use of the Mandela in Psychological Evaluation and Treatment', *Am. J. of Art Therapy*, 16, 123, 1977.

47. Kenny, V. 'Steering or Drifting: The Organization of Psychotherapeutic Conversations', in Heylighen, Rousal and Demeyere (eds), *Self Steering and Cognition on Complex Systems*, 1990; Kelly, G. *The Psychology of Personal Constructs*, vols I & II, Norton, New York, 1958.

48. Van der Hart, O. (ed.) *Trauma Dissociations and Hypnosis*, Zeitlinger, 1991.

49. Frank, J.B., Kosten, T.R., Giller, E.L. Jr., and Dan, E. 'A Randomised Clinical Trial of Phenelzine and Imipramine for Post Traumatic Stress Disorder', *Am. J. Psychiatry*, 145, 10, 1289–91, 1988.

50. Dunner, F.J., Edwards, W.P., and Copeland, P.L. *Clinical Efficacy of Alprazolam in Post Traumatic Stress Disorder Patients. Abstracts: New Research*, American Psychiatric Association, 138th annual meeting, Los Angeles.

51. Davidson, J., and Nemeroff, C.B. 'Pharmacotherapy in PTSD Historical and Clinical Considerations and Future Directions', *Psychopharmacology Bulletin*, 25, 422–5, 1989; Friedman, M.J. 'Towards Rational Pharmacotherapy for Post Traumatic Stress Disorder: An Interim Report', *American Journal of Psychiatry*, 145, 281–5, 1988.

52. McDougle, C., and Southwick, S. 'An Open Trial of Fluoxetine', *PTSD Research Quarterly*, 7, Summer 1990.

53. Davidson, J.R., Roth, S., and Newman, E. 'Treatment of Post Traumatic Stress Disorder with Fluoxetine', *Journal of Traumatic Stress*, 4, 419–23, 1990.

54. Van der Kolk, B. 'The Drug Treatment of PTSD', *Journal of Affective Disorders*, 13, 203–13, 1987.

55. Bleich, A., Siegel, B., Garv, R., and Lerer, B. 'Post Traumatic Stress Disorder Following Combat Exposure: Clinical Features and Psychopharmacological Treatment', *British Journal of Psychiatry*, 149, 365–69, 1986.

56. Shapiro, F. 'Eye Movement De-sensitization: A New Treatment for Post Traumatic Stress Disorder', *Journal of Behavioural Ther. and Exp. Psychiatry*, 20, 3, 211–17, 1990.

57. Puk, G. 'Treating Traumatic Memories: A Case Report on the Eye Movement Desensitization Procedure', *J. Behav. Ther. and Exp. Psychiatry*, 22, 2, 149–51, 1991; Wolfe, J., and Abrams, J. 'Post Traumatic Stress Disorder Overcome by Eye Movement Desensitization', *J. Behav. Ther. and Exp. Psychiatry*, 22, 1, 39–43, 1991.

58. Rottea, J.M., and Silman, M.E. 'Livenants: Internal vs External Locus of Control of Reinforcement: A Major Variable in Behaviour Study', in N.F. Washburne (ed.), *Decisions, Values and Groups*, Pergamon, London, 1962.

59. Miller, T.W., Kamenchenko, P., and Krasniasnski, A. 'Assessment of Life Stress Events: The Etiology and Measurement of Traumatic Stress Disorder', *Int. J. Soc. Psychiatry*, 38, 3, 215–27, 1992.

60. Browne, I., and Kenny, V. 'How Psychotherapy Works', in F. Flach (ed.), *Psychotherapy*, Norton, 1989.

61. Moscarelloro, 'PTSD After Sexual Assault: Its Psychodynamics and Treatment', *J. Am. Acad. Psychoanalysis*, 19, 2, 235–53, 1991.

62. Kaufman, I., Peck, A., and Tagiura, C.K. 'The Family Constellation and Overt Incestuous Relations Between Father and Daughter', *Am. J. Orthopsychiatry*, 24: 266–77, 1954.

63. Brown, G.W., and Harris, T. *Social Origins of Depression*. Tavistock Publications, London.

64. Robinson, P.W., and Foster, D.F. *Experimental Psychology: A Small-N Approach*, Harper & Roe, New York, 1979.

65. Van der Kolk, B., Greenberg, M., Boyd, H., and Krystal, J. 'Inescapable Shock, Neurostransmitters and Addiction to Trauma: Towards a Psychobiology of Post Traumatic Stress', *Biol. Psychiatry*, 20, 314–25, 1985.

66. Boehnlein, J.R. 'The Process of Research in Post Traumatic Stress Disorder', *Perspectives in Biology and Medicine*, 32, 3, 455–65, 1989; Horowitz, M.J.,

and Becker, S.S. 'The Compulsion to Repeat Trauma', *J. Nerv. Ment. Dis.*, 152, 32–40, 1971.

67. Vivekananda, S. *Raja-Yoga or Conquering the Internal Nature*, 16th edition, Sun Lithographing Co., Calcutta, 1976.

68. Grof, S. Realms of the Human Unconscious: Observations from LSD Research, Souvenir Press Ltd, 1975; Grof, S. *Beyond the Brain: Birth, Death and Transcendence in Psychotherapy*, State University of New York, Albany, 1985.

29. Breaking the Mould:
Spirituality and New Developments in Science
and the Psychology of Consciousness

This paper was never published, but I have been developing these concepts over the past ten years for presentations at various training courses for psychotherapists.

MY INTENTION in this paper is to attempt to contrast the Newtonian mechanistic scientific viewpoint with some recent, more open-minded scientific developments in the psychology of consciousness, brain function, memory and information storage, etc.

These are quite separate endeavours going on in various centres around the world, but I believe they are all moving in the same direction. In a short paper such as this, it is not possible for me to describe these in detail. Rather, I think these endeavours provide a glimpse of a much more advanced evolution of human understanding that is coming in the not too distant future and they all point towards a convergence of science and spirituality. Certainly this seems to be what Babuji Maharaj is telling us in 'Whispers from the Brighter World'.

Professor Gary Schwartz, who is working in Arizona and is involved in some of these new developments, has stated that there are three main scientific world views:

- Matter is primary and Energy is secondary and only an aspect of this. (Newton)
- Matter and Energy are equivalent and are interchangeable. (Einstein)
- Energy is primary and what we call Matter is simply organized Energy. (Heizenberg)

It is the latter view that would be generally accepted by the scientists involved in these recent scientific developments.

The Renaissance

A major revolution in European thinking was made possible by the rediscovery in the twelfth and thirteenth centuries of a large body of Greek manuscripts. It was at this time that the ancient Greek writings of the atomists Leucippus and Democritus resurfaced and this led Galileo to make the statement which changed the western approach to science from then onwards:

> Scientists should restrict themselves to the essential properties of material bodies – size, shape, number, weight and motion. Only by means of an exclusively quantitative analysis could science attain certain knowledge of the world. (Tarnas 263)

This statement made possible the extraordinary technological achievements which we see all around us in the world today. But, as R.D. Laing pointed out:

> Galileo's programme offers us a dead world: out goes sight, sound, taste, touch and smell, and along with them have since gone aesthetic and ethical sensibility, values, quality, soul, consciousness, spirit. Experience as such is cast out of the realm of scientific discourse. Hardly anything has changed our world more during the past 400 years than Galileo's audacious programme. We had to destroy the world in theory before we could destroy it in practice. (Capra 40)

Francis Bacon (1561–1626), in England around the same time, went even further. He is said to be the father of empirical science and stressed the importance of direct experiment. If Socrates had associated knowledge with 'virtue' in his search for wisdom, Bacon equated knowledge with 'power'. This had profound implications for the nature and purpose of science. A marked divide was now opening up between the east and the west. Where Indian and Chinese thinkers had looked inwards, the new western scientific view was to look outwards, to map and increasingly control the world of nature. This was also a strongly male, patriarchal perspective and women, to this day, have never participated in this to the same extent (Capra 40–1).

The shift in scientific direction brought about by Galileo and Bacon was pivotal for the influence it had on the development of western science and technology. This was brought to fruition by two further towering figures of the seventeenth century – Descartes and Newton.

In Descartes' youth there was a sceptical crisis in French philosophy; the old-world view was crumbling. Struggling with doubt of every kind, at the age of twenty-three he experienced a startling vision, a sudden flash of intuition, in which he saw, the 'Foundations of a marvellous science'. Following this, he felt the only thing to do was to strip away everything, all traditional knowledge, what he could perceive and even his own body, until he reached the one thing he could not doubt – the existence of himself as a thinker. From this came his famous statement: *Cogito, ergo sum* (I think, therefore I am). He decided that the essence of human nature lies in thought and thus he felt he could rebuild his philosophy of knowledge on firm foundations.

This led him to the view that mind and matter are separate and fundamentally different:

> There is nothing included in the concept of body that belongs
> to the mind; and nothing in that of mind that belongs to the
> body.

This fundamental division between mind and matter has had an enormous effect on western thought and plagues medical thinking to this day. Many academics still think of their body as something simply that carries their head. For Descartes, the material universe was a machine and nothing but a machine. There was no purpose, life or spirituality in matter. Descartes was a brilliant mathematician and is said to be the father of analysis – i.e. understanding achieved by breaking things into their parts and seeing what they are made of; reductionism. In the seventeenth century, people were fascinated by the development of clocks and 'lifelike' machinery. Descartes considered that plants and animals were merely machines and the human body was also a machine (Capra 44–8).

The conceptual framework created by Galileo and Descartes was completed by Isaac Newton (1643–1727), who developed a consistent mathematical formulation of the mechanistic view of nature. From the second half of the seventeenth century to the end of the nineteenth century, the Newtonian, mechanistic model of the universe dominated all scientific thought. Newton created a new mathematical method (differential calculus) to describe the motion of solid bodies. He used this to formulate the exact laws of motion of all bodies under the influence of the force of gravity. The great significance of these laws lay in their universal application. The universe was seen as a vast machine operating according to exact mathematical laws. Einstein described this as 'perhaps the greatest advance in thought that a single individual was ever privileged to make'.

Newton saw time as a separate dimension, which was absolute, having no connection with the material world: 'Absolute, true and mathematical time, of itself and by its own nature flows uniformly, without regard to anything external.' Descartes' view of the world as a perfect machine now seemed to be fully vindicated by Newton's mathematical system (Capra 48–52).

By the nineteenth century, God's creation of the world had dropped out of the picture. It was felt that it was only a matter of time until a complete scientific understanding of the entire universe would be attained. The natural sciences as well as the humanities and social sciences all accepted this mechanistic view as the correct description of reality and modelled their own theories accordingly. To this day, whenever psychologists, sociologists, or economists want to be scientific, they always turn to these basic concepts of Newtonian physics and base their research on them.

In this regard I should mention that the mechanistic scientific paradigm reaches its final arrogant expression in the work of authors like Steven Pinker and Richard Dawkins. In the latter's recent book, *The God Delusion*, he fails to even mention, and appears to be unaware of, any of the recent genuine scientific developments which I want to go into here.

Let us now summarize some of the main tenets of the Newtonian view which relate to the scientific developments that I want to briefly describe in this paper:

> *Reductionism*: Understanding is achieved by breaking things into their parts and seeing what they are made of.
>
> *Determinism*: The doctrine that all events, including human actions and choices, are fully determined by preceding events and states of affairs, so that freedom of choice is illusory.
>
> *No purpose*: 'Chance alone is at the source of every innovation, of all creation in the biosphere' (Jacques Monod).
>
> *The heart*: The heart is simply there to pump the blood around the body.

The brain: There are a fixed number of neurones in the brain and when they die they are not replaced.

DNA: This a completely closed system which is not affected by the environment.

The New Physics

The dawn of the twentieth century heralded an even greater revolution in scientific thought than that of Copernicus and Galileo in the sixteenth century. In 1905, Albert Einstein produced two papers. One dealt with the theory of relativity and the other with a new way of looking at electromagnetic radiation, which was to form the foundation of quantum theory. The material world, which had been viewed as a comfortably ticking clockwork mechanism, was now transformed into a complex of indeterminate, interweaving and interdependent relationships. These new developments in physics brought about fundamental changes in our understanding of cause and effect, of time and space, of matter and objectivity, and to many scientists this came as a great shock.

Following this, in the first three decades of the twentieth century, quantum theory was formulated by an international group of physicists. These scientists were eagerly building into their experiments the human relational features of consciousness, intentionality and subjectivity. In dealing with sub-atomic particles, it became clear that the answer, when obtained, depended critically on the initial conditions, the way the experimenter framed his question, and his position as participant–observer.

I want now to list some of the recent, innovative scientific work which, as I mentioned at the beginning, is going on in various centres around the world. These separate developments are as follows:

The whole is greater than the sum of its parts and represents a new 'emergent' reality.

Living systems are self-organizing, indeterminate and characterized by change, instability and continual fluctuation. (Prigogine)

Epigenetics – The entire cell must be considered; it has 'switches' that can turn genes off and on.

The genetic system can be affected by the environment.

The plastic brain – The brain changes in response to experience, through fresh connections or the generation of new neurones.

The brain is seen as an 'antenna receiver': memory and information are stored in 'morphic fields' (feedback loops) outside the brain.

Heart–lung transplants – The recipient can have dreams, memories and experiences of the donor.

The after-life experiments – Controlled studies.

Near-death experiences – Consciousness can exist outside the brain.

A paradox arises here. Over the past 400 years since Galileo made his prophetic statement about concentrating on those things which could be measured, highly sophisticated technology has been developed and it is because of this very technology that scientists are now able to examine complex questions, which was simply not possible before.

What is more, the technology is getting lighter and lighter, increasingly non-material, dare one say 'spiritualized'. Just compare a nineteenth-century steam engine to a microchip. The latter contains a tiny amount of material and an enormous amount of information. Thus, the recent scientific developments I am concerned with in this paper are only possible because of this.

Self-Organizing Systems

Ludwig von Bertalanffy first proposed a comprehensive theoretical formulation of the principles of organization of living systems in 1968. He recognized that living creatures are open systems that cannot be described by classical thermodynamics:

> The organism is not a static system closed to the outside and always containing the identical components; it is an open system in a (quasi) steady state . . . in which material continually enters from, and leaves into, the outside environment. (Capra 48)

In the latter half of the twentieth century, Prigogine and others were bringing about the same kind of radical change in our thinking at the macroscopic level that the quantum physicists did during the early years of that century. In 1977, Prigogine was awarded the Nobel Prize for his work on the thermodynamics of non-equilibrium systems but perhaps his greatest achievement was to show that such self-organizing systems were characterized by 'change, instability and continual fluctuation' (Capra 86–9; Prigogine 142–3).

Prigogine showed that the behaviour of a dissipative structure existing far from equilibrium no longer follows any deterministic, universal law but is unique to the system itself. He showed that, as the input of energy into such a dissipative structure is increased, and as it moves further from equilibrium, it is likely to be characterized by continual fluctuation. This in turn can give rise to increasing turbulence and now and then may cause a fluctuation so powerful that it destabilizes the pre-existing organization. This is what Prigogine refers to as a 'bifurcation point', at which time it is inherently impossible to determine in advance in which direction the system will move. It may disintegrate into a chaotic state or suddenly reorganize itself into a fresh, more differentiated, higher level of organization, which then takes on the characteristics of irreversibility.

It is in this sense that Prigogine reflects: 'Today, the world we see outside and the world we see within are converging. This convergence of two worlds is perhaps one of the important cultural events of our age.' And further: 'Our vision of nature is undergoing a radical change towards the multiple, the temporal and the complex.'

Epigenetics

It was the triumphal announcement by James D. Watson and Francis Crick in 1953 which convinced biologists not only that genes are real molecules but also that they are constituted of nothing more mysterious than deoxyribonucleic acid. This established DNA as the molecule that not only holds the secrets of life, but that also executes its cryptic instructions – it was, in short, the 'Master Molecule' (Keller 51). In the colloquial paraphrase of the 'central dogma' formulated by Francis Crick in 1957, 'DNA makes RNA, RNA makes protein, and proteins make us'. James Watson, the first director of the Human Genome Organization (HUGO), set the tone: 'We used to think that our fate was in the stars. Now we know, in large measure, our fate is in our genes.'

Unfortunately for this simple view, as Evelyn Keller has pointed out: 'Every molecular biologist now knows, the secrets of life have proven to be vastly more complex, and more confusing, than they had seemed in the 1960s and '70s' (Keller 54–5).

Mae-Wan Ho says, further:

> The notion of an isolatable, constant gene that can be patented as an invention for all the marvellous things it can do is the greatest reductionist myth ever perpetrated . . . There is no simple, linear, one-directional instruction proceeding from the gene to RNA to protein.

In their attempt to find a way out of this dilemma, neo-Darwinians, such as Richard Dawkins, have proposed the existence of 'genetic programmes' but, as Keller states, 'this is precisely the ambiguity that plagues the term "genetic program". Does the genetic refer to the subject or the object of the program? Are the genes the source of the program, or that upon which the program acts?' (Keller 87). What this comes down to, then, as Capra says, is:

> The growing realization that the biological processes involving genes – the fidelity of DNA replication, the rate of mutations, the transcription of coping sequences, the selection of protein functions and the patterns of gene expression – are all regulated by the cellular network in which the genome is embedded. This network is highly non-linear, containing multiple feedback loops, so that patterns of genetic activity continually change in response to changing circumstance . . . The very remarkable stability and robustness of biological development means that an embryo may start from different initial stages but will nevertheless reach the same mature form that is characteristic of its species. Evidently this phenomenon is quite incompatible with genetic determinism. (Capra 151–2)

Recent work in the field of epigenetics strongly suggests that the conventional view that DNA carries all our heritable information and that nothing the individual does in their lifetime will be biologically passed to their children is incorrect. Marcus Pembrey (professor of Clinical Genetics, in London) and Swedish researcher Lars Olov Bygren, working in isolated areas in northern Sweden, have found evidence of an environmental effect being passed down the generations. This work suggests that genes have a 'memory'. That the lives of our grandparents can directly affect one decades later, despite one never having experienced these things oneself. Epigenetics proposes a control system of 'switches' that turn genes on and off – and suggests that things people experience, like nutrition and stress, can control these switches and cause heritable effects in humans (Pembrey).

So it would seem that Lamarck's original idea of acquired characteristics is not so far off the mark as was thought following Darwin's emphasis on gradual evolutionary changes with chance mutations honed and perfected by natural selection. As Mae-Wan Ho says:

> Lamarck's theory, on the other hand, is of transformation arising from the organism's own activities and experience of its environment during epigenesis or development. This requires a conception of the organism as an active, autonomous being, which is open to the environment. It would seem now that biological form and behaviour are emergent properties of the epigenetic network and this will only become clear when complexity theory and non-linear dynamics are applied to the new discipline of epigenetics.

Finally, as Lynn Margulis states, 'Cell heredity, both nuclear and cytoplasmic, always must be considered for the entire cell, the entire organism' (Margulis 29).

The Plastic Brain

A decade ago the dogma in neuroscience was that the brain contained all of its neurons at birth and that this was unchanged by life's experience. We now know that, from Professor Richard Davidson's and others work, the new watchword in brain science is 'neuroplasticity', the notion that the brain continually changes as a result of our experience – whether through fresh connections or through the generation of utterly new neurons (Davidson 21).

In his lab at the university of Wisconsin, Davidson has established the latest, highly sophisticated technology for studying the brain:

1. A turbocharged version of the Elechoencephalogram (EEG), which enables him to pinpoint activity at locations deep within the brain.

2. The functional Magnetic Resonance Imaging (MRI), which offers a video rendition, so that researchers can track the changes the brain goes through during a given activity.

3. The Position Emission Tomography (PET) scanner, which allows researchers to measure which of the brain's several

hundred neurochemicals are involved in a given mental activity. (Davidson 180)

'One of the most exciting discoveries of the last few years is that certain areas of the brain – the frontal lobes, the amygala and the hypocampus – change in response to experience. They are the parts of the brain dramatically affected by the emotional environment in which we are raised and by repeated experience' (Davidson 187–91). The amygdala nuclei play a key role in the circuitry that activates emotion, particularly fear, while the hypocampus is essential for our appreciation of the *context* of events. The prefrontal cortex on the other hand is critical for regulating emotions – the left prefrontal cortex enhances positive emotions, while the right prefrontal area tends to increase negative or destructive emotions.

To pursue this question, the brain activity of a Buddhist monk meditating was recorded, comparing the ratio of his right to left frontal lobe activity with 170 ordinary individuals who had been tested over the years using identical measures. He was found to have the most extreme, left-sided positive value of the entire group (Davidson 339).

In another study a group of young American students were given four months' meditation training. Four months after the training ended, they showed a significant increase in left-sided activation from before they began, compared to a control group (Davidson 344).

Memory and Information Storage Outside the Brain

'The concept of morphogenetic fields is now widely accepted by developmental biologists and is used to explain how your arms and legs, for instance, have different shapes in spite of the fact that they contain the same genes and proteins. The problem is, no one knows what morphogenetic fields are or how they work.' Rupert Sheldrake believes 'they are new kinds of fields for which I have proposed the term *Morphic fields*'. He continues:

> Morphic fields are not fixed but evolve. They have a kind of built-in memory. This memory depends on the process of Morphic resonance, the influence of like upon like through space and time. (Sheldrake 76–7)

As Gary Schwartz has pointed out, in any communication between two things, A and B, a network comes into being and a 'feedback' loop is created. A memory of the relationship is formed and 'emergent properties' arise. In this way, permanent storage of information can occur and this can circulate indefinitely: 'It is not in something or out of something but circulates between both' (Schwartz).

In *Whispers*, Babuji says:

> In centuries to come, scepticism on this point will not exist anymore as these means will be widely used on the Earth. Mankind will make great progress in knowledge, and in the perception of vibratory waves surrounding the planet. It will be less populated than it is now. Another race of individuals will live in these places, being more advanced and receptive to the reality of the 'beyond'. (Babuji 491)

This storage of information outside the brain happens in all kinds of situations:

1. between one person and another
2. between the heart and the brain
3. between cells and atoms
4. between a substance and the fluid in which it is dissolved (For the first time this may provide a scientific rationale for how homeopathy can work. Sceptics say that, by the time full dilution has taken place, nothing of the original substance remains in the fluid in which it was dissolved and therefore the remedy can have no effect. However, if a 'feedback' loop between the substance and the fluid has been established, then the potion could still be effective.)

This hypothesis may for the first time provide an explanation of how heart, and more specifically heart–lung, transplant patients have memories of the donor. Reports of these patients having experiences, dreams, likes and dislikes of the donor are being reported with increasing frequency around the world (Schwartz).

After-Life Experiments

Neuroscientists study brain function in three main ways:

1. Correlation studies – relating visual experience to EEG readings and seeing the correlation between these
2. Stimulation studies – areas of the brain are stimulated with electrodes; e.g. in the occipital area one evokes visual experiences

3. Ablation studies – when an area of the cortex is damaged, in animals, or in the case of humans where there is injury to the brain – where the occipital area is damaged – there will be blind spots

From these three types of study, one can conclude that consciousness is created in the brain. If the brain is the creator of consciousness then, when there is 'brain death', consciousness should disappear. The logic here is that if you knock out the transistors in a television set, this proves that the programmes originate in the set. The television signal is not created by the television set, it is an 'antenna receiver'. The second hypothesis is that the brain too is an 'antenna receiver'. Correlation, stimulation and ablation studies are consistent with either hypothesis. The only way to determine which of these is correct is to apply additional research methods.

Research with mediums is a critical way of testing this.

The second way is to study 'near-death' experiences.

Professor Gary Schwartz has carried out double-blind and triple-blind studies with experienced mediums and has demonstrated that connections with some of those who have already died are statistically significant. These two approaches demonstrate pretty convincingly that consciousness does exist outside the brain and even continues after death.

The messages in *Whispers* are communicated through a sensitive medium and in one of these Babuji says:

The simplicity of heart will enable them to advance on the real ways of knowledge, which is out of reach of the highest universities, however famous they are. First of all, humility must grow in them enabling them to realize that they ignore important concepts. The majority has to discover everything about the 'after-life,' the possible means to communicate with genuine mediums, the reality of parallel worlds – the existence of which science, imbued with alleged superiority, laughs at. (Babuji 573)

Certain great inspired mediums left, and will leave, a very enriching teaching worthy of faith, since it comes from the source. (Babuji 535)

Near-Death Experiences

Some people report a near-death experience (NDE) after a life-threatening crisis. This can occur in many circumstances: cardiac arrest in myocardial infarction, shock after loss of blood, septic or anaphylactic shock, electrocution, coma resulting from traumatic brain damage, intracerebral haemorrhage, attempted suicide, near-drowning or asphyxia.

Identical experiences to NDE, those involving fear of death where death seemed unavoidable, are reported, such as mountaineering accidents, serious traffic accidents or shipwreck.

The effects of near-death experiences are similar worldwide, across all cultures and times. People who have had an NDE are psychologically healthy and do not differ from controls with respect to age, sex, ethnic origin or religion.

The patient's transformational processes after an NDE encompass life-changing insight, heightened intuition and disappearance of fear of death, and also specific elements such as out-of-body experience, pleasant feelings, and seeing a tunnel, a light, deceased relatives or a complete life review.

Most studies have been retrospective and very selective with respect to patients. In these studies about 45% of adults and up to 85% of children were estimated to have had an NDE. These showed varying definitions of the phenomenon and inadequate methods of research.

More recently, a number of prospective studies – Dutch, English and American – have been carried out. They defined clinical death as a period of unconsciousness caused by insufficient blood supply to the brain because of inadequate blood circulation, breathing or both. If, in this situation, cardiopulmonary resuscitation is not started within 5–10 minutes, irreparable damage is done to the brain and the patient will die. The results show that medical factors cannot account for the occurrence of NDE; although all patients have been clinically dead, most did not have NDE. Furthermore, the seriousness of the crisis was not related to the occurrence or depth of the experience. If purely physiological factors resulting from cerebral anoxia caused NDE, most of the patients should have had this experience. The patient's medication was also unrelated to the frequency of NDE. Psychological factors are unlikely to be important, as fear was not associated with NDE.

In these studies, only 18 to 20% of patients had a near-death experience, and of these only 12% had a core NDE. The process of change after NDE tends to take several years to consolidate. Furthermore, the long-lasting transformational effects of an experience that lasts for only a few minutes of cardiac arrest is a surprising and unexpected finding (Lommel).

Scientific Paradigms

These several recent but quite separate developments in science, which are either not accepted or ignored by mainstream science, raise the question of how science changes and develops new ideas. The usual notion is that science develops step by step as one idea and experiment replaces another. But Thomas Kuhn questioned that this is how it happens. He defined a scientific 'paradigm' as: 'a constellation of achievements – concepts, values, techniques, etc. – shared by a scientific community to define legitimate problems and solutions'. He claimed that science, like the evolution of life, tends to move by fits and starts – 'paradigm shifts'. 'Far from subjecting the existing paradigm to constant testing, scientists avoid contradicting it by reinterpreting conflicting data to support it, or by neglecting such awkward data altogether' (Tarnas160–1).

In this regard, Babuji says in *Whispers*:

> Ignorance on Earth is extreme, it is maintained by beings who think they are highly intelligent. It is not easy to get ideas accepted, to admit facts that cannot be verified. Minds are not ready. They would need to be put in a state of shock in order to realize how much they are ignorant of the reality that surrounds them. They delude themselves and want to see and hear nothing that is not allowed in their culture. (Babuji 543)

What tends to happen then is that, as more and more data accumulates which doesn't fit, sooner or later the old model will burst its banks and then a 'paradigm shift' must occur. In this way the various innovative scientific developments, some of which I am describing here, are chipping away at the periphery of mainstream science and inevitably it must give way at some point, when it will be replaced, hopefully, by a more open 'paradigm' (Tarnas160–1). But if one is to listen to the messages of Babuji Maharaj in *Whispers*, these are only glimpses of what is to come, and we are only seeing the future 'through a glass darkly':

> Scientists are very often mistaken in their assertions. In a century these assertions will be outdated. Man will have taken a step forward in his understanding of the laws governing the universe. (Babuji 487)

> Men have a high opinion of themselves. Scientists believe they are the only ones to possess the truth, whereas they are still at the level of kindergarten – no more no less. (Babuji 492)

> A new world is in the offing. You cannot imagine it. It is beyond your comprehension. Your current civilization is built on a few principles that will no longer prevail in the future. A civilization that moves away from its true values is a lost civilization. It condemns itself. (Babuji 509)

> Electricity, oil and its by-products, which are used in the present system, will be considered antiques or simply forgotten. (Babuji 494).

> A natural energy will replace all that is currently used . . . These secrets will be revealed to men of good will, who will look into an inspired scientific research. (Babuji 485)

As our Master Chariji has often said, 'Insights which have been part of the perennial wisdom of the east for thousands of years are, late in the day, being discovered by science' (Chariji, personal communication).

Back to the Heart

Finally, I want to return to the heart, which is central to our spiritual and emotional life. When I was told in India that the heart was the real centre of our emotional life, the location where all the impressions were laid down, I felt it was a figurative way of describing things. However, more and more I realize the literal truth of this statement and that the heart is absolutely central.

The remarkable thing is that now research has demonstrated that the heart is more than just a pump. The atrium of the heart produces a hormone – ANF (atrial natriuretic factor) – that interacts with other hormones, has a controlling influence over the whole cardiovascular system and dramatically affects every major organ in the body. It impacts on the limbic area of the brain and determines the action of the thalamus and its relationship with the pituitary gland. ANF is involved in the immune system and affects the pineal gland, regulating the production and action of melatonin (Wiedemann *et al.* 1; Pearce 104).

With the identification of this atrial hormone, it becomes clear that the heart plays a key role in our emotional life, memory and learning. Indeed recent work is revealing that there are networks of neurones in the heart showing evidence of 'mind' and that the heart is the real centre of our emotions, reflecting back on the brain.

It is interesting that Joseph Chilton Pearce, in his remarkable book *Evolutions End*, has described in very similar terms this centrality of the heart and how it can potentially operate at several levels. He speaks of how we have:

> both a physical heart and a higher universal heart . . . just as our physical heart maintains our body, the non-localized intelligence governing the heart in turn maintains synchrony with the universal consciousness at large.

He goes on to describe how:

> The three major stages of life are heart-centred in this sense:
> 1. The development of a heart–mind synchrony, needed for physical life . . .
> 2. A later 'post-adolescent' development which synchronizes the developed physical self and the creative process.
> 3. A final 'highest heart' which moves us beyond all physical emotional systems. Two poles of experience lie within us, our unique, individual self generating through the brain; and a universal, impersonal intelligence generating through the heart.

Joseph Chilton Pearce goes on to say that his meditation teacher once told him:

> You must develop your intellect to the highest possible extent, in order that it be a proper instrument for the intelligence of the heart but only the intelligence of the heart can develop intellect to its highest level. (Pearce 105)

The medical view is that emotions are really controlled by the brain and that the heart is simply there to pump the blood. Now, after all, here is this work indicating the total unity of our being and that the heart is really central to this unity, the emotional driving force of our character and morality. The intellect is merely an amoral instrument to assist our understanding but is a poor guide as to how we should behave. To open up this third level – the 'spiritual heart' – is the main task of spirituality. Even in the west we speak of someone being 'soft-hearted', 'kind-hearted' or 'heartbroken', showing that this awareness of the centrality of the heart was there in the language of our forebears.

In this regard it is worth remembering what Babuji said:

> People generally think of the heart as made of flesh and blood only . . . This is one of the limitations in viewing the heart region in its broader sense. It is really a vast circle covering everything inner and outer. The things after the first mind all belong to the region of heart. (Ram Chandra 139)

The question is, are we now on the threshold of a much greater and more fundamental period of human change, which is quite unique and of a different order to anything which has happened before? With the development of all kinds of telecommunications, millions of messages are swirling around the surface of the planet. It could be that we are on the verge of the biosphere becoming conscious of itself. It would follow that, the more complex the interactions in any living system, the more 'mind' will develop and the more conscious the system will become. In this sense, from time immemorial, consciousness has been increasing in the biosphere. De Chardin spoke of human beings pressing up against one another around the globe, and the question is, as the complexity of all kinds of communication between them increases, will the biosphere begin to manifest not only consciousness but self-consciousness.

In the last pages of *The Phénomène Humaine*, de Chardin made a prophetic statement:

> Either the entire construction of the world presented here is an empty theory. Or else somewhere around us, in one form or other, we should be able to detect some excess of personal and extra human energy that reveals the great presence, if we look carefully. (de Chardin 209)

Mainstream science and organized religion are blindly driving this planet towards destruction but, as I said at the beginning, at a deeper level spirituality and recent developments in science are converging. It is time to transcend religion and, if there is to be a new spiritual growth, to move towards a universal spirituality. As de Chardin himself said:

> The day will come when we shall harness for God the energies of love. And, on that day, for the second time in the history of the world, the human beings will have discovered fire.

Perhaps the modern world has lost its awareness of the deep mystical forces that are at work below the surface of a civilization that has gone badly astray. It is perhaps such an awareness of the extent to which this intangible web reaches the boundary of our individuality and involves us at all times in some greater unity that is resonating out across the world, and moving imperceptibly towards a truly human society.

References

Babuji, *Whispers from The Brighter World*, Sahaj Marg Spirituality Foundation, Chennai, 2005.

Capra, F. *The Hidden Connections*, London, HarperCollins, 2002.

—. *The Turning Point*, Flamingo, London, 1983.

—. *The Web of Life*, HarperCollins, London, 1996.

Davidson, R. 'Lama in the Lab', in D. Goleman, *Destructive Emotions*, Bantam Dell, London, 2004.

—. 'The Neuroscience of Emotion', in D. Goleman, *Destructive Emotions*, Bantam Dell, London, 2004.

—. 'The Protean Brain', in D. Goleman, *Destructive Emotions*, Bantam Dell, London, 2004.

Dawkins, R. *The God Delusion*, Bantam Press, London, 2006.

Ho, Mae-Wan, *Genetic Engineering: Dream or Nightmare*, Gateway Books, UK, 1998.

Keller, E.F. *The Century of the Gene*, Harvard University Press, Cambridge, MA, 2002.

Margulis, L. *The Symbiotic Planet*, Phoenix, London, 1998.

Monod, J. *Chance and Necessity*, Knopf, New York, 1971.

Pearce, J.C. 'Evolution's End', in *Heart–Mind Bonding*, Harper Collins, New York, 1992.

Pembrey, M., and Bygren, L.O. *Science and Nature*, Horizon, BBC, 2006.

Prigogine, I. *Order Out of Chaos*, William Heinemann, London, 1984.

Ram Chandra, *Efficacy of Raja Yoga*, vol. 1, Shri Ram Chandra Mission, Pacific Grove, CA, 1989.

Schwartz, G. *The After Life Experiments*, Atria Books, New York, 2001.

Schwartz, G., *et al.*, *The Living Energy Universe*, Hampton Roads, Charlottesville, VA, 1999.

Schwartz, G. *Memory Beyond the Brain* CD, Beyond the Brain Conference V1, Scientific and Medical Network.

Sheldrake, R. *Seven Experiments that Could Change the World*, Fourth Estate, London, 1994.

Tarnas R. *Passion of the Western Mind*, Pimlico, London, 1996.

Teilhard de Chardin, P. *The Human Phenomenon*, Sussex Academic Press, Brighton, 2003.

van Lommel, P. 'Near Death Experiences', CD *Memory Beyond the Brain*, Beyond the Brain Conference V1, Scientific and Medical Network.

van Lommel, P., *et al.* 'Near Death Experiences in Survivors of Cardiac Arrest', *Lancet*, 344, 828–30, 1994.

Wiedemann, K., *et al.* 'Effects of Natriuretic Peptides upon Hypothalamo-Pituitary-Adrenocortical System Activity and Anxiety Behaviour', *Pub. Med.*, 2000, 18 September 2005.

30. Northern Ireland – A
Dysfunctional Family?

Written in July 1996, this paper was published in *The Irish Times* as a special article. What I was attempting to do was to describe Northern Ireland as a sick family. Since I wrote this paper, of course, the Peace Process has intervened. It feels strangely prophetic that, at the end of this article, I described as a possibility what has actually happened since then.

'THE NORTH of Ireland? What's to talk about? Honestly I am sick of it. One side is as bad as the other, stuck in their tribalism, none of them willing to compromise. We'd be best to forget about it altogether!'

As a psychiatrist, one knows that a dysfunctional person has to want to change to become healthy. It's like a disturbed family I saw recently. Let's call them the Bulls. I met them because of the younger son, who has been very disturbed and uncooperative for a long time but, the usual thing, you know – he's acting out of a dysfunctional family.

When the parents in this family first met, the young woman – we'll call her Kathleen – didn't want to get involved, but the man, John, wouldn't take no for an answer. He was arrogant and always convinced that he was right about everything. From the beginning he dominated the relationship, trying to convince her that she needed him. She tried to resist marrying him but eventually gave in to his domination and the wedding took place.

It was a disaster from the beginning, with constant discord. Nevertheless, they had two children – two boys. Because it was a mixed marriage, Ian, the older boy, was brought up a Protestant like his father and Gerry, the younger son, a Catholic following his mother. John, the father, favoured the older boy, pampered and spoilt him, giving in to his every whim. Ian made great protestations

422

of love and loyalty to his father as long as he got his own way. By contrast the father rejected his younger son and was constantly nasty and brutal to him, ignoring the feelings of the mother. Kathleen loved her younger son but wasn't able to do much to protect him.

As time went on, the marriage relationship deteriorated further until Kathleen finally rebelled and demanded that the father get out. Eventually Bull agreed to a separation. He left the house and agreed to let the mother have custody of the two children. However, the older boy, who was used to getting his own way, threatened to burn down the house if he was left with his mother. Although the father was about to sign the legal agreement giving custody of the children to their mother, he quickly gave in under the threats and blackmail of the older boy and used his wealthy and powerful legal friends to get custody of both children.

The younger child very much wanted to stay with his mother but he had no say in the matter. At the time the family split up it was as if the younger son had left part of his personality with his mother and could never really separate from her, which weakened him further. He became even less able to stand up to his older brother, who always claimed that, because he was older and stronger, he had the democratic right to make all decisions for both of them. As soon as Ian got his way, he immediately became very sweet and loving to the father, making great protestations of affection and loyalty and blaming the younger son for all that had happened, thus gaining more favour and pampering than ever.

The unsatisfactory agreement that was arrived at then was that the house would be divided into two, the two sons living in a flat upstairs and the mother taking the main part of the house below. As a gesture to the mother, about a third of the space which should have gone to make up the apartment for the boys was left to her. This meant less room for the boys but, because the older boy was bigger and stronger, he took the major share of the space, claiming it as his right because he was older and stronger. Although she was living in the house with them, Kathleen was to have no say over their welfare and management whatsoever, and they were to be completely under Bull's control financially and otherwise, even though he was living elsewhere. Kathleen was very poor and had to get whatever low-level work she could. She had no proper training, having been kept in a very oppressed and subservient state by her husband during all the years of their marriage, so it was always a struggle to make ends meet.

This was the way the situation continued all through the formative years of the two children, the mother watching helplessly as her younger son was brutalized and intimidated by his pampered older brother, who was always believed by the father who consequently blamed Gerry for everything that happened. At another level, the father knew well what was going on, but he took the easy option in supporting his older son's behaviour because he was, in fact, afraid to stand up to him.

As the years went by, the contrast between the condition and behaviour of the two sons became more obvious. The older boy lived in a comfortably furnished room in the upper flat with everything he wanted supplied to him, was sent to a superior school and whenever he wanted anything could manipulate or threaten his father into giving it to him. His father even allowed him several expensive guns, which he said he wanted for game shooting but which he actually hid away carefully in his room. The older son had all the appearance of a sleek, well-fed and well-mannered youth who, on the surface, appeared to be very cooperative and well behaved and was praised by the father for his model behaviour. Under the surface he was petulant, arrogant and quite intolerant unless he got his own way in everything. In fact, Ian was not really developing the skills and competence to be able to take on a true independent life for himself as an adult.

Behind the scenes, Ian's behaviour towards his younger brother was very different. He beat and bullied him viciously when there was no one around and often smashed up his belongings. By contrast, the younger brother looked as if he came from a different family. Everything he had, the bit of space at the top of the house, the secondhand furniture, were cast-offs from his brother.

The younger lad was full of anger. He tried to resist and fight back when his brother bullied him, but he would always be blamed by the father, because his older brother would accuse him of having started it and of course was always believed. He learned very little in his miserable school and indeed often didn't go at all. When I met him, he had taken on the characteristics of a young delinquent who had been deprived of love or warmth from either parent and who responded with viciousness and hate, for which he received further retribution.

Kathleen insisted that she loved him and would like to have him living with her (indeed, she always claimed that she should have had custody of both children). Nevertheless, she did nothing to help or protect him. She was having such a difficult struggle to support herself, and anyway was so afraid of the father, that she colluded with the arrangement that had been established and never did anything effective to help either of her children. Gerry started feeling resentment towards her, whom he perceived as 'standing idly by'.

As the boys grew older, the younger boy, seeing how other youths were treated in their families, became less accepting of his lot and started to protest and argue both with his brother and his father. He demanded what he described as his civil rights. The father, who prided himself on being fair-minded and a guardian of democracy, made feeble efforts to put things right but every time he tried to make some gesture the older son would become ugly and threatening. Bull knew that he would make a vicious scene if he did not leave things exactly as they were. All of this finally came to a head when the younger son started to shout and rattle bin lids outside the house and let everyone know the way he was being treated. Ian responded by attacking him viciously and there was a real danger that he would kill him with one of his 'sports' guns. Finally, when the younger lad was badly beaten and injured, the father had to intervene and he sent an employee, who had served under the father when he was an officer in the British Army, to live in the flat with the two boys to keep order.

After this things settled down for a time but inevitably the older boy, who knew his father's employee well, was able to convince him that all the trouble was the younger boy's fault. To make matters worse Gerry, who understandably always hated his father and anyone who had anything to do with him, started to become belligerent and aggressive towards the supposed protector sent by his father. It is understandable that this would happen as, except for a few token adjustments, he was actually treated as badly as before, with the added problem that he was now regularly physically ill-treated and pushed around by the fellow whom his father had sent to keep the peace. He was locked up for long periods by his 'protector' in his room, on the pretext that this was the only way to maintain peace in the house.

Over and over again, when the injustice of the situation became too obvious and couldn't be ignored because everyone was talking – the boys' rich and powerful uncle Sam in America, a brother of their mother's, realized what was happening – Bull attempted to take a stand and face up to the blackmail and bullying tactics of his older son. However, each time this happened Ian would become disruptive, threaten to create total chaos and the father would give in. Then when Gerry responded to this obvious injustice by turning violent, the 'protector' was allowed to bring the situation under control with vicious retribution meted out to the younger son. The father would wring his hands, as if he were some sort of honest broker, saying 'What can I do with these two impossible boys? All I can do is hope they'll learn, somehow or other, to live at peace with each other. I've tried and tried and I'll go on trying. I'd like to cut them loose to do whatever they want, if they would only agree among themselves, but I can't force them to do anything.'

When dealing with a family like this, it is not useful to think in terms of blame. In a sense all of the participants are victims of the situation and are caught up in a repetitive cycle from which they can see no way out. This is where it is essential to go back to the point where things went wrong in the first place, and ask who had the power and authority to resolve the problem at that time. Clearly at the time of their legal separation, John Bull, who had agreed to Kathleen having custody of her children, was in that position but he failed miserably to exercise that authority and backed down in the face of the threats and blackmail of his older son. It is as though Ian became more like the father than John himself and, in that event, the latter was no match for him. And so this family has been caught in a time-warp ever since.

The father still has the economic muscle and power to take effective control of the situation if he only has the courage to do so. He simply has to make his economic support contingent on his two sons getting down to the job of working out a reasonable accommodation so that they can live in peace together. And of course he must also declare a definite time-limit as to how long he will continue to manage their affairs, after which he will leave them free to take on full adult independent control of their lives. Undoubtedly the older son will do everything he can to prevent this happening, will huff and puff and threaten to bring the house down and create chaos but, if the father once and for all stands up to him and doesn't give in to his threats and bluster, it's been my experience that, like any spoilt child, he'll eventually accept the inevitable. In fact he's already given way on a number of contentious issues, and at heart he's always been an industrious and practical lad. Once he realizes that he's not going to get his own way, I'm convinced he'll accept the situation.

Equally, in this event, it would no longer be appropriate for them to return to live with their mother, so she must also relinquish any thought of this. She should agree to relinquish the part of the house which should have been part of their apartment originally, thus leaving her younger son in a stronger position to negotiate an equal relationship with his brother. It might be suggested that the two brothers should separate and get separate living accommodation but this would not be economically feasible; the only way they could manage once they become independent is to share the top of the house together.

It is this view which I have been attempting to get across to both the parents, and light is perhaps appearing at the end of the tunnel. There is some sign that the boys are starting to hear each other. If only Kathleen would confront John with his responsibility for all this mess, if only he would fully grasp the nettle and take a stand, and if both parents were prepared to withdraw from the situation, then this would allow space for the two sons to work things out between themselves. They have to live together after all. I also understand that the uncle in America and an aunt who is living in Europe have made it clear that they would be willing to supervise this arrangement and even help financially where necessary.

'That's very interesting. I wish you luck and I hope that your plans to help this family work out successfully. But listen, to come back to the North of Ireland, what do you really think about it?'

'As I said at the beginning, one side is as bad as the other. If none of the people concerned are prepared to accept the possibility of change and work at it, then it will just go on forever, won't it?'

31. After the War, Reconciliation?

Written in November 1997, this paper was presented at a conference in Derry under the title 'Reconciliation and Community: The Future of Peace in Northern Ireland'. On the first page of this paper, I refer to four headings which would need to be dealt with if any significant peace and reconciliation in the North of Ireland were to be achieved.

AT THE conference Reconciliation and Community: The Future of Peace in Northern Ireland, Dr Óscar Arias said: 'We have learned that peace is not the signing of a treaty or the shaking of hands. We cannot define peace as the cessation of war.' Recently Gerry Adams echoed these words when he said, 'Peace is not simply the absence of conflict. Rather it is the existence of conditions in which the causes of conflict have been eradicated.' Nor will simply talking and discussing, as happened at this conference recently in Belfast, be enough. If reconciliation is really to take place in the communities in the north, which have been divided for so long, it will have to reach down into the hearts and experience of the persons and groups who have been involved. It is at this level that they will have to meet each other if they are to be reconciled.

If work of this kind is to be undertaken and to be effective, it will have to operate at several different levels:

1. The internal reality within each individual.
2. The personalized human group – the family, the extended family, neighbourhood, local community, etc.
3. The wider community – town or city, government departments, city councils and other institutions, transnational companies, trade unions, etc.
4. Larger aggregations of society – regions, nation states, supranational entities (e.g. the European Union), etc.

Of course, all of these levels are interconnected, as well as being partially separate. Of central importance here is the concept of boundedness, of the interfaces between these various realities, and the interaction and transactions which take place between them. Before going on to describe the kind of work towards reconciliation which we feel can be undertaken at each of these levels, I believe it is essential to have some understanding of living systems theory.

What is a living system? A cell, a human being, a dog or a cat, a beehive or a group of human beings, all these are living systems. The following definition, derived from the work of a number of creative scientists in recent years, such as the Chilean biologists Maturana and Varela, the chemist Ilya Prigogine, Fritjof Capra and others, can be applied to all these levels.

DEFINITION OF A LIVING SYSTEM

1. A living system contains a number of elements.

2. These elements are involved in a dynamic process of interaction and interrelationship.

3. A living system is separated from its environment by a boundary of its own elements such as permits transactions of import and export across the boundary; i.e. it is an 'open system'.

4. It maintains and renews its own elements by its own internal processes. Living organisms continually renew themselves, their cells breaking down and building up tissues and organs in continual cycles of regeneration. The components of the living system are continually renewed and recycled but the pattern of organization remains stable.

5. The 'locus of control' is within the system itself. This is the most essential aspect of 'self-organization'. If the management of a living system moves outside into the environment, then that system is becoming sick and will eventually die.

6. Living systems show a tendency to transcend themselves. Thus they not only tend to change and adapt but also to reproduce themselves and thus ensure the survival and evolution of the species.

The next matter for consideration is that there are things within things, bodies within other bodies, one system within another. The essential thing to understand is that, while one system or body may form the basic unit or building block of another system, this does not mean that the energy is simply merged or that this first-order system loses its boundary and therefore ceases to exist as a separate entity. It remains as a system within a system. Nevertheless, it is now as a unit under influence from the higher-order system and transactions or movements of its energy may take place across its boundary under the influence of the higher-order system. The degree to which this happens will depend on the overruling power of the higher-order system and the degree to which the boundaries of the units are lowered or weakened by this influence; i.e. the strength of the group and the weakness of the boundaries of the persons within it.

The same fundamental principles would appear to be operating in all of reality, whether it be living cells, insects or humans, or atoms or molecules. In all of these, frightening energies are released if they are allowed to merge and coalesce. The forming of higher-order systems out of the delicately balanced, bounded units is fine so long as the energy is contained and properly controlled at each level. When this fails for any reason, then the energy would seem to coalesce and flow upwards to throw pressure on the boundary at the next level, where it must be held if it is not to flow onwards like water bursting a dam or a river overflowing its banks.

Having examined at some length the underlying theoretical principles of living systems, let us now return to look at the sort of restitutive work we feel could be undertaken at each of the levels already mentioned.

The Internal Reality Within Each Individual

Thousands of people in the North of Ireland have been traumatized during the twenty-five years of armed struggle – victims, relatives of victims, paramilitaries, members of the security forces, and their relatives. All of these, those who have carried out the violence, those who have been victims of it, those who have been, or are now, in prison, all have been traumatized in one way or another. As David Rice has said, 'you die at either end of the gun, the price of killing is dying, you die inside'. No attempts at reconciliation can succeed as long as all this traumatic experience is suspended within individuals, groups and separated communities.

The full significance of this cannot be realized unless we understand the way in which human experience is processed and integrated into the person to create memory. It is important to realize that we are our memories; the human personality is nothing without memory, nor could we function in the world without it. In those cases where the ability to process experience is destroyed, the person lives in an eternal present. To put it in its simplest form, when an event takes place in the external world, we do not fully experience it as it happens. We do undoubtedly record an impression of the raw experience as it is taking place but, for an experience to go from perception to storage, it must go through the primitive brain – that ancient part of the brain which we share with other mammals and which manages all our survival functions, controlling the feelings and the endocrine and autonomic nervous systems.

The evidence for this is that, many years after afterwards, a traumatic event may be recalled in complete detail, in what Horowitz termed a 'videotape of the mind'. In other words, experiencing something fully and turning it into memory is a process which takes place over time. This involves a lot of neurophysiological and somatic work by the individual which will be proportional to the degree of disturbance and threat that the traumatic event poses to the integrity of the person concerned. It means that, when a person is subjected to a serious trauma, an immediate, primitive biological reaction is invoked, suspending the experience, either partly or completely, blocking further processing and integration into long-term memory.

The degree to which an event is threatening or traumatic does not depend simply on the nature of the external event but is also a function of the internal set of the individual at the time the event occurred. This is a function of all the learning and experience of that individual up to that moment, including of course other previous insults or experiences of a similar kind which were blocked or suspended, or indeed other predisposing life events. The traumatic event is the meeting-point of the external event and the internal set of the individual, involving all of the learned past up to that time.

It is now as if a piece of the external world is within the person but not part of that person. The experience remains as a frozen present, as alive and real as at the time it happened. This internalized 'stressor' now exists outside of time in a potentially unstable state. It can resurface at any time in terrifying ways and can make life a living death. In Michael Polanyi's terms, there is no movement from the parts to the whole. By this biological refusal to integrate the particles of the encounter, the person may never consciously identify the threatening experience; it is as if it had never happened. In situations such as this, where an experience is suspended, it may be held in that state for years or even a lifetime. Where an earlier experience has been inhibited or suspended, later events of this kind will also be blocked in like manner, thus building up increasing pressure on the primitive brain until activation occurs.

If activated later by some related life event, the experience leaks, breaks through and causes 'flashbacks' on the screen of perception. In spite of attempted denial, this triggers painful emotional responses (symptoms) which once again the individual attempts to block and suspend, as with the original event, but now only partially successfully.

The following are actions that can be taken to assist in such cases:

1. In the new intervention centre, a wide range of therapists and counsellors should be available on a part-time, sessional basis to provide:
    (a) psychotherapy and counselling on an ongoing basis
    (b) various alternative health strategies – such as acupuncture, bio-feedback, different forms of body work and deep massage, guided imagery, reflexology, etc.
    (c) hypnosis, saccadic eye movements, colour therapy, movement and music, creative dance, artwork and creative expression, etc.
2. Periodic experiential workshops should be provided. The important thing here is that traumatic experiences which surface during the workshops should be worked through and integrated as part of the ongoing psychotherapy/counselling and other alternative strategies already mentioned.

The Personalized Human Group

There are a number of forms of intervention which are applicable in the family, the extended family, neighbourhood, local community:

different forms of group work, drama and family therapy. Having reviewed these types of intervention over a number of years, we have found two ways of working to be particularly valuable:

(a) Return to Innocence

As described by Garret O'Connor:

> Alcoholism has been a major public health problem among Irish Catholics for centuries. Until recently, however, the aetiology of this phenomenon has been poorly understood. Heavy drinking among Irish Catholics . . . was strongly influenced by negative stereotypes of cultural inferiority generated by the British in Ireland as a way of justifying their continued occupation of the country . . . In short, the Irish Catholics drank, first, because they were expected to do so and, second, because, for them, drinking served a protective purpose in the struggle for ethnic survival.

These historical, religious and cultural antecedents should make therapists alert to the fact that contemporary Irish Catholic psychology continues to be influenced and shaped by the consequences of nineteenth-century politics. In Ireland after 1850, to paraphrase McGoldric, original sin, sexual repression and eternal damnation were incorporated into a grim theology of fear that led Irish Catholics to believe that they were born bad, were inclined towards evil and deserved to suffer for their sins. Today, Irish Catholics coming for treatment for alcoholism are frequently crippled by shame, guilt and a mortal fear of being exposed as inherently bad or perpetually wrong.

A general knowledge of how and where these feelings may have originated can be helpful to therapists in establishing a working alliance with individual patients or families. Ethnic history, when skilfully used as a therapeutic tool to identify and underscore positive Irish characteristics such as humour, generosity, loyalty and courage, can help the therapist to understand and penetrate the family culture of denial and concealment that is the most destructive part of the post-colonial legacy for Irish Catholics. It has been our experience that misconceptions of cultural inferiority may still cause Irish Catholics to compulsively re-enact in their daily lives the most destructive and degrading themes of Irish colonial history. These re-enactments are most likely to occur during struggles for political power within the family. Shaming strategies, such as ridicule, teasing, contempt and public humiliation, are clearly rooted in the historical reality of political oppression.

(b) Learning for Leadership

A.K. Rice coined the term 'learning for leadership' to describe a method of exploring the dynamics of group and organizational behaviour. These experiential conferences were pioneered by the Tavistock Institute of Human Relations in London. The fundamental difference in this way of working to other forms of group therapy is that it focuses on the behaviour of the group as a living system (as already described in this paper) rather than on the individual within the group. A group is not simply a multiple of individuals but forms a separate living system, a different organism with a life of its own. As part of our early development in the family and as a result of the karmic tendencies we carry into this life, each of us tends to have a predisposition for a role which we enact repeatedly in later life when we become part of various groups.

Typically, we are quite unaware of this and think we are just the same as our experience of ourselves as individuals. However, when we become part of a group we are surprised to find ourselves behaving, thinking and feeling quite differently. In these circumstances, we usually convince ourselves that we have simply changed our view in the light of what is happening in the group, although we typically feel confused and have an uneasy feeling in regard to what is going on. Once away from the influence of the group, we would often like to reverse our position but feel committed by what we have already done. There are many situations in life where we see this kind of process at work. Of course, there are big individual differences in how likely one is to be colluded with in this way, depending on the strength of one's personality and ability to manage one's individual boundary.

Once we are 'entrained' within a group, our individual boundaries tend to dissolve and inevitably some degree of merging between individuals takes place within the newly formed boundary of the higher-order system. Then shifts of energy can occur and unwanted parts, thoughts and emotions can be deposited in one individual from other members of the group. This is usually a combination of the tendency of that person to accept a certain role, or desire for a position of leadership, and the others in the group using this to rid themselves of unwanted aspects of their personality. These then locate in that person, filling him or her with disturbed energy so that they become emotionally upset or even psychotic.

I know of no better way to learn to understand and to manage these phenomena than the experiential conferences developed by W.R. Bion and A.K. Rice at the Tavistock Institute. As part of the work of the Irish Foundation for Human Development and the North West Centre for Learning and Development in Derry, we gained valuable experience over the years in running these conferences and have modified considerably both the theory and the method, so that it is now more applicable to the task of reconciliation.

The Wider Community

The same methods of intervention – that is, 1. and 2., p. 432 above – will be appropriate here also, although with a somewhat different focus. Here again the work of intervention and study, in addition to trying to understand how these function, would be on the relation of the individual and/or the personalized group to these larger institutions and the management of the boundary between them.

It is important to understand that what we term the 'culture' – that is, the attitudes, emotions and behaviour – of a human group is what the inner world of thought, fantasy, emotion and physiological activity (what Claude Bernard called the 'internal milieu') is to the individual. The question which has haunted me for many years is, where is this inner life of the group? In what form does it exist?

The usual answer to this question is to say that the life of the group exists within each individual member, or that the notion of a group mind, or collective unconscious, is only symbolic, only an analogy. However, if we are serious about the definition of a living system, and that this can apply just as realistically to higher-order systems as to individuals, and are saying a human or animal group can be a true living organism, then these answers are not satisfactory. Only the work of Rupert Sheldrake and his concept of morphic resonance throws any real light on this question. His notion of morphic fields, which underlie and organize form and behaviour at all levels of complexity, whether of cells, individuals, groups or species, at last opens up the possibility of real progress in understanding this question.

Larger Aggregations of Society

If the work of reconciliation is to mean anything, it needs to involve an understanding of much more than the differences between the two communities in the north and not see these in isolation from similar divisions and conflicts around the world. Nor are these community and religious differences the only kind of splitting and division we see affecting society at the present time. Since the Industrial Revolution and the development of a mechanistic and materialisic technological society, there has been a separation of mind and body, a separation of work from living, of sexuality from human relationships, of spirituality from so-called practical living and of the past from the present and the future.

Many of the boundaries we have erected around fields of knowledge, different belief systems, academic disciplines such as health and economics, etc., have become far too rigid and are making further human progress difficult. In the traditional academic institutions and universities, people have become closed off within their own disciplines, learning more and more about less and less.

If we turn to the problems of real life and face the question of how we are going to deal with our increasingly threatened biosphere, it is in the interface between these disciplines and divisions in society that the hope of real progress lies; it is through the sharing of understanding and movement of information across these lines of demarcation. What we need is to find a context where this can begin to happen, where sufficient personal growth and change can develop to create openness and greater flexibility in crossing these boundaries, and where a sense of the wholeness and interrelatedness of all aspects of human life can come through.

It seems to us that there are likely to be only a few places in the world where integrated work of this kind can begin and Derry is one of these. Derry is in many ways a unique community, for it still retains much of its semi-tribal, rural past. At the same time, Derry is a true city with an urbanized population in excess of 100,000. It is probably now about the same size as a number of the great European cities were in the past, at the point of their highest cultural achievement, such as Venice, Florence, London, Paris or Dublin. These rather unique characteristics are largely due to the fact that, because of political and economic deprivation, Derry virtually missed the Industrial Revolution, so that it moved directly from a pre-industrial culture to a post-industrial one. It missed out on the Victorian notion of the job as a separated function from living and therefore exists to this day as a manifestation of its 'being' rather than 'doing'; i.e. it is not, like most cities today, dominated by economics.

Over twenty years ago we initiated a social experiment with the young people of Derry which started originally as a separate project. This has now grown to become the catalyst or energizing principle of the whole city, with many community projects active throughout the entire area. Another aspect which makes this social experiment rather unique is that, while on the one hand it is an endeavour to bring about social transformation in one local area, Derry is at the same time forging links with cities and local communities in other parts of the world that are also struggling with social change. If further development can now take place along the lines suggested in this paper, then we will have here an example of a movement which is truly local in character, centred on personal and communal development, but which is at the same time a part of a worldwide activity involving similar projects in cities and communities scattered across the globe. To my knowledge, nowhere has there been a human development project concerned with reconciliation, conflict resolution and intervention working at the four levels suggested here, in the same place, at the same time, up to now.

What is suggested then, is that Derry has the potential to become an international centre of learning, so that if for example people come from across the world to an international conference (such as the Beyond Hate conference held in Derry some time ago), the members attending would also become involved in personal development and/or experiential group work during the same period, in this way bringing about a real change in the persons and groups who come to learn – a real change in what they 'are' and in what they 'do' as a result of the educational process to which they are exposed.

Finally, I feel that a centre of excellence to carry out research should be established in Derry to monitor the human development and learning activities of the International Centre for Learning. It would also provide a means of giving feedback on the local community activities in Derry. This would provide valuable material for those coming to learn from other countries but would also provide a way for the people of Derry to look at and review the changes that are happening to them at some remove from their direct participation in these activities on the ground.

It should be stressed that any attempt to assess outcome and results of these learning enterprises should be directed to evidence of real change in the participants themselves and what they do differently when they return to their home environments, rather than asking whether they have gained this or that piece of intellectual knowledge.

32. Suffering and the
Growth of Love

Written in March 1997, this paper was presented at a scientific/ spirituality conference in Israel. This is the first of five papers that present my thoughts on spirituality, which have been developing over the past thirty years.

Change is central to our existence in this reality, in this material world. Humankind has changed the world out of all recognition and yet it remains true that the only lasting positive change anyone can make is within him/herself. Change oneself and one's world changes. If you become a different person, obviously your world is different, and so are any dealings you have with it. If we examine the question of change, that is of bringing about change and growth in ourselves, it is clear that this can apply at a number of levels. I want to examine this, first of all in regard to our biological and human development, secondly in terms of the question of change in relation to psychotherapy, and lastly regarding what change means in terms of spirituality and the relationship at each of these levels to the growth of love.

Even at its simplest, any change involves two things – work and suffering. The deeper the change to be accomplished, the greater the amount of work and effort, pain and suffering, involved. People resist change for this very reason, even when they realize that change will have a positive benefit. Because of the mechanistic attitudes which have accompanied the enormous advances of science and technology, the western mind has succumbed to the illusion that there is a remedy for every ill and we expect to be able to avail of this without any effort or suffering on our part whatsoever.

At the most superficial, gross level, when someone comes to a doctor or therapist feeling they have problems, with symptoms like depression or anxiety, or simply feeling they can no longer manage, they usually come expecting the doctor to do something to relieve them. With the development of technological medicine during this century, we have all been conditioned to accept the current concepts as to the nature of health and illness. The belief has grown up, particularly in the west, that it is the doctor who cures. The body is seen as a machine with which something has gone wrong, and the doctor's job is to fix it by giving medicine, by operating, or whatever.

Certainly doctors can often relieve symptoms in this way, when the patient appears to have made little contribution to the change in their condition.

The fallacy of this view has been exposed in many areas in recent years, none more so than with the advent of AIDS. This has made it only too clear that, without the natural healing power of the body, medicine and doctors are virtually helpless. Even if we take as simple an example as a fracture, the surgeon only realigns the bones in approximation to each other so that healing can take place. It is the body which heals and joins the bones together, and this takes effort and work on the part of the body and the immune system. It also involves considerable pain and suffering for the patient while the fracture is healing.

Biological Development

If we look at the development of living creatures, right from the moment of conception there is active change and growth. The inherent potential to grow and develop is there in the organism but this can only happen within the surrounding nurturing and warmth of the womb, with everything it needs supplied to it by the mother. Then the push towards maturation will happen in a purely natural way. There is now ample evidence that prenatal infants are sensitive and cognitive, and research confirms various forms of learning and memory both in the foetus and the newborn. In a valuable paper which reviews this recent work by direct observation of infants in the womb, David Chamberlain,[1] who has described much of this work, has said, 'As the light of research reaches into the dark corners of prejudice, we may thank those in the emerging field of prenatal/perinatal psychology'. He goes on:

> Is a baby a conscious and *real* person? To me it is no longer appropriate to speculate . . . when so much is known. The range of evidence now available in the form of knowledge of the foetal

440

sensory system, observations of foetal behaviour in the womb, and experimental proof of learning and memory . . . amply verifies that a baby is a real person . . . Babies are like us in having clearly manifested feelings in their reactions to assaults, injuries, irritations, or medically inflicted pain. They smile, cry and kick in protest, manifest fear, anger, grief, pleasure or displeasure in ways which seem entirely appropriate in relation to their circumstances. Babies are cognitive beings, thinking their own thoughts, dreaming their own dreams, learning from their own experiences, and remembering their own experiences.

Not only is there clear evidence of learning and memory going back into the womb and even to conception but there is the strange phenomenon that these recollections have the characteristic of being like those of an adult. As Chamberlain puts it, 'I have always been impressed by the fact that memories, at whatever age you tap into them, always show mature and humane qualities'.[2]

Given these recent insights, what are we to say now of the infant who is rejected by its mother in the womb? It may be because the baby was conceived as a result of rape, or because of the mother's own misfortunes in life, but consider the infant who experiences being unloved in the womb, and continues unloved and often brutalized after birth by both parents. The most difficult patients I've had to deal with come into life in this way and grow up feeling loveless and unwanted, incapable of even loving themselves. We are only now beginning to appreciate the vital role that maternal influences and relationships play during the prenatal period.

After birth the same process continues but now the effort and work on the part of the creature itself is more apparent. This applies whether it is a lion cub, a baby gorilla, an elephant or a human. Every step, whether it is to learn to walk, to feed itself, or in the case of the human to acquire language, is accompanied by enormous work and struggle. Much of this happens as a part of play. Unless it is literally starving or brutally ill-treated, an infant will play and struggle to learn. One will often notice that a child who has begun to say a few words will temporarily lose the speech when it is struggling to walk, as if this new activity has to take all its concentration for the moment.

As we develop and get older, the same principle holds true. Whether it is in school, taking exams, learning a language or the struggle of attending our first dance, all new learning is associated with pain. When we accept the pain and achieve some success, then we feel a deep satisfaction. Even if we take as simple an example as the contrast between leaving the warmth of a fire and a comfortable living room to go for a walk in the hills on a cold winter's day and sitting all afternoon watching television: if we are honest, I think anyone would have to admit that we feel much more contented and satisfied after the walk than if we had spent the afternoon taking it easy – even though at the time it seemed preferable to take the easy option.

The point I want to stress is that the learning and healthy development of an infant only takes place when grounded in the constant love and care of the mother, whether a lioness with her cubs, an elephant, or a human mother. It is always surprising to see the constant preoccupation and watchfulness of a mother as she fosters the growth and learning of her infant. Nor is she always soft and loving but rather will impose discipline when necessary in the service of her infant's learning. If this needed any confirmation, it was made only too clear in the unpleasant experiments of Harlow with his monkeys, where he isolated them from any love and relationship with others and showed how they were permanently damaged and incapable of learning as a result.

I've seen the same result so often with children separated from their mothers at or near birth and raised in institutions or orphanages. Here, there was no shortage of discipline or moral training yet, the crucial ingredient of love being missing, the result was children with severe personality deficits and an inability to learn, particularly in terms of being able to relate normally to others.

Psychotherapy and Personality Change

The principle here is the same as that in development. The person has to undertake the work of change, and this change involves pain and suffering. I should point out here, however, that there are two contrasting forms of change or learning involved in both development and therapy. On the one hand there is the pain involved in taking action – to learn a new skill, to take an examination, or whatever. On the other hand there is the emotional work necessary, with its quantum of pain and suffering, in integrating an experience such as feeling the grief over the loss of someone dear, or experiencing the effects of a trauma. It is important to realize that the response must be appropriate to the challenge facing us, whether the emphasis be to 'feel' or to 'act'.

This necessary relationship of 'suffering' to 'change' becomes all the clearer when we turn to emotional problems, which give rise to symptoms like anxiety and depression. Because the concept of therapy or treatment, and hence of 'therapist', has been derived from medicine, we have tended to fall into the same trap of thinking that the 'therapist' carries out the 'treatment'; i.e. undertakes some activity which cures the patient. When applied to psychotherapy, this is clearly quite an erroneous notion. In psychotherapy, or for that matter in psychiatry generally, there is no treatment that you can apply to the person which brings about real change in them.

Sadly, orthodox psychiatry seems to have missed this point almost entirely, believing that, by giving tranquillizers or neuroleptics and temporally relieving symptoms, something has been achieved. Whereas in fact no real change has taken place and sooner or later the person will slip back to where they were, with a recurrence of their symptoms. The issue here is not the giving of a drug: many of the psychoactive drugs are very useful; indeed, if we are honest, no psychiatrist could manage nowadays without them. No, the question is whether they are given as a treatment in themselves or as an aid to working in relationship with the patient. Often the pharmaceutical is the only way of making the initial contact so that therapy can begin, where a person is so psychotic or over-anxious that it is not possible to work with them until they have settled down.

As in development, the primacy of learning being grounded in relationship applies here also. In psychotherapy too, the relationship of person to person, of heart to heart, is absolutely fundamental. If this is absent, then there is no context within which the therapy can begin. I think there is a good deal of confusion in regard to this. A therapeutic relationship is a real relationship, like any other, between two human beings. Indeed, it is a genuine friendship and, where it is deep, can often turn into love. By 'love' in this context I mean a love which has only concern for the other, not seeking its own self-interest. Perhaps the best analogy is the love of a mother for her child. Her preoccupation is to nurture and care for the child but also to watch over and foster its growth and development. In a similar way, the therapeutic relationship is not simply to care and feel concern for the patient: it is a relationship established for a purpose – i.e. to help the client with their problems. Like any friendship between two persons, there is naturally a desire to help the person who is in trouble, to care for that person, but in any truly therapeutic friendship there is also a desire to care for their learning: to help them to learn what they need to know to overcome their difficulties. Therefore in a therapeutic setting there also has to be objectivity and the relationship has to be managed.

I feel there is considerable confusion amongst psychotherapists about this. When it is said that therapy should be non-directive, this is essentially correct; it is generally useless to tell a person what to do, or to do it for them, nor can you force them to do something. Nevertheless the therapy has to be managed: if the client is left to feel and behave as they have always done, then they will control the therapy and there will be no change. There is an apparent paradox here. What is often misunderstood is that it is the task of the therapist to manage the context of the therapy. What the client feels or does within this context is still their personal responsibility.

Traditionally in psychotherapy the question of the therapeutic relationship is usually dealt with in terms of the transference. No doubt transference is a reality and the management of it is of considerable importance, but the first thing to be said is that the relationship of therapist and client is a real relationship of one human being to another. The feelings and other manifestations which occur are not something to be simply understood as 'transferred' from some other significant relationship in the past – parent, family, or whatever. This undoubtedly occurs and has to be dealt with. But any relationship between two persons is also a real relationship with real feelings, which has to be managed. Carl Jung was once again ahead of his time in pointing this out:

> In psychotherapy, even if the doctor is entirely detached from the emotional contents of the patient, the very fact that the patient has emotions has an effect on him. And it is a great mistake if the doctor thinks he can lift himself out of it. He cannot do more than become conscious of the fact that he is affected. If he does not see that, he is too aloof and then he talks beside the point. It is even his duty to accept the emotions of the patient and to mirror them. This is the reason why I reject the idea of putting the patient upon a sofa and sitting behind him. I put my patients in front of me and I talk to them as one natural human being to another, and I expose myself completely and react with no restriction.[3]

The notion that, because the therapist sits behind the patient on the couch, out of view, and does not relate, what emerges is purely transference is manifest nonsense. Relationship is not simply verbal or visual, or even non-verbal but, once we are in relationship, a direct exchange of feelings and energy, and also information, takes place (often even at a distance), whether we see each other or not.

So for therapy to provide a context in which real change can take root, it is essential that it be grounded in a genuine relationship; a relationship which will provide the support and trust necessary for the patient to go through the pain and suffering that are an inevitable accompaniment of any fundamental change.

Unexperienced Experience

I want to turn now to something which I feel is a deep principle within nature: that is, the primacy of the need to 'experience'; the absolute necessity to fully experience and integrate into the self whatever challenges, painful traumas and suffering come our way.

When, as living creatures, we are faced with a threatening experience, something which causes a serious disturbance or perturbation and which raises the question of change, we have to suffer that experience and integrate it into ourselves. We have to do this in order to re-establish our internal coherence, to re-orientate and balance once again our internal reality. Because of the failure to understand the painful effort and time involved in the integration of experience, particularly serious traumatic experience, the failure to recognize all the work that goes into the formation of memory, it was assumed, until recently, that everything that happens to us is taken in directly and becomes part of our permanent memory. It has been taken for granted that even overwhelmingly traumatic events are experienced and integrated automatically into the self.

From research carried out during this century to try to understand the nature of memory and how it is formed and retrieved, there is now ample evidence demonstrating the dynamic nature of long-term memory. As the psychologist Endel Tulving has pointed out:

> one of the most widely held, but wrong, beliefs that people have about memory is that 'memories' exist, somewhere in the brain, like books exist in a library, or packages of soap, on the supermarket shelves and that memory is equivalent to somehow

retrieving them. The whole concept of repression is built on this misconception.[4]

The present view of the nature of long-term memory was well described by Bartlett, who said, as far back as 1932:

> some widely held views have to be completely discarded and none more completely than that which treats recall as the re-excitement in some way of fixed and changeless 'traces' . . . [remembering is] an imaginative reconstruction, or construction, built out of the relation of our attitude towards a whole mass of organized past reactions or experience.[5]

While this undoubtedly seems to be true of our permanent memory system, there is another important area of research which has been growing over the past thirty or forty years on the role of the primitive brain in the formation of memory (what Arthur Koestler referred to as the 'horse brain'), known as the 'limbic system' or 'medial temporal lobe'. It is important to stress that this part of the brain has not only connections with higher brain centres but also has intimate connections with the vegetative nervous system, through our hormones and endocrine glands, etc., to our entire emotional response, which is a function of the whole body. It is clear from this work that our whole being is involved in the process of experiencing. This is not simply a function of the brain, indeed the notion of the brain and body as separate realities is no longer sustainable. Nothing which happens to us, therefore, gets into long-term memory without first working its way into this totally unified network which is the human being.

The Unity of Our Being

Recent work by Candace Pert[6] and her colleagues at the National Institute of Mental Health has raised the fascinating prospect that the peptides – a family of about seventy macromolecules, which were originally described in terms of three traditionally separate disciplines, neuroscience, endocrinology and immunology – really form one single network. These 'molecular messengers', which were given different names – hormones, neurotransmitters, endorphins, growth factors, etc. – actually constitute a single family. 'We discovered,' she said, 'that the receptors (for neuropeptides) were scattered throughout not only the brain but also the body . . . In the beginning of my work,

I matter-of-factly presumed that emotions were in the head or the brain. Now I would say they are really in the body as well.' Capra has described succinctly this revolution in our thinking in his recent book, *The Web of Life*:

> In the nervous system, peptides are produced in nerve cells and then travel down the axons . . . to be stored in little balls at the bottom, where they wait for the right signals to release them. These peptides play a vital role in communications throughout the nervous system. Traditionally, it was thought that the transfer of all nervous impulses occurs across the gaps, called 'synapses' between adjacent nerve cells . . . Most of the signals that come from the brain are transmitted via peptides emitted by nerve calls. By attaching themselves to receptors far away from the nerve cells in which they originated, these peptides act not only throughout the entire nervous system but also in other parts of the body. Another fascinating aspect of the newly recognized psychosomatic network is the discovery that peptides are the biochemical manifestation of emotions. The entire group of 60–70 peptides may constitute a universal biochemical language of emotions.
>
> Traditionally, neuroscientists have associated emotions with specific areas in the brain, notably the limbic system. This is indeed correct. The limbic system turns out to be highly enriched with peptides. However, it is not the only part of the body where peptide receptors are concentrated. For example, the entire intestine is lined with peptide receptors. This is why we have 'gut feelings'. We literally feel our emotions in our gut . . . In other words, all our perceptions and thoughts are coloured by emotions. This, of course, is also our common experience. As Candace Pert puts it, 'White blood cells are bits of the brain floating around the body'. Ultimately, this implies that cognition is a phenomenon that expands throughout the organism, operating through an intricate chemical network of peptides that integrates our mental, emotional and biological activities.

To put this in its simplest form, when an event takes place in the external world we do not fully experience it as it happens. We do undoubtedly register it in some way and take an impression of the raw experience as it is taking place, otherwise the event would no longer exist within us once it has happened in the external world. This is why experiences of this kind, if they are activated many years later, are not only true but are also accurate as to detail which is quite often irrelevant to the traumatic experience itself. I believe it is because of the extraordinary detail and accuracy of blocked experiences of this kind that the myth grew up that everything we perceive is taken in and stored somewhere in the mind. In fact, much of what happens around us we do not register at all and of course it no longer exists.

It has long been recognized that, when a living creature is faced with a threat to its physical integrity, it responds to the challenge with the 'fight or flight' response. In situations where attack or evasive action are not possible, it appears that an organism has at its disposal an equally ancient and basic strategy for survival: that is, the capacity to 'freeze' or 'play dead'. This involves the operation of a primitive biological, adaptive response which acts at the level of the limbic system (outside of conscious awareness or control) and blocks, partially or completely, the processing and integration of the experience.

Similar to other survival mechanisms in lower animals, this 'freeze response', while present in human beings, appears to have been modified to serve a somewhat different purpose in modern human conditions. As well as being a way of avoiding external danger it may now be used to deal with the threat of internal destabilization. Whenever we are faced with an overwhelming experience which we sense to be potentially disintegrative, we have the ability to suspend it in an unassimilated form and to maintain it in that stage indefinitely. Our biological structure seems to be able to specify in advance that to fully experience the meaning of the threatening encounter would destroy or disintegrate its core organization. It is now as if a piece of the external world is within the person but not part of that person, existing outside of time in a potentially unstable state.

This is a completely different concept from that of repression, for the experiences we are dealing with in this instance are not long-term memories, nor indeed memories in the accepted sense at all, but the suspended 'frozen present'; that is, experiences which have never been integrated into memory and which in an emotional sense have not yet been experienced.

One reason for this confusion lies in historical factors surrounding the early work of Freud. Because there was little or no understanding of neurophysiology, or of the nature of memory formation, at that time, he understandably, when faced with the problem of 'amnesia' for traumatic events, came up with the concept of 'repression', which was accepted by everyone. And this, as an 'apparent' explanation, has dogged all of psychotherapeutic development ever since. In fact, a little earlier than Freud, the French philosopher/psychiatrist Pierre Janet[7] had developed the concept of 'dissociation' ('desaggregation', which had originally been introduced by Jacques Moreau) and had raised the notion of 'unassimilated happenings',[8] but all of this thinking was swept away by the ubiquitous spread of psychoanalysis, so that Janet's work was almost forgotten.

It was also compounded by the ordinary way we think and our everyday use of language; by the assumption that everything which happens to us is immediately taken in and integrated. In all the descriptions of natural disasters, accidents, child sexual abuse, kidnappings, rape, etc., we repeatedly find the supposed traumatic 'memories' described as being 're-enacted', 're-experienced' or 'relived'. The fundamental error here is all contained in the prefix 're' and in the use of the term 'repressed memory' for, once we use these words in this way, we are already making the assumption that the traumatic event has been fully experienced and is now integrated into the self as memory.

To understand fully the necessity to experience completely the insults, trauma and suffering which afflict us during life, it is essential to grasp the reality of this 'frozen present'; to realize that in therapy we are never dealing with the past, only with what is there now. This is true even though what is suspended may have taken place in the external world many years ago. The work of integrating this 'frozen present' is not, as I used to think, a question of processing a piece of information through the primitive brain, as we would programme a computer. No, it is a matter of integrating the raw experience, in all its emotional richness, into the total self; of re-establishing the coherence and state of balance of our internal reality.

This is why I referred to the work of experiencing as a deep principle within nature. My belief is that this principle extends far beyond the individual integration of experience. I also feel that it transcends this material state of embodiment and resonates out into the wider sphere of reality. If this is so, it would mean that any action or trauma which takes place in the external world would have to be experienced by someone at some time, if not in the present, then at some point in the future.

In Sahaj Marg and the eastern tradition there is, especially for westerners, the difficult concept of Bhog (Bhoga or Bhogam), which in sanskrit is literally translated as 'enjoyment', but in this context is defined as undergoing the effects of impressions (samskaras). As Clark Powell, an American who wrote *The Natural Path: A Companion to Sahaj Marg*, has described it: 'When a samskara is formed, it can be likened to a tightly wound coil, waiting for its kinetic energy to be released by the process of bhogam whenever the environment provides the appropriate conditions.'[9] This appears to be similar to the activation of an unresolved traumatic experience, which is then available to be suffered, fully experienced and integrated into the self.

At this point I feel a little out of my depth, but this would seem to relate to the Judaeo-Christian concept of praying or suffering for one another, as on the day of atonement – Yam Kippur, or the Christian idea of the mystical body, where all souls are thought to be interconnected and suffering can be shared. It also raises the question whether great incarnations like Buddha, Mohammed or Christ, or in recent times Ram Chandra (Babuji), the special personality who founded our mission, can suffer and thus experience and clean away 'impressions' (samskaras) for all of us. When I started meditation in the Sahaj Marg system and I was told that the heart was the real centre of our emotional life, the location where all the impressions (samskaras) which drive our behaviour are laid down, I thought this was simply a nice poetic and figurative way of describing things. However, in this system the heart is absolutely central. To quote our great Master, Babuji Maharaj:

> People generally think of the heart as made of flesh and blood only . . . This is one of the limitations in viewing the heart region in its broader sense. It is really a vast circle covering everything inner and outer. The things after the first Mind all belong to the region of heart. All the lotuses or chakras are set within its limits.

The remarkable thing is that now, research which has been developing over the past thirty years has demonstrated that the heart is more than simply a pump. The atrium of the heart produces a hormone – ANF[10] (atrial natriuretic factor) – that interacts with other hormones and dramatically affects every major organ in the body. It impacts on the limbic system and determines the action of the thalamus and its relationship with the pituitary gland. ANF is involved in the immune system and affects the pineal gland, regulating the production and action of melatonin. Given what was said about the peptides forming a unified network throughout the body, and now with this atrial hormone, it becomes clear that the heart plays a key role in our emotional life, memory and learning.

Here once again we find the phenomenon which our living spiritual Master, Chariji, has often referred to, that insights which have been part of the perennial wisdom of the east for thousands of years are, late in the day, being 'discovered' by science. This has already happened in physics, nearly a hundred years ago now, with the discovery of quantum physics and the interconnectedness of all reality once we enter the subatomic world. It has been happening more recently in biology, with the development of 'living system' theory and the principle of indeterminism in complex systems, the growth of 'chaos' theory and so on. Now, here, once again, this time in the understanding of our human physiology, we find science painfully catching up with what was ancient human intuition. Even in the west we speak of someone being 'soft-hearted' or 'kind-hearted; we say someone is 'heart-scalded' or is a 'sweetheart', showing that this awareness of the centrality of the heart was there in the language of our forebears.

Spirituality and the Growth of Love

This brings me finally to spirituality and what change and growth mean in this regard. Once again, the same principles emerge which we have already seen operating in biological development and as part of psychotherapy – that change involves work and effort, and inevitably is accompanied by pain and suffering. But the change which one embarks on now is at a much deeper and more subtle level; also it is essential that the suffering involved is now accepted in the service of spiritual growth.

In the Sahaj Marg system (which simply means 'natural path'), there is a major emphasis on cleaning out the impressions (samskaras) which have formed around our heart over the long struggle of evolution. Also, if you accept the proposition that we have, as humans, had many lives then these impressions too have to be cleared off. The view here is that deep in the core of our heart the spirit (soul) is pure, close to the condition it was in at the time of creation, when this universe first emerged from the Ultimate Source of All. As Babuji Maharaj has said:

> When the time of creation came the latent thought came into action and the subtlest particles got heated up. Thus the pre-liminary covering set in from the very first day. By the effect of continuous heating, the particles began to come into motion. Its intensity went on increasing adding veils after veils to it. Grossness began to develop by the effect of the growing inten-sity of the vibrations. The action of every particle started and went on multiplying till the Reality was completely wrapped up within, like a silkworm in the cocoon.[11]

It is interesting that Joseph Chilton Pearce,[12] in his remarkable book *Evolution's End*, has described in very similar terms this cen-trality of the heart and how it can potentially operate at several levels. He speaks of how we have 'both a physical heart and a higher "universal heart"' and how, 'just as our physical heart maintains our body, the non-localized intelligence governing the heart in turn maintains synchrony with a universal "consciousness at large"'. He goes on to describe the three major stages of life which are heart-centred in this sense:

1. the development of a heart–mind synchrony, needed for physical life . . .
2. a later 'post-adolescent' development, which synchronizes the developed physical self and the creative process; and
3. a final 'highest heart' which moves us beyond all physical–emotional systems. Two poles of experience lie within us, our unique, individual self generating through the brain; and a universal, impersonal intelligence generating through the heart.

Of course, the traditional medical view is that emotions are really controlled by the primitive brain, the limbic system, and that the heart is simply there to pump the blood. Now, after all, this work is indicating the total unity of our being and that the heart is really central to this unity, the emotional driving force of our character and morality. The intellect is merely an amoral instrument to assist our understanding but is a poor guide as to how we should behave.

Although it is not the main purpose of our spiritual practice, what I have found, to my surprise, is that, as my heart has been opening up spiritually, my practice of psychotherapy has been transformed. I find that I often experience and understand things in the very first interview with a client which would have taken weeks or months to achieve formerly. The more the ego is cleared out, the more sensitive one becomes and the more available one is to be of service to the person one is dealing with. I now see psychotherapy more and more as rough work to remove gross impressions. This prepares the way for more subtle cleaning and for further spiritual development. Of course, not everyone is willing to continue further on this path, and that is their right. However, it remains true that the only real deep change is when this further step is undertaken.

To open this third level or the 'spiritual' heart is the main task of spirituality. To unravel and clear away these coverings around one's heart means hard work and inevitably involves pain and suffering. Sahaj Marg is a system of practical training in spirituality. It is in essence the well-known Raja Yoga (yoga of the mind) but has been remodelled and simplified to suit the needs of modern life. Its goal is inner perfection – God realization. As our present Master, Chariji, has put it: 'God is infinite, yet simple and therefore the way to reach Him must be as simple. By proper regulation of the mind through meditation, under the practical guidance and support of a spiritual master, one can evolve to the highest.'

Babuji Maharaj has clarified what he means by this 'regulation' of the mind:

> In order to control our thoughts and actions we have to look to the proper working of the mind which is never at rest even for a moment. I have often heard religious teachers railing at it in bitterest terms, ascribing all bad names to it and proclaiming it to be our worst enemy. The reason is quite plain. They think it to be the cause of all evil within us, and consequently they advise people to crush it and not to follow its biddings . . . I, no doubt, agree with those who say that every evil has its origin in the mind . . . at the same time I may remind them that it is the very same mind that leads us to virtue and also helps us to realize our highest self. So it is not every evil alone that proceeds from the mind but also every good . . . What is actually required is not the crushing or the killing of the mind but merely its proper training.[13]

This can only be accomplished through the growth of love but because we are human we can only love in a human way. This is another reason why it is necessary to have a capable master. We cannot love an abstract idea of God, nor can we easily have any direct contact with God, who is beyond all our conceptions. If love is to grow and to be genuine, it has to be in relation to a human being, one who has himself been absorbed in the divine. Then, through this channel, love of God can ultimately develop. It is important to stress, however, that love (*Bhakti*), as Babuji has said, 'is the means of achieving the goal, not the goal itself'. Love is not the goal but rather provides the ground on which we progress towards the goal. The goal is 'Realization'; that is, quite simply, to 'realize' our original nature, which is divine. Nevertheless, if we can become absorbed in love, the goal will take care of itself. The goal of meditation is not to achieve something outside ourselves, some reward, but through the process of cleaning to remove the coverings which have blocked our 'realization' of the original condition which we have lost sight of, but which was once ours. This method of spiritual practice does not offer the acquisition of better health, or wealth, or power, or any other material benefit.

One often hears, when human beings behave in deplorable ways, that unfortunately it's 'human nature', but when we behave in cruel, aggressive ways, and this is particularly true of men, this is not our 'human' nature'. It is behaving distortedly, as less than we are capable of being. It is not true to say that it is behaving like an animal, for animals do not show these excesses of depravity, because their behaviour is disciplined by nature and they are behaving in a way that is natural to them. What we have failed to realize is that true 'human' behaviour, the natural state of the human being, only exists when our spiritual nature is awakened, for we are spiritual beings. This is the third stage of flowering of the 'highest heart', as Joseph Chilton Pearce has described it, which unfortunately so few of us achieve.

The crucial difference from the mundane levels of biological development, or issues of therapy, which we have looked at already, is that, in spirituality, it is extremely difficult to make real progress simply by our own efforts. This is again where a capable spiritual guide or Master, who is himself absorbed in the divine, is so essential. It is not sufficient at this level to have simply a guide, or even a loving support.

In the Sahaj Marg system there is the direct assistance of divine energy – '*Pranahuti*' – which the Master, as a channel from the Ultimate (God), pours into the heart through transmission. This directly opens up our internal spiritual reality. The task we have is that of moulding our character and external behaviour to match this internal spiritual growth. Unless our behaviour outside changes to mirror the internal growth, the whole development would become a contradiction, a hypocrisy. It is impossible to give anyone else the understanding of what this journey means for me. To know its benefits one must practise to experience it. In the experience lies the hope of spiritual growth. The pace at which one journeys is irrelevant but sooner or later every human being will have to tread this path back to the Ultimate. The ultimate goal of 'Realization' then has the quality of infinity, so there is really no end to how far this spiritual journey can go, nor is there any final reaching of such a goal. This is why Babuji Maharaj said 'spirituality begins where religion ends, and Realization begins where spirituality ends'. What more is there to say?

References

1. Chamberlain, D.B. 'Babies Are Conscious', in J. English (ed.), *Caesarian Voices*.
2. Chamberlain, D.B. 'The Expanding Boundaries of Memory', *ReVision*, 12, 4, Spring 1990.
3. Jung, C.G. *Analytical Psychology (The Tavistock Lectures)*, Routledge & Kegan Paul Ltd, 155, 1976.
4. Tulving, E. *Elements of Episodic Memory*, Clarendon Press, New York, 1983; Tulving, Endel., *Organization of memory*, N. Y. Clarendon Pr., 1972.
5. Bartlet, F.C. *Remembering: A Study in Experimental and Social Psychology*, Cambridge University Press, Cambridge, MA, [1932] 1977.
6. Pert, C., *et al.* 'Neuropeptides and Their Receptors: A Psychosomatic Network', *Journal of Immunology*, 135, 2, 820–6, 1985; Pert, C. 'The Chemical Communicators', interview in Bill Moyers, *Healing and the Mind*, Doubleday, 1993.
7. Janet, P. *L'Automatisme psychologique: Essai de psychologie expérimentale sur les formes inférieures de l'activité humaine*, Felix Alcan, Paris, 1889; Société Pierre Janet/Payot, Paris, 1973.
8. Janet, P. *Psychological Healing: Historical and Clinical Study*, Macmillan, New York, 1925.
9. Powell, Clark, *A Sahaj Marg Companion: The Natural Path*, Ram Chandra Mission, 1996.

10. Cantin, M., and Genest, J. 'The Heart as an Endocrine Gland', *Scientific American*, 254, 2, 76, 1986.

11. Ram Chandra, *Reality at Dawn, Complete Works of Ram Chandra*, Book I, Shri Ram Chandra Mission, Shahjahanpur (U.P.) 242001, India, 1989.

12. Pearce, J.C. 'Heart–Mind Bonding', in *Evolution's End*, Harper Collins, New York, 1992.

13. Ram Chandra, *Reality at Dawn*.

33. 'Spirituality Begins Where
Religion Ends'

'Spirituality Begins Where Religion Ends' was published in a book called *Soul Searching*, edited by Kieran McKeown and Hugh Arthurs (Columbia Press, 1997).

I think my first awareness of spirituality came from my mother. She was a simple, gentle woman who was herself genuinely spiritual without even being consciously aware of it. She was Church of Ireland simply because of her upbringing but had no prejudice whatsoever. I remember, as an example of her simplicity, that one day I found her reading a book on the Blessed Virgin and I asked: 'Why don't you become a Catholic?' 'I wouldn't mind,' she said, 'but I wouldn't like to offend Mr Collins.' He was her local vicar at the time. All through my childhood, she read medical books. Perhaps she dreamed that some day she might study medicine but she was before her time for choosing a career, especially after marriage, and my father was a traditionalist and could never have imagined a wife with other interests than him and his children.

My mother and father were married in the Church of Ireland, not because my mother wanted it, but because of his insistence. He was a complex man and many of his actions were in the service of his rebellion against his family. He was afterwards reconciled with the Catholic Church by his brother, who was a priest. He refused to sign the *Ne temore* decree and decided that his sons would be raised as Catholics and the girls as Protestants. So on Sundays my father, my brother and I would head off to mass with my father while my sister and mother went to the local Church of Ireland. This seemed clear enough until one day, after attending mass for several years, I was glancing dreamily around the Church and, lo and behold, I became aware that there were women and girls there! Until that day I had assumed that all men were Catholics and all women were

Protestants. I was undoubtedly a rather dreamy child but this did nothing to relieve my confusion of identity.

I was born at 12:30 midnight on 18 March 1929, half an hour late for St Patrick's Day, and so missed being called Patrick. I would have liked to be called Patrick but instead I was christened William Ivory Browne. The name William Ivory sounds innocent enough, but, although I didn't realize it at the time, this was the beginning of my confused identity, for this was the name of the Cromwellian soldier who was given the lands of the Brownes at Mulrankin when these were confiscated after Cromwell crushed the rebellion. William Ivory must have been one of the most detested men in south County Wexford at that time and of course the hatred of him would have lived on in folk memory in that part of Wexford right down to my father's time.

The choice of my name was part of my father's life-long rebellion against his conservative Catholic, Irish Republican family, as was partly his reason for marrying a Protestant. I have no doubt he loved my mother but undoubtedly his unconscious motivation in marrying her was part of that protest. Although he did this, in 1922 it did not alter his underlying Catholic conditioning, which was revealed in his rejection of all my mother's relatives.

As a child I regularly heard him say, 'I'm afraid Ivor was a mistake. I don't think we'll ever be able to rear him.' Now, of course, I understand how my birth must have intensified his anxiety about providing for his family, for he was beyond middle age when I was born. His form of family planning had been to sleep in a shed in the garden until the night he ended up in my mother's bed in the house and I was conceived.

Not having wanted a third child, he identified me with the Protestant side of the family and always referred to me as a Fitzmaurice (my mother's maiden name). In light of this, I came, eventually, to understand the personal significance of 'William Ivory' and that his choosing the name of the hated Cromwellian was clearly no accident.

My first experience of Holy Communion was a spiritual awakening for me. I recall the strong feeling, as the host melted in my mouth, that Jesus was inside me. Of course, the experience was tainted by all the guilt and nonsense about not touching the host with your teeth, fear of it sticking to the roof of your mouth and not touching food or water for twenty-four hours beforehand. Still, that experience of Communion lasted for many years; the clear, raw feeling of the morning air when attending mass early and the experience of Jesus Christ was, in some sense, a genuine spiritual awakening.

But perhaps the first real spiritual opening of my heart was my introduction to jazz, hearing the spontaneous warmth and innocence of recordings like Louis Armstrong's 'Westend Blues' for the first time. I can still respond to them, even though the emotion is less intense, and even after more than fifty years their freshness remains. This was for me the first dawning of a personal awareness. Until then, although I was not consciously aware of it, I was in a state of deep identity confusion, with a father who was Irish Catholic but, in the service of his rebellion against his family, had adopted a pro-British, anti-Catholic view, a mother who was Protestant but innocent and self-effacing, so that I did not know what I was or where I belonged. Perhaps by making a strong identification with jazz and Afro-American culture I, feeling an outsider, identified with a suppressed minority who felt themselves to be outsiders in the white, WASP-dominated culture of the United States. If so, I certainly wasn't aware of it at the time.

One more reflection from my childhood should perhaps be mentioned. As a child, particularly if I was resting in bed in the daytime trying to be sick to avoid going to school, if I heard church bells or the sound of children playing in the distance I would be overcome by a strange, wistful sadness that seemed to come from another world. When I hear church bells far away, to this day, I still get this feeling, although it is now not so intense. However, this feeling does not accord, nor did it then, with any experience of mine from this life and my strong impression from this and other experiences is that I must have been a monk or in some form of religious order in a former life. I have always felt a strong pull in that direction and, after my recovery from a period in bed with tuberculosis, I seriously contemplated joining the Cistercians for a time.

From my father's individuality and oddball way of doing things I learned to think for myself and be my own person no matter what criticism I encountered. He spent his life working in the bank but his real life was outside the bank, working in the field at the back of the house, hauling seaweed from the beach to the house on a rope to grow the potatoes, and playing his mandolin. He planted potatoes in his ninety-first year, although his lazy-beds went back and across in opposite directions. I used to catch crabs under the rocks in Sandycove and my father would roast them on a primus stove in the College Green branch of the Bank of Ireland. One can imagine the smell that wafted through the bank when Browne was preparing his lunch but there was no stopping him. As for the mandolin, he played at every party we ever had or went to, sometimes for too long before anyone else got a chance to perform, and he trained my mother to sing along with him. Every year he lived after retirement delighted him, if only for the fact that the Bank of Ireland was having to pay him for doing nothing! And before he died I heard him say, 'Faith, I'm not sure that Ivor hasn't turned out better than any of them'.

When I reached adolescence I went through the usual disenchantment with organized religion. Then, when in medical school, I contracted TB and was put to bed for a year and so had time to think and read. I once again went into a religious phase. This lasted for a number of years but gradually the irreconcilable contradictions in orthodox Catholicism left me disillusioned once again and I felt quite lost, still feeling the need of a spiritual direction but not knowing where to turn.

In 1973 I finally reached a critical turning-point. I can remember the day quite clearly; it was in the Catholic church in Ballybrack. I was still attending mass for the sake of the children, my marriage was breaking up and I was sitting there feeling quite hopeless and lost, not knowing where to turn. In desperation I began to pray from the heart, asking Jesus to show me the way to go, what direction to take. I didn't know it then but I have learnt since that in those rare moments when we really pray for what we need, not simply for what we want, our prayers are always answered, and I have no doubt that my prayer that day was answered, although it took some time for it to happen. Not long after this I decided to try meditation and started practising Transcendental Meditation as the only method with which I was familiar. Like so many others I have come across since then, I found it very helpful at first. Almost immediately I could feel huge amounts of stress flowing out of me. But then, as I went on, I felt there was no progress in a spiritual sense, simply stress relief. Still, for several years, I went on with it, in spite of feeling rather disillusioned.

Then in 1978 I heard about Sahaj Marg. The remarkable thing about this is that the chance of my hearing about this spiritual system at that time must have been one in a million. Even though the Shri Ram Chandra Mission was established back in 1945 by Shri Ram Chandra (who is affectionately called Babuji), he was an obscure, humble old man living in Shahjahanpur, a remote rather primitive town in northern India, a place seldom even visited by Europeans, and in a country where there are hundreds of thousands of gurus and spiritual masters, many of them charlatans. Although Sahaj Marg had already spread quietly to a number of countries outside India, it was completely unknown in Ireland. What happened was that I had set up the Irish Foundation for Human Development in the early 1970s and an Irish woman, Bairbre Madden, came to work there. She was married to an Indian, K.V. Reddy, and he, after travelling all over India for about ten years in search of a genuine spiritual master, had finally, when he was about to give up (by another coincidence), come upon Babuji Mahara. It was he who introduced me to the system and gave me my initial sittings to start.

As I say, this was apparently an extremely unlikely coincidence, but I believe these things do not happen by chance. My conviction is that, if you are genuinely searching for a spiritual path, then it will find you, and I am convinced that my desperate prayer in 1973 was eventually answered and I was shown the direction I needed to follow. Of course, the question that always arises at this point is, why this particular spiritual system of all those that are available? And I am certainly not saying that this is the only spiritual path, or that it is right for everyone, but I have found it to be mine.

I think it is important to stress, however, that this system is not simply another religious practice imported from the east, lock stock and barrel, like so many before it. With the breakdown and general disillusionment of so many in the west with the mainstream, orthodox Christian religions, both Catholic and Protestant, and also with the failure of materialistic science to deliver the promise it held out at the turn of the century in solving the problems of mankind, there has been an extraordinary upsurge of spiritual longing among people all over the west. One result of this, ever since Vivekananda made his extraordinary journey to Chicago in 1893 to speak to the World's Parliament of Religions, has been the phenomenon of wave after wave of eastern and Yogic spiritual practices, the various forms of Buddhism and so on, flowing into the west from India, Japan and elsewhere. The difficulty has usually been that these ancient forms of eastern religious practice have been adopted without discretion by westerners, with robes, mantras and other rituals that are often poorly understood and lead at best to a form of superficial imitation.

Carl Jung, whose thinking was deeply influenced by his studies of eastern mysticism, was acutely aware of this danger of unthinkingly taking on the trappings of ancient eastern culture, of what he described as the attempt 'to put on, like a new suit of clothes, ready-made symbols grown on foreign soil', for 'if we now try to cover our nakedness with the gorgeous trappings of the east, as the theosophists do, we would be playing our own history false'.

By contrast, Sahaj Marg (which simply means the 'natural path'), although it originated in India, is no more Indian than it is French, Irish or American. Indeed, in many ways it is closest to Christ's original teaching, with its emphasis on working through the heart. It is probably the first truly international, global spiritual system whose aim is to bring a simple method of spirituality to all human beings in the world, so simple that there are no rules, just suggestions for one's own benefit. It is offered to anybody over eighteen years and without charge. Babuji said that the only requirement to begin this form of meditation was to be a human being and to want to do it.

The extraordinary thing about this spiritual system is its simplicity. Ram Chandra (Babuji) was a gentle, humble man, with only a primary-school education, living, as I have said, in a primitive remote town in northern India, but has this not been the very characteristic of great incarnations of the past, like Lao Tsu or Christ, who was an obscure carpenter from a tiny village in Israel and yet shook the very foundations of the Roman Empire. And yet Babuji personally carried his spiritual message to all five continents. Having achieved his purpose, he departed from this world in 1983. Since he established this mission fifty years ago, it has spread quietly, without any publicity, to virtually every country in the world, even though the numbers practising it in any one place are usually relatively small.

Babuji perfected an ancient method of spiritual training, which is in essence the well-known Raja Yoga (yoga of the mind), by remodelling and simplifying it to suit the needs of modern-day life. The system is based on transmission of divine energy and cleaning of past impressions. It depends critically on the continuance of a living Master, who, having been guided towards the spiritual goal by his

Master, can assist the aspirant on his or her spiritual journey. The present spiritual guide is Parthasarathi Rajagopalachari (who is affectionately known as Chari) of Madras, He is a man of high intellect, sensitivity and intense seeking after reality. At the age of thirty-two he met his Master in Shahjahanpur and became his most faithful and competent disciple. As he travels all over the world, giving his talks, informal conversations, many books and, above all, his spiritual service to people everywhere, he serves his Master as Ram Chandra served his Master. This service is vital to this system, for Chariji has himself said that, if at any time Sahaj Marg fails to produce a living Master, it will then simply turn into a religion.

Whatever about that, I have found this method of meditation to be of great benefit to me personally, even though the going is rough at times, and for this reason I stick at it. I began practising in 1978, almost twenty years ago, and still feel as if I am only just beginning, but then it is impossible to gauge the ground covered in a journey towards infinity.

This method of spiritual practice does not offer the acquisition of better health, or wealth, or power, or any other material benefit. It is impossible to give anyone else my understanding of this journey. To know its benefits one must experience it. In the experience is the hope of spiritual development. The pace at which one journeys is irrelevant. Every aspirant has his or her own pace. It is a life-long journey, starting with a single sitting. I have found Sahaj Marg to be a spiritual adventure. This is why Babuji said, 'Spirituality begins where religion ends, and Realization begins where spirituality ends.' What more is there to say?

34. All in One

This paper was written in November 1997. It was presented at a public meeting, but I cannot recall the date.

The inspiration for this talk was a beautiful statement that I found in the oldest of the Upanishads, which are part of the Vedic scriptures from ancient India.

> There is a light that shines beyond all things on earth, beyond us all, beyond the heavens, the very highest heavens. That is the light that shines in our heart.
>
> (Chandogya Upanishad)

Sahaj Marg provides us, as individuals, with a unique method of developing our inner spiritual lives. Nevertheless, as our Master has stressed many times, it is the abhyasi's responsibility to develop character and to mould external behaviour, which is essential if we are not to fall back, creating new samskaras through reactivating our old habits and behaviours.

This aspect has been dealt with ad nauseam by Master and we should all be sufficiently familiar with the concept, even though we fail to live up to it most of the time. But there is another dimension about which I feel there is not sufficient awareness among abhyasis. This relates to the problems which arise when we come together in groups and even more so in large gatherings.

In the late twentieth century, particularly in the west, most of us have a fairly clear awareness of who we are as individuals. However, we are much less aware of the roles we take on as part of a group, of the way in which group energy can make us behave. Our earliest experience in this embodied existence is not that of a separate individual, but rather as an intimate part of a group, i.e. the family. The individual personality only emerges later as we develop into adult life.

My point is that a group is not simply a multiple of individuals but forms a separate living system, a different organism with a life of its own. As part of our early development in the family and as a result of the karmic tendencies we carry into this life, each of us tends to have a predisposition for a role which we enact repeatedly in later life when we become part of various groups. Typically we are quite unaware of this and think we are just the same as our experience of ourselves as individuals. However, when we become part of a group we are surprised to find ourselves behaving, thinking and feeling quite differently. In these circumstances we usually convince ourselves that we have simply changed our view in the light of discussion, although we typically feel confused and have an uneasy feeling in regard to what is happening.

For example, most of us, I think, will recognize the situation where we agreed a policy with someone, and a direction to be followed, before going into a meeting. Then, to our amazement, not only did our colleague not support the view we had agreed but actually spoke against it and voted for the opposite point of view. It is important to understand such occurrences not as disloyalty or dishonesty but as an instance of the person taking on a role given them by the group. Once away from the influence of the group, they would often like to reverse their position but feel committed by what they have already done. There are many situations in life where we see this kind of process at work. Of course, there are big individual differences in how likely we are to be colluded in this way, depending on the strength of one's personality and ability to manage one's individual boundary.

This is where, I believe, living systems theory can be of some help to us. What is a living system? A cell, a human being, a dog or a cat, a beehive, or a group of human beings, all these are living systems. The following definition, derived from the work of a number of creative scientists in recent years such as the Chilean biologists Maturuna and Varela, the Chemist Ilya Prigogine, Fritjof Capra and others, can be applied to all these levels.

DEFINITION OF A LIVING SYSTEM

1. A living system contains a number of elements.
2. These elements are involved in a dynamic process of interaction and interelationship.

DEFINITION OF A LIVING SYSTEM (*cont.*)

3. It is separated from its environment by a boundary of its own elements such as permits transactions of import and export across the boundary; i.e. it is an 'open system'.

4. It maintains and renews its own elements by its own internal processes. Living organisms continually renew themselves, their cells breaking down and building up tissues and organs in continual cycles of regeneration. The components of the living system are continually renewed and recycled but the pattern of organization remains stable.

5. The 'locus of control' is within the system itself. This is the most essential aspect of 'self-organization. If the management of a living system moves outside into the environment, then that system is becoming sick and will eventually die.

6. Living systems show a tendency to transcend themselves. Thus they not only tend to change and adapt but also to reproduce themselves and so ensure the survival and evolution of the species.

The next matter for consideration is that there are things within things, bodies within other bodies, one system within another. The essential thing to understand is that, while one system or body may form the basic unit or building block of another system, this does not mean that the energy is simply merged or that this first-order system loses its boundary and therefore ceases to exist as a separate entity. It remains as a system within a system. Nevertheless, it is now a unit under the influence of the higher-order system and transactions or movements of its energy may take place across its boundary under the influence of the higher-order system. The degree to which this happens will depend on the overruling power of the higher-order system and the degree to which the boundaries of the units are lowered or weakened by this influence, i.e. the strength of the group and the weakness of the boundaries of the persons within it.

The same fundamental principles would appear to be operating in all of reality, whether it be living cells, insects or humans, or atoms or molecules. In all of these, frightening energies are released if they are allowed to merge and coalesce. The forming of higher-order systems out of the delicately balanced, bounded units is fine so long as the energy is contained and properly controlled at each level. When this fails for any reason, then the energy would seem to coalesce and flow upwards to throw pressure on the boundary at the next level, where it must be held if it is not to flow onwards like water bursting a dam or a river overflowing its banks.

Wherever we look in this reality, whether inside an atom or inside a human being, we find opposing positive and negative forces. This appears to be the natural order of things, at least in this world. This was the underlying principle discerned in ancient times by the Taoist sages and in eastern philosophy generally. In very early times these ancient scientist-philosophers in India and China came upon this principle of a balance of forces or energy within all reality. These energies have been given various names – positive/negative, right/left, male/female, good/bad, light/dark, etc.; always changing, always balancing, always attempting to resolve and unify but always dividing. Behind this, as the Taoists would say, there is an unchanging reality on which our effervescent dualistic reality rests, but, as Chari (the present living Master of the Saha Marg system of meditation) has said, this is not something we can ever perceive directly, although we can experience it.

During this century fundamental changes have been taking place in scientific understanding of the world and of the nature of reality. Fritjof Capra describes this change in our scientific world view in the following way:

> The material world, according to contemporary physics, is not a mechanical system of separate objects but rather appears as a complex web of relationships. Sub-atomic particles cannot be understood as isolated, separate entities but have to be seen as interconnections, or correlations, in a network of events. The notion of separate objects is an idealization which is often very useful but has no fundamental validity. All such objects are patterns in an inseparable cosmic process and these patterns are intrinsically dynamic. Sub-atomic particles are not made of any material substance. They have a certain mass but this mass is a form of energy. Energy, however, is always associated with processes, with activity: it is a measure of activity. Sub-atomic particles, then, are bundles of energy or patterns of activity . . . The

world view of modern physics is holistic and ecological. It emphasizes the fundamental inter-relatedness and interdependence of all
phenomena and also the intrinsically dynamic nature of the physical reality. To extend this view to the description of living
organisms we have to go beyond physics.

The more we understand the clearer it becomes that everything
is interconnected, that there is no such thing as a separate human
individual or community. If we apply this view to society, as for
example joy-riding, gang rape, vandalism, or vicious attacks on old
people, these must be ultimately related and interconnected with
what is happening in other sectors that we ordinarily think of as
normal healthy society – the apparently genteel life which goes on
in upper middle-class suburbs. If there is any merit in such a view,
then we must all have a share in the responsibility for the negative
activities which are daily going on in some of the more deprived
and disadvantaged sections of our society. We have to ask how far
each one of us is dumping the negative aspects of ourselves into
others and using certain persons and groups in society as scapegoats.
This should in no way be interpreted to mean that these people
have not their individual share of responsibility for what they are
doing or that there are not some very vicious human beings around,
but nevertheless we still have to ask in what way have we all, society,
contributed to this viciousness. How do we maintain it?

If one looks around the world at all the attempts over the last half
century to bring about real change in human society, we will see how
often what looked like hopeful and enthusiastic experiments withered away after a time and merged back eventually into the same old
status quo. So, looking at the situation from this aspect brings one
back relentlessly to the conclusion that real human change is impossible. No part can change unless the whole changes and the whole
cannot change unless there is change in the parts. This is the human
merry-go-round on which we appear to have been stuck for thousands of years. Is there any way out of this impasse?

This is where we see the greatness of the Sahaj Marg system, as
revealed to us by Babuji Maharaj; the effectiveness of constant
cleaning, utilizing the wonderful gift of transmission which can
free us as individuals from endlessly replicating our samskaras. In
this way, with Master's help, real change can take root in us as
individuals.

I feel there is not sufficient awareness among abhyasis of what happens to us when we become part of a higher-order group system. Once we are 'entrained' within a group, our individual boundaries tend to dissolve and inevitably some degree of merging between individuals, within the newly formed boundary of the higher-order system, takes place. Then shifts of energy can occur and unwanted parts, thoughts and emotions can be deposited in one individual from other members of the group. This is usually a combination of the tendency of that person to accept a certain role, or their desire for a position of leadership, and the others in the group using this to rid themselves of unwanted aspects of their personality. These then locate in that person, filling him or her with disturbed energy so that they become emotionally upset or even psychotic. This can be seen at work every time there is a large Sahaj Marg gathering, when one or more abhyasis usually show disturbance of this kind, causing disruption and sometimes even having to be sent home. This may not be the only reason for this kind of disturbance occurring, as special cleaning is also involved, but I am sure it is a significant factor.

This highlights the important emphasis that has been placed on constant cleaning but it also stresses how vital is the frequent exhortation of our Master for us to be 'alert' and to watch any projection of negative tendencies or even negative thoughts about others. Often in gatherings of the mission that I have attended I have noticed an unfortunate tendency towards gossip and loose thinking. It is up to each individual to control his or her own boundary and to take responsibility for the positive and negative forces that exist within each of us. To put it quite simply, we need to realize and accept that each of us contains both good and bad, is capable of aggression or gentleness, and that the task of each human being is to manage and own all of these painful and conflicting emotions, attitudes, pleasant and not so pleasant behaviours of ourselves, all of which go to make up the human condition.

I have no doubt that Master is working at all these levels, not just with us as individuals, but also at the level of communities, of countries and of society as a whole. The least we can do as abhyasis is to try not to contribute to his burden and to take responsibility for our individual selves, as I have tried to describe.

35. Love and Respect
for Freedom

The following paper was published in a locally circulating journal entitled *Constant Remembrance* as part of the Sahaj Marg meditation method that I have been practising for many years.

IF YOU think about it, were we to design a universe we would want it to be as perfect as possible, to be under our control so that there would be no chaos or disruptive behaviour. Interestingly, this is just the way Newton conceived the universe to be organized. However, this view of the world did not begin with Newton. With the advent of the renaissance, Galileo (1564–1642) in Italy and Francis Bacon in England brought about a fundamental change in the direction of science. Galileo stated:

> Scientists should restrict themselves to the essential properties of material bodies – size, shape, number, weight and motion. Only by means of an exclusively quantitative analysis could science attain certain knowledge of the world.

This prophetic statement set in motion a revolution in science which ultimately made possible the extraordinary technological achievements that we see all around us in the world today. But this emphasis on mechanistic progress is not the whole of reality, as R.D. Laing made clear in the following comment: 'Galileo's programme offers us a dead world – out goes sight, sound, taste, touch and smell, and along with them have since gone aesthetic and ethical sensibility, values, quality, soul, consciousness, spirit . . . We had to destroy the world in theory before we could destroy it in practice.'

Around the same time Francis Bacon (1561–1628) introduced the idea of experiment, which was an important contribution to the progress of science. He is said to be the father of empirical science. However, as Fritjof Capra has pointed out, from ancient times the goal of science had been the pursuit of wisdom, understanding the natural order and living in harmony with it. Bacon took a radically different view. He equated the goal of science with the acquisition of knowledge and power, to enable 'man' to dominate and control nature. He said nature had to be 'hounded in her wanderings', 'bound into service', 'made a slave' and that we should 'torture nature's secrets from her'. It was this more than anything else that gave rise to all the horrors of colonialism – that white men could ride roughshod and destroy whole races and cultures, simply because their skin was of a different colour. It is this view too which has led ultimately to the widespread destruction of nature, the elimination of thousands of species, threatening the very existence of life on this planet.

The great French philosopher Descartes made a further significant contribution to the development of mechanistic science. He was a brilliant mathematician and developed the concept of 'analysis' – the 'whole' is always to be explained by the parts of which it is composed. He doubted the existence of everything except that he could think, annunciating the famous statement: *Cogito ergo sum* – (I think, therefore I am), thus mind and matter were fundamentally different. It is this notion that has had such a detrimental effect on our thinking ever since he stated: 'There is nothing included in the concept of body that belongs to the mind and nothing in that of mind that belongs to the body.' To this day, we have no language to describe a human being as a unity, and the best we can do when we want to look at illness from a broader perspective is to use the term psychosomatic.

The conceptual framework created by Galileo and Descartes was completed by Isaac Newton (1643–1727). He developed a consistent mathematical formulation of the mechanistic view of nature – the world as a perfect machine governed by exact laws of cause and effect. His theory of gravity is a classic example. It is embodied in one simple equation, which says that two bodies will experience a mutual attraction that increases with their masses and decreases as the square of the distance between them. It was the centrepiece of his *Principia* (1687). He saw time as a separate dimension, which was absolute, having no connection with the physical world. In the seventeenth century, Newton used his theory calculus to describe all possible motions of solid bodies in terms of a set of differential equations. Einstein described this achievement as 'perhaps the greatest advance in thought that a single individual was ever privileged to make'.

From the second half of the seventeenth century to the end of the nineteenth century, the Newtonian, mechanistic model of the universe dominated all scientific thought. By the nineteenth century, God's creation of the world had dropped out of the picture. It was felt that it was only a matter of time until a complete scientific understanding of the entire universe would be attained. The universe operated like comfortably ticking clockwork, where everything was determined, so the notion of freedom was illusionary. This mechanistic scientific paradigm realizes its final arrogant expression in the work of people like Christopher Hitchens and Richard Dawkins. In the latter's recent book, *The God Delusion*, he fails to even mention, and appears to be unaware of, any of the recent, genuine scientific developments that I am attempting to describe here.

In 1905 Einstein produced two papers, one of which dealt with the theory of relativity and the other with a new way of looking at electromagnetic radiation, which was to form the foundation of quantum theory. This represented an even greater revolution in scientific thinking than that of Galileo in the sixteenth century. Since then, physicists have realized that Newton's conception of the universe is flawed, that there is an inherent indeterminacy, at the deepest level, in the sub-atomic world, and that the uncertainty principle 'is operating throughout every aspect of the universe'. The material world was now transformed into a complex of indeterminate, interweaving and interdependent relationships. These new developments in physics brought about fundamental changes in our understanding of cause and effect, of time and space, of matter, of subjectivity and objectivity, and to many scientists this came as a great shock.

It appears, then, that the 'Source', the centre, from the beginning when the universe was set into motion, whether this was through the 'Big Bang' or in some other way, was showing an extraordinary respect for freedom. This is utterly different from the way we, as humans, would have thought of creating it.

From the beginning, once creation commenced, the universe set about developing itself. From the simplest elements like hydrogen, through combination and increasing complexity, the whole array of the atomic world took shape, until matter appeared and stars and galaxies began to form, separating out. Water, which of course is the basis of all life, appears to have been present in space from the very earliest stages.

As our planet formed, like other planets around stars, this beginning would seem to have been very chaotic, with intense volcanic activity, earthquakes and so on, until the solid crust formed itself and settled down around the molten centre encased within it. At first the planet was dark and forbidding. As the oceans swarmed and life first appeared, these early cellular organisms, bacteria, and viruses, etc., were anaerobic. At some point they began to produce oxygen, which was toxic to them, and they were facing extermination. However, this enabled other life forms to appear that were able to utilize oxygen. The anaerobic forms of life were able to continue to exist but they retreated into the bowels of the earth and ultimately into our own bowels, where they are present to this day and indeed are essential for the existence, and continuation, of all oxygen-utilizing forms of life.

So, when we view the evolution of the myriad kinds of living creatures, animals, plants, trees and all the other forms of vegetation, it appears that the world of light, sunshine and clouds has been produced by life itself and has been in partnership with nature from the very beginning. James Lovelock's Gaia theory shows that there is an interlocking system at work between the planet's living parts – plants, micro-organisms and animals – and its non-living parts – rocks, oceans and the atmosphere – that has produced the whole wonderful landscape within which we now have our existence.

In this way, freedom has been inherent in the development of the universe and of this planet from the start. Every form of experiment of vegetation and living creatures has been tried, some more successful than others, many becoming extinct and being eliminated, while others have thrived and multiplied. The growth of life has often appeared to be directionless and chaotic but a deeper insight can be discerned in that, as life forms have become more complex, consciousness too has appeared and become ever more manifest. This was the wonderful insight of Teilhard de Chardin, which he called 'complexity-consciousness'.

Living Systems

Over the past thirty or forty years, a new science of living systems has been developing which, put quite simply, is reversing the traditional view of causality, whereby the whole is always explained by studying the parts which make it up. This recent view is saying that, when a new 'whole' emerges, it is a completely new reality. To take a simple example, water is composed of hydrogen and oxygen but water is something quite different, a completely new reality, and is the basis of all life on this planet. Hydrogen and oxygen are two gases, which you can't see, feel or taste, and these in no way explain the many new properties of water.

Self-Organization

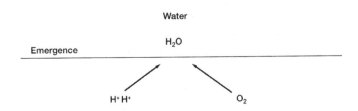

To turn now to ourselves as human beings, we are composed of trillions of cells, which are living creatures in their own right. A human being, on the other hand, as the Russian chemist Ilya Prigogine has shown, is a quite distinct, self-organizing system, a totally new reality. No doubt, through the long process of evolution, we came into being by the merging of cells, which were once separate living creatures but, once we emerge as distinct living systems, we are much more than the sum of our parts and are in no way fully explainable by understanding these.

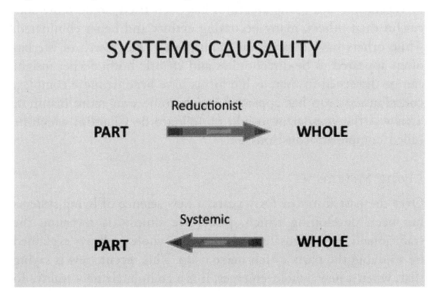

In the latter half of the twentieth century, Prigogine and others were bringing about the same kind of radical change at the macroscopic level that the quantum physicists had done during the early years of that century. In 1977 Prigogine was awarded the Nobel Prize for his work on non-equilibrium systems but perhaps his greatest achievement was to show that such self-organizing systems were characterized by change, instability and continual fluctuation. He showed that the behaviour of a dissipative system no longer follows any deterministic, universal law but is unique to the system itself. As the input of energy into such a system is increased and as it moves further from equilibrium, it is likely to be characterized by continual fluctuation. This in turn can give rise to increasing turbulence and now and then may cause a fluctuation so powerful that it destabilizes the pre-existing organization. This is what he called a 'bifurcation point', at which time it is inherently impossible to determine in advance in which direction the system will move. It may disintegrate into a chaotic state or suddenly reorganize itself into a fresh, more differentiated, higher level of organization.

Prigogine says that, 'Today the world we see outside and the world we see within are converging. This convergence of two worlds is perhaps one of the most important cultural events of our age . . . Our vision of nature is undergoing a radical change towards the multiple, the temporal and the complex.' Thus it is clear from the work of Prigogine and others on the characteristics of self-organizing systems that, at the human level with the emergence of self-consciousness and the ability to discern past, present and future, we have a much greater degree of freedom than most other animals, which are largely controlled by instinct and therefore avoid the excesses of behaviour and destructiveness to which we are so sadly prone. Of course, that is the problem: we also have a much greater freedom to abuse this wonderful gift we have been given and our destructive behaviour has now reached a point where we are threatening the continued existence of this planet.

Accepting then that freedom has been inherent in the universe from the very beginning, the 'Absolute' (God), having set this subtle creative force in motion, could have left it to itself, utilizing its freedom in a sort of partnership with nature, to experiment in developing every possible form of life, to learn by its mistakes and, hopefully, to eventually develop in a more harmonious direction.

This may already have been happening in many other worlds and planets throughout the universe, some of which, as Babuji Maharaj has stated in *Whispers*, are probably much more highly developed and successful than what has been taking place here. Unfortunately, all that we have any knowledge of is what has been happening here on the surface of this planet.

However, this may not be the reality. If we take the spiritual dimension into consideration, another possibility arises: that God doesn't just leave the creation to its own devices but is constantly imminent and working, albeit in a most subtle manner, to bring us back into a harmonious balance with nature and redirect us again and again, to continue the inevitable evolution of this planet back towards the Source. This is achieved from time to time by the incarnation of special human personalities such as, in the sphere of history with which we are familiar, Krishna, Buddha, Jesus Christ, Mohammad and many other lesser saints, whose function appears to be to rebalance our deviant excesses and behaviours and bring about necessary changes for the future of this world.

Once again here, however, we find this extraordinary respect for freedom by the Source of everything, never forcing anything and only influencing change when we show willingness to accept it. Our living Master Chariji, and Babuji Maharaj before him, have continually stressed that they can do little to help us unless there is willingness on our part to change and develop. God can, of course, utilizing the power of nature, bring about radical change in the organization of the planet, which will leave us with little alternative but to accept the painful reality that is coming and to mend our ways.

This brings into focus the question of how we utilize the freedoms we have been given. If you think about it, every time we use our freedom in a selfish way, seeking pleasure through drugs, abuse of alcohol or sexual licence at the expense of others, we end up enslaved, hopelessly addicted, trapped and miserable; or, if we seek the greedy pursuit of power, money and so on, which are usually used to control and oppress others, this too inevitably leads to misery and disaster, for both the perpetrators and the recipients. If we take this to its logical conclusion, the only way our freedom can actually work is when we avail of it to harmonize with nature and, to put it bluntly, to do the will of God.

This is where love enters the picture. The only way we can truly use our freedom successfully is through the development of love: developing love for the 'Absolute' through the heart as the centre of everything. As our living Master, Chariji, has said:

> Love when it is personalized towards oneself, becomes selfish – love for the self for the sake of the self. When this is thrown outward it becomes universal love, where we can love each other, with a pure impartial love, there is no partiality in it . . . A human being is a human being wherever he may be born and by virtue of being a human being, he or she is my brother or sister . . . But if we understand it correctly, we find love is giving and the more one gives, the more one loves, and we can therefore say with confidence that one gives totally when one loves totally . . . So my Master used to say 'Do not love, do not seek to be loved. Try to become love. Because when you become love, everybody will come to you like bees to a flower'.

In the second volume of *Whispers from the Brighter World*, Babuji has this to say:

> Love attracts love as the flower's chalice attracts the bee; it's in the nature of things. It's a natural act, but it's also an act of love, of complicity between two created forms. All has its raison d'être in this vast world. Love is the nectar, which must emanate from you. Your heart totally open must give this divine food plentifully to where it is needed. It's an inexhaustible treasure which you can let flow freely since it will be returned to you from other sources. It's a magic and divine circle.

This raises the question: what is the nature of the transmission that is flowing out continually from the Source. It has been called *Pranahuti* (*prana* meaning life and *ahuti* meaning offering), 'life force', but it is clear from *Whispers* that Babuji Maharaj is saying that this emanation is quite simply 'love'. He says that love is the highest and most subtle form of energy, that this is the ultimate source of everything in the universe. Perhaps it is as simple as that: that love is the 'singularity' that scientists have been seeking in their search for the 'Theory of Everything' (TOE).

Finally, Babuji Maharaj says at the end of the second volume of *Whispers*:

Love is a vibration both subtle and powerful, it is capable of thwarting the unhealthiest plans . . . This form of love can soften the most impenetrable hearts. Divine love manifests itself across the entire creation. It is like beneficial dew, which heals the wounds of mankind.

36. Human Potential

In this paper I ask the question 'Can we exercise our free will without causing damage to everything around us?' It seems to me there is only one way and that is to use our freedom to hand over, to become a humble part of nature. In struggling to envisage how this could happen I point to the way the cells in our body combine and co-operate to make possible the emergence of a new 'holism'; that is the human being.

> 'He that findeth his life shall lose it: and he that loseth his life for my sake shall find it.' (Matthew 10:39)

WHEN human beings behave in a degraded and depraved manner – young girls or men falling about drunk on a Saturday night or assaulting one another, or avaricious and greedy developers or bankers grasping everything they can, depriving others around them of the wherewithal to survive or, even worse, the behaviour of paedophiles, whether clerical or a parent in the family – at such times one often hears it said: 'Ah sure it's only human nature' or 'That's what human beings are like'! But the truth is that these behaviours are much less than we are capable of. It's also often said in these circumstances: 'He's behaving like an animal' or 'That fellow's just an animal'. But animals don't behave like this. They are quite strictly controlled by their instincts and don't go to excesses like this. They behave in a natural way that is appropriate to their stage of evolution.

Once human beings achieved self-awareness and could survey the past, present and future, the way was opened to the possibility of all these excesses. We can see something and say: 'I could have that', and then proceed to grab it. It could be someone else's girlfriend or some material gain that we don't deserve but we want to grasp these things no matter who gets hurt.

I've been trying to wrestle with this problem, trying to understand why we continue to behave in this way, causing all the pain and suffering that fills our lives. Human beings frequently try to justify their behaviour by appealing to science. I feel that, in our attempts to explain this sort of selfish and avaricious behaviour, we have availed of a distorted view of evolution. This is derived from the over-emphasis that Darwin placed on chance mutations, natural selection and survival of the fittest as the main vehicle through which evolution developed. Darwin himself is not to blame for this bias, for he accepted the idea that characteristics of an organism modified during its lifetime could be inherited.

The latter view was suggested by Lamarck, who was also the first to put forward the theory that living creatures evolved. As Mayr states in his book, *Evolution and the Diversity of Life* (1976):

> It seems to me Lamarck has a much better claim to be designated the 'founder of the theory of evolution' . . . he was the first author to devote an entire book primarily to the presentation of a theory of organic evolution. He was the first to present the entire system of animals as a product of evolution.

Lamarck was already an old man when Darwin wrote his great work, *The Origin of Species*, fifty years later. It is rather the neo-Darwinians, like Richard Dawkins or Jacques Monod – it was the latter who said: 'Chance alone is at the source of every innovation, of all creation in the biosphere' – who have been pushing this narrow view that evolution is all about natural selection, competition and survival of the fittest. This gives an apparent scientific rationale to justify the ruthless behaviour, over the past several centuries, of colonial exploitation of the third world. More recently, the same reasoning has been used to justify the greed and selfish behaviour of laissez faire, neo-liberal capitalism, whose dictum is that the only way to advance oneself is by trampling others into the ground and that it is quite acceptable to selfishly grasp what you want at the expense of others.

The truth is that by far the greater part of evolution involves co-operation and symbiosis, what Lynn Margulis refers to as symbiogenesis. Natural selection and survival of the fittest, although a necessary part of evolution, plays a lesser role. In his book *The Biology of Belief*, Bruce Lipton has this to say:

Lamarck's theory suggested that evolution was based on an 'instructive', cooperative interaction among organisms and their environment that enables life forms to survive and evolve in a dynamic world. His notion was that organisms acquire and pass on adaptations necessary for their survival in a changing environment. Interestingly, Lamarck's hypothesis about the mechanisms of evolution conform to modern cell biologists' understanding of how immune systems adapt to their environment.

Mae-wan Ho, in her book *Genetic Engineering: Dream or Nightmare*, puts this perhaps more clearly than anyone else:

The stability of organisms is diametrically opposite to the stability of mechanical systems. Mechanical stability . . . is a closed, static equilibrium, maintained by the action of buffers or buttresses, which return the system to fixed or set points . . . Organic stability, on the other hand, is a state of dynamic balance that is attained in open systems far away from thermo-dynamic equilibrium . . . it is radically democratic, as it works by intercommunication and mutual responsiveness of all the parts, so that control is distributed throughout the system.

When creatures first emerged out of the sea, they had to develop an immune system to protect them from all sorts of organisms that would threaten their existence. This was the first primitive form of immunity (TH2). Then other micro-organisms, such as worms, etc., began to combine and co-operate with us in helping our further evolution. In order that we would not eliminate them, they found a way to reduce our immunity but not too much, so that we, acting as their hosts, would survive (TH1). I am indebted to my old friend Professor Austin Darragh for these insights. He is one of the world authorities on the neurological disease Myalgic Encephalomyelitis (ME) and other auto-immune conditions.

Thus billions of commensal bacteria live on our skin and in our bowels, protecting us from infection, enabling us to digest our food, and these are absolutely essential to our survival. As Lynn Margulis points out in her book *The Symbiotic Planet*:

That animal and plant cells originated through symbiosis is no longer controversial. Molecular biology, including gene sequencing, has vindicated this aspect of my theory of cell symbiosis. The permanent incorporation of bacteria inside plant and animal cells as plastids and mitochondria is the part of my serial endosymbiosis theory that now appears even in high school textbooks.

In this way, bacteria invaded our cells, becoming the mitochondria – a form of DNA in the body of the cell, quite separate from our own DNA in the nucleus. These mitochondria are the powerhouse of the cell, essential to its metabolism and the working of the Krebs cycle. When we are stressed over a long period, we continue to produce cortisol and its precursor DHEA until these are exhausted. Then the body has no alternative but to revert to the primitive form of immunity (TH2) to protect itself from viruses and other infections, such as, for example, glandular fever. Unfortunately, this primitive form of immunity now often attacks our own cells, giving rise to the various forms of auto-immune disorder, such as fibromyalgia or ME. Recently it has been found that roundworms in our gut can operate in a similar way, reducing our immunity to a more subtle level so that we develop fewer allergies. Such allergies have become increasingly prevalent in recent years, with the overuse of antibiotics and a variety of hygienic interventions.

All of these examples, as well as many others, show that much of evolution has been a co-operative endeavour, and not simply a matter of ruthless competition on the part of nature. This has crucial implications for our need to learn to co-operate with each other and to harmonize with nature. If there is to be any hope for human beings, and for this planet to survive, it is essential that we take this to heart. The question is, how can such a radical transformation of human society take place so that we can realize our full potential as human beings.

In struggling to envisage how such a paradigm shift might occur, it struck me that there is an analogous situation in the way the cells in our bodies combine and cooperate in all sorts of ways, to make possible the emergence of the new 'holism' that is the human being. In the long-distant past, each of the cells in my body was a free agent, an amoeba doing its own thing, swimming about in a pond or in the sea. It had freedom but what it could do was painfully limited: it could swim towards light or a food source, retreat from a predator or, if that was not possible, 'play dead'. Then these single cells combined, initially to form primitive creatures like jellyfish or sea anemones and then, as evolution progressed, to become incorporated in more complex plants and animals, until finally becoming part of the full complexity of a human being.

In all of this long evolutionary journey, the cell gradually had to relinquish its freedom and increasingly come under the control of the higher-order living systems of which it was now a part, until finally reaching the human stage. In the process of relinquishing its freedom, however, the different cells have taken on ever more complex functions. Consider, for a moment, the complexity of a liver cell, a kidney cell or, even more so, the extraordinary specialization of a neuron or a cardiac cell. Then we have some idea of the enormous possibilities for development inherent in the original simple cell to realize the full potential of which it is capable. Once it becomes an integral part of a higher-order system such as a human being, it can realize these extraordinary specialized manifestations. We now have fifty trillion tiny cells in our bodies, serving us in all sorts of ways to make us what we are.

Nevertheless, as human beings, we still have to realize that each cell in our bodies is a separate living creature, responsible for its own internal functions, even though in their manifold specializations they are also serving our needs. This is why we should have respect for each and every one of them, as well as for all the billions of commensal bacteria that also serve to protect us, aid our digestion and help us in so many ways.

Perhaps this analogy of the relationship of our individual cells to our being as a whole may help us to discern the direction in which we need to move if we are eventually to realize our full potential as human beings. We, too, will have to relinquish some of our freedom as individuals if a healthy, peaceful society is to emerge out of the present chaos. We, too, will have to make a contribution to the whole of society, and to the welfare of the planet, if we are to progress as individuals in this way. At present, people lay great stress on their right to exercise their freedom in any way they want: 'I've a right to drink or smoke, to take drugs, or to grab as much material wealth as possible, no matter who else suffers.' We do all this in our endless search for happiness but, all too often, all we achieve is to become addicted to one substance or another, with all the misery that this entails.

The question arises, then: how can we exercise our free will without causing damage to everything around us? It seems to me that there is only one way and that is to use our freedom in order to become a humble part of nature, and surrender to the ultimate, the Source of the universe. There is no better illustration of this than the agonized cry of Jesus Christ in the Garden of Gethsemane: 'Nevertheless not my will, but thine, be done' (Luke 22:42). As I have already said, what is needed is to harmonize with nature and treat all other species and each other with respect and love. We must rid ourselves of the illusion that we are in control and surrender some of our selfish individuality. Nowadays one hears a lot about human rights, the charter of human rights, and so on. But who gives human beings the power and control to confer these rights? There seems to be an assumption that we have control over nature, that somehow we can prevent an earthquake or a volcanic eruption. The truth is, we control little or nothing of the workings of this planet, and our attempts to do so are only a manifestation of our infantile arrogance. Sooner or later we all have to suffer in this life but we only grow when we accept suffering and the challenges that life throws up. When we refuse to accept these and rail against the pain, the suffering becomes all the greater. When something pleasant comes our way, we should enjoy it. However, we can also be joyful even when we suffer if we accept it.

The strange thing is, although everyone is searching for pleasure and happiness, the only people I meet who are actually joyful are those who have 'handed over' like this. If you have had the opportunity to meet some of those little Tibetan monks, they are always bubbling over with laughter. When the Dali Lama was here last year, not only was he full of love but everyone around him and all those who met him were filled with joy and happiness. The same was true of my spiritual Master, Babuji, in India, who has had such a major influence on my life. He too was always joking and laughing, and his successor, Chariji, is just the same. Contrast this with the red face of Pope, Benedict, and the downcast faces of our Irish bishops when they were summoned to meet him in Rome some time ago. They all looked miserable, still trying to cling on to some of their outdated power and status.

The problem now is how to get the majority of human beings to accept with humility that to utilize our freedom to hand over to the divine is the only way. An increasing number of people are already understanding this and adapting their lives to take this onboard but they are, as yet, only a small minority. This change began in the latter years of the last century. At first it was only a trickle but now, in the twenty-first century, as the effects of our disastrous behaviour are pressing in on us, it is becoming a river. What is vital at the moment is that as many people as possible find their own spiritual path. This will help to prepare the ground for the advent of a new civilization.

Sadly, I see no evidence that the majority of the human race will heed or understand this message before we reach the tipping point and this whole civilization collapses. Perhaps it will only be when this happens, and we come face to face with a catastrophic situation, with terrifying natural eruptions and millions of people facing death and disaster, that we will come to our senses. Only then, perhaps, will the majority of those who are left finally accept that there is no alternative but to change their ways. I remain optimistic, however, as I do not believe that all life on the planet will be destroyed. What I feel will happen is that a much simpler, more wholesome civilization, based on spirituality, will supervene and arise out of the ashes of this one. This may not happen until towards the end of this century but it will come. It was this that I had in mind when I chose the subtitle for this paper. I feel it was this that Jesus meant when he said: 'For whosoever will save his life shall lose it: and whosoever will lose his life for my sake shall find it' (Matthew 16:25).

References

Ho, Mae-Wan. *Genetic Engineering: Dream or Nightmare*, Gateway Books, Bath, UK, 1998.

King James Bible.

Lipton, B. *Biology of Belief*, Hay House UK Ltd, 11, 2005.

Margulis, L. *Symbiotic Planet*, Phoenix, London, 8, 1999.

Mayr. E. *Evolution and the Diversity of Life: Selected Essays*, Belknap Press of Harvard University Press, Cambridge, MA, 1976.

37. Management of Stress Resulting from the Celtic Tiger

This paper was presented at the Irish Management Institute for the Master's in Organization Behaviour. It was written in February 2001.

Introduction

SO FAR in this conference you have heard eloquent descriptions of the pressures in the workplace, and in contemporary life generally, which cause us to be stressed. What I want to focus on is the question of why it is that these pressures and external circumstances cause us to be stressed? Before I attempt to answer this question, I would like to refer briefly to what has been happening in our situation here in Ireland with the advent of the so-called Celtic Tiger. These developments here in Ireland are of relatively recent origin. We missed out on many of the damaging effects of the Industrial Revolution during the nineteenth century and the early years of the twentieth century in Britain, some of Europe and in the United States. However, over the past thirty or forty years there have been enormous developments in this country, with rapidly growing industrialization and cultural change which have fundamentally altered our way of life beyond anyone's expectations.

There are many good things which can be said about these changes. Young people are freer than they ever were to travel the world – this is even more significant for young women, who have more freedom to decide their own destiny than ever before – and, when young people reach late adolescence, the world is literally their oyster. We have freed ourselves from a conservative, narrow-minded religious domination and from a post-Famine, post-colonial oppression which saw no future for expanding or developing the personality. Also, many women now find they can have a second stage in their life when they have reared their children: taking degrees as mature students in university, which they may have missed earlier in life, or developing a career in business outside the home. With the Celtic Tiger, the economy is booming. For the first time since the formation of the state, we have virtually full employment, emigrants are returning and the population is growing.

However, the other face of freedom is responsibility for our behaviour and how we manage our newfound affluence. It is here that I see some ominous trends. It is hard to believe now but when I went to the United States in 1960 I had never seen a supermarket or a television. Our way of life here at that time was so different, I was overwhelmed by the strange world I had landed in. All this has now changed. Someone going to the States for the first time will experience little difference from the life they already know. To see America now, one has merely to cross the street. All that we associate with the American way of life is already here.

When I returned from America in 1962 it was clear to me even then that, if we followed a laissez-faire market-oriented system, dominated by economics, we would inevitably, as night follows day, eventually have all the other negative aspects of American society, which were present when I was there. At that time there was already rampant drug abuse (under the control of organized crime), breakdown of community and family life, daylight rape, juvenile violence and guns in the schools, daily murder and stabbings on the streets, and so on.

Sadly, what I predicted then has come to pass. Here in Ireland we have caught up. Not only is much of what is happening in other countries now commonplace here but also in some ways we have moved even further on. Suicide is now the commonest cause of death in young men. Last year 400 young people died in this way. Elsewhere in the west, it is only the second commonest cause after accidents. We are also seeing a marked increase in violence; almost daily one reads of people being shot or stabbed on the streets. Two young men were beaten to death not long ago in an affluent part of Dublin by gangs of rugby enthusiasts. What is alarming about all of this is the anonymous nature of it. Most young people who are attacked are just making their way home from a disco and are assaulted by others who don't even know them. I know several people myself who have been attacked in this way, completely out of the blue. These attacks are not perpetrated in order to get money or drugs or to settle arguments but simply to satisfy meaningless aggression. There seems to be a great deal of undirected frustration and anger here among the young. No doubt much of this aggression is drink-related. With our newfound prosperity, the consumption of alcohol is spiralling out of control. This is particularly true where young people are concerned. A recent study has shown that Ireland is top of the league for underage drinking. Spending on alcohol here has increased by almost 70% since 1990. According to the Central Statistics Office, €3.2 billion was spent on alcoholic drinks in 1999, compared to 2.2 billion in 1990. What makes this all the more sinister is that some of the discos are selling drink at greatly reduced prices to increase sales. Is it any wonder that aggression is flowing out on to the streets? Television, and the media generally, subject us to a constant barrage of advertising to encourage drinking. Accident and Emergency services in the hospitals are reporting that as many as 50% of casualty admissions are for alcohol-related injuries. As one consultant remarked:

> binge drinking has the most serious effect on our hospital services and provides so many of the admissions to our emergency services, particularly at night and at weekends . . . Hospital staff tend to be alienated by drunks because of their antisocial and self-destructive behaviour. The inevitable stress, particularly among A&E nurses, leads to serious loss of staff and difficulties of recruitment.

The amount of stress caused by abuse of alcohol must be enormous, in families and in the population generally, but here one comes up against the double-think in regard to alcohol that goes on in Irish society. If any attempt is made to curtail alcohol consumption or drink advertising in this country, we will soon be reminded of the effect this would have on the loss of jobs in the drink industry. Employment in licensed premises throughout Ireland now stands at an all-time high of 78,000 – an increase of 28% in the past five years.

The situation is even more serious as we now have young women and girls drinking. In previous generations, drinking in Ireland was mainly a male preserve and women seldom went into pubs. All this has now changed and, if anything, young women are smoking and drinking even more heavily than boys.

In a similar vein, there is now widespread abuse of other substances. Heroin addiction is still increasing. This is true not only in the inner city but in the better-off suburbs and in other areas of the country as well. Cocaine use is also on the increase, particularly in the affluent sections of society. There is widespread use of cannabis in its various forms all over the country. This is probably the least harmful form of substance abuse. Nevertheless chronic hash smoking undoubtedly has adverse effects on motivation and personality development. More worrying and dangerous, however, is the widespread abuse of ecstasy in discos and other places of entertainment. Already there have been several deaths of teenagers and young adults due to the use of this drug and it is now well established that any prolonged use of 'E's, as they are called, can cause severe brain damage. Also, ecstasy is the drug most likely to precipitate a psychosis. Out of every one hundred people taking ecstasy, four are likely to suffer from psychosis, even where there has not been prolonged use.

As has been pointed out in many studies on stress, the excessive use of alcohol and an increase of smoking among the young as well as the abuse of other drugs are typical maladaptive ways of coping and are major indicators of a high level of stress in a population. With the advent of the Celtic Tiger, the sort of phrenetic, yuppie lifestyle which typified and dominated life in London and New York in the late 1980s, is now more obvious here. The recession which affected both Britain and America since then quietened this behaviour to some extent but, here in Ireland, particularly in Dublin, this kind of arrogant, selfish, individualistic behaviour is now at its height.

A survey of those attending the Dublin County Stress Clinic found that 80% suffered work-related stress. These included a high number of company directors, business owners and senior managers. As social and organizational psychologist Professor Eunice McCarthy commented, 'people can often be their own worst enemies by collaborating in a culture that encourages long working hours. A culture comes into an office, one or two people work long hours and then others feel under pressure if they leave at 5pm'. She went on to say that a 'lack of recognition for your work is a very big factor in burnout and stress'.

A young executive, the father of a young family, working in the financial services sector, spoke of how he gets up at 5.40am to be in the office at about 6.45. Most of his colleagues are at their desk when he arrives. Few workers leave the office before 7pm. Taking a three-week holiday is unheard of, as 'so-called "face-time" is a big issue'.

'Face-time' is an American term for the importance of being seen around the office as much as possible. He believes that the quality of work must suffer over a fourteen- or fifteen-hour day.

Particularly in Dublin, but also in other urban centres, there is constant traffic chaos and people are spending longer and longer in their cars trying to get to and from work. Young couples are moving further and further out of the city centre, often travelling up to fifty miles to get to work. This adds several hours on to the length of a working day. Again mainly in Dublin but also elsewhere, house prices have soared. The cost of mortgages means that both partners must work outside the home and this in turn involves the additional cost of childcare, let alone the loss of quality time spent with the children that is so important in terms of their development.

The degree to which the stressful lifestyle of the new millennium in cities like Dublin has got out of hand was illuminated some time ago in an article in *The Irish Times* on working life. The endless round of working, commuting and still trying to care for the family simply became too much for one highly successful businesswoman. 'It just got longer and longer, getting into town, getting home, organizing childcare, the job got better . . . I just thought what am I doing all this for. I am trekking into town. I have two small kids.' She was spending forty hours a month travelling from Johnstown in County Kildare to her office in Stephen's Green, where she was working for a major market-research company. She was well paid and highly successful as a senior manager in the company but she found herself increasingly asking the question – *what is it all for?* Women, she said, 'get into a life stage where they start having kids and then you are left with this dilemma, do you keep moving up the ranks working sixty hours a week or do you move elsewhere . . . It's people reaching the wall of the Celtic Tiger, commuting.' She moved and set up a new consultancy-based research agency with a colleague who also has a child. Her new office is a ten-minute drive from home. She drops her son off at playschool at 9.20 and is in the office ten minutes later. Three evenings a week she is home before 6pm, which means she has more time at home as a result. She concluded: 'money and title can't improve the quality of life'.

Like many others, I have noticed in recent times a marked change in attitude here; the loss of friendliness, even of common politeness, which is now widespread here in Dublin, particularly among young people. This is not just my impression but is frequently commented on in the media and elsewhere. What seems most strange to me is that people didn't see this coming. We have a multimillion-pound tourist industry whose main platform is the traditional, friendly and welcoming nature of the Irish people – 'Ireland of the Welcomes'.

Other western countries have been gradually transformed over the past 200 years since the advent of the Industrial Revolution. Out of this has emerged the total dominance of the free-market economy. With the collapse of socialism in the Communist countries, this is now accepted with almost religious fervour as the only correct economic philosophy; this in spite of the fact that there is absolutely no proof that it is a sane or appropriate way for human society to behave. While other western countries have had almost 200 years to try to adjust to this inhuman belief system, here in Ireland we have taken this enormous change onboard and swallowed it hook line and sinker within one generation.

Is it any wonder, then, that the new Ireland of the Celtic Tiger is showing all the signs of enormous 'stress and strain' and the rapid breakdown of community, family and spiritual values?

Human Nature

I want now to return to the question that I raised at the beginning: why is it that these pressures and external circumstances of modern society cause us to be stressed? Unless we can answer this question, I don't think we can ever really understand what 'stress' is. If we were made differently, sitting in a car for two hours in traffic, for example, wouldn't affect us. It seems to be something to do with our essential human nature that makes these things affect us as they do. Ultimately, all we know about our environment and the outside world is through our experience of it. So stress is essentially an internal event. I feel, therefore, that it is necessary to understand as fully as we can the nature of our physiology and the way we perceive, experience and integrate what happens to us in the outside world and how it affects us.

Our physiological make-up was formed over millions of years of evolution, thus our internal organization hasn't changed for thousands of years from a time when we had to adapt rapidly to an alien hostile environment. In his book *The Turning Point*, Capra describes the paradoxical situation in which we find ourselves:

The anatomical evolution of human nature was virtually completed some 50,000 years ago. Since then the human body and brain have remained essentially the same in structure and size. On the other hand, the conditions of life have changed profoundly during this period and continue to change at a rapid pace. To adapt to these changes the human species uses its faculties of consciousness, conceptual thought and symbolic language to shift from genetic evolution to social evolution, which takes place much faster and provides far more variety. However, this new kind of adaptation was by no means perfect. We still carry around biological equipment from the very early stages of our evolution that often makes it difficult for us to meet the challenges of today's environment.

In the late 1920s Walter Cannon carried out pioneering work on the bodily changes that occurred when an animal or human being is faced with a threat to its physical integrity involving pain, hunger, fear or rage. He demonstrated how a living creature responded to such challenges with what he called a 'flight or fight' response. He termed these phenomena homeostasis. This involved immobilization of the neuro-endocrine system (with an outpouring of adrenaline) and of the sympathetic nervous system. The organism was thus prepared for fight or flight with a general physiological arousal – exaggerated respiration, dilation of the arteries to the skeletal muscles, increased heart rate and cardiac output and so forth. For some reason, he paid little attention to an equally ancient and basic strategy for survival that is seen in many species. This is the impulse, when faced with an overwhelming external threat against which there would be no possibility of either fight or flight, to 'freeze' or 'play dead' – that is, a state of inhibition in which all reaction that would normally be appropriate is suspended.

This process of homeostasis, whether it involves a fight or flight reaction or freezing, depends on the cybernetic phenomenon of negative feedback. This phenomenon of negative feedback is not only a basic characteristic of our physiology as individuals but is widespread throughout nature. It has been absolutely fundamental to the balance of nature since the first beginnings of life on this planet. This cybernetic process of negative feedback has been absolutely fundamental to the balance of nature since the first beginnings of life on this planet. For millions of years the ecological balance and stability of the biosphere was maintained in this way and, more recently, but still stretching back over several million years, the delicate balance of human settlement *vis-à-vis* the natural environment was maintained in the same way, through cycles of negative feedback.

It is essential, then, to understand this cybernetic principle. A feedback loop is a circular arrangement of causally connected elements, so that each element has an effect on the next until the last 'feeds back' the effect into the first element of the cycle. Thus, the first link (input) is affected by the last (output), which results in self-regulation of the entire system. Our entire physiology works on this basis and the fairly recent development of psycho-neuro-endocrinology has been mainly concerned with working out the details of the various pathways of communication through which this happens in the human body.

In light of these insights, if we return now to the question of stress, the first thing that should be emphasized is that stressful events or challenges to which we are exposed throughout life are not in themselves negative phenomena. Often, this being so if, from the moment of conception onwards, we did not have to meet and overcome life crises and stresses of various kinds, we simply would not develop at all. No, the issue is not that we shouldn't have to face stress but rather how we deal with, fully experience and integrate such events into ourselves as they arise.

Thus a number of factors must be taken into consideration in estimating whether an event is stressful or not and particularly whether it is likely to have a negative impact. The degree to which an event is threatening or stressful does not depend simply on the nature of the external event; it is also a function of the internal set of the individual at the time the event occurs. This is a function of all the learning and experience of that individual up to that moment. The stressful event therefore is the meeting-point of the external world and the internal set of the individual, involving all of the learned past up to that time. How this challenge affects us depends crucially on whether there have been previous insults or crises of a similar kind that were blocked or frozen at the time they occurred and were never dealt with. I refer to this as 'the frozen present'. This would seem to involve the operation of a primitive, non-conscious, biological, adaptive response which is registered and recorded in an unassimilated form at the time but then blocked and never integrated into the self. By this biological refusal to integrate the encounter, the person may never consciously identify the threatening experience; it is as if it had never happened. This internalized 'stressor' now exists outside of time in a potentially unstable state. Hence, the person will be unable to deal with the current situation without activating and dealing with these frozen experiences from the past at the same time. Naturally this can greatly increase the amount of stress involved in dealing with the current situation.

The way we react to a stressful event will also be affected by our basic constitution or personality type: whether we are of an obsessive or rigid personality type, introvert or extrovert. We do not live in isolation and the way we deal with stressful events will be helped or hindered by our relationship with those around us: family, friends or neighbours, colleagues at work, etc. These may encourage healthy adaptive responses but in other instances may collude with our avoidance of facing the challenge or procrastination or, as in the case of loss or grief, reinforce our tendency to deny, or help us to emotionally experience, the pain involved.

In dealing with stress, two factors are of major significance – the *information* available to understand the situation one is facing and the degree to which we have *control* to be able to deal with it. The importance of sleep and dreaming has tended to be underestimated in relation to stress. Shakespeare wrote of 'Sleep which knits up the ravelled sleeve of care' and much of the work of integrating experience and dealing with the effects of stress is carried out during sleep. Unfortunately, people who are feeling stressed frequently have difficulty either in getting off to sleep or with waking in the early hours and ruminating over their problems. An old saying regarding sleep is that 'one hour before midnight is worth two afterwards'. This has been validated by research. Researchers have identified two main kinds of sleep: rapid eye movement (REM) sleep, when we dream, and non-REM sleep (stage 3 and 4 sleep), which is more tranquil. Stage 3 is a period of deep and restful sleep, when the muscles relax and the blood pressure drops. Stage 4 is the deepest form of sleep. Most stage 3 and 4 sleep occurs during the early part of the night. Non-REM sleep seems to play a greater part in restoring physical energy, while REM sleep and dreaming seems to be more concerned with the integration of experience and the formation of memory.

Prolonged loss of sleep affects alertness, performance and mood. People deprived of sleep have difficulty concentrating and are poor at tasks needing sustained attention. They are irritable and depressed, their powers of perception may be affected and they may hallucinate if they are getting too little REM sleep, as the dream world can break through into the day. This is where a vicious circle may supervene; because of stress the person may have difficulty sleeping and this in turn increases their stress reaction, so things go from bad to worse. At this point, it may be necessary to engage in effective psychotherapy to break the pattern in which we are stuck.

38. Redrawing the City

A SENIOR planner with Dublin Corporation and an Israeli architect have put together an imaginative volume about Dublin to which they have given the interesting title, *Redrawing Dublin*. It is beautifully produced and asks many questions about the nature of the city, such as 'Where does your city begin and end?' They point out that this is a notoriously difficult question. They do not provide many answers and perhaps that is wise.

They then open the debate to the general public, again asking a number of questions such as: 'Would you live in Dublin's inner city?' 'Is Ranelagh urban?' 'Is the Phoenix Park underused?' This discussion was then brought to a public meeting on Bloomsday 2011 and they asked me to comment on the general responses from the public. This was followed by a walkabout through the inner city.

In trying to think what I could say at this meeting, it seemed to me that all I could do was to go back to first principles and ask the question: 'What, as human beings, are our fundamental "needs"?' This is as distinct from our 'wants'. Present-day society is full of wants; we are assailed by television advertizing about things we didn't even know we 'wanted' or 'needed'.

In considering this question it is essential to remember that we are not some sort of disembodied cerebral mechanism. We are mammals with the attribute of self-awareness, able from the standpoint of the present to look back on the past and forward to the future. At the same time, we share with other animals the same basic physiology. The primitive part of our brain with all its somatic connections (what Arthur Koestler called 'the horse brain') has not changed for at least the past 100,000 years. This still manages all our survival functions: our fight–flight responses, the ability to freeze in the face of overwhelming trauma, and so on.

Our essential needs, then, are few in number but, in my opinion, are absolutely necessary if we are to remain sane and healthy as human beings:

1. Physical needs – oxygen, water, food, shelter, etc.
2. Relationship to the natural environment – vegetation, trees, other animals, etc.
3. Relationship to each other as persons – involving all age groups, the old and the young, and full equality between women and men
4. Relationship to a human-sized community, small enough to allow face-to-face personal relationships and direct contact with nature, thus to make possible the first two criteria above; this implies some new form of neighbourhood or village-type community of manageable human size
5. Direct experience of a spiritual relationship to the Source, the Universal Absolute

In my opinion, unless these essential needs are satisfied, while we can continue to survive for a time, it is not possible for us to maintain a sane and healthy existence indefinitely. If this is true for us as adults, how much more vital is it for the young, to ensure their healthy development. I have never forgotten the first time I brought my children to Connemara. They literally rolled about in the grass in sheer joy. This was their first real contact with nature and nobody had to tell them about our instinctive need for this direct feeling of contact with the natural world. One can see the result of our current neglect of these essential needs in the relentless deterioration of society. Each generation is becoming more and more alienated and disturbed, sinking into abuse of alcohol, drugs, crime, violence and suicide, while the selfish lust for power and control by the wealthy continues unabated.

In the responses from the public, and even in the book itself, there were a lot of contradictory views and inconsistencies, to the point where one could be forgiven for describing them as schizophrenic. I mean this in the literal etymological sense of the word: to 'split' (from the Greek *skhizein*) and 'mind' (Greek *phrenos*). I feel there are good reasons for this because, on the one hand, there seems to be a tacit assumption and acceptance that globalization, the offspring of neo-liberal capitalism, is here to stay – 'it's the only game in town'. On the other hand, many of the comments are a plea for more open space, parks, allotments to grow vegetables and so on, for more spacious apartments, and to be able to walk the streets without the threat of violence, drunken behaviour or people shooting up drugs.

What seldom seems to be realized is that this form of neo-liberal capitalist globalization is a spectrum that stretches from the selfish, immoral greed of the wealthy at one end, to the poor and deprived at the other. One is predicated on the other. At one pole there are the rich and powerful who reserve to themselves most of the wealth and control of society. At the other pole we find the impoverished, the powerless, where often the only outlet is through organized crime, alcohol and drug abuse, violence or suicide. This form of globalization, with its overuse and abuse of the resources of the earth and its total disrespect for other species, is what is bringing this planet to the brink of destruction.

What has been happening is that all the personal clusters of society have been disappearing, the villages and small towns, the city neighbourhoods, extended families and so on, while a dominant materialistic view of society has supervened, where the only values are economics and ruthless competition. This is not to say that these traditional forms of community were perfect; far from it. They suffered all the problems integral to human relationships but they were *personal*. With the advent of the Industrial Revolution, there has been a relentless progression from the small and personal to the large and anonymous, from rural to urban. For the first time in human history there are now more people living in urban environments than in rural settings. This mechanistic world is now populated by giant corporations, state departments, transnational companies and all other kinds of mass organizations, where one meets only anonymous individuals in numerous roles and functions and the human person has virtually disappeared.

However, below the surface there is another form of globalization that keeps trying to emerge. During the same period that this economically elitist, materialistic form of globalization has become dominant, intermittent attempts to create genuine democratic forms of community keep struggling to emerge. One of the earliest and, for a time, most successful experiments of this kind was the kibbutz movement in the new state of Israel but even this, in recent times, has little attraction for the young and is struggling to survive. In Central and South America during the twentieth century several countries elected democratic governments that attempted to introduce land reform and alleviate poverty but over and over again these efforts were subverted by the wealthy and powerful elites, usually with the aid of the United States through the CIA, for example in Chile* and Guatemala**. They then replaced these democratic leaders and governments with vicious dictators who tortured and murdered thousands of innocent people and maintained a reign of terror, often lasting for many years. Fortunately in recent years there has been a more positive change of direction and most of these dictatorships have been swept away. A number of countries have elected left-wing, more democratic governments once again, and this time the USA has been less involved. Since then we've seen the ill-fated student revolt in Tiananmen Square in China, which was brutally suppressed by the communist government, not just to preserve its conservative dictatorship but rather to allow the introduction of neoliberal capitalism into China. More recently, there have been the spontaneous revolutions by ordinary citizens in a number of Arab countries that have become known as the 'Arab Spring', where ordinary people are refusing to accept any longer the dictatorial regimes to which they have been subjected for so long.

Unfortunately, all of these efforts are eventually either viciously suppressed or tend to drift back to the status quo, as capitalism takes hold once again and the new leadership falls prey to the same old egoistic tendencies and power corruption that characterized the dictators they replaced. This is essentially because there has been no real change of heart or consciousness at the individual level and the same old human behaviours tend to revert back to produce more of the same.

What this comes down to in the end is the question of the appropriate balance between *being* and *doing*. For the vast bulk of human history, the main priority for human beings was the struggle to 'be', to 'exist'. They formed their settlements on the banks of rivers, on the coast, or on hilltops for protection against attack, or wherever gave them the best prospect of survival. With the advent of the

---

*Church Report, Covert Action in Chile 1963–1973, Staff Report of the Select Committee to Study Governmental Operations with Respect to Intelligence Activities. U.S. Government Printing Office 63–372, Washington, 1975.

**The Use of Covert Paramilitary Activity as a Policy Tool: An Analysis of Operations Conducted by the United States Central Intelligence Agency, 1949–1951 – Major D.H. Berger, USMC – 22 May 1995.

Industrial Revolution, however, a marked change took place. As industries developed, with the exploitation of coal and steam power, of iron and steel, we saw the emergence of the great industrial entrepreneurs – the 'robber barons' as they came to be known – like Carnegie, Vanderbilt, Rockefeller and others. Then came oil, the motorcar and air travel, the ever-escalating mad rush to produce goods and services, most of which we do not need. With all this, the human communities that were primarily concerned with 'being' were rapidly replaced by an orgy of 'doing', where human beings became units of production. This was followed by the emergence of giant corporations, transnational companies, government departments and so on, with ever-increasing anonymous urban conurbations, suburban sprawl and the loss of virtually any sense of community. The very word 'community' has lost any real meaning: we now hear of the 'golfing community', the 'business community' and so on – groups that are organized around a function, not communities in any organic sense at all.

Let me describe just two quite different examples of what I mean by a real sense of community. A good many years ago I went with a group to Israel. We stayed for a few days in a hotel near Tel Aviv. This was a commercial hotel but the difference was that it was managed by a kibbutz. They were running the hotel as a commercial enterprise to provide the material wherewithal to maintain the kibbutz, just as another kibbutz might produce fruit or vegetables for sale to support their separate life, but the essential point is that they went on with their separate way of life celebrating their 'being' as a community.

A good many years ago my wife and I went on a break to Forte dei Marmi, at that time a small seaside resort on the west coast of Italy. We were fortunate enough to stay in a small hotel overlooking the main square of the town. Every evening the townspeople would gather, promenading around the square. There were all age groups: mothers wheeling infants in their prams, families with children, teenagers and elderly people, all mingling together peacefully and good-humouredly. This would continue until often as late as midnight, until they gradually drifted away home to bed. The sad thing is that, when we returned there some years later, commercial tourism, with high-rise apartments and all that goes with that type of development, had taken over and all sense of a personal neighbourhood community had disappeared. I hope these examples give a sense of what I mean by a personalized community way of life, one that satisfies the essential basic human needs that I described earlier.

As I have already pointed out, with the arrival of the Industrial Revolution there was a major movement away from the smaller rural settlements into the cities, which grew exponentially. Part of this was to serve the rapidly growing need for workers in the developing industries. Thus young people were drawn into the cities, hoping for better opportunities and greater freedom and also often to escape from the close, suffocating familial relationships and restrictive traditional mores of rural life. Much of this hoped-for freedom and economic opportunity, however, was an illusion and they typically found themselves trapped in soulless occupations, in crowded, impoverished conditions that were even worse than the traditional rural situations from which they had fled.

More recently, as a result of the stifling environment of enormous urban conurbations, with their surrounding anonymous suburban estates, as well as the inevitable economic collapse of neo-liberal capitalism with its uncontrolled greed and avarice, we are seeing a significant movement in the opposite direction. This started as a small stream of independent-minded individuals, in the late twentieth century, setting up what have become known as 'eco-villages' in highly developed areas like California. These are quite different from the earlier hippy communes of the 1960s who, thinking they had found perfection, closed themselves off from the outside world and predictably died. In these recent developments we find highly conscious, educated persons – physicists, architects and others – freely choosing to leave our current stressful society and setting up small, personal human communities. These are open systems, linking with other like-minded developments, utilizing modern technological means of communication – mobile phones, computers, the internet and so on – to keep in touch with each other. They are also availing of the latest developing technology for sustainable living, growing their own food, creating ecological and energy-saving environments and so forth.

What began as a small stream is now turning into a river that, although still peripheral to the dominant society, is spreading in both developed western societies and also in the so-called under-developed world, in India, other parts of Asia and Africa. I don't believe myself that this movement will succeed in the last years of the

501

present civilization, which is on the brink of destroying itself, but it is a beginning, pointing a way to the future and, after a probable period of enormous destruction following the break-up of our present society, it is likely to become the dominant force in a much simpler, more holistic civilization, built on a spiritual basis, not in the near future but perhaps towards the end of the present century. I suspect that, if and when such a civilization does emerge out of the ashes of the present chaos, human beings will have mutated to a much higher level of consciousness, where they will be able to commune much more directly through telepathic and other means so that they will no longer require the present unwieldy technological methods of communicating.

If, as have I stated already, this type of small, human-sized village or neighbourhood community is essentially what human beings require for a sane and healthy life, what then is the need for a city? It seems to me that a larger type of urban centre or city will only be required for a few specific reasons. First of all, there are likely to be a limited number of economic functions that require a greater degree of centralization than can be provided by a small neighbourhood-type of community setting. This would in all probability become much clearer once a decentralized, cellular form of society has been established as the main form of human organization. The main need for a city is for cultural activities. In a small community you can't have the kind of facilities that only a city of reasonable size can provide – the cafés and restaurants, concert halls and art galleries, museums, theatres and cinemas, colleges and universities, the full range of shopping facilities, etc.

The city of the future, as I would envisage it, however, would be an assemblage of discrete neighbourhoods, each of them sub-serving all the needs of *being* – of the full life cycle: development of the young, care of the old, etc. In many ways this would be similar to the great cities of the past – Paris, Verona, Venice, London or Dublin, at their high point, before they became overgrown and depersonalized. These neighbourhoods would be similar in every way to the eco-villages already described, dispersed in a more rural setting.

In a city of this kind there would be parks and open spaces, streets and walkways, where people could walk and promenade in peace and safety, and engage in all the activities of healthy communal living. One can envisage a city of this kind surrounded by rural eco-villages linked by rapid-transit systems, so that one could spend the day in a rural village setting but be in the city the same evening to participate in all the cultural activities that are only possible in an urban centre.

I realize all this sounds hopelessly idealistic but I don't believe it is as unrealistic as it sounds if we conceive of a future society where there has been a real change in the level of human consciousness and human beings have achieved the full humanity of which they are capable. This can only happen in the context of a vast reduction in the population. James Lovelock has predicted that, by the end of the century, this will have been reduced to less than one billion. It can only happen, too, with the emergence of a much simpler civilization based on true spiritual values, where human beings learn to live in harmony with nature, learn to respect all other forms of life, to respect all the other living creatures who have an equal right to inhabit this planet. If all of this can come to pass, and there is no absolute reason why it cannot, then I don't think what I have written is as unrealistic as it may appear at first sight.

39. Mental Illness — The
Great Illusion?

This paper was presented at the 'Mad Medicine Seminar' held in University College Cork on 24 September 2011. It has since been published on the internet.

I AM WELL aware that the title of this paper may appear to be provocative but my hope is that those who are prepared to read it will bear with me and see for themselves the context within which I am asking this question.

The world is a sea of troubles and we all have to face suffering in various ways as we go through life. We have to adapt to these circumstances as best we can. People use all kind of ways to try to manage; some work better than others, while some are counter-productive and land us in trouble. The latter are usually ways of attempting to avoid suffering by taking the easy way out, rather than by accepting the situation and trying to deal with it.

This avoidance and failure to accept what life throws at us usually only leads to greater suffering in the long run. Before and after birth, on to adult death, human beings experience things that cause them suffering. But this is a fact of life which is often overlooked. The simple truth is, it is only when we suffer and accept it that we grow and develop as persons.

There is a current notion in society that we are entitled to happiness and, when this is not our experience we feel something is wrong that must be put right. Some can bear more than others but suffering may become so unbearable that we want to be rid of it. It is often at this point that we seek help. This is usually from one of the agencies of the health services. In the majority of cases, this will be our general practitioner.

A Process of Definition

What happens when a person who is emotionally troubled goes to their general practitioner seeking help? If, for example, you are feeling depressed as a result of some reverse in your fortunes, or because of some unresolved trauma in the past, you may struggle on for a time hoping that things will improve. If this doesn't happen, sooner or later someone is likely to say, 'I think you need help. Perhaps you should go and see a doctor'. If, in the first instance, you present with a physical symptom that is crying out to draw attention to an underlying emotional problem, the GP may miss this connection altogether and go off in a wrong direction, initiating a lot of physical investigations that reveal nothing. More often, he may sense there is an underlying problem. Then a process of definition is set in train. When you see the GP, he says that he thinks you may be suffering from 'depression' and refers you to a psychiatrist. Now the definition is raised to a new level, as the doctor has made a diagnosis that you are suffering from a 'depressive illness', a case of 'clinical depression'. This is seen as an objective mental illness, presumably the result of a biochemical imbalance, that is partly due to genetic influences and is a true medical illness, just like diabetes or tuberculosis. This is not the ordinary depressed feeling we all suffer from, periodically, in dealing with the difficulties and troubles of life.

Typically, if a person is 'clinically depressed', they are told that, whenever they feel a depression descending on them, they must contact their psychiatrist and commence the appropriate 'treatment'. It is because of this, more than anything else, that many people are gradually entrained into a pathway of sickness. Perceiving themselves as 'ill' and helpless, they gradually move into a state of chronic ill-health. The situation is now taken out of their hands, as it is the psychiatrist's or doctor's job to prescribe the appropriate treatment – antidepressant medication, mood stabilizers, ECT, or whatever. This strikes at the very heart of the principle of 'self-organization' and one's responsibility for the management of one's own health. Later, if, as a result of the continuing antidepressant medication, one becomes elated, the diagnosis may be elevated further to that of bi-polar disorder and so it goes on, with a relentless drift into chronicity. This has reached its logical end-point, in that these drugs have now drifted onto the streets, where they are becoming a major part of illicit drug abuse, often in combination with the existing drugs of addiction – heroin, cocaine, etc. Addiction workers are finding it even more difficult to detox addicts from these substances than the more traditional street drugs, and it takes even longer because of the side-effects.

What we are waking up to now is the phenomenon of 'rapid cycling', which didn't exist prior to the introduction of psychiatric medication. Manic-depression (bi-polar disorder) was once considered a rare phenomenon. In fifty years of practising as a psychiatrist, I have seen only a small handful of people with a strong cyclothymic tendency, who were subject to spontaneous powerful mood swings. These would fit the picture of bi-polar disorder, although I would prefer myself not to use that term, as I believe that even these people, with proper help and support, can learn to manage their mood swings and achieve a more balanced lifestyle. All the rest – and I find every third person who comes to see me now has been given this diagnosis – are mainly suffering from the effects of long-term use of antidepressants.

A similar process of definition, and the movement of the person along a pathway towards chronic illness, can be seen where there is an acute psychotic breakdown. This leads on, through successive hospitalizations and the long-term use of heavy medication, to increasing chronicity. The tragic thing here is that, in the process, the person drops out of work, college or whatever, loses contact with friends and other key relationships and withdraws into an isolated, motivationless life within their family. This eventually results in a diagnosis of schizophrenia. We find the same thing happening with various other conditions – eating disorders, chronic anxiety, phobias, ADHD, and so on; always the diagnosis of a supposedly 'biological' illness. This ushers in the 'appropriate' medication, usually on a long-term basis, thus compounding the problem and leading on to an inevitable deterioration, and a life of chronic illness. The use of the term 'biological', so frequently used in this context, troubles me greatly. My understanding of the essential definition of 'biological' refers to the interaction between a living organism and its environment. As used by psychiatrists, 'biological' has come to mean the internal physiology and biochemical activity going on within the person, which is out of relation to the world around them. This is what Francisco Varela referred to as seeing the person as a 'decoupled monad'.

Reductionist Versus Systemic View of Reality

To understand these two fundamentally different views as to the nature of mental disturbance it is necessary to make a clear distinction between a reductionist and a systemic view of reality. I would like to describe as best I can what is involved here. When a surgeon is carrying out a hip or knee replacement, or a coronary bypass operation, this is essentially treating the body as a machine just as, when the engine in a car lets us down, we find the part which is not functioning and replace it. This is an appropriate reductionist approach which has served us well. However, even if you take an intervention as extreme as a heart–lung transplant, it is still true that when this is completed the person has to take back control of their health if they are not to remain sick and a burden on the health services for the rest of their life, or indeed to succumb to a premature death. However, when we put this limited view within the context of the whole person, then a much wider, more comprehensive reality opens up. The well-known statement that 'the whole is more than the sum of the parts' is the simplest way of stating this. What this means is that, for the first time, we now have a definition of what it is to be alive. The bedrock of this holistic view is the principle of 'self-organization'. We say something is alive when it has the characteristic of maintaining itself in existence, constantly renewing itself – building up and breaking down its constituents, yet preserving its overall pattern of organization.

There is, however, much more to it than this. When molecules or cells join together to form a new combination, a completely new reality emerges that is not explainable in terms of the parts that make it up. What is even more important, the direction of causality now reverses. Where, in a historical sense, the parts came together to form this new reality, once it is there it now takes on the crucial responsibility of controlling and managing all the organs, cells, molecules and biochemistry of which it is composed. At the physical level, this is what we know as our 'immune system' but of course the same principle also applies at the psychological level. Indeed, this separation into physical and mental is just an illusion; there is simply one totally integrated human being and this totality has the task of managing its overall relation to the surrounding environment.

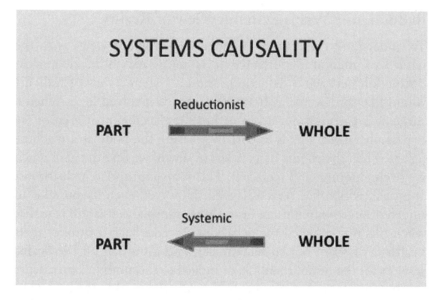

SYSTEMS CAUSALITY

When considering the reductionist as against the systems view of reality, it is important to stress once again that it is not a question of one approach being right and the other wrong but rather of when and in what circumstances each approach is appropriate. Nevertheless, it is essential to point out that while 'living systems' theory is able to encompass the 'reductionist' approach all the way down to subatomic particles, the reverse is not true. Reductionism is incapable of incorporating the systemic approach in the same way. In a reductionist epistemology there is no concept of 'holism', therefore it is simply not possible for this view to take into account all that is involved in a 'systems' perspective.

The History of Psychiatric Interventions

If anyone doubts the truth of this statement, let them just look back at the history of psychiatry over the past couple of hundred years. Whenever medical doctors have taken over the management of the mentally ill, the results have been truly appalling. In the eighteenth century, it was physicians who ran the small private mental institutions. They instituted a range of 'treatments' that amounted to a regime of torture – bleedings, purgings, beatings, dropping people into freezing water, swinging chairs and so on. Then in the nineteenth century, when a spiritually based lay movement spearheaded by William Tuke and his son Samuel, who set up the

York Retreat in 1792, and the work of Pinel in Paris following the French Revolution, of Chiarugi in Italy and Muller and Reil in Germany became dominant – the so-called 'Moral Movement' – there was an extraordinary improvement. (Pinel was a doctor but his mentor, Jean Baptiste Pussin, who was a lay superintendent of the hospital, had already begun the reforms before Pinel arrived.) As Quakers, the Tukes believed that 'to encourage the influence of religious principles over the mind of the insane is considered of great consequence as a means of cure'. Patients were treated with respect and the discharge rates were even better than today, with less relapses. This movement spread into mental hospitals, such as the Pennsylvania Hospital opened in 1841 by the Quaker Dr Kirkbride, and the Metropolitan State Hospital in Massachusetts and, to take just one local example, Grangegorman in Dublin – in the 1850s, every patient in the hospital was attending a national school programme. There was very little disturbance or need for restraint and many patients were discharged back to normality.

However, towards the end of the century, the psychiatrists took over once again. The search for an organic medical cause of mental illness was ushered in and the social and more liberal programmes gradually disappeared. The mental hospitals became grossly overcrowded, there was a marked deterioration in the level of care and the general environment became dirty and delapidated. The early years of the twentieth century saw the advent of the Mental Hygiene movement in the United States. In 1883, Galton coined the term 'eugenics' as a name for the science that 'would improve the human stock'. This was founded on the absurd and now totally redundant notion that the mentally ill, criminals, mentally handicapped and other undesirables were genetically inferior and should, if possible, be eliminated or at least prevented from reproducing their kind. This was espoused enthusiastically by several states, particularly California. Between 1907 and 1927, about 8,000 eugenic sterilizations were performed. There was considerable debate at the time as to whether this activity was unconstitutional. However, the US Supreme Court ruled that it was constitutional and the number of eugenic sterilizations markedly increased, averaging more than 2,200 annually during the 1930s. By the end of 1945, 45,127 Americans had been sterilized, 21,311 of whom were patients in state mental hospitals.

It was in Germany, impressed by the American experience, that eugenics ran its full course. Hitler came to power in 1933 and over the next six years Germany sterilized 375,000 of its citizens. This German thoroughness was greatly admired by eugenicists in the USA. The hateful rhetoric of American eugenicists in the 1920s and 1930s, which characterized the mentally ill as 'social wastage', 'malignant biological growths' and 'poisonous slime', also implicitly suggested that perhaps society should find a way to get rid of them.

It was then that Nazi Germany took eugenic treatment of the mentally ill to its ultimate conclusion. By 1939, the plan to murder many mental patients, and mentally handicapped, was put into operation with the support of most of the professors of psychiatry and senior psychiatrists. 'By September 1941 over 70,000 mental patients had been killed with carbon monoxide . . . the total figure for Germany alone is well over a quarter of a million.' The entire procedure, which was later used in the Holocaust, had already been developed by psychiatrists. As Robert Whitaker stated in his book *Mad in America*:

> Hitler called a halt to this systematic killing of the mentally ill on August 24, 1941; the gas chambers were dismantled and sent to concentration camps in the east, where they were reassembled for the killing of Jews and others 'devoid of value'. A path that had begun seventy-five years earlier with Galton's study of the superior traits of the English elite, and had wound its way through the corridors of American science and society, had finally arrived at Auschwitz.

The Mental Hygiene movement was followed by a series of barbarous 'treatments' that were introduced, one after the other: deep insulin coma therapy; epileptic seizures induced by the injection of metrazol which, after about a minute of terror, triggered a major convulsion that resulted in spinal and other fractures; then the horrors of lobotomy, which produced thousands of living vegetables. In the first six months of my intern year in 1955 after graduating, I worked in the neurosurgical unit of the old Richmond Hospital. In my book *Music and Madness*, I referred to this: 'Nearly every Saturday morning one or two patients would be sent down from Grangegorman to have their brains "chopped".' This was the major lobotomy procedure developed by Freeman and Watts, where burr holes were drilled on each side of the temples and a blunt instrument inserted to sever the frontal lobes almost completely from the rest of the brain. At that time, in 1955, there were literally hundreds of very disturbed patients, both women and men, in St Brendan's Hospital, as Grangegorman was renamed, and this operation was seen as an almost miraculous method of calming their disturbance. Indeed, it did succeed in doing this but in the process many patients were turned into vegetables. When I think of standing there, Saturday after Saturday, assisting the surgeon as he happily whistled tunes while carrying out this drastic procedure, I feel shame and regret. But it is senseless, in retrospect, to react with such emotions of guilt, nor does it make sense to blame the surgeon, for neither of us knew any better. This was an accepted procedure at the time, recommended by supposed experts and the senior psychiatrists who ran Grangegorman.

Later, Freeman simplified this operation, as Robert Whitaker described in *Mad in America*:

> Freeman attacked the frontal lobes through the eye sockets. He would use an ice pick to poke a hole in the bony orbit above each eye and then insert it seven centimeters deep into the brain. At that point he would move behind the patient's head and pull up on the ice pick to destroy the frontal-lobe nerve fibers.

He drove all over the country carrying out hundreds of operations in this way and even training psychiatrists, who had no surgical experience, to do it. Over the next decade, more than 20,000 underwent the operation in America alone.

One prominent psychiatrist in New York spent years removing teeth and other organs from patients on the crazy notion that their mental illness was due to toxicity. Even worse, in Canada, Dr Ewen Cameron at McGill University's Allen Memorial Institute introduced a method of 'complete depatterning' of the personality of his patients (often without their consent) to bring their minds to a state of 'tabula rasa'. He then used continuous electroshock, giving a terrifying 360 shocks to each patient, and an array of drug therapies and sensory deprivation in a failed attempt to create an entirely new personality for the person. At the time that he was involved in this programme, he was at the pinnacle of his profession, being at various times president of the American Psychiatric Association, the

Canadian Psychiatric Association and the World Psychiatric Association. This cruel programme was funded by the CIA and the methods pioneered by Cameron, a man who was highly respected in his field, have formed the basis of the interrogation and torture techniques still used by American intelligence to this day.

All of these intrusive interventions were eventually shown to be destructive or ineffective, or both. Since then we have the more modern electro-convulsive therapy (ECT), which is still being engaged in and defended by orthodox psychiatrists, although the evidence is mounting that this too gives rise to long-term damage. Over many years, studies of ECT have shown no long-term benefit, only a temporary relief of symptoms due to confusion and brain damage. Some early studies utilized a simulated ECT control group and found no significant difference between the two groups but later studies justified the exclusion of any control group on the plea of 'ethical difficulties', i.e. of witholding a treatment 'known' to be effective, thus begging the question and deciding the very result that required to be demonstrated. In my opinion, this damaging therapy will eventually go the same way as all the others.

The current version of this same approach of 'medical' interventions is that patients are being subjected to a range of psycho-active medications, on which they are being maintained long-term, with eventually equally damaging results. This is a more subtle use of psychiatric power by which people can be maintained in the community but nevertheless is just as real a form of control as the older methods of institutionalization. Every week, people turn up at my clinic who are on six or seven different drugs. This is simply bad medical practice. How can you tell what, if any, effect a given drug is having if the patient is taking several at the same time? By giving tranquillizers and relieving symptoms, something may be achieved temporarily but in fact no real change will have taken place and sooner or later most will slip back to where they were, with a recurrence of their symptoms. It is important to remember that most of these pharmaceuticals are derived from natural neurotransmitters that we produce ourselves. Because we are self-organizing systems, the body responds to the intrusion of the drug by cutting down or increasing its own production of the neurotransmitter concerned. While there is no evidence of a biochemical imbalance prior to the introduction of the medication, if an attempt is made to disontinue it then a genuine imbalance will ensue, as it takes some time for the body to reorganize its own production of the substance.

Many of these drugs are useful on a temporary basis but, let us be clear, they are not treatments for specific 'psychiatric disorders'. However, no psychiatrist who deals with the full range of psychiatric disturbance could manage completely without them. The question is rather whether they are given as a treatment in themselves, or as an aid to working in psychotherapy with the person. At times, the drug is the only way of facilitating the initial contact so that therapy can begin. There is also the situation where a person who has a reasonably competent and functioning personality, and is normally managing well, comes up against an acute life crisis and is temporarily destabilized. If given an appropriate psychiatric medication, this may kick-start them into recovery. However, even in this case, the drug is not curing anything; it is simply giving them a break so that they are able to take up their normal routine again.

One may well ask the question, how has psychiatry got itself into such a sorry mess, where mental illnesses are actually being invented and the person is entrained into a pathway of chronic sickness and deterioration; all this, instead of helping people to solve their problems in life. Part of the answer is undoubtedly that, with all the alternative forms of psychotherapy, body therapies, acupuncture and many others that have developed in recent years among non-medical practicioners, psychiatrists, particularly in the United States, have retreated into a sort of siege mentality. They have been struggling desperately to establish themselves as real doctors, who can prescribe medication, carry out physical treatments and have the power to hospitalize patients, even against their will. They desperately want to be accepted by the rest of the medical profession on an equal basis; to have their psychiatric unit in the general hospital (even if it is hidden away, out of sight, down the end of a long corridor). In the end, they don't really find themselves accepted by their peers and are often the butt of jokes about headshrinks, etc., but they keep trying nevertheless, hoping eventually to be accepted as real physicians and be treated with respect by their colleagues.

Someone reading this could well be forgiven for thinking that I am simply rehashing yet again the views of Thomas Szasz in his polemic *The Myth of Mental Illness*, which was published more than fifty years ago in 1961, but this would be a quite wrong assumption for, while I share with him the view that psychiatric illnesses are largely an illusion, he bases this opinion on the position that the problems of 'living' that we call mental illness are not 'disorders of the brain', that they are not physical illnesses, which he does accept as real. For example, he maintains that 'the scientific definition of illness is the structural or functional alteration of cells, tissues and organs'. In stating the problem in this way, he is joining with the main body of psychiatrists at the present time in taking a nineteenth-century definition of medicine, which is based on the 'germ theory of disease', which I have already alluded to at length. Thus he is basing his argument on this premise, rather than upholding the view I am taking in this paper that medicine as a whole should be much more centred on immunity and a role supportive of people's self-management of their health. My view is therefore virtually the polar opposite to the position he is espousing.

The sad thing is that this view of medicine, whereby psychiatrists are desperately seeking to be accepted as respected colleagues, is already out of date and is essentially that dominated by the germ theory of disease. This is clearly demonstrated by the language used by psychiatrists when describing the various pharmaceutical therapies. In medicine there are 'antibiotics', anticonvulsants, antidiuretics and so on, and in psychiatry we have antidepressants, antipsychotics, etc., which illustrates how inappropriate this kind of language is when applied to psychiatric problems.

The American *Diagnostic and Statistical Manual* (DSM), which has now taken on an almost biblical status as the voice of orthodox psychiatry, not only in the USA but throughout psychiatry generally, personifies this medical approach. This didn't happen by accident. The earlier versions of the document took a psychodynamic approach but then a small elite of conservative psychiatrists, like Spitzer and others, with the collusion of the pharmaceutical multinationals, quite consciously led a coup d'état and took over control of the DSM III manual. This gives a cross-section of psychiatric symptoms which it is claimed describe a multitude of discrete psychiatric illnesses. These are said to be true, objective, medical illnesses. However, clusters of symptoms tell one little about the cause, or the natural history, of these so-called 'disorders'. They have a more ominous significance, however; for, once you can name a cluster of symptoms as a 'disease' due to some, as yet, unidentified biochemical abnormality, then you have created an apparent reality. If you have a specific illness, then there should be a specific remedy to deal with it. This is a closed delusional system that suits the pharmaceutical industry perfectly. Unfortunately, most psychiatrists have taken this great falsehood onboard.

What, then, are the the implications of this for psychiatry? What it comes down to is that there is no treatment a psychiatrist can perform on a patient that will bring about real change in them. The person has to undertake the work themselves, with the help and support of a therapist. All that drugs can do is temporarily relieve symptoms to make life bearable. No drug can teach you what you need to know to manage life or to have a personal identity. Often in life we cannot see how we got to where we are, or why we continue to make the same mistakes no matter how hard we try. If a person could undertake whatever change is necessary to successfully manage their life, there would be no need for a psychiatrist or therapist. Of course, the person who can help us need not be a professional therapist – indeed, a lot of helpful intervention is carried out by primary care workers and self-help organizations – but in many situations a friend is not enough and the objectivity and understanding of a person with experience and training is necessary.

A New Direction for Psychiatry

Now, the rest of medicine is already moving away, be it unwillingly, from this preoccupation with pathogenic organisms. From now on its activity will be much more centred on immunity, and a role supportive of people's self-management of their health. This is why it is so counterproductive for psychiatrists to be trying to be accepted, as 'real' doctors, into a concept of medicine that is already many years out of date. Far from trying to be accepted in this way, psychiatry should be at the forefront of the change to a more holistic approach, with the main emphasis being on human beings taking responsibility for their own health.

Thus psychiatrists could be in an excellent position to foster 'wellness' rather than concentrating on controlling 'sickness'. To have a medical degree as well as a profound psychotherapeutic understanding would place them in a unique position to be trailblazers in moving the whole of medicine forwards. In a public health system with its main emphasis on primary care, which is now government policy, psychiatrists could for the first time have an opportunity to be 'genuine' doctors, and have a supporting role in dealing with the totality of the human being, encompassing all aspects of health, both physical and psychological. This too would place them in a pivotal position to open up a dialogue between traditional medicine and all the alternative forms of health care. Some of these are from ancient sources like Ayurvedic or Chinese medicine but there are also all the body therapies, herbal treatments, homeopathy, energy therapies, and so on. To cite just one example of the limited horizons of our thinking, take the question of the placebo response. Most studies and therapeutic trials are seeking ways to eliminate this effect. However, seeing that it is such a significant and remarkable factor in so many situations, surely it would make more sense to try to find ways to strengthen this response and avail of it. After all, is this not just one more aspect of our unique capacity to control our health and heal ourselves?

Thus, in this way psychiatrists could have a key role in helping to create a much more broadminded approach to all aspects of health, bringing together the three great therapeutic streams of allopathic medicine, the complementary therapies, and the insights of holistic psychotherapy. This would be in line with the government policy document put forward in 'A Vision for Change'. This was adopted as the official blueprint for the development of psychiatric services in this country in 2006. The mission statement of this national policy framework emphasizes that services should from now on be 'person-centred' and should make a radical shift from the current 'medical' orientation and preoccupation with mental ilness to a much more holistic approach to mental health and recovery.

The Training of Psychiatrists

There is one serious difficulty, however, in considering the possibility of a major change of direction for psychiatry along these lines. In their training at present, psychiatrists get virtually no direct experience or training in psychotherapy. Thus, even when they give credence to its importance with certain clients, they depend on others – i.e. psychologists, social workers, etc. – to carry it out. If you compare this to the experience that non-medical therapists undergo in a typical four-year training programme – personal psychotherapy, group therapy, regular supervision of their work with clients, personal exposure to deep experiential therapy, as well as intensive theoretical study of a wide range of different forms of psychotherapy – one can see what is so lacking in the training of psychiatrists.

Even apart from being directly involved in psychotherapy with their patients, as leaders in the field this kind of personal experience and self-awareness is essential in any comprehensive psychiatric assessment of a patient. Certainly, if they are to take on an innovative role along the lines I have described above, then a total reorganization of their training would appear to be absolutely essential.

When will psychiatrists finally accept that we are dealing with sensitive, delicately poised human beings, not machines to be tampered with? When will they accept that the very definition of human life is one of self-management and self-organization, and that, therefore, the only real change comes about when we help a person to undertake the painful work of changing themselves from within?

References

Bernard, C. *An Introduction to the Study of Experimental Medicine*, first English trans. by Henry Copley Greene, published by Macmillan & Co., Ltd., [1865] 1927; reprinted in 1949.

Bleuler, E. *Text Book of Psychiatry*, trans A.A. Brill, The Macmillan Co., New York, 1924.

Canon, W.B. *Bodily Changes in Pain, Hunger, Fear and Rage: An Account of Recent Researches into the Function of Emotional Excitement*, 2nd edition, Appleton-Century-Crofts, New York, 1929.

Pasteur, Louis. 'The Germ Theory and Its Application to Medicine and Surgery', in *Comptes Rendus de L'Académie des Sciences*, 1878.

—. 'On the Extension of the Germ Theory to the Etiology of Certain Common Diseases', in *Comptes Rendus de L'Académie des Sciences*, 1880.

Scull, A. *Madhouses, Mad-doctors, and Madmen: The Social History of Psychiatry in the Victorian Era*, University of Pennsylvania Press, Philadelphia, PA, 1981.

Szazs T. *The Myth of Mental Illness: Foundations of a Theory of Personal Conduct*, Hoeber-Harper (rev. ed. Harper Collins, 1974), [1961] 2000.

Whitaker, R. *Mad in America: Bad Science, Bad Medicine, and the Enduring Mistreatment of the Mentally Ill*, Perseus, Cambridge, MA, 2002.

40. *Turning Medicine*
Upside Down

Medicine at present is functioning upside-down. What do I mean by this? Traditionally, the medical profession is organized on a hierarchical basis. The elite at the top are the specialist physicians and surgeons. They work in our hospitals and private clinics and expect to be treated with the greatest deference and respect. In a recent paper, David Healy referred to the 'Cardinals of Psychiatry'. With his indulgence, I feel it is appropriate to extend this metaphor to cover all the 'Cardinals of Medicine'.

We have exposed the feet of clay of the church authorities. Since then, elite developers and our politicians have also been exposed for what they are: addicted to greed; corrupt and dishonest. They are now regarded with the same distrust as the bishops and cardinals of the Church. Only the legal authorities, senior councils and judges, and the medical specialists are still regarded with any respect by society, although the former are already under scrutiny for the fortunes they have made from the tribunals and the exorbitant fees they have been charging. One can only wonder how long it will be before people feel the same way about the elitist medical specialists who are showing the same tendencies.

In attempting to understand how medicine has come to be organized on the present hierarchical basis, controlled by an elite group of medical and surgical specialists, we need to ask what is the prevailing view of most doctors in terms of their understanding of the nature of health and disease? In order to do this, I would like to look at the way medicine has developed over the past 200 years. There is an historical perspective to all this, about which I feel it is important to remind ourselves.

Prior to the emergence of germ theory, surgery was conducted without gloves, masks or antiseptic. Surgeon's gowns and smocks were only used to keep blood from staining their clothing and these were not changed between operations. Infections were so common that more than half of the patients for some procedures died afterwards as a direct result of them. Germ theory was to change all that.

During the nineteenth century, Louis Pasteur demonstrated that fermentation is caused by micro-organisms and that the emergent growth of bacteria was due to biogenesis, not spontaneous generation. Thus the germ theory of disease was born. He was not, in fact, the first person to propose this idea but he demonstrated it beyond contradiction and, as so often happens, its time had come. Three of Pasteur's five children had died from typhoid and this personal tragedy inspired him to try to a find a cure for diseases such as this.

Fig. 40.2. Louis Pasteur (1822–1895)

Fig. 40.3. Claude Bernard (1813–1878)

By coincidence – if there is any such thing as coincidence – another Frenchman, Claude Bernard, made an equally significant contribution to our understanding of health and disease. He was a celebrated physiologist and a contemporary of Louis Pasteur. Pasteur was born in 1822 and Claude Bernard in 1813, so their work was carried out during the same period of the nineteenth century, but Bernard approached the question of the management of our health from the opposite direction. He was fascinated by, and emphasized, our inner ability to manage our health and to resist disease. He was the first to define the term *milieu intérieur*; of this major insight he wrote: *La fixité du milieu intérieur est la condition d'une vie libre et indépendante* (the constancy of the internal environment is the condition for a free and independent life). This is still the underlying principle of 'homeostasis', a term that was coined by Walter Cannon in 1928. It is the term used more recently to describe the way we maintain our physiology in a balanced state and manage our immune responses in general. In this sense, Bernard could be said to be the father of the whole concept of immunity. A historian of science,

Bernard Cohen of Harvard University described Claude Bernard as 'one of the greatest of all men of science'.

I remember reading somewhere, I think it was in G.K. Chesterton, that a heresy is not something which is untrue or false but rather the emphasis on one aspect of truth at the expense of other equally valid aspects of reality that are neglected or ignored altogether. This is what happened to medicine during the nineteenth century. The vital contribution of Claude Bernard to our understanding of health was virtually obliterated by the wholesale change of direction of medicine to concentrate almost entirely on the elimination of pathogenic organisms. There is no doubt that great advances were made by this change of emphasis. The introduction of clean water and sewage systems, and other public health measures, virtually eliminated many of the infectious diseases which plagued society. The later introduction of antibiotics greatly enhanced these advances. So it seemed for a time that we were on the brink of conquering disease and that we would all enjoy perfect health into perpetuity.

This development caused a major paradigm shift across the whole of medicine. Interest now focused on finding the organisms, bacteria, later viruses and other pathogens that cause disease and searching for ways to eliminate these. Human activity in science and medicine, etc., is subject to fairly abrupt changes of direction in this way, where the whole human endeavour moves over to concentrate on one aspect of understanding to the relative neglect of other equally relevant areas.

However, there are good reasons why this failed to be realized. First of all, when you introduce a drug to kill pathogenic organisms there are always a few who survive. These reproduce and the new population tends to be more resistant. A simple understanding of evolution and natural selection would have made this obvious, yet antibiotics were grossly abused, often applied where there was no indication for their use, and each new drug was hailed as the final solution to all our problems.

As time elapsed, it became more and more expensive to produce new antibiotics and fewer and fewer are coming on-stream. The result is that we now have whole new generations of organisms that are resistant to virtually everything. If further proof were needed the advent of AIDS, where the virus strikes at the heart of our immune system, has demonstrated only too clearly how little doctors can do when the natural healing power of the body is not functioning.

Secondly, as the numbers dying of infectious diseases declined, other problems took their place – cancer, heart disease, hypertension, stroke, psychiatric problems and so on. These result mainly from our patterns of living: diet, sedentary life, the stresses of modern society, and lifestyle generally, where pathogenic organisms are minimally involved, if at all. Thus the situation has come full circle.

Now at last the question of our immunity, and ways to strengthen this, is coming into its own, with the realization that, in the end, each of us has to take ultimate responsibility for the management of our own health. There is a growing awareness of this reality among the lay public, in the media and all the health supplements in newspapers and magazines, particularly women's magazines. Medicine too is gradually moving in this direction – surgery is becoming less invasive and more procedures are being used in the service of the self-maintenance of health.

Tragically, if the view proposed by Claude Bernard had only been given equal emphasis to the germ theory of disease back then, think how much our understanding of what is involved in the management of health and illness would have progressed by now. When I was studying as a postgraduate in the mental health programme of the Harvard School of Public Health, I came upon an English translation of Bernard's *Introduction à l'étude de la médecine expérimentale*. Reading it was a revelation and it changed fundamentally my understanding of the nature of health and disease.

We need to understand that the legacy of Pasteur's germ theory is the hierarchical system that exists in the medical world as we now know it. If we are unable to manage our own health then we are forced to turn to the 'experts'. Most doctors in training positions work mainly under the supervision of these specialists, and indeed in the hospitals carry out most of the work. The general hospital, therefore, including psychiatric units, where these exist, is seen as the centre of the health service.

At the most fundamental level are the general practitioners. They constitute the majority of all doctors on the medical register, greater than all of the specialists – physicians, surgeons, psychiatrists, radiologists, etc. – combined. They also see the majority of patients coming to the doctor seeking help in the first instance. Yet they are seen as at the lowest level in terms of status in the hierarchical structure of medicine at the present time.

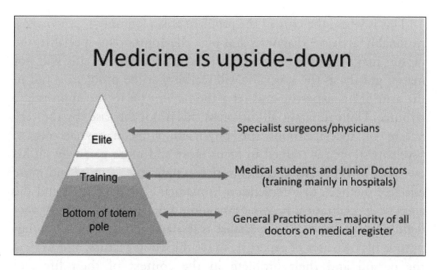

Having made an assessment and diagnosis of the patient, the GP may manage the care and treatment of the person themselves. This will usually be true where the problem the person is complaining of is not too serious or life-threatening – such as a case of 'flu, sore throat or the common cold, mild depression or anxiety, etc. – and these probably constitute the majority of patients coming to see them. However, if the problem is more serious or life-threatening, the GP may feel it necessary to refer the patient to a specialist.

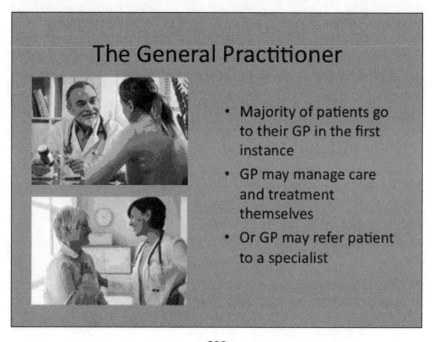

This is where the crux of the problem arises for, unless they make a reasonably accurate diagnosis and pick the appropriate specialist, the person may end up in the wrong hands. You may say this will not matter greatly, as the specialist will realize that the problem is not in the area of his expertise and refer the patient on to the appropriate resource. Unfortunately, all too often this is not the case. By the very nature of specialization, the physician, surgeon, gynaecologist, psychiatrist, etc., is trained to focus more and more narrowly on his own area of expertise, and this is increasingly true as more and more effective methods of intervention in medicine are developed and the areas of specialization become ever more finely demarcated. By very definition, therefore, the specialist is less and less able to see things outside his own area of expertise: to see the whole picture, and to view the person and their problem in the context of their life and adaptation generally. Perhaps I can illustrate this by a somewhat factitious description of the difference between an architect and an engineer: an architect is someone who knows less and less about more and more, until he knows nothing about everything; while an engineer is someone who knows more and more about less and less, until he knows everything about nothing. You can see the point!

The Nature of Specialisation

- Narrow focus on field of expertise
- Specialist less able to see outside his own area of expertise – the 'whole' picture

Architect

Knows less and less about more and more until he knows nothing about everything

Engineer

Knows more and more about less and less until he knows everything about nothing

An analogy may help to explain what I am trying to say here. When a building is being created, the architect is like the 'generalist' and the artisans who do the building work would correspond to the specialists – the electricians, plasterers, plumbers and bricklayers, etc. The architect has the overall vision or design of what the building will become but he does not have the specific skills of any of the artisans. This is not in any way to denigrate the specific craftsmen; they have their special expertise in their own areas but don't tend to see the overall picture. What this analogy doesn't cover, of course, is that in the actual health services, much of the work and therapeutic intervention is already carried out by general practicioners themselves before there is any question of referral to a specialist.

GENERALIST vs. SPECIALIST

- Architect = Generalist
  - Overall vision and design
  - Not the specific skills of artisans

- Artisans = Specialists
  - Specific craftsmen
  - Expertise in own area
  - Not able to see 'big picture'

Perhaps an actual living example of how things can go wrong may help to clarify, at this point, what I mean. A good friend of mine was suffering from severe lower back pain. She was referred to a gynaecologist, who tragically decided to remove her womb and both her ovaries. Following the operation, her pain was just as severe as before. She then was advised to see an alternative body worker, an experienced rolfer. After a few sessions, her pain completely disappeared and she has had no trouble since. It would be comforting to think that this was a rare occurrence but unfortunately in my experience this kind of tragedy happens all too often. The cases where there is this kind of misdiagnosis and where the doctor is successfully sued are only a minority, as most people just accept what has happened and put up with the consequences.

That doctors can make mistakes is understandable but this kind of tragedy is too common to be explained simply as human error. It is much more a structural problem and in my opinion arises specifically because of the way medicine is organized. The simple fact is that there is no seeing eye in our health services at present.

After many wasted years, the health authorities here in Ireland have at last decided that the central axis of the health services should be a comprehensive primary health clinic. These are to be developed all over the country and a number of them are already coming on-stream. They are to be centred on a group of general practitioners, with the support of nurses, physiotherapists, social workers and psychologists or psychotherapists. They should also liaise with public health nurses in the community. It is essential, however, that this service should be free to all, otherwise it will be ineffective and will not achieve the result hoped for. I understand that the Department of Health has decided to bring in this innovation as soon as possible.

PROGRESS IS BEING MADE

- Policy is changing
- Comprehensive primary health clinics are being developed
- Centred on a group of general practitioners, with support of nurses, physiotherapists, social workers and psychotherapists

Portarlington Primary Healthcare Team

Mallow Primary Healthcare Centre

There is no doubt that, when these clinics are fully developed, they will do much to relieve the present overcrowding and chaotic situation in our A&E departments and will also have a major impact on the number of people requiring hospitalization in general. Clinics of this kind have been functioning for many years in Canada and have made a major contribution to the effectiveness of health services there. An old friend of mine who emigrated to Canada many years ago was one of the pioneers involved in setting up one of the first of these clinics. He told me that, once it was up and running, very few patients were referred on to medical, surgical or psychiatric specialists. One reason for this was that they saw people earlier, before the problem had become too serious, so much of their work was preventative in nature.

If the current situation is true of medicine and surgery, it is even more so in the case of psychiatry. Here the majority of referrals from GPs are unfortunate, because psychiatrists by and large are making diagnoses which have little basis in reality. Their thinking is now dominated by the influence of the American system of classification of psychiatric illness – the *Diagnostic and Statistical Manual* (DSM) – and to a lesser extent the International Classification of Diseases (ICD). The former, in my opinion, is a disastrous document that, with each new edition, provides longer and longer lists of supposed psychiatric illnesses. The claim is that these are real illnesses, just like those in other branches of medicine. Thus they give to the patient, and to the pubic at large, an apparent certainty that has little basis in reality and is essentially an exercise in mythology. Even worse is the fact that their view of treatment is almost completely confined to the administration of psychiatric medication.

This is the tragedy of psychiatry at the present time and why it is doing so much damage to those who seek help. Even more unfortunate is the fact that most general practitioners have, understandably, accepted these views as true and are now themselves handing out these spurious diagnoses and routinely prescribing antidepressants and other dangerous psychiatric drugs to their patients.

In my opinion, the planned move to primary health clinics will not be sufficient to solve the real problems in our health services, for they will do nothing to alter the hierarchical elitist structure of medicine that I referred to at the beginning of this paper. They will do nothing to change the relatively low status of the general practitioner as against his God-like specialist colleague in the hospital, nor will they avoid the tragedies of misdiagnosis and inappropriate therapeutic intervention that are all too frequent at present. This is where I see the role of a key person, whom I am referring to as a 'generalist'.

I can't think of a better way to describe the core function of a 'generalist' than to quote what Arnold Mindell says at the beginning of his recent book, *The Quantum Mind and Healing*:

> Training awareness, not curing illness, is the most basic task of medical practitioners. Body symptoms are not only problems to be solved. Chronic symptoms are *koans* – apparently unanswerable questions meant to increase our consciousness. Many such symptoms require dropping our everyday thinking and using awareness to perceive the force of silence in our bodies.

It is important to understand what he means by 'the force of silence'. This gives our life its specific meanings; by going down into silence we are forced to increase our awareness of chronic symptoms, long-term behavioural patterns and relationship difficulties. This gives us the opportunity to take responsibility for all of these and to heal ourselves.

It is not so much that the 'generalist' should be elevated to the highest status, such as with the specialist, but rather it is to be hoped that the whole hierarchical structure in medicine would be phased out and a more democratic approach would supervene, where all doctors would be more or less equal, seeing themselves simply as human beings like their patients.

As more and more women succeed in taking up the higher posts in medicine, they will naturally bring about a shift to a more egalitarian relationship between the different kinds of doctors. The very fact that women see that conceiving a child and bringing it through pregnancy and birth to deliver it into the outside world is a far more significant achievement than taking up a high-status post in medicine means that they are less likely to perpetuate this notion of an 'elite' group of medical specialists.

These then are the difficulties that lie at the heart of appropriate diagnosis and referral to specialists, and this is where I see the creation of a 'generalist' as absolutely essential. S/he would have to have real authority to ensure that s/he has command over the direction of where people are likely to end up. Thus the 'generalist' would require a broad training, to be able to scan across the entire health field, not only alopathic (western) medicine but also all of the complementary therapies as well. Some of these are from ancient sources like Ayurvedic or Chinese medicine but there are also all the body therapies, herbal treatments, homeopathy, energy therapies and so on. In addition s/he should have a broad grasp of the insights of holistic psychotherapy. At first sight this might seem an impossible task but it would be quite feasible provided it was undertaken without going into the details or specialist interventions in any specific area.

A NEW ERA FOR MEDICINE

- Bring together the three great
  therapeutic streams:

  – Allopathic medicine
  – Complementary therapies
  – Holistic psychotherapy

This ability to see the 'wood' rather than the 'trees', to apply 'common sense' and to be able to select out what is important from all the background possibilities is the one unique quality left to human beings. This is so even in the face of all the technical information now available from computers, biochemical analysis and all the other highly specialized imaging techniques and sophisticated methods of assessment that are now available.

At the moment all of this assessment technology is located in hospitals and is therefore only accessible to specialists. In this regard, I feel it would be essential – if the idea of a 'generalist' were taken up and as the policy of putting in place the comprehensive primary developed – that there should be in each health ___ ___ ogical hub where all of the assessment technology is ___ to the 'generalist' and the primary health clinics, as ___ alists. This would provide the 'generalist' with all the ___ cessary to make the overall diagnosis for the purpose ___ referral to a specialist or to an alternative professional where ___ considered preferable. The specialists would then only have the more specialized technology required for their specific interventions located in the hospitals

This then is the idea I am suggesting, however unlikely it may seem that it would ever be taken up. This has been the story of my life – suggesting directions many years too early for anyone to take seriously – but there is an old saying that, when someone suggests an innovation, people first say 'It's not true!' then, when the idea has been around for a while, they say 'It's not new'. Eventually, when the idea is being implemented, they say 'It's not you'! Perhaps one simply has to accept that that's the way life is.

41. Psychotherapy:
What is it?

The word 'therapy' comes from the greek – *therapeia*,[1] meaning to treat, or alternatively to be of service, to attend on, but it is usually understood as referring to 'Medical treatment'. In medicine this is understood as meaning to 'treat', that is, the main activity rests with the doctor, to do something; to carry out some precedure on the patient. In this way psychiatrists too, because of their obsession with being accepted as 'real' doctors, have no other conception than that they are there to administer treatment; to prescribe medication, or like the rest of medicine, to carry out some precedure such as ECT or whatever.

But as psychotherapy too has derived from medicine and evolved out of psychiatry, this concept has unfortunately been carried over into psychotherapy and, to this day, has penetrated deeply into the very way we think of therapy as something that we deliver to the client. You can see this in the way language is used. You will hear therapists speak of giving someone ten sessions of Cognitive Behaviour Therapy (CBT), or providing a course of 'short-term' psychotherapy, and so on.

This stikes me as being at the heart of what is wrong with psychiatry, and to a lesser extent with psychotherapy at the present time. Perhaps it would be better if we had taken onboard the other translation of *Therapeia*, meaning: 'to attend on, service'. This could mean to be there as a guide and support and to provide a context, where the person feels held in a trusting relationship, that enables them to do the work they have to do, to bring about necessary changes in themselves for the better. If this is something like the real task, then perhaps we need to ask once again – what is psychotherapy?

In order to do this I feel it is necessary to go back to the origins of psychotherapy. The three great pioneers who began this development were Sigmund Freud, Alfred Adler and Carl Jung. It is not my intention to attempt to cover all the writings of these three masters which are enormous. Freud's complete works alone must run to twenty volumes or more, as well as several biographies of him by others, and the writings of C.G. Jung are also vast. The same is true to a lesser extent of Alfred Adler. My purpose is simply to try to elucidate what are, in my opinion, the salient and most useful contributions that each of them made to the art of psychotherapy as I understand it and try to practice it today.

Sigmund Freud

Of these three great pioneers Freud was undoubtedly the first and therefore the most significant. Whatever criticisms and reservations there may be about him and his theories, no one can take that away from him.

Even if everything he said were wrong, our world was different after Freud. Like Darwin, he brought about a fundamental change in human consciousness and understanding. Before Freud there was a dim awareness of these depths of human personality among philosophers, sages and others. But Freud approached this question from a biological standpoint and it was only through his insights that it finally broke through into the clear light of day. Our awareness of ourselves was deepened, and with this came the realization that much of what we are, is happening at an unconscious level. As an example of this general change of consciousness, I often think of my own father. He was born in 1883 and in this sense was pre-Freudian. He had no awareness whatsoever of the unconscious depths of his being and operated at what he would have thought was a purely rational level.

Freud was essentially an introvert, whose life-long mission was as a seeker of the truth: as Ernest Jones says in his biography of Freud 'He had a veritable passion to understand'.[2] Even if many of his theories - his over-emphasis on infant sexuality, his preoccupation with libido, wish fulfillment and the pleasure principle; and his piling up of one hypothesis on top of another, without any demonstrable proof – have been rightly criticized and superceded, it seems to me that in the midst of all this he did make major contributions to our understanding that have stood the test of time.

It was he who was the first to clearly identify the major significance of traumatic experience and its long-term effects. Freud was in Paris from October 1885 until February 1886, a relatively short time. But while there he was influenced by the great neurologist Charcot, who had drawn attention to the traumatic origin of hysteria in a preliminary way. On his return to Vienna he began collaboration with Joseph Breuer, who was much older, and for a time was a sort of father figure to Freud. It was then that they began serious work on the traumatic origin of the neuroses. At that time hysteria was the term covering what we would now understand as the neuroses, and/or post-traumatic stress disorder. They were the first to appreciate the long-term effects of traumatic experiences. In 'Studies in Hysteria' (1893),[3] Freud and Breuer stated: 'Hysterics suffer mainly from reminiscences.' They also stressed that: 'These memories were found to be astonishingly intact, to possess remarkable sensory force and when they returned they acted with all the affective strength of new experience.' They realized too that it was not possible to resolve these experiences unless the emotion connected to the trauma was fully experienced:

> We found to our great surprise . . . that each individual's hysterical symptom immediately and permanently disappeared when we had succeeded in bringing clearly to light the memory of the event by which it was provoked and in arousing its accompanying affect, and when the patient had described that event in the greatest possible detail and had put the affect into words. Recollection without effect almost invariably produces no result.[4]

Unfortunately he made two tragic errors. He correctly pointed to the importance of sexual abuse and incest in little children and it was on this issue that he broke with Joseph Breuer. But even he didn't realize it was as common as it has turned out to be since the revelations of recent years. In one of his early papers, 'The Aetiology of Hysteria',[5] he said: 'Whatever case and whatever symptom we take as our point of departure, in the end we infallibly come to the field of sexual experience.' In an earlier paper in a French Journal: *Revue Neurologique*,[6] Freud stated: 'In none of these cases was an event of the kind above (seduction in childhood) missing. It was represented by a brutal assault committed by an adult or by a seduction less rapid and less repulsive but reaching the same conclusion.' This became known as the 'seduction theory'.

Then in 1897, as recounted by Ernest Jones,[7] in his biography of Freud, he confided in a letter to his friend Fliess: 'The great secret of something, which in the past few years has gradually dawned on me . . .' Ernest Jones continues: 'It was the awful truth that most – not all – of the seductions in childhood which his patients had revealed and on which he had built his whole theory of hysteria, never occurred.' Speaking about this change of heart in 1914 in 'The history of the psychoanalytic Movement', Freud stated:

> When this ideology broke down under the weight of its own improbability and contradiction in definitely ascertainable circumstances, the result at first was helpless bewilderment. Analysis had led back to these infantile sexual traumas by the right path and yet they were not true . . . if hysterical subjects trace back their symptoms to traumas that are fictitious, then the new fact which emerges is precisely that they create such scenes in fantasy and this cyclical reality requires to be taken into account alongside practical reality. This reflection was soon followed by the discovery that these fantasies were intended to cover up the auto-erotic activity in the first years of childhood, to embellish it and raise it to a higher plane and now, from behind the fantasies, the whole range of a child's sexual life came to light.[8]

For many years I could find no answer as to why Freud changed his mind; there didn't seem to be any evidence to justify such a volte-face. It was only when Jeffrey Masson's book – *Assault on Truth*[9] appeared in 1985, with the hidden letters written to Fliess during 1896 that were never published, that it was clear at last what severe pressure Freud was under in conservative catholic Vienna during that year. I dealt with the background to all this in some detail in my book *Music and Madness*. In denying the ubiquitous reality of sexual abuse and blurring the distinction between fantasy and reality Freud made his second tragic error. This has caused serious confusion in both psychoanalysis and in turn in much of psychotherapy, and this confusion persists to this day.

In my opinion Freud's second great contribution was that he refused to be diverted from the painful realities of human life. He stuck relentlessly to the core relationships within the family, between parents and their children, and he refused to be diverted from the less pleasant aspects of early development. There is no doubt that much of the emotional disturbance that comes across our path as therapists arises in these primary relationships between parents and their children. And this indeed extends farther back than even Freud realized. The work of Melanie Klein on projective identification[10] with infants from shortly after birth to the first couple of years was highly significant in this regard, and these insights were developed further by others in the Tavistock Institute who demonstrated their revelance in many areas of human life. More recently there has been increasing emphasis on the far reaching effects of the prenatal relationship of mother and infant in the womb.[11] The father can also be involved even as far back as this. If, for example, you have a drunken and violent husband causing severe anxiety and stress to his wife, she may then pass this disturbance on to the infant in her womb. It is influences like this that gives rise to how some babies at birth seem to be born already anxious and distressed, crying all the time.

If there is a loveless atmosphere in the family, a depressed mother who is unable to bond and relate, alcoholism, or to a lesser extent drugs, in one or both parents, violence and many other situations of this kind, these kind of influences can have disastrous and long-term effects on the children growing up in such a home. This is so even where there are not specific traumas such as loss or abuse, etc.

Here again, however, we find another fundamental problem with psychoanalysis. This relates precisely to Freud himself and his messianic aspirations. As Ernest Jones said he had a veritable passion to understand, to elucidate the universal principles underlying human nature and the behaviour of human beings. It was this ambition which lay behind his theories, such as infantile sexuality, the oedipus complex and so on. As an example, just witness once again his statement in 1914: '. . . This reflection was soon followed by the discovery that these fantasies were intended to cover up the auto-erotic activity in the first years of childhood, to embellish it and raise it to a higher plane and now, from behind the fantasies, the whole range of a child's sexual life came to light.'

The difficulty with this is that such universal principles have to be applied to everyone, everywhere, at all times. Given this, it is not possible to make distinctions between one situation and another; where, for example, there is a reasonably happy and loving atmosphere in one family and awful distress, violence and lack of love in another. And this, of course, is the crux because it is these very differences that we have to work with in real life. There is all the difference in the world between the oedipus complex of a little girl flirting with her daddy in a happy relationship and a father who is indulging in systematic incest and brutallity, raping his daughter three or four times a week.

The third major contribution made by Freud was his elucidation of the human 'defence mechanisms'. It is hard to exaggerate the importance of these in the understanding of neurosis and psychosis. How would we make sense of a psychotic paranoid reaction without understanding 'projection'? This is something not only used by individuals to protect them from having to take responsibility for themselves but also by families, and even nations, as Hitler did in projecting all evil onto the Jews. How would we understand addiction without the mechanism of 'denial'? It is not necessary for me to list all of these 'defences' as they are well known but the important thing to be stressed here is that, unlike the other two great contributions Freud made, these 'defence mechanisms' do have a general application to all of us; we all use them to a greater or lesser extent to avoid facing the truth about ourselves, and to look honestly at our real motivations behind our thoughts and actions.

Alfred Adler

I will turn now to the second of these great early innovators. As a true pioneer, and years ahead of his time, Alfred Adler was the first rebel to depart from Freud's inner circle. He was a very different type of personality from Freud. Adler was by contrast very much an extravert. He saw himself as a doctor, he had an intense desire to try to help those in trouble. He related to others as human beings rather than as patients and had little interest in formal psychiatric diagnoses.[12] He dealt with the person's whole life, and their struggles to overcome the handicaps from their early life. He took into account their total relationships with others and all the interconnections of their life in general. All of this was encapsulated for him in the German word – *Gemeinshaftsgefühl*,[13] which is almost impossible to translate into English, but is perhaps best roughly described as a sense of community. In this sense he could be said to be the grandfather of community and social psychiatry,[14] although he is not given any credit for this and has been virtually written out of history.

Yet it was he who started the first child guidance clinics,[15] he would deal with whole families, teachers and other concerned relatives at the same time. It was he too who pioneered family and group therapy, and was therefore a pioneer of preventive psychiatry. He could also be said to be the father of ego-psychology and felt the present was as important as the past. In this sense he anticipated much of what has now become fashionable under the mantle of Cognitive Behaviour Therapy (CBT), although here again there is no awareness that he frequently employed similar methods in dealing with those who came to him for help. He always tried to find the 'goal', that would help to give the person a direction through which they could achieve a full and creative life.[16] This is essentially the 'Recovery Model', that is being put forward as the main direction psychiatry should follow from now on.

In more recent years many Freudians, dissatisfied with Freud's rather restricted view of sexuality and the libido theory of orthodox psychoanalysis, have opened up a number of innovations in both neurosis and psychosis and introduced a range of new approaches to psychotherapy. But because, following his break with Freud from 1911 onwards, Adler and his ideas had been effectively eclipsed by the ubiquitous spread of psychoanalysis, there is little or no awareness that he had already anticipated many of these developments. Thus the major contributions he made have been virtually ignored by all those who followed him.

He was also one of the first to work successfully with psychotic patients,[17] although he preferred to think of them as human beings rather than as patients; and in this sense, he anticipated much of the recent activity that is currently being developed in Scandinavian countries, Finland, and in some places in the USA. But here too there seems to be little or no awareness on the part of those doing this work, that Adler had been sucessfully addressing many of these issues in the early decades of the twentieth century, and that much could be learnt from examining the work he was doing then.

The one serious lack in Alfred Adler's thinking was that he largely neglected the question of trauma, traumatic neurosis, or what is now usually dealt with under the heading of 'Post Traumatic Stress Disorder' (PTSD). He had little to say about this. He did like, when he started with someone, to ask them what was their earliest memory but this was to asertain what defects or disabilities they might have started out with and had to struggle to overcome.[18] His purpose in this was to identify the drive to grow towards independence and what goal in life they would really like to achieve.

Although he was right in seeing any traumatic event in terms of the total development of the person, he failed to appreciate the long-term effects that shock and trauma can have when the experience is too much to deal with at the time and is frozen. It then becomes the 'frozen present', in that it remains fully present in the person but not part of them and has never been integrated into long-term memory.

C.G. Jung

Adler, as I noted already, departed from Freud's inner circle in Vienna in 1911. Carl Jung was in Zurich at that time and was not involved in this rift, which Freud found very unpleasant. Jung was president of the 'International Psycho-analytic Association' at the time and was still closely associated with Freud and orthodox psychoanalysis. Indeed, Freud saw him as the great hope for the spread of psychoanalysis internationally. Yet several years earlier than this Jung was already having doubts about Freud's view of infantile sexualty as the basis of libido and hence of psychoanalysis as a whole. By 1911, when the rift with Adler was at its height, Jung's book – *Transformations and Symbols of Libido*,[19] was published and this revealed for the first time the degree to which their paths were diverging. This parting of the ways finally came to the surface during 1912, and they met acrimoniously at the association meeting for the last time in 1913. As Ernest Jones stated in his biography, this was a bitter disappointment for Freud as he had such high hopes of Jung, almost as his son and heir. Jung saw this very differently; he didn't see his relationship with Freud as the main inspiration of his work. For example, in an unpublished article in the 1930s he said: 'I in no way exclusively stem from Freud. I had my scientific attitude and the theory of complexes before I met Freud. The teachers that influenced me above all are Bleuler, Pierre Janet and Theodore Flournoy.'[20]

Before he even commenced the collaboration with Freud, Carl Jung had already developed the 'word association test'. This was a genuinely scientific attempt to identify the 'complexes',[21] or 'theme', underlying our deeper behaviour. Freud was pleased with this work but later difficulties in the relationship began to emerge. Like Adler, Jung could not accept sexuality as the total basis of libido. He gradually developed a much broader concept of libido as a subtle psychic energy underlying all human activity.

From then on he made several unique contributions to our understanding. He developed the idea of the 'complexes' from the original work on the 'word association tests'. From this point it was a natural evolution for him to begin to identify 'themes' in people's lives. By this I mean a life pattern that tends to keep repeating itself. For example some people suffer one serious loss after another, while others who have been sexually abused as children, get raped or mugged as adults. These repetitive events keep happening until something takes place that breaks the cycle. But Jung went one step further; that no one has adverted to until recently, when he wrote his three remarkable essays on 'synchronicity'.[22] What he pointed out here was that, in certain situations, the environment actually matches the internal state of the individual. This takes place as if by chance but happens too often for this to be a reasonable explanation. It is as if there is an interconnectedness in all of reality. This, of course, is what quantum physisists like Neils Bohr or David Boehm had already been pointing out that everything at the subatomic level behaves like a totally interconected web but to my knowledge Jung never directly referred to their work.

This led to his formulation of different types of personality: he identified four main types and these could be reworked in various combinations. But, to my mind, the most useful aspect of these is the separation into 'introversion' and 'extraversion'. The advantage of this is that there is no pejorative implication of something being wrong or of these personality traits being symptoms of an illness. They are simply two basically different types of personality, each of which can have a favourable or unfavourable outcome depending on the direction of development.

By the end of the First World War Jung began to find a clearer direction to his thinking. He saw that the future or goal of the person was often more important than their past but he felt he could not understand this direction without looking at their developmental background. Thus he developed a psychological theory that involved looking at the person simultaneously from opposite directions, from the past to understand how they were formed, and from the future to ascertain the goal they were striving to achieve. In this his thinking was remarkably similar to that of Adler, who also tried to identify the goal that would help to give a person the direction that would enable them to achieve a full and creative life. But he never seemed to advert, at least consciously, to the fact that he was following very much along the lines that Adler had already developed.

Initially, he accepted as a starting point Freud's view that part of the ego-self was unconscious but his explorations went much further and deeper. He saw that beyond the ego there was a more real personal self that was unconscious. From there he went on to discern a much wider and more fundamental view of the 'self' and the unconscious was subsumed in this: he took the view that this deeper 'self' was universal, taking this concept much further than anyone else has done before or since. In *The Archetypes and the Collective Unconscious*,[23] Jung had this to say:

> A more or less superficial layer of the unconscious is undoubtedly personal. I call it the 'personal unconscious'. But this personal unconscious rests upon a deeper layer which does not derive from personal experience and is not a personal acquisition but is inborn. This deeper layer I call the collective unconscious. I have chosen the term 'collective' because this part of the unconscious is not individual but universal; in contrast to the personal psyche, it has contents and modes of behaviour that are more or less the same everywhere and in all individuals. It is, in other words, identical in all men and thus constitutes a common psychic substrate of a suprapersonal nature which is present in every one of us . . .The contents of the personal unconscious are chiefly the feeling-toned complexes, as they are called; they constitute the personal and private side of psychic life. The contents of their collective unconscious, on the other hand, are known as archetyes.

Having identified this archetypal dimension Jung's explorations went further and deeper. The crucial period when this happened was during the years 1912–1913 when his relationship with Freud had effectively ended. But it seems that the termination of their relationship had little to do with what was taking place inside him at the time.

It was no accident that Jung was led to penetrate deeper into the unconscious. He was always interested in mythology and had assembled a vast library of esoteric literature. After retiring from the Burgholzli in 1909, he set about writing the *Transformations and Symbols of the Libido*. This represented for him a return to his true intellectual roots, his preoccupation with cultural and spiritual realities. Later in 1935 he described this in this way: 'It seemed to me I was living in an insane asylum of my own making. I went about with all these fantastic figures: centaurs, nymphs, satyrs, gods and godesses as though they were patients and I was analysing them.'[24]

Until this change he had considered himself a rational scientist and had felt an aversion to fantasy: 'As a form of thinking I felt it to be altogether impure, a sort of incestuous intercourse, thoroughly immoral from an intellectual viewpoint.'[25] Now he began to realize that there are two forms of thinking – 'directed' thinking and 'fantasy' thinking, one verbal and logical, the other passive, associative and imagistic; the former characteristic of 'science' and the latter of 'mythology'. 'Directed' thinking was a modern phenomenon; when directed thinking was put aside fantasy thinking came to light. In this way his: *Transformations and Symbols of the Libido* was essentially a study of 'fantasy' thinking, that it: 'could be taken as myself and that an analysis of it leads inevitably into an analysis of my own unconscious processes.' He felt completely lost and as time went on he began to have visions and dreams about vast destruction, floods with thousands dying, a sea of blood covering the northern lands. At first he thought these fantasies applied to him personally and he feared that he was going mad, that he was on the way to becoming schizophrenic. Then on 28 June Archduke Ferdinand was assassinated and on 1 August 1914 war was declared. To his great relief, Jung realized that all he had been experiencing was a precognition of the destruction that was about to overtake Europe and was not something to do with him personally after all.[26]

Many years later in 1957, speaking of this crucial period of his life when he went down for the first time into the recesses of his unconscious mind, Jung recalled:

> The period of which I have spoken to you, when I pursued the inner images, were the most important time of my life. Everything else is to be derived from this. It began at that time and the later details hardly matter any more. My entire life consisted in elaborating what had burst forth from the unconscious and flooded me like an enigmatic stream and threatened to break me. That was the stuff and material for more than only one life. Everything later was merely the outer classification, the scientific elaboration, and the integration into life. But the numinous beginning, which contained everything, was then.[27]

But perhaps in the end of all, the most significant service that Carl Jung made to psychology and psychotherapy was to open up, in his tentative way, the relationship to the inner world of spirituality. He made the connection to the deeper wisdom of the ancient Rishies and Sages of India and China, and the Christian and Suffi Mystics This is something that Freud didn't address as he was part of the nineteenth-century scientific and materialistic view current at that time. Adler, towards the end of his life, did make some moves in this direction but didn't manage to go into it in any depth. Since then many others have developed this relationship to spirituality that Jung pointed to. People like Otto Rank,[28] Viktor Frankl,[29] Mazlow,[30] Buber,[31] Erich Fromm[32] Assagioli[33] and so on, have made this a central part of their therapeutic approach. It is also true that an increasing number of people around the world are opening up their hearts and taking up various forms of meditation.

Having got this far in this rather long detour through the history of psychotherapy and the early pioneers, I want to turn now to another great psychiatrist who has undoubtedly been the main influence in my therapeutic life.

Joshua Bierer has been, like Adler, largely written out of history. As a true pioneer, and years ahead of his time, Bierer rejected the current medical model of psychiatry. He was a pupil of Alfred Adler, but Bierer was by no means a slavish follower of his mentor. In saying this he fully acknowledged his debt to Alfred Adler but he was his own man and it was often said of him that he was 'more Bierian than Adlerian'. Like Adler he related to others as human beings, rather than as patients, and took into account their total life and relationships. He developed much further the work Adler had begun in community and social psychiatry. As he said in his autobiography, 'I believe there is no "cure" without change, there is no change without incentive, there is no incentive without meaning, the new meaning of life has to be experienced, and there is no experience unless patients are helped into a position where they can do things for themselves and carry the responsibility for their own mistakes.'[34]

But, like Freud in his early work, he also realized the importance of the long-term effects of traumatic experience; and in groups and with the aid of LSD, he brought people back directly into the traumas they had suffered, to bring them through the full emotional experience of what had happened to them. In his autobiography he sums up his view of the situation in psychotherapy generally, as it has developed out of psychoanalysis:

> As I see it one of the shortcomings of the more traditional forms of psychotherapy, derived from psychoanalysis, has been to attempt to work out all this purely in the context of the therapeutic relationship, in what is often described as 'talk therapy', dealing with transference and counter transference.

In his autobiography Joshua spoke about the dangers of this:

> The mentally ill can, and should, be shown how to help themselves and each other . . . nor am I convinced that purely individual treatment is always a healthy thing. For sixty years the 'transference situation' has been the basis of psychotherapy. Put in plain language, you not only associate your early childhood and relationships with your analyst, you 'transfer' all your worries, doubts and fears to your analyst. You become dependent on him (or her), you almost fall in love with your analyst and the relationship between analyst and patient becomes 'libidinous'. This has been so much taken for granted that few people have dared investigate what happens afterwards, namely how you teach the patient to stand on his or her own feet. 'Dissolving the transference', i.e. 'ending the love affair' and restoring the patient's independence and freedom is such a delicate and complicated task, that many sufferers are so wrecked by it that their last state is worse than their first, and both patient and psychiatrist are disillusioned and disappointed.[35]

It was only when I had the opportunity to read Joshua Bierer's autobiography that I had the rather humiliating realization that most of the ideas and methods I thought I had personally developed were already to be found there in the work of Bierer himself and his great teacher Alfred Adler. All I could do was to try, as best I could, to bring Joshua's dream of a community mental health service that would eliminate the old custodial mental hospital system entirely, to fruition. I'm afraid I met with only partial success.

More importantly, I have tried to find simpler and more effective ways of bringing people down directly to experience their traumas from the past, and also to do this in the light of a better understanding of the way we integrate traumatic experience into memory. Much more is understood now than in Bierer's day about the neuro-physiology underlying this process.

In the years that he was working during and after the Second World War, the new science of living systems, and the concept of 'self organization' which is the central defining characteristic of life, had not yet developed. Yet he intuitively understood this and refused to deal with those who are defined as mentally ill as objects to be manipulated and controlled. He insisted on dealing with each person simply as a human being, relating to them with love and under-standing on a basis of equality and self-respect. This was the real gift he offered to the understanding of psychiatric disturbance that sadly has been almost totally ignored. The setting up of day and night hos-pitals, hostels, therapeutic social clubs and so on were simply vehicles to enable the application of this central message.

If self-organization is the essence of what it is to be healthy and alive, then to deprive a person of the very quality of being in control of him or herself is the worst thing that can be done to them. Yet, in spite of all that, Bierer tried to get across that this is what is happening every day of the week in psychiatric hospitals and clinics. It is because of this, more than anything else, that many people are gradually led into a pathway of illness. Seeing themselves as ill and helpless, they move imperceptively into a state of chronic mental ill health.

One day, when I arrived at Bierer's rooms in Harley Street for my session of psychoanalysis with him which I underwent throughout the year while I was there, he broke off to see a young teenage girl who had been brought by her mother and was in a mute, totally with-drawn, psychotic state. To my amazement, in less than an hour Joshua had broken through this 'glass wall' so that the girl was talking and relating freely. This was the wonderful unique quality that Bierer had. He could break through into the inner world of a patient in a way that showed how utterly misguided and pessimistic the psychiatric estab-lishment's view of illnesses such as schizophrenia could be.

Conclusion

My idea in writing this paper was to ask what could we learn from the work of the first great pioneers and many of those who have fol-lowed in their footsteps? The contribution of these more recent innovators has been merely to further elaborate and develop what the first three great pioneers of the art of psychotherapy had initiated. My purpose has been to try to draw out what were the main contributions that each of the three made, that were each specific to one of them but were not emphasized to the same extent by either of the others. Then to see if, by combining and learning from the best of what each had to offer, it is possible to envisage what might be more effective forms of psychotherapy for the future.

First of all in attempting this, I want to return to the very beginning where I quoted the definition of the Greek term – *therapeia*. As I said, the usual interpretation of this is to 'treat', that is, something the doctor or therapist does to the patient, some procedure that s/he carries out. But the other translation of this term is: 'to be of service, to attend on, to heal . . .' It would follow from this latter interpretation that the role of the therapist is an indirect one; to guide, to help to identify the nature of the problems the person is suffering with and, even more important, to provide the context of safety and trust that will enable them to undertake the work.

The notion therefore that the job of the psychotherapist is to 'Treat' is, to my mind, the most profound error that has plagued all forms of psychotherapy right up to the present day. The plain fact is, IT IS THE PERSON, WHO HAS COME TO SEEK HELP WITH THEIR PROBLEMS, WHO HAS TO UNDERTAKE THE WORK OF CHANGE THEMSELVES, nobody can do this for them. As I said in my book *Music and Madness*: 'it inevitably involves pain and suffering.' I don't wish to labour this point any further, but I believe it is of vital importance because it follows that, if the person is not willing or able to undertake the work that is necessary to change for the better, then the therapist can be the most celebrated and skilful professional in the world but s/he won't be able to do a damn thing to help.

Secondly, as has been stressed so often, the establishment of a therapeutic relationship is fundamental if anything useful is to happen in therapy. But I mean something quite specific by this. Following on from what Alfred Adler insisted on so often and which I learnt from my mentor Joshua Bierer, this should always be a relationship of one human being to another, on a basis of equality and respect, a relationship of person to person; of heart to heart. But to say this is not sufficient, as I said in *Music and Madness*: 'this is a real relationship, like any other, between two human beings. But it is not simply that; it is a relationship established for a purpose, which is to help the client with their problems. Therefore there also has to be objectivity and the relationship has to be managed.[36] I feel there is an urgency about this, however, and if it is at all possible this feeling of friendship and trust should be established in the very first interview. This is very important because without this feeling of warmth and trust a person is not going to open up and tell you the truth about him or herself. But, once this is established, they may now tell you things they have never divulged to another living soul.

The way is open then without further delay to move on to the next step. If there is a lot of unresolved trauma, or a very disturbed early development, parental separation, alcohol abuse, or just a loveless family background, etc., then it is essential to bring the person directly down into this experience as early as is feasible. This is achieved by helping them, by whatever means, to move into an altered state of consciousness, so that the traumatic experience then becomes available to them to work on. I often commence this work as early as the second interview if the basic trust and the context of safety has been established. There are two aspects to this question of trust, first that they feel a sufficient sense of trust in you to let it happen but, even more important, that they feel that whatever frightening experience comes to the surface, you will be able to handle it. Many therapists are afraid of 'madness', of the situation getting out of control, and intuitively the person is immediately aware of this and won't allow their defences to dissolve.

There is another quite different dimension of psychotherapy to be considered in relation to the person's contemporary surroundings, their relationship to others, to their environment and to their world in general. It was Adler who emphasized this aspect of the work. This is what he had in mind when he used the term '*gemeinshaftsgefühl*'. This really means a person's sense of community, their relation to others and to work, etc., Joshua Bierer carried this further; he would intervene in a person's environment in any way he could that would help to improve their situation. This should never be done, however, in such a way as to interfere with a person's proper autonomy and responsibility for themselves but only where an intervention can help them to realize themselves for the better. Such interventions can often be quite crucial in enabling a person to move on when they are stuck in a rut and can't see any way to progress.

What this essentially means is that when someone comes to us looking for help all these connections to their past relationships, to their family of origin, their work environment, their current partner or family and their present relationships, etc., are all there present in the room with them, and need to be taken into consideration. By contrast in traditional psychotherapy one doesn't get involved in anything outside the therapy room. But to my mind this is simply not good enough and it is often necessary to intervene in a practical way, in the wider aspects of their life, work and relationships, to help them break out of a vicious cycle in which they are trapped.

It is here that I find the traditional approaches to psychotherapy are far too passive. If a person has been subjected to severe trauma like early loss of a parent, particularly the mother, or a beloved grandparent; or if they have been subjected to serious physical or sexual abuse, or again, if they have spent their early years with an alcoholic parent or in a family where there is no love and only criticism and rejection, they will typically, in order to survive, build a wall of defence around themselves to protect them from the pain of all they have suffered. People like this show an extraordinary strength of character and courage over the years as they struggle to survive but it is at a high cost for it prevents them from getting any access to the traumatic experiences which caused the problems in the first place. It is for this reason that it is extremely difficult in therapy to loosen these defences to enable the person to do the experiential work necessary to find relief.

The classical method in psychoanalysis of free association will not touch such highly defended persons, they can freely associate until the cows come home and it will not even make a dent in their defences. The same is true of the passive forms of psychotherapy where there is creative listening and patient waiting for the person to open up but in these highly defended people this simply won't happen. However, once a basic trust and safety is established in my experience people move fairly easily into their frozen experiences and will do the necessary work to resolve them.

It is thus essential to understand the reason why it is important for a person to move into their unresolved experiences directly. The concept in traditional psychotherapy, because it has derived from psychoanalysis, has been that everything has to be worked out in the relationship between the client and therapist, in terms of transference and counter transference. Nothing else is really important outside the therapy room. The problem with this is that the person tends to become overly dependent and attached to the therapist. This makes it very difficult to dissolve the transference and to conclude the therapy, enabling the person to return to independent living. Joshua Bierer dealt with this problem in some detail in his autobiography and I quoted what he had to say about this on p. 543. By contrast when a person moves directly into their own experience, the therapist becomes less central, other than to maintain the context of safety and love. The person is fully engaged in working on their own unresolved material and this makes the problem of handling the transference much less difficult. This is illustrated in a slightly humorous way in that quite frequently towards the end of therapy a person may say to me: 'I have to admit I feel a lot better, than when I first came to see you, having worked through all this suffering, but I don't know what you've been doing all the time!'

Indeed, as time goes on and I become increasingly open I find that those who come to me for help move into their unresolved experiences more and more easily without me seeming to do very much directly. It is as if I'm simply there for them to use as they wish. Without in any way dissenting from what I've already said of the need for a person to work directly with his or her own experience, I do feel now that if one could only open one's heart completely then the subtle energy of love and compassion would flow through you and it would appear as if the work was happening automatically. I think it is unlikely now that I will ever reach such a state of total openness. But this was certainly true of my great spiritual guide Babuji Maharaj. Just to be in his presence was sufficient for extraordinary things to happen, without his appearing to do anything. He often used to say, 'it is not enough to love; one has to become love'.

I should stress here that in this work we are never dealing with the past, which has already happened and is gone. We are always working with what is there now, suspended in a frozen state, and the work is about integrating these unresolved experiences into normal long–term memory. It is important to remember, however, that this work of direct experiencing is still only the first part of any therapeutic process. Once the unresolved traumas have been dealt with and fully experienced, the question of the present and the identification of the goal to be pursued comes to the fore, and in many cases where there is not a serious traumatic background, this becomes the main focus of therapy. Adler was the first to stress the importance of this. As I stated earlier he always tried to find the 'goal' that would help to give a person a direction: 'through which they could achieve a full and creative life.'

C.G. Jung also emphasized the importance of assisting a person to find the goal they should strive to achieve. In the section of this paper dealing with Jung I said – He saw that the future or goal of the person was often more important than their past, but he felt he could not understand this direction without looking at their developmental background, thus he developed a psychological theory that involved looking at the person simultaneously from opposite directions, from the past to understand how they were formed, and from the future to ascertain the goal they were striving to achieve. For Viktor Frankl too this was of supreme importance. He put it in terms of a man's search for 'meaning'.[37] But all three of them saw this search in terms of finding the goal as part of a person's practical life and it was seen as mainly a cerebral operation and, of course, there is no doubt that this can be important.

It is only in this century, however, that the centrality of the heart is coming into its own. More and more the evidence is pointing to the fact that the heart is the real centre of our being, All of our emotions are related to the heart and to the body generally, and it has now been found that the heart has its own neurones, in a sense its own nervous system. The heart also influences and has control over the cardio-vascular system as a whole, as well as the rest of the body including the brain.[38] My spiritual Master Babuji has said over and over again that: 'The heart is the seat of the soul.' This means that at the deepest level the goal to be reached is inside us, and it is through opening the heart that we can come to experience the subtle transmission coming from the 'Source'. This is nothing other than love and is the most subtle form of energy in the entire universe. For those who seek a spiritual path this constitutes the ultimate goal to be reached.

It may appear strange that I have said nothing about the current infatuation among psychiatrists with Cognitive Behaviour Therapy (CBT). The reason is that this form of therapy has developed out of a quite separate tradition and it was not therefore central to my purpose in writing this paper. But even here, although psychiatrists are enthusiastic about the efficacy of this form of therapy, most of them still don't undertake it themselves. They expect someone else to do it for them and refer the patient on to a psychologist, social worker or whoever. This can only make one wonder what exactly they are doing themselves. The other reason why I did not go into this in any depth is that Alfred Adler and Viktor Frankl already anticipated much of what happens in Cognitive Behaviour Therapy and, together with my mentor Joshua Bierer, undertook many of the things that would nowadays be thought of as CBT.

The origins of CBT come from the inspirational work of the great Russian physiologist Ivan Petrovich Pavlov.[39] His study of conditioned reflexes in dogs influenced Behaviourism, and the clinical implications of this were later developed by Behaviourists like Skinner,[40] Wolpe[41] and others. This approach was initially very narrow and materialistic and gave rise to what became known as 'Behaviour therapy', and for a time we were flooded with 'Behaviour Therapists.' Although this was a very limited view of therapy, some positive developments did result from it and in *Music and Madness'* the point was made that: 'Even though the theoretical concepts of the early Behaviourists were over-simplified and don't stand up to critical examination, their emphasis on the fact that true insight only exists when there is a real change in behaviour has been a valuable contribution.'[42] But then the realization that we don't respond to life's challenges simply in terms of conditioned reflexes meant that some deeper view of reality had to be introduced.

It was then that Aaron Beck[43] and others developed the concept of Cognitive Behaviour Therapy. There is no doubt that this is a valid part of psychotherapy, that is very useful in certain situations, but it is only one dimension. What needs to be stressed is that if you are dealing with someone who has been profoundly traumatized and is highly defended, to subject them to CBT, and to try to get them to change their negative attitudes when they are filled up with unresolved frozen experiences, is not only ineffective but can be actually damaging. As the realization of these limitations is slowly becoming clearer various efforts are being made to extend the range of these behavioural techniques. We now hear about third stage CBT, Dialectal Behaviour Therapy and Cognitive Analytic Therapy. One can only hope that eventually the realization will come that what is really required is to accept and become involved in the full range of holistic psychotherapy.

Finally I want to say that increasingly in my own clinical practice I have found that at the deepest level many of the emotional problems that people come with are spiritual in nature. Over and over again I find that below the level of all the problems that life throws up, there is the question of meaning: 'Why am I here? Is there any purpose to all this struggle?', and so on. This is where the insights of Carl Jung come into the picture, for he was the first to raise this aspect and this is what made his work, in opening up the wider and deeper dimensions of the self so valuable. Viktor Frankl in his logotherapy developed these insights much more fully and made this question of 'meaning' central to his whole approach. In *Man's Search for Ultimate Meaning* he states:

> Today, man's will to meaning is frustrated on a worldwide scale. Ever more people are haunted by a feeling of meaninglessness which is often accompanied by a feeling of emptiness – or, as I am used to calling it, an 'existential vacuum'. It mainly manifests itself in boredom and apathy .While boredom is indicative of a loss of interest in the world, apathy betrays a lack of initiative to do something in the world, to change something in the world.[44]

Not everyone wants to delve down to this level, even if they have a dim awareness that this deeper question remains unanswered, and of course that is there right. But I find that with all the problems that people are assailed with since the economic collapse of capitalism, more and more of them are now being forced to ask this question – 'Is there not something more to life than just striving to succeed economically and just keeping your head above water?' It seems that with the immanent collapse of this civilization more and more hearts are opening up and searching for some deeper meaning to life.

References

1 Collins, English Dictionary.

2 E. Jones, *The Life and Work of Sigmund Freud*, Vol. 1 & 2, Basic Books, 1953.

3 S. Freud, 'Studies in Hysteria', *Complete Psychological Works*, Vol. 18, London: trans. & ed. I. Strachey, Hogarth Press, 1954.

4 Ibid.

5 S. Freud, *Complete Psychological Works*, London: trans. & ed. I. Strachey, Hogarth Press, 1954.

6 S. Freud, *Revue Neurologique*, 1896.

7 E. Jones, *The Life & Work of Sigmund Freud*, Vol. 1 & 2, Basic Books, 1953.

8 S. Freud, 'Complete Psychological Works', *Complete Psychological Works*: trans. & ed. I. Strachey, Hogarth Press, 1954.

9 J. Masson, *The Assault on Truth*, Middlesex: Penguin Books, 1985.

10 M. Klein, 'Notes on Some Schizoid Mechanisms', 1946.

11 B. Lipton, *The Biology of Belief*, Hay House, Inc., 2008; D.B. Chamberlain, 'The Expanding Boundaries of Memory', Re*Vision*, pp. 11–20, Spring 1990.

12 J. Bierer, *Peddlar of Dreams*, in publication.

13 A. Adler, *Uber den nervosen Charakter*, Munich: Verlag von J.F. Bergmann, 1919.

14 J. Bierer, *Peddlar of Dreams*, in publication.

15 A. Adler, *The Education of Children*, New York: Greenberg, 1930; P. Bottoms, Alfred Adler, *A Biography*, New York: G. P. Putnam's Sons, 1939.

16 A. Adler, *What Life Should Mean to You*, Boston: Alan Parker (ed.), Little, Brown & Co., 1932.

17 A. Adler, *Problems of Neurosis, A Book of Case Histories*, New York: Phillipe Mauret (ed.), 1930.

18 A. Adler, *Social Interest: A Challenge to Mankind*, London: Faber & Faber Ltd., 1938.

19 C.J. Jung, 'Symbols of Transformation', *Collected Works*, Vol. 5, 2nd Ed., Princeton & London, 1967.

20 C.J. Jung, Unpublished article, 1930.

21 C.G. Jung, 'Psychological Types'. *Collected Works*, Vol. 6, Princeton & London, 1971.

22 C.G. Jung, 'Synchronicity: An Acausal Connecting Phenomenon,' in *The Structure and Dynamics of the Psyche*, Princeton University Press.

23 C.G. Jung, *The Archetypes and the Collective Unconscious*, New York, N. Y.: Bollingen Foundation Inc., 1959.

24 C.G. Jung, *Analytical Psychology: Its Theory & Practice* (1935), London: Routledge and Kegan Paul, 1976.

25 Ibid.

26 Ibid.

27 C.G. Jung, *The Red Book*, Liber Novus, 500 Fifth Avenue, New York, NY 10110: W. W. Norton & Company, 1957.

28 O. Rank, P*sychology and the Soul: A Study of the Origin, Conceptual Evolution, and Nature of the Soul*, Leipzig: Franz Deuticke, 1930.

29 V. Frankl, *Man's Search for Meaning*, 1959.

30 A. Maslow, *Religions, Values and Peak-Experiences*, New York: Penguin Books Inc, 1970.

31 M. Buber, I and Thou, Berlin: Shocken Verlag, 1923.

32 E. Fromm, *Psychoanalysis and Religion*, Binghampton, New York: Vail-Ballou Press Inc., 1950.

33 R. Assagioli, 'Self-realization and Psychological Disturbances', *Psychosynthesis Research Foundation*, no. Issue No. 10.

34 J. Bierer, *Peddlar of Dreams*, in publication.

35 Ibid.

36 I. Browne, *Music and Madness*, Cork, Ireland: Atrium, An imprint of Cork University Press, 2008.

37 V. Frankl, *Mans Search for Meaning*, Beacon Press, 1959.

38 J. C. Pearce, *Evolution's End*, New York: Harper Collins, 1992; P. Pearshall, *The Heart's Code*, 77–85 Fulham Palace Road, London: Broadway Books, 1998.

39 Collins Dictionary.

40 B.F. Skinner, *About Behaviorism*, Vintage Books, 1974.

41 J. Wolpe, *The Practice of Behavioral Therapy*, New York: Pergamon Press, 1969.

42 I. Browne, *Music and Madness*, Cork: Atrium: An imprint of Cork University Press, 2008.

43 A.T. Beck, *Cognitive Therapy and the Emotional Disorders*, International Universities Press, 1975.

44 V. Frankl, *Man's Search for Ultimate Meaning*, London: Rider , 2011.

Index